READINGS
IN CHILD
DEVELOPMENT

READINGS IN CHILD DEVELOPMENT

Edited by

Harry Munsinger

University of California, San Diego

HOLT, RINEHART AND WINSTON, INC.
New York Chicago San Francisco Atlanta
Dallas Montreal Toronto London Sydney

Copyright © 1971 by Holt, Rinehart and Winston, Inc.
All rights reserved
Library of Congress Catalog Card Number: 78-143319
ISBN: 0-03-078610-X
Printed in the United States of America
1 2 3 4   074   9 8 7 6 5 4 3 2

To those trying to understand children

PREFACE

How did I come to pick these particular studies? My biases were for experimental rather than observational evidence, human rather than animal subjects, and theory rather than data. However, I included experimental *and* observational studies to cover all important areas, animal *and* human materials for a balanced picture of current knowledge, and theory and data to give the flavor of contemporary child psychology.

A book of readings should do two things: acquaint the student with *how* we know and excite the imagination of future professionals. These particular readings represent compromises among scientific rigor, good teaching doctrine, and currently popular notions of child development. The compromises were necessary because it is impossible (given the present state of the field) to present anything that resembles a finished picture of the child. In these readings we see faint outlines of several children: a newborn, a child learning, a child thinking, a child interacting with his peers, a child afraid, and a child playing. To present a clear, coherent picture of *the* child would be science fiction—so I present the happy confusion and healthy conflict of current child psychology.

I included recent rather than classic studies, short rather than long articles, and relevant rather than tedious writing. I edited all articles to make their difficulty comparable, their messages clear, their style lively, and their length commensurate with the particular point I was trying to make.

Studies are ordered along a chronological base paralleling rapid or important changes in the growing child. The readings fit into two main sections. The first eight chapters cover basic processes; the others explore relations between the child and his family, school, and culture.

THE INDIVIDUAL CHILD

The first half of the book covers biological substrate, sensory input, operations, and performance. Chapter One deals with the relations between genetics and behavior. The studies present evidence for the effect of environment on the intelligence of identical twins, the maturation of phylogenetic behavior patterns (walking, running, grasping), and the interaction of nature and nurture. Chapter Two considers questions of physical growth—the norms of early development, biological regulatory mechanisms that govern growth rate, the relation of body build to self-perception, and the effects of early or late maturity on one's self-concept. Chapter Three presents a survey of the infant's sensory capacities; it looks at the methods of measurement and the effects of visual, auditory, and olfactory stimuli. Chapter Four covers perceptual abilities of the older child with particular attention to depth perception, the development of shape and size constancy, whole-part perception, and recognition of briefly presented stimuli. Chapter Five outlines the basic facts of learning. In particular, it shows that newborns can be conditioned, that the child can learn to discriminate without seeing the same stimulus, that learning situations are problems to think about, and that correlation is a difficult notion for the young child. Chapter Six deals with thinking—the relation between thinking and visual imagery, acquisition of the notion that matter does not change under transformations in shape, and the results of concept learning in children. Chapter Seven considers emotions. It begins with a theoretical discussion of pain, anxiety, and distress, outlines children's fears, shows that isolation leads to emotional arousal, and ends with a discussion of curiosity, complexity, and cognitive change. Chapter Eight treats in more detail the human processes of choice and conflict. We note first that children have preferences for color or form; then we explore cheating, the effect of effort on preference, and the development of morality.

THE INTERACTING CHILD

The other readings cover infant-mother interactions and the child's relations with family, culture, and society. Chapter Nine covers prenatal influences, with particular attention to the effects of maternal anxiety, foetal reactivity, prematurity, and neonatal trauma on later development. Chapter Ten outlines the effects of early experience on later development. The chapter covers imprinting, early sensory stimulation, maternal love, and the effect of mothering on a child's later social behavior. Chapter Eleven looks at sensory-motor coordination, in particular the development of visually directed reaching and the results of inverting and distorting prisms. Chapter Twelve treats parent-child relations as they affect children's adjustment; the effects of differing childrearing practices on intellectual abilities and the childrearing practices of various social classes are presented. Chapter Thirteen asks how a child names things and how he learns syntax. Chapter Fourteen views the measurement of intelligence and creativity. Beginning with an historical note by Terman about the Binet test, the chapter includes longitudinal data on the predictability of IQ and ends with a theoretical analysis of the many factors of intellect. Chapter Fifteen covers social relations—the roles of anxiety and idea in children's play, the child's perception of others, and the effect of social climate on productivity and group satisfaction. Chapter Sixteen examines the child's personal development—identification is outlined, the results of therapy are reviewed, and the notion that dreams express desires is revealed.

The organization will enable an instructor to cover the individual child (for example, genetics, growth, motivation, association, thinking, sensation, and perception) and then his more complex interactions (for example, with his mother, family, culture, and society). Alternatively, the instructor may want to follow a chronological sequence. In this case, he can alternate between the individual and the interacting child—first, genetics and growth, then paranatal influences and early experience. After this the instructor would present sensation and perception followed by sensory-motor integration and parent-child relations. The next section could outline association and thinking and cover language and complex intellectual and creative processes; the following section could present motivation and emotion, and be followed by the social relations of the child and his personality development. This flexibility should appeal to a variety of teaching styles.

H. L. M.

San Diego, California
February 1971

CONTENTS

READINGS
IN CHILD
DEVELOPMENT

CHAPTER ONE
GENETICS

The study of relations between genetic endowment and environmental influences has had a long and stormy history. The "heredity-environment" controversy created a flurry of interest in the relative importance of genetic as opposed to environmental factors in the child's development. However, to determine *how much* each influences development is a difficult problem. The current question is *how* genetic endowment interacts with environmental conditions to form the individual.

Because of prejudices over the last 50 years, scientific opinion is skeptical of claims for genetic differences among groups. The first article discusses the effects of different educational opportunities on the intellectual development of several pairs of identical twins who were separated soon after birth and reared apart. R. S. Woodworth shows that ratings of the educational advantages of each twin correlate quite nicely with their subsequent intellectual development, suggesting that there is an environmental component to the development of intelligence. Once we know that environment can influence intellectual development, we can look for the causal mechanisms involved.

An experimental analysis of learning and maturation in identical twins is studied in the next selection. Gesell and Thompson show that by giving one identical twin experimental training while leaving the other to his usual experiences, we can compare the relative effects of training and maturation on the development of motor skills. The authors show that although one member of a pair of identical twins can be trained to perform stair climbing at a slightly earlier age than the other member, the untrained twin will catch up very quickly when he has matured. There was no permanent difference between the twins in ability to climb stairs.

In the final paper of this section, Anastasi considers the historical and logical problems involved in the study of heredity and environment. Her conclusion is that we cannot ask the question "How much?" Instead we should ask the question "How does it work?" She proposes a continuum of directness between the actions of heredity and environment and suggests several examples of direct and indirect actions for both components. Several lines of research that offer promising leads on the problem of how genetic factors and environmental influences interact are outlined in the last part of her paper.

1 Resemblances Between Identical Twins Reared Apart

R. S. WOODWORTH

Identical twins have exactly the same hereditary characteristics; any differences between identical twins must therefore be due to differing environmental influences. This paper investigates the effects of differences in educational and social opportunities upon the intellectual development of several pairs of identical twins who were reared apart from an early age. The study of these twins shows how individuals with the same genetic inheritance develop under differing environmental circumstances.

Nothing is more certain, after a little consideration, than the statement that heredity and environment are co-acting factors in the development of any living individual and that both are absolutely essential. If the individual's hereditary potencies could somehow be annulled he would immediately lose all physiological and mental characteristics and would remain simply a mass of dead matter. If he were somehow deprived of all environment, his heredity potencies would have no scope for their activity and, once more, he would cease to live. To ask whether heredity or environment is more important to life is like asking whether fuel or oxygen is more necessary for making a fire. But when we ask whether the *differences* between human individuals or groups are due to their differing heredity or to differences in their present and previous environments, we have a genuine question and one of great social importance. In a broad sense both heredity and environment must be concerned in causing individuals to be different in ability and personality, but it is a real question whether to attach more importance to

Adapted from *Heredity and environment*. New York: Social Science Research Council Bulletin #47, 1941.

the one or the other and whether to look to eugenics or euthenics for aid in maintaining and improving the quality of the population.

TWINS

Though the investigation of human heredity is beset with difficulties, due in part to the long interval between generations and in part to the lack of well-controlled matings such as are used by the geneticist in his experiments on plants and animals, enough is known to justify the carrying over of certain fundamental laws and concepts. We know that certain human traits are dominant, and certain others recessive. We know that certain traits are genetically simple, and many others complex. We know, too, that in any mixed population—and every human population is decidedly mixed in comparison with the "pure lines" of the geneticist—it is practically impossible for two matings of the same parents, even, to result in offspring having the same heredity. The chromosomes of the parents are combined differently in their several children. The same parents can

3

produce a considerable variety of children, though the variety is not so great as it is in the population as a whole.

But it sometimes happens that a pair of twins comes from a single fertilized ovum, that is, from a single ovum fertilized by a single spermatozoon. The embryo in this case, after starting life as a single individual, divides at a very early stage of development and gives rise to two individuals. Now as all daughter cells derived from the same fertilized ovum have exactly the same assortment of genes, the two (or sometimes more) individuals derived from the same fertilized ovum are exactly alike in genic constitution. They are truly identical as far as heredity is concerned. They are often indistinguishable in appearance. They are necessarily of the same sex. These "identical" or monozygotic twins thus afford perfect material for the study of the differentiating effects of environment. Since they are genetically identical any difference which develops between them must be due to some sort of environmental factor.

The remaining twins, called fraternal or dizygotic, are derived from two different eggs or ova, fertilized by two different spermatozoa. Genetically they are no more alike than other siblings. Being conceived and born at the same times does not make them any more alike in heredity. But their environment, both prenatal and postnatal, must on the whole be more alike than that of other siblings.

IDENTICAL TWINS REARED APART

The first pair of separated identicals to be tested and carefully studied was that reported by H. J. Muller (1925). The principal series of such pairs was gathered with much labor over a period of years by the Chicago group, Newman, Freeman and Holzinger, and reported in their book on *Twins* (1937). They discovered, measured, and tested 19 pairs of identicals who had been separated in infancy or early childhood and reared in different families and communities. Another

pair has been added by Gardner and Newman (1940). And a British pair, reared apart up to the age of nearly ten years, has been studied by Saudek (1934). Diagnosis of monozygosity was carefully made in all these cases.

Table I presents certain data for each of the separated identicals. With regard to prenatal and natal environment, the case histories of the pairs numbered 1 and 8 suggest the possibility that the twin with lower IQ in each of these pairs got a poor start and perhaps suffered a slight but permanent handicap.

For the most part the environment in which the twins of the same pair were brought up did not differ extremely—not more than would be true of children brought up in the same community. In a few instances the difference was rather large. The greatest difference in education occurred in the case of two girls, one of whom was reared in a good farming region and who went through college and became a school teacher, while her twin grew up largely in the backwoods and had only two years of regular schooling. This girl however obtained employment later in a large city and became a general assistant in a small printing office where she performed a variety of duties including typesetting and proofreading. On being tested her IQ came out at 92, while that of her college-educated twin sister was 116. This difference of 24 points in IQ was the largest found in any case.

Another pair of young women had been separated in infancy and one had been reared on a good farm and had gone to school only for the eight grades, while the other had lived in a small town, gone through high school, studied music, and engaged in clerical work. The town girl's IQ as determined by the test was 106 while the farm girl made only 89. In spite of this large difference in the tests the country girl gave the impression of being fully as intelligent, or competent, as her twin sister.

A pair of young men from Tennessee had been brought up, the one in a small town where he went through high school

TABLE 1   Some Data from Identical Twins Reared Apart (Newman, Freeman, and Holzinger; Muller; Gardener and Newman; Saudek)[a]

| Case Number | Sex | Age at Separation | Age at Testing | Environmental Differences | | | IQ Difference |
				in Years of Schooling	in Estimated Educational Advantages	in Estimated Social Advantages	
11	f	18 mos.	35	14	37	25	24
2	f	18 mos.	27	10	32	14	12
18	m	1 yr.	27	4	28	31	19
4	f	5 mos.	29	4	22	15	17
12	f	18 mos.	29	5	19	13	7
1	f	18 mos.	19	1	15	27	12
17	m	2 yrs.	14	0	15	15	10
8	f	3 mos.	15	1	14	32	15
3	m	2 mos.	23	1	12	15	− 2
14	f	6 mos.	39	0	12	15	− 1
5	f	14 mos.	38	1	11	26	4
13	m	1 mo.	19	0	11	13	1
10	f	1 yr.	12	1	10	15	5
15	m	1 yr.	26	2	9	7	1
7	m	1 mo.	13	0	9	27	− 1
19	f	6 yrs.	41	0	9	14	− 9
16	f	2 yrs.	11	0	8	12	2
6	f	3 yrs.	59	0	7	10	8
9	m	1 mo.	19	0	7	14	6
Muller	f	1 mo.	30	9	?	?	− 1
Gardner and Newman	f	1 mo.	19	0	2	?	− 3
Saudek	m	1 mo.	20	0	?	?	± 4

[a] The estimated differences in educational and social advantages are in "points" with a maximum possible of 50. From the case material, each of five judges rated the environmental differences between every pair of twins on a scale of 10 points, and the figure given in the table is the sum of these five ratings. A minus sign before an IQ difference means that the twin who received the higher rating for educational advantages obtained the lower IQ.

and engaged in business, the other back in the mountains with irregular schooling amounting to eight grades at the most. Tested at the age of twenty-five, the mountain boy obtained an IQ of 77, the town boy of 96.

When the IQ differences are averaged with account taken of sign, the twin having the advantage in educational opportunities usually surpasses the other. On the average the IQ was 6.0 points higher for the better educated twin. This difference is statistically reliable, being over three times its standard error. It seems safe to conclude that when one of a pair of identicals has been afforded better educational advantages than the other, the better educated one will on the whole do better in the intelligence tests.

However, there were only six pairs differing very much in the amount of formal schooling received. These six show an average difference of 13 points in IQ. The remaining pairs show only a small and unreliable IQ superiority for the better educated twin (3 points on the average, and only 1 point when the two cases of possible prenatal handicap are omitted). It appears, then, that rather a large educational advantage is required to give any dependable superiority in tested intelligence.

Years of schooling are of course not an adequate measure of educational advantages. Newman (1937) and his colleagues endeavored to do a little better by going over the case histories of their 19 pairs and estimating the educational difference between the twins by aid of a rating scale. The ratings are given in our table. There is a correlation of +.79 between the estimated educational difference and the obtained difference in IQ. This substantial correlation depends largely but not wholly upon the few pairs whose education was very unequal.

CONCLUSIONS FROM THE TWIN STUDIES

If we consider the results on the intelligence of identical twins reared apart, two conclusions seem probable even though the sample is still far too small to make either conclusion sure. In the first place, radical differences in education can create substantial differences in intelligence, so far as intelligence is measured by our tests. Differences in IQ as great as the standard deviation of the population have been found in several instances, corresponding to large differences in educational advantages. We can conclude that the educational environment, taken in a broad sense, has a marked effect on such intelligence as we are now able to measure.

In the second place, however, the differences between identical twins reared apart are remarkably small except in those cases where the contrast of educational advantages was very great. For the majority of the separated identicals the IQ difference was no greater than for identicals reared together. When individuals of identical heredity are subjected to environments differing about as much as those of the children in an ordinary community, such identical twins differ much less than the children of such a community. Therefore the differences found among the children of an ordinary community are not accounted for, except in small measure, by differences in homes and schooling. To repeat—if the differences in intelligence found among the children of a community were mostly due to differences in home and school environment, these differences would remain almost in full force even if the heredity of all the children were made identical. But when a trial is made of this hypothesis by placing identical twins in different families not too different in environment, the twins show only a small fraction of the difference found in the community at large.

These two statements—(1) that differences in environment can produce substantial differences in intelligence, and (2) that the differences actually present in a community are *not* due mostly to differences in environment—may appear mutually contradictory. That they are not contradictory has been emphatically pointed out by several students of the nature-nurture problem.

REFERENCES

Gardner, I. C., & Newman, H. H. Mental and physical traits of identical twins reared apart, case XX. *Journal of Heredity,* 1940, **31,** 119–126.

Muller, H. J. Mental traits and heredity. *Journal of Heredity,* 1925, **16,** 433–448.

Newman, H. H., Freeman, F. N., & Holzinger, K. J. *Twins: A study of heredity and environment,* p. 369. Chicago: University of Chicago Press, 1937.

Saudek, R. A British pair of identical twins reared apart. *Character & Personality,* 1934, **3,** 17–39.

2 Learning and Maturation in Identical Twins: An Experimental Analysis by the Method of Co-Twin Control

ARNOLD GESELL
HELEN THOMPSON

Investigators have long been interested in the effects of experience on the development of relatively simple motor behavior. This study outlines a method of study (co-twin control) and illustrates how the method may be used in the study of stair climbing. One twin was given extensive training in stair climbing at an early age while the other twin was not allowed to explore stairs until relatively late in her development. The difficulty of early training and the relative ease with which the later control twin learned to climb stairs suggests a strong genetic component for this activity.

Our own studies of twins have a point of departure similar to that of Galton's paper. We used a pair of twins to explore experimentally the interrelations of learning and growth. These interrelations lie at the basis of the so-called "nature-nurture" problem. For some time we had been interested in the remarkable correspondences both physical and mental exhibited by identical twins. These correspondences were highly interesting in themselves; but what did they signify? What was the origin of the identities and disparities of similar twins?

The biologist would prefer to call such twins "monozygotic" or "one-egg" twins, because it is possible even for twins derived from a single egg cell to be extremely non-identical. Twinning is a process of bilateral doubling. In some measure this process is also manifested in the genesis of the single

Adapted from Learning and maturation in identical infant twins: An experimental analysis by the method of co-twin control. *Genetic Psychology Monographs*, 1929, **6**, 5–124.

individual derived from a single zygote, producing his paired organs and the right and left halves of his unpaired organs. He, the singleton, is a product of developmental duplicity. In the case of true, complete monozygotic twins, this process of duplication is carried to such a degree that two offspring result from the single ovum. A perfectly symmetrical bilateral individual, on the one hand, and a perfect pair of duplicated individuals, on the other, represent the ideal extremes of the process of twinning. Between these extremes there are many gradations and deviations, some of them benign, others monstrous, in character. With abnormal conditions even a monozygotic twin may lack all semblance to a co-twin.

It happened that the mother of a pair of fair-haired Italian twins had died when they were a month old. This necessitated the removal of the twins to a child-caring institution. This made it possible to keep them under systematic observation. The twins were virtually indistinguishable in physical appearance. By ordinary observation they were also extremely alike in their patterns and modes of activity. Once more we were intrigued by the phenomena of similarity.

We made repeated physical and mental measurements at six, eight, sixteen, twenty-four, twenty-eight, thirty-two, thirty-six, thirty-eight, forty, forty-two, and forty-four weeks of age. We were so engrossed with the study of similarities that we almost overlooked the potential significance of twins as methodology.

But when the twins were about nine months of age we said to ourselves, "Why not capitalize these remarkable similarities and utilize them for making an experimental analysis of the developmental processes which are producing such impressive correspondences?" We shifted our angle of approach and outlined a method of comparison which we later designated "the method of co-twin control."

The twins were rebaptized alphabetically. Almost at random we selected one twin for differential training in specific functions—Twin T (T = trained twin). The co-twin was reserved as a comparative control. She was not trained or stimulated in the specific functions. We called her Twin C.

By extraordinary good fortune we have been able to maintain investigatory contact with these twins over a period of 14 years. Throughout this period numerous comparisons were made, Twin C being consistently reserved as a standard for comparison. We sought light on the origin and fate of individual differences which we experimentally produced through the device of limiting certain types of specific training to one twin, Twin T.

THE METHOD OF CO-TWIN CONTROL

A brief statement of the nature and philosophy of the method of co-twin control is in order at this point. In essence the method consists in using the complexities of one individual to elucidate the complexities of another under highly controlled conditions; i.e., differential training in some specific function is confined to one of a pair of identical twins whose behavior before training is highly similar. By comparing the twins at the end of such a training period, we can determine how effective the imposed training has been in modifying what would have been the natural behavior of the twin. We are able, in effect, to compare the individual with himself as we would have been if not trained.

A control co-twin has had a highly equivalent prenatal and postnatal life career, except for divergences which are experimentally created and recorded or naturalistically observed. When one contemplates the almost infinite number of variables which enter into the shaping of any life career, it must be granted that an "identical" co-twin who brings these variables into finite and manageable range is indeed an extraordinarily powerful statistic in his own integral person. His individuality is unique but by definition it is almost a replica of the individuality which is being assayed.

The method of co-twin control requires that a basic parity and identity should be established by careful measurements *prior* to the period of comparative observation and experiment.

This methodological requirement was amply fulfilled in the case of T and C. Daily determinations of weight and temperatures and frequent measurements of height and body diameters, periodic observations of dentition, and records of the skin patterns yielded evidence of a remarkably stable developmental correspondence with respect to physical characteristics.

At the age of forty-six weeks they had arrived at virtually the same level of maturity with respect to both mental and physical characteristics. At this age both twins were at the threshold of climbing ability. This was a particularly favorable juncture for initiating a training program designed to make Twin T an expert in stair climbing. There were no staircases in the institution for C to climb.

Therefore she was for the time being denied all specific experience in stair climbing. This experimental differential gave *T* a double advantage, particularly since she was from the beginning very slightly accelerated in her general motor development.

THE STAIR-CLIMBING EXPERIMENT

The training period The purpose of the experiment was to investigate the effects of daily training upon the locomotor behavior of *T*, measuring these effects by comparison with the untrained co-twin, *C*, who was used as a control. Every morning for 6 days a week over a 6-week period, beginning when she was forty-six weeks old, *T* was given definite stimulation and guidance in the following locomotor activities: (*a*) stair climbing on the four-tread staircase leading to the crib; (*b*) creeping for an interesting object placed at a near enticing distance; (*c*) pulling herself to a standing position; (*d*) walking by holding on a chair or crib; (*e*) walking by holding experimenter's hand. Of all these activities, stair climbing was under the most complete training control. Accordingly, after the first 3 days, an attempt was made to entice *T* to climb the stairs as many times as possible, the experimenter using her judgment as to when it would be unwise to press the stair-climbing feat. Each training period lasted for 10 min.

Comparisons of the behavior of the twins were made at various stages of the primary experimental period. At the end of this period, at the age of fifty-two weeks, the results proved so interesting that it was decided to widen the range of comparison by subjecting the control twin, *C*, to a brief course of training in stair climbing. This course began when Twin *C* was fifty-three weeks old, continued 6 days a week for 2 weeks, each session being 10 min. long.

The purpose of this special training period was to check the results of the previous experiment by determining the trainability of Twin *C* at a more advanced age than Twin *T*.

Comparative results At forty-six weeks, just before the training period began, the twins behaved as follows when placed before the experimental staircase. Each twin lifted one foot, but neither went further in an effort to climb. On the floor they crept with equal facility. Each walked if held by both hands. Each pulled herself to standing position. There was no apparent difference between the twins in locomotor performance.

It will be noted that in the early stages of the training period, *T* mounted the stairs only three or four times during the 10-min. session, with fluctuations which could be clinically explained. Well-defined enjoyment in climbing came into prominence in the fourth week. The number of successful scalings per session increased, until it reached the maximum of 10 on the twenty-fifth session during the fifth week. This record may be taken as representing the peak of her performance, regarded from the point of view of spontaneity and of speed. All told, she had, at this particular session, scaled the stairs 115 times. At the end of the 6-week period the total number of successful scalings increased to 156.

Turning now to the record of Twin *C*, it will be noted that she scaled the stairs seven times at the very first session, *even though she had not been trained at all*. Her maximum record of 10 successful scalings was reached in 1½ weeks, at the ninth session. It took her from 10 to 18 sec. to make each successful mounting of the stairs. This speed is approximately equal to that of Twin *T*, who did not, however, attain that score until 5 weeks of training had elapsed.

Perhaps the most striking event which happened during the course of this investigation was the successful climbing of the stairs by Twin *C* at the age of fifty-three weeks, without previous specific training and without any environmental opportunity to exercise the function of climbing. When the stair-climbing behavior of the twins is compared for their 56-week performance, (after *T* was trained for 6 weeks, *C* for 2 weeks), it appears that on a first trial *T* climbs the flight of stairs in 11.3 sec., C in 14.8 sec.; but that on a second trial T climbed in 13.8 sec. and C in 13.9 sec., an almost identical performance.

Most significant is the simple fact that Twin C, when her time was ripe, climbed the stairs altogether without tuition. Of similar significance is the fact the Twin T's response to early training was indifferent and impassive. Not until the fiftieth week did she seem in full possession of a climbing proclivity. It should also be noted that the early form of the behavior pattern for climbing was somewhat distinctive for Twin T because it was grafted on creeping rather than on walking. Her climbing was a creeping upward rather than an ordinary mounting. This observation suggests that the form as well as the incidence of behavior pattern is governed by existing neural counterparts, determined by maturational factors.

3 | Heredity, Environment, and the Question "How?"

ANNE ANASTASI

The heredity-environment question is still very much alive, but we have replaced the question "Which is more important?" with the question "How do they interact?" Both hereditary influences and environmental factors vary along a continuum of directness in their effects. More indirect connections between these factors and behavior produce a wider range of variation.

Several current lines of research offer promising techniques for exploring the interaction between heredity and environment. Among these approaches are studies of (1) hereditary conditions that underlie behavioral differences between selectively bred groups of animals; (2) relations between physiological variables and individual differences in behavior, especially in the case of pathological deviation; (3) the role of prenatal physiological factors in behavior development; (4) the influence of early experience upon eventual behavioral characteristics; (5) cultural differences in childrearing practices in relation to intellectual and emotional development; (6) mechanisms of somatopsychological relationships; and (7) the psychological development of twins from infancy to maturity, together with observations of their social environment. These approaches vary in subjects used, psychological functions studied, and experimental procedures followed. But this variety of methods is demanded by the diversity of ways heredity and environment can interact in development.

Two or three decades ago, the so-called heredity-environment question was the center of lively controversy. Today, on the other hand, many psychologists look upon it as a dead issue. It is now generally conceded that both hereditary and environmental factors enter into all behavior. The reacting organism is a product of its genes and its past environment, while present environment provides the immediate stimulus for current behavior. To be sure, it can be argued that, although a given trait may result from the combined influence of hereditary and envi-

ronmental factors, a specific difference in this trait between individuals or between groups may be traceable to either hereditary or environmental factors alone. The design of most traditional investigations undertaken to identify such factors, however, has been such as to yield inconclusive answers. The same set of data has frequently led to opposite conclusions in the hands of psychologists with different orientations.

Nor have efforts to determine the proportional contribution of hereditary and environmental factors to observed individual differences in given traits met with any greater success. Apart from difficulties in controlling conditions, such investigations have usually been based upon the implicit assumption that hereditary and environmental factors combine in an additive fashion. Both geneticists and psychologists have repeatedly demonstrated, however, that a more tenable hypothesis is that of interaction. In other words, the nature and extent of the influence of each type of factor depend upon the contribution of the other. Thus the proportional contribution of heredity to the variance of a given trait, rather than being a constant, will vary under different environmental conditions. Similarly, under different hereditary conditions, the relative contribution of environment will differ. Studies designed to estimate the proportional contribution of heredity and environment, however, have rarely included measures of such interaction. The only possible conclusion from such research would thus seem to be that both heredity and environment contribute to all behavior traits and that the extent of their respective contributions cannot be specified for any trait. Small wonder that some psychologists regard the heredity-environment question as unworthy of further consideration!

But is this really all we can find out about the operation of heredity and environment in the etiology of behavior? Perhaps we have simply been asking the wrong questions. The traditional questions about heredity and environment may be intrinsically unanswerable. Psychologists began by asking *which* type of factor, hereditary or environmental, is responsible for individual differences in a given trait. Later, they tried to discover *how much* of the variance was attributable to heredity and how much to environment. It is the primary contention of this paper that a more fruitful approach is to be found in the question *"How?"* There is still much to be learned about the specific modus operandi of hereditary and environmental factors in the development of behavioral differences. And there are several current lines of research which offer promising techniques for answering the question "How?"

VARIETY OF INTERACTION MECHANISMS

Hereditary factors

If we examine some of the specific ways in which hereditary factors may influence behavior, we cannot fail but be impressed by their wide diversity. At one extreme, we find such conditions as phenylpyruvic amentia and amaurotic idiocy. In these cases, certain essential physical prerequisites for normal intellectual development are lacking as a result of hereditary metabolic disorders. The individual will be mentally defective, regardless of the type of environmental conditions under which he is reared.

A somewhat different situation is illustrated by hereditary deafness, which may lead to intellectual retardation through interference with normal social interaction, language development, and schooling. In such a case, however, the hereditary handicap can be offset by appropriate adaptations of training procedures. It has been said, in fact, that the degree of intellectual backwardness of the deaf is an index of the state of development of special instructional facilities. As the latter improve, the intellectual retardation associated with deafness is correspondingly reduced.

A third example is provided by inherited susceptibility to certain physical diseases, with consequent protracted ill health. If environmental conditions are such that illness does in fact develop, a number of different behavioral effects may follow. Intellectually, the individual may be handicapped by his inability to attend school regularly. On the other hand, depending upon age of onset, home conditions, parental status, and similar factors, poor health may have the effect of concentrating the individual's energies upon intellectual pursuits. The curtailment of participation in athletics and social functions may serve to strengthen interest in reading and other sedentary activities. Concomitant circumstances would also determine the influence of such illness upon personality development. And it is well known that the latter effects could run the gamut from a deepening of human sympathy to psychiatric breakdown.

Finally, heredity may influence behavior through the mechanism of social stereotypes. A wide variety of inherited physical characteristics have served as visible cues for identifying such stereotypes. These cues thus lead to behavioral restrictions or opportunities and—at a more subtle level— to social attitudes and expectancies. All of these influences eventually leave their mark upon his abilities and inabilities, his emotional reactions, goals, ambitions, and outlook on life.

Realistic examples are not hard to find. The most familiar instances occur in connection with constitutional types, sex, and race. Sex and skin pigmentation obviously depend upon heredity. General body build is strongly influenced by hereditary components, although also susceptible to environmental modification. That all these physical characteristics may exert a pronounced effect upon behavior within a given culture is well known. It is equally apparent, of course, that in different cultures the behavioral correlates of such hereditary physical traits may be quite unlike. A specific physical cue may be completely unrelated to individual differences in psychological traits in one culture, while closely correlated with them in another. Or it may be associated with totally dissimilar behavior characteristics in two different cultures.

It might be objected that some of the illustrations which have been cited do not properly exemplify the operation of hereditary mechanisms in behavior development since hereditary factors enter only indirectly into the behavior in question. Closer examination, however, shows this distinction to be untenable. First it may be noted that the influence of heredity upon behavior is always indirect. No psychological trait is ever inherited as such. All we can ever say directly from behavioral observations is that a given trait shows evidence of being influenced by certain "inheritable unknowns." This merely defines a problem for genetic research; it does not provide a causal explanation. Unlike the blood groups, which are close to the level of primary gene products, psychological traits are related to genes by highly indirect and devious routes. Even the mental deficiency associated with phenylketonuria is several steps removed from the chemically defective genes that represent its hereditary basis. Moreover, hereditary influences cannot be dichotomized into the more direct and the less direct. Rather do they represent a whole "continuum of indirectness," along which are found all degrees of remoteness of causal links. The examples already cited illustrate a few of the points on this continuum.

It should be noted that as we proceed along the continuum of indirectness, the range of variation of possible outcomes of hereditary factors expands rapidly. At each step in the causal chain, there is fresh opportunity for interaction with other hereditary factors as well as with environmental factors. And since each interaction in turn determines the direction of subsequent interactions, there is an ever-widening network of possible outcomes. If we visualize a simple sequential grid with only two alternatives at each point, it is obvious that there are two possible outcomes in the one-stage situation, four outcomes at the second stage, eight at the third, and so on in geometric progression. The actual situation is undoubtedly much more complex, since there will usually be more than two alternatives at any one point.

A large portion of the continuum of hereditary influences which we have described coincides with the domain of somatopsychological relations, as defined by Barker et al. Under this heading, Barker includes "variations in physique that affect the psychological situation of a person by influencing the effectiveness of his body as a tool for actions or by serving as a stimulus to himself or others" (1953, p. 1). Relatively direct neurological influences on behavior, which have been the traditional concern of physiological psychology, are excluded from this definition, Barker being primarily concerned with what he calls the "social psychology of physique." Of the examples cited in the present paper, deafness, severe illness, and the physical characteristics associated with social stereotypes would meet the specifications of somatopsychological factors.

The somatic factors to which Barker refers, however, are not limited to those of hereditary origin. Bodily conditions attributable to environmental causes operate in the same sorts of somatopsychological relations as those traceable to heredity. In fact, heredity-environment distinctions play a minor part in Barker's approach.

Environmental factors

Organic Turning now to an analysis of the role of environmental factors in behavior, we find the same etiological mechanisms which were observed in the case of hereditary factors. First, however, we must differentiate between two classes of environmental influences: (a) those producing organic effects which may in turn influence behavior and (b) those serving as direct stimuli for psychological reactions. The former may be illustrated by food intake or by exposure to bacterial infection; the latter, by tribal initiation ceremonies or by a course in algebra.

Like hereditary factors, environmental influences of an organic nature can also be ordered along a continuum of indirectness with regard to their relation to behavior. This continuum closely parallels that of hereditary factors. One end is typified by such conditions as mental deficiency resulting from cerebral birth injury or from prenatal nutritional inadequacies. A more indirect etiological mechanism is illustrated by severe motor disorder—as in certain cases of cerebral palsy—*without* accompanying injury to higher neurological centers. In such instances, intellectual retardation may

occur as an indirect result of the motor handicap, through the curtailment of educational and social activities. Obviously this causal mechanism corresponds closely to that of hereditary deafness cited earlier in the paper.

Finally, we may consider an environmental parallel to the previously discussed social stereotypes which were mediated by hereditary physical cues. Let us suppose that a young woman with mousy brown hair becomes transformed into a dazzling golden blonde through environmental techniques currently available in our culture. It is highly probable that this metamorphosis will alter, not only the reactions of her associates toward her, but also her own self-concept and subsequent behavior. The effects could range all the way from a rise in social poise to a drop in clerical accuracy!

Among the examples of environmentally determined organic influences which have been described, all but the first two fit Barker's definition of somatopsychological factors. With the exception of birth injuries and nutritional deficiencies, all fall within the social psychology of physique. Nevertheless, the individual factors exhibit wide diversity in their specific modus operandi —a diversity which has important practical as well as theoretical implications.

Behavioral The second major class of environmental factors—the behavioral as contrasted to the organic—are by definition direct influences. The immediate effect of such environmental factors is always a behavioral change. To be sure, some of the initial behavioral effects may themselves indirectly affect the individual's later behavior. But this relationship can perhaps be best conceptualized in terms of breadth and permanence of effects. Thus it could be said that we are now dealing, not with a continuum of indirectness, as in the case of hereditary and organic-environmental factors, but rather with a continuum of breadth.

Social class membership may serve as

an illustration of a relatively broad, pervasive, and enduring environmental factor. Its influence upon behavior development may operate through many channels. Thus social level may determine the range and nature of intellectual stimulation provided by home and community through books, music, art, play activities, and the like. Even more far-reaching may be the effects upon interests and motivation, as illustrated by the desire to perform abstract intellectual tasks, to surpass others in competitive situations, to succeed in school, or to gain social approval. Emotional and social traits may likewise be influenced by the nature of interpersonal relations characterizing homes at different socioeconomic levels. Somewhat more restricted in scope than social class, although still exerting a relatively broad influence, is amount of formal schooling which the individual is able to obtain.

METHODOLOGICAL APPROACHES

The examples considered so far should suffice to highlight the wide variety of ways in which hereditary and environmental factors may interact in the course of behavior development. There is clearly a need for identifying explicitly the etiological mechanism whereby any given hereditary or environmental condition ultimately leads to a behavioral characteristic—in other words, the "how" of heredity and environment. Accordingly, we may now take a quick look at some promising methodological approaches to the question "how."

Within the past decade, an increasing number of studies have been designed to trace the connection between specific factors in the hereditary backgrounds or in the reactional biographies of individuals and their observed behavioral characteristics. There has been a definite shift away from the predominantly descriptive and correlational approach of the earlier decades toward more deliberate attempts to verify explanatory hypotheses. Similarly,

the cataloguing of group differences in psychological traits has been giving way gradually to research on *changes* in group characteristics following altered conditions.

Among recent methodological developments, we have chosen seven as being particularly relevant to the analysis of etiological mechanisms. The first represents an extension of selective breeding investigations to permit the identification of specific hereditary conditions underlying the observed behavioral differences. When early selective breeding investigations such as those of Tryon (1940) on rats indicated that "maze learning ability" was inherited, we were still a long way from knowing what was actually being transmitted by the genes. It was obviously not "maze learning ability" as such. Twenty—or even ten—years ago, some psychologists would have suggested that it was probably general intelligence. And a few might even have drawn a parallel with the inheritance of human intelligence.

But today investigators have been asking: Just what makes one group of rats learn mazes more quickly than the other? Is it differences in motivation, emotionality, speed of running, general activity level? If so, are these behavioral characteristics in turn dependent upon group differences in glandular development, body weight, brain size, biochemical factors, or some other organic conditions? A number of recent and ongoing investigations indicate that attempts are being made to trace, at least part of the way, the steps whereby certain chemical properties of the genes may ultimately lead to specified behavior characteristics.

An example of such a study is provided by Searle's (1949) follow-up of Tryon's research. Working with the strains of maze-bright and maze-dull rats developed by Tryon, Searle demonstrated that the two strains differed in a number of emotional and motivational factors, rather than in ability. Thus the strain differences were traced one step further, although many links still remain to be found between maze learning and genes. A promising method-ological development within the same general area is to be found in the recent research of Hirsch and Tryon (1956). Utiliz-ing a specially devised technique for mea-suring individual differences in behavior among lower organisms, these investigators launched a series of studies on selective breeding for behavioral characteristics in the fruit fly, *Drosophilia*. Such research can capitalize on the mass of available genetic knowledge regarding the morphology of *Drosophilia,* as well as on other advan-tages of using such an organism in genetic studies.

Further evidence of current interest in the specific hereditary factors which in-fluence behavior is to be found in an ex-tensive research program in progress at the Jackson Memorial Laboratory, under the direction of Scott and Fuller (1951). In gen-eral, the project is concerned with the be-havioral characteristics of various breeds and cross-breeds of dogs. Analyses of some of the data gathered to date again suggest that "differences in performance are pro-duced by differences in emotional, moti-vational, and peripheral processes, and that genetically caused differences in central processes may be either slight or non-existent" (Scott & Charles, 1953, p. 225). In other parts of the same project, breed dif-ferences in physiological characteristics, which may in turn be related to behavioral differences, have been established.

A second line of attack is the explora-tion of possible relationships between be-havioral characteristics and physiological variables which may in turn be traceable to hereditary factors. Research on EEG, autonomic balance, metabolic processes, and biochemical factors illustrates this ap-proach. A lucid demonstration of the proc-ess of tracing a psychological condition to genetic factors is provided by the identi-fication and subsequent investigation of phenylpyruvic amentia. In this case, the causal chain from defective gene, through metabolic disorder and consequent cere-bral malfunctioning, to feeblemindedness and other overt symptoms can be de-scribed step by step. Also relevant are the recent researches on neurological and bio-chemical correlates of schizophrenia. Ow-ing to inadequate methodological controls, however, most of the findings of the latter studies must be regarded as tentative.

Prenatal environmental factors provide a third avenue of fruitful investigation. Especially noteworthy is the recent work of Pasamanick and his associates (1956), which demonstrated a tie-up between socioeconomic level, complications of pregnancy and parturition, and psycho-logical disorders of the offspring. In a series of studies on large samples of whites and Negroes in Baltimore, these investigators showed that various prenatal and paranatal disorders are significantly related to the oc-currence of mental defect and psychiatric disorders in the child. An important source of such irregularities in the process of childbearing and birth is to be found in de-ficiencies of maternal diet and in other conditions associated with low socio-economic status. An analysis of the data did in fact reveal a much higher frequency of all such medical complications in lower than in higher socioeconomic levels, and a high-er frequency among Negroes than among whites.

Direct evidence of the influence of prenatal nutritional factors upon subse-quent intellectual development is to be found in a recent, well controlled experi-ment by Harrell et al. (1955). The subjects were pregnant women in low-income groups whose normal diets were generally quite deficient. A dietary supplement was administered to some of these women dur-ing pregnancy and lactation, while an equated control group received placebos. When tested at the ages of three and four years, the offspring of the experimental group obtained a significantly higher mean IQ than did the offspring of the controls.

Mention should also be made of ani-mal experiments on the effects of such factors as prenatal radiation and neonatal asphyxia upon cerebral anomalies as well as upon subsequent behavior development. These experimental studies merge imperceptibly into the fourth approach to be considered, namely, the investigation of the influence of early experience upon the eventual behavioral characteristics of animals. Research in this area has been accumulating at a rapid rate. In 1954, Beach and Jaynes surveyed this literature for the *Psychological Bulletin,* listing over 130 references. The variety of factors covered ranges from the type and quantity of available food to the extent of contact with human culture. A large number of experiments have been concerned with various forms of sensory deprivation and with diminished opportunities for motor exercise. Effects have been observed in many kinds of animals and in almost all aspects of behavior, including perceptual responses, motor activity, learning, emotionality, and social reactions.

In their review, Beach and Jaynes pointed out that research in this area has been stimulated by at least four distinct theoretical interests. Some studies were motivated by the traditional concern with the relative contribution of maturation and learning to behavior development. Others were designed in an effort to test certain psychoanalytic theories regarding infantile experiences, as illustrated by studies which limited the feeding responses of young animals. A third relevant influence is to be found in the work of the European biologist Lorenz (1952) on early social stimulation of birds, and in particular on the special type of learning for which the term "imprinting" has been coined. A relatively large number of recent studies have centered around Hebb's (1949) theory regarding the importance of early perceptual experiences upon subsequent performance in learning situations. All this research represents a rapidly growing and promising attack on the modus operandi of specific environmental factors.

The human counterpart of these animal studies may be found in the comparative investigation of child-rearing practices in different cultures and subcultures. This represents the fifth approach in our list. An outstanding example of such a study is that by Whiting and Child (1953). Utilizing data on 75 primitive societies from the Cross-Cultural Files of the Yale Institute of Human Relations, these investigators set out to test a number of hypotheses regarding the relationships between child-rearing practices and personality development. This analysis was followed up by field observations in five cultures, the results of which have not yet been reported.

Within our own culture, similar surveys have been concerned with the diverse psychological environments provided by different social classes. Of particular interest are the study by Williams and Scott (1953) on the association between socioeconomic level, permissiveness, and motor development among Negro children, and the exploratory research by Milner (1951) on the relationship between reading readiness in first-grade children and patterns of parent-child interaction. Milner found that upon school entrance the lower-class child seems to lack chiefly two advantages enjoyed by the middle-class child. The first is described as "a warm positive family atmosphere or adult-relationship pattern which is more and more being recognized as a motivational prerequisite of any kind of adult-controlled learning." The lower-class children in Milner's study perceived adults as predominantly hostile. The second advantage is an extensive opportunity to interact verbally with adults in the family. The latter point is illustrated by parental attitudes toward mealtime conversation, lower-class parents tending to inhibit and discourage such conversation, while middle-class parents encourage it.

Most traditional studies on child-rearing practices have been designed in terms of a psychoanalytic orientation. There is need for more data pertaining to other types of hypotheses. Findings such as those of Milner on opportunities for verbalization and the resulting effects upon reading readiness represent a step in this direction.

Another possible source of future data is the application of the intensive observational techniques of psychological ecology developed by Barker and Wright (1953) to widely diverse socioeconomic groups.

A sixth major approach involves research on the previously cited somatopsychological relationships (Barker & Wright, 1953). To date, little direct information is available on the precise operation of this class of factors in psychological development. The multiplicity of ways in which physical traits—whether hereditary or environmental in origin—may influence behavior thus offers a relatively unexplored field for future study.

The seventh and final approach to be considered represents an adaptation of traditional twin studies. From the standpoint of the question "How?" there is need for closer coordination between the usual data on twin resemblance and observations of the family interactions of twins. Available data already suggests, for example, that closeness of contact and extent of environmental similarity are greater in the case of monozygotic than in the case of dizygotic twins. Information on the social reactions of twins toward each other and the specialization of roles is likewise of interest. Especially useful would be longitudinal studies of twins, beginning in early infancy and following the subjects through school age. The operation of differential environmental pressures, the development of specialized roles, and other environmental influences could thus be more clearly identified and correlated with intellectual and personality changes in the growing twins.

Parenthetically, I should like to add a remark about the traditional applications of the twin method, in which persons in different degrees of hereditary and environmental relationships to each other are simply compared for behavioral similarity. In these studies, attention has been focused principally upon the amount of resemblance of monozygotic as contrasted to dizygotic twins. Yet such a comparison is particularly difficult to interpret because of the many subtle differences in the environmental situations of the two types of twins. A more fruitful comparison would seem to be that between dizygotic twins and siblings, for whom the hereditary similarity is known to be the same.

In Kallmann's (1953) monumental research on psychiatric disorders among twins, for example, one of the most convincing bits of evidence for the operation of hereditary factors in schizophrenia is the fact that the degrees of concordance for dizygotic twins and for siblings were practically identical. In contrast, it will be recalled that in intelligence test scores dizygotic twins resemble each other much more closely than do siblings—a finding which reveals the influence of environmental factors in intellectual development,

REFERENCES

Barker, R. G., Wright, Beatrice A., Myerson, L., & Conick, Mollie R. Adjustment to physical handicap and illness: A survey of the social psychology of physique and disability. *Social Science Research Counsel Bulletin*, 1953, No. 55 (rev.).

Beach, F. A., & Jaynes, J. Effects of early experience upon the behavior of animals. *Psychological Bulletin*, 1954, **51,** 239–263,

Harrell, Ruth F., Woodyard, Ella, & Gates, A. I. *The effect of mothers' diets on the intelligence of the offspring.* New York: Teachers College of Columbia University, 1955.

Hebb, D. O. *The organization of behavior.* New York: Wiley, 1949.

Hirsch, J., & Tryon, R. C. Mass screening and reliable individual measurement in the experimental behavior genetics of lower organisms. *Psychological Bulletin*, 1956, **124,** 429–430.

Kallman, F. J. *Heredity in health and mental disorder; principles of psychiatric genetics in the light of comparative twin studies.* New York: Norton, 1953.

Lorenz, K. *King Solomon's Ring*. London: Methuen, 1952.

Milner, Esther A. A study of the relationships between reading readiness in grade one school children and patterns of parent-child interaction. *Child Development*, 1951, **22,** 95–112.

Pasamanick, B., Knobloch, Hilda, & Lilienfeld, A. M. Socioeconomic status and some precursors of neuropsychiatric disorder. *American Journal of Orthopsychiatry, 1956,* **26,** 594–601.

Scott, J. P., & Charles, Margaret S. Some problems of heredity and social behavior. *Journal of Genetic Psychology,* 1953, **48,** 209–230.

Scott, J. P., & Fuller, J. L. Research on genetics and social behavior at the Roscoe B. Jackson Memorial Laboratory, 1946–1951—a progress report. *Journal of Heredity,* 1951, **42,** 191–197.

Searle, L. V. The organization of hereditary maze-brightness and maze-dullness. *Genetic Psychology Monographs,* 1949, **39,** 279–325.

Tryon, R. C. Genetic differences in maze-learning ability in rats. *Yearbook of National Social Studies Education,* 1940, **39,** Part I, 111–119.

Whiting, J. W. M., & Child, I. L. *Child training and personality: a cross-cultural study.* New Haven: Yale University Press, 1953.

Williams, Judith R., & Scott, R. B. Growth and development of Negro infants: IV. Motor development and its relationship to child rearing practices in two groups of Negro infants. *Child Development,* 1953, **24,** 103–121.

CHAPTER TWO
HUMAN GROWTH

The study of human growth was an early interest of child psychologists. Gesell was a strong proponent of the theory that preset genetic mechanisms guide the infant's early physical growth. As an antidote to the often exaggerated claims of behaviorists, his maturational conceptions of growth were influential in guiding the study of children. How the body grows is an important topic in its own right, but the self-concept a child develops is dependent to some extent on how a child views his own body and how others react to him. Interest in human growth also comes from attempts to understand basic developmental processes —whether maturation controls the child or whether he develops through experience.

In the first article Gesell presents evidence that some response systems of the infant and young child (for example, stair climbing, prehension) are controlled by maturational processes. He claims that an understanding of genetic limitations on possible variation is the key to a child's growth.

The idea of "target-seeking" or self-stabilizing processes is introduced from the field of cybernetics by J. M. Tanner; he notes that children who are retarded in size because of disease or malnutrition increase their rate of growth following the insult. They regain their normal growth pattern as a result of this spurt in maturation. Although the mechanism is based on speculation, it is consistent with results from several careful studies. There is good reason to believe that the child does possess regulatory mechanisms of the sort Tanner describes.

The last two articles on human growth trace the relation between the child's conception of himself and his body build. Walker studied the effects of various physiques on parents' ratings of their children. He found several interesting relations. Children who are muscular are seen as social and energetic; those who are thick in trunk and limb are viewed as low in anxiety and more cooperative; while the thin child is seen as anxious and uncooperative. These studies show that others' conceptions of a child are determined to some extent by how they view his body. Thus, the child's conception of himself is determined partially by feedback from others.

Mussen and Jones explored another aspect of the same question: How is the child's level of physical maturation related to his self-concept? They compared the self-conceptions of children who mature early (reach puberty before 13 years in the case of boys) with children who mature later. Groups of early- and late-maturing boys were identified and followed longitudinally. After three years, when their self-concepts were more fully formed, they were tested by means of projective techniques (Thematic Apperception Test). The authors believe that the child's physical maturity in relation to his peers profoundly influences his self-concept. In particular, they found that the boy who matures early (and thus acquires a strong body and mature social interests before his peers) sees himself in a positive way when compared with the boy who matures later. The late-maturing boy is physically weak and awkward; the result of this physical immaturity is a negative self-concept.

4 | Maturation and Infant Behavior Pattern

ARNOLD GESELL

The fight between proponents of maturation and supporters of learning generated strong feelings and considerable activity during the early part of this century. This selection presents some well-reasoned arguments by a predeterminist, stressing the notion of preset maturational mechanisms which control the sequencing and timing of motor activities. In support of his proposition that a good deal of behavior is genetically determined, Gesell presents evidence from (1) the development of prehension, (2) the correspondence between identical twins, (3) the limitations of training, (4) the restricted influence of physical handicap, and (5) the developmental progression of emotional behavior. As a healthy antidote to extreme claims made for conditioning, the maturational approach was very influential in establishing developmental psychology as a separate field of study.

The influence of conditioning on the human infant has been so forcibly asserted from the standpoint of behaviorism, that it may be desirable to examine the influence of sheer maturation on his patterns of behavior.

The behavior of the infant, by nature, is obedient to pattern. Never does the picture of normal behavior become as diffuse and formless as a drifting cloud. Even the random movements of the month-old child are not utterly fortuitous. The closer one studies them the more configuration they assume. There is indeed no such thing as utter randomness in infant behavior. Accordingly the "random activity" of the two months infant is distinct from that of the month-old. It is distinctive because it has its own pattern.

Likewise with the foetus. Its behavior is in no sense amorphous, but, as the studies of Minkowski have shown, manifests itself

Adapted from Maturation and infant behavior pattern. *Psychological Review*, 1929, **36**, 307–319.

in fairly well-defined reflexes—long, short, diagonal, and trot reflexes; postural reflexes; rhythmical and inhibitive phenomena. These patterns of behavior follow an orderly genetic sequence in their emergence. Genetic sequence is itself an expression of elaborate pattern. And the relative stability of both prenatal and postnatal ontogenesis under normal and even unusual conditions must be regarded as a significant indication of the fundamental rôle of maturational factors in the determination of behavior.

Again take the foetus. The uterus is the normal environment of the foetus till the end of a gestation period of 40 weeks. But birth with survival, may exceptionally occur as early as 24 weeks and as late as 48 weeks, an enormous range of variation in natal age amounting to 6 lunar months. Variation with a range of 3 lunar months is common and yet this considerable variation does not impose a corresponding deviation on the complex of behavior. Our normative studies of both premature and postmature infants have shown repeatedly that the growth course of behavior tends to be obedient to the regular underlying pattern of genetic sequence, irrespective of the irregularity of the birth event. Refined studies will doubtless reveal that such irregularity does subtly modify many details of behavior; but as a point of departure for the discussion of maturation, nothing is more comprehensive in implication than the general stability of the trend and the tempo of development, in spite of precocious or postponed displacement of birth. The patterns of genetic sequence insure a basically similar growth career for full term, pre-term, and post-term infants. It is as though Nature had provided a regulatory factor of safety against the stress of extreme variations of environment. In the mechanisms of maturation this regulation operates.

The term *growth* may be construed to embrace the total complex of ontogenetic development. Maturation refers to those phases and products of growth which are wholly or chiefly due to innate and endogenous factors. It is our purpose to assemble in a summary manner, diverse evidences of behavior maturation, based upon our clinical, experimental and normative observations.

These evidences are drawn from several sources as follows:

(1) The development of prehension.
(2) Developmental correspondence in identical twins.
(3) The limitations of training.
(4) The restricted influence of physical handicap.
(5) Developmental progression in emotional behavior.

THE DEVELOPMENT OF PREHENSION

The development of prehension throughout the first year of life displays significant progressive changes in behavior pattern. These changes raise searching doubts concerning the influence of experience and training upon these patterns. We have studied these changes with particular reference to a pellet 8 millimeters in diameter. The characteristic eye-hand reactions of an infant confronted with this tiny pellet may be recapitulated in the following which is a genetic order:

(a) No visual regard for the pellet.
(b) Transient regard for the pellet.
(c) More prolonged and definite fixation upon the pellet with slight postural changes (16 weeks).
(d) Visual fixation with crude bilateral or unilateral hand approach (20 weeks).
(e) Unilateral pronated hand approach with scratching in vicinity of the pellet (24 weeks).
(f) Pronated hand approach with occasional raking flexion resulting in palmar prehension (28 weeks).
(g) Pronated hand approach with extension of index finger and partial suppression of other digits resulting in poking or prehension by index finger with partial thumb opposition.
(h) Rotation of wrist in hand approach, with pincer-like prehension of pellet by index finger and thumb (40 weeks).
(i) Perfection and further delimitation of pincer-like response.

All these changes mature with subtle but significant accompanying changes in head posture, body posture, hand and arm attitude and associated visual behavior. It seems quite erroneous to say that the child learns to prehend the pellet in the traditional sense of the learning process. Crudely, but nevertheless effectively, he prehends the pellet by gross palmar approach as early as the age of 28 weeks. The refinement of his eye-hand behavior comes not by the alleged utilization of snatches of successful random activity, but by the progressive acquisition and consolidation of a hierarchy of behavior patterns which are the result of developmental decrements and increments rather than the stamping in or chaining of satisfying, successful reflexes. The defective child shows retardation in the acquisition of these patterns even though he may, in a durational sense, have a larger fund of prehensory experience. It is not improbable that many of these developmental changes in the pattern of prehension would be realized even if the prehensory hand were altogether swaddled and deprived of activity. When the prehensory mechanism is damaged by restricted birth injury to the brain, resulting in extensive athetosis,[1] the propensity to prehend or reach may still assert itself at the proper genetic level. Even though the propensity is aborted its presence is highly suggestive of the potency of maturational determination.

DEVELOPMENTAL CORRESPONDENCE IN TWINS

During the past year we have gathered extensive detailed data on the development of prehension in a pair of identical infant twins. These twins were identical not only with regard to their skin patterns but also to a remarkable degree, with regard to their behavior patterns. Nowhere was this more objectively shown than in their prehensory reactions to cubes and pellets under controlled observational conditions. At 28 weeks both of these twins, being somewhat retarded in their development, were visually unheedful of the pellet, though they definitely regarded a cube. At 38 weeks they addressed themselves in an identical manner to the pellet. The hands were in full pronation, the fingers, spread apart in a fan-like manner, were fully extended. The thumb was fully extended almost at right angles. The photographic record of their attack upon the pellet, in the motion pictures, shows an almost uncanny degree of identity in the details of postural attitude, hand attitude and mechanism of

[1] Athetosis is a type of brain injury marked by slow, weaving movements of arms and legs, and by facial grimaces. [Ed.].

grasp. Time does not permit the further specifications of these details.

At 40 weeks each twin made a crude raking attack upon the pellet, with occasional awkward but completed prehension in which the palm and all of the digits participated. The form of the prehension pattern was again remarkably similar in the two children. At 42 weeks they were again examined in the same situation. Although there had been no special instruction or conditioning in the interval, these 2 weeks imposed a palpable and strikingly similar change upon the prehension picture. Simultaneous flexion of the digits was very neatly displaced by a preferential flexion of the index finger. The raking approach was replaced by a poking with the tip of the index finger. Such an interesting inflection of the prehensory pattern surely could not have been induced so precisely and so simultaneously in both of these children without the presence of controlling factors of organic maturation. Of similar significance is the fact that comparable changes in prehension pattern appeared coincidentally throughout the course of their development.

The correspondences in behavior patterns in these twins were literally uncountable. However, the records of 13 developmental examinations were analyzed and 612 separate comparative ratings of behavior items were made from these records in order to determine items of correspondence and disparity. There were 99 items of minor disparity and 513 items of identical or nearly identical correspondence. The parity of behavior patterns was overwhelming.

Many convincing examples of behavior correspondence might be cited. We content ourselves with a few much abbreviated illustrations. Here is one which seems to us to have experimental control, even though it deals with nothing more than the reaction of two infants when placed in exactly the same manner upon a flat platform to observe their postural control in the sitting position. Both children showed precisely the same kind and degree of difficulty in equilibrium at the age of 28 weeks. In both there was a tendency to sway to the right; in both it was impossible, even by spreading the legs, to make the body lean forward sufficiently to establish a passive balance. In the case of each child there was an antagonistic tension which made the body rebound backward in an automatic manner resembling a sharp spring-like action of a knife blade snapping into position. We have never seen precisely this kind of reaction in an infant at this age. It is inconceivable that the response arose out of some identical conditioning factor in the environment. It is reasonable to suppose that this distinctive behavior pattern reflected a maturity level and a synchronous neural organization shared by both children because of their common genetic origin.

Within a week this reaction disappeared. Four days later the twins were placed upon a large blotter on the platform of a clinical crib and maintained the sitting position by leaning forward. Simultaneously they attacked the blotter with the hand in full pronation, and simultaneously, with vocalization, they continued to scratch the blotter, leaving visible marks. Here again was a dramatic bit of correspondence all the more impressive because displayed simultaneously. The complexity and nature of these two behavior patterns again suggest the determining rôle of maturation. If it is argued that extrinsic factors determine the form and the time incidence of these simultaneous patterns it is necessary to demonstrate in detail the cunning arrangements of environment and of conditioning stimuli which could design so precisely, and in duplicate, the configuration of behavior. How can the environment, even of twins, accomplish such architectonic miracles?

A brief example of behavior correspondence may be cited from the 44 weeks examination record. The twins were confronted with a test performance box with its three holes. The common method of approach of the two children, their preferred regard for the edge of the performance box, the fleeting regard for the holes, the exploitation of the vertical surface of the performance box by a scratching, simultaneous flexion of the digits, the failure to place a round rod into any of the holes, the brushing of the surface of the performance box with the rod, the transfer of the rod from one hand to the other, and finally an almost simultaneous peculiar, clicking vocalization in both twins—altogether constituted a very complicated behavior pattern, but one which bristled with numerous identities of spatial and dynamic detail. One can give due weight to the significance of this correspondence only by reflecting on the myriad of behavior exploitations of the situation which the twins *might* have adopted. But in spite of this multitude of exploitational possibilities, the twins were apparently under a common inner compulsion to adopt those very similarities of behavior which have been noted.

Still another, and very pretty example of identity was disclosed in the pellet and bottle test at 48 weeks. This test involved a bit of learning as well as perception and prehension. Three trials were made with each child. The examiner dropped a pellet into a small glass bottle and then gave the bottle to the child. Both children watched the dropping of the pellet with the same transfixed attention. Both children, on the first trial and on the second trial too, seized the bottle apparently heedless of the contained pellet. Both children on the third trial pursued the pellet by poking at it against the glass. Here the details of behavior pattern extended even into the marginal zone of adaptation through learning.

In passing it should be noted that although these observations on twins are comparative, they are objective. They have an objective, quantitative validity. It must be insisted that it would be very difficult to devise a more complicated and in some senses a more delicate instrument of behavior measurement than one twin used in juxtaposition with an identical co-twin as a standard of reference and comparative observation.

LIMITATIONS OF TRAINING

While the positive results of training and conditioning have somewhat obscured the factors of maturation, the limitations of training may be adduced to show the existence of these factors. Such limitations were put to experimental study in the same pair of twins (Twin T and Twin C) whom we have just cited. At the age of 46 weeks, when the thorough-going mental and physical identity of the twins had been well established, it was decided to determine the influence of training confined to one twin, by using an experimental method which we have designated *the method of co-twin control.* T became the trained twin; C was reserved as a control.

Very briefly, Twin T was systematically trained for 20 minutes daily over a period of 6 weeks, in two fields of behavior, stair climbing and cube behavior, including prehension, manipulation and constructive play with a dozen one-inch red cubes. An experimental staircase arrangement of 5 treads was used, and for 10 minutes daily Twin T was put through her paces. At 48 weeks she scaled the stairs for the first time with slight assistance. At the conclusion of the 6 weeks training period (age one year) she was a relatively expert climber. At that age her untrained Co-twin C, would not yet scale the staircase, even with assistance. At the age of 53 weeks however, when C was again confronted with the staircase she climbed to the top without any assistance and without any previous training whatsoever. In this sense the form and the efficiency of her pattern of climbing were almost purely a function of the maturation of the appropriate neural counterparts.

Twin C was then given an experimental course of training in stair climbing, two weeks in length. At the end of this period (age 55 weeks) she approached Twin T in her climbing skill. By means of the motion picture it was possible to make a comparison of the climbing ability of C at 55 weeks (after 2 weeks of training) with that of T at 52 weeks (after 6 weeks of training). This comparison introduced an interesting form of relativity into the investigation and brought out the significant fact that although T had been trained three times longer and seven weeks earlier, this advantage was more than overcome by the three weeks of C's added age. Again the powerful influence of maturation on infant behavior pattern is made clear. Early training altered slightly the form of the pattern, and hastened the acquisition of facility, but left no considerable or decisive locomotor advantage in favor of Twin T.

In the field of cube play the experiment clearly showed that training had no significant effects upon the patterns of prehension, manipulation and constructive exploitation. Although Twin C had enjoyed no special opportunities in the handling of cubes, her cube behavior was fully equal to that of T after a 6 weeks training period. The similarity in temporal and spatial details of pattern was confirmed in this case by a time-space analysis of the behavior patterns by means of the cinema record. This does not mean, however, that there were no changes in the patterns of cube behavior during the training period from 46 weeks to 52 weeks. On the contrary, the records, when analyzed, show consistent and incontrovertible weekly increments. Indeed, a day by day analysis of the diurnal records of cube behavior satisfied us that there was a daily drift toward progressive changes in the cube performance patterns. These changes were developmentally achieved by steady processes of decrement and increment rather than by a saltatory or zigzag course. There may be spurts and plateaus and rhythms in the development of other fields of behavior, but at this stage of the life cycle there was a relatively constant trend toward daily change. This progressive daily changing apparently occurs by a process of continuous emergence which tends to lift the level of development slowly and steadily as though by tide action rather than by rhythmic spurt. We would explain the resistance of the patterns of cube behavior to the influences of training and conditioning by the fact that these patterns are basically under the stress and the regulation of the intrinsic organic factors of maturation. The very fact that there is a growth trend toward daily change of pattern makes the behavior less susceptible to stereotypy and to conditioning.

THE RESTRICTED INFLUENCE OF PHYSICAL HANDICAP

This subject opens up the vast field of experimental etiology in which the conditions of disease and environmental abnormality may be analyzed to determine the influence of extrinsic factors upon the complex of growth. In many instances these extrinsic factors seem to be much less powerful than one might suppose. Even grave degrees of malnutrition, correlated with excessive subnormality of weight, are usually incompetent to inflict any drastic changes upon the forms of fundamental behavior patterns and upon the genetic order of their sequence. While it must be granted that certain food deficiencies, for example in the field of calcium metabolism, may definitely influence the general picture of behavior, the nervous system itself is remarkably resistant to general adversity, even to malnutrition. When certain areas of the nervous system are actually damaged by disease or injury, maturation cannot make amends, but the maturation of the nervous system seems to proceed toward the optimum in the areas unimpaired, even though lacking the stimulus of exercise of the functions controlled by the

impaired areas. It is for this reason that certain clinical types of profound motor disability attain none the less considerable approximation to normality in certain patterns of behavior.

In this context we may also mention the high degree of autonomy which the nervous system maintains even in extreme cases of *puberty praecox*. We have investigated one case in which there was a precocious displacement of puberty amounting to a whole decade. This girl became physiologically mature at the age of 3½ years. In spite of this extreme developmental alteration, the course of her behavior development in the fields of intelligence, language and locomotion has been relatively normal and stable.

Here, also, should be mentioned the general developmental course of the healthy infant born after an abnormally short or an abnormally long gestation period. A premature postnatal environment and a protracted uterine environment must be considered as drastic deviations from normal environmental influence. The relative immunity of the behavior patterns from these environmental deviations again bespeaks the potency of maturational factors.

DEVELOPMENTAL PROGRESSION IN EMOTIONAL BEHAVIOR

The rôle of maturation in the control of emotional behavior has had scant recognition. The primary emotions have been discussed as though they were elementary stable phenomena subject only to the changes of social conditioning. This is the implication in much that has been written concerning the emotion of fear. It seems to us that the problem has been over-simplified. Fear may be an original tendency, but it is subject to the genetic alterations of organic growth as well as to organization by environmental conditioning. Such conditioning may determine the orientation and reference of fears, but the mode of fearing undergoes change as a result of maturation. Fear is neither more nor less of an abstraction than prehension. It is not a simple entity. It waxes and alters with growth. It is shaped by intrinsic maturation as well as by experience, certainly during the period of infancy.

Consider for example the reactions of an infant to confinement in a small enclosed space, approximately 2 x 3 x 4 feet. In a physical sense the situation is entirely harmless. The space is ample in size, it is ventilated, it is illuminated, it is open at one end. In a personal sense however, the space may have elements of novelty and unusualness. The infant is not accustomed to lie in such a small space which shuts him off from his accustomed environment. What are his reactions, even when he is gently introduced into this enclosed chamber? At 10 weeks he may accept the situation with complete complaisance; at 20 weeks he may betray a mild intolerance, a dissatisfaction, persistent head turning and social seeking which we may safely characterize as mild apprehension; at 30 weeks his intolerance to the same situation may be so vigorously expressed by crying that we describe the reaction as fear or fright. Here then are three gradations of response: first, no disquietude; second, mild disquietude; third, robust disquietude. Is not this a genetic gradation of fear behavior which is based upon maturational sequence rather than upon an historical sequence of extrinsic conditioning factors? Such factors may account for specific aspects of fear behavior, but not for the organic pattern beneath such behavior. This pattern, we would suggest, is as much the product of organic growth as the various stages in the elaboration and perfection of prehension. Incidentally it may be said that the observation of duplicate twins will tend to substantiate the existence of maturational factors in the development of emotion. Although the tendency toward developmental divergence in identical twins is probably greater in the field of personality make-up than in any other sphere of behavior, there is, during infancy, an impressive tendency toward identity of emotional behavior. Twins T and C, already referred to, showed a highly significant degree of correspondence in their manifestations of initial timidity, in their responsiveness to social games, in their reactions to the mirror image, in their gestures of avoiding and refusing, in their seeking and begging gestures, in their laughter and crying. The relatively simultaneous and progressive nature of these changes in the field of emotional behavior suggests the influence of organic maturational factors as opposed to purely extrinsic factors in the determination of behavior pattern.

The extreme versions of environmentalist and conditioning theories suffer because they explain too much. They suggest that the individual is fabricated out of the conditioning patterns. They do not give due recognition to the inner checks which set metes and bounds to the area of conditioning and which happily prevent abnormal and grotesque consequences which the theories themselves would make too easily possible. Although it is artificial to press unduly a distinction between intrinsic and extrinsic factors, it must after all, be granted that growth is a function of the organism rather than of the environment as such. The environment furnishes the foil and the milieu for the manifestations of development, but these manifestations come from inner compulsion and are primarily organized by inherent inner mechanics and by an intrinsic physiology of development. The very plasticity of growth requires that there be limiting and regulatory mechanisms. Growth is a process so intricate and so sensitive that there must be powerful stabilizing factors, intrinsic rather than extrinsic, which preserve the balance of the total pattern and the direction of the growth trend. Maturation is, in a sense, a name for this regulatory mechanism. Just because we do not grant complete dichotomy of internal and external factors, it is necessary to explain what keeps the almost infinite fortuities of physical and social environment from dominating the organism of the developing individual.

The organismal concept requires that the individual shall maintain an optimum or normal integrity. The phenomena of maturation suggests the stabilizing and inexpugnable factors which safeguard the basic patterns of growth. Just as the respiration of the organism depends upon the maintenance of constant hydrogen-ion concentration, so probably on a vastly more intricate scale, the life career of the individual is maintained by the physiological processes of maturation—processes which determine in such large measure the form and the sequence of infant behavior pattern, that the infant as an individual is reasonably secure against extreme conditioning, whether favorable or unfavorable.

5 | The Regulation of Human Growth

J. M. TANNER

For some time we have known about variations in an infant's growth rate. Tanner suggests that these variations are not random fluctuations, but the result of a human infant's own self-stabilizing processes. He suggests that an animal has a strong tendency to return to its natural growth curve after being deflected from this pattern by disease or starvation. Illustrations of growth in height are given which show an excellent fit to the "normal" growth curve. A central control mechanism is proposed to explain how the body knows when to catch up and when to slow its growth rate. Tanner assumes that there is a time-tally mechanism which represents the normal growth of the organism. The central nervous system is assumed to sample this tally regularly and to increase or decrease the body's rate of growth in proportion to the difference between the projected size of the organism at any given time and its actual size. If there is a large discrepancy, the body grows faster; when the difference decreases, so does the rate.

The most striking and perhaps most fundamental characteristic of the growth of an animal is that it is self-stabilizing, or, to take another analogy, "target-seeking." Children, no less than rockets, have their trajectories, governed by the control systems of their genetical constitution and powered by energy absorbed from the natural environment. Deflect the child from its natural growth trajectory by acute malnutrition or a sudden lack of a hormone and a restoring force develops so that as soon as the missing food or hormone is supplied again the child catches up towards its original curve. When it gets there it slows down to adjust its path onto the old trajectory once more.

Let me illustrate how regular is the growth of a healthy, well-nourished child. The upper section of Figure 1 shows the measurements of height of a boy in the Harpenden Growth Study taken every six months from age 4 to 10. Note that none of the measurements deviates more than 4 mm from this line, although the experimental error of measuring height may be 3 mm even in experienced hands. A curve of this form fits height data very well from about six months to around 10 years. If there were any periods of acceleration common to most children during this time, then they would be shown by the deviations from the fitted curves being mostly positive at that age, and negative before and after. When we average the deviations for 19 boys and 13 girls each fitted from 4½ years to 9 years we find no age at which these averages depart significantly from zero. In other words we can find no satisfactory evidence of a midgrowth or juvenile spurt in height occurring at 6 or 7 to 8.

Seasonal Effect

A number of children show greater deviations from the fitted curve than does the

Adapted from The regulation of human growth. *Child Development*, 1963, **34,** 817–847.

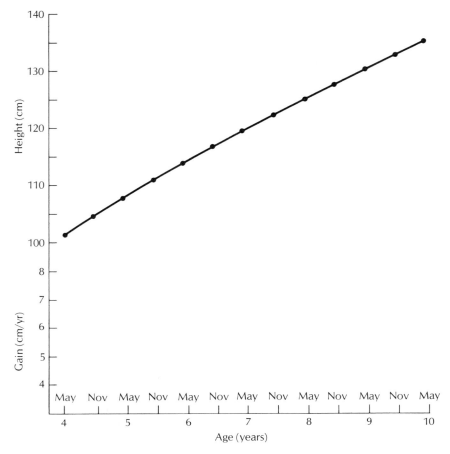

FIGURE 1 Growth of a boy in the Harpenden Growth Study measured every six months by R. H. Whitehouse. "Distance" plot of height achieved at each age. [From Tanner, in F. Gross (Ed.), *Protein metabolism.* Berlin: Springer, 1962.]

child in Figure 1, but when they are investigated most of the deviations turn out to be regular. The fluctuations of velocity from 6½ onwards represent the effect that season of the year has on growth in height of many, but not all, children.

The cause of the seasonal effect is not known. Presumably the endocrine system is affected by light or temperature or some other climatic or just possibly some nutritional factor. The most likely endocrine mediators are probably the thyroid and the adrenal cortex, with thyroxine possibly accelerating growth and increased cortisol secretion possibly decelerating. We have

no sure evidence however that a seasonal change in rate of secretion of either of these hormones takes place in man. Growth hormone could be another possibility and perhaps insulin a fourth. All we can say for certain is that there are marked individual differences in this response to seasonal change.

Illness

Similar individual differences in the ability to regulate growth seem to occur in response to illness. We have fitted curves to six-monthly height measurements of children who have suffered relatively minor illness, but omitted the first measurement following the illness. We then tested whether the post-illness measurement was significantly below the fitted non-illness curve. In the great majority of cases it was not; either the illness had had no effect or the catch-up had been complete within a few months. But in a few children the post-illness point was depressed, and these children were not apparently any sicker than the others, nor were they apparently eating less or behaving in any obviously different way in the uniform environment of the children's home where all were resident. Some children seem to be less well regulated, or canalized, in Waddington's (1957) terminology, than others.

CATCH-UP GROWTH

More severe diseases, or acute malnutrition, cause a retardation in growth. In each case a period of what we call catch-up growth follows restoration of the child's physiological state towards normal.

Figure 2 shows the effect on growth of a young child of two periods in which food intake was much reduced for psychological reasons. The curve represents body length at successive ages. The velocity during each period of catch-up reached more than twice the average velocity for the chronological age; it was nearly twice average for the skeletal age, which was retarded in parallel with the retardation in

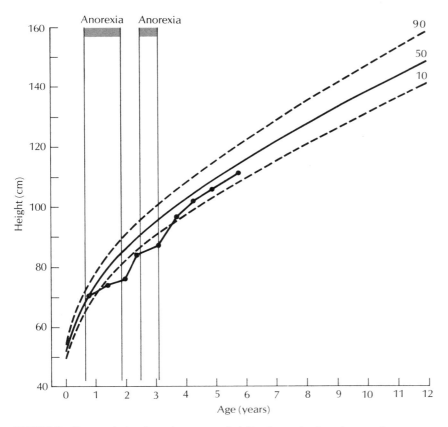

FIGURE 2 Two periods of catch-up growth following episodes of anorexia nervosa in a young child. For explanation of charts see text. (From Prader, Tanner, & von Harnack, 1963.)

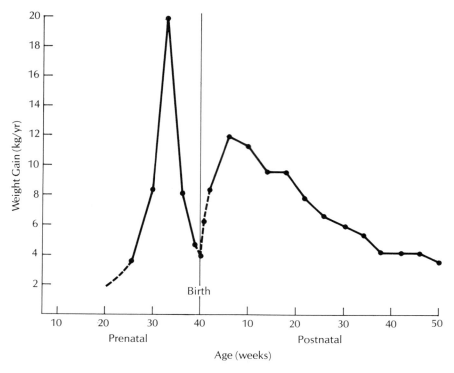

FIGURE 3 Velocity of growth in weight of singleton children. Prenatal curve is derived from the data of McKeown and Record (1952) on birth weights of live-born children delivered before 40 weeks of gestation. Postnatal data is from the Ministry of Health (1959) mixed longitudinal data (their table VII). Dotted line indicates the estimate of velocity immediately before and after birth, showing catch-up.

length and caught up as the length caught up. The catch-up is apparently complete in that the child is quite normal in both length and velocity of length growth by age 5.

Birth Catch-up

This capacity to catch up in growth seems to be used normally around the time of birth in man. There is evidence that the growth rate of the foetus, at least in weight, slows down during the last four weeks of pregnancy, as illustrated in Figure 3. The prenatal values are calculated from McKeown and Record's (1952) data on birth weights of live children born after a shorter gestation than average. In using them we are assuming that these early-

delivered children's weights are the same as the weights of foetuses of the same age as yet still in the uterus; in other words, that amongst healthy singletons the early-born are not specially big or small children for their gestational age. Such an assumption may be challenged. But there is good evidence of a catch-up occurring after birth, particularly in small babies.

Thus there is a negative correlation between birth weight and weight gain from birth to three months, or from birth to six months of the order of about −0.15 (Thompson, 1955). The negative correlation is still present, though lower, by the time one year is reached. Norval, Kennedy, and Berkson (1951) give figures for the correlation of birth weight with the birth-to-one-year increment of −0.15 in boys and −0.05

in girls. The catch-up occurs also in length, indeed, probably to a greater extent than in weight.

Thompson (1956) found correlations of the order of −0.4 in both sexes between birth length and the length increment from birth to six months in some 4,500 babies in Edinburgh. By one year the correlation had somewhat dropped, but was still appreciable (average correlation −0.35).

The catch-up mechanism at birth is of much genetical importance. It seems to be the chief means by which variability in adult size is maintained in the population. Most of the adult size variability is established by two years after birth, since by then the individual's adult size is to a large extent fixed (presuming adequate environmental conditions). The correlation coefficient between length of child at 2 years and length of the same child when adult, is nearly 0.8; it approaches 0.7 even at age 1. (Genetical differences in the time and intensity of the adolescent spurt account for the remainder of the adult variability.) Thus there would be many genetically large children developing in the uteri of small mothers and constituting a problem at the time of birth unless selection for assortative mating were very strong, a solution which would produce other genetically undesirable effects. The problem is solved by birth size being controlled almost entirely by uterine factors (Penrose, 1961), the correlation of birth length and adult length being only about 0.2. The catch-up after birth does the rest.

CONTROL OF CATCH-UP

In all the examples of catch-up growth the velocity of growth was rapid at first, became less as the child approached what we can reasonably assume was its pre-illness curve, and finally settled down to a normal value as the child regained the trajectory of his natural curve. A major problem that remains quite unsolved at present is the manner in which the organism knows when to stop the catch-up phase.

During a typical catch-up the whole organism grows rapidly and in at least approximately its proportionate manner. . . . It is difficult (though not impossible) to see how this could happen unless the stimulus to catch up is a systemic one circulating with the blood to all parts of the body. In everything that follows it must be remembered that we are dealing with growth in *size* and not in *shape*. So far as our present data goes shape in the human is little affected by a slow-down and subsequent catch-up of growth. Differential effects of malnutrition on limbs and trunk, for example, have never been proved to occur, though they have been suggested by analogy with some results on cattle. Growth in shape must clearly be regulated by peripheral mechanisms rather than the central mechanism for size postulated here.

We do not know what the catch-up stimulus is: growth hormone alone is not it, for one of the features of the catch-up is that skeletal maturity, retarded along with size, catches up also. Human growth hormone does not cause an increase in skeletal maturity when administered to hypophysectomized children (at least to those with bone ages of about 12), although it causes growth. Given to bone-age-delayed, insulin-sensitive dwarfs however (with bone ages of 4 to 10), it does cause advancement in bone age along with growth (personal observations). These dwarfs have apparently normal functioning of their ACTH and TSH mechanisms, and we must attribute the bone age result to an increase in one of these secretions (of a degree not detectable on present tests), or else to an unknown pituitary factor. We cannot identify ACTH with the catch-up factor because it does not cause growth in preadolescent children; indeed, in dwarfed children with evidence of ACTH deficiency, administration of ACTH to restore normal 17-hydroxycorticoid values does not result in either growth or skeletal age catch-up (Tanner & Clayton, unpublished). Thyroid hormone might possibly be the catch-up stimulus, but we cannot detect any increase in protein-bound iodine during growth hormone-dependent catch-up, and administration of thyroid causes only a transient effect on growth unless there is a definite thyroid deficiency. On the whole it seems more likely that the catch-up factor is not a single substance, but a balanced response involving several hormones, all dependent on the pituitary.

The factor or factors must be released in response to a signal, and it seems likely that this signal acts either on the brain or the pituitary since its mode of operation is to cause a whole-body catch-up in response to a whole-body delay. Lack of growth of a limb, as in poliomyelitis, or hypertrophy of a limb, as in arterio-venous aneurysm, does not cause any catch-up or slow-down of the body as a whole (though in certain organs, such as the liver and kidney, local factors are additionally operative, causing hypertrophy of the corresponding organ alone following removal or disease of part of it).

The characteristics of catch-up require, it seems to me, that this signal represents the degree of mis-match between the actual size (or, for the sake of clarity, actual height) of the organism and the size (or height) required at that age by the hypothetical built-in or "target" growth curve. As the target curve is approached, the mis-match diminishes and the catch-up slows down. For the mis-match to be read both actual size and target size must somehow be represented in the organism. At present we do not know how either representation is made. It is possible that the mis-match is a peripheral phenomenon and occurs in all cells in all tissues, the cells themselves each carrying the code for their own maturity. The catch-up in treated hypothyroidism might indeed be explicable on this basis. But it seems an unlikely hypothesis for explaining most catch-ups and for explaining the normal control of growth in size, which is our ultimate objective. I

should like to suggest a possible and, I believe, more plausible hypothesis for investigation.

Consider "target" size. Suppose that somewhere in the brain a tally is kept of the time passed since conception, or rather since the age (perhaps about three months after conception), when the mechanism of the tally begins to function. This tally can represent the target curve, for both are fundamentally series of signals made against a continuing time base. Suppose, purely for simplicity's sake, that the tally consists of a steady increase in the amount of a substance in certain nerve cells; then the form of the growth curve may be represented at any time by (some function of) the concentration of this substance.

Now as to actual size—it is scarcely conceivable that the body can represent its actual extension in space. Suppose, instead, that the organism measures its actual height or size by the concentration of some form of circulating substance produced by cells as an inevitable accompaniment to the process of growth or protein synthesis. In this supposition I follow the most provocative and stimulating ideas of Paul Weiss, except that he envisages these substances —which he calls anti-templates—as numerous, tissue-specific, and acting directly on peripheral cells, whereas I prefer to think primarily of a single substance acting at the brain level. In the simplest model then, the concentration of this substance (which we will call the "inhibitor") would be proportional to the size of the organism. Its actual concentration can be measured against the concentration expected on the basis of the time tally and the discrepancy can be used as the mis-match signal for release of the growth-stimulating factor. If, for simplicity's sake, we suppose that the time tally consists of a steady increase in the number of receptive sites for the growth-inhibitor substance, then the mis-match signal would consist of the number of unoccupied sites.

Suppose that the inhibitors develop in proportion to the sites of synthesis used

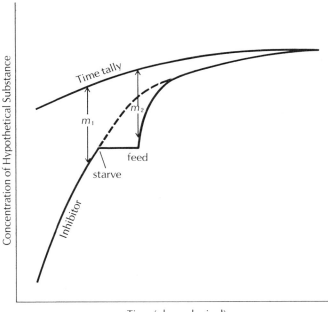

FIGURE 4   Velocity expected in catch-up growth. Catch-up velocity is proportional to the mis-match m_2, which is greater than the mis-match when starvation began and equal to the mis-match at an earlier age, as represented by $m_1 = m_2$.

up in the cells as they pack in more protein, each turn of the RNA wheel, as it were throwing off a molecule of inhibitor. Then the inhibitor concentration would rise in an exponential fashion, fast at first and slowly later. The mis-match (m) between these two concentrations would be large at first and decrease after the manner of the growth velocity curve. In this simple model the concentration of growth-stimulating factor is directly proportional to the mis-match, and the velocity of catch-up is supposed to be directly proportional to the concentration of growth-stimulating factor. (Really one or other of these relationships might well be logarithmic.)

As Figure 4 shows, the model represents the chief feature of catch-up correctly. The catch-up velocity seems usually to be not only greater than the velocity expected at the age of catch-up, but also greater than the velocity expected at the age at which

growth stopped (see Prader et al., 1963). The model predicts that the mis-match and hence the catch-up velocity will be the velocity appropriate to a younger age than this, how much younger depending on the relative curvatures of the time tally and inhibitor lines. The model also predicts that catch-up growth, following a given time of growth arrest, will be more intense at young ages than at older ones. This is generally thought to be the case, although our own data give no direct evidence for it.

FACTORS AFFECTING THE REGULATORY SYSTEM

The regulatory system is evidently built in to the organism and we would expect its characteristics, such as precision, speed of response, and so forth to be mainly genetically determined. Such indeed is the case.

Two factors are known which affect the system: heterozygosity and sex. In animals hybrids seem to be better regulated, or canalized, than inbred strains, at least in a number of instances. Hybrid mice for example vary less than inbred in weight and in tail length either in a normal or a hot environment (Harrison, Morton, & Weiner, 1959). Nothing is as yet known about this in the human. The effect of sex however is becoming well documented in man (see Tanner, 1962, p. 127). Girls are apparently less easily thrown off their growth curves by adverse circumstances than boys. Greulich (1951) first drew attention to this, after studying the effects on growth of wartime hardships in Guam and of the atomic bombing in Hiroshima and Nagasaki. The same sex difference seems to occur in response to malnutrition in rats.

CONCLUSION

We have apparently ended rather far into physiological and genetic technology, but I think this an appearance only. One reason that I chose to speak about regulation in growth was because it is a general problem. By this I mean that formal, model solutions may be applicable not only to the problems of physical growth but in several different fields. It is an old and entirely justified complaint that the great majority of so-called interdisciplinary studies of child growth fail in their endeavour to link the psychology and physiology of development. The mistake was to suppose that the child was the integrating factor; that when psychologists and physiologists applied their techniques not to different children but to the *same* child, that integration would follow. An integral view can be obtained only when both groups use a common, and because common, more

fundamental language than their present ones, and I have a feeling that that language in so far as child development is concerned will be cybernetics.

REFERENCES

Greulich, W. W. The growth and developmental status of Guamanian school children in 1947. *American Journal of Physical Anthropology,* N.S., 1951, **9,** 55–70.

Harrison, G. A., Morton, R. J., & Weiner, J. S. The growth in weight and tail length of inbred and hybrid mice reared at two different temperatures. *Philosophical Transcripts* (Series B), 1959, **242,** 479–516.

McKeown, T., & Record, R. G. Observations on foetal growth in multiple pregnancy in man. *Journal of Endocrinology,* 1952, **8,** 386–401.

Ministry of Health (Great Britain). Standards of normal weight in infancy. *Ministry of Health Report on Public Health, No. 99.* London: H.M.S.O., 1959.

Norval, M. A., Kennedy, R. L. J., & Berkson, J. Biometric studies of the growth of children of Rochester, Minnesota. The first year of life. *Human Biology,* 1951, **23,** 274–301.

Penrose, L. S. *Recent advances in human genetics.* London: Churchill, 1961.

Prader, A., Tanner, J. M., & von Harnack, G. A. Catch-up growth following illness or starvation; an example of developmental canalization in man. *Journal of Pediatrics,* 1963, **62,** 646–659.

Tanner, J. M. *Growth at adolescence* (2nd ed.) Oxford: Blackwell, 1962.

Thompson, J. Observations on weight gain in infants. *Archives of Diseases in Childhood,* 1955, **30,** 322–327.

Waddington, C. H. *The strategy of the genes. A discussion of some aspects of theoretical biology.* London: Allen & Unwin, 1957.

6 | Body Build and Behavior in Young Children: II. Body Build and Parents' Ratings

R. N. WALKER

This study is one of a series describing relations between young children's body build and their behavior characteristics as judged by different observers. Earlier studies showed that there are significant associations between ratings of body build and judgments of the children's behavior by a nursery school teacher. The present paper describes relations between the physique of the child and ratings of home behavior made by mothers. The results depict the endomorphic girl (thick trunk, "chubby") as more cooperative, low in tenseness and anxiety, and socially extroverted. The mesomorphic girl (muscular, heavy boned) was seen as energetic, and the mesomorphic boy as energetic, cheerful, and social. The ectomorphic girl (tall and thin) was depicted as uncooperative, not cheerful, anxious, and aloof. The ectomorphic boy was depicted as similarly unsocial, but cooperative and unaggressive. These results show that the type of physique one develops influences the way others perceive him.

METHOD

Subjects

The sample consists of 147 nursery school children. The 2-year-olds actually ranged in age from 2–6 to 2–11, the 3-year-olds from 3–6 to 3–11, the 4-year-olds from 4–6 to 4–11. The parents of these children are predominantly of upper-middle class background. Each child was rated for manifest level of endomorphy (roughly speaking, the roundness and plumpness of his physique), mesomorphy (his muscularity), and ectomorphy (his linearity and attenuation of physique). These ratings were made by

three judges independently classifying standard, nude photographs of the children in front, side, and back views. Two of the judges, never saw the children in person; the third, the author, photographed and was acquainted with most of them.

For each physique variable the ratings of each judge were converted to standard scores for each age group, scores for the three judges were averaged, and the averages reconverted to somatotype-like scales with a mean of 3.5 and a standard deviation of 1.0 for boys and girls combined at each age. The reliability of the average of the standard scores (Peters & Van Voorhis, 1940, formula 113) approximated .90 for endomorphy and ectomorphy for each sex at each age. For mesomorphy the reliability of the average was closer to .85 for the boys, .75 for the girls.

Adapted from Body build and behavior in young Children. II. Body build and parents' ratings. *Child Development*, **34**, 1–23.

Parents' Adjective Check List

A form was devised on which parents could record their judgments of a variety of behaviors in their children quickly and easily. As in the case of the Nursery School Behavior rating scales, the items composing this check list were assembled from a variety of sources, in hopes of covering a broad spectrum of temperament variables. The resulting list resembles the usual adjective check list in that it lists a series of 68 descriptive adjectives and phrases and the rater is asked to underline those characteristic of the child being rated. Instructions also indicate, however, that traits clearly uncharacteristic of the child may be circled and that a double underline or double circle may be used when emphasis seems called for. Thus, though similar in format to a check list the list can also be scored as a 5-point rating scale. For dichotomous comparisons this gives the advantage that the contrasted groups can be made more nearly equal in size by moving the cutting point when ratings pile up on one side of the scale. (For example, the great majority of parents noted by underlining that their children were affectionate, energetic, enthusiastic, talkative, imaginative, friendly, and cheerful, but fairly equal groups were formed when single and double underlines were separated.)

Procedure

Before the check lists were distributed to the children's mothers, predictions were made by the author concerning the probable direction of relation between each check list item and each physique variable. For example, it was predicted that good appetite would be positively associated with both endomorphy and mesomorphy and negatively associated with ectomorphy. These predictions were based on Sheldon's findings for 200 college men (1942). For some items no prediction could be made but between 52 and 56 predictions from the 68 items were made for each physique variable. The same predictions were made for both boys and girls.

The mother of each eligible child (white, not physically handicapped, of average intelligence or higher) attending the Nursery School during the three-year period was asked to fill out the check list. For the 170 eligible children, 147 forms (86 per cent) were returned completed. Parents were not informed that their ratings were to be used in connection with physique data. Though all parents knew that "growth pictures" were taken of their children during the school year, these were presented as one of many ongoing research efforts rather than as a focus of comparison with behavior.

Once both physique ratings and behavior ratings were obtained, several types of comparisons were made. First, the predictions made for individual items were tested to see how many could be confirmed, either in direction alone or at statistically reliable levels. Second, significant associations between single physique variables and individual behavior items were determined, regardless of whether or not they conformed with predictions made. Third, the single physique variables were correlated with the behavioral cluster scores. And finally, the three physique variables jointly were compared with the behavior clusters by means of a graphic technique, in an effort to see if physique pattern had greater meaning than the physique variables considered singly.

RESULTS

Predictions and Outcomes

For boys and girls separately, the array of scores for each physique and each behavior variable was dichotomized as close to the median as possible and fourfold tables of association between physique and behavior items were set up. The probability of association between the two scores was then tested by x^2.

For the total number of predictions made, two thirds were in the direction predicted and 12 per cent were confirmed beyond the .05 level in contrast with 2 per cent disconfirmed beyond the .01 level. However, it is clear that the degree of confirmation differs considerably in relation to both sex and physique variable. Compared with the boys, the girls showed 12 times as many predicted associations confirmed at a significant level. And among the girls the great majority of predictions for endomorphy were confirmed in direction, about half of these at statistically significant levels; predictions for ectomorphy were intermediate; and predictions for mesomorphy fell close to purely chance levels of confirmation.

For the boys the number of predictions confirmed significantly did not exceed chance expectation for any physique variable, though well over half their predictions were confirmed in direction alone. Predictions for endomorphy were generally less well confirmed than those for mesomorphy or ectomorphy.

Endomorphy Just nine traits showed relation to endomorphy in the boys and practically none of them had been predicted. Perhaps the main element that these nine have in common is low social desirability. Together they give a picture of a boy who is aggressive and provoking (bossy, quarrelsome, impudent, etc.), but awkward and defeatist (not well coordinated, jealous, easily discouraged).

On the other hand, out of 68 assorted behavior descriptions by mothers, 32 showed relation with endomorphy in the girls. None of these associations contradicted predictions made, 28 of them confirmed previous predictions, and the four for which no predictions had been made seem clearly to belong with the remaining

28. Collectively, the traits give a picture of robust good adjustment, portraying a child who is loving, cooperative, relaxed and easy-going, stable, extravert, expressive and cheerful, open and trusting, social, unaggressive, and not fearful.

Mesomorphy The findings for mesomorphy are few, with the boys and the girls each showing just 10 traits associated beyond the .10 level. Eight of the 10 associations in each list, however, had been predicted, and both lists seem mainly to indicate an abundance of energy. In the boys this energy appears associated with bossy, bold, impudent, destructive, disorderly behavior; the mesomorphic girls appear more cooperative but not more affectionate.

Ectomorphy Ectomorphy showed association beyond the .10 level with 17 of the behavior traits for the boys and with 27 traits for the girls. A majority of these associations had been predicted in the case of the boys, only a minority in the case of the girls. The composite picture of the latter group, nevertheless, is a coherent one.

The ectomorphic girls were viewed by their mothers as tense and unstable (tense and high-strung, unpredictable, has tantrums), uncooperative (not eager to please, lacks concern over misdeeds, not well-mannered or orderly or conscientious), aggressively fault-finding (criticizes, destructive, fights physically, quarrelsome, impudent), anxiously dependent (dependent and clinging, afraid of failure, worries, jealous, feels unloved), and yet distant (does not love physical contact, stays away from home), desurgent (often moody and sad, suspicious of others, reserved and quiet, complains of aches and pains), and underenergized (lacks good appetite, slow moving). The boys showed some similar aspects of this picture but also some important differences. Like the girls they seemed to show social reserve (can entertain self, not friendly or sociable, likes to spend time alone, bashful and shy), but this was combined with low rather than high aggressiveness (not bossy, destructive, impudent, or quarrelsome), and, quite contrary to prediction, with a greater than average ability to give and accept intimate affection (eager to please, does not stay away from home, affectionate, loves physical comfort). They were also seen as having other sources of strength (well coordinated, not easily discouraged, and even mischievous).

DISCUSSION

These results may be compared with findings obtained for different samples of children and with findings for the same children as viewed by different observers. Apparently only one other study, that of Davidson, McInnes, and Parnell (1957), has compared behavior traits and somatotype-like variables in girls. Seven-year-old English children were rated by a psychiatrist from their mothers' reports. The endomorphic girls were reported to be not sad and not on the defensive, the mesomorphic girls to be not submissive, not shy, and not dreamy, and to communicate feelings easily, and the ectomorphic girls to be fussy, meticulous, and conscientious. Their findings for endomorphy and mesomorphy seem parallel to those reported here; for ectomorphs "fussy" likewise seems to describe the girls in the present study but the meticulous, conscientious behavior of their girls is explicitly contradicted here.

The energy and aggressive assertiveness of the mesomorphic boys in the present study and the shy reserve of the ectomorphic boys appear repeatedly as prominent correlates of male mesomorphy and ectomorphy, whether viewed in 7-year-old English boys by their mothers (Davidson, et al., 1957), in 11-to 16-year-old nondelinquents by psychiatrists (Glueck & Glueck, 1956), in junior-high-school boys by their peers (Hanley, 1951), or in college men by

themselves (Child, 1950). It is in describing endomorphy that other studies tend to disagree with this study and with each other or else to have little conclusive to say. Hanley (1951) reports no findings for endomorphy, and the fewest predictions were confirmed for endomorphy in Child's study (1950), as here. There is general agreement (Hanley, 1951; Davidson, et al., 1957; Glueck & Glueck, 1956), however, with Sheldon's finding (1942) that endomorphs tend to be socially outgoing and amiable. The absence of this association in the present study may derive in part from the lack of balanced endomorphs. Most of the boys high in endomorphy were also high in mesomorphy; the aggressiveness in their reported behavior may be a result of this correlated variable.

Whatever the explanation, this study suggests that physique-behavior associations rise from many sources and have force at different levels of personality. Several variables appear likely as primary, near-physiological sources. If the individual differences ordered in the physique ratings reflect underlying differences in body composition and function, then certain relations may be presumed to lie primarily within the physical organism. An example would be energy level, a variable obviously affected by situational factors—emotional, nutritional, etc.—yet plausibly seen as basically intra-organismic. Energy level would seem to play an important role in such psychological variables as surgency, the child with high energy having at least greater opportunity for lively, expressive cheerfulness. Bodily differences in such variables as thresholds, drive strengths, capacities, etc., may likewise contribute to such behavioral variables as tenseness-relaxedness.

Variations in relatively directly physique-linked traits may have far-reaching consequences for individuals, setting the conditions of their learning. The mesomorph has greater probability of successful outcome in aggressive attempts than the ectomorph; his aggressive assertiveness appears to reflect his experience. Others' evaluations play an important role in physique-behavior association. The boy with high energy level comes into frequent contact with his surroundings, human and inanimate, and often finds himself in conflict with its demands and prohibitions; then he gets called uncooperative by parents and teachers. Still further evaluations of his physique and his behavior by others and the expectations and roles assigned to him must contribute to shaping the associations between his body and his behavior, both in the general patterns described and in more individual, idiosyncratic ways. The associations seem to lie not alone in biological makeup nor in learning, not just within the subjects' bodies nor just in other's stereotyped perceptions, but in a complex interplay among all these levels.

REFERENCES

Child, I. L. The relation of somatotype to self-rating on Sheldon's temperamental traits. *Journal of Personality*, 1950, **18,** 440–453.

Davidson, M. A., McInnes, R. G., & Parnell, R. W. The distribution of personality traits in seven-year-old children: a combined psychological, psychiatric and somatotype study. *British Journal Educational Psychology,* 1957, **27,** 48–61.

Glueck, S., & Glueck, E. *Physique and delinquency.* New York. Harper, 1956.

Hanley, C. Physique and reputation of junior high school boys. *Child Development.* 1951, **22,** 247–260.

Peters, C. C., & Van Voorhis, W. R. *Statistical procedures and their mathematical bases.* New York. McGraw-Hill, 1940.

Sheldon, W. H. *The varieties of temperament.* New York. Harper, 1942.

7 | Self-Conceptions, Motivations, and Interpersonal Attitudes of Late- and Early-Maturing Boys

P. H. MUSSEN
MARY C. JONES

As part of the work associated with the University of California Oakland Growth Study, Mussen and Jones examined the relation between an individual's rate of physical growth and his self-perceptions. The study was longitudinal, allowing the assessment of early and late maturation and the later testing of these same individuals for self-perceptions and attitudes. The results suggest that early maturation accompanies positive attitudes and self-perceptions in boys, and is related with negative self-perceptions in the case of girls (Jones & Mussen, 1957). The article also shows the strengths and weaknesses of the longitudinal method of child study.

While many intensive case studies show that personal and social adjustment during adolescence may be profoundly influenced by rate of physical maturation, there is a scarcity of systematic data on the relationship between the adolescent's physical status and his underlying motivations, self-conceptions and interpersonal attitudes. There is, however, a small body of evidence which demonstrates that greater physical maturity is associated with greater maturity of interest among girls and that early-maturing boys differ from their late-maturing peers in both overt behavior and reputational status. In one study (Jones & Bayley, 1950) in which a staff of trained observers assessed a large group of adolescents on a number of personality variables, boys who were consistently retarded in physical development were rated lower than those who were consistently accelerated, in physical

attractiveness, grooming, and matter-of-factness; and higher in sociability, social initiative (often of a childish, attention-getting sort), and eagerness. Reputation Test (Tryon, 1939) data indicated that classmates regarded the late-maturing boys as more attention-getting, more restless, more bossy, less grown-up, and less good-looking than those who were physically accelerated.

On the basis of these findings, it may be inferred that adult and peer attitudes toward the adolescent, as well as their treatment and acceptance of him, are related to his physical status.

The present study was designed to investigate the relationship between maturational status and certain important, covert aspects of personality during late adolescence. Personality structure was assessed by means of the Thematic Apperception Test (TAT) which seems to be the most appropriate and sensitive instrument for this purpose. More specifically, on the basis of

Adapted from Self-conceptions, motivations, and interpersonal attitudes of late- and early-maturing boys. *Child Development*, 1957, **28**, 243–256.

the literature reviewed above and other general works on the psychology of adolescence, we formulated and tested a series of propositions relating to differences between the physically retarded and the accelerated in self-conceptions, underlying motivations, and basic interpersonal attitudes. These variables were translated into TAT categories—needs (*n*), press (*p*), and descriptions (defined briefly in Table 1)—and the scores of early- and late-maturers in each of these categories were compared. The propositions and the rationale underlying them, together with the TAT variables involved, follow.

1. In view of their obvious physical retardation, relatively unfavorable reputations and disadvantageous competitive position in many activities, the late-maturing boys are more likely to have feelings of inadequacy. Hence, more boys in this group than in the early-maturing group are likely to have negative self-conceptions (TAT category: *negative characteristics*).

2. The adolescent in our culture generally desires some independence and adult status. This may be the source of a major problem for the late-maturer, however, since he is often regarded and treated as a small boy by adults and peers and is not likely to be granted independence as early as physically accelerated boys. Therefore, it may be anticipated that more late- than early-maturers regard adults, particularly their parents, as dominating, forcing them to do things they don't want to or preventing them from doing things they want to do (high scores in *p Dominance*). Moreover, the parental treatment these boys experience and parental refusal to grant them independent status may be interpreted as personal rejection. Hence, we predicted that more late-maturing boys would score high in *p Rejection.*

3. These feelings of being dominated and rejected may result in attitudes of rebellion against the family and in feelings of hostility. We therefore expected that more of the late-maturing group would reveal strong aggressive needs (high scores in

n Aggression) and desires to escape from (*n Autonomy—leaving parents*), or to defy, the family (*n Autonomy—defying parents*).

4. On the basis of the data indicating that slow-maturers showed a great deal of social interest (although often of an immature kind), we hypothesized that more members of this, than of the early-maturing group would reveal strong interests in friendly, intimate interpersonal relationships (high scores in *n Affiliation*).

5. Assuming that, as Jones and Bayley (1950) suggest, the social initiative and attention-getting devices of the late-maturers are of a compensatory nature, we would expect this group to be basically dependent and to have strong needs for support from others. These should be manifest by higher scores in TAT *n Succorance* and *p Nurturance.* The latter may be considered a more indirect measure of dependence, a kind of wish-fulfilling view of the world as helpful and friendly.

6. The early-maturer, being regarded and treated as more adult, is more likely to become self-confident, and to acquire high status goals. For these reasons, we predicted that more of the physically accelerated would give evidence of high achievement goals (high scores in *n Achievement*) and concern with personal recognition (high scores in *n Recognition*).

7. Late-maturing boys in our culture probably face more problems of personal adjustment than do their early-maturing peers. As a result of this, they may become more aware of their problems, and, as the high degree of flexibility of young adults who had been retarded in maturing suggests, more insightful. Hence we predicted that they would be more willing and able than early-maturers to face their own feelings and emotions (low scores in the TAT variable *denial of feeling*).

In summary, we attempted to test seven propositions related to differences in the personalities of early- and late-maturing boys. It was hypothesized that more late-maturers would score high in variables relating to negative self-conceptions, dependence, aggression, affiliation, rebelliousness, and feelings of being dominated and rejected. More early-maturers, on the other hand, were expected to reveal strong achievement and recognition needs, feelings of personal success, and tendencies toward denial of feelings.

PROCEDURE

The 33 seventeen-year-old male subjects of this investigation were members of the Adolescent Growth Study which included a normal sample of boys in an urban public school system. The subjects of the present investigation represented two contrasting groups, selected on the basis of their physical maturity status: 16 of them had been among the most consistently accelerated throughout the adolescent period; the other 17 had been among the most consistently retarded. All of them took the Thematic Apperception Test, which provides the basic data of this study, at age 17.

The TAT consisted of 18 pictures: nine from the Murray set which is now standard (cards 1, 5, 6, 7BM, 10, 11, 14, 15, 17); five pictures from the set generally used in 1938 when these data were collected (a man and woman seated on a park bench; a bearded old man writing in an open book; a thin, sullen, young man standing behind a well-dressed older man; a tea table and two chairs; an abstract drawing of two bearded men); and four designed especially for this investigation (the nave of a large church; a madonna and child; a dramatic view of mountains; a boy gazing at a cross which is wreathed in clouds).

The tests were administered individually. Each card was projected on a screen while the subject told a story which was recorded verbatim. Standard instructions were given for the Murray cards, and subjects were asked to describe the feelings elicited by the other four pictures. Most of the stories were brief, consisting of only one or two sentences.

As we noted earlier, each of the personality variables involved in the seven propositions was translated into a TAT scoring category. The scoring scheme involved counting the relevant needs, press, and descriptions of the heroes of the stories, the assumption being that the story-teller has identified with the hero: the hero's needs are the same as the boy's; the press that impinge upon the hero are the ones that affect the boy telling the story. A total of 20 needs, press, and descriptive categories, each defined as specifically as possible, was developed in the analysis of the protocols. A score for each subject for each TAT category was derived by counting the number of stories in which it appeared. A list of the categories used, together with brief descriptions of them, is found in Table 1.

To test the reliability of this analysis, one of the authors (PM) and another psychologist independently scored 15 complete protocols (300 stories). The percentage of interrater agreement was 90, computed by the usual formula (number of agreements divided by number of agreements plus number of disagreements).

In order to eliminate bias, the scoring used in the present study was done "blind," that is, independently of knowledge of the subject's maturational status.

RESULTS

Frequency distributions of the scores of all subjects were made for all the TAT variables. Each distribution was then dichotomized at the point which most nearly enabled the placing of half of the 33 subjects above, and half of them below, the dividing point. Subjects having scores above this point were considered high in this particular variable; those with scores below this point were considered low in this variable. Chi square tests were used to test the seven propositions, i.e., to ascertain whether or not high scores in certain TAT variables were in fact more characteristic of one

TABLE 1   Number of Early- and Late-Maturers Scoring High in TAT Variables

TAT Variable	Definition of Variable	High Early-Maturers	High Late-Maturers	Chi Square Value	p
Proposition 1					
Negative Characteristics	H is described in negative terms (e.g., imbecile, weakling, fanatic)	5	13	6.80	<.01
Proposition 2					
p Dominance 1	H forced by parents to do something he doesn't want to	4	8	1.73	.09
p Dominance 2	H prevented by parents from doing something he wants to	6	8	.31	>.30
p Dominance 3	Total instances of H's being forced by parents to do something and/or prevented from doing something	7	11	1.46	.11
p Rejection	H rejected, scorned, or disapproved of by parents or authorities	5	11	3.69	.03
Proposition 3					
n Aggression 1	H is aggressive in physical, asocial way	8	3	3.88	.02
n Aggression 2	H is mad at someone, argues	7	4	1.52	.10
n Aggression 3	Total of all H's aggressive actions	11	8	1.26	.10
n Autonomy 1	H leaves home	7	10	.75	.20
n Autonomy 2	H disobeys or defies parents	7	11	1.46	.11
n Autonomy 3	Total of instances in which hero leaves and/or defies his parents	3	9	4.16	.02
Proposition 4					
n Affiliation 1	H establishes good relations with his parents	8	8	.00	>.50
n Affiliation 2	H falls in love, has a romance, marries	9	14	2.66	.05
n Affiliation 3	Total instances in which H establishes and/or maintains friendly relations	8	12	1.46	.11
Proposition 5					
n Succorance	H feels helpless, seeks aid or sympathy	7	12	2.43	.06
n Nurturance 1	H is helped, encouraged, or given something by parents	5	8	.93	.18
p Nurturance 2	H is helped, encouraged, or given something by someone else (not parents)	8	14	3.88	.02
Proposition 6					
n Achievement	H attempts to attain a high goal or to do something creditable	9	10	.02	>.50
n Recognition	H seeks fame and/or high prestige status	9	8	.28	>.30
Proposition 7					
Denial of Feeling	S states that picture elicits no thoughts or feelings	9	5	2.43	.06

group (late- or early-maturers) than of the other.

Table 1 shows that, as had been predicted, more late-maturing than early-maturing boys revealed feelings of inadequacy and negative self-concepts, i.e., scored high in the TAT variable *negative characteristics*. Hence proposition 1 was confirmed. This finding is consistent with the frequently made clinical observation that retardation in physical maturation may be an important source of personal maladjustment and attitudes of inferiority.

Proposition 2 stated that more late-maturers regard their parents as highly dominating and rejecting. The evidence summarized in Table 1 substantially supported this proposition. While the difference was not statistically significant, more late-than early-maturers scored high in p Dominance by parents (total). There was a marked difference between the groups in the variable which involves parental domination by forcing the child to do something he does not want to do (p Dominance by parents, forcing). However, examination of the data with respect to the variable p Dominance by parents (prevention) makes it necessary to reject that part of the proposition which maintains that late-maturers are more likely to view their parents as highly restrictive of their activities.

The hypothesis (part of proposition 3) that more late-maturers would be highly aggressive was rejected on the basis of the evidence given in Table 1. In fact, the differences between the two groups on all the TAT aggression variables were in the opposite direction from the prediction. High scores in the variables relating to aggression of the most overt and violent type were significantly more frequent among the early-maturers, and more members of this group also scored high in measures of milder (verbal) aggression and of total aggression. While late-maturers may experience more problems of adjustment and greater frustrations than their early-maturing peers, they apparently do not manifest greater aggressive motivation.

Proposition 4 stated that, compared with their early-maturing peers, more late-maturers would manifest strong needs for establishing close social contacts with others. While there was some confirmatory evidence, the results were not clear-cut. When all affiliative needs were considered together (score for n Affiliation—total), the group differences were in the predicted direction, but not statistically significant. Examination of the protocols revealed that almost all instances of affiliation concerned either parents or the opposite sex; there were very few stories involving close, friendly associations between like-sexed peers. The two major types of affiliation were scored separately. As Table 1 shows, late-maturers did not differ from early-maturers with respect to need for affiliation with parents, but a significantly greater proportion of the former group displayed strong motivation for heterosexual affiliation.

The data were generally supportive of proposition 5 which stated that late-maturers are likely to have strong underlying dependent needs. A higher proportion of this group than of their early-maturing peers scored high in n Succorance, the difference between the two groups approaching statistical significance ($p = .06$). Furthermore, high scores in the category involving receiving help and support from others (not including parents) (p Nurturance—non-parents)—an indirect measure of dependent needs—were significantly more characteristic of the physically retarded than of the physically accelerated. In view of the late-maturers' attitudes toward their parents, discussed above, it is not surprising to find that perceptions of parents as kindly and supportive (high scores in p Nurturance—parents) were not significantly more common in this group than in the early-maturing group.

On the basis of the data involving the TAT variables n Achievement and n Recognition, we rejected proposition 6 which stated that more early-maturers would be self-confident and have high needs for achievement and personal recognition. In our culture there is strong pressure to develop needs for achievement and personal recognition, and, according to our results, these needs and feelings may become intense regardless of—or perhaps in spite of—the child's maturational status, feelings of personal adequacy, dependency, and adjustment to parents.

Proposition 7, which stated that relatively few of the physically retarded boys are unwilling or unable to face their own feelings and emotions, received some support from the TAT data summarized in Table 1. A smaller proportion of the members of this group than of the physically accelerated group specifically denied that the pictures evoked any feelings or emotions (e.g. "It doesn't make me think of anything"). While this variable may not adequately measure *denial of feeling* as a major defense mechanism, this result seems to indicate that late-maturers are more sensitive to their own feelings and more ready to admit and face them openly. Since these qualities are basic to the development of psychological insight, it may be inferred that late-maturers, as a group, are more likely to become insightful individuals.

DISCUSSION

The results of the study support the general hypothesis that, in our culture, the boy whose physical development is retarded is exposed to a sociopsychological environment which may have adverse effects on his personality development. Apparently, being in a disadvantageous competitive position in athletic activities, as well as being regarded and treated as immature by others, may lead to negative self-conceptions, heightened feelings of rejection by others, prolonged dependent needs, and rebellious attitudes toward parents. Hence, the physically retarded boy is more likely than his early-maturing peer to be personally and socially maladjusted during late adolescence. Moreover, some of his attitudes are likely to interfere with the process of identification with his parents, which is generally based on perceptions of them as warm and accepting (Payne & Mussen, 1956). This, in turn, may inhibit or delay the acquisition of mature characteristics and attitudes which are ordinarily established through identification with parents. Fortunately for the late-maturers' subsequent adjustments, they seem more willing and able to face their feelings and emotions. This may be a result of their awareness of others' attitudes toward their immaturity or their feelings of personal inadequacy and dependency.

The physically accelerated boys, on the other hand, are likely to experience environmental circumstances which are much more conducive to good psychological adjustment. Hence, their psychological picture, as reflected in their TAT stories, is much more favorable. By the time they were 17, relatively few early-maturers harbored strong feelings of inadequacy, perceived themselves as rejected or dominated by parents or authorities, or felt rebellious toward their families. As a group, they appeared to have acquired more self-confidence and had probably made stronger identifications with mature adults. Hence, they perceived themselves as more mature individuals, less dependent and in need of help, and more capable of playing an adult male role in interpersonal relationships.

Insofar as our results permit generalization, they suggest that some important aspects of motivation, such as needs for achievement and personal recognition, are not significantly affected by maturational status. It may be that among subjects whose achievements are strongly encouraged and rewarded from very early childhood, the need to achieve becomes powerful and resistant to change even in the face of feelings of helplessness and inadequacy. The latter may inhibit the achievement-oriented overt behavior of some late-maturers, but the underlying motivation to achieve seems as strong in this group as it is among the physically accelerated.

In conclusion, it should be noted that, although rate of maturing and associated factors may affect personality development, the relationship between physical status and psychological characteristics is by no means simple. A vast number of complex, interacting factors, including rate of maturation, determine each adolescent's unique personality structure. Hence, in any specific instance, the *group* findings of the present study may not be directly applicable, for other physical, psychological, or social factors may attenuate the effects of late- or early-maturing. For example, an adolescent boy who is fundamentally secure and has warm, accepting parents and generally rewarding social relationships may not develop strong feelings of inadequacy even if he matures slowly. Analogously, the early-maturing boy who has deep feelings of insecurity, for whatever reasons, will probably not gain self-confidence simply because he matures early. In summary, in understanding any individual case, generalizations based on the data of the present study must be particularized in the light of the individual's past history and present circumstances.

REFERENCES

Jones, M. C., & Bayley, N. Physical maturing among boys as related to behavior. *Journal of Educational Psychology,* 1950, **41,** 129–148.

Payne, D. E., & Mussen, P. H. Parent-child relations and father identification among adolescent boys. *Journal of Abnormal and Social Psychology,* 1956, **52,** 358–362.

Tryon, Caroline M. Evaluation of adolescent personality by adolescents. *Monograph of Society for Research in Child Development,* 1939, **4,** No. 4.

CHAPTER THREE
SENSORY ABILITIES

These four articles explore the newborn's ability to fixate, to follow the contour of a form, to differentiate among auditory stimuli, and to habituate to olfactory sensations. Three main questions are asked: To what is the newborn sensitive? How can we ask the newborn infant what he sees, hears or smells? What changes occur in his sensory abilities during the first days of life?

The first study outlines the method of pair-comparisons and reports an investigation which shows that the newborn is sensitive to a dimension of brightness. Exploration of the baby's sensitivity to complexity of stimulation, his perception of the human face, and his interest in the information in forms yielded either insignificant differences or suggestive hints of what he sees. The main import of the first article is methodological; the authors point out that only by using at least three stimuli and determining whether there are significant differences among them all can we know the dimensionality of an infant's sensory world.

How the neonate comes to construct his perceptual world is the theme of the second article. The authors outline a photographic method which enables them to measure (within five degrees of visual angle) where the infant is looking. They report that infants look at either a contour or a corner; they are not able to follow the contour and thus reconstruct the entire figure. The newborn infant either is too young to link his perceptual elements or cannot analyze the solid triangular figure into elements, or cannot integrate the elements of the large figure used in the present study. The authors state that the infant may be responding to brightness differences, he may have a mechanism specifically tuned to angles, or, finally, he may respond only to transitions in brightness near the contours of a figure.

The next study shows that infants are sensitive to the duration of auditory stimuli but that they are not sensitive to either pitch or interval of presentation. The measure used was cessation of non-nutritive sucking. Other studies have shown that older infants are sensitive to pitch and loudness as well as to duration.

Engen and Lipsitt presented infants with compounds of olfactory stimuli for several trials. Following the administration of the compound stimuli, they presented the same newborn infants with pure olfactory stimuli. Their reasoning was that if the infant has habituated (learned inhibition of response) to the compound stimulus, he will respond again when the pure sensation is presented because he still senses the difference. However, if the baby's sensory apparatus has adapted to the stimulation (decreased receptor sensitivity), then changing to a pure stimulation should produce no effect. The pure stimulus did have an effect, suggesting that his reactions result from response inhibition and not sensory adaptation.

8 | Pattern Perception in the Human Newborn: A Close Look at Some Positive and Negative Results

MAURICE HERSHENSON
WILLIAM KESSEN
HARRY MUNSINGER

How is it possible to ask the human newborn what he sees? This investigation suggests some of the problems that occur when psychologists begin a dialogue with the neonate. Hershenson, Kessen, and Munsinger outline the method of pair-comparisons and describe four studies that show some of the sensitivities and limitations of the newborn's sensory apparatus. The authors make two points of some importance: Many of the stimuli which have been presented to the human newborn are in fact multidimensional, and for that reason the results derived from conventional unidimensional methods are suspect. Also, the minimum requirements for assessing the dimensionality of perception are the presentation of three stimuli and the finding of differences among all three. Only in rare cases have these conditions been met, making the results from studies using newborns of limited value in understanding their perceptual world.

Our attempt to evaluate the perceptual abilities of the newborn reflects our interest in the nature of the processes which underlie perceptual development. It further reflects our belief that speculation as to the nature of such mechanisms based on data obtained from adults—or from children—is risky, at best, and that the newborn *can* be studied if the proper techniques are applied.

Our particular methodological posture derives from the conviction that the study of perceptual development in nature will be fruitful only when perceptually mediated responses—"perceptual indices" as they have been called—are somehow related to organization or structure in the stimulus field. That is to say, a theory of perceptual development must be based on an analysis of *perceptible stimulus structure*. Otherwise, generalization to classes or orders of stimulus elements is impossible, whether it be in terms of dimensions of stimulation or attributes of objects as we know them, or some organization of the stimulus array with which we are not familiar. We say not familiar because one may not assume that the newborn is sensitive to perceptual arrays similar to those to which adults respond, and we should be prepared for this contingency. At any rate, unless this analysis is accomplished, it is difficult to see the gain from speculation about mechanism.

Adapted from Pattern perception in the human newborn: A close look at some positive and negative results. In W. Wathen-Dunn (Ed.), *Models for the perception of speech and visual form.* Cambridge, Mass.: MIT Press, 1967. Pp. 282–290.

Thus the problem resolves itself to one of detecting perceptible dimensions for a nonverbal, essentially immobile organism when stimulus prepotency cannot be assumed. How, then, to begin? Fortunately, Stevens, in the very first chapter of the *Handbook* (1951), supplies us with part of the answer: The minimum information necessary to establish a linearly ordered set involves an analysis of *relations* among at least *three elements*. That is, if a response, ocular orientation, for example, could be interpreted to indicate how three stimuli are "related" to one another, then we might have a basis for establishment of a scale. The requirements which a system must satisfy if it is to be classed as ordered are given by Huntington's postulates. These demands are as follows:

1. If a $\neq$ b, then either a $<$ b or b $<$ a.
2. If a $<$ b, then a $\neq$ b.
3. If a $<$ b and b $<$ c, then a $<$ c.

The properties *asymmetric, transitive, connected,* and *irreflexive* are implied by these postulates.

Now in order to apply the postulates of serial order to our problem a definition of the relations is necessary in terms of observable responses. Let a $\neq$ b denote the relation of inequality when "a is fixated for a *significantly* different number of frames than b," and let a $<$ b denote the relation of order when "a is fixated for fewer number of frames than b." (We may abbreviate the latter relation by saying "b is preferred to a.") The relation "preferred" may now be measured by means of ocular orientation and if an ordered set can be derived, then we may index perception in the newborn by means of precisely this operation while at the same time proposing that the ordered set obtained represents a perceptible dimension. Thus we can assume discriminable stimulus structure if, and only if, a serially ordered set of responses obtains. The task of determining the aspects of stimulus structure which correlate with those of the ordered response set can be simplified by using unidimensional stimuli with any given set of responses.

There are, of course, further problems relating to the organism being studied and also to specific stimuli. We shall return to these later. For the present, let us briefly describe the method and then plunge into an analysis of the results.

Babies were seen in the second, third, or fourth day of life in a small room on the Maternity Service of Grace-New Haven Community Hospital. The relevant apparatus and procedures have been described in detail elsewhere (Hershenson, 1964). We should indicate, perhaps, that in each of the studies three points on a single dimension were selected as stimuli to be presented in a paired-comparison procedure and that photographs of eye fixations served as the basic measure.

HOMOGENEOUS STIMULI

In the study of homogeneous stimuli (Hershenson, 1964), light from the projector lamps was reduced by achromatic filters to produce three levels of illumination at the stimulus screens. Twenty newborns each saw six pairs of stimuli. The scale scores of orientation are shown in Figure 1. The medium intensity was more

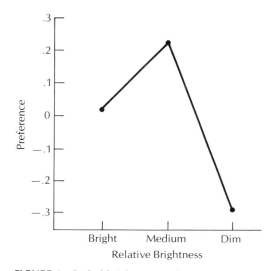

FIGURE 1   Scaled brightness preferences.

often fixated than either the bright or the dim, and the bright stimulus was more often fixated than the dim one. All comparisons were significant over the entire group of babies. Moreover, child-by-child analysis shows a large number of infants with significant individual differential fixations. These data, then, meet the demands of Huntington's postulates and we may conclude that newborn humans can perceive brightness.

PATTERNED STIMULI

Sixteen infants were observed in a study of "complexity" defined as number of brightness transitions (Hershenson, 1964). This dimension correlates with the perimeter of solid figures. The stimuli used were checkerboards of 4, 16, and 144 alternately blackened squares. As can be seen from Figure 2, the differences in scale scores are much smaller than for brightness and, in fact, only the difference between the least complex and the most complex stimuli was statistically stable. We should also note that an apparently inordinate number of babies showed, individually, a texture of significant preferences.

For the group, transitivity was not demonstrated; only the superiority in number of fixations of one of the stimuli. Although one might be inclined to conclude, on such data, that the two stimuli have been discriminated—that the responses were related to the dimension on which the two stimuli are points—this conclusion is clearly unwarranted. All that has been demonstrated

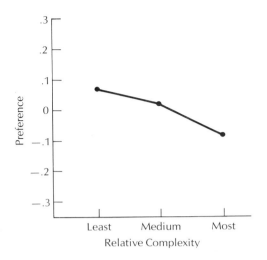

FIGURE 2   Scaled complexity preferences.

in this case is that the infants *attend* to one of the stimuli; the other stimulus may not be available to them at all but may be part of the background. Recall, if you will, our earlier argument essentially emphasizing the importance of just this differentiation—between "They discriminate A from B" on the one hand and "They attend to A" on the other—between discrimination on the one hand and attention tropisms on the other.

The second pattern study, of 20 infants, is the hardest to name and we have oscillated between calling it "organization" and "faceness." As can be seen in Figure 3, the stimuli show Joan Crawford in nature and in two states of facial disorder. The scale scores shown in Figure 4 indicate no differences in preference among the stimuli;

(a) Real Face   (b) Distorted Face   (c) Scrambled Face

FIGURE 3   Stimuli in "organization" or "faceness" experiment.

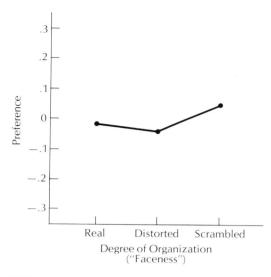

FIGURE 4 Scaled "faceness" preferences.

the differences for the group are indeed small or nonexistent. But again we must note the very large number of infants who, considered individually, show significant preferences. For the group, there is no transitivity, no single preferred stimulus.

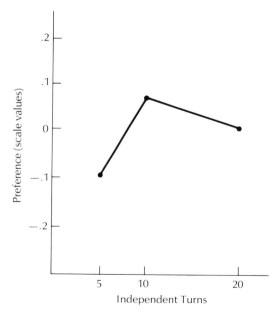

FIGURE 5 Scaled "turns" preferences.

In a third study of patterned stimuli, the "turns" study, 17 babies were presented with solid black figures which differed in the number of independent turns (Hershenson, Munsinger, and Kessen, 1965). This dimension approximates information value. Although the scaled preferences produced the interesting pattern shown in Figure 5, once again only one comparison was significant while a great many babies showed individual preferences.

CONCLUSION

Now the problem is "Where do we go from here?" Do we continue using a methodology based on unidimensionality until, by chance, we hit upon a perceptible dimension, or would it be more profitable to turn immediately to a multidimensional approach? We feel certain you would be easily convinced that the solution is not apparent if we had time to discuss in detail some of the ramifications of these studies which bear directly on this problem. We have learned a good deal about the behavior of the newborn including those things we like to talk about, as, for example, his ability to fixate and to move his eyes in a coordinated fashion; and those we would prefer to ignore, such as his tendency to prefer looking to one side, or his tendency to manifest behavioral extremes which severely limit his workday and in effect restrict his usefulness as a subject in complex designs.

We have also been forced to learn more about the stimulus materials which present themselves as possible candidates in unidimensional studies and perhaps what we have learned is that they are multidimensional. At any rate, the list of possible dimensions is growing so rapidly that we are tempted to let the newborn himself supply the structure. This consideration forces us closer and closer to large matrix designs.

These, then, are the main counterforces with which we are presently grappling. We hope to attack the former by being able to obtain measurements of relative states of wakefulness and to use many babies as one subject. We hope to attack the latter by applying multidimensional scaling techniques with appropriate modifications to accommodate the newborn.

In summary, then, it would appear that for models of perceptual development to advance beyond the stage of speculation, the exciting first glances into the "perceptorium" of the human infant must be succeeded by parametric analysis and the use of conventional psychophysical procedures in somewhat more sophisticated designs.

REFERENCES

Hershenson, M. Visual discrimination in the human newborn. *Journal of Comparative and Physiological Psychology,* 1964, **58,** 270–276.

Hershenson, M., Munsinger, H., and Kessen, W. Preference for shapes of intermediate variability in the newborn human. *Science,* 1965, **147,** 630–631.

Stevens, S. S. Mathematics, measurement, and psychophysics. In S. S. Stevens (Ed.), *Handbook of experimental psychology.* New York: Wiley, 1951. Pp. 1–49.

9 Visual Scanning of Triangles by the Human Newborn

PHILIP SALAPATEK
WILLIAM KESSEN

Another technique for the study of sensory and perceptual development is to photograph the newborn's eyes as he follows the contour of a triangle. The authors report that the baby almost immediately finds either an angle or a contour of the figure and centers his attention there.

Ten human newborns were shown a homogeneous black visual field and ten newborns were shown a large black triangle on a white field. Ocular orientation to within approximately ±5° of visual angle was measured by scoring infrared photographs of corneal reflections. The infants showed much less dispersion of scanning in the presence of the triangle than in the presence of the homogeneous field. Moreover, ocular orientations were directed toward a vertex of the presented triangle. The results were related to Hebb's theory of perceptual development, to analyzer theories of discrimination, and to studies of complexity and preference in the human newborn.

It is only through a detailed study of ocular responses in the newborn child that critical questions about the nature of perceptual development can be resolved. Recent studies (for example, Fantz, 1961, 1963; Hershenson, 1964; Hershenson, Munsinger, and Kessen, 1965) have indicated that the human infant will usually look longer at certain visual patterns than at others during the first few days of life. These findings have generally been explained as representing a preference for differing levels of stimulus complexity; unfortunately, different Es have found that preference is greatest for low complexity, for moderate complexity, and for high complexity. Variation in empirical outcome may be accounted for in part by variation from study to study

Adapted from Visual scanning of triangles by the human newborn. *Journal of Experimental Child Psychology*, 1966, **3,** 155–167.

in the stimulus dimensions that were under investigation. Of more consequence, however, is the difficulty in determining with the procedures used in these studies whether or not the infant was responding to the dimension defined by the *E*. For example, in studies of preference for visual forms, the child may have been responding to the preferred figure as a whole or only to certain parts of it; that is, the preferred figure may have more of what the infant wants to look at or the preferred figure may have something uniquely attractive which the less well preferred figure does not have. In addition, although the finding of differential orientation in a paired-comparison design indicates a discrimination of the preferred figure from its surround, lack of preference does not necessarily indicate a lack of discrimination (Kessen and Hershenson, 1963). This paper describes a procedure which permits more detailed specification of the ocular orientation of human infants than has been available heretofore with dichotomous left-right or yes-no judgments of orientation. A measure of looking accurate to within a few degrees of visual angle will illuminate the processes that underlie preference and discrimination of form in the human newborn.

A large solid black triangle in the center of a white field was shown to human newborns in the present study. It was expected that a central stimulus would capture the infant's regard and that a solid figure on a contrasting field would not demand fine acuity. Further, if the contours of a figure influence ocular orientation, orientations toward the contours would be more readily discernible if the figure was large, i.e., if the contours were at some distance from the center of the field. Of the many figures that might have been selected for initial study, the triangle was chosen because it has received detailed consideration in theoretical treatments of perception in the newborn (Hebb, 1949).

METHOD

Subjects

Subjects for the experiment were 20 awake alert newborn infants under 8 days of age from the nursery of the Grace-New Haven Community Hospital. The Ss were randomly selected from the babies available and awake in the nursery at the time of observation. Records obtained from 49 other babies could not be used either because the infants fell asleep during the observation or because the film was badly processed and unscorable. Observations on the ten babies in the experimental group were completed before observations on the ten babies in the control group were begun. The experimental group was made up of five males and five females ranging in age from 23 to 177 hours with a mean age of 68.1 hours. The control group was made up of six males and four females ranging in age from 23 to 137 hours with a mean age of 77.6 hours.

Apparatus and Procedure

All Ss were observed approximately 20 minutes before their regular feeding at 9:30 A.M. or their regular feeding at 5:30 P.M. in a quiet room under moderate illumination. Each S was brought into the observation room by a nurse, placed in a head-restraining cradle (Hershenson, 1964) and given a pacifier. The experimental group was shown a solid black equilateral triangle 8 inches on each side. The triangle was painted on wire window screen and was centered in a circular white background of aluminum 23 inches in diameter. The stimulus was approximately 9 inches above the infant's eyes. From the baby's side, the wire-screen triangle appeared solid in color. However, enough light passed through the screen to permit photography of the eyes by a camera directly behind the wire screen. Figure 1 shows a schematic drawing of the apparatus. Infrared marker lights, invisible to adult observers from the position of the baby's eyes, were placed behind the stimulus panel at each vertex of the triangle.

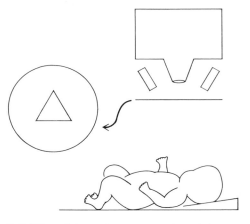

FIGURE 1 Schematic representation of the apparatus used in determining ocular orientation.

Once each second during each observation a picture of the infant's centered eye was taken through the wire screen stimulus; in 19 cases, the right eye was photographed. The noise of the solenoid in the camera which advanced the shutter permitted E to count the number of pictures taken. At least 100 pictures of the infant's open eye were taken with the triangle in an upright position. The camera was then stopped, the triangle was rotated 180°, and at least 100 pictures were taken of the infant's open eye with the triangle inverted. Order of rotation of triangle was balanced across Ss. If S fell asleep during an observation, E stopped the camera and tried to wake S up. If he was successful, a note was made of the interruption in the record and the observation continued until 100 pictures had been taken of S's open eye. The procedure did not produce an equal number of pictures for all Ss or a constant duration of observation; the observation continued until at least 100 frames of film had been taken of each rotation of the triangle with S's eye open.

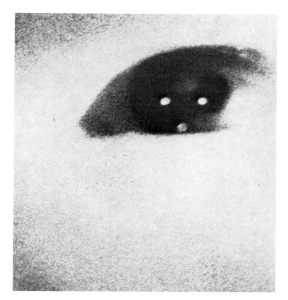

FIGURE 2 Infrared photograph of the newborn's eye. The three white dots in the form of a triangle are the reflections of the infrared marker lights from the cornea.

The control group was treated just like the experimental group with these exceptions. Instead of being shown a black triangle on a white field, the control group was shown a homogeneous circular black field 21 inches in diameter. The infrared marker lights remained mounted behind the stimulus panel at the vertices of a hypothetical equilateral triangle, 8 inches to a side. After at least 100 pictures had been taken of S's open eye (at the standard rate of one frame per second) with the marker lights in one rotation, the camera was stopped, S's eye was covered for a second or two, and the marker lights were rotated 180°. Then, at least 100 pictures were taken of S's open eye with the marker lights in the second rotation.

RESULTS

Scoring

Figure 2 is a photograph of an infant's eye obtained in the way described earlier. Ocular orientation was determined by calculating the deviation of the corneal reflections of the infrared marker lights from the center of S's pupil. The distance from a given marker light to the center of the pupil changes as S looks at different parts of the field. The relative position of the center of the pupil was obtained for each film frame by subtracting the marker light coordinates for a particular frame from the pupil-center coordinates for the same frame. The first 100 successive positions of pupil orientation obtained in this way were fed to an EAI Dataplotter which plotted the points with a reference marker light as origin and joined them to provide a record of visual scanning. Therefore, all records of visual scanning were based on exactly 100 positions of pupil orientation.

Scoring with both instruments yielded inter- and intra-scorer reliability coefficients (r) of over $+.90$. Both instruments were also calibrated to detect a change in ocular orientation of less than 1 inch on the stimulus panel (approximately 5° of visual angle). Ocular orientation could be measured as far as 45° from the center of the stimulus panel.

Patterns of Ocular Orientation

Eight records of ocular orientation for the babies in the control group—those who were shown a homogeneous black field—are presented in Fig. 3. The triangle shown in each record is a hypothetical one, 8 inches on each side, formed by joining the positions of the infrared marker lights behind the field; the triangle is drawn in to permit easy comparison with records of ocular orientation in experimental Ss. Ocular orientations among control Ss were generally widely distributed through the field; there was no evidence that the infrared marker lights systematically influenced the orientation of control Ss. Eight records of ocular orientation for the babies in the experimental group—those who were shown a black equilateral triangle in a white field—are presented in Fig. 4. The inner triangle in each record is again a hypothetical one drawn to indicate the positions of the invisible infrared marker lights; the outer triangle, 8 inches on each side, represents the stimulus actually shown to the infants. As can be seen, when Ss were presented with a solid black triangle on a white field, their ocular orientation tended to cluster, and more, tended to cluster near the vertices of the triangle. Relatively few orientations were directed toward the center of the triangle. It seems clear, from a comparison of Figs. 3 and 4, that the ocular orientation of the human newborn is to some degree controlled by visual form.

As inspection of Figs. 3 and 4 indicates, this overall effect is largely an expression of the experimental group's orientation toward the vertices of the triangle.

The division of contour for scoring purposes into angular components (vertices) and linear components (sides) gave considerably greater total area for linear components. Of course, the linear components (sides) were also nearer the center of the visual field than were the vertices and, presumably, more easily accessible to ocular orientation. In spite of these possible biases in favor of linear components of the figures, it was the vertices and not the sides that significantly attracted ocular orientation in the experimental group. Figure 4 also shows that experimental Ss typically looked toward a *single* vertex although the particular vertex chosen varied both between and within Ss.

Dispersion of Ocular Orientation

The tendency of babies to orient their eyes toward the vertices of the presented triangle is part of a more general characteristic of ocular orientation in the experimental group. As an examination of Figs. 3 and 4 will indicate, babies in the experimental group showed much less dispersion of orientations through the stimulus field. To put the finding another way, the presence of a triangular form reduced the tendency of the baby's eye to wander.

SUMMARY AND DISCUSSION

When infants under 8 days of age were shown a homogeneous black field, their visual scanning tended to be widely dispersed with a greater dispersion in the horizontal than in the vertical dimension. This selective dispersion suggests that horizontal scanning is easier for the newborn than is vertical, although it should also be noted that the infants were able to scan widely in both dimensions. The introduction of a large, solid, central triangle into the infant's field of view markedly reduced the overall dispersion of scanning and also reduced the predominance of horizontal over vertical scanning. Of greatest consequence for perceptual theory, the infants responded to only part of the figure. The ocular orientations of the infants were not distributed haphazardly over the triangle but tended to cluster at the vertices. Not only did their orientations cluster at vertices; there were extremely few orientations in the center of the triangle, the region

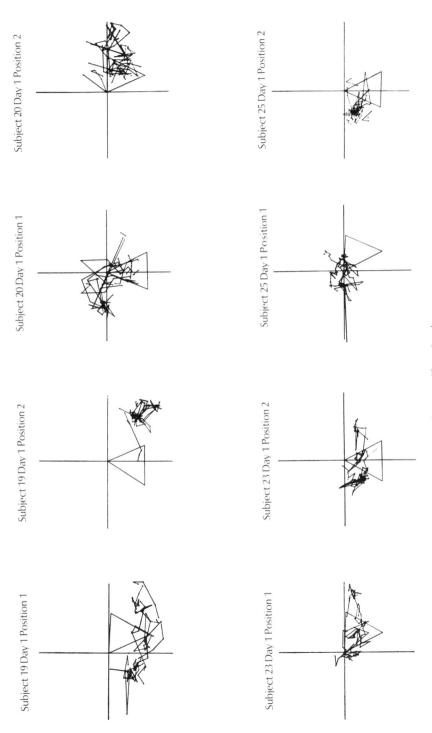

FIGURE 3 Records of ocular orientation for Ss in the control group. The triangle on each record is a *hypothetical* one metrically equivalent (8 inches on each side) to the triangle presented to the experimental Ss.

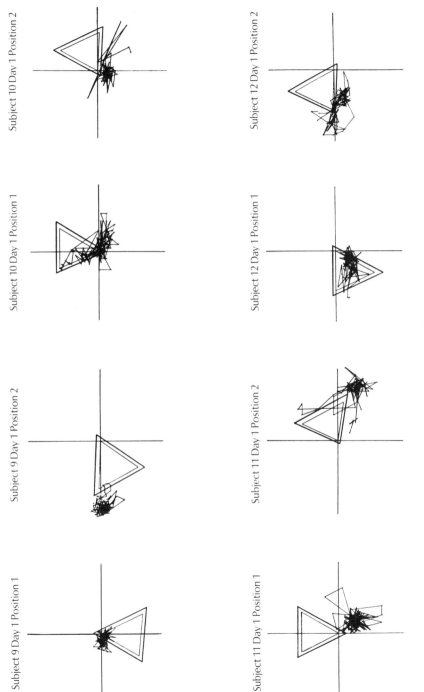

FIGURE 4 Records of ocular orientation for Ss in the experimental group. The outer triangle on each record represents the outline of the solid black equilateral triangle, 8 inches to a side, presented to the experimental Ss.

in which it would be expected that a substantial number of orientations would lie if the infants were responding to the figure as a whole. Moreover, *S*s typically looked toward a single vertex of the figure, the preferred vertex varying from *S* to *S*. There was little indication that, for any particular *S*, orientation was toward more than one 'element' of the figure, e.g., orientations divided between two vertices or between a vertex and a side.

If one tries to explain the obtained results in the light of Hebb's (1949) theory about the acquisition of the concept of 'triangle' by linkage through visual scanning of the 'elements' comprising the figure, one is lead toward one or another of the following conclusions:

1. The newborn *S*s, either because of a lack of maturation or of experience, were at a 'pre-linkage' stage, capable of responding to elements but incapable of linking the elements through scanning.

2. A *solid* triangular figure is defined by contour and may not be analyzed by the visual system into the elements—sides and angles—that are fundamental to Hebb's theory.

3. The figure used in the present study was too large to permit the integration of elements. Obviously, the influence on ocular orientation of age, visual experience, and the size and nature of the figure must be studied before the role of scanning in the construction of form can be fully assessed.

What mechanism may underlie the response of the newborn to vertices of a triangle? The obtained results are compatible with at least three interpretations. It is possible that newborns respond to transitions in brightness and that the orientation toward a vertex is directed by the presence of two brightness transitions. Secondly, the infants may respond to vertices through a mechanism specifically tuned to angles. This interpretation is congruent with analyzer theories of discrimination (for example, Sutherland, 1959; Deutsch, 1960; Dodwell, 1964), and may suggest the presence

in young infants of neurophysiological coding mechanisms analogous to the contour operators described for the visual system of cats (Hubel and Wiesel, 1962, 1963). Thirdly, it is possible that the infants were responding to an optimal level of brightness (Hershenson, 1964) that is only to be found near a vertex.

REFERENCES

Deutsch, J. A. *The structural basis of behavior.* Chicago: University of Chicago Press, 1960.

Dodwell, P. C. A coupling system for coding and learning in shape discrimination. *Psychological Review,* 1964, **71,** 148–159.

Fantz, R. L. The origin of form perception. *Scientific American,* 1961, **204,** 450–463.

Fantz, R. L. Studying visual perception and the effects of visual exposure in early infancy. Paper read at meetings of American Psychological Association, Philadelphia, August, 1963.

Hebb, D. O. *The organization of behavior.* New York: Wiley, 1949.

Hershenson, M. Visual discrimination in the human newborn. *Journal of Comparative and Physiological Psychology,* 1964, **58,** 270–276.

Hershenson, M., Munsinger, H., & Kessen, W. Preference for shapes of intermediate variability in the newborn human. *Science,* 1965, **147,** 630–631.

Hubel, D. H., & Wiesel, T. N. Receptive fields, binocular interaction and functional architecture in the cat's visual cortex. *Journal of Physiology,* 1962, **160,** 106–154.

Hubel, D. H., & Wiesel, T. N. Receptive fields of cells in striate cortex of very young, visually inexperienced kittens. *Journal of Neurophysiology,* 1963, **26,** 994–1002.

Kessen, W., & Hershenson, M. Ocular orientation in the human newborn infant. Paper read at meetings of American Psychological Association, Philadelphia, August, 1963.

Sutherland, N. S. Stimulus analyzing mechanisms. In *Mechanization of thought processes.* London: Her Majesty's Stationery Office, 1959, vol. II.

10 | Effects of Auditory Stimuli on Sucking Behavior in the Human Neonate

RACHEL KEEN

Psychologists are interested in what the newborn can hear. It is clear that we cannot just ask him if he is aware of a particular sound; more subtle ways of measuring his sensitivity are required. It is also interesting to know which particular characteristics of sound affect the baby. Can he detect differences in the length of a sound, or its pitch?

The present study used starting and stopping of non-nutritive sucking as an index of sensitivity to sound. A moderately intense (90 db) auditory stimulus was presented to 48 full-term, newborn infants. Frequency of tone (400 and 4000 cps), stimulus duration (2 and 10 seconds), and interval between trials (2 and 10 seconds) were varied. Infants who received longer stimulus durations (10 seconds) responded significantly more to the stimuli initially than did the 2-second group. No significant effect of interval or frequency was found.

A series of Soviet studies by Bronshtein, Antonova, Kamenetskaya, Luppova, and Sytova (1958) indicate that cessation of sucking, in response to an auditory stimulus, could be rapidly habituated in the neonate, and that sucking increased in response to some types of stimulation. Sucking is an activity with natural pauses and resumptions which occur in the absence of any apparent external stimulus. The problem of determining when cessations in sucking are associated with stimuli and when they are "natural" pauses is not easily solved. The Soviet studies did not specify the criteria for a response, leaving unanswered such crucial questions as minimum length of pause considered as a response, and how

Adapted from Effects of auditory stimuli on sucking behavior in the human neonate. *Journal of Experimental Child Psychology,* 1964, **1**, 348–354.

soon after stimulus onset responses were scored. Further, if left to the experimenter's discretion, stimulus presentations could capitalize on natural rhythms in sucking. The present study used objective methods of recording and scoring responses, and stimuli were presented automatically at fixed, predetermined intervals.

In addition to attempting to reproduce habituation of sucking cessation and initiation, the present study investigated the effects of intertrial interval and stimulus duration on the rate of habituation. Several investigations have indicated that these stimulus characteristics are important variables affecting habituation. The early work of Stubbs (1934) indicated that 15-second durations of tones evoked greater body activity, increased rate of respiration, and more shallow breathing than did shorter durations of 1, 3, or 5 seconds. Irwin's (1946) review stated that discontinuous auditory stimulation produced rapid decrements in circulatory and respiratory responses when presented repeatedly. With shorter inter-stimulus intervals the amount of response per stimulus decreased. More recently, Bartoshuk (1962a) found that shorter in-tertrial intervals produced faster habitua-tion of the heart rate acceleration response in infants, and Bridger (1961) also found that habituation of the startle response was similarly affected. In the same study Bridger reported that longer stimulus durations re-sulted in faster habituation to a tone of moderate intensity.

METHOD

Subjects

The Ss were 24 male and 24 female full-term, normal, newborn infants from the Minneapolis General Hospital nursery, and were 3–5 days of age. Infants who could not be aroused by stroking the mouth with the pacifier ($N = 3$) or who accepted the pacifier but sucked at a mean rate of less than 20 sucks per minute during the first 2 minutes ($N = 2$) were not included. Ex-perimental sessions occurred from 8:00 to 9:00 P.M. The infants were on a 4-hour feed-ing schedule, and the previous feeding had occurred at 5:00 P.M.

Procedure

The Ss were tested in their own cribs in a room adjoining the nursery. The E offered a nipple to the infant by lightly stroking the lips with the nipple, then placing it in the mouth. A warm-up period (1 minute of sucking followed by removal of nipple for 1 minute) preceded a 2-minute Base Rate Period, presentation of tones for 50 trials, and a 2-minute Base Rate Period. The Ss were randomly assigned to one of four tone-presentation groups, each containing six males and six females. The groups were:

Group 2I- 2D: 2-second intertrial interval with 2-second stimulus duration

Group 10I- 2D: 10-second interval with 2-second duration

Group 2I-10D: 2-second interval with 10-second duration

Group 10I-10D: 10-second interval with 10-second duration

For half of the Ss in each group, the 400-cps tone was presented on the first 20 trials, the 4000-cps tone on trials 21–40, and the 400-cps tone on trials 41–50; this series was Order I. For the other half of the Ss, the frequencies were presented in reverse order, i.e., 4000, 400, and 4000; this series was Order II. Three males and three females composed each order subgroup.

Definition and Scoring of Sucking Response

Intrasubject consistency was indicated by a positive correlation of 0.75 between mean rate of sucking during the Base Rate Period and mean rate during the remainder of the session. There was only a slight decrement in mean rate from 57 sucks per minute initially to 53 sucks per minute at the end of the longest experimental session of 20 minutes in Group 10I–10D. However, rate of sucking did not remain completely stable for any group, but tended to fluctuate minute by minute around the mean rate. A recent study by Levin and Kaye (1963) offers further evidence for stability of suck-ing rate.

Cessation of sucking was scored as the response to a tone stimulus if a pause of at least 2 seconds duration interrupted a se-quence of at least two sucks. Most pauses were of longer duration than 2 seconds, but a brief minimum time for defining a pause was arbitrarily selected. A minimum of two sucks occurring prior to the pause attempted to insure against mistaking a single random sucking motion for the beginning of a new sequence. Initiation of sucking was scored as the response to a tone if an infant who had not been sucking for at least 2 seconds prior to a tone made at least three sucks following the tone. In the case of both cessations and initiations, a response was scored only if the change in sucking behavior occurred within 2 seconds after tone onset. This latency was selected as the criterion since two thirds of all responses on the first trial occurred within this time interval. In addition, a brief time limit for scoring responses decreased the probability of including changes unrelated to the experimental stimulus.

The effects of stimulus variables on sucking behavior were determined for (a) sucking-changes, the total number of cessations and initiations either in blocks of ten trials or for fixed periods of time; (b) cessations, the proportion of times a sucking sequence was interrupted, in blocks of ten trials; and (c) initiations of sucking.

RESULTS AND DISCUSSION

Comparison of Base Rate, Tone, and Post-Tone Periods

Since natural pauses occur in the sucking patterns of every infant, the question may be raised as to whether cessations and initiations occurring during the Tone Period were responses to the stimuli or whether they were natural variations which would have occurred in the absence of stimuli. To test this, comparisons between Base Rate Periods, Tone Periods, and Post-Tone Periods were made for each group. The 2-minute Base Rate Period and Post-Tone Period for each S were scored for cessations and initiations at the points where stimuli would have occurred if they had been presented. To keep the amount of time constant for comparison of various periods, only the first 2 minutes and the last 2 minutes of the Tone Period were used. These are labeled "Tones Early" and "Tones Late,"

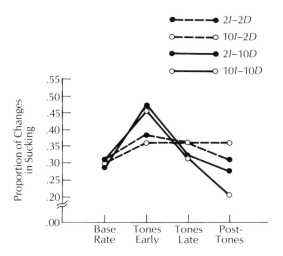

FIGURE 1 Changes in sucking behavior for different experimental periods.

respectively (Figure 1). The groups had the following number of stimulus presentations for any single 2-minute period: (a) Group 2I–2D had 30; (b) Groups 2I–10D and 10I–2D had 10; and (c) Group 10I–10D had 6. Group differences in number of stimuli presented necessitated the conversion of sucking changes for each S to a proportion score.

Figure 1 shows that Base Rate changes in sucking behavior were similar for all groups, with mean proportions ranging from 0.29 to 0.31. The proportions increased in all groups during the Tones Early Period, but the difference was significant only in Group 2I–10D ($t = 3.11$, $p < 0.05$) and Group 10I–2D ($t = 1.81$, $p < 0.05$). The failure of the relatively large change shown by Group 10I–10D to achieve significance ($t = 1.51$, $p < 0.10$) is due to the greater variability associated with the smaller number of stimulus presentations occurring within the 2-minute periods for this group. No group showed a significant difference in responses between Base Rate and Tones Late. Following the Tone Period, there was no further significant decrease except in Group 10I–10D ($t = 2.02$, $p < 0.05$), the group with the greatest variability. A possible explanation for no differences in the other groups is that most responses during Tones Late occur by chance, i.e., unrelated to any external stimulus, and so do not contrast with random pauses during the Post-Tone Period. This explanation is supported further by the fact that there were no differences in any group between random Base Rate responses and Tones Late responses.

These results are in line with Bridger's (1961) finding that longer durations (20 seconds) were more effective in producing habituation of the startle response than were 5-second durations. Bridger's data also indicated that short intervals produced habituation faster than did long intertrial intervals. Lack of a significant interval effect in the present study could be due to the particular intervals used and the response being habituated. Bridger found differences between 3-second and 10-second intervals, while Bartoshuk (1962b) found no differences between 15-, 30-, and 60-second intervals. However, in a later study (1962a) Bartoshuk reported differences between 6-second and 1-minute intervals. Discrepancies in results may be explained by the fact that Bridger used the startle response, Bartoshuk employed decrement in heart rate acceleration, and the present study considered cessation and initiation of sucking as the response. The phenomenon of habituation may vary depending upon the particular response habituated.

Two main differences can be noted between the report of Soviet research by Bronshtein et al. (1958) and the present study. First, the Russian report implied that a high percentage (82%) of cessation of sucking occurred upon initial presentation of the stimulus. In the present study the highest mean proportion of cessations made by any group in the first block of ten trials was 0.52, or about half of the tone presentations. The total range of proportions was from 0.58 to 0.22. Although repeated application of the stimuli resulted in fewer cessations, the number was never zero. The nature of the sucking response itself, due to the frequent occurrence of

natural pauses, produced some artifactual pauses throughout all portions of the experimental session.

A second discrepancy is between the rate of habituation displayed by the Russian infants and the rate shown by the subjects in the present study. Bronshtein et al. reported that most infants (exact number not specified) required only 4–5 stimulus presentations before they ceased to respond. Such rapid habituation was not found in the present work. Habituation should be measured in terms of change in proportions of pauses following stimulation, without the expectation that the subject will initially respond to every stimulus and later show no responses at all. Comparison of the present study's findings with the Russian studies is difficult because of the absence of information concerning duration of stimuli, length of intertrial interval, and number of trials used in the Soviet investigations.

In summary, the present study suggests that changes in non-nutritive sucking can be used as an indication of infants' responses to auditory stimulation. Durations of 10 seconds produced greater changes in sucking initially, but as trials continued a decrement in responding occurred. The 2-second duration groups responded less to the tones throughout all trials, except in the last block when a slight increase over the 10-second groups was shown. There was no evidence that the infants discriminated between the two frequencies used.

REFERENCES

Bartoshuk, A. Human neonatal cardiac acceleration to sound. *Perceptual and Motor Skills,* 1962, **15,** 15–27. (a)

Bartoshuk, A. Response decrement with repeated elicitation of human neonatal cardiac acceleration to sound. *Journal of Comparative and Physiological Psychology,* 1962, **55,** 9–13. (b)

Bridger, W. Sensory habituation and discrimination in the human neonate. *American Journal of Psychiatry,* 1961, **117,** 991–996.

Bronshtein, A. I., Antonova, T. G., Kamenetskaya, A. G., Luppova, N. N., & Sytova, V. A. On the development of the function of analyzers in infants and some animals at the early stage of ontogenesis. In *Problems of evolution of physiological functions.* OTS Report No. 60-51066. Translation available from U. S. Dept. of Commerce. Moscow: Acad. Sci., 1958.

Irwin, O. C. Infant psychology. In P. L. Harriman (Ed.), *Encyclopedia of Psychology.* Philosophical Library, Inc., New York, 1946. Pp. 272–285.

Levin, G. R., & Kaye, H. Non-nutritive sucking by human neonates. Paper read at Eastern Psychological Association, New York, April, 1963.

Stubbs, E. M. The effect of the factors of duration, intensity and pitch of sound stimuli on the responses of newborn infants. *University of Iowa Studies in Child Welfare,* 1934, **9,** 75–135.

11 | Decrement and Recovery of Responses to Olfactory Stimuli in the Human Neonate

TRYGG ENGEN
LEWIS P. LIPSITT

The infant and child soon come to ignore sustained stimulation of moderate intensity. There are two main hypotheses advanced to explain this. One suggests that the effect results from response inhibition; the other hypothesis attributes it to fatigue of sensory receptors. The present study tries to decide which hypothesis is correct in the case of infants' responses to sustained olfactory stimulation. The investigators used differential breathing patterns following the administration of the stimuli. The newborn infants quickly adapted to a compound of amyl acetate and heptanal diluted in diethyl phthalate. Following adaptation to the compound stimulus, they were administered one of the two odors in pure form.

If response decrement is due to sensory fatigue (adaptation), then the change from the compound stimulus to the pure stimulus should not produce response recovery—that is, a change in respiration. On the other hand, if response decrement is due to habituation, then the change from first to second stimulus should produce response recovery in the form of respiratory change. Their findings support the conclusion that habituation rather than sensory adaptation was operating.

Engen, Lipsitt, and Kaye (1963) have demonstrated with recordings of activity and respiration: (a) differential reactions of human newborns to different odorants, (b) a decrement in this response after repeated stimulation by asafoetida and anise oil, and (c) recovery of the diminished response following repetitive presentation of either of these stimuli by the introduction of the other.

Adapted from Decrement and recovery of responses to olfactory stimuli in the human neonate. *Journal of Comparative and Physiological Psychology,* 1965, **59,** No. 2, 312–316. Copyright © 1965 by the American Psychological Association, and reproduced by permission.

The decrement and recovery of such responses have been reported with olfactory stimulation in newborns by Disher (1934), who also cites Kussmaul's very early experiments, by Bridger (1961) and Bartoshuk (1962a, 1962b) with auditory stimulation, and by Bronshtein, Antonova, Kamenstkaya, Luppova, and Sytova (1958) with both olfactory and auditory stimuli. Brackbill (1962) has reported the use of the technique by Zonova for determination of color discrimination in the newborn. In these experiments, the definition of recovery involves the introduction of a different stimulus (S_2) following decrement of the response to a previous stimulus (S_1).

Engen et al. (1963, p. 76) have called attention to the distinction between sensory adaptation (fatigue of receptor organs produced by repeated stimulation) and response habituation (extinction of response to an originally effective stimulus). When recovery of response upon presentation of S_2 takes place, this could result either because sensory adaptation or response habituation has occurred to S_1. Previous studies of olfactory recovery have involved the presentation of a new or qualitatively different stimulus (S_2); consequently the recovery could not be attributed solely to sensory adaptation or to habituation. It is our purpose to demonstrate here that recovery of response may occur to an olfactory S_2 even when this stimulus is simply a component of S_1. Under such conditions, recovery of response upon presentation of S_2 would suggest that the response decrement obtained to S_1, just preceding, is more likely response habituation and less likely sensory adaptation. Our previous olfactory experiments with newborns have suggested that such component "novel" stimulation can reinstitute the diminished response.

METHOD

Subjects

Seventy apparently normal infants, slightly more girls than boys, were Ss. Their average age was about 55 hr with a range of 27–77 hr. Each was used only in one session and had not been an S in any other olfactory experiment.

Apparatus

The apparatus (Lipsitt & De Lucia, 1960) and the method (Engen et al., 1963) have been described and only the pertinent details will be stressed here. Breathing was recorded on a Grass polygraph (Model 5A) from a Phipps and Bird infant pneumograph attached around the abdomen.

The odorants were anise oil (Anethol USP), tincture asafoetida, amyl acetate, heptanal, and a mixture of anise oil and asafoetida and a mixture of amyl acetate and heptanal. The diluent was diethyl phthalate. All chemicals were the purest obtainable commercially.

One cubic centimeter of each odorant was kept in a 10 x 75 mm Pyrex test tube stopped with a cork wrapped in aluminum foil. Stimuli were presented to the infant on a piece of cotton wrapped around a glass rod with the other end of the rod attached to the cork. The cotton was partially immersed in the liquid odorant when not in use.

Procedure

The experiment was performed in a quiet air-conditioned laboratory room at the Providence Lying-In Hospital at a temperature of about 78°F. All infants were tested individually between 10:00 and 11:00 A.M. Infants were fed about 9:30–9:45 A.M. The infant was placed on its back in the experimental crib and the pneumograph was attached. The Es waited until the infant appeared to be asleep with no activity indicated on the stabilimeter (recorded on the polygraph), eyes closed, and a steady regular breathing. Since the infant had been fed beforehand, this condition would normally be reached within a few minutes. Less than 1 in 10 infants were discarded for failure to quiet.

A test trial consisted in holding the cotton between and about 5 mm from the infant's nostrils for 10 sec, and the duration of the trial was recorded on the polygraph. A trial was presented every minute. Occasionally it was impossible to maintain the cotton in place for 10 sec for the S responded by moving during the trial. Occasionally, also, more than a minute was required before the infant quieted to the pretrial criterion following response to the previous trial. A response was defined as a change in the regular breathing record as in a previous study (Engen *et al.*, 1963) in which reliability of *E*s' judgments of the records was found satisfactory.

RESULTS

Experiment 1

Ten trials were administered to each of ten infants with a 50-50% mixture of undiluted anise oil and asafoetida. Then half of the group was tested with a 50% concentration dilution of asafoetida and the other half with 50% anise oil on Trials 11 and 12. The average results are presented in Fig. 1, which shows a very regular decrement in response with the mixture over the ten trials, and a recovery of the response to asafoetida but not to anise. Average blocks of two trials present a smoother but unaltered picture of the results. The curve drawn in the figure was obtained with the method of least squares and fits the data very well as indicated by a value of *r* of −0.99.

To study the intensity and quality of these odorants and help clarify the results, one of two groups of ten *S*s was given two trials with the 50% asafoetida stimulus and another group of ten *S*s was given two trials with the 50% anise stimulus. These results are also shown in Fig. 1 for the first block of trials, and show that asafoetida is the stronger of the two stimulus components of the mixture. Note that the response of the asafoetida component in the posttest is at a level just below its value without prior exposure to the mixture. Anise on this basis should have a value of about 0.4 in the posttest, for the slope of these decrement curves (as will be shown below) has been found to be relatively constant with variation in chemicals (Engen *et al.*, 1963).

It has been shown that the amount of information human *O*s are able to transmit about multidimensional olfactory stimuli depends primarily upon variations in quality and is not appreciably affected by the intensity of the stimuli (Engen & Pfaffmann, 1960). To evaluate this possibility, similarity judgments of the quality of the three odor stimuli were obtained with the method of similarity estimation (Ekman, Goude, & Waern, 1961) from a group of 12 graduate students in psychology. Briefly, the procedure consisted in presenting on a rack the three possible pairs of the three stimuli used with the infants (the 50-50% mixture, the 50% anise, and the 50% asafoetida) to each individual *O*, counterbalancing the order of presentation to different *O*s. The task was to judge the similarity of the quality only of the smells of each pair on a scale from 0 ("not at all similar") to 100 ("identical") with 50 designated as halfway between these extremes, etc. The means of the judgments were: anise-mixture, 60.8; asafoetida-mixture, 39.2. That anise and asafoetida are clearly discriminable from one another was indicated by a mean value of 27.5 assigned to that comparison. The standard deviation of the judgments was about 20.0. These results show that anise was decidedly more similar subjectively to the mixture than was asafoetida. This supports the hypothesis that whether or not a posttest response occurs depends upon the similarity of the

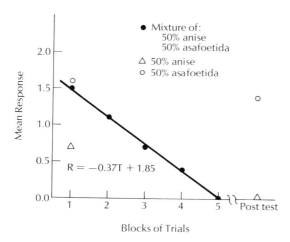

FIGURE 1 Average number of responses as a function of trials and posttest stimulus presentation. (Circles and triangle at left show level of response to odorants without prior mixture presentation.)

component to the mixture (i.e., the novelty of the posttest stimulus). This finding is in line with the fact that anise produced no response in the posttest while asafoetida did.

In summary, the supplementary tests suggest that another mixture with two (psycho-physical) characteristics is needed to establish recovery of response with *both* components of a two-chemical mixture. First, the components should be of equal intensity and, second, the quality of component odors should be different from each other but equally similar to the mixture. To satisfy both criteria is generally difficult, and in the case of some mixtures impossible; for example, to accomplish both conditions in the case of the mixture of anise and asafoetida would require an even smaller proportion of anise in the mixture, but that would reduce the intensity of the anise component which Fig. 1 shows was already of marginal intensity. However, satisfactory stimuli were obtained after several preliminary attempts with amyl acetate and heptanal.

Experiment 2

Twenty infants were divided at random into two groups of ten. Each group first received ten trials with a mixture consisting of 33.3% amyl acetate, 16.7% heptanal, and 50% diluent. In the posttest one group was tested with 33.3% amyl acetate, Fig. 2, and the other group with 16.7% heptanal, Fig. 3. The data were treated as above and curves fitted with the method of least squares. The curve shown in Fig. 3 is the poorer fit but is still good with $r = -0.96$ and a standard error of estimate of 0.13 which suggests that the heptanal component in posttest is a significant distance away from this regression line. A fit of the data trial by trial rather than for blocks reduces r to -0.90 but would not affect the interpretation of the results for the present purpose.

It can be observed from these figures that the slope is very similar for the three

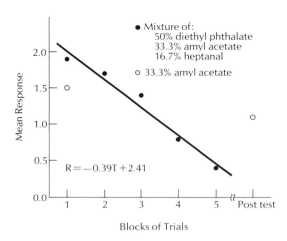

FIGURE 2 Average number of responses as a function of trials and posttest stimulus.

sets of data, but the y-intercept is higher for the two present figures which shows that even when diluted 50%, this mixture is stronger than the undiluted mixture of anise and asafoetida. In this case both components produce a response in the posttest, but more to amyl acetate (Fig. 2) than to the heptanal component (Fig. 3).

Again two groups of infants were used to obtain a measure of the intensity of each component without the prior exposure to

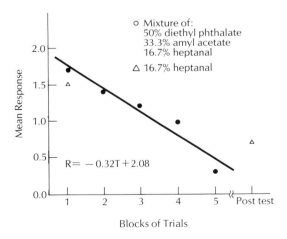

FIGURE 3 Average number of responses as a function of trials and posttest stimulus.

the mixture. The results from these two groups are also included in Figs. 2 and 3 and indicate that the two components are of equal psycho-physical intensity, although the amyl acetate stimulus is of higher concentration. This verifies our pilot data.

A group of 12 psychology undergraduate students judged the three pairs of these stimuli as described previously. This resulted in means of 61.9 for 33.3% amyl acetate paired with the mixture, 73.3 for 16.7% heptanal paired with the mixture, and 50.9 for the pair of components. The standard deviation for a pair is about 26, and in general the data of Experiment 2 are more variable than those of Experiment 1. However, these posttest stimuli do satisfy the requirement of equal intensity and at the same time are not too different on the similarity scale, but once more the component which is more similar to the mixture (heptanal) is the less effective stimulus in the posttest. The similarity of both these components to their mixtures is greater than the similarity value for asafoetida and its mixture, and they also have lower posttest response values. Finally, the data also indicate some of the complexity of mixing odorants; this is an important psychophysical problem although not of primary interest here (cf. Geldard, 1953).

DISCUSSION

Habituation has been defined by Thorpe (1956) as the waning of a response resulting from repeated stimulation not followed by reinforcement. If the decrement is of a relatively enduring nature, and can be demonstrated to be different from sensory adaptation or fatigue, Thorpe regards the phenomenon as learned behavior. Martin (1964), on the other hand, makes a plea for the parametric study of response-decrement phenomena per se, and argues that "No useful purpose can be found for distinguishing habituation as an independent term from adaptation [p. 40]." Concerning habituation and its similarity to other response-decrement processes, Rheingold and Stanley (1963) also take the view that: ". . . any suggestion that neonatal habituation is similar to extinction, Pavlov's internal inhibition, or Hull's inhibition would be premature indeed [p. 3]." Much remains to be discovered about the neural mechanisms underlying such habituatory processes (Hernandez-Peón, 1960; Thompson & Welker, 1963).

The data of the present experiments clearly demonstrate response recovery. That is, the infant responds to a stimulus, S_2, which is a component of another stimulus, S_1, to which response decrement has just been obtained. From Thorpe's distinction, response habituation rather than sensory adaptation, or fatigue of receptors responding to S_2, accounts for our decrement, and the reactions in posttest trials constitute dishabituation. This conclusion is supported by the finding that the degree of response recovery is inversely related to the degree of similarity between S_1 and S_2, or the degree of novelty of S_2 following the exposure to S_1 (assuming congruence of similarity data of adults and infants).

Concerning the "novelty" aspects of the present data, a recent review (Cantor, 1963) of studies of attending and manipulative responses in infants and children to complex and novel stimulation stated:

In view of the ubiquity of these types of phenomena and the relative ease with which they can be studied, it is surprising how little systematic investigation of the novelty-familiarity variable and its relation to infant or child behavior has occurred [p. 21].

Cantor cited four child studies dealing with such effects, all of these done with children of preschool age and older, and asserted that novelty cannot be considered independently of the individual organism's past experience, unlike some other stimulus attributes such as complexity. What is novel for a given S depends to some extent on the recency of his exposure to either that stimulus or one similar to it.

Viewed in this way, studies of response-decrement and recovery (or habituation and dishabituation) in neonates constitute procedures for investigating effects of novel stimulation in inarticulate, immature organisms. Quantitative variations in amount of response recovery to posttest stimuli, following decrement, could yield gradients of generalization which are essentially gradients of novelty.

Under what conditions may response decrement be taken as evidence for a learning process? Another way to ask the same question is: when is response to novelty evidence for an S's having *learned not* to respond to a familiar stimulus? Thorpe (1956) seems to argue that when adaptation and fatigue have been ruled out as the basis for diminution of response to the "familiar" stimulus, learning is left.

Hinde (1954) says there may be as many as four different mechanisms underlying decrement to repetitive stimulation. When response is found to wane specifically to an evoking stimulus, when the waning seems temporary, and when the response can still be evoked by other stimuli, Hinde favors calling this selective process adaptation and keeping it distinct from habituation. Martin (1964), on the other hand, asserts that *all* response decrement phenomena resulting from repetitive stimulation are of a learning nature and should not be arbitrarily separated. Bridger (1961) says that the startle decrements in neonates to tones of a given frequency are changed, do not constitute phenomena usually referred to as learning, but are rather indicative of ". . . some sort of primitive sensory discrimination [p. 994]." In contrast, Bartoshuk (1962a, 1962b) labels his heart-rate decrement to auditory stimuli, and subsequent recovery to changed stimulation, as a kind of discrimination learning. He also shows that repetitive presentation of a changing tone (from low to high frequency over an 8-sec period of stimulation) produces response-decrement and that when the change is temporally reversed (now high to low frequency over an 8-sec

period), the response recovers. Barring the possibility that the auditory receptors are influenced physiologically and differentially under the two conditions of tone-order, the only determinant remaining for the recovery is novelty. Similarly, in the present study, barring the possibility that the olfactory receptors for S_2 are changed somehow by their interaction with receptors for S_1 (consisting of both stimuli), the remaining determinant for the recovery is the novelty of S_2.

Assigning the term "novelty" to a stimulus on the basis of the organism's increased reaction to it implies a perseverative effect of previous familiarization with another stimulus. Whether this familiarization effect should be regarded as a learning phenomenon or not (Lipsitt, 1963) depends upon arbitrary definitions of learning and on what particular parameters control the process that also control (other) learning processes. Since the present study rules out strictly sensory fatigue, the decrement and recovery must surely be classified as habituatory and, according to the Thorpe terminology, as a learning phenomenon.

REFERENCES

Bartoshuk, A. K. Human neonatal cardiac acceleration to sound: Habituation and dishabituation. *Perceptual and Motor Skills,* 1962, **15,** 15–27. (a)

Bartoshuk, A. K. Response decrement with repeated elicitation of human neonatal cardiac acceleration to sound. *Journal of Comparative and Physiological Psychology,* 1962, **55,** 9–13. (b)

Brackbill, Y. Research and clinical work with children. In R. A. Bauer (Ed.), *Some views on Soviet psychology.* Washington, D. C.: American Psychological Association, 1962, 99–164.

Bridger, W. H. Sensory habituation and discrimination in the human neonate. *American Journal of Psychiatry,* 1961, **117,** 991–996.

Bronshtein, A. I., Antonova, T. G., Kamenstkaya, A. G., Luppova, N. N., & Sytova, V. A. [On the development of the functions of analyzers in infants and some animals at the early stage of ontogenesis.] In *Problemy evolyulaii fisiolgicheskikh funktsii.* [Problems of evolution of physiological functions.] Office of Technical Services Report No. 60–61066, 1960. Pp. 106–116. (Translation obtainable from the United States Department of Commerce, Office of Technical Services.) Moscow-Leningrad: Academiya Nauk USSR, 1958.

Cantor, G. N. Responses of infants and children to complex and novel stimulation. In L. P. Lipsitt & C. C. Spiker (Eds.), *Advances in child development and behavior.* New York: Academic Press, 1963. Pp. 1–30.

Disher, D. R. The reactions of newborn infants to chemical stimuli administered nasally. In F. C. Dockeray (Ed.), *Studies of infant behavior.* Columbus: Ohio State University Press. 1934. Pp. 1–52.

Ekman, G., Goude, G., & Waern, Y. Subjective similarity in two perceptual continua. *Journal of Experimental Psychology,* 1961, **61,** 222–227.

Engen, T., Lipsitt, L. P., & Kaye, H. Olfactory responses and adaptation in the human neonate. *Journal of Comparative Physiological Psychology,* 1963, **56,** 73–77.

Engen, T., & Pfaffmann, C. Absolute judgments of odor quality. *Journal of Experimental Psychology,* 1960, **59,** 214–219.

Geldard, F. A. *The human senses.* New York: Wiley, 1953.

Hernandez-Peón, R. Neurophysiological correlates of habituation and other manifestations of plastic inhibition. *EEG and Clinical Neurophysiology,* 1960, Suppl. No. 13, 101–114.

Hinde, R. A. Factors governing the changes in strength of a partially inborn response. *Proceedings of the Royal Society of London, Series B,* 1954, **142,** 306–358.

Lipsitt, L. P. Learning in the first year of life. In L. P. Lipsitt & C. C. Spiker (Eds.), *Advances in child development and behavior.* New York: Academic Press, 1963. Pp. 147–195.

Lipsitt, L. P., & DeLucia, C. A. An apparatus for the measurement of specific response and general activity in the human neonate. *American Journal of Psychology,* 1960, **73,** 630–632.

Martin, I. Adaptation. *Psychological Bulletin,* 1964, **61,** 35–44.

Rheingold, H. L., & Stanley, W. C. Developmental psychology. *Annual Review of Psychology,* 1963, **14,** 1–28.

Thompson, R. F., & Welker, W. I. Role of auditory cortex in reflex head orientation by cats to auditory stimuli. *Journal of Comparative and Physiological Psychology,* 1963, **56,** 996–1002.

Thorpe, W. H. *Learning and instinct in animals.* London: Methuen, 1956.

CHAPTER FOUR
PERCEPTUAL GROWTH

Perceptual processes are more complex than sensory abilities and they develop later in the child's life. The developmental course for perceptual processes is of considerable interest because many theorists believe they are the foundation for later cognitive abilities. Piaget, for example, feels that the sensory-motor abilities of very young infants are incorporated into the perceptual processes of the child, and that these perceptual processes mature into the cognitive mechanism's of the adult.

This set of studies shows that the young infant possesses depth perception, demonstrates cross-cultural variation in people's abilities to perceive depth in two-dimensional photographs, traces the early growth of shape constancy and part-whole perception, and outlines tachistoscopic recognition by young children and adults.

The "visual cliff" takes advantage of our fear of falling and uses it to examine depth perception in the infant. Six-month-old babies were placed on the center of a table covered with glass; one side of the table appeared to drop about five feet (deep side), while the other (shallow-side) seemed level with the center platform. Babies routinely crawled toward their mothers on the shallow side of the visual cliff, but only a rare infant ventured onto the deep side. Six-month-old babies perceive depth; however, the course of development for depth perception is open to conjecture.

Depth perception is a part of how we see photographs. We are so familiar with three-dimensional scenes represented in two-dimensions that we may be surprised to find that this ability is not universal. Hudson shows that Africans with little or no experience in seeing two-dimensional pictures do not view them as we do; the culturally isolated African views the photographs in two dimensions.

The next article shows that shape constancy (the ability to recognize shape as identical over spatial transformations) exists at 50 days of age in the human infant. Age variation in this ability is probably the result of changes in the infant's total processing capacity (his ability to do more than one thing at the same time) and is not the result of differing sensitivity to cues.

Piaget holds several expectations about the development of part-whole perceptions; his notion of decentering suggests that the prelogical child is governed by perceptions. Later, when the child is able to logically consider several alternative interpretations of the same input, he is able to see parts *and* wholes. These predictions were tested and confirmed by Elkind, *et al.* They presented children from four to nine years of age with pictures that contained both a meaningful whole and meaningful parts. Both part and whole perceptions increased with age.

A classic method used to study perception in the adult and child is to present a stimulus for some short interval. In this way we can examine the growth of a percept. One easy way to vary the information an observer receives is to change the time during which the stimulus is shown. At very short durations (tachistoscopically) he makes many interesting mistakes that tell us something about how he sees. The final article of this section discusses the use of this method to study the effect on recognition of varying complexity and redundancy (predictability) of stimuli. The results show that simple figures are easier to see than complex ones, that redundant information is easier to recognize, and that the child and adult process varying levels of information differently.

Visual Depth Perception in Infants

RICHARD D. WALK
ELEANOR J. GIBSON

The visual cliff offers a natural test of depth perception. If the infant possesses depth perception, he will choose not to fall off the deep side; instead, he will tend to crawl toward the other side of the apparatus, which appears to drop only two inches. However, this test requires that the infant crawl; by that age he will have had considerable experience in falling and in coordinating his perceptual abilities. Although the test is a valuable aid in studying the infant's abilities, the use of this method does not allow us to know the course of depth perception from birth to six months of age.

One of man's strongest fears is the fear of high places and falling. The paratrooper standing in the door of his airplane waiting to jump and the steel worker on the girders of a rising skyscraper are dramatic cases of fearful situations. Nearly all adults have felt apprehensive of height when looking down from a tall building or into a gorge, when balanced at the top of a high ladder or preparing to jump from a high diving board.

The problem with which this monograph is concerned is the discrimination, by vision alone, of depth downward at an edge. Some of the questions to be answered are the following: When is the discrimination present in children? Can it be detected by tendency to avoid a drop-off? What conditions or cues are actually operative in making the discrimination? And what is the role of visual experience in promoting the discrimination?

The apparatus designed for the present experiments, which we named the "visual

Adapted from Visual depth perception in infants. *Psychological Monographs,* **75,** 1961. Copyright © 1961 by the American Psychological Association, and reproduced by permission.

cliff," uses the principle of a drop-off or graduated heights, but gives the child a *choice* between a short drop-off on one side of a center board and a long drop-off on the other side. A child, if it detected the difference, should prefer the short drop-off at a safe depth to the long drop-off at a dangerous depth. To eliminate nonvisual cues that might permit detection of the difference, such as auditory, olfactory, or temperature differentials from near or distant surfaces, a sheet of glass was inserted under the center board where the organism was placed, so as to extend outward across both the shallow ("safe") drop and the deep ("dangerous") one. The glass was placed over the shallow side as well as the deep side to equate stimulation produced by the glass itself, if any (e.g., reflections), and to equalize tactual cues for locomotion.

Patterned material (wallpaper, linoleum, etc.) could be placed directly under the glass on the shallow side and on the floor below, at any desired distance, on the deep side. Information in the light coming to the eye from the patterns on either side, in combination with stimulation produced

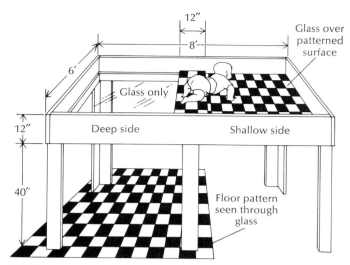

FIGURE 1 Drawing of the visual cliff, *Model III.* An infant is starting from the center board toward the shallow side. The entire floor of the room is covered with the checkered linoleum identical with that on the cliff.

by the child's own motion and ocular equipment constituted the stimulus basis for visually differentiating the two sides. Figure 1 shows diagrammatically the situation created by the apparatus.

APPARATUS AND PROCEDURE

This model of the visual cliff was designed to test larger animals and human infants. A table was constructed of 2″ × 4″ pine, measuring 8′ long, 6′ wide, and 40″ high. Supporting legs were placed at each corner and in the middle of each long side where an additional supporting cross beam was also used. Two large pieces of Herculite glass 4′ × 6′ × ⅜″ formed the surface of the table. Under the shallow side a 46″ × 68½″ × ¾″ piece of composition plywood ¼″ below the glass was placed to support a textured surface, an irregular green and white pattern of linoleum tile that matched the floor. The same tile pattern was laid over the center board which measured 6′ × 11½″ × 1″.

The cliff table was entirely surrounded

by an 8″ high board of ¾″ pine to protect the subject from accidentally falling off the cliff.

The standardized procedure evolved was as follows: The mother stood twice at each side, alternating, some mothers starting at the shallow side, some at the deep. The mother stood for 2 minutes at each side unless the child got off the board and reached a lure. If this happened, the child was put back on the board and the mother switched sides. An experimenter stood at each end of the board so as not to influence the way the infant crawled. If the child crawled away from the mother the experimenter went toward the infant to safeguard him.

RESULTS

The use of this standardized procedure clearly showed that the babies discriminated depth. They crawled toward the mother when she stood at the shallow side and refused to cross the glass to her when she stood at the deep side. Many infants crawled to the shallow side when the mother stood at the deep side and urged him to come to her. Eleven subjects did this; no subject crawled away from the mother across the deep side when she stood at the shallow. Some of the babies cried when the mother stood at the deep side and would not go to her. In such cases, the 2-minute observation period from the deep side was usually terminated at 1 minute.

Once the procedure was standardized, from Subject 10 on, the infants tended to behave very consistently. They crawled to the shallow side twice; in only two cases did the child go but once to the shallow side. The three negative cases, all boy infants, were also consistent; each child crawled twice to the mother across the deep side, twice to her at the shallow side.

When 30 subjects had been run, there were five subjects in the youngest (6–7 month) age group. Of these infants, three had not moved from the center board, one had gone to the shallow side only and one to both sides. Even though two cases is not a large sample, one of the two had crawled across the deep side and it seemed possible, a trend that had to be checked, that very young infants could not discriminate depth as adequately as older ones. Consequently telephone calls were made to mothers in the city with infants 6–7½ months old. Very few of these infants were crawling, but five subjects were added to the youngest group. Of these five children, two remained on the shallow side. The indication was, therefore, that younger infants

have as adequate depth perception, if they can be tested, as the older ones.

The results on the first 36 subjects run are shown in Table I. The only age trend is the inadequate locomotor ability of the younger subjects. They evidently crawled at home but not in a strange place. One must recognize that Table I is not a random sample of babies at the indicated ages, but a sample of infants whose mothers say they crawl. It is probably slightly skewed toward younger developers in the 6–7 months old group.

There is much interesting behavior to be observed in this situation. The babies were attracted by the lure and when they reached it, played with it eagerly. They peered down through the glass, sometimes patted it or leaned on it with their faces, yet refused to cross. Some used the deep side for support with one knee, others *backed* partly out across it (in first locomotion in the human infant the child often goes in reverse when he means to go forward), yet they still refused to cross. It was as if the infant could not recognize the consequences of his own actions, since he had already been where he now refused to go. The attitudes of the mothers were interesting as well. The predominant impression among mothers seemed to be that the child had failed the "test" because he did not have enough sense to realize the glass was safe to crawl over. The glass on the deep side was banged with hands and fists; cigarette boxes, lipsticks, purses, crumpled bits of paper, and other releasers of infant

TABLE I   Behavior of Human Infants on the Visual Cliff

Response of S	Age of Infant (months)				Total	Percentage
	6–7	8–9	10–11	12–14		
Did not move off center board	5	2	1	1	9	25
To shallow side only	4	7	8	5	24	67
To deep side only	0	0	0	0	0	0
To both sides	1	1	1	0	3	8
Total	10	10	10	6	36	100

approach behavior were proffered—but the babies still refused to go across the glass of the deep side.

These data show that the average human infant discriminates depth as soon as it can crawl. By the time the locomotion is adequate, which is the time when depth discrimination is necessary for survival, the infant can discriminate depth. In this the human infant fits with other late maturing species we have studied, the rat and the cat. But the human infant does not have quite the same marked apprehension of depth as the goat or the sheep, and a few crawled across the deep side. One also notes the relative clumsiness of the human infant at this age. Despite adequate depth discrimination many babies would have fallen but for the glass on the deep side to protect them.

But there is no evidence from these data that apprehension of height is learned from prior experience with falling. The avoidance and apprehension of height seems in general to be present as soon as an infant has adequate locomotion.

13 | Pictorial Depth Perception in African Groups

W. HUDSON

Western man is very familiar with photographs and other pictorial representations of the world; he is likely to assume that the understanding of depth represented in pictures could not possibly offer difficulty to anyone. The present study used pictures constructed to provide two- or three-dimensional perception of object size, superimposition, and perspective. This type of depth perception is quite different from the perception of deep and shallow sides of a table. The purpose of the present study was to show that the perception of depth in two-dimensional arrays is not a universal characteristic, but must be learned through experience. Eleven groups, six of them school-going (three white, three black) and five of them non-school-going (one white, four black) saw the pictures. School-going groups saw the pictures as three-dimensional, the others as two-dimensional. Formal schooling and informal training combined to supply the exposure necessary for three-dimensional perception. Cultural isolation was effective in preventing or retarding the process, even in persons possessing advanced formal education.

Western culture is book-learned, characterized by dependence upon the written word, illustration, diagram, photograph. Visual presentation is a common mode in the classroom. Educational and training programs, advertisements, safety, and health propaganda, and much current didactic literature make use of pictorial material. Certain characteristic perceptual habits have become normal for Western culture, and for the groups professing it. Pictorial representation of a three-dimensional scene requires the observance and acceptance of certain artistic or graphic conventions. Pictorial depth perception depends upon response to these conven-

Adapted from Pictorial depth perception in African groups. *Journal of Social Psychology*, 1960, **52,** 183–208. Used with permission.

tional cues in the two-dimensional representation. There are three such cues concerned with form only, viz., object size, object superimposition or overlap, perspective. In the visual world, of two objects of equal size, that object nearer the observer is larger. When one object overlaps another the superimposed object is nearer to the observer. Parallel lines tend to converge with distance from the observer. In the two-dimensional representation of the three-dimensional scene, foreground objects are depicted larger than background items. Superimposed objects are perceived as nearer. Pictorial structuring by perspective technique is accepted as a convention for depicting distance. The incidental evidence furnished by African samples indicates that these pictorial conventions are not familiar to such subcultural groups.

The present investigation is limited to the study of the perception of three dimensions in pictorial material by subcultural groups in southern Africa.

METHOD

Test Material

Test material was constructed to isolate the pictorial depth cues of object size, object superimposition and perspective. Six outline drawings and one photograph were constructed. The experimental situation is simple to construct. Pictures 1-6 were designed to obtain the responses of observers to depth cues of size, overlap, and perspective in horizontal pictorial space. Each picture is similarly structured. The elephant is positioned centrally between a human

figure and an antelope. In this "hunting scene," the elephant is depicted smaller than the antelope. This object size depth cue occurs in each of the six pictures. Pictures 2 and 3 carry the additional depth cue of overlapping. Pictures 4, 5 and 6 have perspective lines representing a road vanishing in a horizon. In all pictures the hunter's assegai is aligned on both elephant and antelope.

A similar picture was made using modeled objects. Human figure, elephant, and antelope were modeled to scale and subsequently photographed to reproduce a scene similar to Picture 1.

Testing Procedure

Pictures were presented separately to individual candidates in the given order. Questioning was done orally in whatever tongue

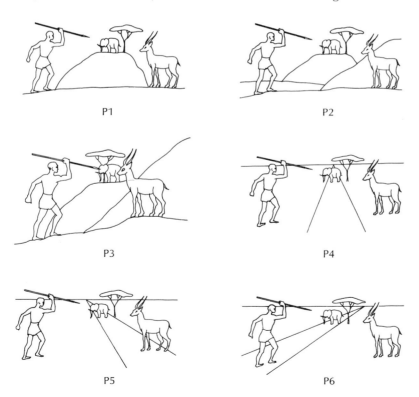

P1   P2

P3   P4

P5   P6

FIGURE 1   Horizontal pictorial space.

was mutually intelligible to both candidate and tester. Where this practice was not feasible (with illiterate samples from different territories in southern Africa), an interpreter was used. Answers were recorded seriatim. Complete picture sets were not administered to the first four samples.

Candidates were asked the following questions while viewing each picture:

1. What do you see?
2. What is the man doing?
3. Which is nearer to the man, the elephant or the antelope?

In addition candidates were required to identify each object in each picture, viz., man, assegai, elephant, tree, hill, antelope.

If a candidate reported that the man was aiming or throwing the spear without specifying his quarry, an additional question was asked to clarify whether he was aiming at elephant or antelope. In the majority of cases, this additional question was unnecessary.

Scoring Method

For reasons to be discussed later, responses to Question 3 were taken as indicative of the type of dimensional pictorial perception possessed by a candidate. If candidates reported the antelope in the "hunting scene" to be nearer the man than the elephant, their responses were classified as three-dimensional (3D). Similarly, for Question 2, if candidates reported the hunter to be aiming at the antelope, these responses were classified as three-dimensional. All other responses in the scenes were characterized as two-dimensional (2D).

Samples

The test was administered to 11 samples which fell into two main types, a non-school-attending group (Sample a-e) and a school-attending group (Sample f-k). The nonschool-attending group contained no children and consisted of four black and one white sample. The school-going group consisted of children mainly except for one sample of adult teachers. Three of the samples in this group were black, and three white. All samples were tested in the Union of South Africa. Samples a-d contain candidates whose territorial origins cover the Union of South Africa, South West Africa, High Commission territories, Federation of Rhodesias and Nyasaland, East Africa, Mozambique, and Angola. Age and educational data are lacking for two cases in Sample e.

RESULTS

Intersample Differences in Depth Perception for Photographs and Drawings

Percentage number giving 3D responses to Question 3 with respect to the photograph are listed for samples taking this test (Table 1).

Illiterate mine workers do not see the pictures three-dimensionally. The remaining samples, where a high proportion of candidates perceive three-dimensionally, are all school-going samples, both black and white. There are minor differences within this second group. White school beginners and black pupils at the end of their primary course perceive the photograph three-dimensionally less frequently than do white pupils at the end of their primary course. But the main intersample difference in depth perception in photographs lies between the illiterate black sample and the school-going group, both black and white.

TABLE 1   Percentage Candidates with 3D Responses

Samples	n	Percentage
d	45	0
f	42	72
g	113	85
h	34	76
i	25	92
j	52	81
k	32	100

Object Identification as a Factor in Dimensional Perception

Since pictorial depth perception depends upon the perception and the appropriate cues there must be a direct relationship between object identification and dimensional perception.

In all pictures, except Picture 3, the man and the animals were correctly identified. In Picture 3, the depth cue of overlap was introduced and as can be seen from Figure 1, objects were superimposed over the central figure of the elephant in order to enhance the perception of depth. With the illiterate Sample d, this technique defeats its own object by complicating the representation of the elephant to such an extent as to render it unrecognisable to the candidates. This finding does not apply to Picture 2 where overlap is also used. In this instance superimposition is restricted to contour lines, so that the animals and objects retain their definition.

DISCUSSION

White and black school-going samples perceive depth more frequently in pictorial material than do illiterate black samples, and samples both black and white, which have terminated their school course and live in isolation from the dominant cultural norm. As expected there is no direct relationship between incorrect identification of items, in the drawings, and two-dimensional perception, but correct identification does not predicate three-dimensional perception. Outline drawings making use of perspective depth cues are less frequently seen three-dimensionally than those using overlap or size depth cues. This finding holds particularly in the case of white primary school pupils. School-going samples perceive three-dimensions in a photograph more readily than in an outline drawing, but this finding does not apply to illiterate samples. Intersample differences are less pronounced with photographic material than with outline drawings.

There are three hypotheses which can be set up on these results: (1) that the results are artifacts of the test, (2) that the results are culturally determined, (3) that the results are genetically determined.

Test Artifacts in Dimensional Pictorial Perception

This hypothesis has two aspects to it: (a) How far has the perceptual structure of the test influenced results? (b) How far has the semantic structure of the test influenced results?

Outline drawings were used to provide the simplest and least graphically contaminated medium for the representation of the appropriate depth cues in a standard scene. Such drawings have representational drawbacks. Perspective cues in particular tend to become symbolic and unrealistic, and the high proportion of incorrect identifications, particularly in the illiterate samples, lends support to this view. But responses to the photographic reproduction of the same pictorial scene modeled show that with that form of two-dimensional representation, which is least symbolic and most realistic of three-dimensions, the illiterate sample continues to perceive two-dimensionally. Work by Smith et al. (1958) on perceived distance as a function of the method of representing perspective showed that judgments of distances in drawings do not vary with the amount of detail included.

What do candidates understand the tester to mean when he asks the question —Which is nearer to the man, elephant or antelope? There is evidence to show that 2D responses are not semantically dependent on the wording of the question. With all samples except high school pupils (black) and graduate teachers (black) responses, whether 3D or 2D, were immediate.

Following their identification of objects in the pictures candidates were asked what the hunter was aiming at in the "hunting scene," prior to being questioned on relative proximity of animals to hunter. Candidates in all samples, choosing the elephant as the hunter's quarry, were those who perceived the elephant as nearer the hunter than the antelope. This means that the whole manifest content of the picture tended to be perceived two-dimensionally, and appropriately interpreted. The occurrence of this phenomenon is considered to be a function of perceptual organisation and not merely a semantic evaluation. The hypothesis postulating the influence of the semantic structure of the test on candidates' responses is rejected.

Cultural Factors in Dimensional Pictorial Perception

There are two levels of cultural factors to be considered viz., (a) formal education, (b) informal training.

The white primary groups' (Samples f, g, k) 3D perception is associated with educational level. The higher the educational standard, the more frequent is the occurrence of 3D pictorial perception.

This finding does not apply to black samples, otherwise markedly superior performances would be expected from black high school pupils (Sample j) and graduate teachers (Sample i). Candidates in Sample b (mine laborers) possess a primary school level of education, but their pictorial perception is entirely two-dimensional and does not differ from that of the illiterate mine workers. In addition the 3D perception of the white laborers (Sample e), the majority of whom have had primary schooling, is markedly inferior to that of the white school beginners (Sample f).

Training in pictorial perception is not included in the formal school curriculum. It is gradually acquired by white children between the ages of 6 and 12 years (Samples f, j, k). During that period, there is an informal process of almost continuous exposure to pictorial material in the school

and in the home, so that by the age of 12 years, most white children have learned to perceive pictures three-dimensionally.

But pictorial depth perception is not learned by the white laborers in Sample e, although they attended school. Mundy-Castle and Nelson (1960) have described this subculture elsewhere. It is an isolated group living under conditions of sheltered employment, closely intermarried, and centripetal. Families are large, and homes are poorly supplied with pictures, books, magazines, and newspapers. Consequently school-going children are not exposed in the home to the informal training necessary for the three-dimensional perception of pictorial material. School is equally isolated, and, as an agency by which the outside world may attempt to invade the community, is resisted by the elders of the group. There is little opportunity for scholars, unstimulated perceptually in the home, to acquire new depth perceptual organization with respect to pictures.

The black samples are also isolated. This is particularly true of Samples a-d, which are migratory and rurally orientated. The black urban samples (h, i, j) are ethnocentrically isolated. They have been urbanised for one generation only. Homes, even of graduates, are poorly furnished with pictures and illustrated reading matter. The women-folk seldom read and then mainly literature in the vernacular. Most books owned by the men are of the nature of textbooks. Daily and monthly magazines are taken, but most of these are sparsely illustrated with photographs. During the early years, however, when the white child is obtaining his informal training in pictorial material, the black child, even in an urban home, suffers from lack of exposure to pictures. He may acquire the skill at a later stage, but there is little opportunity for stimulation, particularly where formal schooling is presided over by teachers, many of whom perceive pictorial material two-dimensionally. Hence it does occur that a black graduate of London University perceives a picture flat. It also happens that a black teacher sees a picture flat, and his pupil perceives it three-dimensionally.

Such results are not unexpected. African art is essentially volumetric. Where it is pictorial as in wall decorations or body tattooing, it is either diagrammatic or two-dimensional naturalistic. Haselberger (1957) reports on a long continuous history of two-dimensional mural art in Africa. Jeffreys (1957) describes tattooing in Nigeria as the African counterpart to abstract pictorial art in Europe and America. Such evidence emphasises that the critical feature for pictorial depth perception appears to be adequate exposure to the appropriate experience.

REFERENCES

Haselberger, H., Die Wandmalerei der afrikanischen Neger, *Zeitschrift für Ethnographie,* 1957, **82,** 209–237.

Jeffreys, M. D. W., Negro Abstract Art or Ibo Body Patterns, *South African Museums Association Bulletin,* 1957, **6,** 219–229.

Mundy-Castle, A. C., & Nelson, G. K. Brain Rhythms, Personality and Intelligence in a Socially Isolated Community," *Nature,* 1960.

Smith, O. W., Smith, P. C., & Hubbard, D. "Perceived Distance as a Function of the Method of Representing Perspective," *American Journal of Psychology,* 1958, **71,** 662–674.

14 Slant Perception and Shape Constancy in Infants

T. G. R. BOWER

Three experiments investigated shape constancy in human infants between 50 and 60 days of age. Babies were first conditioned to respond to a standard shape. They were then tested for their generalization of the initial response to other shapes, which were either (1) in the original position, (2) rotated 45 degrees, (3) a trapezoid in the frontoparallel plane, or (4) a trapezoid that presented the infant with exactly the same retinal image as the original stimulus. The first study showed that infants possess some capacity for shape constancy. The second study confirmed this finding and showed that the capacity is not attained by correlation of perceived projective shape with perceived orientation.

Earlier (Bower, 1964; 1965) I presented evidence that human infants between 40 and 70 days of age display some degree of size constancy. The research I now report was designed to discover whether such infants are also capable of shape constancy; the problem is of theoretical interest. Strong empiricist theories of perception (Helmholtz, 1935) tend to assume that shape constancy only becomes possible when the organism has become familiar with all possible retinal projections of an object; they assume that one learns how an object looks in various orientations, and that one infers from seeing a recognized "look" of an object that one is seeing that object x in some particular orientation. Obviously these theories would be refuted by any demonstration of shape constancy with infant subjects and unfamiliar shapes. A second major class of theory[1], which assumes that shape constancy is attained by correlation of projective or retinal shape with perceived orientation, has not been confirmed with adult subjects (Stavrianos, 1944); its adherents claim that this is because by adulthood the correlation process has become so automated that its components cannot be separately reported. If the hypothesis were true, it should surely be demonstrable with infant subjects. My results indicate that 50- to 60-day-old infants do manifest some degree of shape constancy and that it does not result from correlation of perceived projective shape with perceived orientation.

The first experiment used eight infants 50 to 60 days old. The infant under test reclined in an infant seat placed on a brown,

Adapted from Slant perception and shape constancy in infants. *Science,* 1966, **151,** 832–834.
[1] For example, J. Piaget, *Les Mécanismes Perceptifs* (Presses universitaires de France, Paris, 1962); S. Klimpfinger, *Arch. Ges. Psychol.* **88,** 599 (1933). My discussion and experiments are aimed only at those theories of shape perception that assume that projective shape and perceived orientation precede shape constancy in perceptual development, and that projective shape, orientation, and real shape are separately registrable attributes of an object in space. Some projective shape-slant correlation models are not committed to the position of separate registration.

wooden table, at 45 deg. His head was clasped between two yielding pads, the left pad containing a microswitch whose closing operated an event recorder placed beneath the table. Immediately before each infant seat an experimenter was stationed beneath a gap in the table. When the event recorder closed, the experimenter emerged and 'peek-a-booed' at the infant. Two meters from each infant's eyes a wooden board, 25 by 50 by 2.5 cm, was placed on a turntable. The board, of unfinished white wood, stood on its long edge, turned 45 deg anticlockwise from the infant's fronto-parallel plane; its center of rotation lay in the infant's medial plane. The room was otherwise unfurnished; the walls were of coarsely textured brick. Illumination was provided by a roof light of the same length as the table, which minimized shadows. The experimenter could introduce a screen between himself and the infant for stimulus changes and rest periods.

During training, the board in the above orientation served as conditioned stimulus (CS); the leftward head movement, as conditioned response (CR); and the "peek-a-boo," as reinforcement. Initially the infants were trained to respond only in the presence of the CS. After this was accomplished, behavior was shaped in daily 30-minute sessions until the infants were working at a rate of one response per 2.0 seconds on a variable-ratio schedule on which every fifth response, on average, was reinforced, the exact interval between reinforcements varying randomly. The training procedure is described in greater detail elsewhere (Bower, 1964; 1965).

After 1 experimental hour at this level, generalization testing was begun. Four stimuli were presented during testing: (i) the CS in its original 45 deg orientation; (ii) the CS in the fronto-parallel plane; (iii) a trapezoid in the fronto-parallel plane, whose retinal projection was then equal to that of the CS at 45 deg; (iv) this trapezoid at an angle of 45 deg. Each stimulus was presented for four 30-second periods in counterbalanced order. No reinforcement was given during testing. In terms of difference from the CS the four presentations may be classified as follows: (i) no change; (ii) same objective shape, different projective shape, different orientation; (iii) different objective shape, same projective shape, different orientation; (iv) different objective shape, different projective shape, same orientation.

The mean numbers of responses elicited by the four presentations were (i) the CS, 51.00; (ii) the same objective shape in a different orientation, 45.13; (iii) that which projected a retinal shape identical with that of (i), 28.50; and (iv), 26.00. The difference between (i) and (iii) was highly significant ($t = 12.08$; df, 7; $P < .01$). It is obvious that these infants had not learned to respond to a projective or retinal shape but to an objective shape, which could be recognized in a new orientation; to this extent they showed shape constancy. Also in line with this interpretation is the fact that (iii) and (iv) elicited equally few responses ($t = 0.47$; not significant), indicating that they were responded to as if equivalent.

Although this experiment clearly rules out the strong empiricist explanation of shape constancy described above, it is neutral in respect to the second hypothesis: that shape constancy develops out of the correlation of two perceptually prior variables, projective shape and apparent slant. This hypothesis was not confirmed in the following experiment.

Each of nine infants, aged 60 to 63 days after the test, was trained to make a head movement as CR to the rectangle used in experiment 1, presented at a 5-deg anticlockwise orientation, as CS in the manner described above. Behavior was shaped to the same criterion level of responding on a variable-ratio schedule. Then in three successive sessions each infant performed once on each of the following three tasks (see Table 1).

(1) The rectangle described was ex-

posed in four orientations, turned 5, 15, 30, or 45 deg anticlockwise. Each orientation was presented 30 times in random order for 5-second periods. Only responses made while the rectangle was at 5 deg from the frontal plane were rewarded, and these were rewarded continuously. Reinforcement time was not included in presentation time, so that several 15-second reinforcements could be obtained during a 5-second presentation.

(2) This condition was exactly like the first except that the stimuli used were only projectively equivalent to those used in condition 1. Four trapezoids casting the same retinal image as the rectangle at 5, 15, 30, or 45 deg were all shown in the fronto-parallel plane[2].

(3) This condition differed from the others in the nature of the stimuli used. An opaque cardboard screen, 1 by 1 m, was placed 10 cm before the rectangle. An aperture, 10 by 20 cm, was cut in it so that, while the body of the rectangle was visible, its edges were not. Thus only orientation per se was available to differentiate presentations of the rectangle in its four orientations. Order of testing was counterbalanced across infants.

In all conditions only stationary positions of stimuli were ever visible; transitions were never seen. These three conditions were designed to present the infant with, respectively, a form in space (having objective shape, projective shapes, and orientations with only the first invariant); a set of projective shapes with orientation invariant; and finally a set of orientations, with projective shape invariant. The developmental hypothesis being tested asserts that at this stage of development, shape judgments result from deduction from two perceived components, projective shape and orientation. This should

[2] To ensure that the trapezoids used were pictorially equivalent to the rectangle in its various orientations, the latter was photographed in all four positions, and matte enlargements were pasted on the visible surfaces of the corresponding trapezoids.

mean that discrimination performance, shown by the difference between the numbers of responses elicited by rewarded and unrewarded stimuli, should be best under condition 1, where the infants had both projective shape and orientation as differentiating features. This prediction was not confirmed. Discrimination performance was poorer under condition 1 than condition 2 ($t = 6.06$; $P < .01$) or condition 3 ($t = 4.97$; $P < .01$) (6). In fact, examination of performance in condition 1 indicates very little discrimination between the four presentations; only one presentation, the rectangle at 45 deg, was significantly differentiated from the rewarded presentation ($t = 1.08$; $P < .1$).

The putative advantage of the last experiment was that every subject served as his own control. The training conditions and the stimulus situation were such that discrimination in condition 1 should have been easier than in the other two conditions. As I have pointed out, there are two differentiating variables available in condition 1 to only one in conditions 2 and 3.

In addition, all infants were trained with a condition-1 CS, which fact should have facilitated discrimination in condition 1; in fact it did not. This can be interpreted to mean that the subjects showed such a high degree of shape constancy that the same shape in different orientations literally looked the same, or so very similar that discrimination was too difficult to be

TABLE 1 Proportions of Responses Elicited by Rewarded Stimulus That Were Elicited by Unrewarded Stimuli in the Three Presentation Conditions Described in the Text

Condition	Proportion at Orientation			
	5°	15°	30°	45°
1	1.0	1.04	0.98	0.90
2	1.0	.70	.64	.55
3	1.0	.86	.78	.77

formed in the time given. However, there are objections to this interpretation: it could be argued that little response strength transferred from training to conditions 2 or 3 because the rewarded stimuli differed so much in the three conditions that the data are not truly comparable. In order to meet this objection a third experiment was run.

Three groups of five infants were each run through one condition of experiment 2. One group was trained with the rectangle at 5 deg as CS; the second, with a projectively equivalent trapezoid in the frontal plane as CS; and the third, with the 5-deg orientation of the surface behind the screen as CS. The groups were equated for total number of reinforcements received. After response rate reached a criterion of one response per 2 seconds, the four stimuli in each condition were each presented for four 30-second periods, in counterbalanced order, without reinforcement, after the paradigm of experiment 1. The results (Table 2) show that significantly more responses were elicited by the novel stimuli in condition 1 than in condition 2 or 3 ($P < .01$ by the t-test), whereas there was no significant difference between the numbers of responses elicited by the three CS. If one accepts the basic logic of the generalization experiment, this can only mean that the infants in condition 1 perceived the novel stimuli as more like their CS than did the infants in the other two

conditions; that variations in orientation of the same object, with projective shape and orientation variant, and only real shape invariant, produce a higher degree of identity or "sameness" than do variations in projective shape alone, with orientation invariant, or variations in orientation, with projective shape invariant.

These three experiments taken together strongly indicate that young humans possess the capacity for shape constancy, the capacity to detect the invariants of shape under rotational transformation in the third dimension. The data of experiments 2 and 3 seem in fact to show that response to a shape invariant is more primary than response to a simple variable such as orientation. In both experiments it was shown that rotation of an object into the third dimension did not produce the response decrement that was produced by rotation of a surface without limiting contours. In the latter case there was of course no shape invariant to respond to.

It thus seems that the capacity-limited perceptual machinery of the infant is set to respond to high-order invariants, and to ignore low-order variables such as orientation, when both are present, so that in these experimental situations it is difficult for the infants to respond to the low-order but differential variable orientation.

The notion that invariants and variables may compete for central access within the perceptual system is useful in the present context: it may also explain the paradox that adult subjects may show perfect shape constancy while hopelessly misjudging orientation, and vice-versa (Eissler, 1933).

This explanation constitutes a reformulation of the problem of the development of shape constancy; it shifts the emphasis from an attempt to understand how infants learn to compute "real shape" from projective shape and orientation to an attempt to understand how the ability to *simultaneously* register orientation and real shape develops. It shifts the emphasis from de-

TABLE 2 Mean Numbers of Responses Elicited in Experiment 2

Orientation (Deg)	Responses under Conditions (No.)		
	1	2	3
5	50	48	56
15	48	40	40
30	46	35	30
45	44	30	31

velopment of specific local functions, such as the constancies, to development of a general capacity to simultaneously handle multiple variables and invariants.

This shift may have some merit in that it points to a resolution of the apparent contradiction between the fact that perceptual capacities undoubtedly do change with age, and the fact that many local functions make their appearance very early in life.

REFERENCES

Bower, T. G. R. *Psychonomic Science,* 1964, **1,** 365. *Science* **149,** 88 (1965).

Helmholtz, H. *Physiological Optics III.* Optical Society of America, 1935.

Eissler, K. *Archives of Gestalt Psychology,* 1933, **88,** 487.

Stavrianos, B. *Archives of Psychology,* **61,** 5 (1944).

15 Studies in Perceptual Development: II. Part-Whole Perception

DAVID ELKIND
RONALD R. KOEGLER
ELSIE GO

In this study children from four to nine years of age were tested for their ability to perceive both parts and wholes in drawings; both the parts and wholes had independent meanings. Results showed that (1) there is a regular increase with age in ability to perceive part and whole, (2) parts are perceived at an earlier age than wholes, (3) part-whole integration is present in a majority (75 percent) of children by age nine, and (4) whether parts or wholes are seen is partially a function of the stimulus. The results are interpreted from the standpoint of Piaget's genetic theory of perception.

This is the second in a series of studies devoted to the systematic exploration of Piaget's (1958) theory of perception as it applies to meaningful materials. According to Piaget, the perception of the young child is "centered" in the sense that its organization is dominated by the Gestalt-like principles of proximity, closure, and good form, etc., which Piaget calls *field effects*. With age, however, and the development of new mental structures, the child's perception is progressively freed from its domination by field effects and becomes increasingly logical in form. (That is, the older child is able to differentiate the elements of a configuration and can organize and reorganize them as if he employed operations analogous to those of logic and mathematics.) Piaget's decentering theory was originally formulated in relation to illusions and constancy phenomena, but it has also been found to apply to figure ground reversal involving the identification of meaningful figures (Elkind & Scott, 1962). The present study seeks to determine whether the decentering of perception can also be demonstrated in the development of part-whole perception when both parts and wholes have different and independent meanings.

Although a number of studies have investigated part-whole perception, only one, a study by Meili-Dworetzki (1956) used figures in which both parts and wholes had different meanings. For example, in one of her drawings Meili-Dworetzki had a number of fruits drawn so that in their entirety they resembled a man. Meili-Dworetzki presented her figures to both children and adults and found a regular increase with age in the percentage of subjects who saw both parts and wholes. She also found that, for her figures, wholes

Adapted from Studies in perceptual development: II. Part-whole perception. *Child Development,* 1964, **35,** 81–90.

were perceived at an earlier age than were the parts and that a majority of her subjects (75 per cent) did not perceive both part and whole until adulthood.

Despite the fact that Meili-Dworetzki's study was not carried out in relation to Piaget's theory (she was concerned with the genetic analysis of Rorschach responses), her results do bear on Piaget's position. The increased ability with age of Meili-Dworetzki's subjects to perceive both part and whole is in keeping with Piaget's de-centering hypothesis which would also predict that the ability to attribute different meanings to the same perceptual form should develop gradually with age. On the other hand, Meili-Dworetzki's finding that it was not until adulthood that a majority (75 per cent) of subjects perceived both parts and wholes conflicts with Piaget's hypothesis that perceptual regulations, permitting the perception of both part and whole, are well developed by middle childhood. Likewise, her finding that wholes were perceived earlier than parts does not necessarily support the Piaget position. According to Piaget's theory, whether wholes or parts are perceived is determined by the field effects produced by the stimulus configuration and not by whole or part tendencies in young children.

In the present study the figures used (Figure 1) contained parts which were taken from nursery school books, were clearly drawn with all identifying characteristics, were not superimposed, and were generally (as determined by pilot studies with nursery school children) easier to recognize than the wholes. Using these figures with children at different age levels, three questions were asked: (a) Is there a regular increase with age in the ability of children to perceive both parts and wholes? (b) With figures in which the field effects favor part perception, will parts be perceived earlier than wholes? (c) With figures containing parts and wholes which are familiar and easily identified, will both parts and wholes be perceived by a majority of children (75

per cent) during middle childhood? Control tests for sex and IQ differences were also carried out.

METHOD

Subjects

Two groups of subjects were used. One group consisted of a nursery school class and the first three grades of the University elementary school at UCLA, a total of 95 children. The nursery school youngsters were of the same socioeconomic (and presumably the same intellectual) level as the elementary school children. For the elementary school group as a whole, the mean IQ (Stanford-Binet) was 122. Mean ages for the four age groups were: 63 months, 79 months, 91 months, and 103 months, respectively.

The second group of subjects were the first four grades, a total of 100 children, of an elementary school in a lower-middle class neighborhood of Los Angeles. The mean IQ of this group was 100. Mean ages for the four age groups in this sample were: 78 months, 91 months, 104 months, and 115 months respectively.

Tests

The figures used in the study are shown in Figure 1. We call the set as a whole the Picture Integration Test (P.I.T.). The figures were pretested on groups of nursery school children (not those used in the study), and it was found that the parts were easily recognized by a majority of 4- and 5-year-old children.

Procedure

Each child was tested individually. The cards were shown one at a time in the order indicated by the numbers in Figure 1. The child was instructed, "I am going to show you some pictures one at a time. I want you to look at them and tell me what you see, what they look like to you." After the child's response to the first card, he was asked (if he had not seen either the parts of the whole), "Do you see anything else?" Thereafter no further questions, other than to clarify a response, were asked, and only spontaneous responses were recorded.

Scoring

The child was given a W for every whole response, a D for every part response (regardless of the number of parts mentioned), and a W + D for every whole and part response.

RESULTS

Age and Perception

Age increase in part-whole perception There was a regular increase with age in the percentage of children who perceived both parts and wholes.

Age sequence of whole-part perception Contrary to Meili-Dworetzki's results, children of average and above average intelligence perceived parts more readily than they perceived wholes.

Age of part-whole integration Although Meili-Dworetzki did not find part-whole integration in a majority of her subjects until adulthood, a majority (78.6 per cent) of the 9-year-old children in this study were able to make such an integration, and close to a majority (60.2 and 62.6 per cent) of 8-year-olds were also able to make such an integration.

Control Measures

Gross socioeconomic and intellectual factors Despite the socioeconomic and intellectual differences between the two groups used in the present study, there were no significant differences between them

(by χ^2 tests) with respect to the age at which part and whole were perceived nor with respect to the order of part and whole responses.

IQ and part-whole perception To test the relation between part-whole perception and intelligence more directly, the scores of the University elementary school subjects, for whom Stanford-Binets (Form LM) were available, were translated into numerical scores. Each part response was given a score of 1, each whole response was given a score of 2 (since nursery school children saw parts and not wholes we assumed wholes were more difficult to see and so gave them a higher numerical score), and each part and whole response was given a score of 3. The rank difference correlations at the three age levels were: age 6, + .41; age 7, −.01; age 8, −.05. The average was .11.

Sex differences Sex differences for order and age of part-whole perception were checked at each age level by means of χ^2. No significant differences between boys and girls with respect to part-whole perception were found at any of the age levels studied.

DISCUSSION

The results of our study have shown that: (a) There is a regular increase with age in the ability of children to perceive parts and wholes involving the identification of meaningful figures. (b) When the figures are such that the laws of closure, good form, etc., favor the perception of parts, the parts will be perceived at an earlier age than the wholes. (c) When the parts and wholes are easily identified and familiar even to nursery school children, the perception of both parts and wholes can be accomplished by a majority (75 per cent) of 9-year-old children. Each of these findings will be commented on in the present section but we will take them up in reverse order.

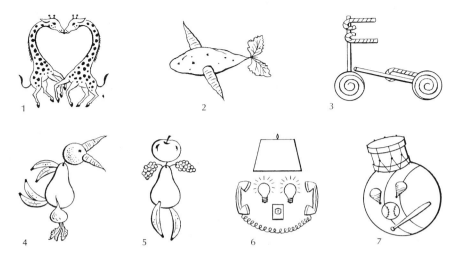

FIGURE 1   Drawings used in the study of part-whole perception.

Age of Part-Whole Perception

According to Piaget, the decentering of perception comes about in middle childhood as a consequence of the development of perceptual regulations which free the child's perception from its earlier domination by field effects. In our study, we found that 78.6 per cent of the 9-year-old children were able to perceive both part and whole in agreement with Piaget's position and with the results of our other studies (Elkind, Koegler, & Go, 1962; Elkind & Scott, 1962) which have also shown that the 7- to 8-year level is the point of most abrupt perceptual improvement.

In view of this finding, that part and whole can both be perceived by a majority of youngsters in middle childhood, it seems plausible to attribute Meili-Dworetzki's results (part and whole perceived only at the adult level) to factors other than an incapacity of children to integrate meaningful parts and wholes. The finding that children of average and above average intelligence perform in a similar fashion and that there is little correlation between IQ and part-whole perception also seems to rule out intelligence as the condition making for the difference between Meili-Dworetzki's findings and our own. Cultural differences are also probably not the answer because a number of studies (Elkind, 1961a,b,c,d) have shown that there is considerable similarity between European and American children in the age stages of conceptual development and presumably in stages of perceptual development as well. In sum, it seems reasonable to conclude that the differences between Meili-Dworetzki's findings and our own with regard to the age of part-whole integration are attributable to differences in the stimulus materials and not to differences in the subjects.

Sequence of Part and Whole Perception

The theory of perceptual decentering holds that the perception of the young child is determined by Gestalt-like laws of closure, good form, etc. According to this theory, whether a child perceives parts or wholes, depends upon the configural character of the stimulus materials. In our study the parts, which were more closed and had better (more recognizable) form than did the wholes, were perceived at an earlier age. In view of these results, Meili-Dworetzki's finding that wholes were perceived earlier than parts cannot be attributed to inborn tendencies to perceive wholes. On the contrary, her findings seem most reasonably ascribed to the fact that her figures favored whole over part perception. It may be that in perception, as in embryology and development generally, growth is sometimes from whole to part and sometimes from part to whole and that generalizations regarding the sequence of part-whole perception cannot be made without adding some specific information as to the characteristics of the stimuli employed. At any rate, this is the implication of Piaget's theory, and it is supported by Meili-Dworetzki's results as well as our own.

Age Increase in Part and Whole Perception

Centering, as it is used by Piaget, implies not only a domination by field effects but also a kind of fixation on the dominant figure and an inability spontaneously to shift perspective so as to perceive the configuration in a new way. Decentering is in fact the spontaneous shift of focus from one perceptual organization to another which is made possible by the development of perceptual regulations. In part-whole perception, decentering involves a shift of focus from whole to part or vice versa. Our finding that there is a general increase with age in the ability of children to perceive both part and whole is therefore in accord with the decentering position. It remains, however, to describe the regulational mechanisms of this decentering in part-whole perception, and that is the task of the present section. Unfortunately, Piaget has not dealt with the problem of part-whole perception involving the identification of meaningful figures, and the interpretation given below is our application of his theory to this new situation. To paraphrase a popular slogan, what follows is not necessarily the view of Piaget.

From the regulational standpoint, the problem of perceiving both whole and part would seem to be analogous to the problem of forming disjunctive classes on the plane of conception. Disjunctive classes are formed by means of the operation of logical multiplication. Logical multiplication requires, from the standpoint of intension, the formation of a new property by the joining of the properties of two independent classes. For example the logical multiplication of the property "Protestant" and the property "American" results in the new property "Protestant American." Looked at from the standpoint of extension, logical multiplication requires the subject to attribute two properties to the same object at the same time. For example, the subject must be able to attribute to one and the same person the properties of being "Protestant" and "American."

Now, it seems to us, that with respect to part and whole perception somewhat the same requirements hold true. The child must be able, from the standpoint of intension, to combine say the percept of a head with the percept of an apple, the percept of a banana with that of an arm, etc. He must also, from the standpoint of extension, be able to attribute both percepts to one and the same perceived form. Put differently, the perception of both part and whole would seem to involve the formation of a new percept just as the recognition of an "American Protestant" requires the formation of a new concept. If this analysis of part-whole perception is correct, we would expect to find stages in the development of logical multiplication in perception analogous to those found in the realm of conception. Such stages were indeed found.

REFERENCES

Elkind, D. Children's discovery of the conservation of mass, weight and volume. Piaget replication study II. *Journal of Genetic Psychology*, 1961, **98,** 219–227.(a)

Elkind, D. The development of the additive composition of classes in the child. Piaget replication study III. *Journal of Genetic Psychology*, 1961, **99,** 51–57.(b)

Elkind, D. The child's conception of brother and

sister. Piaget replication study IV. *Journal of Genetic Psychology,* 1961, **99,** 269–276.(c)

Elkind, D. The child's conception of right and left. Piaget replication study V. *Journal of Genetic Psychology,* 1961, **99,** 269–276.(d)

Elkind, D., Koegler, R. R., & G. E. Effects of perceptual training at three age levels. *Science,* 1962, **137,** 755–756.

Elkind, D., & Scott, L. Studies in perceptual development: I. The decentering of perception. *Child Development,* 1962, **33,** 619–630.

Meili-Dworetzki, G. The development of perception in the Rorschach. In B. Klopfer (Ed.), *Developments in the Rorschach technique.* New York: World Book, 1956. Pp. 108–176.

Piaget, J., & Morf, A. Les isomorphismes partiels entre les structures logiques et les structures perceptives. In J. Piaget (Ed.), *Etudes d'épistémologie génétique.* Vol. VI. Paris: Presses Universitaires de France, 1958. Pp. 51–116.

16 | Symmetry, Development, and Tachistoscopic Recognition

HARRY MUNSINGER
RODERICK FORSMAN

Children and college adults were presented random shapes for tachistoscopic recognition on four successive days. The sets of stimuli differed in amount of variability (5, 10, or 20 turns) and form (symmetrical and asymmetrical). The results supported the following generalizations: Recognition accuracy at tachistoscopic durations is facilitated by age, by experience with the task, and by reduction in the variability of the stimulus. [Less variability was achieved either by decreasing the number of coordinates used in generating the random shape (for example, 5 vs. 20) or by adding bilateral symmetry to otherwise randomly generated shapes.] The addition of symmetry to random shapes facilitates the recognition of 5- and 10-turn shapes, but interferes with the recognition of 20-turn shapes. This finding suggests that the addition of symmetry to shapes at or near the person's (S's) processing limit facilitates recognition. However, in the case of shapes of high variability (20 turns), adding symmetry introduces perceptual noise, which disrupts the sampling strategy necessary for recognizing high-variability shapes.

Recent studies by Munsinger and Kessen (1966) have suggested that children and adults may differ in their ability to process classes of information. These studies have centered around the notions that human beings are sensitive to variability of stimulation, that there is a limit on the amount of information which they can simultaneously process, and that by the formation of coding rules through experience Ss can surmount this limit on their ability to process.

Munsinger (1965) has shown that in the tachistoscopic recognition of random shapes, figures of low variability (5-turn) are more easily recognized than are figures of high variability (20-turn). It was also suggested that human beings learn to recognize shapes of differing variability through practice without external reinforcement or feedback.

Adapted from Symmetry, development, and tachistoscopic recognition. *Journal of Experimental Child Psychology*, 1966, **3,** 168–176.

There are several types of structure which may be imposed on stimulus variability. In the study previously cited (Munsinger, 1965) the stimulus structure was manipulated through repetition of the same random shapes. Another common type of structure which may be built into stimuli is symmetry. Most people have had considerable experience with this type of redundancy, since much of the perceptual world is symmetrical. Bilaterally symmetrical shapes contain approximately half as much stimulus variability or information as asymmetrical random shapes of the same number of turns. Combining the notions of human sensitivity to stimulus variability and a limit on their ability to process information (a limit somewhere between 5 and 10 independent turns), we had certain expectations about the effect of bilateral symmetry on tachistoscopic recognition of classes of stimulus variability. One expectation was that bilateral symmetry will not uniformly facilitate the recognition of shapes at all levels of stimulus variability. Specifically, only when bilateral symmetry shifts a class of random shapes from above to within the S's ability to process will there be a facilitating effect on recognition accuracy.

If the variability of the stimulus is well above the S's ability to process (e.g., 20-turn figure), he may use a strategy of partial information processing. This sampling strategy allows recognition of a many-turn figure, since parts of the figure are unique and sufficient for differential classification. However, a sampling strategy does not allow the development of a category unique to that shape. Only those stimuli within the S's processing limits will allow the development of unique categories. Therefore, the addition of structure to a stimulus may affect the S's recognition accuracy differentially depending upon the processing procedure required (i.e., perceptual vs. sampling). For example, if the stimulus is well within the S's ability to process, and structure is added, S's recognition accuracy should increase, since he has a unique category for the stimulus, and the structure only adds redundancy or overdetermination to the classification procedure. However, if the same structure is added to stimuli which are well above the S's ability to process (i.e., 20 turns), the redundancy may interfere with the development of probabilistic classes, thus *decreasing* the recognition accuracy of high variability stimulus. Evidence on the relations of symmetrical structure of random shapes, levels of stimulus variability, and the effects of age and training is presented in this study.

METHOD

Subjects

Three groups of six children each from the first, third, and sixth grades of Bottenfield Elementary School in Champaign, Illinois, served as Ss in this study. In addition, six college students from the introductory psychology classes at the University of Illinois comprised the adult group.

Stimulus Materials

Six sets of four random shapes each were presented to Ss by means of a two-field tachistoscope. The sets differed in level of stimulus variability (5, 10, 20 turns) and in form (asymmetrical and symmetrical). Thus, there were six sets of four shapes each for a total of 24 shapes. The stimulus shapes were black on white glossy prints occupying one-quarter square inch and appeared 18 inches in front of the S in the tachistoscope. Six small posterboards, each containing the four stimuli of a set, were used by the S as a sample to which he matched the tachistoscopically exposed stimulus shape. These sample shapes were approximately 3 × 3 inches.

Apparatus

Subjects were presented a lighted inspection field which contained a ¼-inch X as a focus. A second field containing the stimulus shape was illuminated during each trial while the inspection field was simultaneously darkened. All intervals were controlled by a precision solid-state timing mechanism built by the Electronics Shop of the University of Illinois Department of Psychology. This timing mechanism produced a linear time function from 0 to 1000 mseconds, measured by a Tektronix oscilloscope. The S used a microswitch trigger which allowed self presentation of each trial.

Procedure

A 20-minute session on Day 1 was used to acquaint S with the procedure, measure initial thresholds for the sets of shapes (to define the range of exposure durations to be used in the data gathering sessions), and screen any person with visual difficulties. Subjects were given the following instructions:

I am going to show you some little shapes, one at a time. Each one will be shown for only a very short time, so sometimes you may not be able to see the shape very well at all. Each figure will be one of the four you have here in front of you (the sample set) and you are supposed to pick the one you think you saw inside the box. You'll notice that these four shapes have numbers that go with them. Look at them now and see what number goes with what figure. The figures you see inside the box are the same shapes as these but very much smaller. You will know exactly when the shape is going to flash on because it will come on when you squeeze this button. But don't squeeze this button until after you hear this buzzer (demonstrate). This is a signal for you to go ahead any time. The little X you see inside there is a marker. The shape will always appear just to the left of it each time so you will know exactly where to look. Do you have any questions before we start?

Fifteen trials with each set of shapes were presented each day for four successive days. The order in which the six sets of shapes were presented to each S was determined by a 6 × 6 Latin square and remained the same for each S. The final 10 trials from each stimulus set each day were included in the analysis.

Analysis of Results

A derived score was used to obtain a more sensitive estimate of S's recognition accuracy than would have been possible by using either a constant exposure duration or an arbitrary percentage of correct recognition. Each of these two measures of recognition accuracy presents problems when used separately. By using a constant exposure duration, Ss' percentage of correct recognition may vary from chance to 100%. In the extreme cases, the validity of the recognition estimate is doubtful. On the other hand, if one selects an arbitrary percentage of correct recognition threshold, the practice effect due to repeated exposures required to attain

that threshold are confounded with learning effects. Learning was of primary interest in this study. Therefore, we combined the duration of exposure (which varied from 5 to 60 mseconds for adults and 6 to 200 mseconds for children) and percentage of correct recognitions (which varied from 40 to 100% for both children and adults) into a single measure. The exposure duration for each S was set on the basis of his initial threshold. Each S was presented stimuli at an exposure duration which should produce approximately 50% correct recognition. The exposure duration for each S was changed from day to day to maintain the percentage of correct recognitions in the range from 40% to 100%. This measure is defined as:

$$\text{Recognition Accuracy} = \left[\frac{\sqrt{\% \text{ correct}}}{\text{Exposure Time (ms.)}} \right] \times 100.$$

This derived score assumed a monotonic relation between increases in presentation duration and percentage of correct recognition, an intuitively reasonable assumption. As an investigation of the characteristics of this derived score, a family of curves was generated for several exposure durations at differing percentages of correct recognition. In general, these curves are parallel within the range of recognition percentages and exposure durations used in this study.

In summary, the overall design of the experiment included four age levels (first-, third-, and sixth-grade children, and college adults). Each S was presented for tachistoscopic recognition six sets of random shapes, which were symmetrical or asymmetrical and contained either 5, 10, or 20 turns. All Ss were presented these stimuli on four consecutive days.

RESULTS

The derived scores for both adults and children were combined in a mixed design analysis of variance to assess the effects on recognition accuracy attributable to age,

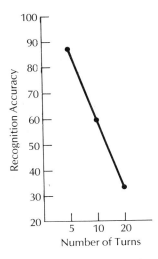

FIGURE 1 The relation between recognition accuracy and levels of variability of random shapes.

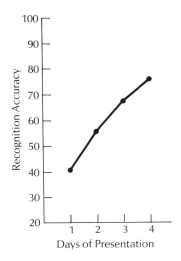

FIGURE 2 The relation between recognition accuracy and days of recognition experience.

symmetry-asymmetry, stimulus variability, and successive daily trials. All main effects were significant. Recognition accuracy improved as a linear function of age ($F = 10.2$; $df = 3, 20$; $p < .001$). Stimulus variability had a profound effect on recognition accuracy, as shown in Fig. 1. Recognition accuracy for the random shapes was a decreasing linear function of the logarithm of number of turns ($F = 232.4$; $df = 2, 40$; $p < .001$). This finding is very consistent with the notions of information processing, which suggest that S's performance should show a linear relation to the logarithm of the number of stimulus alternatives. Symmetrical shapes were more easily recognized than asymmetrical shapes.

Figure 2 shows the significant relation ($F = 12.7$; $df = 3, 60$; $p < .001$) between recognition accuracy and days. Both children and adults improved their recognition accuracy although they received no feedback from E regarding correctness of individual trials. This suggests that *experience* alone is sufficient for Ss to structure perceptually a series of stimulus events which are exposed for very brief durations. The learning mechanism here must involve an active structuring of stimulus variability by the S, and does *not* require external reinforcement or feedback.

One of the most interesting findings was the interaction of symmetry-asymmetry by level of stimulus variability, shown in Fig. 3. This interaction ($F = 30.9$; $df = 2, 40$; $p < .001$) shows that recognition is facilitated by the addition of symmetry to shapes of low and intermediate variability (5 and 10 turns), but recognition is hindered in the case of high variability stimuli (20 turns). The effect seems to reside in the change from asymmetrical randomness to symmetrical structure in the case of 10-turn shapes. Ten turn asymmetrical shapes are slightly above the S's ability to process. Bilateral symmetry reduces the variability of a random shape by making about half the variability of the shape redundant. Thus a 10-turn *symmetrical* shape is roughly equivalent to a 5- or 6-turn *asymmetrical* shape in terms of variability. However, the fact that 5-turn asymmetrical shapes are still recognized more easily than 10-turn symmetrical shapes, even though the information construct would make them approximately equivalent in amount of variability

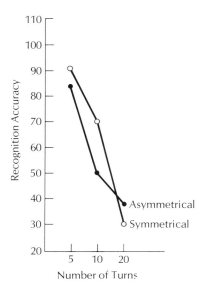

FIGURE 3 The relation between recognition accuracy and level of stimulus variability for symmetrical and asymmetrical random shapes.

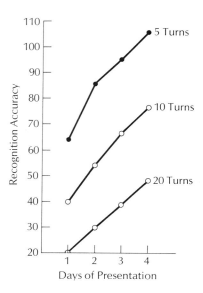

FIGURE 4 The relation between recognition accuracy and daily trials for the three levels of stimulus variability.

(Attneave, 1955), probably indicates that bilateral symmetry not only reduces stimulus variability, but also introduces perceptual noise into the discrimination problem. The interaction of symmetry-asymmetry by number of turns shows that this perceptual noise has little effect on discrimination when stimulus variability is within the human processing ability. However, the reduction in number of unique discriminable characteristics attendant upon the addition of symmetry to 20-turn shapes, which are *well above* the S's processing limit, hinders their discrimination on a stimulus-sampling basis.

Figure 4 shows the significant interaction of stimulus variability by days. This result ($F = 5.0$; $df = 6, 20$; $p < .001$) replicates a previous finding (Munsinger, 1965) which showed that the recognition of high-variability stimuli did not improve as rapidly as that of low-variability stimuli. It is interesting to note that the recognition-accuracy curve for 10-turn shapes over days matches

exactly the curve shown in Figure 2 (which represents data averaged across all three levels of variability).

DISCUSSION

It is apparent that the relation of stimulus variability and recognition accuracy is a complex function of age, experience, stimulus variability and stimulus structure. The finding that children have higher recognition thresholds for shapes than adults has been assumed for some time and is not surprising. Of somewhat more interest is the observation that human beings, both children and adults, can learn through experience to recognize forms with no external information feedback or reinforcement. This finding suggests that the general observer is *not* a passive recipient of contingencies from the outside world. The linear decreasing function of recognition accuracy and stimulus variability supports strongly the sensitivity of S's performance to this variable.

The interaction of symmetry-asymmetry by level of stimulus variability can be subsumed easily under the notion of a limit on the ability of human beings to process stimulus variability. Bilateral symmetry is presumed to reduce the variability of the asymmetrical 10-turn shape enough that the subject can process it (i.e., it is now within his processing ability). Bilateral symmetry facilitates the recognition of 5- and 10-turn shapes but interferes with the recognition of 20-turn shapes. Twenty-turn shapes are presumed to be well above the S's ability to process, and the addition of structure to these shapes does not help. To facilitate recognition, the structure must reduce the stimulus variability to *within* the S's ability to process. If the stimulus variability is too high, the S will find that symmetrical structure hinders recognition because of the perceptual noise which it adds to the shape.

A differential rate of learning to recognize figures of few as opposed to many turns suggested that two processes may be contributing to the learning of shape recognition. For figures of few turns, there may be a simple perceptual process which presents an immediate precept. Kaufman, Lord, Reese, and Volkmann (1949) discussed this process as "subitizing." However, for figures more variable than 5 turns, a process of estimation and partial information-processing probably occurs. This sampling or partial processing allows recognition of a many-turn figure, since *parts* of the figure are unique and sufficient for differential recognition. However, the sampling procedure does not allow the development of a category unique to that shape (Bruner, 1957). Instead, what probably occurs is the building of probabilistic categories on the basis of cues from the many-turn figures, with a weighting of these cues in terms of both their validity (Brunswik, 1956) and probability of occurrence. However, in the case of high variability stimuli, the addition of symmetry may add perceptual noise which interferes with recognition, although the amount of information in the 20-turn symmetrical shape is much *less* than in the 20-turn asymmetrical shape.

REFERENCES

Attneave, F. Symmetry, information, and memory for patterns. *American Journal of Psychology*, 1955, **68,** 209–222.

Bruner, J. S. On perceptual readiness. *Psychological Review*, 1957, **64,** 123–152.

Brunswik, E. *Perception and the representative design of psychological experiments*. Berkeley: University of California Press, 1956.

Kaufman, E. L., Lord, M. W., Reese, T. W., & Volkmann, J. The discrimination of visual number. *American Journal of Psychology*, 1949, **62,** 498–525.

Munsinger, H. Tachistoscopic recognition of stimulus variability. *Journal of Experimental Child Psychology*, 1965, **2,** 186–191.

Munsinger, H., & Kessen, W. Stimulus variability and cognitive change. *Psychological Review*, 1966, **73,** 164–178.

CHAPTER FIVE
LEARNING

Learning by the association of stimuli and responses has fascinated American psychologists. However, a new conception of this fundamental process is being developed. Rather than the simple bonds of early theories, complex mediation and subtle strategies are now included to explain the learning abilities of children. The infant learns by rote, but simple notions of association cannot explain the child's behavior as he matures.

Lipsitt, Kaye, and Bosack explored early learning in the baby. They presented infants (aged three to six days) with dextrose either immediately following a sucking response, or 30 seconds after a sucking response. Their results show that the very young infant can learn the association between sucking and reinforcement.

White changed the positive and negative cues from trial to trial in a discrimination learning situation to show that children can learn a simple discrimination when there is no single stimulus to connect with a response. Most children solved the problem by using the rule that the stimulus closest to the correct one on the last trial also was correct this time.

In a probability learning task (in which the child is presented with two or more responses, one of which is reinforced on a random basis with some specified probability), the child seeks a solution even when there is none. He devises differing strategies to handle this problem. The lower the child's expectation of a reward (and the younger the child), the more likely he is to probability match (respond with the same probability as he is reinforced). Older children try to solve the problem (to find a solution that will give them 100-percent reinforcement), even though it is impossible.

The final study of this section shows that children are not sensitive to correlation among cues, and suggests that the probability matching we see in many learning situations is due to the complex strategies children develop.

17 | Enhancement of Neonatal Sucking through Reinforcement

LEWIS P. LIPSITT
HERBERT KAYE
THEODORE N. BOSACK

When is the newborn first able to learn? Lipsitt, *et al.*, demonstrated that when sucking is followed by reinforcement with a dextrose solution, the infant's sucking rate increases, while cessation of such reinforcement leads to a decrease in his response rate. The infants used in the study ranged in age from 35 to 94 hours. One group (experimental) received a dextrose solution during the last few seconds of their conditioning trial, while another group (control) did not receive a solution of dextrose until 30 seconds after the nipple had been removed from their mouths. The experimental group increased their rate of sucking following reinforcement, while the control group did not change. This arrangement of reinforcements allows us to say that reinforcement following a response is effective in producing learning, while reinforcement given some time after the response does not produce learning.

Recently, Lipsitt and Kaye (1965) demonstrated in human newborns sucking non-nutritively that (a) an ordinary commercial rubber nipple elicits a faster sucking rate than does a length of ¼-inch (diameter) rubber tubing, and (b) experience with one of these intraoral stimuli affects the infant's sucking rate to the other. These differences in sucking rate to the two stimuli occurred both within and between Ss. Moreover, sucking on the tube was temporarily enhanced by immediately previous sucking experience with the nipple, thereby enabling the prediction that appropriate reinforcement of sucking behavior will induce conditioned enhancement of tube-sucking rate. A parallel procedure with newborn dogs, utilized by Stanley *et al.*

(1963), has shown such sucking-rate increases after milk reinforcement and rate decreases after administration of a quinine solution.

SUBJECTS

Twenty infants, aged 35 to 94 hours, were studied. An experimental group (Group E) had six males and four females, with mean age of 68 hours and mean weight of 7 lb 5 oz (*SD*'s of 18 hours and 17 oz, respectively). A control group (Group C) had five infants of each sex, with mean age of 70 hours and mean weight of 7 lb 4 oz (*SD*'s of 8 hours and 18 oz, respectively). These infants were selected for participation in the study by means of a pre-experimental sucking test, which insured an actively sucking population. On the basis of previous work by Levin and Kaye (1964),

Adapted from Enhancement of neonatal sucking through reinforcement. *Journal of Experimental Child Psychology,* 1966, **4**, 163–168.

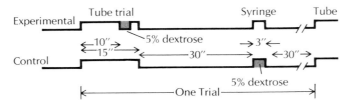

FIGURE 1 Temporal arrangement of tube and liquid presentations for the experimental and control groups representing a single trial during the Conditioning and Reconditioning periods.

a 1-minute nipple-rate criterion of 30 responses was adopted. Three *S*s did not meet this criterion and were replaced with *S*s until the two groups described above were achieved.

Apparatus

The *S*s were placed in a stabilimeter crib (Lipsitt & DeLucia, 1960), with a Phipps and Bird pneumograph attached around the abdomen, and throughout the experiment the infants were swaddled to prevent their touching of the face with hands. A brace made of a folded sheet cradled the head loosely at midline position. All responses were recorded on a Grass multichannel polygraph.

The sucking stimulus consisted of a 6-inch length of ¼-inch (outside diameter) surgical tubing connected to a 4-oz bottle by a T tube, the other arm of which was connected to an air pressure transducer (Statham Laboratories, p22s, 3 psi). Pilot data indicated that when pressure changes were recorded polygraphically utilizing this device, infants often had difficulty in forming an adequate pressure seal. Consequently, some sucking movements did not produce a recordable signal. Two observers, independently of one another and of the polygraph, therefore counted sucking movements, and the data of the present study are taken from these reliable (.95 +) counts. A 5-cc syringe was used for presentation of the dextrose solution to Group C, as described below.

Procedure

Baseline trials with the tube were begun 2 minutes after a 1-minute sucking pretest. All trials consisted of placing the tube about 1 inch into the *S*'s mouth for a 15-second period, followed by an approximate 80-second intertrial interval. The sequence of trials was as follows: six Baseline, ten Conditioning (or comparable Controls), ten Extinction, five Reconditioning, and five Extinction. Groups E and C were treated identically except for the manner and timing of dextrose presentation. Group E received 1 cc of 5% dextrose-water solution during the last 5 seconds of each Conditioning and Reconditioning trial, this being administered by manually tilting the bottle over a 3 second period, starting on the eleventh second of these trials. Group C received 1 cc of solution through the syringe 30 seconds after the withdrawal of the tube from *S*'s mouth, on trials comparable to the Conditioning and Reconditioning trials of Group E. The syringe spout was placed against the *S*'s upper lip and was emptied over a 3-second period. Group E also received a tactile stimulation from the syringe, but without liquid.

For Group E, the bottle contained 10 cc during Conditioning, and was refilled with 5 cc just prior to Reconditioning, thus assuring that Group E would not receive more liquid than Group C. Figure 1 compares a single trial for Groups E and C during Conditioning and Reconditioning trials.

Response-Assessment Procedure

The numbers of sucking responses to the tube during the first 10 seconds of each trial, as recorded by the two observers, were averaged. The intent at the outset was that the six Baseline trials would include an initial "warm-up" trial (following the nipple pretest), the data from which would be discounted to provide a five-trial Baseline period. However, since there was no difference between first- and second-trial responding, all six trials were included in the determination of Baseline performance. As the data analysis progressed, moreover, it was realized that response on the first trial of any period (e.g., in Conditioning) was affected by the trial preceding it. The final analysis therefore was made as follows: (a) Baseline—six trials and the first Conditioning trial; (b) Conditioning—trials 2–10, plus the first Extinction trial; (c) Extinction—trials, 2–10, plus the first Recon-ditioning trial; (d) Reconditioning—trials 2–5, plus the first Re-extinction trial; and (e) Re-extinction—four trials.

Because of considerable individual variation in numbers of sucking responses during the Baseline period, each S's responses were averaged for blocks of trials in each experimental period, then were divided by the mean number of responses per trial for the Baseline period. These ratios, as in previous work of Stern and Jeffrey (1965), were converted to percentages, a procedure resulting in the equating of scores for individuals with different basal sucking rates.

RESULTS AND DISCUSSION

Figure 2 shows the change in percentage of responses over the course of the experiment for Groups E and C. The effect of differential treatments was first assessed by an analysis of variance, which revealed a

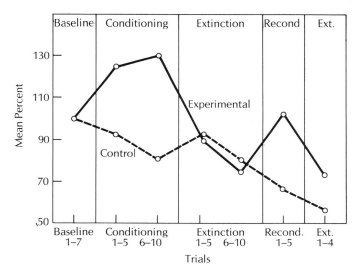

FIGURE 2 Changes in sucking rate for experimental and control groups represented as the mean ratio of number of sucks per trial in each of the periods divided by the number of sucks per trial during the baseline period. A trial consisted of the first 10 seconds of tube presentation prior to reinforcement for the experimental group and the data is averaged over trials as indicated on the abscissa.

significant Groups × Trials interaction ($F = 2.31$, $df = 6,108$, p, $< .05$). Simple tests at each of the trial-blocks points showed no differences, as expected, during Extinction and Re-extinction, but did reveal a significant effect at the second block of the initial Conditioning period ($t = 2.66$, $df = 18$, $p < .02$). Moreover, tests of the difference between Group E and Group C for the two Conditioning blocks combined produced a reliable effect ($t = 2.227$, $df = 18$, $p < .05$). The differences between groups on the first Conditioning block alone, or upon Reconditioning, approached but did not attain reliability ($t = 1.69$, $df = 18$, $p < .15$, and $t = 1.81$, $p < .10$, respectively).

These data provide evidence in neonates of enhancement of sucking through delivery of reinforcement associated with that behavior. Since response level was enhanced in a group which received reinforcement associated with tube-sucking, relative to a group which did not receive the reinforcement contingent upon that response, it may be argued that the effect obtained is based upon a conditioning process. There are two alternative interpretations to such a learning interpretation, however. The first is that Group E, having received reinforcement through the same tube as was used to elicit the sucking behavior, showed increased response during Conditioning and Reconditioning simply because there remained on the tube traces of dextrose solution from the immediately previous delivery of reinforcement. That is, Group E may have been sucking on a sweeter tube than Group C when counts were taken. The second argument is that responses of Group C during Conditioning and Reconditioning were suppressed by the administration of the solution through the syringe at shorter intervals preceding the 10-second sucking-measurement periods; the dextrose was given 30 seconds before for Group C, whereas Group E received dextrose 60 seconds preceding tube-sucking counts.

Two additional control experiments therefore were conducted, the results from which argue against each interpretation. First, a group of 10 Ss, comparable in weight-age-sex characteristics to Groups E and C, was administered a set of conditions identical to those of Group C, except that the sucking-tube was flushed with dextrose solution after each trial of the "Conditioning" period. There was no essential difference between the obtained results and the behavior of Group C during "Conditioning"; thus the difference between Groups E and C, with reliably higher response for Group E, cannot be attributed to traces of dextrose remaining on the tube.

The second additional control experiment determined whether more responses to the tube would occur 60 seconds after dextrose delivery (as in Group E) than 30 seconds after (as in Group C). Two groups of ten infants, comparable physically to previous groups, were given ten 10-second opportunities to suck on the tube. The first group was given five such trials, each 60 seconds after receiving 1 cc of dextrose via syringe, then another five trials, each 30 seconds after dextrose. The second group received five trials involving 3-second intervals first, then five trials at the 60-second interval. Comparison of the first five-trial series yielded response means per trial of 10.36 and 10.10 for the 60- and 30-second intervals, respectively. Response averages for the 20 Ss after 60- and 30-second intervals regardless of presentation order, were 9.21 and 9.88, respectively. Thus, the 30- and 60-second intervals after dextrose delivery do not differentially affect sucking rate, and this possibility cannot account for sucking-rate differences between Groups E and C.

The enhancement effect found in Group E may, therefore be considered a result of the reinforcement contingency. It should be pointed out that the changes taking place in sucking rates for Group E during "Conditioning" and "Extinction" were quite rapid. This may indicate that newborns are extremely "sensitive" to changes in feeding contingencies. Others have suggested (Kessen, 1963) that the processes producing short-term changes in infants be given labels other than "learning." It would seem, however, that these terms should be operationally based, and the paradigm on which the above experiment was designed was the general model for respondent conditioning. Until it is shown that this model is inadequate to integrate these data into the general framework of the analysis of behavior, parsimony requires that these operational concepts be employed.

REFERENCES

Kessen, W. Research in the psychological development of infants: an overview. *Merrill-Palmer Quart.,* 1963, **9,** 83–94.

Levin, G. R., & Kaye, H. Nonnutritive sucking by human neonates. *Child Development,* 1964, **35,** 749–758.

Lipsitt, L. P., & DeLucia, C. A. An apparatus for the measurement of specific response and general activity of the human neonate. *American Journal of Psychology,* 1960, **73,** 630–632.

Lipsitt, L. P., & Kaye, H. Change in neonatal response to optimizing and nonoptimizing sucking stimulation. *Psychonomic Science,* 1965, **2,** 221–222.

Stanley, W. C., Cornwell, A. C., Poggiani, C., & Trattner, A. Conditioning in the neonatal puppy. *Journal of Comparative and Physiological Psychology,* 1963, **56,** 211–214.

Stern, E., & Jeffrey, W. E. Operant conditioning of the non-nutritive sucking response in the neonate. Paper delivered at SRCD, Minneapolis, March 26, 1965.

18 | Variables Affecting Children's Performance in a Probability Learning Task

HAROLD W. STEVENSON
MORTON W. WEIR

A probability learning task has no solution. The typical situation presents a child with what appears to be a discrimination learning problem; in fact, the "correct" response is only rewarded some percent of the time on a random basis. The child may approach this task with one of several strategies. (1) The best strategy, if he wants to gain the most reinforcement, is to always make the response that is reinforced most often. However, many children find this a bore. (2) Another possible strategy is to try outguessing the random-reinforcement contingencies to win more often. This is a statistically less effective strategy but is more interesting to the child and is often adopted. (3) The final strategy (usually adopted by older children and adults) is to try various complex solutions in the hope that one can be found to yield 100-percent reinforcement. The various strategies result in probability matching (the child responds with the same probabilities as the reinforcement). The present experiments show that older children and children with higher expectations of reinforcement try to solve the problem and do not probability match as often as do younger children.

It was found in a recent study (Stevenson & Zigler, 1958) that children's performance in a probability learning task differed for normal and institutionalized feeble-minded children and for normal children given pretraining on games involving high and low degrees of success. It was hypothesized that these differences were related to the children's different expectancies for frequency of reinforcement. These expectancies were assumed to affect performance by determining the degree to which the child would accept a solution in the probability learning task which yielded less than 100% reinforcement. It was predicted that Ss with low expectancies would show a greater frequency of choice of the reinforcing stimulus than would Ss with higher expectancies. This would result from the attempt by Ss with higher expectancies to seek, through variable behavior, a means by which they could obtain a frequency of reinforcement corresponding to the frequency which they expect.

In the present study two experiments are reported investigating the effects of two variables on probability learning in children: CA, and incentive conditions. It is assumed that older children have expectancies for a higher percentage of reinforcement than do younger children and that the performance of these groups will differ in the manner outlined. In the experiment involving incentive conditions, the same general hypothesis is tested; however, it is assumed that the degree to which the child will accept a particular frequency of reinforcement is a function in part of the value of the reinforcement to S. The hypotheses tested in each experiment are discussed in greater detail in later sections.

EXPERIMENT I

The purpose of this experiment was to investigate the behavior of young children of different chronological ages in a probability learning task. There is some basis for assuming that performance in such a task would differ as a function of CA. It has been suggested (Goodnow, 1955) that one of the conditions influencing performance in a probability learning task is the level of success S will accept in the task. It seems reasonable to assume that older Ss' greater familiarity with soluble problems and their greater desire to master adult-controlled tasks would result in their being less likely than younger children to accept low levels of success. It is assumed that when less than 100% reinforcement is available older children would seek a solution which would provide a level of success more acceptable than that attainable by the consistent choice of the reinforcing stimulus. The variable behavior resulting from their attempts would reduce the frequency of choice of the reinforcing stimulus below that found with younger Ss. It is predicted, therefore, that with levels of reinforcement below 100% there is an inverse relationship between frequency of choice of the reinforcing stimulus and chronological age. It is further predicted that under conditions of 100% reinforcement the asymptotic frequency of correct response will be comparable at all CA levels, since 100% reinforcement provides a level of success acceptable to all Ss.

Method

Subjects   The Ss were 120 children attending nursery and elementary schools in Austin, Texas. The Ss were selected at random from among children of the appropriate CA's enrolled in the schools. Children at four age levels were used: 3-0 to 3-11, 5-0 to 5-11, 7-0 to 7-11, and 8-9 to 10-2. There were 30 Ss at each CA level.

Apparatus   The apparatus has been described previously (Stevenson & Zigler, 1958). It consisted of a yellow panel containing a horizontal row of three knobs. Above the knobs was a signal light and below the knobs was a delivery hole for marbles. The marbles fell into an enclosed plastic container.

Procedure   The S was seated in front of the apparatus and was told that he was to play a game. The E demonstrated the apparatus, and said, "When the light comes on, you push one of the knobs. If you push the correct knob a marble comes out here, like this. Now every time the light comes on you push the knob that you think will get you the marble. Remember, just push one knob each time the light comes on." The S was told that he was to get as many marbles as he could and when the game was over he could choose two toys from a selection of toys including balloons, plastic figures, etc., which E showed him.

Three conditions which differed in the percentage of reinforcement of correct response were used. For each S, one of the three knobs (either L, M, or R) was designated as the correct knob. The knob which was to be correct for a particular S was determined by a prearranged random sequence. An equal number of Ss was tested with each knob. The correct knob yielded reinforcement; choices of the other two knobs were never reinforced. Depending upon the condition, the correct knob yielded 100%, 66%, or 33% reinforcement. In other words, a contingent procedure of reinforcement was employed whereby S was reinforced for a certain percentage of the times, that he chose the correct knob. For example, in the 33% condition reinforcement was delivered on 33% of S's choices of the correct stimulus rather than on 33% of the trials. Ten Ss at each CA level were assigned at random to each of the three conditions. In the 66% and 33% conditions the trials on which a choice of the correct knob was reinforced were determined by a random sequence of 30 trials. This sequence was repeated when S pressed the correct knob on more than 30 trials. The Ss were given a total of 80 trials each.

Results and Discussion

The average numbers of correct responses in blocks of 10 trials for the four age levels and the three percentages of reinforcement are presented in Fig. 1. An examination of the curves for the 33% and 66% groups re-veals that performance differed as a function of CA. As predicted, there is a tendency for older Ss to choose the reinforcing stimulus less frequently than younger Ss. An analysis of variance of the results of the total 80 trials indicates a significant difference associated with CA ($F = 4.43$, $df = 3$ and 72, $P < .01$). A significant difference is found also for percentage of reinforcement ($F = 7.37$, $df = 1$ and 72, $P < .01$). The interaction between CA and percentage of reinforcement is not significant ($F < 1$).

Performance in the groups receiving 100% reinforcement was similar at each age level. It was predicted that asymptotic level of response would be comparable in all four groups. This was found to be true, for all but six Ss chose the correct stimulus on all of the last 20 trials. There were two Ss in each age group except CA 3 who did not consistently choose the correct knob during the last 20 trials.

There are several additional features of

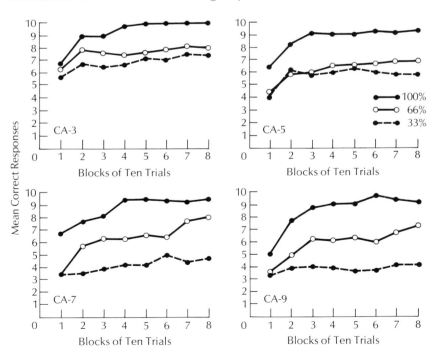

FIGURE 1 Mean number of correct responses for blocks of 10 trials: Exp. I.

Ss' performance which are of interest. The Ss initially had strong position preferences. On Trial 1, 15% of the Ss chose the left knob, 50% the middle knob, and 35% the right knob. As a control for possible knob preferences, each knob was correct for an equal number of Ss at each CA level. Knob preferences did not operate throughout all the trials, however, for of the total number of correct responses made on the 80 trials, .33 were made when the left knob was correct, .35 when the middle knob was correct, and .32 when the right knob was correct.

In order to determine whether the poor performance of older Ss was a result of their developing patterns of response, each individual's performance was examined. A high frequency of LMR and RML patterns of response appeared. The Ss at CA 3 had an average of 8.4 repetitions of these patterns, Ss at CA 5 an average of 14.8, Ss at CA 7 an average of 14.5, and Ss at CA 9 an average of 14.0. No other patterns of response were readily apparent. The behavior of Ss at CA's 5, 7, and 9, therefore, was not random since approximately 50% of the responses were made in the form of one of the patterns analyzed. This may indicate that the performance of these Ss is attributable in part to the fact that they were more likely than were the youngest Ss to form complex hypotheses resulting in the patterning of their responses.

The high level of performance of the three-yr.-old Ss indicates that a task of this type is within the level of ability of young nursery school children. These Ss, as are most children attending private nursery schools, were highly selected. The older children, however, were also from private schools and were above average in their performance on group intelligence tests.

EXPERIMENT II

The purpose of this study was to investigate the effects of two incentive conditions upon performance of children in a probability learning task. The hypothesis to be tested was that, under conditions of less than 100% reinforcement, the frequency of choice of the reinforcing stimulus will vary inversely with the value of the incentive. The hypothesis is derived in the following manner. In simple probability learning tasks such as the one used, children should learn rather quickly that the reinforcing stimulus does not pay off 100% of the time. If S accepts this frequency of reinforcement, S should choose the reinforcing stimulus with a high degree of consistency. If this frequency of reinforcement is not acceptable, S must attempt to find a solution to increase the frequency with which he is rewarded. This attempt leads to variable behavior, with the result that the frequency of choice of the reinforcing stimulus is lower than that occurring if such an attempt is not made. It is assumed that incentives affect performance by determining the degree to which S would attempt to find such solutions. It is further assumed that if incentives are of high value S is more likely to seek a solution yielding consistent reinforcement than if incentives are of low value. In this manner incentives of high value would produce more variable behavior than would incentives of lower value, with the consequence that there would be an inverse relationship between frequency of choice of the reinforcing stimulus and incentive value.

Under conditions of 100% reinforcement no differences between incentive groups should appear, except perhaps in the rate at which an asymptotic level of response is approached.

Method

Subjects   The Ss consisted of 60 five-yr.-old children attending nursery schools in Austin, Texas. The Ss were selected at random from among children of the appropriate CA enrolled in the schools.

Apparatus   The apparatus was the same as that described in Exp. I.

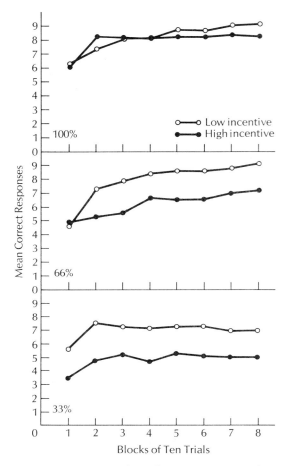

FIGURE 2   Mean number of correct responses for blocks of 10 trials: Exp. II.

Procedure   High and low incentive conditions were used. In the high incentive condition, the choice of the reinforcing knob resulted in the delivery of a trinket. A wide assortment of small plastic trinkets was provided. In the low incentive condition, the choice of the reinforcing knob resulted in the delivery of a marble. The S was told that at the end of the experiment the marbles could be exchanged for three trinkets of the types used in the high incentive condition.

As in Exp. I, reinforcement was delivered on 33%, 66%, or 100% of the choices of the correct knob. The procedure was the same as that in Exp. I except for the reinforcement used.

Results

The average numbers of times that the correct knob was selected in each incentive condition under the three percentages of reinforcement are presented in Fig. 2. The curves for the 100% reinforcement groups are highly similar and do not differ significantly ($t = .12$). The data in Fig. 2 support the prediction that the low incentive groups in the 66% and 33% conditions would choose the correct knob more frequently than the high incentive groups. An analysis of variance of these data results in an F of 6.71 ($P = .05$, 1 and 36 df). The difference in frequency of choice of the correct knob in the groups receiving 66% and 33% reinforcement is not significant ($F = 2.70$, $P > .05$, $df = 1$ and 36). The interaction between percentage of reinforcement and incentive condition is not significant ($F < 1$).

The higher level of performance in the low incentive, compared to the high incentive groups in the 33% and 66% conditions is an inversion of the results typically found in learning situations. It has been noted earlier (Stevenson & Zigler, 1958) that even though Ss in the present type of problem may not choose the reinforcing stimulus consistently, they do know which stimulus has provided reinforcement. This suggests that performance in this situation does not mirror the learning that has taken place; rather, it indicates the degree to which S will accept the percentage of reinforcement provided by the reinforcing stimulus.

The two incentive conditions appeared to operate in the anticipated manner; Ss in the high incentive groups seemed to be much more pleased to get the trinkets than were Ss in the low incentive groups to get the marbles.

These results differ from those of Messick and Solley (1957), who report exploratory data indicating an increase in frequency of choice of the reinforced stimulus when candy was compared to verbal reinforcement as the incentive. It is difficult to compare the results of the two studies because of differences in procedure and because of the descriptive nature of their results.

The results may be interpreted as providing support for the suggestion by Goodnow (1955) that one of the conditions affecting the distribution of choices in a probability learning task is *S*'s ability to overlook losses. If the reward has significance for *S*, he may be less likely to overlook loss than when the reward has less significance. The *S*'s inability to overlook losses, as Goodnow suggests, would lead to more variable behavior than when *S* is less concerned about the failure of a response to lead to reinforcement. Behavior would become more variable as *S* attempts to seek a solution to minimize the frequency of nonreinforced responses.

REFERENCES

Goodnow, J. J. Determinants of choice distribution in two-choice situations. *American Journal of Psychology,* 1955, **68,** 106–116.

Messick, S. J., & Solley, C. M. Probability learning in children: Some exploratory studies. *Journal of Genetic Psychology,* 1957, **90,** 23–32.

Stevenson, H. W., & Zigler, E. F. Probability learning in children. *Journal of Experimental Psychology,* 1958, **56,** 185–192.

19 | Discrimination Learning with Ever-Changing Positive and Negative Cues

SHELDON H. WHITE

Early learning theories suggested that the child associates a particular stimulus with a particular response during discrimination learning; he is assumed to attach approach tendencies to the positive stimulus and avoidance tendencies to the negative stimulus. What would happen if the particular positive and negative stimuli changed from trial to trial and the child was reinforced when he responded to the stimulus most like the positive stimulus on the preceding trial? Could children learn this discrimination with ever-changing positive and negative cues? White tested this notion by presenting fourth- and fifth-grade children with a discrimination task in which the positive and negative cues changed from trial to trial. The changes were unsystematic. The task may be conceived as a complex concept formation situation; the concept to be learned is the similarity of the positive and negative stimuli with those from previous trials. Following several trials, all the children were able to learn this relatively subtle concept, showing that the association of a particular stimulus with a particular response is not necessary for discrimination learning in children.

House, Orlando, and Zeaman (1957) and White (1965) have reported studies in which children were given two-choice simultaneous discrimination problems involving varying cues. Under a *varying-negative* condition, the correct choice on each trial was to a constant cue, but the incorrect choice was to cues which changed from one trial to the next. Under a *varying-positive* condition, the positive cue changed from trial to trial, while the negative cue was constant. To produce their varying stimulus conditions, House *et al.* interchanged a set of 5 stimuli; White, a set of 20. Under such conditions, normal and retarded children were able to learn.

Learning theories generally assume, in one way or another, that learning takes place

through some combination of approach tendencies attached to a positive cue and avoidance tendencies attached to a negative cue. If learning takes place when there is no fixed positive or negative cue then, apparently neither cue-approach nor cue-avoidance connections are absolutely necessary to the process. It can happen when there is only the possibility of one or the other type of connection.

The present study grew out of curiosity: could learning be demonstrated when both positive and negative cues constantly changed from trial to trial?

METHOD

Subjects

The *S*s were 80 children drawn from fourth and fifth grade classes at the Baker School

Adapted from Discrimination learning with ever-changing positive and negative cues. *Journal of Experimental Child Psychology*, 1965, **2**, 154–162.

in Brookline, Massachusetts. The children were taken without selection from four classrooms and randomly assigned to the four experimental conditions to be described below. Group intelligence test scores were available in the school records of most of the Ss, and the mean Kuhlman-Anderson IQ for all Ss in the sample for whom there were scores was 120.2.

Apparatus

The apparatus was a slide projector arrangement for the presentation of simultaneous discrimination problems, described in some detail elsewhere (White & Plum, 1964). Stimuli were presented by back-projections of 35-mm slides on two 4-inch diameter circular projection windows. Slight pressure by S against either hinged window would cause a chime to sound if a correct response had been made, or a brief buzzer sound if an incorrect choice were made, and in either case turn off the choice stimuli.

Stimuli

Two series of 80 stimuli were prepared for use in the experiment; the design of these series may best be explained with the aid of Fig. 1. Each series was designed by beginning with a black-on-white line drawing and imposing sequential variation in succeeding drawings. The changes were not systematic, in the sense that they did not tend in any direction—the drawing of a step in a series might occur by addition, subtraction, rotation, or superimposing drawn material on the preceding step. A systematic attempt was made to completely remove any traces of a given step within the next five or six steps. A systematic attempt was also made to insure that the two series had no characteristics as series which differentiated one from the other, i.e., that one series had no more circularity, filled-in figures, complexity, etc. than the other.

After the series were drawn, they were mixed and photographed. One set of photographs was prepared by taking Step 1 of Series A and Step 1 of Series B and photo-graphing them together, once in left-right and once in right-left arrangement; the two resulting photographs were used for the control condition. Another set was prepared by taking the first drawing of Series A and photographing it together with each step of Series B; the A member and the B members were alternated from left to right according to an unsystematic sequence. These 80 photographs were then used for varying-positive and varying-negative conditions. A final set of photographs was prepared by taking Step 1 of Series A together with Step 1 of Series B, Step 2 of Series A with Step 2 of Series B, etc. until all 80 members of each set had been paired. Again, the sequence of 80 pictures alternated Series A and Series B members from left to right according to a balanced sequence. All photographs were developed to black-and-white negatives and mounted, so that when projected the stimuli appeared as white figures against a dark background (see Figure 1).

Procedure

Instructions were kept simple. Under all conditions, the S was shown the stimuli for the first trial and shown which choice "rang the bell" and which "rang the buzzer." He was told that he would see this pair and others and that he was to try to ring the bell every time. His appropriate sequence of stimuli was then presented in order; if he made a wrong choice on a given trial, he was told, "I'm going to show you that again," and the trial was re-presented until he got it right. The procedure was therefore essentially a correction procedure.

There were four groups, each consisting of 20 Ss. The Ss in the Double-Variation group were given the double-variation condition without any preliminary training. The Varying-Positive group learned a varying-positive condition followed by the double-variation condition. The Varying-Negative group learned a varying-negative condition before double-variation learning. The Control group learned a simple two-choice discrimination, with a constant positive and

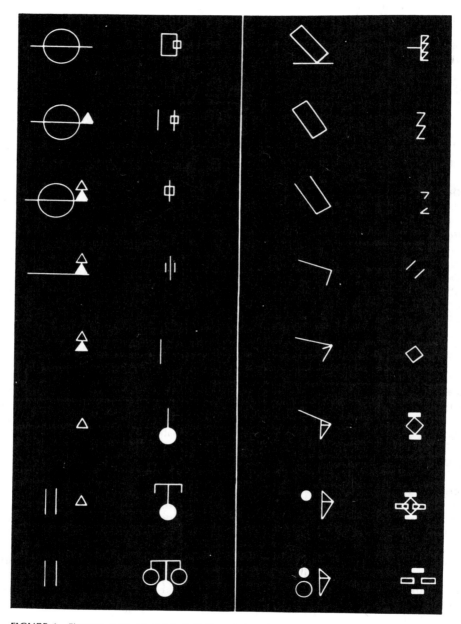

FIGURE 1 Figures seen on Trials 1–8 (two left columns) and Trials 36–44 (two right columns) of the double-variation condition. The first and third columns are Series A drawings; the second and fourth, Series B drawings.

negative stimulus, before double-variation learning.

Transfer from one condition to the other was always consistent and overlapping with what had gone before, that is, the S who was switched from varying-negative to double-variation learning was presented with exactly the same series of negative stimuli, but now the positive cues varied as well.

Counterbalancing in the Double-Variation and Control groups insured that half the Ss in these groups learned their double-variation problems with Series A correct and half with Series B correct.

Any condition was completed only when S gave 10/10 correct responses, or when 80 trials had been given.

RESULTS

The question of interest in undertaking the study was whether children could solve a discrimination problem under the double-variation condition. The results show that 12/20 children solved that condition without pretraining of any kind, 16/20 after pretraining with a varying-positive condition, 15/20 after pretraining with a varying-negative condition, and 16/20 after pretraining with a control condition. With or without pretraining, then, a majority of the Ss was able to learn the problem.

Analysis of presolution performance during double-variation learning suggested something like a "twostep" learning process —one step to an above-chance level which was consistently maintained before solution, a second step to criterion, i.e., during successive blocks before criterion, those Ss who solved averaged 67, 64, 65, and 70% correct—followed by 100% critical performance. (During successive blocks of 20 trials, nonsolvers averaged 58, 53, 59, and 57% correct.)

The pretraining groups were introduced in an attempt to shed some light on how a double-variation problem is solved. Some of the groups found their initial learning

condition much easier than others [$F(3,76)$ = 3.35; $p < .05$]. The Varying-Positive group took appreciably fewer trials in first learning than the Double-Variation group [$t(76)$ = 6.38; $p < .01$] but more trials than either the Varying-Negative or Control groups [$t(76)$ = 2.28; $p < .05$].

Differences among the four groups in number of trials to solve their double-variation conditions were not significant [$F(3,76)$ = 1.76; $p < .20$]. The difference between the Varying-Positive and Double Variation groups' performance on double-variation was large enough to be significant by t test [$t(76)$ = 2.25; $p < .05$); however, the significance of this statistic must be held questionable in view of the nonsignificance of the over-all F.

One might explain such a pattern of results by asking what recurrent regularity of a learning situation an S will "track" from trial to trial. Under the control condition, he must track a stable stimulus from trial to trial, and this is quite easy for him. Under the double-variation condition, he has no choice but to track a constantly changing stimulus set from trial to trial; this is relatively more difficult but possible. Under the varying-negative condition, he has a choice between tracking a stable stimulus or a varying set. Apparently, he chooses to track the stable stimulus because he learns as easily as under the control condition and, like Control Ss, he derives little benefit from his first learning when he turns to his second learning. The Varying-Positive Ss are faced with the same choice, and they meet it in almost the same way, but not quite. Some of the time, they choose the varying set to track; this slightly hinders their original learning and it slightly benefits them in transfer.

Answers to Queries

All children were queried after completing their learning. They were asked how they had known how to choose the right window each time. Most of the time, but not always, the children who had been able to solve their double-variation condition were those who could explain the principle by which the stimuli changed. Of 59 children who had solved their double-variation task before 80 trials, 56 were able to verbalize the way in which the stimuli changed from trial to trial in a way that was judged adequate, and 3 gave ambiguous statements which were neither clearly right nor wrong. Of 21 nonsolvers, 7 were able to verbalize the principle of change, and 14 were not.

Explanations of the principle were in statements like the following. "You added on something and you subtracted something." "I followed the one that you took off a bit and then added some." "They were adding on bits or having bits taken away." "You'd first see an arrow and then it was camouflaged." "[It was] by having parts put on and taken away." "Pieces of the one before were in the next."

Perhaps the most interesting feature of the query material was the considerable number of Ss who could verbalize the principle of change but who denied, or were uncertain, that the principle applied to the incorrect stimuli as well as the correct in the double-variation problem. Six of the Ss stated that they weren't paying attention to, didn't know, or "could never decide" what was happening in the windows other than those they were following. Seven others stated that something different was happening in the wrong windows, but gave uncertain account of what that something different was. Thirteen Ss asserted that the stimuli in the wrong windows changed more completely, that they were radically different each time, and that there was not continuity in the wrong windows as there was in the right windows. In all, then, 26 of the Ss (7 in the Double-Variation group, 5 Varying-Negative, 7 Varying-Positive, and 7 Control Ss), asserted in some way either that they were not following the series of wrong windows or did not recognize clearly what was happening in them.

The other Ss who could explain the principle of change recognized that it applied to both correct and incorrect windows in the double-variation condition. But the comments given in the above paragraph are an indication that children tended to handle the double-variation condition by tracking the positive series, and apparently to such an extent that they could be completely unclear about, or could misconstrue, the negative series.

DISCUSSION

The double-variation condition is interesting in a theoretical sense, because it cannot be learned using many of the processes conventionally used to explain children's learning. It cannot be solved through the buildup of cue-approach or cue-avoidance connections because, of course, the cues keep changing. For the same reason, it cannot be solved by attaching a response to configurations of cues. It cannot be solved by the buildup of an approach response to a common element; any element (a circle, a square, a pair of parallel lines, etc.) in Series A or Series B appeared and was gone within five or six trials, and was as likely as not to reappear as part of the other series. The problem is not solvable through the more commonly conceived sorts of mediating responses (the labels attached to particular cues, elements of cues, or perceptual relations) because all these were inconstant.

There is a kind of mediating response to which an approach response might be consistently attached and solution be achieved. The child might always label the correct stimulus on each trial "the one most like the last one which was right." But the identification of such a mediating response, if it were used, would not solve the problem of how learning occurs. The meat of the issue would then remain as the question of why the S selects this peculiarly appropriate label for use above all others, and the question of how he is able to consistently identify the object to be so labeled on each trial.

Logically, solution of a double-variation problem might proceed through a tactic involving models. The S might form an inner model of the correct stimulus on a given trial, as an image or in words, and store this model until the next trial. On the next trial, the two presenting cues would be scanned and somehow matched against the stored model as template. Comparisons of cues and template would determine which cue was a better fit to the model. This cue would be selected for choice and would at the same time be stored as a model for use on the next trial.

Such a process could include a similar modelling process applied to the series of negative cues, but Ss' responses to queries suggested that many of them ignored the possible connections among their negative series of cues, and several aspects of the study as a whole make one wonder how much Ss generally dealt with both positive and negative cues in forming their choices.

The postulated modelling process is hypothetical but apparently quite reasonable. The common human ability to recognize implies, of course, that some kind of model of an input stimulus is readily formed and stored. Modelling is also implied by the fact that slight changes in repeated familiar cues cause "perceptual disparity responses" (Grings, 1960). John has provided evidence suggesting inner modelling of flickering inputs to animals by analyzing evoked potentials at various brain sites to find those which follow the frequency of the flickering input and those which do not. Some sites follow input frequencies immediately others do so only after training (John, 1962). If, after training with one input frequency, a new frequency is presented, the new input is followed in sensory-specific structures (sensory cortex), while nonsensory-specific structures (hippocampal and reticular sites) emit the trained frequency. John (1962) has sug-

gested possible pathways by which these models of the old and new stimuli might be brought together for comparison.

The kind of learning in the double-variation condition apparently differs considerably from that involved in simple two-choice learning. It is significantly more difficult. It benefits little from previous two-choice discrimination learning, and one might perhaps ascribe that degree of benefit to little more than simple warmup. What is being learned? Perhaps the child spends his trials seeking and finding the relatively subtle principle connecting his series of positive and/or negative stimuli. Perhaps what is learned is a tactic, the tactic of model use.

REFERENCES

Grings, W. W. Preparatory set variables related to classical conditioning of autonomic responses. *Psychological Review,* 1960, **67,** 243–252.

House, B. J., Orlando, R., & Zeaman, D. A. Role of positive and negative cues in the discrimination learning of mental defectives. *Perceptual and Motor Skills,* 1957, **7,** 73–79.

John, E. R. Some speculations on the psychophysiology of mind. In J. M. Scher (Ed.), *Theories of the mind.* New York: Free Press, 1962.

White, S. H. Age differences in reaction to stimulus variation. In O. J. Harvey (Ed.), *Flexibility and creativity: Nature and determinants.* Volume in preparation, 1965.

White, S. H., & Plum, G. E. Eye movement photography during children's discrimination learning. *Journal of Experimental Child Psychology,* 1964, **1,** 327–338.

20 | Developing Sensitivity to Correlated Cues

HARRY MUNSINGER

In an earlier selection we saw that younger children seem to probability match when they are trying to solve a problem. The present study suggests that probability matching is not the result of children's sensitivity to probabilities and correlations among events, but comes from producing various strategies and hypotheses while trying to solve the puzzle. This study used children of two grade levels and adults; they were presented random shapes of varying numbers of turns for tachistoscopic recognition. The relation between number of turns of the shapes and color of the shapes was either 1:1 or random. The children treated the correlated relation as a random pairing of cues. However, adults were sensitive to correlation; they showed significant improvement in their estimation of the shapes with correlated colors.

Brunswik (1956) speculated that children and adults are sensitive to the validity of stimuli and that they can use correlated cues to increase their perceptual accuracy. In addition, Piaget and Inhelder (1951) suggest that between the period of concrete operations (around 7–11 years) and formal operations (adolescence) the child comes to distinguish between chance events and associated ones. The purpose of this study was to explore these speculations; in particular, to examine the ability of children and adults to use correlated cues to help them correctly categorize stimuli.

Two sets of stimuli were developed. Four colors (red, blue, yellow, and green) were randomly associated with four classes of stimuli (5-, 10-, 20-, and 40-turn random shapes) in one set, while in the other set only one color was associated with each class of stimuli. Specifically, in the second set of stimuli 5-turn random shapes were associated with red, 10-turn shapes with blue, 20-turn shapes with yellow, and 40-turn shapes with green.

Adapted from Developing sensitivity to correlated cues. *Psychonomic Science,* 1968, **10,** 149–150.

Groups of children and adults were repeatedly presented (for tachistoscopic recognition) the sets of random or related stimuli. Each group received only one type of stimuli. If the subjects are sensitive to correlated cues, the estimation of cue-correlated stimuli should differentially improve over trials when compared with randomly related cues and stimuli. A developmental view might suggest that adults would profit more from experience than would children, so that we might find an interaction among age, correlated or random cues, and pre-post measurement.

METHOD

Subjects

Forty-eight introductory students from the University of Illinois, 48 second and third grade children, and 48 fifth and sixth grade children from the Chicago Public School System served as Ss in this study. An equal number of Ss at each age level were unsystematically assigned to the experimental groups, with the restriction that the number of second and third grade, and fifth and sixth grade children should be equated within the age groupings and that the sexes should be balanced.

Stimulus Materials

Twenty-four random shapes were constructed according to a procedure described in Munsinger and Kessen (1964). Each shape was a black figure on a white background. Transparent plastic tape was put over the entire slide to introduce appropriate background color. Preliminary investigations showed that the red, yellow, green, and blue tape used in this study did not differentially mask the shapes during tachistoscopic estimation. The four colors were easily distinguished.

Procedure

Six examples of four levels of complexity of random shapes (5, 10, 20, and 40 turns) were presented at 200 msec exposure duration to all Ss. The order of presentation of the 24 stimuli was randomized within blocks of eight shapes. The stimuli were presented in this randomized order; the order was reversed and then changed on subsequent presentations. The Ss were instructed to estimate (guess) the number of angles (points) contained in each shape. The children wrote the numbers 5, 10, 20, and 40 at the top of their answer sheets to help them remember the four possible responses. All Ss were asked to use only these four categories in responding; they were shown examples of each type of figure and were instructed to guess whenever they were not sure of the number of turns. The Ss received a four-page booklet with 24 lines on each page.

Each shape was projected tachistoscopically, by means of a Compur mechanical shutter monitored by a Tektronix oscilloscope, to the front wall of a room in which small groups of Ss were seated. All groups were told to pay particular attention to the relation between the shapes and colors because this relation would improve their estimation accuracy. The interval

between presentations was approximately 10 sec. All Ss were shown the complete set of 24 figures four times.

The ability of Ss to estimate the number of turns of the shapes was assessed by calculation of transmitted information according to Garner's bivariate uncertainty analysis (Garner, 1962). A 4 by 4 confusion matrix was constructed with the four types of stimuli representing rows and the four possible responses representing columns. The six examples of each level of complexity (one trial of 24 shapes) were pooled for greater reliability. The contingent uncertainty of the first and last 24 presentations was computed separately and entered into a repeated measures analysis of variance as pre- and post-measurement.

RESULTS AND DISCUSSION

Figure 1 shows a monotonic relation between grade in school and bits of trans-

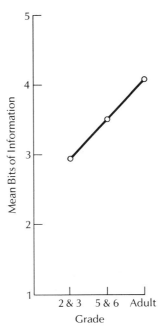

FIGURE 1 The relation between grade in school and amount of transmitted information.

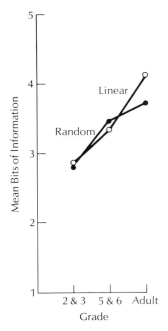

FIGURE 2 The relation between grade in school and amount of transmitted information plotted separately for the linear and random contingent conditions.

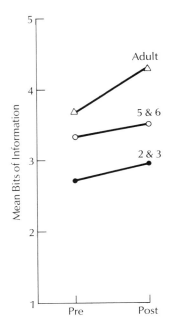

FIGURE 3 The relation between pre- and post-measurement and amount of information transmitted plotted separately for the three grade levels.

mitted information. This significant effect (F = 48.9, df = 2/138, p < .001) demonstrates that the ability to estimate number of turns of random shapes increases with age, a not surprising finding (Munsinger & Kessen, 1964; 1966a, b). Estimation accuracy also increased from trial one to four (F = 21.3, df = 1/138, p < .001, suggesting some learning. Figure 2 shows a more interesting result. This significant interaction (F = 5.6, df = 2/138, p < .01) between the two types of relations (correlated and random) and age of Ss shows that only the adults were able to take advantage of the correlated cues. For both the second and third grade children and the fifth and sixth grade children there was no difference in estimation accuracy between the random and correlated sets of shapes. Children were *not* sensitive to the association of number of turns and color. For the fifth and sixth

grade children the correlated condition is slightly below the random condition. However, the adults clearly estimated number of turns of the shapes more accurately when they contained correlated colors. Figure 3 (F = 7.8, df = 2/138, p < .01) shows that the difference between adults and children increased between the pre- and the post-measurement period. Figure 4 supports this finding, showing a significant (F = 7.3, df = 1/138, p < .01) interaction between the linear correlation and random conditions and the pre- and post-measurement periods.

The conclusion is that college adults are sensitive to a simple correlation among cues, but without better instructions, or much more experience, young children cannot use correlated cues to improve their estimation accuracy. The children's insensitivity to correlated cues may be due to the

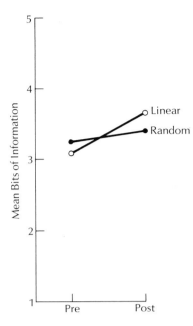

FIGURE 4 The relation between pre- and post-measurement and amount of information transmitted plotted separately by linear and random contingent conditions.

quired children to store and integrate a contingent relation. At present, it is impossible to know where the younger children are deficient; it may be memory overload; it may be inability to integrate contingencies over time; or it may be lack of understanding of the notion of contingency itself. Further work can examine these particular points. Simultaneous presentation of cue-correlated stimuli seems promising. A gradual building of the notion of correlation may also be a productive approach. Trial and error learning is inefficient; the children should be tutored.

small amount of experience given. Alternatively, it may be that children are not able to integrate over time. If the latter notion is correct, simultaneous presentation of several cue-correlated stimuli should produce much better performance among children. This simultaneous presentation would give the child the information all at once and not require him to integrate information over time. The present study re-

REFERENCES

Brunswik, E. *Perception and the representative design of psychological experiments.* Los Angeles: University of California Press, 1956.

Garner, W. R. *Uncertainty and structure as psychological concepts.* New York: Wiley, 1962.

Munsinger, H., & Kessen, W. Uncertainty, structure, and preference. *Psychological Monographs,* 1964, **78,** 1–24 (Whole No. 586).

Munsinger, H., & Kessen, W. Stimulus variability and cognitive change. *Psychological Review,* 1966, **73,** 164–178. (a)

Munsinger, H., & Kessen, W. Structure, variability, and development. *Journal of Experimental Child Psychology,* 1966, **3,** 20–49. (b)

Piaget, J., & Inhelder, B. *La genèse de l'idée de hasard chez l'enfant.* Paris: Paris University Press, 1951.

CHAPTER SIX
OPERATIONS: THOUGHT

Thought concerns the acquisition and use of rules (operators) which may be applied to several situations. Specific stimulus-response associations are of no interest; only the understanding of relations that transcend a particular task are important. Problems in thought include the relation between symbolic imagery and thought, the way children come to conserve weight and substance under transformations in form, and the relation between stimulus structure and concept formation.

Dr. Inhelder suggests that some kinds of operational thinking may be helped by symbolic imagery. She suggests that the child is better able to reproduce the stages through which a tube passes during a somersault when he has seen them than when he must construct the stages by thought alone.

Smedslund considers the problem of how children acquire conservation of weight and substance. A child of six does not appreciate the invariance of weight and substance under transformations in form or size; he is perceptually bound. Only later, at about eight years of age, is he free of perceptual ties and can he understand weight invariance under transformations of form. Several theories have been proposed to explain these findings; the notions of Piaget seem most compelling.

How do children of varying ages react to stimulus structure (rules that allow coding of stimulus input)? The final selection presents data showing that very young children solve concept formation tasks by rote association. However, older children are able to use rules.

21 | Operational Thought and Symbolic Imagery

BARBEL INHELDER

Although several investigators (for example, Binet) have shown that imageless thought is possible, there may be situations in which images are not only helpful but absolutely necessary for thinking. Dr. Inhelder suggests that the operations we perform on perceptual input may be of this type. She suggests that symbolic imagery and operational thought develop concurrently and are influenced by the same variables. However, the types of mistakes a child makes trying to reproduce certain perceptual transformations (such as the stages through which a tube goes in a somersault) suggest a certain independence of symbolic imagery and operational thought. There are times when the child can reproduce (through perceptual imagery) transformations that he cannot construct by operational thought. If the child is shown a series of transformations, he will reproduce them with much greater accuracy than on the basis of thought alone. This leads to the conclusion that symbolic imagery is supplementary to, and probably ahead of operational thought during the early development of the child; only later is he able to supply more by thought than by imagery.

There is a large domain that language is not competent to describe except in devious and complex ways: the domain of everything that is perceived (as opposed to conceived). Sometimes it is useful to communicate things perceived, but, above all, it is necessary to retain a large part of them in the memory if future action is to be possible. Recourse to symbolic imagery would thus be necessary every time that past perceptions are to be evoked or future perceptions anticipated.

The importance of symbolic imagery varies according to the type of operation it is called upon to support. It is inadequate for symbolizing logical and arithmetical operations, which, at the higher level, rely on arbitrary sign systems; never-

Adapted from Operational thought and symbolic imagery. *Monographs of SRCD*, 1965, **30,** No. 2, 4-18.

theless, it provides an important adjunct for the so-called geometrical intuitions, since in these there is partial isomorphism between signifiers and signified, the former consisting of spatial figures, themselves imagined, and the latter consisting of spatial relations on which geometrical operations are performed.

The techniques and results to be set forth in this paper are part of a larger study on the genesis of mental imagery that we carried out in Geneva under the leadership of Jean Piaget. Experiments involving reproductive, evocative, and anticipatory images were carried out. It is the intention here to concentrate especially on the last group, which bears more particularly on our problem: the relation between the development of operativity and the development of symbolic imagery. Children were asked to anticipate the results of the displacement of one figure in respect to another and to imagine successive transformations of one and the same figure.

METHODS

The development of symbolic imagery can, of course, never be grasped directly but must be approached through actualizations, such as drawings, gestures, selections from among a series of drawings representing both correct solutions and typical errors of children of different ages, and verbal comments. Along these lines, starting from consonant or contradictory indices, we tried to make inferences about the various kinds of anticipatory imagery. Following our genetic method, we put the same problem to children of different ages, and, from comparisons and the hierarchical arrangements of their ways of symbolization, as well as from the increasing frequency of successful solutions, we tried to extract the laws governing the development and modification of symbolic representation.

Displacement and Transformation of Figures

Translation of a square in relation to another square which is kept immobile (a) The children (aged 4 to 9 years) were shown two square pieces of cardboard (5-cm. square). The upper edge of the immobile square was parallel to and contiguous with the lower edge of the square that was to be laterally displaced (see Fig. 1).

First we made sure that the child could actually draw the configurations. Then he was asked to anticipate the result of dis-

placing the upper square from left to right. In terms comprehensible to the child we might say, "If I push the upper square a little bit to the right, can you do a drawing to show me what the two squares will be like?" The experimenter made a gesture to suggest the lateral displacement and requested the child (1) to draw the result of the displacement without seeing the actual displacement, that is, to anticipate the result; (2) to choose from a set of drawings the one that seemed best to represent the actual displacement; and (3) to draw the result of the displacement, but this time after actually seeing the displacement and the two squares in the new position. We asked the child to comment on his trials and errors in order to gain insight into his special difficulties and into the beginning of representative imagery.

From a qualitative analysis of how young children try to arrive at figurative symbols (see Fig. 1) one may educe that the symbol long remains static even in as simple a case as the displacement of one figure in relation to another. The child did indeed indicate clearly by gesture the direction followed by the upper square, but this was only a global, all-encompassing image. When he tried to represent details, however, he sometimes drew the upper square as if it was detached from the lower one, or else—and this was more frequent from 4 to 7 years—he refused to go beyond one of the two frontiers. Thus, instead of conserving the surface sizes, he "conserved" a frontier, that is to say, he rigidly maintained its original position. This kind of "pseudo-conservation," which we encountered several times, was not caused simply by difficulties of drawing. This is shown by the fact that in choosing a drawing from among those presented to him the child picked the one that was like his own drawing of the anticipated result. The drawings of the final configuration, after the experimenter had actually performed the displacement, presented no difficulties from about 5½ years onward, although among 4-year-old children the drawings showed the same

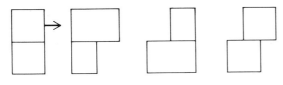

FIGURE 1

peculiarities as those of the anticipated results among children of 5 to 7 years.

Folds: Rotating a figure through 180° (a) The child was presented with a transparent sheet to be folded along its vertical axis. On the left side, which was to remain stationary, a 5-cm. square was drawn adjacent to the axis. On the right side, which was to be rotated through 180°, a small round figure (or square) was placed successively at different distances from the axis in such a way that, after folding, the small figure would appear outside, or inside, or on the frontier of the larger figure (see Fig. 2). The child was requested to draw what he expected would be the result of the folding. He was asked, for example, "Where will the little circle be when the book is closed?"

(b) The same experiment was done with a square frame placed on a background surface.

(c) The child was asked to imagine the paper being folded in a straight line at an angle of 45° or 90°, etc., to the vertical folding axis (see Fig. 3).

Two results struck us as particularly interesting.

1. Children from 5 to 7 years showed considerable reluctance to place the small figure inside or on the frontier of the larger one, but the problem became much easier to solve if the large square had an opening (a hole), thus depriving it of the figural quality manifested in the small circles or squares.

2. The representative imagery of topological relations of interiority or exteriority came long before the imagery of the transformation of Euclidian figures, such as changes of direction of straight lines in relation to a frame of reference. The latter form of representation did not become general until fairly late, that is for children between 9 and 11 years. The figurative symbolism seemed to be closely related to the corresponding geometric operations.

Transformations of arcs into straight lines and vice versa A supple piece of wire in the shape of an arc (10, 13, or 24 cm. long) was presented to children aged 5 to 9 or 10 years, and they were asked,

(a) To draw a straight line showing the length of the wire if it were straightened out (by gesture, the experimenter suggested the action of pulling the wire straight by its extremities); to cut lengths of wire equal to the result of straightening the arc; and

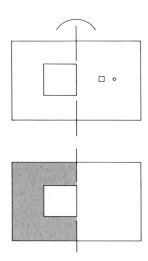

FIGURE 2

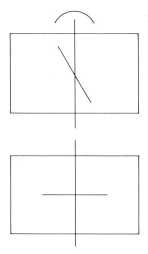

FIGURE 3

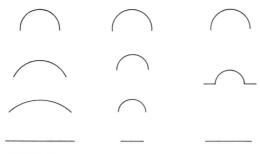

FIGURE 4

(*b*) to draw successive intermediate stages of the transformation.

The drawings by the young children (see Fig. 4), as well as the cutting of the lengths of wire, were evidence of an initial difficulty of representing the result of a transformation and of a much more persistent inability to symbolize successive stages of the transformation. Centering his attention on the extremities of the figure, the child first behaved as if the result of the straightening would be equal to the chord of the arc, in other words, as if he had to "conserve" the ordinal relations of the figure's frontiers. Only very gradually, along with the development of operativity, did older children succeed in more or less correctly imagining the straight lines result-ing from arcs. When this first obstacle was overcome, there remained the difficulty of representing intermediate stages of the transformation. This symbolization required an operative understanding of the ordinal change of the extremities, the seriation of intermediate stages, and the conservation of length. With progress in operative think-ing, it would seem that a new form of imagery developed which captured successive moments of a continuous transformation (like the frames of a film) in order, as it were, to represent the continuity of the transformation in a schematic way.

The somersault A tube with its extremities painted different colours was placed on a horizontal support in such a way that part of the tube projected beyond the support. By striking it on the projecting end, the tube could be made to perform a somersault (translation as well as rotation through 180°), so that it arrived in the inverse position on a lower support. After having rapidly performed this movement before the child, the experimenter removed the tube and asked the child to reproduce very slowly the same movement and then to draw the tube in its initial position, in its final position, and in intermediate positions. Finally, the child was asked to draw the trajectories traveled by the two extremities of the tube during the somersault.

From observing the rich variety of symbolic images provided by children aged 4 to 9 years, we would have concluded that, generally, the symbolic representation of the result of a transformation preceded the symbolic representation of the transformation itself. This seemed to command the over-all development of imagery. The drawings (see Fig. 5) show the clumsy way that the children tried to represent the ordinal change of the extremities resulting from this movement. The lag between symbolization of results and symbolization of transformations would seem to be explained by the fact that the child needs to understand what happens during the trans-

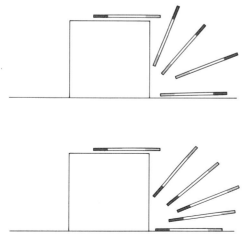

FIGURE 5

formation before he can symbolize it in detail; the transformation image thus seems to be subordinate to operational activities.

The Development of Imagery

The origin of symbolic imagery   It is certainly difficult to say exactly when the child's first images appear. Piaget's studies on the origins of sensorimotor intelligence and the genesis of the permanent object would invalidate the hypothesis that imagery appears early, as certain psychoanalysts have contended. Piaget's observations of the development of spontaneous symbolic behaviour in his own children, which have since been confirmed experimentally by our team, lend colour to the hypothesis that imagery is linked to symbolic function, and symbolic imagery arises by genetic filiation from imitative mechanisms.

The earliest observed behaviour implying evocative images is linked to deferred imitation. The child evokes physical as well as human models in their absence. His means of evocation are gestures, attitudes, and movements. Imitative movements seem to become interiorized subsequently in the form of incipient schemes that, in our experiments, are seen as movements and drawing gestures that enable the child to symbolize the models figuratively. This filiation from imitation is, moreover, part of the general process of the development of symbols. From the second year onward, we witness a great development of symbolic function that is marked by the progressive differentiation of signifiers and signified. On the one hand are the multiple signification and the elastic extension, which the child attributes to symbols in his imaginative play, verbal (prelogical) concepts, and evocative imagery; this signification and extension result from assimilative processes of nascent thought. On the other hand, however, the accommodating mechanisms of imitation play a striking role in the constitution of the forms and contents of signifiers.

The fact that the genesis of elementary forms of imagery—far from constituting an isolated process—takes in a series of linked filiations that lead from imitation to symbol formation, strongly supports the modern conception according to which images have the status of symbols.

The relation between elementary forms of symbolic imagery and preoperative thought   An essentially static quality was seen to dominate symbolic imagery that corresponds to the level of preoperative thought. This quality generally determines the difficulties of the child in passing from a reproductive image, itself frequently deformed, to an anticipatory image. The static quality of the image is seen particularly in the child's efforts to conserve certain features of the figure while neglecting others and by his incapacity to symbolize the continuous transformations of shapes and movements. Retaining certain typical features of the figure leads the child toward what one might call pseudoconservations and to a certain reluctance to exceed or cross the frontiers.

A whole set of converging indices point to the importance that the child attaches to certain figure frontiers: the translation of a square in relation to another gives rise to a pseudoconservation of the terminal frontier at the expense of surface conservation. As a complement to the conservation of the outer frontier, the child refuses to draw the inner frontiers of a figure when transparent squares are partially superimposed and thus neglects the intersection of the figures. In the experiments on folding, the child similarly refuses to represent the envelopment of a small circle in a square or the intersection with the frontier of the latter as long as the square is a figure and not a background surface. The almost insurmountable difficulties of imagining the intermediate stages between the arc and the straight line will be recalled, as will the children's clumsy efforts at symbolizing the successive positions of a somersaulting tube.

In conclusion, we shall consider the relation between operative thought and its symbolic imagery from both the functional and the structural points of view. From the point of view of the functioning of cognitive activity, it would seem that there is, concurrently, a complementary relation and a certain interdependence between the operative and figurative aspects of thought. According to the distinction established by Piaget, operativity consists in transforming, by action or in thought, a piece of reality considered as an object of knowledge. Thanks to a series of reversible operations, the child discovers, for example, the invariability of the quantity, although the matter is transformed. The figurative aspects of thought, on the other hand, are limited to copying, or, more precisely, to imitating in a schematic way the piece of reality. At each moment of development, operativity directs the formation of symbolic imagery by providing it with meanings, and the figurative signifiers, once they have been built up, favor the acquisition and the fixation of information that is food for thought.

By considering the development of operative structures and symbolic imagery, we are entitled to suppose that their modes of construction do not enjoy an equal degree of independence from outside influences. The successive structures of operative thought, as Piaget has shown, are engendered one from the other according to a constant and integrated order. They may be accelerated or inhibited by many external factors; their mode of construction, however, does not seem to be modified by such factors.

The development of symbolic imagery, we believe, depends to a large extent on external contributions. It is as if, in the initial phases, symbolic imagery bore the imprint of motor-imitation schemes from which it stems; as we have shown, the later evolution of figurative symbolism is modified through the progress of operativity.

22 | The Acquisition of Conservation of Substance and Weight in Children

JAN SMEDSLUND

How do children come to ignore perceptual changes in an object and understand that weight or substance is not changed by a transformation of shape or form? Smedslund reviews the history and logic involved in testing this notion. He shows that the child of six does not appreciate the invariance of substance and weight under transformations; however, by the time the child is eight or nine, he understands conservation. Several theories have been proposed to explain this change: (1) nativism—the human nervous system is organized in such a way that the child immediately recognizes conservation when he has sufficient knowledge; (2) learning theory—the child discovers empirically that as long as nothing is added or taken away, the weight remains constant; (3) maturation—the logical structure develops as a result of physiological maturation; (4) equilibration theory—the logical structure develops as a function of experience and activity through the process of equilibration.

Smedslund reviews several studies showing that nativism and maturation cannot account for the findings; this leaves only learning theory and equilibration as serious contenders. After discussing two critical tests of the theories, he concludes that the equilibration theory can handle the findings with ease, while theories of learning have considerable difficulty.

This series of articles will be concerned with the following specific problem: What processes are involved in children's acquisition of conservation of substance and weight? These phenomena are defined as follows. A subject has conservation of substance when he thinks the amount of substance in an object must necessarily remain unchanged during changes in its form, as long as nothing is added or taken away. Similarly, a subject has conservation of weight when he thinks the weight of an object must necessarily remain unchanged during changes in its form, as long as nothing is added or taken away.

The classical test for the study of conservation of substance and weight employs pieces of plasticine. The child is presented with two equal balls of plasticine and is told that they are equally heavy. Then one of the balls is changed into a sausage or something else, and in the test of conservation of substance the following standard question is asked: "Do you think there is more plasticine in the ball, or the same amount in both, or more in the sausage?" The corresponding question in the test of conservation of weight is: "Which is heavier, the ball or the sausage, or do they weigh

Adapted from The acquisition of conservation of substance and weight in children. *Scandinavian Journal of Psychology*, 1961, **2**, 11-20.

139

the same?" After the child has answered the question he is asked: "Why do you think so?"

Children with conservation of substance answer that the objects contain the same amount of plasticine because they contained the same amount in the beginning; because only the shape is changed; or because nothing has been added or taken away. Children with conservation of weight answer that the objects weigh the same, and use the same arguments as in the case of conservation of substance. Children who do not have a principle of conservation usually rely on perceptual features of the objects: The sausage contains more because it is longer; the ball weighs more because it is thicker and rounder, because it looks a little bigger, etc.

TRANSITION AGES

Several earlier studies have established the generality of the developmental transition from non-conservation to conservation in the domains of substance and weight. The classical study of Piaget & Inhelder (1941) first drew attention to these phenomena. These writers did not report the exact number and ages of their subjects, but stated that conservation of substance is reached on the average around 7–8 years, and conservation of weight around 9–10 years. Furthermore, their data seemed to indicate that conservation of substance and weight are invariably acquired in this order, i.e. subjects with conservation of weight always have conservation of substance but not vice versa.

The generality of this sequence seemed to be confirmed in parallel studies of children's interpretations of the melting of sugar in water and of the swelling of popcorn on a hot plate. In each situation they observed some children who asserted conservation of substance and denied conservation of weight, but they observed no children who asserted conservation of weight but denied conservation of substance. This early study was conducted by means of Piaget's *méthode clinique,* which consists of flexible and intuitively directed conversation and play. This method has proved very fruitful in the initial steps of research, but has the drawback that it cannot be exactly replicated, and it allows for unknown degrees of subjectivity in the procedure and interpretations.

A study by Inhelder (1944) verified the substance–weight sequence and indicated that these tests, together with those of conservation of volume and transitivity of weight, may have considerable diagnostic utility in practical application. The general developmental level of feeble-minded children and adults was reported as being clearly reflected in the test-responses.

A large scale standardization by Vinh-Bang (1957) has provided reliable and exact information on the transition ages in the population of Geneva. Nearly 1500 children between 4 and 12 years of age were given a battery of some thirty objective tests, including conservation of substance and conservation of weight. The 50 per cent level for the acquisition of conservation of substance is at 7½ years, and the corresponding level for conservation of weight is at 8 years. See also Vinh-Bang (1959). The study of Lovell (1960) in England gave approximately the same results. On the other hand, Smedslund (1959) found somewhat earlier transition ages in a group of children (sons and daughters of delegates to the international committees and organizations) from a socio-economically superior milieu in Geneva.

The studies of conservation of number by Slater (1958) in England and by Hyde (1959) with European and non-European subjects in Aden further support the hypothesis that the rate of development of concepts of conservation is influenced by environment.

POSSIBLE INTERPRETATIONS

Historically, the diverging interpretations of the phenomena of cognitive development may be traced to the conflict between the classical philosophical schools of *empiricism* and *rationalism*. Briefly stated, the former assumes that everything that is in the mind comes from experience. The latter asserts that there are certain structures and categories which impose themselves by necessity upon the human mind and which exist independently of any experience. In contemporary psychology one may discern at least four major interpretations of the type of developmental phenomena to be studied here (and combinations of them).

Nativism

According to this point of view, the human nervous system is organized in such a way that the intrinsic validity of the inference of conservation is immediately recognized at the moment when the child has acquired a knowledge of the empirical elements involved. This line of thought assumes that even very small children are always logical *within those limited areas where they have sufficient knowledge*. Development is seen as a process where appropriate inferential behavior is immediately applied to every new domain of experience.

Learning Theory

This continues the old empiricist tradition and assumes that the child acquires the concepts of conservation as a function of repeated external reinforcements. According to this point of view, the subjective validity and necessity of the inference of conservation derives from an *empirical law*. The children discover empirically that as long as nothing is added or taken away, objects maintain the same amount of substance and the same weight, irrespective of changes of shape.

Alternatively, learning theorists may interpret the development transition as resulting from *social* reinforcements. The sanctions from adults and older children may gradually lead to the "correct" behavior relative to physical substance and weight. The training in the rules of language

may contribute in various ways to the same outcome.

Maturation Theory

This theory asserts that logical structure may not be present from the beginning in children's behavior, but that it develops as a function of nervous maturation and independently of experience. No amount of experience can bring about a given type of inferential behavior in a child who is not mature enough, and once he has reached a sufficient degree of nervous maturation his experiences are immediately integrated into a logical framework. Small children may be "illogical," but there is nothing one can do about it, just wait for nature to take its course.

Equilibration Theory

This is the position of Piaget and his co-workers (Piaget, 1950; 1957), who assert that logical structure is not originally present in the child's thinking, but that it develops as a function of an internal process, equilibration which is heavily dependent on *activity* and *experience*. This point of view differs radically from that of learning theory, since practice is not assumed to act through external reinforcements, but by a process of mutual influence of the child's activities on each other. Logical inferences are not derived from any properties of the external world, but from the placing into relationship (*mise-en-relation*) of the subject's own activities. The process of equilibration is not identical with maturation, since it is highly influenced by practice which brings out latent contradictions and gaps in mental structure, and thereby initiates a process of inner reorganization. The theory is somewhat similar to Festinger's theory of cognitive dissonance (1957) and Heider's theory of balance (1958), but is more general.

These are, briefly, the four main theories of the mechanisms of cognitive development. Needless to say, many psychologists may choose intermediate positions, e.g., by postulating some kind of *interaction* of learning and maturation.

Nativism and learning theory represent opposite positions with respect to the role of experience, but they share the idea that children's thinking is essentially similar to that of adults. Both theories assume that in situations with insufficient knowledge adults will behave like children, and that in situations with sufficient knowledge children will behave like adults.

CRITICAL DISCUSSION

The well-established findings of Piaget and his collaborators in a variety of fields seem to have excluded *nativism* as a serious possibility. (For a summary of many of these findings see Piaget, 1950, pp. 129–147.) Children below a certain age do not, for example, have notions of conservation, and they seem to acquire these notions at a relatively late stage of their development. Young children show amazingly "illogical" behavior even in situations where they seem to be in possession of all the relevant knowledge necessary for a correct conclusion. A child may know that nothing has been added to or taken away from a piece of clay, and still assert that the amount of clay and the weight has increased or diminished when the form is changed from ball to sausage. Even when every possible precaution is taken to ensure that the child has grasped the essential elements of the situation, one may observe the same type of perception-bound, "irrational" behavior.

We must conclude that the available evidence is clearly against the theory that logical structure follows automatically when the elements of a situation have been understood.

It is most tempting to apply some variant of *learning theory* to the developmental process. However, this application encounters a number of obstacles, some of which stem from the fact that it is so difficult to

imagine how conservation can be established by external reinforcements in the normal life of children.

Let us begin with conservation of substance. According to Piaget and Inhelder (1941) this notion is established before conservation of weight and volume, i.e. before there exists any unequivocal empirical criterion of conservation. The subject cannot observe the conservation of substance during changes in form. On the contrary, his perceptual schemata lead him to suppose that the amount changes, and he has to fight to overcome the impact of how things "look." "It *looks* as if there were more in the ball, but I *know* it can't be." Thus, the child acquires conservation of substance by learning to *ignore* the appearance of things and his own direct experience.

In the experiment of melting sugar in water (Piaget & Inhelder, 1941), some children with conservation of substance asserted that the melted sugar was still there, even though they thought that the glass with the sugar would weigh exactly the same as the other glass with pure water, and that the water level would be the same in the two glasses. In this case, the child ignores the visual disappearance of substance, and asserts conservation without relying on a single empirical support. Even the taste is supposed to disappear after some time. It is difficult to imagine by what means children in normal conditions could be led by their observations to assume exact conservation of substance.

There are at least three possible auxiliary hypotheses, which depart more or less from a strict learning theory interpretation, but which nevertheless attribute a crucial role to external reinforcement.

1. The subject may have learned empirically that objects become larger when something is added to them and smaller when something is taken away. This may be generalized in some complex way to the class of situations where nothing is added or taken away and where consequently no change is assumed.

The difficulty with this explanation is that even very young children understand that nothing has been taken away or added in the conservation test, and still think that the amount of substance has increased or decreased. They do not appear to regard the absence of adding and taking away as a relevant argument for conservation, and this is really the crucial problem. Why does this argument suddenly become relevant and lead to the idea that conservation is logically necessary?

2. It may be thought that the discovery of *empirical reversibility,* i.e. the fact that one may return to the point of departure after a deformation, would be sufficient to induce conservation. More generally, the set of expectancies associated with other possible deformations remain unchanged by any given deformation, and by some complex mechanism this might lead to the notion of conservation.

A large amount of evidence shows that empirical reversibility cannot explain the acquisition of conservation. Even very young children know practically always that one may return to the starting point; the sausage can be remade into a ball that contains exactly as much plasticine as the unchanged standard. Even so, the sausage is seen as containing *more* or *less* plasticine than the standard! Finally, it should be noted that in the experiment with the melting of sugar, children assert conservation of substance even though the melting process is not empirically reversible in their field of experience.

3. One may assume that the lack of conservation of substance stems from a *difficulty of recall,* and that this can be improved upon by a process of "learning to learn." Perhaps the small child is unable to recall the initial state of equality, after just one presentation? This hypothesis is clearly contradicted by the available evidence, since the children, with few exceptions, do remember the initial state. However, they do not feel that the initial state of equality is relevant for the judgment of the state after the deformation, and learning theory probably cannot easily provide an explanation of how this is changed.

The preceding considerations are equally valid for conservation of weight. In this case, however, learning theory might seem to be in a somewhat better position, since weight is a directly observable factor. Perhaps children learn directly that weight does not change with changes in form? Again the answer seems to be negative. It is well known that the direct kinesthetic–tactile impression of weight is highly unreliable and extremely sensitive to irrelevant visual stimuli. We have repeatedly observed how children *confirm* their idea of non-conservation by weighing the objects in their hands. "Yes, I can feel that the sausage is heavier than the ball"; "the ball is much heavier now," etc. Again, we must conclude that the children acquire conservation *against* the perceptual appearance of things.

It has been suggested that children learn conservation of weight by means of scales. The answer to this is that children relatively seldom play with scales. Furthermore, the scales designed for children and available in the nurseries are technically rather primitive and do not easily lend themselves to any test of the principle of conservation.

A direct learning interpretation of the acquisition of conservation of weight also fails to explain why conservation of substance seems regularly to precede it genetically, although conservation of substance has no unambiguous observable referent.

Learning theorists may also try to explain the transition from non-conservation to conservation as a result of accumulated direct and indirect *social reinforcements.* We are aware of no evidence pointing to any direct training in these matters in the homes, and the sequential development of the various notions does not have any obvious connection with the teaching program in nurseries and schools. On the other hand, as mentioned above, several recent studies have shown an effect of children's socio-economic and cultural backgrounds on the speed of acquisition of the various concepts of conservation. This is in accordance both with a learning theory interpretation and an equilibration theory interpretation. The former would attribute the acceleration to a higher frequency of direct and/or indirect reinforcements, whereas the latter would assume that certain environments more frequently than others confront the child with complex intellectual problems, thus forcing him to organize his thinking.

Altogether, we may conclude that, despite apparent difficulties, one cannot discard the possibility of a learning theory interpretation of the acquisition of notions of conservation. Among recent authors on this subject, Apostel (1959) apparently believes in this possibility, whereas Berlyne (1960) introduces so many new assumptions into the Hullian framework that it becomes almost indistinguishable from the equilibration theory.

The *maturation theory* is in some ways a relatively plausible one. It takes account of the general observations of pre-logical behavior and of the absence of evidence for direct learning. The great difficulty from this point of view is (a) to explain the *time lag* between the occurrence of the various notions of conservation (Piaget, 1950; Vinh-Bang, 1959), and (b) to explain the accelerating v. retarding effects of the various elements. These two types of observations show that the maturation hypothesis is invalid as a general explanation, and that maturation can at most be a necessary condition for certain other processes to occur. The main problem is to discover the nature of these other processes.

Most of the arguments so far presented are not only *against* the three other interpretations, but also *for* the equilibration theory. The following tentative conclusions may be drawn from the preceding discussion: that the existing evidence seems to exclude nativism as a possible interpretation, and that maturation can at most be a contributing factor in providing the necessary neurological conditions for the acquisition of the successively more complex cognitive levels.

The respective validities of learning theory and equilibration theory remain undetermined, although many findings seem to point against the former. In what follows, we will focus on the problem of how experience influences cognitive development, and on the question of learning v. equilibration. A brief review of some relevant earlier studies will conclude this introductory paper.

The direct predecessor of the present investigations was a study by Smedslund (1959). It was designed to show the effects of direct external reinforcement on the acquisition of conservation and transitivity of weight.

The experiment on conservation learning included three groups of subjects between 5;10 and 7;1, who consistently asserted non-conservation. Group A ($N = 8$) went through a series of 30 empirical controls on a pair of scales, permitting direct observation that objects do not change weight during deformation. Group B ($N = 8$) likewise had 30 controls on the scales, but 11 of the items of deformation were exchanged for items of addition and subtraction.

It was thought that if the learning theory interpretation were true, group A should learn more and faster than group B, since A had only direct reinforcements of the response category to be learned. On the other hand, equilibration theory would lead one to expect more improvement in group B, since this involved practice on the operations of addition and subtraction, whose combination is assumed to lie beneath the concept of conservation. ("Nothing is added and nothing is taken away.") Finally, there was a group C ($N = 5$) which did not take part in any practice sessions, and which functioned as a control.

There was a considerable amount of learning in both the experimental groups and no significant difference between them, although group A had slightly better results. Taken at their face value these results seemed to indicate that a concept of conservation of weight may be acquired as a function of external reinforcements. Furthermore, the slight advantage of group A over group B was in the direction of confirming the learning theory interpretation and went against the equilibration theory.

However, there are at least two alternative interpretations of the findings which, if true, would radically change the conclusions.

1. It is quite possible that what occurred was a simple response learning leading to a *pseudoconcept* without the quality of insight and necessity that accompanies the genuine concept. The genuine concept of conservation is inaccessible to experimental extinction, whereas the outcome of simple response learning would presumably be easy to extinguish. In article III of this series the outcome of an experimental test of this possibility will be reported.

2. The possibility of an easy response learning in group B (the majority of the items involved simple deformations which were identical to those in Group A), may have inhibited any tendency to active cognitive reorganization induced by the small number of addition/subtraction items; cf. the discussion of Gréco's experiments below. A more crucial test would be to compare a condition with only addition/subtraction items with a condition with only deformation items. The outcome of such an experiment is described in article II of this series.

The experiment of Wohlwill (1959) on the acquisition of conservation of number is highly relevant for our purpose. A subject has conservation of number when he thinks that the number of objects in a collection must necessarily remain unchanged during changes in the spatial arrangement of the collection, as long as nothing is added or taken away.

Wohlwill posed the problem of whether conservation of number develops from the operations of adding and subtracting by means of some inferential process, or

whether it results from direct reinforcement. He decided to check this by comparing the outcome of direct external reinforcement of conservation with the outcome of reinforcement of the operations of adding and subtracting.

The results show a not quite significant but highly suggestive superiority of the group trained on additions and subtractions as compared with the group trained directly on conservation over deformations. Since ordinary S-R learning principles would lead one to expect more learning in the latter group, this experiment represents a very suggestive strengthening of the equilibration theory. Wohlwill's data are at variance with our own, reported above, and this provided further encouragement to repeat our experiment with a more clearcut design involving only addition/subtraction items v. only deformation items.

The study of Gréco (1959a) concerns the learning to understand successive spatial rotations. The materials were a cardboard tube and a wooden rod to which were fastened a black, a white, and a red bead, in that order. The rod with the beads is moved into the tube until it is completely hidden and the child is asked: "Which color comes out first at the other end?" This simple question is answered correctly by most children at the age of 5–6 years. The tube with the rod inside is then rotated slowly and horizontally 180 degrees, once or twice, and the question of which color comes out is again asked. Gréco was interested in whether young children could learn to understand the meaning of the successive rotations of the tube. To the adult the rotations form a kind of logical grouping. The rotations may be combined with each other to deduce the effect, and the outcome is considered as *logically necessary*. If red is expected to come out in the direct order, then black must come out after one rotation and red again after two rotations.

Gréco's design involved two main experimental groups, D and S. The subjects in group D learned one rotation and two rotations separately to perfection, before they were presented with a mixed set of items containing both one and two rotations. The subjects in group S were mainly trained on the mixed set of items. The subjects in both groups learned to anticipate correctly the outcome of both one and two rotations. After a period of between one and three months a post-test was given to test the stability of the achievements. Furthermore, the *generalization* to *n* rotation was studied and the *transfer* to an analogous situation (a rotating disk with red and black placed in diametrically opposite positions). The data show a striking difference between the two groups. The children in group D had forgotten practically everything they had learned, whereas the children in group S had retained almost everything. The children in S also showed a considerable, but not complete generalization to *n* rotations and some transfer to an analogous situation.

Gréco's conclusion is as follows: In this situation it is possible for most pre-school children to learn behavior that is seemingly equivalent to the performance of older children. However, this learning seems to proceed in two ways which lead to quite different results. The subjects in group D seemed to have learned the outcome of one and two rotations separately as empirical laws and with no understanding of their "necessary" character. The subjects in group S never had a possibility to learn in this way; directly confronted with the more complex mixed set of items, they were probably forced into an intense "structuring activity." Apparently this led them to understand that two rotations represent the outcome of one rotation and another rotation.

These findings seem to strengthen the hypothesis that situations which permit simple response learning are detrimental to the occurrence of more profound cognitive reorganizations. Unfortunately, the two experimental conditions differed in several other respects, such as standardized v. clinical procedure and massed v. distributed practice. This makes the interpretation very uncertain.

The experiment of Morf (1959) concerned the acquisition of certain operations of class-inclusion. In a typical test the subject is presented with a collection of wooden beads, most of which are brown and a few are white. The subject is led to acknowledge explicitly that all the beads are made of wood and that most of them are brown and only a few are white. Finally, the following question is asked: "Can you tell me whether there are more brown beads or more beads made of wood?" The typical answer of the 5–6 year old is; "There are more brown beads because there are only two or three white ones."

No amount of reformulation or rearrangement of the material seems to bring these children to understand the correct answer. Morf wanted to find out whether it was possible for children to acquire the operations of class-inclusion as a function of some kind of training or practice.

Very briefly, the findings were as follows: With a method of various empirical controls and with several concrete materials the outcome was completely negative as far as the correct answer was concerned. The outcome of a method of free play was likewise negative. A third technique tried to make the relations between the total class and the subclasses directly visible, but again there was no real learning. Finally, some success was obtained with a technique involving exercise of the operations of *logical multiplication*.

The children were trained in seeing objects as being simultaneously members of two or more classes, and this induced learning in 7 of 30 subjects. These results, as far as they go, are more in accordance with equilibration theory than with ordinary learning theories.

Churchill (1958) in a study of the acquisition of conservation of number, apparently succeeded in inducing conservation to a considerable extent, but the exact procedure is not given in the summary that has been available.

TENTATIVE GENERALIZATIONS

The preceding experiments are mostly very complex and exploratory and have served to raise questions rather than answer them. Nevertheless, they permit us to formulate certain tentative generalizations, which may act as a frame of reference for further research.

1. The possibility of inducing a cognitive reorganization depends on the subject's already available schemata. If he has a structure which already approaches the given notion, the probability of the desired reorganization is high, whereas if he is still far from the notion, the chances are small that he will change sufficiently during a limited series of experimental sessions. Gréco (1959b) was able to show that children of the same age as those in the experiment with the rotating tube were unable to learn an exactly analogous but purely empirical and arbitrary problem. The probable reason was that the subjects in the former experiment already had a beginning "intuition" about the rotations, whereas, the subjects in the latter experiment had to start from scratch. The studies of children's learning at different age levels by Gréco (1959b), Goustard (1959), and Matalon (1959) all demonstrate directly how the ability to profit from experience depends on the initial developmental level.

2. Situations which permit immediate and simple response learning with empirical control are unlikely to lead to any profound cognitive reorganization. This is exemplified by Gréco's group D and by our own groups A and B. For evidence supporting this interpretation see article III of this series.

3. Situations stressing empirical control, which do not permit simple response learning, may or may not induce a cognitive re-organization, which probably depends on the conditions mentioned under 1. Morf's groups with empirical control and our own experiment on learning of transitivity of weight (Smedslund, 1959) gave completely negative results. Correct inferences of transitivity and class-inclusion involve different stimuli and different responses in each new situation, and thus would be expected to yield little learning on the basis of current learning theories. These situations would also be expected to yield little improvement on the basis of equilibration theory, since they emphasize the empirical outcomes instead of the activities of the subject. Positive results were found in Gréco's group S.

4. Direct exercise of the relevant operations is likely to induce cognitive change to the extent that the conditions mentioned under 1 are favorable. This is exemplified by Morf's group, trained on the multiplication of classes, and by Wohlwill's addition/-subtraction group.

These are only vague statements with little predictive value. In the subsequent articles attempts will be made to determine the exact conditions for the acquisition of conservation of substance and weight and to construct a more specific theory.

REFERENCES

Apostel, L. Logique et apprentissage. *Études d'Épistémologie génétique*, 1959, **8,** 1–138.

Berlyne, D. E. Les équivalences psychologiques et les notions quantitatives. *Études d'Épistémologie génétique*, 1960, **12,** 1–76.

Churchill, E. M. The number concepts of the young child. Leeds: *Leeds University Research Studies*, 1958, **17,** 34–49; **18,** 28–46.

Festinger, L. *A theory of cognitive dissonance.* New York: Row, Peterson, 1957.

Goustard, M. Étude psychogénétique de la résolution d'un problème (Labyrinthe en T). *Études d'Épistémologie génétique*, 1959, **10,** 83–112.

Gréco, P. L'apprentissage dans une situation à

structure opératoire concrète: les inversions successives de l'ordre lineaire par des rotations de 180°. *Études d'Épistémologie génétique*, 1959, **7,** 68–182. (a)

Gréco, P. Induction, déduction et apprentissage. *Études d'Épistémologie génétique*, 1959, **10,** 3–59. (b)

Heider, F. *The psychology of interpersonal relations*. New York: Wiley, 1958.

Hyde, D. M. An investigation of Piaget's theories of the development of the concept of number. Unpublished doctoral thesis, University of London, 1959.

Inhelder, Bärbel. *Le diagnostic du raisonnement chez les débiles mentaux*. Neuchâtel: Delachaux & Niestlé, 1944.

Lovell, K., & Ogilvie, E. A study of the conservation of substance in the Junior School child. *British Journal of Educational Psychology*, 1960, **30,** 109–118.

Matalon, B. Apprentissages en situations aléatoires et systematiques. *Études d'Épistémologie génétique*, 1959, **10,** 61–91.

Morf, A. Apprentissage d'une structure logique concrète (inclusion). Effets et limites. *Études d'Épistémologie génétique*, 1959, **9,** 15–83.

Piaget, J. *The psychology of intelligence*. London: Routledge ? Kegan Paul, 1950.

Piaget, J. Logique et équilibre dans les comportements du sujet. *Études d'Épistémologie génétique*, 1957, **2,** 27–117.

Piaget, J., & Inhelder, Bärbel. *Le développement des quantités chez l'enfant*. Neuchâtel and Paris: Delachaux & Niestlé, 1941.

Slater, G. W. A study of the influence which environment plays in determining the rate of which a child attain Piaget's "operational" level in his early number concepts. Unpublished dissertation, Birmingham University, 1958.

Smedslund, J. Apprentissage des notions de la conservation et de la transitivité du poids. *Études d'Épistémologie génétique*, 1959, **9,** 85–124.

Vinh-Bang. Evolution des conduites et apprentissage. *Études d'Épistémologie génétique*, 1959, **9,** 3–13.

Vinh-Bang. Elaboration d'une échelle de développement du raisonnement. Genève: Institut des Sciences de l'Education. Proceedings of the 15th International Congress of Psychology, 1957, 333–334.

Wohlwill, J. Un essai d'apprentissage dans le domaine de la conservation du nombre. *Études d'Épistémologie génétique*, 1959, **9,** 125–135.

23 | Structure and Strategy in Concept Learning

SONIA F. OSLER
ELLIN KOFSKY

Many assume that children of varying ages approach concept learning with differing strategies and that maturation influences the child's sensitivity to stimulus structure. The present study investigated sensitivity to structure among three age groups, using a concept learning task. The complexity (information content) of the task was varied to see whether the form of information affected the manner in which children solve problems.

The authors suggest that very young children (four years old) learn concepts by rote associations, while older children learn rules which make the task easier to solve. The authors used a task that could be either memorized or solved by a rule. If children memorized instances, they would show little difference in performance between the situation with stimulus structure and the situation without. However, if they used rules, stimulus structure should facilitate solution. Their results show that older children use rules, while younger children learn by rote associations.

The aim of this investigation was to determine the effect of stimulus structure on concept attainment. It has been established that the amount of stimulus uncertainty in a concept task influences the performance of adults and children (Archer, Bourne, and Brown, 1955; Osler and Kofsky, 1965). However, a given level of uncertainty may be obtained in a variety of ways. For example, four bits of stimulus uncertainty may be generated from all possible combinations of four binary dimensions or from combinations of one binary with one eight-valued dimension. There is some evidence from adult Ss to suggest that increasing the number of values on a dimension does not have the same effect on concept attainment as

Adapted from Structure and strategy in concept learning. Journal of Experimental Child Psychology, 1966, **4,** 198–209.

increasing the number of dimensions in a set, despite equal uncertainties (Battig and Bourne, 1961). Hence the two sets described above may prove to be of unequal difficulty.

The study of the effects of stimulus structure may provide a means for discovering some of the strategies involved in concept attainment. An illustration may help to clarify this statement. If S attempts to classify the stimuli according to one of the constituent dimensions, it is obvious that the probability of choosing the relevant dimension will vary with the total number of dimensions in the stimulus set. It follows, that for classifiers the two sets described above, with four and two dimensions, respectively, would be of unequal difficulty. On the other hand, it is possible that S does not classify the stimuli, but rather regards each stimulus independently of the others in attempting to learn the correct response.

In this eventuality, the two problems should be of equivalent difficulty as they each require the learning of correct responses to 16 stimuli.

On the basis of a variety of research findings (Kendler and Kendler, 1959; Osler and Trautman, 1961), it was predicted that both kinds of solution actually occur. Rote learning may characterize the performance of young children; and later, perhaps at six or seven years, classification of stimuli may begin to play a significant role in inductive concept tasks. Young children, who are presumed to be rote learners, should respond to the number of stimuli in a set, rather than to its structure. Older children, who are presumed to classify more frequently, should respond primarily to variations in the number of dimensions within a stimulus set, rather than to the size of set. To test these hypotheses, the following experiment was performed.

METHOD

Subjects

The subjects were 108 white boys, equally divided among kindergartners, third and sixth graders in Baltimore City and County schools. The children were selected randomly from the class rolls. The mean ages of the three groups were 5.6 years (range 5.1–6.0 years), 8.7 years (range 8.0–10.4 years), and 11.8 years (range 10.9–13.0 years). The children came from families in the lower part of the socioeconomic scale, but from stable neighborhoods. They were definitely not in the culturally deprived group, as indicated by an average IQ of 100.5 ($SD = 11.4$, range of 80 to 128), measured by the performance subtests of the Wechsler Intelligence Scale for Children.

Stimuli

Three sets of geometric stimuli were employed. Set A, constructed from all the combinations of four binary dimensions, contained 16 stimuli. Set B also consisted of 16 stimuli, but these stimuli were generated by combining one binary dimension with one eight-valued dimension. Stimulus set C was generated from combinations of two binary dimensions, resulting in a total of four stimuli. Sets A and B contained the same number of stimuli, but differed in the number of dimensions. Sets B and C each contained two dimensions, but varied in size of set. A description of the stimuli used is presented in Table 1.

Procedure

The experimental procedure consisted of four parts: pretesting, pretraining, concept attainment, and intellectual assessment.

Ss were screened individually to eliminate those who could not discriminate each of the colors, sizes, and shapes of the stimuli used in the experiment. In addition, each S was given a sample learning task involving the same procedure and apparatus as the concept task. Failure to learn this task resulted in exclusion from the experiment.

TABLE 1 Stimulus Sets

Relevant Dimension	Irrelevant Dimensions		
Sets A, B and C	Set A	Set B	Set C
Form 1	color, size, number	color	color
Form 2	color, size, number	color	color
Size	color, number, form 1	color	color
Number	color, size, form 1	color	color

Note. Form 1 consisted of circles and squares; form 2 consisted of stars and crosses.

At the onset of the concept task Ss were instructed: "Some pictures give a marble with this handle and some pictures give a marble with this handle. See if you can find out where the pictures belong, so that you can get a marble every time (you press). When you have won enough marbles you can have the . . . [prize S had previously selected]." Responses were elicited until S made 30 correct choices in a block of 32 consecutive trials, or until 160 trials were administered. To prevent fatigue, the screening procedures were administered on one day, the concept task the following day, and the WISC within a week of the first experimental session.

Experimental Design

A 3 × 3 factorial design was employed, with three stimulus conditions and three age groups constituting the two variables. This produced nine experimental groups of 12 Ss each. Three Ss in each group worked with the same relevant dimension.

RESULTS

Response to dimensional structure. Errors to criterion are shown in Fig. 1. Performance on sets A and B was compared by means of an analysis of variance. Since stimulus uncertainty was equal under these two conditions, differences in performance are likely to be the result of dimensional structure (two vs. four dimensions). Three significant sources of variance were found: dimensional structure ($F = 7.47$, $df = 1,66$, $p < .01$), age ($F = 13.04$, $df = 2,66$, $p < .001$), and the structure by age interaction ($F = 3.08$, $df = 2,66$, for a $p < .05$, F must be 3.15). An analysis of the interaction showed that the third graders found problem A to be more difficult than B ($t = 3.53$, $df = 66$, $p < .01$). While the kindergartners found both problems equally difficult, the sixth graders found both relatively easy.

A similar analysis was performed with

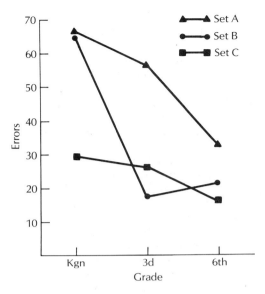

FIGURE 1   Mean errors to criterion.

the data obtained on problems B and C (equivalent in dimensional structure but different in uncertainty). The analysis showed that kindergartners responded to size, as they found problem B more difficult than problem C, while the older children responded to structure, as they found both problems to be of equivalent difficulty. The kindergarten Ss solved problem C quickly, but found problems A and B very difficult. The critical feature for them seemed to be the size of the stimulus set. The third graders found problems B and C easy to solve, but problem A was difficult for them. In fact, despite their equal size, sets A and B were of such divergent difficulty that set A produced three times the number of errors elicited by set B. While the kindergartners responded to the *size* of the stimulus set, for the third graders the crucial factor appeared to be the *number of independent dimensions* in the stimulus set. The sixth graders, too, found problem A more difficult than B or C, but the differences among all three tasks were reduced by the increased competence of the oldest children on the most difficult problem.

DISCUSSION AND CONCLUSIONS

The two experimental predictions that motivated this study were confirmed by the data. Sets that are equivalent in uncertainty may vary in difficulty as a function of their dimensional structure. Thus structure, as well as uncertainty, is an important variable in concept attainment. Secondly, the effect of the structure variable depends on the age of the learner. Differences in structure within a given level of uncertainty produced no effect on the performance of kindergarten Ss, but produced an appreciable effect on the performance of third graders.

Why is one age group more sensitive to the dimensional properties of the stimulus set than another? According to the original hypothesis, sensitivity to structure reflects the child's ability to categorize. Since young Ss are less likely to categorize, their performance is not facilitated by a reduction in the number of dimensions, but by a reduction in the size of the stimulus set. In contrast, older children who can categorize respond differentially to stimulus sets according to their dimensional structure. Subjects may, however, experience some limits to the number of ways in which they can classify. Thus, in our data, it appears that 8-year-olds can categorize sets with two dimensions, but have difficulty with four dimensions. This gradual development is consistent with Piaget's findings of a similar process in the ability to conserve liquids. Children may conserve when a liquid is poured into two beakers, but not when the liquid is divided among three (Piaget, 1952). Finally, Ss whose capacity to categorize is much greater than required by the problems are not likely to differentiate among sets which vary in number of dimensions. Hence the performance of the sixth graders shows less variation across the three problem sets.

As attractive as this interpretation sounds, there are some features of the data that call it into question. So far only criterion Ss have been included among the cate-gorizers; but many failing Ss who persever-ated on irrelevant dimensions were also categorizing. We can determine who these Ss were by using informational analyses (Osler and Kofsky, 1965). If these Ss are included, then age differences in classi-fication are diminished (24-kindergartners, 27 third graders, and 32 sixth graders, as compared with 13, 27, and 31 criterion Ss respectively). It is apparent that the largest discrepancy between number of cate-gorizers and number of criterion Ss occurs among the youngest Ss. It seems, there-fore, that there is more to concept attain-ment than categorizing; memory, attention, and the employment of inductive strategies may also play a role. Each of these abilities develops with age. It is also likely that the attentional requirements of each task, the memory load imposed by each set, and the ease of induction vary as a function of stim-ulus properties of the set. The ability to change criteria seems to be another prereq-uisite for success in concept attainment. Why the younger Ss do not abandon incor-rect response systems is unclear. A suggested hypothesis is that categorizing is a some-what rudimentary ability for 5-year-olds and that they are, therefore, not yet able to see more than one way of classifying a group of stimuli. This limitation would explain the drop in the performance of the young Ss on the complex problems, for increased stimulus complexity reduces the likelihood that the initial hypothesis will be correct.

One factor contributing to persevera-tion is the occurrence of 50% reinforcement with almost any strategy. For young Ss the instruction "try to get a marble every time" may not be inconsistent with success only half the time. Piaget has shown that at this stage the words "all" and "every" are not clearly understood (Inhelder and Piaget, 1964); and Osler and Shapiro (1964) have shown that concept attainment performance in 6-year-olds is not affected by the reduc-tion of rates of reinforcement from 100 to 50%. Both of these factors may contribute to S's willingness to stay with a hypothesis that pays off only 50% of the time.

Another reason for failure, aside from perseveration, may be *S*'s inability to construct classes of the appropriate size. Problems A and B may be too difficult for young *S*s because the tasks require the formation of eight-stimulus groups. As neither the interpretation based on the ability to shift criteria nor the interpretation based on size of class can be verified with the data on hand, an investigation of free classification of the stimulus sets used in the present study is now being conducted.

REFERENCES

Archer, E. J., Bourne, L. E., Jr., & Brown, F. G. Concept identification as a function of irrelevant information and instructions. *Journal of Experimental Psychology,* 1955, **49,** 153–164.

Battig, W. F., & Bourne, L. E., Jr. Concept identification as a function of intra- and inter-dimensional variability. *Journal of Experimental Psychology,* 1961, **61,** 329–333.

Inhelder, B., & Piaget, J. *The early growth of logic in the child: classification and seriation.* New York: Harper and Row, 1964.

Kendler, T. S., & Kendler, H. H. Reversal and nonreversal shifts in kindergarten children. *Journal of Experimental Psychology,* 1959, **58,** 56–60.

Osler, S. F., & Kofsky, E. Stimulus uncertainty as a variable in the development of conceptual ability. *Journal of Experimental Child Psychology,* 1965, **2,** 264–279.

Osler, S. F., & Shapiro, S. L. Studies in concept attainment: IV. The role of partial reinforcement as a function of age and intelligence. *Child Development,* 1964, **35,** 623–633.

Osler, S. F., & Trautman, G. E. Concept attainment: II. Effects of stimulus complexity upon concept attainment at two levels of intelligence. *Journal of Experimental Psychology,* 1961, **62,** 9–13.

Piaget, J. *The child's conception of number.* New York: Humanities Press, 1952.

CHAPTER SEVEN
MOTIVATION AND EMOTION

Motivation and emotion are concerned with variations in the intensity, instigation, and direction of activity and feeling. These selections consider the problem of anxiety and distress, cover the development of children's fears, test two conflicting notions of social isolation and reinforcement, and propose a new theory of cognitive motivation.

The first selection outlines classic conceptions of anxiety. Two sources of anxiety exist: pain and distress. The usual way to inhibit distress is to flee from pain; however, the authors suggest that innate mechanisms exist to inhibit distress. For example, congenital sucking of the newborn and rhythmic sensory input inhibit infant distress. The authors suggest that a consideration of these congenital inhibitors would increase our knowledge about anxiety.

Children are often afraid. How do they learn to fear and how can fears be allayed? The second selection used a series of experimental situations (large dogs, loud noises, heights) to elicit distress in children of various ages. Infants fear loud noises, sudden stimulation, and unfamiliar things. Three-year-old children fear dark forms, being alone, and dealing with a snake. Older children fear imaginary things like witches, the dark, and being alone. Fear is positively related to intelligence, and boys are less fearful than girls. Fears can be overcome by increasing the child's competence in dealing with specific situations.

Conflicting hypotheses exist about why social reinforcement is more effective following isolation. One hypothesis suggests there is a social drive which increases following social deprivation; another argues that children are frightened when they are isolated, and the increased effectiveness of social reinforcement following isolation results from emotional arousal. Authors of the third article isolated fourth-grade boys and girls to test these notions. They obtained measures of arousal and found it accounted for all the variation in effectiveness of social reinforcement.

Children are curious. Explanations for this activity include sensory starvation, curiosity drives, and information flow. Munsinger and Kessen suggest that the human nervous system is constructed so that curiosity must occur. They propose that children (1) are sensitive to information variation, (2) are limited in their ability to process variation, (3) learn rules which help this processing, and (4) prefer to process at or near their abilities. Thus, children should increase their preference for complex figures as a function of experience, and that adults (with more experience) should prefer more complex inputs. The findings support these propositions.

24 | Anxiety, Pain, and the Inhibition of Distress

WILLIAM KESSEN
GEORGE MANDLER

Contemporary theories of anxiety share a dual emphasis: They assume an archetypical evoker (for example, pain) to explain the primary occurrence of anxiety, and they presume that previously neutral stimuli are associated with this anxiety to account for learned symptomatic or secondary anxiety. In addition, they assume that escape or avoidance of anxiety is the main mechanism for control of anxiety. However, there is good evidence that the flight from trauma formulation is incomplete and that pain is not a necessary condition for the development of anxiety. Persons with congenital insensitivity to pain, for example, still develop anxiety.

This paper presents two supplements to current theories of anxiety. First, anxiety often occurs without pain, as in the periodic distress of the human newborn. And second, anxiety may be reduced by specific inhibitors (such as sucking in the newborn). Some symptomatic behavior (for example, thumb sucking) may be understood as the infant's attempt to reduce anxiety by taking advantage of these natural inhibitors.

Theories of anxiety have been developed from evidence as diverse as the avoidance behavior of animals and the symptomatic behavior of human neurotics; the language of these theories ranges from existentialism to learning theory. For all the differences in detail, however, there is remarkable similarity in the approach of different theorists to the problem of anxiety.

We will, in the present paper, examine the proposition that these theoretical communalities do not fully encompass available data about human and animal distress and then go on to present several theoretical propositions supplementary to current theories of anxiety.

Adapted from Anxiety, pain, and the inhibition of distress. *Psychological Review*, 1961, **68,** No. 6, 396–404. Copyright © 1961 by the American Psychological Association, and reproduced by permission.

Briefly and without extenuation, the following shared characteristics of contemporary theories of anxiety can be noted. First, there exists an archetypical event or class of events which evokes anxiety primitively or innately or congenitally. For Freud (1936), this original inciter was overstimulation; for Mowrer (1939), it is pain; for Miller (1951), the "innate fear reaction"; for Rank (1929), birth trauma; for Selye (1956), stress; for the existentialists, it is the very fact of being human and alive. The second communality in theories about anxiety is the postulation that, somehow, the response to the archetypical event is transferred to previously innocuous events, events either in the external environment or in the action of the organism. The typical assumption has been that this association takes place with contiguous occurrence of trauma and neutral event, although the students of human learning have been more detailed than this in discussing the conditioning of fear (see, for example, Dollard & Miller, 1950). Finally, it is assumed that the events terminating or reducing anxiety are closely related to the events which evoke it. Thus, the primitive danger of overstimulation is controlled by a reduction in level of stimulation; similarly, the "fear" of electric shock is reduced by moving away from events associated with shock, presumably in inverse analog to the model of hunger and thirst, where a deficit of some substance (deprivation) is repaired by its replacement (eating or drinking).

These common elements of present day conceptions of anxiety—the archetypical evoker, the mechanism for association to previously neutral events, and the parallelarity of the elicitation and the reduction of anxiety—have produced discernable biases in contemporary psychology. In theory, in research, and apparently in therapy, the problem of anxiety has come to be, on one hand, largely a problem of trauma—that is, what events set off the anxiety—and on the other hand, largely a problem of flight—that is, what responses will lead away from the inciting event. In what follows, we will examine the place of the "trauma" or "archetype" notion by examining in detail the best candidate for primary primitive evoker of anxiety—pain—and then we will go on to a consideration of a position that is alternative to, but not necessarily incompatible with, the common elements of anxiety theory sketched out here.

DEATH OF PAIN

We will defend the position—coming to be widely held in American psychology—that a theory of anxiety based solely on pain as an archetypical precondition is untenable. The evidence at hand suggests two conclusions: first, that pain is not a necessary condition for the development of anxiety and avoidance behavior; and second, that

when pain is apparently a sufficient condition for the development of anxiety, there is at work a variety of factors rather than a single innate link.

There are three areas of evidence that support the conclusion that anxiety can occur even when pain does not occur. First, there are external events other than pain which arouse, without prior experience of association with pain, behavior which bears the marks of distress or anxiety. Of particular interest to our argument in the next section are the startle and distress responses of the newborn human infant to loud noise or to loss of support (Peiper, 1956; Watson, 1919).

Unless a severe twist is given to the behavioral interpretation of "anxiety," these cases, among others, stand against the Original Pain principle.

More striking as a demonstration of the separability of pain and anxiety is the behavior of human beings afflicted with congenital analgesia.

Despite the fact that these patients fail to develop specific adaptive avoidance behavior in the face of many injurious and noxious situations, anxiety toward other—nonpainful—events always seems to develop normally.

The foregoing two points have shown that distress will develop in the absence of pain. A third collection of evidence supports the assertion of the disjunction without conclusively demonstrating the absence of an association with pain, but the data, when seen all in a row, strongly indict an exclusive commitment to a pain-traumatic theory of anxiety. We refer here to the occurrence of anxiety or discomfort when highly practiced and well organized responses are interrupted. The early research of Lewin and his students and that of more recent workers (for example, Lewin, 1935; Marquis, 1943) suggest that the interruption of highly motivated, well-integrated behavior arouses emotional responses much like anxiety. To these data can be added the research on emotional responses of animals to frustration (for example, Marx, 1956).

Similar and perhaps more revealing phenomena can be observed in young infants where, usually after and rarely before the sixth month of life, both the appearance of a stranger and the disappearance of the mother can give rise to signs of extreme distress.

If it can be agreed that pain is not a necessary condition for the development of anxiety, another question comes to the fore. To what degree or in what fashion is pain a sufficient antecedent condition for the development of anxiety? The skeptical answer that appears to be warranted by the evidence is that the relation between pain and anxiety is rarely simple or obvious, and further that attention to the distinction between pain as a sensory event and the distress reaction which usually but does not always accompany pain may clarify the complexity somewhat.

There is some, though admittedly very little, evidence that the appearance of discomfort with painful stimulation requires early experience of as-yet-unknown character. Puppies raised by Melzack and Scott (1957) in a restricted environment showed indifference to stimulation painful to normal dogs and great difficulty in learning to avoid objects associated with pain. These observations are of crucial importance to speculations about anxiety and warrant replication and extension. In human infants, there is a striking temporal difference between the first "defensive" response to painful stimulation (withdrawal or startle) and the second "distressful" response (crying, increased motility, and so on). Peiper (1956) reports that the first response has a latency of 0.2 second while the second response has a latency as high as 5–7 seconds.

Finally, Barber suggests that noxious painful stimulation has wide cortical effects and argues against a neurology of pain based exclusively on specific pain pathways or pain areas. The discomfort-pain association seems to depend on extensive cortical organization—in the words of the present argument, on experience of pain and discomfort.

NATURE OF FUNDAMENTAL DISTRESS

It is our contention that a nontraumatic theory of the sources of anxiety can be defended and, further, that anxiety may be reduced or terminated by devices other than escape from and avoidance of threat. These alternative formulations are proposed as supplements to, rather than as substitute for, the archetypical theories of anxiety.

The schematic model suggested here for the occurrence of anxiety—in distinction from the classical model of the organism fleeing the associations of pain—is the cyclical distress of the human newborn. There may be antecedent events which could account for the crying and increased activity we recognize as distressful in the young infant—for example, food privation, shifts in temperature, and so on—but *it is not necessary to specify or even to assume such a specific antecedent event.* It is a defensible proposition that the strong bent of the archetypical formulations to study those conditions of distress for which a specific evoker could be discerned seriously limits the range of proper investigation. The distress of the human newborn, as obviously "anxious" as a rat in a shuttle box, can be taken as an example of human anxiety and as a starting point for changes in speculations about human emotion, regardless of the absence of known or well-guessed "unconditioned" archetypical evokers.

To see anxiety as fundamental distress raises the ghosts of an old dispute in psychology—that between James and Cannon on the nature of emotion. Let us take a further theoretical step and suggest that the crucial event in fundamental distress is the perception or afferent effect of variable and intense autonomic, visceral activity. This is a rough restatement of James' position that emotions are the result of the perception of visceral events or are those perceptions themselves (James, 1890). Most of Cannon's counter-arguments to such a position are not relevant to the postulation of such an effect during early infancy, since his position depends to a large extent on the identification of external threatening stimuli—a feat beyond the powers of the newborn (Cannon, 1927). But Cannon's major argument that emotional reactions take place with a latency far shorter than the latency of autonomic reactions deserves particular attention here. The delayed emotional response of the infant cited earlier, as well as the variable, badly organized reactions of infants, suggests just such a delayed emotional mechanism as Cannon ascribes to James. If we assume further (cf. Mandler & Kremen, 1958) that these visceral reactions are eventually represented centrally (in other words, that "central" anxiety shortcircuits visceral events), then ascription of a developmental shift from a Jamesian to a Cannonic mechanism becomes plausible.

In short, fundamental distress is held to be a state of discomfort, unease, or anxiety which bears no clear or necessary relation to a specific antecedent event (archetypical evoker). The model or "ideal case" of fundamental distress is held to be the recurrent distress of the human newborn. Examination of the notion of anxiety in the light of these propositions is compatible with a resolution of the conflict between James' and Cannon's views on the nature of emotion. What remains for consideration is an examination of the occasions of reduction or termination of anxiety and the relation of such occasions to fundamental distress.

INHIBITION OF ANXIETY

The second departure from conventional views of anxiety has to do with techniques for the reduction or termination of anxiety. It is proposed that, in addition to the classical mechanisms of escape and avoidance of danger, anxiety is brought under control (that is, diminished or removed) by the operation of *specific inhibitors*. Before moving on to a discussion of the inhibitory mechanism, however, we must emphasize a point that is implicit in the foregoing treatment. The undifferentiated discomfort of the infant which we have taken as an example of fundamental distress may accompany particular conditions of need or drive; that is, the newborn may be hungry *and* distressed, thirsty *and* distressed, cold *and* distressed, and so on. With the removal of the privation or drive, the distress may disappear, but this reduction by the repair of a deficit—which is formally equivalent with escape from danger—is not of primary interest in the present discussion. Rather, our concern is with those responses of the organism and events in the environment which inhibit distress, *regardless of their relation to a specifiable need, drive, or privation.*

Anecdotal evidence of the operation of congenital inhibitors of anxiety in infants abounds, but there has been relatively little systematic exploration of these inhibitors in the newly born, human or animal. However, two recent empirical studies will serve to illustrate the character of the inhibitory mechanism; one of them is based on a response of the infant, the other on a particular pattern in the environment. Research by Kessen and his associates has shown that infant distress, as indicated by crying and hyperactivity, is dramatically reduced by the occurrence of empty—that is, nonnutritive—sucking as early as the fourth day of life. The performance of the congenital sucking response on a rubber nipple stuffed with cloth brings the newborn to a condition of motor and vocal quiescence. Thus, sucking appears to fit the pattern of the congenital inhibitor of distress, or, more broadly, of anxiety. Systematic observation of the effects of sucking on motility in the period immediately after birth will be necessary to demonstrate that the inhibition is not "secondary" to the experience of food. There can be cited the incidental observation that the hungry infant during the first days of life, with little or no experience of feeding, will quiet when given breast or bottle, even though it is unlikely that his hunger has been reduced during the first several sucking responses.

There is a further aspect of the problem of distress-inhibition which will illustrate the relation of fundamental distress and its inhibitors to anxiety of the archetypical variety. If distress is under control by the operation of an inhibitor, what is the effect of withdrawing the inhibitor? What, in other words, are the consequences of disinhibition of distress? For some occurrences of some inhibitors—for example, rocking the hungry and distressful infant—it seems that disinhibition "releases" or "reinstates" the distress. For others—for example, sucking on the hand until asleep—the withdrawal of the inhibitor does not result in the recurrence of distress.

The following proposals can be made to deal with this kind of disjunction. Archetypical evokers (for example, pain, hunger) are accompanied by or lead to distress. This distress can usually be reduced in two quite distinct ways: by action of a specific inhibitor which reduces distress but does not necessarily affect the primitive evoker; or by changes acting directly on the level of the primitive evokers. The best example of how these mechanisms work together in nonlaboratory settings is nutritive sucking. The infant's *sucking* inhibits the fundamental distress accompanying hunger; at a slower rate, the *ingestion of food* "shuts off" the source of distress. It is maintained here that these two mechanisms for the reduction of distress or anxiety are profitably kept separate in psychological theory.

The separation of distress reduction by specific inhibition and distress reduction by changes in archetypical evokers can be defended on other grounds as well. As noted earlier, much infantile (and later) distress is of a periodic variety without obvious relation to specific environmental evokers. Specific inhibitors may serve to tide the organism over the peaks of these distress cycles, whatever their source, until some other occurrence (for example, the onset of sleep) results in a more stable reduction of the level of organismic disturbance.

In short, anxiety is not only the trace of a trauma which must be fled, but is as well a condition of distress which can be met by the action of specific inhibitors. The model of fundamental distress and its inhibition which is proposed here may serve to provide a testable alternative to the current metaphysics of anxiety (May, Angel, & Ellenberger, 1958).

REFERENCES

Cannon, W. B. The James-Lange theory of emotions: A critical examination and an alternative theory. *American Journal of Psychology,* 1927, **39,** 106–124.

Dollard, J., & Miller, N. E. *Personality and psychotherapy.* New York: McGraw-Hill, 1950.

Freud, S. *The problem of anxiety.* New York: Norton, 1936.

James, W. *Principles of psychology.* New York: Holt, 1890.

Lewin, K. *A dynamic theory of personality.* New York: McGraw-Hill, 1935.

Mandler, G., & Kremen, I. Autonomic feedback: A correlational study. *Journal of Personality,* 1958, **26,** 388–399. (Erratum, 1960, **28,** 545).

Marquis, Dorothy P. A study of frustration in newborn infants. *Journal of Experimental Psychology,* 1943, **32,** 123–138.

Marx, M. H. Some relations between frustration and drive. In M. R. Jones (Ed.), *Nebraska symposium on motivation: 1956.* Lincoln: University of Nebraska Press, 1956.

May, R., Angel, E., & Ellenberger, H. F. (Eds.) *Existence: A new dimension in psychiatry and psychology.* New York: Basic Books, 1958.

Melzack, R., & Scott, T. H. The effects of early experience on the response to pain. *Journal of Comparative and Physiological Psychology,* 1957, **50,** 155–161.

Miller, N. E. Learnable drives and rewards. In S. S. Stevens (Ed.), *Handbook of experimental psychology.* New York: Wiley, 1951.

Mowrer, O. H. A stimulus-response analysis of anxiety and its role as a reinforcing agent. *Psychological Review,* 1939, **46,** 553–566.

Peiper, A. *Die Eigenart der kindlichen Hirntätigkeit.* (2nd ed.) Leipzig: Thieme, 1956.

Rank, O. *The trauma of birth.* New York: Harcourt, Brace, 1929.

Selye, H. *The stress of life.* New York: McGraw-Hill, 1956.

Watson, J. B. *Psychology from the standpoint of a behaviorist.* Philadelphia: Lippincott, 1919.

25 | Studies of Children's Fears

ARTHUR T. JERSILD

Of what are children afraid? How do these fears develop? How can we help children overcome their fears? These questions are answered in this classic study of children's fears. Dr. Jersild observed hundreds of children; he asked them to state their fears, observed them in a variety of situations, and asked their mothers and nursery school teachers to follow them around for 21 days.

His results show that infants are afraid of intense stimulation (particularly loud noises), unfamiliar objects, and new persons. During the second year, children fear the dark and being left alone. The child of four or six is most afraid of going into a dark room alone, mounting a high board, and dealing with a snake. The eight- or twelve-year-old child fears imaginary creatures, witches, the dark, and being alone.

Fears are related to intelligence; brighter children express more fears than do their duller peers. In addition, girls express more fears than boys. Children's fears can be overcome by increasing their competence in dealing with the fear-arousing situation. Love and understanding from the parent and getting the child to deal actively with the fear stimulus also helps. Procedures that do not help in dealing with fear include coercion, ridicule, and ignoring the child's fears.

INTRODUCTION

This chapter gives an account of a series of investigations of the fears exhibited by children at various age levels and of the factors that contribute to the development as well as the overcoming of fear.

The term "fear," as used in everyday speech, denotes a large variety of experiences, ranging from overwhelming terror to milder forms of apprehension. By virtue of the complexity of what is known as fear, several different approaches were used in these investigations. In one approach attention was given primarily to signs of fear as revealed by the child's overt behavior—such as fleeing, cringing, running to an adult, crying or vocalizing, coupled with other symptoms of distress, efforts to avoid or

withdraw, etc. This method of *direct observation* was utilized in one study in which parents, teachers, nurses, and others cooperated by keeping records of fears exhibited by children during their everyday lives. The method was employed also under more rigidly controlled experimental conditions.

These procedures involving the use of direct observation had certain limitations. It is not possible in an experiment, or in observations extending over a limited period of time, to obtain information concerning the almost countless circumstances that elicit fear in everyday life. Moreover, children may be subject to fears and yet fail, especially as they become older, to reveal their emotion through actions that an observer can readily detect, even though they may still be willing to report such fears to a friendly person. In the present series of investigations reports from individuals them-

Adapted from Studies of children's fears. *Child Development Monographs*, 1935, **20.**

selves were obtained through a series of *interviews* with children, through interviews with adults, through the use of a *check-list procedure* with children, and by way of *written anonymous reports* of fears recalled from childhood by adults.

NONEXPERIMENTAL PROCEDURES

Fears Reported by Parents and Other Adult Observers

Procedures The parents of 136 children cooperated by keeping records, for one or more periods of 21 days at a time, of the fears displayed by children when at home or in the care of their elders (Jersild & Holmes (1935a). The data included 153 such 21-day records.

Each parent was provided with mimeographed forms for recording observed fears and with a mimeographed set of instructions. The forms and the directions stressed the importance of describing as objectively as possible the situation in which the child gave signs of being afraid (place, time, what child was doing, persons present, apparent cause of fear, etc.) and of providing an account of the behavior of the child (words spoken, cries, other vocalizations, jumping, starting, withdrawing, running away, etc.) as distinguished from simply stating that the child showed fear. The parents were also asked to give information concerning such matters as the child's physical condition, his appetite, departures from the child's routine, etc., and to report the number of hours during which the child was observed each day.

In addition to the foregoing, 52 parents, teachers, and nurses who had children in their care cooperated by recording, on forms prepared for that purpose, evidences of fear that had come prominently to their attention without, however, aiming to make systematic observations over a period of 21 days.

Subjects The children who thus were observed ranged in age from less than one year to ninety-seven months. A majority of the children lived in a large city, but there was

also a representation of children from the suburbs, small towns, and rural areas. The families included a larger representation in the higher socioeconomic levels than is true of the general population.

Treatment of the data The categories used in classifying the data were based upon the data themselves. Rough compilations were made of situations that elicited fear, as described by the observers. Situations that seemed to have elements in common were grouped together and a tentative set of categories was devised. Further portions of the data were then analyzed and the categories were reexamined and revised as the need arose. The final set of categories included 23 major headings.

Reports by Children and Other Individuals Concerning Their Own Fears

Interviews with children The subjects interviewed were 398 children, aged five to twelve years, and included 25 boys and 25 girls at each yearly level, with two exceptions (Jersild, Markey, & Jersild, 1933).

Check-list approach Instead of simply being asked to recall and describe their fears (as in the interview study), 1,100 fifth- and sixth-grade children were presented with small booklets which contained brief one-sentence descriptions of 25 situations which, according to earlier findings, had frequently been named by children in describing their fears (Jersild, Goldman, & Loftus, 1941). Each child was asked to check whether he *often, sometimes,* or *never* "worried" about each of these situations. The percentage of children who will testify that they have "worried" about a given circumstance —such as failing on a test at school—when they are specifically asked to report concerning this item will be considerably larger than the percentage of children who happen to mention failure on a test when they simply are asked, without prompting or leading questions, to describe their fears. The interview procedure is likely, however, to give a better indication of the range and variety of conditions feared by children.

Anonymous reports by adults of their own childhood fears Written anonymous reports of fears recalled from childhood were submitted by 303 undergraduate and graduate college students, ranging in age from eighteen years upward. The adults were provided with mimeographed forms that included a number of detailed questions and directions.

This part of the study was undertaken to obtain incidental information on certain points, including the nature of childhood fears when viewed in retrospect by adults or when interpreted in the light of later experiences, as compared with the fears displayed by children themselves in the presence of adult observers or as compared with the account children themselves give of their fears when questioned during interviews.

EXPERIMENTAL STUDIES OF FEAR

The aim in these studies, conducted by F. B. Holmes (1935), was to observe and record evidences of fear shown by young children under controlled experimental conditions. In the main experiment the subjects included 105 preschool children ranging in age from twenty-four to seventy-one months. Smaller numbers were employed in supplementary studies of methods of overcoming children's fears.

Behavior of Children in Controlled Situations

The fear situations Eight situations were employed in the main body of the study. Among other considerations that were taken into account in selecting and arranging these situations were the following:

a. The situations represented stimuli or circumstances which, according to information obtained in earlier studies, were likely to be feared by a substantial proportion of children.

b. They were selected with a view to avoiding, as far as possible, the necessity of deliberately scaring the child (the aim, rather, was to observe his behavior when confronted with circumstances that might elicit fear but which he was free to cope with or to withdraw from as he chose).

c. The situations were designed to be of such a nature that it would be possible to present them in substantially similar form to all the children involved in the study.

d. They were designed to make it possible to obtain an objective record of each child's behavior.

A brief description of the situations follows. All the experiments were conducted in rooms set aside for that purpose.

1. *Being Left Alone.*—When the child is seated at a table playing with a toy, the experimenter names a pretext for leaving the room (which until the time of the experiment was unfamiliar to the child). The experimenter remains outside the room for 2 min. The child's behavior is recorded by concealed observers.

2. *Sudden Displacement or Loss of Support.*—A bridgelike piece of apparatus, consisting of two boards laid end to end at a height of about 2 in. above the floor, was used. The first board is securely supported, but when the child steps onto the second board, which is supported only at the middle, it gives way and descends to the floor. (The situation did not strictly fulfill all the requirements mentioned above, but the procedure called for asking the child whether he voluntarily would walk on the board a second time.)

3. *Dark Room.*—While playing ball with the child, the experimenter seemingly inadvertently throws the ball into a dark passageway, 18 ft. long, leading from one corner of the room. The child is asked to retrieve the ball.

4. *Strange Person.*—While the child was temporarily withdrawn from the room an assistant, dressed in a long gray coat, a large black hat, and a veil that obscured

her features, seated herself in one of the two chairs near the entrance. When the child returned his reactions were observed when he noticed the stranger and when he was asked to obtain toys placed near the stranger's chair.

5. *High Place* (possible danger of falling).—A board 12 in. wide, about 8 ft. long, and 2 in. thick, held firmly in place at the ends by two stationary ladders, was arranged at various heights from the ground and the child was asked to walk from one end of the board to the other to obtain a box of brightly colored toys. The board was first placed at a distance of 4 ft. from the floor; it was subsequently lowered if the child refused to walk across at this height and was raised if he performed at the 4-ft. level.

6. *Noise.*—An iron pipe 2 ft. in length and 2¼ in. in diameter, suspended from the ceiling in a corner of the room behind a screen, was struck a sharp blow with a hammer while the child and the experimenter were seated at a table containing toys. The child's response to this unexpected noise from an unseen source was first observed and then, pointing to the screen, the experimenter asked the child to "Go and see what made that noise."

7. *Snake.*—The snake, a harmless garter snake 22½ in. long (later replaced by a harmless ribbon snake, 24 in. long, which closely resembled the garter snake) was placed in a box deep enough so that it could not immediately climb out when the top was removed. In the box was placed a small colored toy. The child's attention was directed to the box, the lid was uncovered, the child was allowed to look in, if he raised any questions the experimenter simply said, "It is a snake," and then pointed to the toy and asked the child to reach in and get the toy.

8. *Large Dog.*—While the child was seated at a table containing toys a large collie dog was brought into the room on a leash by a familiar person. The dog was led to a certain point in the room and, after preliminary comment by the experimenter, the child was asked to go and pat the dog.

A small number of children were similarly exposed to a small dog. As it turned out, this little mongrel was livelier and more fear-provoking than the collie. This situation was discontinued early in the study by reason of the accidental death of the little dog while off duty.

A horned toad about 5 in. in length, rather ugly in appearance according to adult standards, was presented in the same manner as the snake described above. The use of this creature was discontinued when it appeared that most of the children were unaffected by it.

FINDINGS

Findings will be presented in the following order: age trends in children's fears; fear as related to sex and intelligence in early childhood; factors in a child's everyday experience that contribute to his susceptibility to fear; factors in overcoming children's fears.

Age Trends

The findings showed definite age trends in children's fears. Before noting these in greater detail, two points should be emphasized. First, at all age levels it was apparent that children differ decidedly in their susceptibility to fear. Second, at any age level, in the case of the *same* child, the circumstances that elicit fear are likely to be quite complex. A given noise, for example, may provoke no fear if the child is with a familiar adult or is already engaged in noisy horseplay; but a similar noise may elicit fear in a different setting (such as when the child is in the company of an unfamiliar person or if he is suddenly startled). Accordingly, when it is noted below that a large proportion of children's fears at a given age level are shown in response to noise, for example, or in response to something that is new or unfamiliar to the child's experience, it does not necessarily mean that the fears in question can be accounted for solely in terms of noise or unfamiliarity as such. It does mean, however, that these features, as far as could be ascertained, were predominant in the total situation that confronted the child when he was afraid.

Fears in infancy In early infancy, according to the observations of parents who kept records for periods of 21 days, fears are exhibited primarily in response to (a) intense or sudden stimuli that impinge directly upon the individual, (b) unexpected happenings, and (c) events which a child is able to recognize as new or unfamiliar but with which he has not yet learned to cope.

During the first year of life the fears that were observed were shown preponderantly in response to noises and events previously associated with noise, falling or displacement, sudden or unexpected movements, lights and flashes, persons or objects previously associated with pain, animals, and strange persons, objects, or situations. Fears in response to these latter situations appear when the child has achieved some measure of ability to notice differences

between objects and persons in his environment and some ability to discriminate between familiar and unfamiliar events.

During the second year a large proportion of children's fears continued to be exhibited in response to noises, strange events, and falling or danger of falling. There was a decline in fear of sudden unexpected movements and of lights, flashes, and reflections. There was a slight increase in fear of animals and of objects or persons previously associated with pain. During the second year some children exhibited fears of the dark and of being left alone that were not exhibited during the first year.

Fears in the age range from two to six years Some of the major trends with respect to the situations in response to which fear is shown at various age levels from two to six years are shown in abridged form in Table 1.

It can be noted from Table 1, which is based on findings in the experimental study, that there was a marked decline with age in the percentage of children who showed fear in response to each of the eight experimental situations, with the exception of the snake. This decline was not

TABLE 1 Percentage of Children at Yearly Age Levels Who Showed Fear in Response to the Various Experimental Fear Situations

Situation	Age in Months							
	24–35		36–47		48–50		60–71	
	Number of Children Studied	Percentage Showing Fear	Number of Children Studied	Percentage Showing Fear	Number of Children Studied	Percentage Showing Fear	Number of Children Studied	Percentage Showing Fear
I. Being left alone	33	12.1	45	15.6	14	7.0	12	0
II. Falling boards	33	24.2	45	8.9	14	0	12	0
III. Dark room	32	46.9	45	51.1	14	35.7	13	0
IV. Strange person	32	31.3	45	22.2	14	7.1	13	0
V. High boards	31	35.5	45	35.6	14	7.1	13	0
VI. Loud sound	31	22.6	45	20.0	14	14.3	13	0
VII. Snake	23	34.8	36	55.6	14	42.9	13	30.8
VIII. Large dog	21	61.9	28	42.9	7	42.9	0	0
Total	236	32.0	334	30.2	105	18.1	89	4.5

a regular one, however. The three-year-olds did not find the falling board so menacing as did the younger children, but they were, if anything, more responsive than the two-year-olds to potential or imaginary danger involved in being left alone, going into a dark room alone, mounting a high place, and dealing with a snake.

Fears at the five- to twelve-year level The fears of five- to twelve-year-old children as reported by themselves in private interviews showed many of the characteristics noted in the fears of the older preschool children who were observed by their parents. Fears of imaginary creatures, bogeys, and witches, of the dark, and of being alone represented about one-fifth of all the fears that were reported by five- to twelve-year-old children. Approximately 10 per cent of all fears dealt with criminal characters (robbers, kidnapers, etc.) apart from actual contact with such characters. These categories, plus reported fears of corpses and funereal matters, characters remembered from stories and pictures, and remote animals (such as lions, wolves) constituted 53 per cent of the fears reported by the children. Fears dealing with ostensibly imaginary, supernatural, or remote dangers showed a high frequency at all age levels from five to twelve but on a slightly declining scale (from about 63 per cent at five and six to about 48 per cent at eleven and twelve years).

Relation of Fear in the Experimental Situation to Age and Sex

Fear and intelligence There was a positive correlation between fear scores and intelligence (a correlation of .30 between I.Q. and quantitative fear scores) in response to the eight experimental situations in the case of 51 children for whom similar intelligence ratings were available. This correlation was higher at the younger level (a coefficient of .53 at the twenty-four to thirty-five months range) and declined to almost

.00 by the age of five. This finding is not out of keeping with findings from other studies which indicate that fear in response to certain situations is related to the maturation of intellectual abilities. A bright young child may perceive possible danger in certain situations which are not, as yet, feared by less intelligent children of the same age.

Sex differences In almost every experimental situation the number and percentage of girls who showed fear was found to be higher than the number and percentage of boys. When comparisons were made between 29 boys and girls who were matched with respect to age, a statistically reliable difference, indicating that girls showed more fear than boys, was found. Girls were also described as tending to show more fear than the boys in the nursery-school environment when rated by nursery-school teachers.

Factors Which Contribute to the Development of Fear

The following is a summary of some of the factors contributing to the arousal or persistence of fear, as revealed through records kept by parents and interviews with parents.

Many of the persisting fears that children exhibited could be traced directly to an actual frightening event, as when a child is frightened by the pounding of a radiator and later shows fear of the object when it is silent.

Many fears also appeared to be shown in response to situations that were immediately associated with a frightening event, as when a child, after being struck by an automobile, not only showed fear of oncoming automobiles but also was apprehensive about crossing the street even if there was no automobile in sight.

Other fears had their inception through a more devious process of association with an original frightening event. One child in the study, for example, suffered from nightmares following a traffic accident and following this for the first time exhibited fear of being alone in a dark room (Jersild & Holmes, 1935b,c).

When a child already is frightened, whatever may be the original cause, he may show fright in response to happenings that normally would not affect him. Further, if a state of apprehension already is present, the child may formulate his fear in terms of an imaginary or anticipated danger, such as criminal characters, bogeys, or gorillas or other sinister circumstances which he has encountered in his experience or in connection with his reading or pictures that he has seen. The child's tendency to be afraid or to fix upon this or that condition as something to be feared can be aggravated by the cumulative effect of setbacks or difficulties in his everyday life, such as difficulties in schoolwork, threats and punishments administered by his elders, problems arising in his relations with his parents and with other children, including, among other matters, competition with other children for the affection of his elders.

Findings Concerning the Overcoming of Fear

According to information provided by parents in response to interviews, the most effective means of aiding a child to overcome fear is to help him, by degrees, to become more competent and skillful in coping with the thing or situation that he fears and to enter into active dealings with it. This procedure cannot so readily be applied, of course, in the case of apprehensions of an obscure nature, but, interestingly enough, it was found to be effective in some instances in dealing with fears of imaginary dangers (such as fear of an imaginary dog). If the procedure is to be effective it is important that the adult should try, as far as possible, to understand the background of the child's apprehensions and that he should be sympathetic in his approach. Methods involving a somewhat passive approach (such as verbal explanations and reassurances) were found to be ineffective in a large proportion of instances unless they were supplemented by more active techniques. Techniques that proved to be generally quite ineffective included coercion, ridicule, ignoring, offering palliatives for the child's symptoms of fear.

REFERENCES

Holmes, F. B. An experimental study of the fears of young children. (In) A. T. Jersild, and F. B. Holmes. *Children's Fears*, pp. 167–295. *Child Development Monographs*, 1935, No. 20.

Jersild, A. T., Goldman, Bernard, & Loftus, J. J. A comparative study of the worries of children in two school situations. *Journal of Experimental Education*, 1941, **9,** 323–326.

Jersild, A. T., & Holmes, F. B. Children's fears. *Child Development Monographs*, 1935, No. 20. Pp. ix + 358. (a)

Jersild, A. T., & Holmes, F. B. Methods of overcoming children's fears. *Journal of Psychology*, 1935, **1,** 75–104. (b)

Jersild, A. T., & Holmes, F. B. Some factors in the development of children's fears. *Journal of Experimental Education*, 1935, **4,** 133–141. (c)

Jersild, A. T., Markey, F. V., & Jersild, C. L. Children's fears, dreams, wishes, daydreams, likes, dislikes, pleasant and unpleasant memories. *Child Development Monographs*, 1933, No. 12. Pp. xi + 172.

26 | Emotional Arousal, Isolation, and Discrimination Learning in Children

RICHARD H. WALTERS
ROSS D. PARKE

Gewirtz and Baer (1958) proposed that social deprivation arouses a drive which leads to increased social reinforcement effectiveness. The present selection tests the notion that emotional arousal (fear of being alone) is the cause of increased effectiveness of social reinforcement.

The authors used fourth-grade children in a complex experimental design that included two levels of arousal, two types of reinforcement, the sex of the subjects, and isolation versus nonisolation. Their results conclusively show that arousal level alone accounts for the children's behavior following isolation.

Gewirtz and Baer (1958a,b) reported that children who had experienced a 20-minute period of social isolation conditioned more readily in a simple discrimination-learning task, when verbal approval was used as a reinforcer, than did children who had not been isolated. They attributed their findings to the arousal by isolation of a social drive which motivated behavior "for" a social reinforcer. Walters and Karal (1960) criticized this interpretation on the grounds that the isolation procedure may have aroused "anxiety" in young children and that the findings could therefore be interpreted without the postulation of a social drive. This latter interpretation is consonant with evidence from a variety of studies showing that moderate arousal or moderately heightened drive improves performance in some kinds of learning task (Bindra, 1959; Malmo, 1959).

Adapted from Emotional arousal, isolation, and discrimination learning in children. *Journal of Experimental Child Psychology*, 1964, **1**, 163–173.

Walters and Ray (1960) repeated the conditioning procedures of Gewirtz and Baer by using a 2 × 2 design in which both degree of social contact and "anxiety" level were experimentally manipulated. In this study it was assumed that the placing of Grade 1 and Grade 2 children in a strange environment by a strange adult would be a stimulus for anxiety and that this anxiety would be reduced by the use of a familiar adult as E's assistant. It was assumed also that a 20-minute period of isolation would, in itself, have little influence on responsiveness to social reinforcers. The results indicated that the "anxiety" variable was far more effective than the variable of isolation-interaction in facilitating conditioning.

However, Walters and Ray failed to provide any validating measure of the effectiveness of their manipulation for inducing arousal in young children. Moreover, during the conditioning procedure they employed only social reinforcement of precisely the same kind as that used by Gewirtz and Baer. Since it is crucial to the social-drive hypothesis that this drive increases motivation for *social* reinforcers, the effects of varying the degree of social responsiveness of the experimenter during testing should perhaps also have been investigated.

This paper reports a partial replication of the Walters and Ray study in which a physiological index of emotional arousal was secured and both verbal approval and impersonally dispensed material rewards were used as reinforcers. Children older than those used by Walters and Ray were selected as subjects partly to facilitate the use of a physiological index, and partly to increase the range of subjects with whom the phenomenon under investigation might be demonstrated. The simple discrimination task utilized by Walters and Ray is unsuitable for older children; consequently, a task devised by Miller and Estes (1961) was substituted.

The choice of a physiological index was limited by the necessity of carrying out the study within a school setting. Since there is some evidence that a fall in finger temperature is a concomitant of emotional arousal (Mittelman and Wolff, 1953, Mandler, Mandler, Kremen, and Sholiton, 1961) and equipment for recording this index is battery-operated and easily portable, the finger temperatures of S's were recorded at the same time as the children carried out a discrimination-learning task.

METHOD

Subjects

Subjects were 40 Grade 4 boys and 40 Grade 4 girls from two schools in a single area of metropolitan Toronto. Five girls and five boys were randomly assigned to each of eight conditions in a $2 \times 2 \times 2 \times 2$ factorial design involving high versus low arousal, isolation versus no isolation, material versus verbal rewards, and sex of Ss.

Apparatus

A 35 mm slide viewer was attached to a box containing a transformer, which operated the viewer light. When E pushed a button at the rear of the box, a slide was illuminated. When S pressed either of two buttons on the front of the box, the viewer light was extinguished; at the same time, one of two red lights on E's side of the panel was illuminated, thus indicating to E which button S had pushed.

The stimuli presented to S consisted of line drawings of a pair of faces which were identical except that the eyebrows on one face were drawn close to the eyes, whereas they were high up over the eyes on the other face. Four slides were used, two with the high-eyebrow face on the right and two with the high-eyebrow face on the left. Two pairs of slides were used in order to facilitate presentation.

A Yellow Springs battery-operated telethermometer with thermistor probe was used to record S's finger temperatures during testing. The thermistor probe was tightly secured with adhesive tape to the second finger of S's left hand, which was placed on a table with the probe upwards. Ss were instructed to keep the hand as still as possible through the testing period. The dial of the telethermometer permitted readings accurate to the nearest half degree; these were read by inspection and recorded on a data sheet.

Procedure

High-arousal, isolation condition   A female psychology student (E_1) appeared at the door of the classroom and asked for S. The E instructed S to come with her without offering any explanation of her intentions. No conversation was initiated and any questions were answered in a brief and formal manner. The S was then taken to an unfamiliar room, seated in a chair facing the wall, and told: "I have something for you to do, but the machine is broken. Sit in this chair and do not move until I come back." The E then left the room. Ten minutes later she returned with the second E (E_2), and seated S in front of the slide-viewer cabinet which until then had been concealed from S. The E taped a thermistor probe to S's middle finger, again without explanation of what she was doing, and instructed S to keep his finger in one position on the table. Both Es then left the room. The S was left alone for 3 minutes to allow the finger temperature to stabilize. The Es then returned and commenced the conditioning procedure. E_1 recorded S's finger temperature while E_2, with whom S had had least contact, supervised the learning task and dispensed the reinforcers.

High-arousal, no-isolation condition   The procedure was identical with that used for high-arousal, isolation Ss, except that the 10-minute isolation period was omitted. While the finger temperature stabilized, both Es remained in the room. In order to maintain the presumably stressful atmosphere, their responses to S's questions consisted only of the statement, "Just keep still and wait for a while," and brief sentences and phrases of equivalent meaning. The Ss in the no-isolation groups were tested after mid-morning or noon-hour breaks, during which they had been interacting in play sittings with classmates for a period of at least 10 minutes.

Low-arousal, isolation condition   While E fetched S from the classroom, she maintained a very pleasant and friendly manner. She explained to S that he was going to play a game and kept up a running conversation with him in an effort to make S feel at ease. The S was taken to the experimental room, where E said, "We want to play a game with you, but it is broken right now. I do not want you to miss your turn, so just wait in this room while we fix it. We'll come for you when the game is ready."

After 10 minutes, Es returned, and the thermistor probe was attached to S's finger.

It was explained to S that this would not hurt and that it was just the same as having a thermometer placed in his mouth, except that it would be placed on his finger. The Es then left the room for 3 minutes while the temperature stabilized.

Low-arousal, no isolation condition Ss were treated in the same manner as in the previous condition, except that the isolation period was omitted and consequently no explanation of a delay was needed.

Conditioning procedure   All Ss were given the following instructions: "We are going to show you pictures of two twins, Bob and Bill, in this viewer in front of you, and we want you to try to tell them apart. When the light comes on and you see the two twins, push the button underneath the twin you want to call Bill. You may choose either one the first time. After that, each time you see the twins try to pick that same one which you first called Bill."

Following these instructions, the slides were shown one at a time with the position of the twins varied according to a predetermined, randomly arranged schedule. Stimuli were presented and Ss' responses recorded by E_2 while finger temperature readings were taken every 15 seconds by E_1. The slides were presented for 80 trials or until S had made eight consecutive correct responses.

Rewards

Half the children in each arousal condition were reinforced with verbal approval, while half were given material rewards. Verbal reinforcement consisted in E's saying, "That's good," "That's right," or "That's fine," following every correct response which S gave.

The Ss in the material-reward condition had every correct response reinforced with tokens, which were exchangeable for toys. After the learning instructions, these Ss were told: "Each time you push the right button, that is, the one that is under Bill, you will receive one of these little green disks. If you make enough right choices and collect enough green tokens, we shall give you a prize." The Ss were then shown a tray of the toys that they could win, and the learning task was begun. Whenever S made a correct response, E, who was concealed from S's view by a screen, pushed a token through an aperture, from which it fell into a tray that had been set in front of S. The E made no comment of any kind during the dispensing of these reinforcers. At the end of the game, S was given a disk and told that in about a week's time he could exchange it for a toy. The S was then taken back to his classroom.

RESULTS

Table 1 presents means and SDs of trials to criterion of boys and girls under each of the eight experimental conditions. The table also includes parallel results in terms

TABLE 1 Means and SDs of Trials to Criterion and Errors for All Subgroups[a] of Ss

	BOYS							
	High Arousal, Isolation				Low Arousal, Isolation			
	Trials		Errors		Trials		Errors	
Reward	Mean	SD	Mean	SD	Mean	SD	Mean	SD
Verbal	20.8	17.82	5.8	9.22	50.4	28.76	22.2	17.44
Material	17.0	13.02	3.2	4.93	47.2	27.11	20.2	17.43
	High Arousal, no Isolation				Low Arousal, no Isolation			
	Trials		Errors		Trials		Errors	
	Mean	SD	Mean	SD	Mean	SD	Mean	SD
Verbal	36.4	24.22	15.4	11.88	34.8	31.51	15.4	19.72
Material	24.2	12.07	8.6	6.83	25.4	27.43	7.0	11.56
	GIRLS							
	High Arousal, Isolation				Low Arousal, Isolation			
	Trials		Errors		Trials		Errors	
	Mean	SD	Mean	SD	Mean	SD	Mean	SD
Verbal	20.2	10.81	4.2	3.82	19.6	16.31	5.4	7.86
Material	30.2	26.73	8.8	12.42	47.4	27.16	20.4	16.13
	High Arousal, no Isolation				Low Arousal, no Isolation			
	Trials		Errors		Trials		Errors	
	Mean	SD	Mean	SD	Mean	SD	Mean	SD
Verbal	28.2	24.83	9.6	11.76	53.6	25.29	26.0	11.06
Material	20.8	12.62	6.8	6.79	43.0	27.25	18.0	13.74

[a] N = 5 in each subgroup.

TABLE 2   Finger Temperature Changes

| | High Arousal | | Low Arousal | |
	Isolation	No Isolation	Isolation	No Isolation [a]
Change				
Fall	17	13	7	7
No change or slight rise	3	7	13	12
	Chi-square = 13.87; $p < 0.001$			

[a] The data for one S were lost on account of a loose thermistor probe.

of number of errors. The two measures are, of course, not entirely independent.

A $2 \times 2 \times 2 \times 2$ analysis of variance of trials to criterion yielded a significant main effect for arousal level ($F = 7.20$; $p < 0.01$ for 1 and 64 df). The effects of isolation, sex of subject, and type of reward, and all interactions were nonsignificant. An analysis of variance of number of errors produced a similar result ($F = 7.80$ for arousal, no other significant effect).

The selected criterion of arousal was the direction of change in temperature during the testing period, which could be adequately assessed from the data secured by E_1. Table 2 gives the number of Ss who showed drops in finger temperature during the learning task. Data are based only on the first 2 minutes of learning, since some Ss had reached the criterion of learning by the end of this period and consequently the recording of their finger temperatures was discontinued.

DISCUSSION

The results of this study and those of previous related investigations (Walters and Ray, 1960; Walters, Marshall, and Shooter, 1960) indicate that children learn a relatively simple task more readily when their arousal level is moderately high than when their arousal level is low.

Walters and Ray interpreted similar findings as indicating that *reinforcers are more effective* if the recipient of reinforcers is anxious or aroused. However, there is also evidence that observational learning that occurs *in the absence of reinforcement* is facilitated if the observer is aroused (Bandura and Walters, 1963). Consequently, a more general explanatory principle is required to account for the effects of arousal.

One possible explanation is that under moderate emotional arousal the learner is more attentive to relevant cues (Easterbrook, 1959; Kausler and Trapp, 1960). If this is so, it is reasonable to suppose that children under our high-arousal conditions confined their attention more closely to the visually presented stimuli, so facilitating the recognition of differences, and were also more alert to the associations between their choices and the responses of the experimenter.

According to the social-deprivation theory, it is the nature of approval or attentiveness as a specifically *social* reinforcer that accounts for the heightened susceptibility to social influence of children who are rewarded for conformity following social deprivation. Our failure to find any interaction effects involving isolation and type of reward suggests that this aspect of the theory is mistaken and consequently lends some support to the arousal hypothesis, which demands only that the rewards be appropriate to the age, sex, and socioeconomic status of the recipients. Perhaps the weight of evidence would have been greater if an automatic dispenser had been used to deliver the material rewards. However, the manner in which material rewards were dispensed closely approximates automatic dispensing, except for the fact that the E was quite evidently the controller of resources. It may even be claimed that our procedure is the better parallel to the dispensing of "nonsocial" rewards in real-life situations, in which material rewards are ordinarily perceived as being mediated by socialization agents. In any case, the manner in which the material rewards were dispensed involved a minimum of social interaction and departed radically from the conditions under which, according to Gewirtz and Baer, reinforcer effectiveness should be enhanced.

A fairly lengthy series of isolation studies has thus led to several conclusions. In the first place, there is some evidence to support the hypothesis that isolation may, under some circumstances, be a conditioned stimulus for "anxiety." This conclusion can draw further support from Schachter's (1959) studies of affiliation. Second, isolation may be a condition under which "anxiety" induced by preceding events may mount, again a conclusion that is consonant with Schachter's data. Third, moderate emotional arousal (accompanying or not accompanying isolation) may lead to faster learning, at least of some kinds of discrimination tasks. Finally, it is now proposed that this faster learning is in no way related to changes in reinforcer effectiveness, but rather reflects the improved perceptual organization and cue utilization that appears to accompany moderate emotional arousal.

REFERENCES

Bandura, A., & Walters, R. H. *Social learning and personality development.* New York: Holt, 1963.

Bindra, D. *Motivation: a systematic reinterpretation.* New York: Ronald Press, 1959.

Easterbrook, J. A. The effect of emotion on cue utilization and the organization of behavior. *Psychological Review,* 1959, **66,** 183–201.

Gewirtz, J. L., & Baer, D. M. The effects of brief social deprivation on behaviors for a social reinforcer. *Journal of Abnormal and Social Psychology,* 1958, **56,** 49–56. (a)

Gewirtz, J. L., & Baer, D. M. Deprivation and satiation of social reinforcers as drive conditions. *Journal of Abnormal and Social Psychology,* 1958, **57,** 165–172. (b)

Kausler, D. H., & Trapp, E. P. Motivation and incidental learning. *Psychology Review,* 1960, **67,** 373–379.

Malmo, R. B. Activation: a neurophysiological dimension. *Psychological Review,* 1959, **66,** 367–386.

Mandler, G., Mandler, Jean M., Kremen, I., & Sholiton, R. D. The response to threat: Relations among verbal and physiological indices. *Psychological Monograph,* 1961, **75,** No. 9 (Whole No. 513).

Miller, Louise B., & Estes, Betsy W. Monetary reward and motivation in discrimination learning. *Journal of Experimental Psychology,* 1961, **61,** 501–504.

Mittelman, B., & Wolff, H. G. Emotions and skin temperature: Observations on patients during psychotherapeutic (psychoanalytic) interviews. *Psychosomatic Medicine,* 1943, **5,** 211–231.

Schachter, S. *The psychology of affiliation.* Stanford University Press, 1959.

Walters, R. H., & Karal, Pearl. Social deprivation and verbal behavior. *Journal of Personality,* 1960, **28,** 89–107.

Walters, R. H., Marshall, W. E., & Shooter, J. R. Anxiety, isolation, and susceptibility to social influence. *Journal of Personality,* 1960, **28,** 518–529.

Walters, R. H., & Ray, E. Anxiety, social isolation, and reinforcer effectiveness. *Journal of Personality,* 1960, **28,** 358–367.

27 Stimulus Variability and Cognitive Change

HARRY MUNSINGER
WILLIAM KESSEN

Munsinger and Kessen suggest a type of motivation that is not derived from tissue deficit. Specifically, they propose the existence of a limit on children's processing ability, the extraction of rules from the environment, sensitivity to the information content of stimulation, and a preference for processing information at or near the limit of children's ability. These four propositions generate a motivational system for cognitive learning. In this scheme children and adults learn new materials and become curious about more complex tasks as a result of previous learning. The extraction of rules allows them to move on to more complex variation; they consequently are curious.

Since the publication of Hebb's *The Organization of Behavior* in 1949, psychologists have become increasingly concerned with two closely related problems—the definition of cognitive structure and the specification of a mechanism for cognitive change.

There is great diversity in the definition of cognitive *structure*. Hebb's emphasis has been on the elaboration of perceptual processes as a general model for cognition. Bartlett (1932) discussed schemata as the structures underlying memory and its distortions, while Piaget (1950) used the same word to comprehend a very different range of phenomena—the development of intelligent behavior in children. Two more recent statements have extended the notion that human thought can be conceived as a system of rules. Newell, Shaw, and Simon (1958) discuss the application of computer technology and logic to an understanding of human think-

ing, and Miller, Galanter, and Pribram (1960) propose the mechanism Test-Operate-Test-Exit as the basic unit of cognitive structure. The theme most clearly common to these and other attempts to encompass human thought in structural terms is their rejection of the topographically defined response as a model for cognition. In language that varies from metaphor to mathematics, cognitive theorists propose that man's thought is a system of rules for processing environmental change, for building representations of things, and for ordering these representations to suit the demands of the person and his world.

Variation of opinion about the nature of cognitive *change* also contains a common rejection; almost without exception, cognitive theorists have denounced the use of physiological deficit and its derivatives in explaining the development of human thought. A number of mechanisms have been proposed as substitutes for this traditional view of motivation. Berlyne (1960) has suggested curiosity drive, and Butler

Adapted from Stimulus variability and cognitive change. *Psychological Review*, 1966, **73,** No. 2, 164–178. Copyright © 1966 by the American Psychological Association, and reproduced by permission.

(1953) discusses stimulus hunger, but most recent proposals have contained the notion of discrepancy between sensory input and cognitive structure or discrepancy between two elements of cognitive structure as demanding cognitive change. The removal or reduction of a discrepancy is assumed to be responsible for cognitive change (see Hunt, 1963, for a review of several theoretical positions on this issue).

Even before questions about cognitive structure and change can be addressed, it is necessary to make some statement about the nature of the environment from which cognitive structures must develop. Some psychologists have continued to use the traditional division of the environment into common objects and, rarely, physical quantities under the general term *stimulus* with occasional reference to characteristics of receptor end organs. A somewhat more general procedure for description of the environment has been suggested in the work of Attneave (1957) and Garner (1962), among others. For these psychologists, the environment is seen as a field of variability characterized by relative independence or redundancy of events. They have used modifications of communication theory (Shannon & Weaver, 1949) to develop metrics for the specification of environmental variability.

We have recently reported (Munsinger & Kessen, 1964; Munsinger, Kessen & Kessen, 1964) a series of studies on the structuring of environmental variability. Specifically, we asked subjects to state their preferences for (a) random shapes that varied widely in number of independent elements, and (b) sequences of letters and words that varied from random to fully redundant. Those studies and the ones to be reported here grew out of several general assumptions. The purpose of the present report is to state these governing assumptions briefly, to present four new studies derived from them, and, in the light of the results of these studies, to indicate required modifications and extensions of the assumptions. Our initial assumptions were four.

1. *Variability.* Human beings are sensitive to stimulus variability; this variability may be usefully specified in the metric of information theory (Attneave, 1959).

2. *Limit.* There is an upper limit on the capacity of human beings to process independent environmental events (Miller, 1956).

3. *Structuring.* Human beings are able to break through this limitation on their capacity to process independent events through the development of rules (structure) which reduce the effective stimulus variability (Mandler, 1962).

These first three assumptions can be interrelated in another way. People respond to cognitive uncertainty. In the limiting case, the unrealistic one in which there is no organizing cognitive structure, cognitive uncertainty is a simple function of stimulus variability. However, even for unsophisticated human beings—the newborn infant, at the extreme—rules are available which permit some coding or processing of stimulus variability. Thus we can think of cognitive uncertainty as a joint function of cognitive structure and stimulus variability.

It should be remembered that, in the present studies, we have assumed that human beings have a preference for a certain level of cognitive uncertainty (Munsinger & Kessen, 1964). Cognitive uncertainty reflects the person's ability to impose meaning (cognitive structure) on the array of information available in his environment (stimulus variability). If stimulus variability changes with no change in cognitive structure, then preference should shift. Similarly, if the subject imposes structure on a fixed field of stimulus variability, then his preference will change also. Certainly preference is *not* the only index of cognitive uncertainty; for this reason we have reported relevant evidence on estimation accuracy and categorization. The measure of preference, however, has the advantage of expressing, in part, the motivational aspects of cognitive uncertainty. If the development of structure results in the subject's preference for increasing amounts of stimulus variability, we have a general model for intellectual development. As the person learns to structure variability, he turns toward higher levels of variability.

It is not altogether clear how rules are imposed on random shapes to reduce stimulus uncertainty. Subjects may categorize the figures in terms of previous experience ("They look like something.") or, in the case of the art-student subjects, in terms of an imposed dimensionability (jaggedness or weight), or in terms of specific memorization. However the structuring takes place, it seems clear that it is accompanied by changes in accuracy of estimation, accuracy of categorization, or preference.[1]

4. *Cognitive Change.* A person will be most likely to change his cognitive structure if he is presented with a level of cognitive uncertainty just beyond his present processing ability. If he is presented cognitive uncertainty far beyond his ability to process or no cognitive uncertainty at all, little or no change will take place (Piaget, 1952).

In our first studies derived from these assumptions we decided to examine human preference for variability. In part, this decision grew from our concern with problems of motivation. What aspects of the environment would claim the attention of a person? What parts of the environment would be attractive to him? As Piaget (1952) says ". . . a subject looks neither at what is too familiar, because he is in a way surfeited with it, nor at that which is too new, because this does not correspond to anything in his schemata . . . [p. 68]." Thus, in earlier studies of the structuring of variability, we examined the specific hypothesis that subjects would indicate a preference for random shapes in the middle range of stimulus variability,

and that this level of preference could be changed with the development of rules for coding stimulus variability. These results will be reviewed in the following pages as we examine new evidence on three aspects of the formulation presented here—the limitation on processing ability, the development of cognitive structure, and the role of specific experience in forming cognitive structure.

PROCESSING LIMITS

Miller (1956) has reviewed much of the earlier literature on the existence of an upper limit on the ability of human beings to receive, process, and transmit environmental variability. Garner (1962) has summarized more recent literature on this issue. In studies of preference and variability we found an inflection in the preference-variability function with stimuli of about 10 independent turns.

THE DEVELOPMENT OF STRUCTURE

We have examined three sources of variation in the handling of figures of high variability—long-term experience with complex forms, short-term experience with the random shapes, and age (Munsinger & Kessen, 1964; Munsinger et al., 1964).

Long-Term Experience with Complex Forms

Art students were asked to state their preferences for random shapes varying from 5–40 independent turns in the expectation that their experience with geometrical figures would have led to the development of rules for structuring high variability. The results confirmed the expectation; the preference-variability function for the art students was generally monotonic and positive. It is interesting also that the art students found figures of few turns "dull, plain, and uninteresting."

---

[1] Another interesting example of change in behavior with the assumed development of structure is provided by a study of estimation accuracy in which two groups of subjects ($N = 120$) were asked to look at and to try to remember 5-turn figures (Group 1) or 40-turn figures (Group 2). After 140 presentations at 7 seconds duration, all subjects were asked to estimate four levels of stimulus variability at 200 milliseconds exposure duration. A statistically stable ($F_{3/340} = 4.01$; $p < .01$) interaction reflected the fact that Group 2 was more accurate in estimation of 40-turn figures.

Short-Term Experience with Random Shapes

A group of college undergraduates was asked to state their preferences over and over again for the same figures differing in stimulus variability under the hypothesis that increasing experience with random shapes would lead to the development of procedures for structuring. Preference for figures of high variability was expected to shift upward following 2 hours of paired-comparison preference judgments. Again, the results supported the conclusion that preference for high variability may be changed through development of coding rules. The subjects showed higher preference for figures of many turns toward the end of the session than they had at the beginning.

Age

The changing preferences of children for figures of high variability were explored by means of the same procedures for determining preference used with adults. Children in all grades of an elementary school made preference judgments of the 5- to 40-turn random shapes. The expectation of an age-invariant area of inflection of the preference-variability function near figures of 10 independent turns was confirmed. There is surprising similarity in the shape of the preference-variability function between 5 and 10 independent turns when the responses of human beings from ages 6–22 are compared.

As has already been suggested, no such developmental invariance exists in expressed preference for figures of higher variability (i.e., figures of more than 10 turns). We had expected that children would have less ability to structure figures of high variability and that they would therefore show lower preference for them. However, the children prefer figures of high variability far more than adults do. The decreasing preference for figures of high variability with increasing age is regular; second graders state lower preferences for figures of high variability than do first graders, third graders state lower preferences for figures of high variability than do second graders, and so on.

Sense may be made of the unpredicted preference of young children for figures of high variability if it is assumed that young children and adults process high variability in the following different ways. Young children may sample the high-variability figures, attending only to that part of the figure which they can structure; figures of many turns provide more opportunity for this process of selection than do figures of few turns. Thus, young children could handle and would prefer figures of high variability. Adults, on the other hand, are more likely to attend to the entire figure whatever its level of variability. This strategy places a demand on adults to structure figures of many turns; their inability to do so leads unsophisticated adults to express relative dislike for figures of high variability.

REFERENCES

Attneave, F. Physical determinants of the judged complexity of shapes. *Journal of Experimental Psychology*, 1957, **53,** 221–227.

Attneave, F. *Applications of information theory to psychology.* New York: Holt, 1959.

Bartlett, F. C. *Remembering: An experimental and social study.* London: Cambridge University Press, 1932.

Berlyne, D. E. *Conflict, arousal, and curiosity.* New York: McGraw-Hill, 1960.

Butler, R. A. Discrimination learning by rhesus monkeys to visual-exploration motivation. *Journal of Comparative and Physiological Psychology*, 1953, **46,** 95–98.

Garner, W. R. *Uncertainty and structure as psychological concepts.* New York: Wiley, 1962.

Hebb, D. O. *The organization of behavior.* New York: Wiley, 1949.

Hunt, J. McV. Motivation inherent in information processing and action. In O. J. Harvey (Ed.), *Motivation and social organization:*

Cognitive determinants. New York: Ronald, 1963. Pp. 35–94.

Mandler, G. From association to structure. *Psychological Review,* 1962, **69,** 415–427.

Miller, G. A. The magical number seven, plus or minus two: Some limits on our capacity for processing information. *Psychological Review,* 1956, **63,** 81–97.

Miller, G. A., Galanter, E., & Pribram, K. H. *Plans and the structure of behavior.* New York: Holt, 1960.

Munsinger, H., & Kessen, W. Uncertainty, structure, and preference. *Psychological Monographs,* 1964, **78** (9, Whole No. 586).

Munsinger, H., Kessen, W., & Kessen, M. L. Age and uncertainty: Developmental variations in preference for variability. *Journal of Experimental Child Psychology,* 1964, **1,** 1–15.

Newell, A., Shaw, J. C., & Simon, H. A. Elements of a theory of human problem solving. *Psychological Review,* 1958, **65,** 151–166.

Piaget, J. *The psychology of intelligence.* (trans. by M. Piercy & D. E. Berlyne) New York: Harcourt, Brace, 1950.

Piaget, J. *The origins of intelligence in children.* New York: International Universities Press, 1952.

Shannon, C. E., & Weaver, W. *The mathematical theory of communications.* Urbana: University of Illinois Press, 1949.

CHAPTER EIGHT
WILL

Will is a complex faculty. It includes motivational and emotional states, a child's preferences and desires, his strivings for achievement, and most of all the development of character. These readings match this diversity.

The first article traces children's preference for color and form as they mature. Younger children prefer color while older children prefer form; the median age of transition is about four years, about the age when children become interested in learning to read. Whether they learn to read because they are interested in form, or whether they become interested in form as they learn to read is a fascinating (and unanswered) question.

The education of character has received little attention among contemporary educators; the church and family are considered more traditional guardians of this topic. A classic study by Hartshorne and May showed that ethical behavior is a complicated and often contradictory process for children. They found that children understand ethical differentiations long before they practice them, suggesting that motivation (not information) is more relevant to character training. Knowledge of what is right or wrong does not influence cheating; however, brighter children do not cheat as much as their duller peers. Presumably, bright children are not compelled to cheat; they are competing effectively already. Any system that places such emphasis on achievement in competition must expect to train children to cheat; there may be no other way for them to compete.

Must we work for something before we can appreciate it? This piece of folklore is substantiated in the study by Lewis, who showed that the reinforcement value of poker chips is enhanced by hard work. The data are consistent with several theories of motivation—frustration, cognitive dissonance, or the Protestant Ethic.

How do children learn moral behavior and how is their conception of morality related to judgments of right and wrong? Johnson studied children's conceptions of right and wrong with a series of situations which the children judged by their own moral codes. The test's reliability was high enough to afford some insight into children's moral judgments. He found that the parents' attitude and the child's IQ account for most variation in moral judgments.

28 | Color and Form Preference in Young Children

ROSSLYN GAINES SUCHMAN
TOM TRABASSO

Children's preferences for color, form, and size have been studied for years; the results show that young children (three years of age) prefer color and older children prefer form. The median transition age is about four years, two months. The present study looks at individual differences in these functions in order to differentiate between genuine age trends in color and form preferences and a possible artifact resulting from the groupings of individual data. The authors measured preferences among color, form, and size by 145 three- to six-year-old children; 133 of the 145 children's preferences were unidimensional; they preferred either color or form. The few children with mixed preferences did not increase in frequency with age. There is some evidence for a preference hierarchy; color-preferring children showed an increase in preference for form over size with age; form-preferring children showed no preference for color over size.

The authors suggest that the main determinant of children's shift from color to form is that they are learning to read; at that time form becomes important. Whether they learn to read because they become interested in form, or whether they become interested in form as they are learning to read is an unanswered question.

Children's preferences for either color or form have been studied intermittently for over 50 years (e.g., Descoudres, 1914; Corah, 1964). These studies show a decrease in average preference for color over form with age. In general, nursery school children prefer color, a shift to form preference occurs at about age six (Colby and Robertson, 1942; Corah, 1964). The transition from color to form preference has been regarded as a correlate of cognitive growth: color responses to the Rorschach are termed "primitive" or "immature" (Schactel, 1958); form children have higher mental test scores than color

Adapted from Color and form preference in young children. *Journal of Experimental Child Psychology,* 1966, **3,** 177–187.

children (Brian and Goodenough, 1929); form children are more accurate in classifying stimuli along other dimensions (Suchman, 1966); form preference is related to verbal mediation development (Kagan and Lemkin, 1961).

Despite the interest in the relationship between stimulus preference and other cognitive behavior, these studies have failed to systematically investigate stimulus variation within and between dimensions. In this regard, Huang (1945) suggests that the preference may depend upon the type and complexity of stimulus materials used: children chose that stimulus with the larger number of values (e.g., four colors over two forms), independent of their measured preference.

Also, value characteristics within stimulus dimensions could compete with simple color vs. form preference. For example, Piaget and Inhelder (1956) report that children prefer asymmetrical over symmetrical forms. Finally, the folklore of child rearing suggests that children respond more readily to saturated hues. With the exception of Honkavaara (1958), who used a larger number of color than form values and found that color preference increased with age, experimenters have acted upon this assumption by using predominantly saturated hues as stimuli in preference studies. Therefore, one purpose of the present investigation was to study the stability of a child's preference for form and color under conditions where hue, saturation, form and contour were varied and compared. A second purpose was to see if a child's preference for stimuli is unidimensional by use of a longer test series than previously employed and allowing assessment of individual differences and consistency in preference.

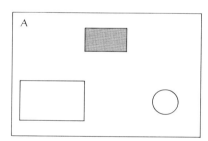
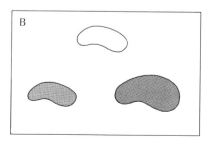

FIGURE 1 Example slides used in test series. In A, color, form and size are varied; in B, color and size are varied and form is constant. See text for a description of their use in the preference test.

METHOD

Preference Test

The stimuli were presented on slides via rear-screen projection. Each slide consisted of three figures arranged in an equilateral triangle (after Doehring, 1960) on a plain yellow background. The slides were photographed from figures cut out from silk screen paper and arranged with one figure above and two below. There were a total of 48 slides; 8 were practice slides and 40 were test slides. Two examples of the test slides are shown in Fig. 1.

As can be seen in Fig. 1, the stimuli differed in binary values of color, form and size. When a dimension varied, two figures had the same value and a third figure had a different value. For example, if the form dimension varied, as in Fig. 1a, two figures (regardless of color and size values) could be rectangles and the third, a circle. When form was constant, as in Fig. 1b, all figures could be asymmetrical and curvilinear, and the form was considered removed as a dimension of choice.

The S's task was to "Point to the two that are the same." The values of the figures on the 40 test slides were arranged so that a pair of figures would match in values from only one dimension but differ in values from the remaining dimensions or could not be matched on any of the varied dimensions. The set of forty slides, with all experimental manipulations, is summarized in Table 1.

As seen in the columns of Table 1, four sets of slides allowed choices for one over either one or two other dimensions. On 16 slides, form, color, and size (FCS) varied; a dimensional choice could be made among these dimensions by choice of any pair of figures. On three sets of eight slides each, a dimensional choice could be made between only two dimensions, either form and color (FC) or form and size (FS) or color and size (CS), respectively. A choice for a third pair on these latter sets was regarded as errone-

TABLE 1   Description of Slides Used for Testing Dimensional Preferences

	Form, Color, Size	Form, Color	Form, Size	Color, Size
Saturated symmetrical (SaSy)	4	2	2	2
Saturated asymmetrical (SaA)	4	2	2	2
Unsaturated symmetrical (USy)	4	2	2	2
Unsaturated asymmetrical (UA)	4	2	2	2
	16	8	8	8

ous since a match could not be based on common values of the varied dimensions (e.g., the two right-hand objects in Fig. 1b cannot be matched on color or size, which vary, while form is constant).

As can be seen in the rows of Table 2, four values of the color and form dimensions were used. For the color dimension, two hues, red and blue (*Color-Aid Swatch Book*, 1962) were presented either in full or next-to-least saturation on a five-point tint scale (white added). For the form dimension, two contours, curvilinear and angular, were used in either symmetrical or asymmetrical equiarea shapes. The two sizes, as projected, were small (15¾ square centimeters) and large (30⅞ square centimeters).

Hue saturation (Saturated, Sa, or Unsaturated, U) and figure contour (Symmetrical, Sy, or Asymmetrical, A) were compared factorily. Within the set of 40 test slides, there were 10 slides each of Sa vs Sy; Sa vs. A; U vs. Sy; and U vs. A. The Sa hues were red

and blue; the U hues were pastel pink and blue. The Sy contours were circles and rectangles; the A contours were trapezium and kidney shapes with no sides or arcs equal in length. The positions of the dimensional pairs and color-form values were varied in three different orders of the test series; Ss were randomly assigned to an order.

The first eight slides shown were practice slides. On these slides, two of the figures were identical in form, color, and size; the third figure differed from the other two in the same three dimensions. For example, in one slide, two figures were small, red circles and the third figure was a large, blue rectangle. A choice, then, could be based on one, two or three dimensions. This task was used to determine whether an S could make choices consistent with the instruction: "Point to the two that are the same." All forms and colors were used in the practice set. Twenty-one Ss (see below) who made three or more errors on the eight

TABLE 2   Choices and Individual Preferences for Form or Color

		Proportion of				
		Group Choices		Individual Preferences		
Age	No. of Ss	Form	Color	Form	Color	Neither
2.10–3.5	12	.42	.58	.33	.42	.25
3.6–3.11	12	.41	.59	.33	.59	.08
3.12–4.5	24	.57	.43	.50	.33	.17
4.6–4.11	54	.71	.29	.74	.24	.02
4.12–5.5	28	.59	.41	.62	.35	.03
5.6–6.1	15	.74	.26	.67	.20	.13
Total Ss	145					

practice slides were not continued onto the 40 preference test slides and were thus excluded from the study.

Testing Procedure

The S was obtained from his school room for testing by either E who asked if S would like to play a game. As an incentive, S was shown a plastic ring, worn by E, and told it was his to keep after the game was over. If the child refused, he was approached once more on another day. The S, upon agreeing, was escorted by E to the test room, where he was seated before the rear projection screen. The S was given a wooden pointer, a practice slide was projected and S was instructed to "Point to the two which are the same." When S made a correct choice between pairs on the practice slides, E said "good" or "that is the idea." If S made less than three errors on the practice slides, testing on one of three different sequences of the 40 slides followed immediately, without any change of instructions. During testing, no comment or reinforcement for any response was given by E, who sat behind the child. The S self-paced his choices and after each response, the next slide was shown immediately. Testing continued until S completed his choices on 40 test slides.

Subjects

The Ss were 166 preschool children from the West Los Angeles area. One hundred forty-five children completed preference testing: 84 were from a private nursery school and 61 were from nursery and kindergarten classes at the University of California Elementary School. There were 76 girls and 69 boys who ranged in age from 2 years, 10 months to 6 years, 6 months. The age distribution was: 24 Ss under 4 years of age; 78 Ss between four and five; 43 Ss over five. The 21 Ss who were unable to perform the practice problem were excluded from further testing; these Ss were generally younger and ranged in age from 2.6 to 4.3 (median = 3.7).

RESULTS

Color versus Form Preference

Twenty-four slides in the test series compared color against form. The choices on these slides were analyzed with respect to age trend and unidimensional preference for individual Ss.

The age trend analysis consisted of summing choices for each dimension over Ss at 6-month age intervals. Table 2 gives the proportion of form and color choices as a function of age. The first and last groupings each include one S 2 months younger and older, respectively.

For group choice data, Table 2 shows that the two youngest groups choose color over form, but that form was more frequently selected by the older groups. The median age at which more children chose form than color is 4 years and 2 months. The choice data were tested for trend by Kendall tau (Siegel, 1956), at the .05 level of significance. The trend for form was significantly increasing; the difference between form and color was also significantly increasing.

The developmental trend in the group data is a reflection of the differing numbers of Ss who reliably prefer one dimension over the other, since both the trend and proportion of group choices are nearly the same as that for the individual preferences for each dimension. The trend for the small number of Ss (8%) showing a mixed preference was not significant. That is, for some Ss, there was a mixed pattern of responses which might indicate that a shift in preference was occurring, but these mixed patterns did not occur more often at a certain age level. Thus, the increase in form preference with age shows that more children respond unidimensionally to the form dimension with age, but does not indicate an increase in form preference responses among children who prefer color. Most children prefer either color or form. It is only by averaging over individuals that a developmental trend is found.

Stimulus Variation

Eight slides each compared either form-size (FS) or color-size (CS). The effect of stimulus variation on the form or color choices for these 16 slides was analyzed in a 2 × 2 × 2 × 2 factorial design with the following variables: (a) preference (83 F and 50 C Ss), (b) hue (Sa vs. U choices), (c) contour (Sy vs. A choices), and (d) slide type (Fs or Cs). The first factor was a preselected between factor; the other three were within factors.

Table 3 summarizes the mean number of choices for form over size and color over size for the only significant main effects and interaction from the analysis of variance ($p < .01$). (Note that the maximum number of choices per cell was eight.)

As can be seen in Table 3, by averaging the column sums, Color Ss chose both form and color over size more often than Form Ss ($F = 7.90$; $df = 1, 131$). Likewise, averaging the row sums, form was chosen more often than color over size ($F = 58.95$; $df = 1, 131$). The interaction between preference and slide type indicates that Color Ss selected color over size and Form Ss chose form over size, a result consistent with the preference classifications ($F = 138.50$; $df = 1, 131$).

Choices between nonpreferred stimulus dimensions were compared for Form Ss and Color Ss. That is, the eight size vs. color choices were examined for Form Ss and the eight size vs. form choices were examined for Color Ss. The analysis of variance showed choice pattern was different between preference groups ($F = 280.83$; $p < .01$). Table 4 compares the percentage of choices for each comparison by preference groups.

TABLE 3 Mean Number of Choices of Form over Size and Color over Size As a Function of Individual Form or Color Preference

Slide Type	Preference	
	Form	Color
FS	7.59	5.26
Cs	3.89	7.52

As can be seen in Table 4, Form Ss chose size as often as color, at all age levels. Color Ss preferred form over size and this preference increased with age. These data suggest an emergence of a second order preference, or choice hierarchy, among Color Ss, but not among Form Ss. The number of responses for individual Ss were too small to analyze individual trends in this second-order preference. These data suggest that one method for studying an individual's preference transition from color to form would be to remove the preferred stimulus, as was done in the FS and CS slides for the Color or Form Ss, respectively. With a longer test series on such slide types, one might be able to detect reliable individual transitions in preference and possibly relate these to environmental variables such as amount of schooling, reading experience, etc.

DISCUSSION

Despite variation between the values within both the form and color dimensions, the results of the present study confirm the general finding that young children tend to prefer color and older children tend to prefer form. It was shown, however, that these

TABLE 4 Proportion of Choices of Color over Size by Form Ss and Form over Size by Color Subjects As a Function of Age

Age	Form Ss:	Color	Size	Color Ss:	Form	Size
2.10–3.11	8	.34	.34	12	.53	.36
4.0–4.11	49	.49	.37	24	.68	.23
5.0–6.1	26	.51	.45	14	.75	.14
Total	83			50		

preferences are mostly unidimensional and the group trends reflect the fact that more *S*s prefer one dimension over another at different ages. Although such evidence indicates that a transition from color to form must occur, the age at which such a transition occurs is not apparent unless one uses averaged data. The small proportion of children who showed a mixed preference may have been individually undergoing a transition but there was no age relation for these *S*s. Undoubtedly, the "critical transition age" and whatever conditions are responsible for the transition vary for individual *S*s so that studies of the present kind are unlikely to detect a sharp transition age. Therefore, further research on this problem might be aimed at an understanding of the specific environmental experiences which could alter color or form preferences. For example, to what extent would discrimination training on forms, with color either irrelevant or constant, affect the color preference of a child? Such procedures could be readily realized by the introduction of reinforcement for opposite preference choices within the present test series. Lee (1965) has suggested that reinforcement for form discrimination in learning to read and other school activities is probably responsible not only for the shift in preference to form but also for differences in learning color and form concepts between preschool- and school-age children. The influence of environmental variables is emphasized by a finding that African children showed no shift from color to form preference by adolescence (Suchman, 1966). Indeed, it is surprising that Euro-American preference studies report such similar preference findings, in view of considerable disparity in procedures, subject sampling, tasks, instructions, and stimulus materials. These disparities could account for the 2-year range reported in various studies for the median transition age of the shift from color to form. Rather than try to reconcile these different findings in median transition age, we wish to emphasize the importance of turning to an analysis of the conditions which are responsible for the transition from color to form preference.

Preference is apparently stable under two kinds of stimulus change. First, it is stable following a choice on slides where the preferred dimension is removed (i.e., constant). Second, despite value changes within the color and form dimension, the child does not shift preference. Color children generalize their preference to a range of hue intensities and do not behave in accord with the folk concept that children prefer only saturated hues. Form children, likewise, generalize their preference to symmetrical, as well as asymmetrical contours and do not evidence a preference for asymmetrical (qua topological) forms as suggested by Piaget and Inhelder (1956). However, there is evidence (Huang, 1945; Vokvelt, 1926) that either color or form preference can be temporarily modified by the discriminability (or embeddedness) of these dimensions in a stimulus configuration; such factors were not studied here. In addition to stimulus characteristics which influence preferences for one dimension over another, questions might be raised as to what effect does a preference have on other behavior? For example, one might ask what other role does stimulus preference play in the child's learning environment? Since preference measurement within certain value ranges is reliable, a knowledge of these preferences might be used to predict learning rates of problems where the role of the preferred stimulus varies. Suppose that the dimensions were of equal discriminability but a preference for one exists. Suppose further that the preference operates as an observing response to cues in a discrimination or concept learning task, then the solution of the problem may be either facilitated or interfered with, depending upon the congruence between *S*'s preference and the relevant dimension of the problem.

REFERENCES

Brian, Clara R., & Goodenough, Florence L. Relative potency of color and form perception at various ages. *Journal of Experimental Psychology*, 1929, **12,** 197–213.

Colby, Martha, & Robertson, Jean. Genetic studies in abstraction. *Journal of Comparative and Physiological Psychology,* 1942, **33,** 303–320.

Color-Aid Co. *Color-aid swatch book.* New York: Author, 1962.

Corah, N. L. Color and form in children's perceptual behavior. *Perceptual and Motor Skills,* 1964, **18,** 313–316.

Descoudres, Alice. Couleur, forme, ou nombre? *Archives Psychology,* 1914, **14,** 305–341.

Doehring, D. Color-form attitudes of deaf children. *Journal of Speech and Hearing Research,* 1960, **3,** 242–248.

Honkavaara, Sylvia. A critical re-evaluation of the color and form reaction and disproving of the hypothesis connected with it. *Journal of Psychology,* 1958, **45,** 25–36.

Huang, I. Abstraction of form and color in children as a function of the stimulus objects. *Journal of Genetic Psychology,* 1945, **66,** 59–62.

Kagan, J., & Lemkin, Judith. Form, color and size in children's conceptual behavior. *Child Development,* 1961, **32,** 25–28.

Lee, Lee C. Concept utilization in preschool children. *Child Development,* 1965, **36,** 221–227.

Piaget, J., & Inhelder, Barbel. *The child's conception of space.* London: Routledge, 1956, Pp. 17–43.

Schactel, E. *Metamorphosis.* New York: Basic Books, 1959.

Siegel, S. *Nonparametric statistics for the behavioral sciences,* New York: McGraw-Hill, 1956. Pp. 213–223.

Suchman, Rosslyn G. Color-form preference, discriminative accuracy and learning of deaf and hearing children. *Child Development,* 1966, **37,** 439–451.

Suchman, Rosslyn G. Cultural differences in children's color and form preferences. *Journal of Social Psychology,* 1966.

Vokvelt, H. Fortschritte der Experimentellen Kinderpsychologie. *Bericht uber d. IX Kongress f. Experimentelle Psychologie in Munchen,* 1926, 80–135.

29 | Studies in the Organization of Character

HUGH HARTSHORNE
MARK A. MAY

How to educate children in character and moral behavior is a difficult and complex question. Investigators considering the development of character not only have the problem of identifying the behavior but also must evaluate the behavior against ethical standards and try to find those processes that lead to more effective character education. American culture has many ethical standards; these complicate the problem for educator, investigator, and child. Although Hartshorne and May investigated character education and practice in 1920, their study is still important today. They developed tests to measure the child's perception of social processes by describing a situation for the child and asking what he would do if it were to occur. Following their measurement of existing social perceptions they placed the child in a test situation that would allow him to cheat. Cheating was recorded by the investigators and compared with social, economic, and other individual variables to find those traits which differentiate children who cheat from those who do not. Knowledge of what is right or wrong did not predict cheating. Also, there was no correlation between age and cheating or sex and cheating. They did find strong positive relations between intelligence and cheating. Brighter children do not cheat as often, probably because they don't have to cheat to keep up in school.

The character education inquiry was launched at Teachers College, Columbia University, in September, 1924, at the request of, and under a grant from, the Institute of Social and Religious Research, and under the general supervision of Professor E. L. Thorndike.

At the outset, several approaches to the study of character were open, but the character testing approach was chosen, for several reasons. Not only is this relatively

Adapted from A summary of the work of the character education inquiry. *Religious Education*, 1930, **25**. Reprinted from the September and October 1930 issues of *Religious Education*. By permission of the publisher, The Religious Education Association, New York City.

neglected approach basic to any fresh scientific research into the nature of character and its manner of growth, but studies of the relative value of current methods of moral and religious education and of experiments to discover improvements in technique depend, to a degree rarely appreciated, on the availability of ways of *measuring results.* Plans and programs which have no experimental basis, and which may be as likely to damage character as to improve it, are produced by the score. Hundreds of millions of dollars are probably spent annually by churches, Sunday schools and other organizations for children and youth, with almost no check on the product—a negligence of which no modern industry would be guilty. Through lack of tests for predicting effective living a vast amount of time and no one knows how much money are probably thrown away on expensive and intricate devices for moral and religious education.

Although the main form of the research was the development of tests for the measurement of progress in character education, it happened, as is often the case in scientific investigation, that the byproducts of the investigation are of greater importance than the main results. This paper thus is concerned not only with the tests developed, but also with the nature of character traits and their concomitants.

THE TESTS DEVELOPED

Tests of Moral Knowledge

One of the most important intellectual abilities in character is that of being able to foresee the social consequences of acts. Accordingly, we devised a test that was intended to measure the child's ability to foresee the types of consequences that might follow from simple types of activity, such as starting across the street without looking both ways, getting into fights on the playground, giving away money that had been saved for another purpose, and similar commonplace activities well within the range of experience of school children.

In the first instance, the children were simply asked to write after each statement of an act all the things they could think of that might happen. They were asked to list both the good things and the bad. This gave a rough measure of what one might call the child's social imagination.

In a second test a situation is briefly described, and the child is asked to check the sentence that tells what is the best thing to do. For example, if you are very hungry at a party when only light refreshments are served, what is the right thing to do: (1) Eat little and say nothing? (2) Try to eat a lot without being noticed? (3)

Leave the party and go to a restaurant? (4) Tell the hostess that her refreshments are too light?

It does not particularly matter, therefore, whether the child gives the answer which he thinks has the approval of the teacher and examiner, or guesses at what he is expected to say, or gives his own personal view. This point has been urged as a criticism against this type of testing, but we have regarded it as precisely that which we wish to measure.

Still another sample of the tests of intellectual factors is what we originally called a provocations test. Presumably there are conditions under which such conduct as lying, cheating, stealing, and the like, might be relatively desirable. What we wish to know is where the child draws the line. For example, under what conditions would the child justify stealing or lying? This is how we attempted to measure it: We told, in simple, one- or two-sentence stories, of things that children have done, describing briefly the circumstances. Then we asked for a vote on whether or not this act under these circumstances was right, wrong or excusable. For example, on the way to Sunday school Jack matched pennies with other boys in order to get money for the Sunday school collection. Was this right, wrong or excusable under the circumstances? We compiled a list of many similar situations and asked the children to vote on them. This gave information on the extent to which and the conditions under which a child will excuse types of action that fall below the ideal standard.

These tests, which we have called, for the want of a better name, moral knowledge tests, have satisfactory statistical reliability and validity. Their scientific quality is on a par with the best intelligence tests and school achievement tests.

Conduct Tests

In the field of actual conduct, we have developed tests covering four types of behavior—deception, co-operation, inhibition, and persistence. Before describing samples of these tests, a word should be inserted concerning the general theory of conduct testing. We have proceeded on the assumption that the only sense in which conduct can be measured is by taking samples of it. If they are representative and there are enough of them, his future conduct may be predicted from them.

In the study of honesty, or rather its opposite, deceit, we sampled the tendencies of children to cheat, steal and lie. Of the cheating type of conduct, we took fourteen samples of classroom situations, four of situations involving athletic contests, three of situations involving parties or parlor games, and two of school work done at home. We also took two samples of the lying tendency and two of stealing. The lying and stealing tests, however, were not widely used.

Examples of situations involving cheating in the classroom are such as copying answers from an answer sheet that was given out for the purpose of correcting papers at the close of the test, of adding answers in a speed test after time had been called, or violating the rules in the solution of a puzzle, or opening the eyes in doing a stunt that was to be accomplished with the eyes closed. The essential feature of these tests is that a child is placed in an ordinary classroom situation and given a task to perform which has in it an opportunity for cheating, but the situation is so arranged that if a child cheats or attempts to deceive the experimenter he unwittingly leaves a record of his conduct.

The next series of behavior tests is in an entirely different area. They represent types of behavior that are ordinarily described as helpfulness, cooperation, self-denial, self-sacrifice, charity and the like. We have used the term "service" to cover all of these. The plan for testing the service tendency is in general the same as that for testing the deception tendency and involves the setting up of a situation with an appeal and at the same time a resistance.

Sample situations involving self-denial or self-sacrifice are these: inviting the child to come to school a half hour early in order to make pictures for hospital children; asking boys to give up their manual training project (in one case the building of a wooden automobile model) to make wooden toys for hospital children; presenting children in an orphan's home each with nineteen cents and asking them to vote how they would distribute it between self, bank and charity (a check-up was made to determine precisely what they did with this money).

Another type of conduct that we attempted to measure is persistence. Here, again, we had two series of tests, one for groups and the other for individuals. The plan was to set up a situation involving a task and note the length of time a child would stick at it. One task was that of solving magic squares; another, that of solving a very difficult mechanical puzzle; another, that of reading a story printed in a confusing manner.

VALIDITY OF THE TESTS

We are now ready to raise the question as to the extent to which we have measured character. It is obvious that no one of these tests is an adequate measure of all there is to character. The question is whether or not any combination of them in any sense adequately measures character. This question can be answered only experimentally.

In order to find out the extent to which the tests measured character, it was necessary to secure data on the conduct, ideals, attitudes, social adjustments, reputation and environmental background of these children, quite apart from the scores derived from the tests themselves. We were fortunate in securing a large body of such data on a sufficient sample of the children who had been tested to enable us to determine the extent to which the character test scores correlate with these character factors.

Two main sources of information against which our tests were checked were: (1) The child's reputation among his teachers, classmates, and leaders; and (2) pen portraits of the character of one hundred children based on all available data, arranged, by sixty-three judges, according to the desirability of the character described.

Reputation

Reputation as a criterion of character has been used by numerous investigators and, on the whole, the results have been disappointing. Profiting by the mistakes of predecessors, we attempted to free our reputation data from the influence of prejudice and gossip so that the results would reflect as true a picture as possible of the facts on which the ratings were based. For example, instead of asking a teacher to give her general impression of the cooperativeness of a pupil, we asked her to check the one of five statements which seemed to her to describe best this behavior. One such group of five statements is as follows: (1) Works with others if asked to do so. (2) Works better alone; cannot get along with others. (3) Works well and gladly with others. (4) Indifferent as to whether or not he works with others. (5) Usually antagonistic or obstructive to joint effort. Similar statements were worked out for twenty-two types of conduct.

We also secured the opinions of pupils concerning the conduct of their classmates by the use of an instrument called the "Guess Who" test. The "Guess Who" test is a series of twenty-four descriptions of types of conduct characteristic of school children. Each child reads over each description and writes after it the names of his classmates who seem to him to be described by it. For example, one of the descriptions is: "Here is a crabber and knocker. Nothing is right. Always kicking and complaining." The children are asked to write down the names of their class-mates who they think are described in these terms. This instrument turned out to have very high reliability and high validity.

In addition to these two devices, three others were used, so that the total reputation score of the child was a composite of the opinions of his teachers, classmates, and leaders. When this score was freed statistically from the effects of prejudice, it showed remarkable correspondence with the scores derived from the objective tests. When all of the conduct scores were combined into a single score, and all reputation scores combined into a single score, the correlation between the two, corrected for attenuation, is .94. These are exceedingly high values and are extremely significant.

But character is more than conduct and more than reputation. When we include in our character score not only conduct but also moral knowledge, social attitudes, the child's background and his reactions to it, all of which are parts of his character, the correlations run even higher. In fact, the raw correlation is .70, which, when corrected for attenuation, rises to .988. In other words, character so far as it is represented in reputation, is completely accounted for by performance on an extended series of tests which measure conduct, culture, social opinion and attitude.

Character Portraits

While these results seemed significant and even somewhat startling, we were not satisfied to let the matter rest here. We pushed the validation procedure a step further, in an attempt to check our character tests against a more unified and concrete criterion.

We took at least one step in the direction of concreteness by developing a scale of character as a whole. That is, we attempted to handle our specific data not in terms of their summation but in terms of their organization. Our technique consisted in the building of character sketches on the basis of our records. We selected one hundred children from one of our populations, on whom we had a rather complete set of data. The data on each child were written up in the form of a pen portrait or a description of his conduct, attitudes, reputation, intelligence and background, including what information we were able to secure regarding the second criterion, namely, the adequacy of the child's social functioning. These one hundred portraits were then ranked by sixty-three judges according to the degree of character exhibited by each. These rankings were surprisingly uniform and yielded a scale of character sketches with a reliability of .98.

The next step in the procedure was to find the correlation between each of the elements in the total composite and this general character scale. The results show that reputation stands in closest relation to total character as measured by this scale. Moral knowledge and social attitudes come next, conduct next, cultural background and personal factors, such as intelligence and age, come last. When all the conduct scores are added together, however, the correlation between conduct and character is about as high as between reputation and character, both being around .8.

Consistency

The consideration of this question led us to construct another type of criterion which resembles the one just described in being built on quantitative data. It differs, however, in one important respect. While both of the criteria described above rely on judgments and opinions, in this one all subjective factors are eliminated, and it is derived from the objective data themselves. The same one hundred cases used in the construction of the pen portrait criterion were also used for the building of this objective criterion, and scores on the moral knowledge tests, conduct tests, tests of emotional instability, home background, school marks, deportment and reputation were classed into twenty-three groups. This gave twenty-three character scores for each of the one hundred individuals.

These scores were treated in two ways: first, they were summed up, as usual, in an average score; and, second, the variability of each individual's scores around his own mean was computed. Thus, for each individual, we have an average score and a variability score. The variability score was called his consistency score.

Our character score represents consistency multiplied by level. An individual who has a high average score but a low consistency score will have a relatively low index or score. But the individual who has a high average score and a high consistency score will receive the highest index or score. That is, the child who is consistently good will receive the highest score, whereas the child who is consistently bad will receive the lowest score.

A character score was thus computed for each of the one hundred children whom we have been discussing. This score, in a sense, represents our final effort as a criterion. It correlates .72 with reputation, which, it will be recalled, was our first criterion, and .81 with the criterion derived by having judges rank the pen portraits of character.

The conclusion reached as a result of our attempts to construct satisfactory character tests is that if a large number of samples of conduct, knowledge, attitude, intelligence, background, and social adjustment are taken, and if the general algebraic level for each individual is determined, and, at the same time, if the variability of each individual's scores around his own mean is computed, a combination of these two values will indeed yield an index or score of character.

THE SPECIFICITY OF MORAL CONDUCT

A great deal of moral education has been built on the assumption that character is a structure of virtues and vices. In our studies in actual conduct, we see that there is very little evidence of unified character traits.

The evidence for the specificity of conduct is (1) the low intercorrelation between sample tests of the same type of behavior, (2) the normal distribution of honesty scores in a population of children, and (3) the tremendous differences in situations in the amount of dishonesty they elicit. If honesty were a trait which you either have or do not have, then we would expect the distribution of honesty scores to be bimodal; that is, at one end of the score we would have a piling up of saints and at the other end of the scale a piling up of sinners, with nothing much in between. The exact opposite of this is the truth. At the dishonesty end of the scale, there are very few. That is, we find very few children who cheated twenty-three times in twenty-three chances. At the honesty end of the scale we also find very few children who are honest twenty-three times in twenty-three chances. Most of them are sometimes honest and sometimes dishonest.

KNOWLEDGE AND CONDUCT

If you ask the same question regarding "rightness" or "wrongness" of conduct of fifty perfectly honest children, that is, children on whom we have no evidence of cheating, they will give you the same kinds of answers in about the same proportion as the cheaters. We made similar studies of four or five hundred questions, and the results were nearly always the same—no differences. Then we tried to determine the relationship between knowledge in general and conduct in a specific situation. Again the correlations were very low. So we finally pooled together all of our moral knowledge scores on each individual, on the one hand, and all the conduct scores, on the other, and correlated these in a very widespread and heterogeneous population, with a resulting coefficient of about .50. Thus we find no specific relations between moral knowledge and conduct, but only general relations.

FACTORS RELATED TO CHARACTER

Age

We can say with considerable certainty that within the limits of the present research there is practically no correlation between age and conduct, except, perhaps, in the case of the scores on the persistence tests. The results of our persistence tests do show that older children are inclined, on the whole, to be somewhat more persistent than younger children. This, however, may very well be accounted for by differences between older and younger children in the amount of interest in the tasks set by our tests. In the case of deception, we found that the older children were, in fact, a little more inclined to be deceptive than the younger children. This is rather significant in view of the amount of money and energy that has been spent on their moral education.

With moral knowledge, however, the case is quite different. Here we do find correlations with age, though of somewhat less magnitude than between moral knowledge and intelligence or school achievement. As children grow older, they become more appreciative of ideal standards, and their opinions and attitudes conform more closely to those of educated adults.

Sex

Our tests show no consistent sex differences in the matter of deception but rather wide and significant differences in service and self-control. In the tests of helpfulness, co-operation and charity, girls are slightly better than the boys. Their teachers, however, rate them very much better than the boys. In the tests of inhibition, the girls are markedly better than the boys and consistently so. In persistence, the differences are very slight and vary with the test situation. In moral knowledge, attitudes and opinions, the differences again are very slight but favor the girls.

Intelligence

Nearly all of the children with whom we have worked were tested with the Thorndike Group Intelligence Test. We estimate that if all honesty tests were combined on a large population of children, the correlation with intelligence would probably run as high as .60. In the case of service, inhibition and persistence, however, the correlations are somewhat lower. Evidently intelligence is more closely related to honesty than to any of these three types of behavior.

As would be expected, the correlations between intelligence and moral knowledge are almost as high as between one intelligence test and another. They are equally as high as between intelligence and school achievement. They run in fact from about .5 to about .9. This close relation between intellect and the abilities measured by these tests indicates what a strong part intelligence actually plays in the development of a child's social concepts and ability to make ethical discriminations.

Socio-economic Background

We find significant differences in honesty between children whose parents are engaged in the professional occupations and children whose parents are unskilled laborers. We take this to indicate that the general social and economic background of the child is an important factor in his honesty. It is also an important factor in his social attitudes and opinions, and also in his knowledge of right and wrong.

A careful study was made in one community of the homes of the fifty most honest and fifty most dishonest children. This revealed certain important differences between home conditions of these two groups of children. The homes from which the worst offenders came might be best characterized as exhibiting bad parental example, parental discord, bad discipline, unsocial attitudes toward children, impoverished community and changing economic or social situation. The homes from which the more honest children came revealed the opposite of these conditions.

Schooling

Turning now to school influences, we begin with the Sunday school. In the matter of honesty, co-operation, inhibition and persistence, we find a general tendency for children enrolled in Sunday schools to exhibit more desirable conduct than the children who are not enrolled in Sunday schools. But, on the other hand, we find (and this is especially true of honesty) that there is practically no correlation between frequency of attendance at Sunday school and conduct. Apparently it is only necessary to be enrolled. It is clear that we have here an excellent illustration of selection. It is the better trained children who are enrolled in the Sunday schools in the first place.

In our studies of the influence of the day school, we found that different types of school experiences are accompanied by differences in the conduct, knowledge, and attitudes of children. For example, children who attend private schools, particularly the more progressive schools, are markedly more honest in their school work than are children who attend conventional public schools. This question was investigated rather thoroughly with a long series of experiments. Aside from the fact that children who attend private schools are a selected group coming from the better homes and better environments, we find that progressive methods are more likely to foster situations in which honest behavior is the natural result than are more conventional methods. Schools, however, differ widely among themselves, and there are enormous differences between different classrooms, indicating an influence of the teacher, an influence of the morale of the group, or both. These phenomena have been investigated, and we find that the attitude of the teacher toward her pupils is a factor of considerable significance. Whenever this attitude is frankly co-operative and sympathetic, the children are likely to be more honest, more co-operative and to show higher degrees of self-control than in cases where the attitude of the teacher is unsympathetic, arbitrary, and dictatorial.

EDUCATIONAL IMPLICATIONS

Contradictory demands made upon the child by the varied situations in which he is responsible to adults not only prevent the organization of a consistent character but actually compel inconsistency as the price of peace and self-respect.

There is introduced, therefore, one conclusion. This relates to the building of a functioning ideal for society which may serve at once as a principle of unified or consistent response and as a principle of satisfactory social adjustment. Such a policy or principle must, therefore, be derived from the inherent nature of social life and growth as experienced by the child himself. It must not only be scientifically sound in the sense that it presents a workable theory of life; it must also emerge in the minds of the children through their own guided experiments in living.

It can hardly be expected that most children can be taught to be responsive to social ideals unsupported by group code and morale. When the individual is made the unit of educational effort, he is so abstracted from life situations as to become more and more of a prig in proportion as his teachers succeed with him, and more and more the victim of a disorganized and detached mind in proportion as they fail. The normal unit for character education is the group or small community, which provides through co-operative discussion and effort the moral support required for the adventurous discovery and effective use of ideals in the conduct of affairs.

30 | Effect of Effort on Value: An Exploratory Study of Children

MICHAEL LEWIS

How does the amount of work we do to earn something affect our preferences for an object once we receive it? Several theories are relevant: (1) Frustration may increase our general drive level, so that the stimuli associated with the successful reduction of this drive would receive greater reinforcement value. (2) Cognitive dissonance theory suggests that when a person obtains insufficient reward relative to the expenditure of energy, he will over-value that reward. (3) The Protestant Ethic claims that work is good, and anyone who works more should enjoy it more.

In the present study, children were asked to turn a crank to obtain chips. The effort required to turn the crank was varied; preference and reinforcement value were assessed. There were no differences between preferences, but effort increased the reinforcement value of the chips for younger children. The data are consistent with all three theories.

The concept of effort was formally introduced by Hull as the psychological variable of work in his *Principles of Behavior* (1943). Hull viewed work in terms of its subtractive effect on performance. His views of effort have been subjected to two different kinds of tests. The first examines whether an organism will tend to choose the less effortful of two responses if both are followed by identical reinforcement. The second test uses extinction data as a measure of the effect of effort on the effective reaction potential ($_sE_R$) of a response. If inhibitory potential ($_sI_R$) is a function of work or effort, then those responses involving greater work would presumably extinguish more quickly than those responses requiring less effort. The majority of subsequent experimentation manipulating the work or effort variable has been primarily in-

terested in the choice and strength (duration) of instrumental responses or paths to a goal, and has had little concern with the value of the object worked for, that is, the reinforcer itself. There are, however, a few studies which have dealt with the value of the goal object. Wright (1937) argued that the presence of a barrier between S and a desired goal increased the positive valence of that goal, and in a series of studies demonstrated this phenomenon. Child and Adelshein (1944) attempted to replicate Wright's findings but in general were unable to do so. In a more recent study Olds (1953) demonstrated that increased effort, or "wanting-practice," affected the value of a secondary reinforcer. Old's experiment, however, confounded expectations with effort; and his results, therefore, could be explained by using frustration concepts. Finally, Aronson (1961) showed that a group expending high effort demonstrated a stronger pref-

Adapted from Effect of effort on value: An exploratory study of children. *Child Development*, 1964, **35,** 1337–1342.

erence for irrelevant aspects of a goal situation than that shown by a low effort group. The literature on the effect of effort is still ambiguous.

The present experiment investigated whether a stimulus-event used as a positive reinforcer (reward) undergoes changes in value as a function of the effort expended during the response that it reinforced. Age was also varied in an attempt to confirm the finding that increased age, representing variable socialization, would result in greater increases in value for objects obtained under high as compared with low effort. Two kinds of indices of value were used: (a) "preference" or "incentive" value—the tendency of the cue aspects of the stimulus-event to elicit approach responses resulting in its attainment, (b) reinforcement value—the effect of presentation of the stimulus-event upon the probability of occurrence of a subsequent new response.

METHOD

Subjects

A total of 110 boys, 52 first graders and 58 sixth graders, from a large urban school system were used in this experiment. The high effort (HE) groups consisted of 26 first and 26 sixth graders; the low effort (LE) groups consisted of 26 first and 32 sixth graders.

Apparatus

The device used to vary effort and deliver reinforcement was a metal box with a crank handle on one side which S was required to turn. A brake inside the box, to which a 2 lb. weight could be attached, was used to vary the difficulty of turning the crank handle. There was an opening in the front of the box from which one chip was automatically dispensed when the subject turned the crank a required number of times. Two chip colors were used, light

and dark blue. Each S received only one color chip during training. The binary choice apparatus was a black metal instrument case with two spring-back levers mounted 7 inches apart.

Procedure

During *training*, S turned the crank handle in order to receive a poker chip. Effort was varied by requiring the high effort group (HE) to turn the handle 18 times with a brake connected, while the low effort group (LE) was required to turn the handle only three times with the brake disconnected. Each S was assigned to one of the two effort and colored chip conditions and worked until he received 20 chips.

A *preference* measure was obtained immediately following this training procedure. Preference was determined by asking S how many chips of the alternative color he would want for five of his training chips. Thus, if S worked for light blue chips and was willing to surrender five of them in exchange for eight dark blue chips, he would be said to value the light blue chips more than the S who was willing to exchange them for a lesser number of dark blue ones. This preference measure was always taken on the chips for which S worked and was always started by presenting S with a pile of five alternatively colored chips.

The two-choice probability learning task was used to determine the *reinforcement* value of the training chip. It has been amply demonstrated that amount or intensity of reinforcement in the two-choice problem affects the asymptotic level at which children choose the more frequently reinforced response (Lewis, Wall, & Aronfreed, 1963). The present experiment used a 70:30 random sequence, where the lever on the left side of the binary choice instrument was reinforced 70 per cent of the time, and the lever on the right side, 30 per cent of the time. The order of occurrence of the two events was randomized within each block of 25 trials, and Ss were run for 150 trials. The reinforcement was a chip of the same color as those for which S had originally worked. S received one of these chips each time that he chose the correct button. On those trials on which S chose the incorrect response, no chip was dispensed. Measures were taken both of (a) asymptotic percentage of responses to the more frequently reinforced side (S_{70}) during the last 20 trials, and (b) over-all percentage of these responses across the 150 trials.

It was predicted that Ss who exerted more effort toward a reward would value it more than Ss who exerted less effort. This would be reflected in the number of alternatively colored chips S surrendered for five of his training chips, and in S's binary choice behavior where the reward was used as reinforcement for the correct response. It was also predicted that there would be no age difference in the effect of effort on value.

RESULTS

Both the utility measure and the reinforcement measure were taken on the color chip received during the training condition. Because of the absence of color differences, the data for both groups were pooled. The utility measure, an indication of S's preference for his training chip, failed to differentiate either the effort conditions or the age groups.

The results of the two-choice task, an indication of the reinforcement value of the training chip, however, did reveal significant differences.

Table 1 presents the mean over-all percentage of responses to the most rein-

forced side (S_{70}) and the mean percentage of responses to S_{70} for the last 20 trials for both age groups and effort conditions.

An analysis of variance for the mean over-all percentage of responses to S_{70} failed to reveal any significant main effects. It did show an age × effort interaction ($F = 4.02$, $p < .05$). A t test applied to the first-grade data revealed that those Ss trained under the high-effort condition performed significantly better than those trained under the low-effort condition ($t = 4.44$, $p < .001$). No significant differences existed for the sixth graders. While an analysis of variance for the mean percentage of responses to S_{70} for the last 20 trials revealed no significant effects, a t test again revealed a significant effort difference for the first graders ($t = 4.20$, $p < .001$) and none for the sixth graders.

DISCUSSION

The results lend support to the hypothesis that effort can increase the value of a stimulus-event used as a positive reinforcer. That the preference measure failed to reflect this phenomenon is, in large part, a function of the particular measure used and the interesting effect that the addition or subtraction of a single chip of the alternative color had on a child's preference. The data indicated that both age groups would readily shift their preference from one pile of chips to the other when only one or two alternative chips had been added or removed. This lack of variability in the preference measure score (i.e., the number of chips the child would exchange for five of the chips he worked for) resulted in an inability to demonstrate any changes

TABLE 1   Group Mean Performance in Binary Choice Learning Task

| | First Graders | | Sixth Graders | |
	HE	LE	HE	LE
Mean percentage of responses to S_{70} for last 20 trials	.64	.52	.68	.65
Mean over-all percentage of responses to S_{70}	.61	.53	.61	.61

attributable to the effect of effort. The lack of an effort effect for the older boys suggests either that while the two effort conditions were discrepant enough for the younger boys, they were not so for the older ones, or that this phenomenon exists only for younger children. The mean data for the last 20 trials indicate that while there were no significant differences for the sixth graders, some effort effect was apparent. That the high and low effort conditions did not constitute real effort differences for the older, more muscular and bigger boys appears, therefore, to be the more parsimonious solution.

That effort can affect the value of a stimulus-event can be accounted for by several theoretical positions. One such theory revolves around the concept of frustration. When viewed as interfering with a goal-directed response, high effort would result in frustration (Sears, Maccoby, & Levin, 1957), and thereby increase the general drive level of the organism. The reinforcer associated with this increased drive might have acquired greater value in the original training because it reduced a higher level of drive. Such an interpretation would maintain that the effort affected drive level and the consequent reinforcement value of drive reduction.

A second interpretation relies on the concept of cognitive dissonance. In a paper by Festinger and Aronson (1960), the authors specifically discuss the theory's relevance to effort and value. They contend that when an organism obtains an "insufficient reward" relative to a particular expenditure of energy, there will be a tendency to discontinue the effortful activity or to attribute additional value to the activity or to its goal consequences. This development of an "extra preference" for the activity or its goal consequences is conceived of as a result of an internal process of dissonance resolution; that is, the receipt of a reward incommensurate with the effort expended in its attainment leads to a state of cognitive dissonance that the organism is motivated to reduce. In a study

by Aronson (1961), following a series of unrewarded trials, preference was directly assessed on tasks which required "considerable expenditure of energy" for one group and were "almost effortless" for another group. The high-effort group clearly preferred irrelevant aspects of the goal situation more than did the low-effort group.

A third position would cite the socialization of values as an explanation. Max Weber, in his classic treatise on *The Protestant Ethic and the Spirit of Capitalism* (1930) and others following him (McClelland in *The Achieving Society* [1961]), have pointed out that work has acquired a special meaning in Western society and that, to some extent, it is valuable in proportion to effort expended and not merely to the consequences of the work. Individuals learn that rewards are scaled, in part, with respect to the effort or difficulty of activities directed toward their attainment. Therefore, they expect increased value from increased work. This Protestant Ethic is reflected in cognitions such as, "I worked harder for it; therefore, it must be more valuable."

Finally, a fourth position stresses the attentional factor. In a series of experiments investigating the effect of effort on value in animals (Lewis, 1964), it was hypothesized that responses requiring large expenditures of effort tended to hamper any movement or activity not directed toward obtaining the goal. One might view effort, then, as inhibiting those responses which are not compatible with obtaining the stimulus-event and, therefore, increasing the probability of the occurrence of the goal-directed response. While this explanation can best account for effort differences in a test situation having a response similar to the training response, as shown by Lewis, it might also be applicable to the present results. Under the high-effort condition, the children may have learned to attend only to the task of getting chips, the effort expenditure having prevented them from looking around, exploring the machine or any other competing response. Thus, the response set of attending to the task of getting chips might have been generalized from the training condition to the binary choice problem. Such learning could lead to superior binary choice performance.

Because all of the theoretical positions can predict the observed results, further investigations of the effect of effort should be directed toward determining the specific mechanisms involved.

REFERENCES

Aronson, E. The effect of effort on the attractiveness of rewarded and unrewarded stimuli. *Journal of Abnormal and Social Psychology,* 1961, **63,** 375–380.

Child, I., & Adelshein, E. The motivational value of barriers for young children. *Journal of Genetic Psychology,* 1944, **65,** 97–111.

Festinger, L., & Aronson, E. The arousal and reduction of dissonance in social contexts. In D. Cartwright & A. Zander (Eds.), *Group dynamics.* Row, Peterson, 1960.

Hull, C. L. *Principles of behavior.* Appleton-Century, 1943.

Lewis, M. Some non-decremental effects of effort. *Journal of Comparative and Physiological Psychology,* 1964, **57,** 367–372.

Lewis, M., Wall, A. M., & Aronfreed, J. Developmental changes in the relative values of social and non-social reinforcement. *Journal of Experimental Psychology,* 1963, **66,** 133–137.

McClelland, D. C. *The achieving society.* D. Van Nostrand, 1961.

Olds, J. Influence of practice on the strength of secondary approach drives. *Journal of Experimental Psychology,* 1953, **46,** 232–236.

Sears, R. R., Maccoby, E. E., & Levin, H. *Patterns of child-rearing.* Row, Peterson, 1957.

Weber, M. *The Protestant ethic and the spirit of capitalism.* Trans. Talcott Parsons. London: Allen & Unwin, 1930.

Wright, H. F. The influence of barriers upon strength of motivation. *Contributions to Psychological Theory,* 1937, **1,** No. 3 (Whole No. 3).

31 | A Study of Children's Moral Judgments

RONALD C. JOHNSON

Piaget's notions of how children develop moral judgments have contributed much to our understanding. In this study, the author develops new tests of moral development much like those originally used by Piaget. These tests were given to a large population of children for standardization. Johnson used a cross-sectional sample (at several age levels) to test the relations between measures of moral judgment and age, intelligence, class, and parental attitude. The reliability of the entire moral judgment scale was approximately .60 (a relatively low reliability). Responses within most of the areas were positively related (often significantly). Abstractness and concreteness were only slightly related to moral judgments; parental attitudes were significantly related to moral judgments. IQ, and to some extent parental occupation, were positively related to moral judgment.

The factors that Piaget assumed would have the most influence on moral judgments turned out to be relatively insignificant; parental attitudes and IQ accounted for most of the variation in children's moral judgments.

The development of moral judgment in the child has been of considerable interest to the social scientist. Among the students of human development, Jean Piaget has been, perhaps, most influential in this area of study (1932). His studies of the child's developing understanding of causality, of physical and temporal reality, and of ethics and moral judgment have been extremely fruitful. This study proposes to test some of Piaget's ideas concerning developmental changes in moral judgment.

Moral judgment, for Piaget, consists of a number of areas. These include: (a) immanent justice—the belief in the existence of automatic punishments which emanate from things themselves; (b) moral realism—a belief that acts should be judged in terms of consequences, not on the basis of the

motive behind the act; (c) belief that punishment should be retributive vs. belief that punishment should be restitutive (merely restore the equilibrium destroyed by the punished act); (d) acceptance or rejection of the idea that the more severe punishment is more efficacious; and (e) choice of collective (essentially, guilt by association) or of individual responsibility for punishable acts.

. . . Piaget sees three forces interacting to produce developmental change in moral judgment: adult constraint, peer group cooperation and reciprocity, and the changing character of the child's mind. He says, ". . . We have three processes to consider: the spontaneous and unconscious egocentrism belonging to the individual as such, adult constraint, and cooperation." ". . . cooperation alone can shake the child out of its initial state of unconscious ego-

Adapted from A study of children's moral judgments. *Child Development*, 1962, **33**, 327–354.

centrism; whereas constraint acts quite differently and strengthens egocentric features of moral realism until such time as cooperation delivers the child both from egocentrism and from the results of this constraint" (1932, p. 184). The interaction of these factors, the changing mind of the child, the amount of adult constraint, and the amount of peer group cooperation and reciprocity, to Piaget, cause developmental differences in systems of responsibility and type of moral judgment used by children of different ages.

This study was concerned first with an attempt to determine the degree of interrelation within and between areas of moral judgment. This study dealt secondly with the relation of various antecedent conditions to moral judgment. There was an attempt to discover the relation of adult constraint, "egocentricity," age, sex, IQ, and parental occupational level to moral judgment.

METHOD

Sample

This study included all the children (all of those present on the day when their classes were tested) in grades 5, 7, 9, and 11 in a midwestern public school system.

Measuring Devices

The major purpose of this study was to determine the degree of interrelation between responses to questions formulated to represent different areas or kinds of moral judgment. The writer's initial problem was that of devising a test of moral judgment within which a number of questions could be found having to do with each of the areas under discussion. A number of stories were made up, modeled quite closely after those of Piaget. The stories illustrated five types of moral judgment: immanent justice, moral realism, retribution and expiation vs. restitution and reciprocity, the

efficacy of severe punishment, and communicable responsibility.

Piaget's questions were generally quite simple, since they were designed for use with 6- to 12-year-olds. The writer wished to use an older sample, so that the moral judgment test could be administered as a paper and pencil test and so that a test of "abstractness-concreteness" might be used. For these reasons, a number of new questions, based on those used by Piaget, were devised.

Procedure

The test of moral judgment was administered to the subjects in May of 1957. When presenting the moral judgment questions to the subjects in their classrooms, the writer introduced himself, passed out the test booklets, and then made the following statement:

> This is a sort of test, but it is not a test in the same way that you might be tested in arithmetic, because, as far as I know, there are no right or wrong answers. No one from the school here will know what you wrote down. The reason that I am asking these questions is this: I am interested in what young people think, because if we know more about what you think, we might be able to understand each other better. There are no right or wrong answers to these questions, so I'd just like you to put down what you think or really feel. I'll read each question while you follow along on your copy of the questions. Then you put down your answer. When you are ready I'll read the next question and we'll go on that way. Don't look at your neighbor's paper; just put down what you think. Be sure and answer every question. Are there any questions? (If so, they were answered.) O.K., let's begin.

The moral judgment test and the Proverbs test were administered in the school. Further data gathering involved contacting the parents of the subjects. The writer wished to determine the relations of adult constraint to abstractness-concreteness and to moral judgment. This required obtaining some measure of adult attitudes toward freedom and constraint.

RESULTS

The data to be presented in the following pages are divided into sections. There are a number of problems to be dealt with, and, for the purpose of clarity, they will be taken up in serial order. The first four sections of the results and discussion deal with responses to the moral judgment questions themselves, and the fifth with the relation of moral judgment to antecedent conditions. The results appear in the following order: (a) reliability of the moral judgment test; (b) intercorrelations of responses to moral judgment questions; (c) correlations of responses within moral judgment areas; (d) correlations of responses between moral judgment areas; and (e) relation of moral judgment responses to antecedent conditions.

Reliability of the Moral Judgment Test

The reliability of the 20-item moral judgment test, and also of the subscales, was not as high as that usually attained in educational tests. Subscale reliabilities were sometimes higher than the reliability of the whole scale, indicating that the various areas of moral judgment are not as closely knit as one would expect on the basis of Piaget's discussion. . . . Statistically, the relatively low reliability values of the subscales and of the whole scale set definite limits to the size of the interrelations that can appear among the so-called varieties or areas of moral judgment.

Intercorrelations of Responses to Moral Judgment Questions

Responses to each item on the 20-item test were correlated with responses to every other item at each of the four age levels—

a total of 760 correlations. Among this many correlations, where no relation of any sort actually existed, one would expect to find, by chance, 38 values significant at the .05 level and beyond. There actually were 294 positive correlations and 79 negative correlations significant at or beyond the .05 level of confidence. It seems clear that responses to moral judgment questions were positively correlated with one another to a far greater extent than one could expect by chance. A larger number of negative correlations were obtained than one could expect by chance. Some questions that seem, logically, to be positively related to other questions were apparently negatively correlated with other questions at one or more grade levels if judged in terms of the responses obtained.

Correlations of Responses Within Moral Judgment Areas

The area of immanent justice showed higher correlations between responses than other areas, but correlations in all areas of moral judgment were such that one is justified in talking about consistency within areas of moral judgment, especially when considering the reliability of the test items.

Correlations of Responses Between Moral Judgment Areas

A more basic problem is the determination of whether there is any consistent correlation between the type of response made in one area of moral judgment and responses made in each of the other areas of moral judgment. It is implicit in Piaget's theory (1950, pp. 106–107) that response tendencies in the various areas of moral judgment (excluding communicable responsibility) are positively related to one another. This is a testable proposition. . . . The correlations of response tendencies between moral judgment areas are presented in Table 1.

Twenty of the 40 correlations between areas of moral judgment were significant. . . . All of the significant correlations shown in

TABLE 1 Correlations of Responses between Moral Judgment Areas

	Moral Realism	Retribution vs. Restitution	Efficacy of Severe Punishment	Communicable Responsibility
Immanent Justice				
Grade 5	.12	.27**	.09	.13
Grade 7	.29**	.18*	.17	.06
Grade 9	.16*	.09	.14	.12
Grade 11	.07	.19*	.27**	.09
Moral Realism				
Grade 5		.23*	.34**	.30**
Grade 7		.33**	.32**	.18*
Grade 9		.20*	.33**	.15
Grade 11		.16	.10	.00
Retribution vs. Restitution				
Grade 5			.18*	.16
Grade 7			.33**	.18*
Grade 9			.30**	.00
Grade 11			.22*	.09
Efficacy of Severe Punishment				
Grade 5				.21*
Grade 7				.06
Grade 9				.08
Grade 11				.04

* Significant at the .05 level.
** Significant at the .01 level.

Table 1 were positive, except for the correlation of moral realism with communicable responsibility at grade 7, where the relation was negative, and the correlation of immanent justice with efficacy of severe punishment at grade 11, where the relation was curvilinear. In this curvilinear relation, both highly mature and highly immature sets of responses to the immanent justice question were positively related to mature responses to questions concerning the efficacy of severe punishment.

The intercorrelations among areas of moral judgment seem to show that mature moral judgments in the areas of moral realism, retribution vs. restitution, and efficacy of severe punishment were the most closely correlated with one another, that responses to questions concerning immanent justice were somewhat less closely correlated to responses in other areas of moral judgment, and that belief or nonbelief in communicable responsibility was even less closely related to other aspects of moral judgment.

Relation of Moral Judgment Responses to Antecedent Conditions

Piaget suggests that changes from immature to mature moral judgment result from changes in the amount of adult constraint and peer group cooperation experienced by the child and from qualitative changes in the child's method of thought. The child's level of development, for Piaget, is best predicted from chronological age. Most students of moral judgment since Piaget have found intelligence and social class to be related to the type of moral judgment made by the child. All of these variables, except peer cooperation, were measured in this study. Each significant relation between these variables and moral judgment responses is presented in Table 2.

From the data in Table 2 it seems that IQ and parental occupation were more closely related to moral judgment than were the other variables studied in the areas of moral realism, retribution vs. restitution, and the efficacy of severe punishment. In general, one can say that brightness, represented by IQ, was more closely related to the type of moral judgment used in those three areas

listed above than was any of the other variables measured in this study. Since parent's occupation and child's IQ were themselves positively correlated, it may well be that the correlations found between parent's occupation and the moral judgment of the child were merely reflections of differences due, basically, to IQ, rather than to cultural differences denoted by occupational level. The results of a determination of class differences in parental attitudes, discussed later in this study, seem to favor this position.

Immanent justice and communicable responsibility responses were less often significantly related to the antecedent condi-

TABLE 2 Significant Correlations of Antecedent Factors with Moral Judgment Responses

Factor	Immanent Justice	Moral Realism	Retribution vs. Restitution	Efficacy of Severe Punishment	Communicable Responsibility
IQ	.17(9)* .23(11)†	.34(5)* .36(7)* .31(9)* .20(11)*	.31(5)* .42(7)* .23(9)*	.24(5)* .30(7)* .30(9)*	
Parent Occupation	.21(9)‡ .22(11)‡	.21(7)‡ .17(9)‡ .16(11)‡	.23(5)‡ .23(7)‡	.18(5)‡	
Age (entire sample combined)	.35§	.35§	.25§	.26§	.12§
Abstractness	.29(9)¶ .26(11)¶	.25(7)¶	.26(7)¶	.34(9)¶ .46(11)‖	
Concreteness		.31(11)**		.36(7)††	.38(9)††
Parent Attitudes					
Ignoringness	.31(9)§§		.39(7)‡‡		.32(7)‡‡
Possessiveness	.53(11)§§				.32(7)‡‡ .52(11)‡‡
Dominativeness				.44(11)§§	.40(11)‡‡
Extremeness of Point of View	.32(11)§§			.40(9)§§	.29(7)§§ .40(11)§§

Note.—Grade level at which correlation was found is indicated in parentheses following each coefficient.
* High IQ positively related to mature judgment.
† IQ related to moral judgment curvilinearly; highest and lowest IQ made most mature responses.
‡ Higher parental occupation positively related to mature moral judgments.
§ Increasing age positively related to mature moral judgments.
¶ High abstractness positively related to mature moral judgments.
‖ High abstractness negatively related to mature moral judgments.
** High concreteness negatively related to mature moral judgments.
†† High concreteness positively related to mature moral judgments.
‡‡ High amounts of the parent attitude positively related to mature moral judgments.
§§ High amounts of the parent attitude negatively related to mature moral judgments.

tions of sex, parental occupation and IQ than were judgments concerning moral realism, retribution vs. restitution, and the efficacy of severe punishment. It may be that the higher degree of association between responses to moral judgment questions in the latter three areas is a result of the fact that response tendencies in these areas were related to the same antecedent conditions.

Chronological age was positively and significantly related in all areas of moral judgment—even "communicable responsibility" where, from Piaget's analysis, one would expect a negative relation in this age range. Age change was by no means saltatory, however—no sudden shifts in response tendencies were evident.

Out of 45 correlations of abstractness with moral judgment, six were significant. If abstractness is indicative of a freedom from egocentricity, one would expect high abstractness scores to be positively related to mature moral judgment. Five of the six significant correlations were in this direction. Only three of the 45 correlations of concreteness with moral judgment were significant. If concreteness is a manifestation of egocentricity, concreteness should be negatively correlated with mature moral judgment. The reverse held true in two of the three significant correlations.

If one scored the parent attitude scale in terms of the amount of ignoringness, possessiveness, and dominance expressed by the parents, one would expect, from Piaget's theory, to obtain the following results: belief in immanent justice, moral realism, retribution, and expiation, as opposed to restitution or reciprocity, and in the efficacy of severe punishment are all learned from the parents. If this is so, possessiveness and dominativeness should be positively correlated and ignoringness negatively correlated with acceptance of these beliefs. On the other hand, acceptance of communicable responsibility is usually learned from the peer group, which uses communicable responsibility as an evidence of group solidarity. Here it would seem probable that the ig-

nored child, more free to interact with peers, should show less mature moral judgment than the child of possessive or dominative parents who presumably would have somewhat fewer peer group contacts. Of the 45 correlations of the parent attitudes of expressed dominativeness, possessiveness, and ignoringness with the level of the child's moral judgment, eight were significant, seven of them in the direction predicted from the above discussion.

Extremeness of point of view on the part of the parent was correlated more frequently with the moral judgment of the child than were Shoben's (1949) subscales of ignoringness, possessiveness, or dominativeness. Extremeness of point of view was not significantly correlated with the type of parental response to any of the three subscales; there was no significant correlation, for instance, between the amount of dominativeness expressed and the number of extreme positions taken—so that the parent's extremeness of point of view seems, in its own right, to be a significant factor in relation to the child's level of moral judgment. The parents who more frequently take extreme points of view tended to have children who are immature in their moral judgments.

The existing significant correlations of parent attitude to moral judgment were not distributed randomly, but occurred most frequently in the areas of immanent justice and communicable responsibility, the very areas that showed few significant correlations with such variables as intelligence and parental occupation.

One can ask whether parent attitudes as measured here may be merely a reflection or indirect measure of social class differences in approach, either to child rearing or to answering questionnaires. The writer attempted to determine whether this might be the case. The responding parents had already been categorized into occupational groups. They were now divided into two larger groupings, those in classes I to III and those in classes V to VII of the Minnesota Occupational Scale. Their responses were divided into those above and below the median in amount of expressed dominativeness, possessiveness, and ignoringness and in the number of extreme points of view. A comparison of the attitudes of these two groups allows one to determine whether the obtained correlations between parent attitudes and moral judgment are actually a result of some occupational group bias in responses. An analysis of the data indicates that this was not the case. There were no significant differences in attitude between the two groups. Parent attitudes, as expressed on the Shoben scale, were not significantly related to parental occupation as measured by the Minnesota Occupational Scale (1950).

DISCUSSION

The primary purpose of this study was to determine the amount of association between responses to moral judgment questions.

The reliability of the test items, as a whole scale, seems to indicate in itself that responses concerning various aspects of moral judgment are related to one another empirically as well as logically, but not to as large an extent as one would expect from Piaget's analysis. Reliability did not change appreciably from one age to another. This seems to indicate (as do the actual correlations between responses) that moral judgment remains consistent in the amount of association from one area to another, contrary to what one might expect.

The reliability of subscales measuring specific areas of moral judgment was often somewhat higher than that of the total scale, suggesting a low association between areas but a higher association within areas. The reliability of the subscales seems rather high, in general, since each subscale consisted of only four items. Although high, when looked at in this fashion, subscale reliability was still so low that one cannot expect inter- and intra-moral judgment area correlations to be as high as they might be with a more

reliable test. It should be noted, however, that the whole scale reliability of this test is equal to that of some widely used measuring devices. . . .

The correlations of responses within moral judgment areas, like the reliability figures, seem to argue for quite considerable consistency within each area. This consistency may be due, in a large part, to the common correlations of items within an area to such things as intelligence and socioeconomic differences.

The results tend to support the idea that there is at least some consistency in response between areas. The correlations between responses in the five different areas of moral judgment indicate that judgments made regarding moral realism, retribution and expiation vs. restitution and reciprocity, and the efficacy of severe punishment were often significantly related to one another. Immanent justice was somewhat less frequently correlated positively and significantly with these three areas, though certainly there were far more positive and significant correlations than one would expect by chance. Communicable responsibility was less closely correlated with other areas of moral judgment; in fact, one of the four significant correlations of communicable responsibility with other areas of moral judgment was negative. The fact that the data were obtained separately at each of four age levels with quite similar results lends support through replication to the findings discussed above.

Piaget assumes, as a result of his logical analysis and of his findings, that response tendencies are similar in all areas of moral judgment (except for communicable responsibility), that there is what we would now call a general factor of moral judgment. The findings above were, in general, the results one would expect on the basis of Piaget's theoretical discussion, except that responses to questions involving communicable responsibility seemed largely unrelated, rather than negatively related, to responses in the other four moral judgment areas. With this exception the correlations were in the expected direction but were considerably lower than one would expect from Piaget's own work. The reliability data, as well as the interarea correlations of the responses, seem to show that what might be called a general factor of moral judgment was present, but with a rather low degree of saturation.

The second purpose of this study was to determine the relation of a number of variables to the type of moral judgment used by the subjects. A number of antecedent conditions were investigated. Some of these factors, such as sex, IQ, and parent occupation were touched on peripherally in Piaget's investigation and discussion of moral judgment. Other factors were discussed more comprehensively by Piaget. These were age (as a sign or indicator of the condition of the organism with reference to the next two factors, rather than a direct cause of change), egocentricity (which the writer attempted to measure, admittedly indirectly, through a test of abstractness-concreteness), and adult constraint. The latter two factors, interacting with one another and with peer group cooperation, were believed by Piaget to be directly causal in producing changes in beliefs concerning moral judgment. Here, too, the results obtained in this study must be judged in terms of the reliability of the measuring instruments.

Of those variables that were not discussed to any extent by Piaget, IQ was clearly the most significant in its relation to responses concerning moral realism, retribution and expiation vs. restitution and reciprocity, and the efficacy of severe punishment. Sex of subjects and parent occupation of subjects also showed a considerable number of significant correlations with responses in these three moral judgment areas. Immanent justice seemed less closely related, and communicable responsibility seemed essentially unrelated to this group of variables.

Age was correlated with the type of response made in all five areas. One would expect on the basis of Piaget's work that increasing age is positively correlated with more mature moral judgment in all areas except that of communicable responsibility, where an increase in peer group solidarity might well cause a greater frequency of immature responses as age increased. Contrary to Piaget's theory, even communicable responsibility showed a very low but significant positive correlation between age and mature moral judgment. Within the age groups studied there was certainly no evidence for any large, sudden change in beliefs concerning moral judgment.

Parent attitudes, as expressed on questionnaire reponses, most often showed significant correlations with responses to questions concerning communicable responsibility and immanent justice. These are the very areas that were less closely correlated with the first group of antecedent conditions. Abstractness and concreteness were related to moral judgment in the direction predicted by Piaget, but perhaps because abstractness is itself related to IQ. None of these variables was closely and consistently related to moral judgment to the extent that it accounted for the major portion of the variance, perhaps because the test of moral judgment was itself less reliable than one would desire.

This writer's general conclusions regarding these antecedent conditions are that IQ and chronological age were the variables most closely correlated to the type of response made with reference to moral realism, retribution and expiation vs. restitution and reciprocity, and the efficacy of severe punishment. Age and to some extent, IQ and parent attitudes, seemed to be correlated with responses to immanent justice items. Only parent attitude items seemed correlated to any extent with type of response made to questions involving communicable responsibility.

This study provided a number of moral judgment questions of known reliability and also information about their relation to one another and to various antecedent conditions. The questions had an additional value in that they evoked a very high degree of interest among subjects within the age groups studied.

It seems to this writer that the next step in research is to develop a more reliable moral judgment test and then to determine the relation of the various aspects of moral judgment to behavior. All the studies of moral judgment done since Piaget's time have limited themselves to testing some aspect of his theory. Knowledge of an individual's beliefs concerning the various areas of moral judgment might have practical as well as theoretical importance. This question, whether an understanding of any individual's concepts of moral judgment has any practical application, is one that has not yet been asked, much less answered. This is an area in which further research may fill a definite gap in our knowledge.

REFERENCES

Minnesota scale for paternal occupations. University of Minnesota Press, 1950.

Piaget, J. *The moral judgment of the child.* New York: Harcourt, Brace, 1932.

Piaget, J. *The psychology of intelligence.* New York: Harcourt, Brace, 1950.

Shoben, E. J., Jr. The assessment of parental attitudes in relation to child adjustment. *Genetic Psychology Monograph,* 1949, **39,** 101–148.

CHAPTER NINE
PARANATAL INFLUENCES

Paranatal influences affect the embryo and foetus before birth and the infant during birth; maternal state, for example, has profound influences on foetal development. In addition, the time of birth (premature or full term) deeply affects the infant's survival and later development, and the type of delivery he endures has lasting results.

The first selection considers relations between the mother's emotional state during pregnancy, infant health, and ease of delivery. Davids, DeVault, and Talmadge measured the stated anxiety of women during pregnancy and shortly after their delivery. Mothers who expressed high anxiety about pregnancy were more likely to experience difficult delivery and to produce children with abnormalities than were women who expressed less anxiety about pregnancy. The authors suggest that this effect comes not because the mothers are aware that they are going to produce abnormal children but because delivery difficulties are caused by the mother's emotional state.

When can the foetus first begin to interact with the outside world? Must he wait until birth before sampling sounds? Bernard and Sontag studied foetal sensitivity to sounds during the eighth and ninth months of pregnancy. They showed that the foetus reacts to loud sounds during this time and that the results cannot be attributed to maternal hormonal reactions or maternal muscle movements. They believe that the foetus hears.

Prematurity results in lower birth weight. Does the smaller child have an easier time because he experiences less trauma passing through the birth canal? Or does his apparent impatience lead to later physical and intellectual problems? The third study in this section shows that the effects of prematurity are almost always bad; there is a strong relation between the infant's size at birth and his later development. Smaller infants experience more physical and motor difficulties, but in particular they show abnormal intellectual development.

Reliable and valid measures of infant trauma are important for diagnosis and later treatment. The final article presents five tests which reliably differentiated groups of traumatized infants from their more normal peers. The authors measured pain thresholds, vision, maturation, irritability, and rated the infant's muscle tension. All the tests differentiated those infants traumatized at birth (by instruments, breach delivery, or oxygen loss) from normal babies. In addition to differentiating traumatized and normal neonates, they found racial differences between black and white infants on the tests of maturation and vision. The black babies were more advanced.

32 | Anxiety, Pregnancy, and Childbirth Abnormalities

ANTHONY DAVIDS
SPENCER DeVAULT
MAX TALMADGE

Are mothers who confess anxiety about their pregnancies more likely to produce abnormal babies at birth? The present study compared measures of manifest anxiety obtained during pregnancy and following childbirth; the authors related these measures to delivery room experiences. In two independent samples of clinic patients, women who later experienced difficulties in the delivery room or gave birth to children with abnormalities obtained significantly higher scores on an anxiety scale than did women who had a "normal" delivery. The retest measures showed that all women produced lower manifest anxiety scores following delivery; however, anxiety scores remained higher for the women who experienced difficulties during labor or produced abnormal children. There is no way of knowing (from these data) if the delivery problems resulted from the mother's anxiety or whether she experienced anxiety because her body "knew" she would experience difficulty. The authors suggest that the relation is between anxiety and later difficulties. This is a reasonable hypothesis; we know that maternal state can affect the baby during his prenatal period.

Since the development of a rather simple instrument for assessing manifest anxiety (Taylor, 1953), there has been an epidemic of psychological studies concerned with the role of anxiety in a wide range of experimental situations. Here, we will not attempt to survey this vast literature. We wish merely to point out that these studies of anxiety have been conducted mainly in laboratory and academic research settings, and little use has been made of the instrument in clinical or "real life" situations. . . .

It seems, then, that the Manifest Anxiety Scale has demonstrated utility as a research instrument and has generated considerable interesting research. However, since most personality theorists place great emphasis on anxiety as a motivating factor in life adjustment, and since it is a well established fact that anxiety plays a crucial role in the formation of psychopathology, it seems worthwhile to conduct further research on the clinical utility of this objective instrument for assessing manifest anxiety.

At present, there appears to be increasing research interest in the effects of anxiety and stress on the psychological course of pregnancy and the influence that emotional turmoil during pregnancy may have on the subsequent adjustment of the offspring. In a study of physical and mental handicaps following disturbed pregnancy, Stott (1957)

Adapted from Anxiety, pregnancy, and childbirth abnormalities. *Journal of Consulting Psychology*, 1961, **25**(1), 74-77. Copyright © 1961 by the American Psychological Association, and reproduced by permission.

suggested that prenatal influences were to blame. In studying a group of mentally defective children, he found that in a large proportion of the cases there had been marked emotional stress during pregnancy, as a result of family conflicts and personal unhappiness. In a recently reported study of the influence of prenatal maternal anxiety on emotionality in rats, Thompson (1957) tested and confirmed the hypothesis that "emotional trauma undergone by female rats during pregnancy can affect the emotional characteristics of the offspring."

The plan of the research program from which the present report derives is to use a variety of psychological procedures to study emotional factors in pregnant women. This report, however, is concerned specifically with findings obtained from the MAS [Manifest Anxiety Scale] administered to a group of women during pregnancy and readministered soon after delivery of their children.

METHOD

The subjects of this investigation were 48 pregnant women who were studied at the clinic of the Providence Lying-in Hospital. They are a representative sample of a larger group of women who were studied in the course of a pilot study conducted by a team of medical and scientific investigators who were engaged in a collaborative project on perinatal factors in child development. The women were seen for individual psychological testing during the course of a routine visit to the clinic, which in most cases was at approximately the seventh month of pregnancy. Of the group of 48 women, 20 returned for a routine physical checkup at approximately 6 weeks following childbirth, while the other 28 women failed to return for this scheduled hospital visit. The 20 patients who were seen twice will be labeled Group I, and the 28 women who were seen only during pregnancy constitute Group II.

In the course of the large scale investigation, voluminous data were gathered for each patient. As part of the assessment, they were administered a comprehensive battery of psychological tests. Included in this assessment procedure was the 50-item MAS, which is the focus of the present report. In Group I, the MAS was administered both during and following pregnancy, while in Group II it was administered only during pregnancy. On the basis of the official hospital records, it was possible to classify each patient's delivery room record as "normal" or as indicating some "abnormality or complication." In Group I, there were 13 patients in the normal category and 7 patients in the abnormal category. In Group II, the subdivisions were 12 normal deliveries and 16 with abnormalities or complications.

The patients in both groups were of "normal" intelligence. As measured by the Wechsler-Bellevue Intelligence Scale, the mean IQ in Group I was 101 and the mean IQ in Group II was 95. Moreover, in both groups the mean age was 25 years and ranged from 17 to 40 years. Thus, although no attempt was made to match the patients in the two groups, it happened that the groups were of very similar age and IQ, and in regard to these two variables it seems probable that they are representative of pregnant women who are being studied at various clinics throughout the country.

RESULTS AND DISCUSSION

Now let us consider the findings from the MAS. In Group I, on the first testing, the normal subgroup obtained a mean manifest anxiety score of 16.5, which is significantly lower ($t = 2.19$, $p = .05$) than the mean of 23.5 in the abnormal subgroup. Examination of the ranges of the manifest anxiety scores in the two subgroups further evidences the greater anxiety in the abnormal group, with their scores ranging from 14 to 37, as compared with scores ranging from 8 to 26 in the normal group. Thus, both the mean scores and the spread of the individual scores reveal the abnormal delivery group to have been relatively high on manifest anxiety according to their own avowal of feelings and symptoms during pregnancy. In analyzing the results from the second testing of the patients in Group I, it is noteworthy that the level of manifest anxiety decreased in both subgroups following pregnancy, with a mean of 15 in the normal subgroup and a mean of 18.3 in the abnormal subgroup. Although the group that experienced difficult deliveries continued to score higher on manifest anxiety than did the group who had normal delivery room experiences, the nonsignificant difference ($t = .70$) was not as pronounced as it was when the women were in a state of pregnancy.

The findings in regard to manifest anxiety in Group II were remarkably similar to those obtained in Group I. In this second group of patients, the mean MAS score in the normal subgroup was 16, which is significantly lower ($t = 2.39$, $p = .05$) than the mean score of 23.6 in the abnormal subgroup. Again, the range of MAS scores from 4 to 30 in the normal subgroup was noticeably lower than the range from 12 to 38 in the abnormal subgroup. Thus, in both samples studied in this research, it was found that women who were later to experience complications in delivery or were to give birth to children with abnormalities tended to report a relatively high amount of disturbing anxiety while they were pregnant.

In considering these findings, it should be emphasized that at present we have no information regarding the causes or reasons underlying the higher MAS scores in the abnormal subgroup. One possibility is that the obstetricians may have anticipated abnormalities or complications and may have conveyed this information to the patients. However, this possibility does not seem too likely, as for the majority of these patients the psychological assessment was conducted during their first visit to the clinic. That is, these women did not have private obstetricians who followed their medical progress throughout the pregnancy, but were being seen for their first medical examination at a rather late stage of their pregnancy. Future examination of sociological, medical, and past history data on these clinic patients may provide some understanding of causative factors, and greater understanding in this regard may well come from comparisons of clinic and private patients. One other point that should be made at this time, however, is that there was no difference between the two subgroups in regard to the number of patients for whom this was the first delivery. The mean number of previous pregnancies and previous deliveries was practically identical in the normal and abnormal subgroups.

It is also interesting to note that the mean MAS scores of about 16, obtained in the normal subgroups both during and after pregnancy, are very similar to the mean MAS scores obtained previously in relatively large samples of female college undergraduates (Smith, Powell & Ross, 1955). The present findings suggest, therefore, that, as a group, pregnant women who will later experience normal childbirth do not differ from normal nonpregnant college females in the avowal of manifest anxiety, but pregnant women who are likely to experience childbirth abnormalities later are significantly higher on manifest anxiety than are other groups of pregnant and nonpregnant women.

The results of this preliminary study, which should be regarded as tentative and in need of further independent confirmation, are quite encouraging. In addition to demonstrating the utility of the MAS in this clinical setting, the positive findings obtained with this objective instrument suggest that even more fruitful results may be obtained through use of projective techniques designed to uncover indices of emotional factors operating at deeper levels in the personality. It is hoped that the intensive program of investigation we have embarked upon will eventually lead to greater psychological understanding of complex relations between maternal psychodynamics during pregnancy and the process of child development.

REFERENCES

Smith, W., Powell, Elizabeth K., & Ross, R. Manifest anxiety and food aversions. *Journal of Abnormal and Social Psychology,* 1955, **50,** 101–104.

Stott, D. H. Physical and mental handicaps following a disturbed pregnancy. *Lancet,* 1957, **1,** 1006–1012.

Taylor, Janet A. A personality scale of manifest anxiety. *Journal of Abnormal and Social Psychology,* 1953, **48,** 285–290.

Thompson, W. R. Influence of prenatal maternal anxiety on emotionality in young rats. *Science,* 1957, **125,** 698–699.

33 | Fetal Reactivity to Sound

JACK BERNARD
LESTER W. SONTAG

The foetus cannot see or feel environmental events; however, the present study shows that external sounds of high intensity can stimulate him. Whether this stimulation occurs through hearing or touch is an open question, but the foetus does react to sounds during the last two months of pregnancy. The authors suggest four alternative explanations of their findings: (1) that maternal hormonal changes affect the foetus, (2) that the mother is anticipating stimulation and triggering hormonal responses which affect the foetus, (3) that the foetus is being mechanically stimulated by maternal tension, and (4) that the cardiac response is directly related to the stimulus. However, the authors found that (1) maternal hormone changes could not be the cause because the time relations were wrong. They also presented false trials, in which the mother anticipated a tone that did not come, and found that (2) maternal anticipation produced no cardiac response in the foetus. And (3) the mothers did not tense (according to their own reports), so that this seems an unlikely explanation. The only remaining possibility was that (4) the foetus heard the sound or that he was sensitive to pressure through touch.

In 1925 Peiper, using a "loud and shrill" automobile horn as the stimulus and fetal movement as the index of reactivity, obtained some fetal responses, but cautiously concluded that the results of his experiment were ambiguous. More recently Sontag and Wallace (1934, 1936) and Sontag and Richards (1938) have produced evidence that the fetus in utero is responsive to a 120-cycle vibratory stimulation applied to the maternal abdomen, responding by cardio-acceleration and by muscular activity in a way which is suggestive of a fetal startle pattern.

In this connection, it is pertinent to consider the fact that infants born prematurely are responsive to sound stimulation. It may be assumed, therefore, that the seven- or eight-month fetus possesses the necessary equipment for hearing. But, within the uterine environment, does the fetus hear?

The possibility that the human fetus in utero is capable of receiving and responding to stimulation, which outside of the mother's abdomen is perceived as sound, opens an intriguing field of inquiry. When the vibratory stimulus used is evaluated as sound stimulation and calibrated for its qualities, such as tonal range and intensity, do we detect a differential response in the fetus in utero? Are sounds in the everyday external environment, such as music, the dropping of heavy objects, the sound of automobile horns, and so on, perceived by the fetus? How does the fetus' sensitivity to vibratory stimulation change with age? Another crucial question—and one which previous

Adapted from Fetal reactivity to sound. *Journal of Genetic Psychology*, 1947, **70**, 205–210.

studies involving vibratory stimulation have failed to settle—is this: To be effective in arousing fetal response, must vibratory stimulation be applied directly to the mother's abdomen, that is, contiguous to the tissue of the mother's body? Or will vibration transmitted through air space be further transmitted through the mother's body to the fetus?

In an attempt to answer some of these questions, the following procedures were initiated.

PROCEDURE

Our experimental procedure involved the weekly presentation of tonal stimulation during the last two and a half months of pregnancy. The tones, relatively pure in character, were generated by a Jackson Audio Frequency Oscillator, amplified by a Setchell-Carlson Amplifier Model 13-B, and brought to the maternal abdomen through a Utah G8P speaker resting on a rubber baffle centered over the head region of the fetus. Thus any vibratory stimulus reaching the fetus would have to pass through an air space and could not be interpreted as being conducted through physical contact with the mother's body.

Fetal cardiac change was used as an index of fetal reactivity. Fetal heart sounds were picked up by means of a Brush microphone strapped to the maternal abdomen at the point where the sound was loudest, suitably amplified, and recorded by means of an ink-writer on a moving tape. A switch broke the microphone circuit as it made the speaker circuit, thus avoiding damage to the recording equipment.

During the weekly experimental sessions, each of which involved the presentation of approximately 10 tonal stimulations, the subjects rested in bed in a relatively soundproof room which the experimenter entered only for the purpose of adjusting the microphone. The frequencies used ranged from 20 to 12,000 dv/sec, and were varied systematically. Each stimulation

lasted five seconds and was preceded by a warning about three seconds before. In the earliest work this warning was verbal; later a small signal lamp was substituted. In the present analysis, we shall consider only frequencies of 6,000 dv/sec and lower, as intensity fell off rapidly above that point with our present apparatus.

RESULTS

Ten-beat intervals were marked off on the records in both directions from the stimulation, measured as to length, and converted by means of a table to beats per minute. This analysis is therefore in terms of beats per minute of 10-beat samples. The 10-beat periods were continuous.

Figure 1 presents three individual curves for Subjects F, H, and I, and a composite curve for 73 stimulations conducted on these three subjects plus a few observations on a fourth subject, Subject J, who had too few stimulation sessions to permit treating her individual data statistically. It will be seen in each of these curves that a high fetal cardiac rate obtains shortly after stimulation. The critical ratio of the difference between the means of the five consecutive 10-beat prestimulation intervals and the three consecutive poststimulation intervals (when the effect of the stimulation was at its height) was highly significant in the case of each subject.

DISCUSSION

Four explanations of the phenomenon of cardio-acceleration visible in each of the curves appear plausible. We shall discuss each of these in turn.

1. Could the observed cardio-acceleratory response of the fetus be due to maternal stimulation with resultant humoral changes in the mother, which are then passed on through the placenta to the fetus to serve as a secondary stimulus? The four graphs in Figure 1 show that the cardio-

acceleratory effect of the stimulation reaches maximum in the second 10-beat period following stimulation, or about 11 seconds after the onset of stimulation. The rapidity of this response eliminates the possibility of its being a maternal stimulus transmitted secondarily to the fetus through passage of newly liberated blood components into the fetal circulation. Any endocrine or other products released into the mother's blood stream as a response to stimulation could not possibly be circulated to the placenta and through the fetal circulation in so little time.

2. If the mother knew far enough in advance just when the stimulation was coming, is it conceivable that her emotional response might occur early enough to permit humoral changes to reach the fetal circulation? To test this possibility, we used suggestion of stimulation during 15 of the experimental sessions. On these occasions warning of impending stimulation was

given, but no tone sounded. There was no significant change in fetal heart rate after such "suggestions." This fact does not rule out the possibility of a *delayed* fetal cardio-acceleration due to the process cited above, but it does eliminate the possibility that the cardio-acceleratory effect as demonstrated in this study is the result of humoral changes in the maternal organism.

3. Could the observed fetal cardio-acceleration be the result of mechanical stimulation caused by tensing abdominal muscles as part of a maternal startle response to the stimulation? No overt startle responses on the part of the mothers were noted during the study, and no mother reported being startled by the sound. Ample time was allowed to permit relaxation before each stimulation, and warning of impending stimulation kept the sound from being unexpected. In addition, the baffle concentrated the sound on the maternal abdomen and reduced the intensity

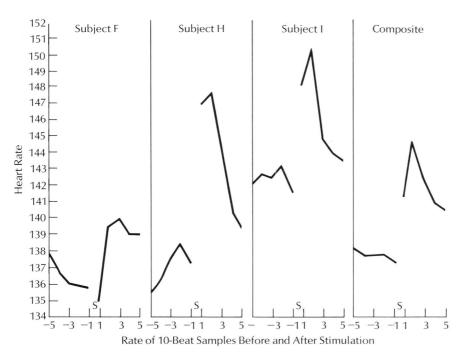

FIGURE 1 Fetal heart rate in three individual subjects and as a group before and after tone stimulation.

reaching the maternal ear. These facts make it appear unlikely that the fetal response stems from *any* maternal reaction, either physical or chemical.

4. Finally, is the cardio-acceleratory response of the fetus a direct response to a stimulus which, evaluated externally as sound, is transmitted to the fetus via the maternal tissues and/or fluids? In the light of the above discussion, this appears to be the logical explanation of the observed results.

The cardio-acceleratory effect shown in the curves is distributed over the full range of frequencies used, and is not the property of any narrow band. The problem of mapping the limits of fetal tonal sensitivity is therefore opened for future investigation.

By referring to Figure 1 it will be seen that the cardio-deceleration precedes cardio-acceleration for Subject *F*. This is in contrast to the direct acceleration in the other curves and is worth comment. Sontag and Richards (1938, p. 49) have interpreted fetal cardio-acceleration following vibratory stimulation as an aspect of a fetal startle response. It is well known that the cardiac response in the human adult startle pattern involves a momentary deceleration followed by acceleration. It is possible that the same pattern obtains in the fetus, the deceleration in Subjects *H* and *I* taking place during the five-second stimulation period and thus not visible in our records, while for some reason not now apparent the deceleration in Subject *F* lasted beyond the stimulation period. This is a point which requires further investigation.

CONCLUSION

The experimental data presented here indicate that the human fetus in utero is capable of perceiving a wide range of tones. This tone sensitivity is such that tones produced by an amplifier loud-speaker arrangement and transmitted through the air to the mother's abdomen elicit a fetal response. Whether such tonal perception is accomplished by means of the fetal auditory apparatus or represents a vibratory perception sense of other parts of the body, has not been established. It may or may not be proper to speak of "fetal hearing." Response to tonal stimulation is expressed in sharp body movements and cardiac acceleration.

REFERENCES

Peiper, A., "Sinnesempfindungen des Kindes vor seiner Geburt," *Monatschrift für Kinderheilkunde,* 1925, **29,** 236–241.

Sontag, L. W., & Wallace, R. I. "Preliminary Report of the Fels Fund: A Study of Fetal Activity," *American Journal of Diseases of Children,* 1934, **48,** 1050–1057.

Sontag, L. W., & Wallace, R. I. "Changes in the Heart Rate of the Human Fetal Heart in Response to Vibratory Stimuli," *American Journal of Diseases of Children,* 1936, **51,** 583–589.

Sontag, L. W., & Richards, T. W. "Studies in Fetal Behavior: I. Fetal Heart Rate as a Behavioral Indicator," *Child Development Monographs,* 1938, Vol. 3, No. 4.

34 | Sequelae of Premature Birth

LULA O. LUBCHENCO
FREDERICK A. HORNER
LINDA H. REED
IVAN E. HIX, Jr.

DAVID METCALF
RUTH COHIG
HELEN C. ELLIOTT
MARGARET BOURG

Are premature babies more likely to have physical and intellectual defects later in their lives or do they develop along the same lines as their more patient peers? Lubchenco et al. showed that very premature infants of low birth weight are much more likely to experience physical and intellectual difficulties than are premature infants only slightly underweight. Both these groups of premature infants experience more difficulties than do normal babies.

This study also shows the blunders that can occur when we try to help the premature infant survive. Common medical practice during the period of this study was to saturate the air around a premature infant with high concentrations of oxygen, causing retrolental fibroplasis (a bursting of the tiny capillaries to the retina), which leads to blindness. This practice has been stopped in every hospital in the world; however, it makes one wonder what other errors we may be committing with our "help" to the premature infant.

The main difficulty in interpreting these data stems from the nonrandom sampling of infants seen at the clinic. There is no way of knowing whether the problems are the result of their social, economic, and genetic background. However, the size of the effects and their relation to birth weight strongly indicate that, even given the sampling bias, the authors' main conclusions are correct.

Until recently, it was considered that premature infants might have an increased possibility of being handicapped but that the total number of such involved children was likely to be small and the severity of handicaps relatively mild or of limited duration. Recent reports (Drillien, 1959; Dann, Levine & New, 1958; Knobloch, Rider, Harper & Pasamanick, 1956) dealing with the growth and development of prematurely born children give an unfavorable prognosis for central nervous system growth.

Adapted from Sequelae of premature birth. *American Journal of Diseases of Children*, 1963, **106,** 101–115.

Since the mid-1950's, reports on the incidence of handicaps found in premature infants show an increased number of children to be abnormal. The predominant type of defect described appears to vary with the experience of the authors. For example, Dann et al. (1958) found a lowering of the intelligence quotient in 44% of the children that they were able to follow, a high incidence of ophthalmologic defects, but very few physical defects except delay in attaining normal stature. Drillien (1959) noted intellectual, behavioral, and physical defects in more than 60% of her group of infants.

This paper presents a detailed survey of abnormalities in premature infants of low birth weights studied approximately ten years after their birth and confirms the discouraging reports of a high incidence of physical and mental defects.

SUBJECTS AND METHODS OF STUDY

All surviving infants with birth weights of 1500 gm (3 lb 4 oz) or less, born between July 1, 1947 and July 1, 1950 (the first three years of the Premature Infant Center's operation) and admitted to Colorado General Hospital Premature Infant Center, were included for study. Admissions included infants born in Colorado General Hospital, as well as those born elsewhere and transferred to the Premature Infant Center. During this time, a total of 187 infants were admitted of whom 87 died in the neonatal period while 6 succumbed in the subsequent 11 months. The 94 who survived the first year of life constituted the sample to be followed.

The examination included medical and neurological examinations, psychological testing, electroencephalography, ophthalmological examination, and evaluation of the social situation of the families of the patients. The children returned to the Out Patient Department of the Colorado General Hospital for these examinations.

Of the 94 children who constituted the group to be re-evaluated at approximately ten years of age, 63 were available for follow-up examinations. Twelve children had been placed in adoptive homes, ten could not be located but pertinent information on them was present in the medical records, and nine children were lost to the study.

Children who had recently been examined in the Out Patient Department at Colorado General Hospital were included in the study without necessarily returning for re-examination. Ten children who were not available at ten years of age had been

examined previously in the various clinics in the Out Patient Department, and adequate data for study were available in their medical records. Eight were mentally retarded, had convulsions and/or residual retrolental fibroplasia. Two children were well at the time of their last evaluation. No attempts were made to locate the 12 children placed in adoptive homes. There was hesitation on the part of the investigators and the social agencies to identify these children and concern about the agencies' role ten years later in providing special services to these families if handicaps were disclosed.

Of the 63 children examined, 20 had no handicap, 31 showed a central nervous system disorder, 25 were slow learners or retarded, having IQs of 89 or less, and 20 had serious eye defects. Of the 20 children classified as normal, some had relatively minor physical findings, such as myopia, strabismus, or behavioral problems of minor degree. One child, though "normal" in all respects, was considerably below the intellectual level of parents and siblings.

The major positive findings were related to the central nervous system and the eyes—43 of the 63 children (68%) available for follow-up examination exhibited such handicaps. Multiple handicaps were present in 26 of the 43 children. In the main, the central nervous system lesions consisted of spastic diplegia and intellectual retardation.

Other characteristics peculiar to this group of children were smallness of stature, plus a variety of social and emotional problems related to the rearing of a handicapped child. Perinatal difficulties were frequent in the histories of these children.

Intellectual Status

The full scale IQ was determined from administration of the Wechsler Intelligence Scale for Children (WISC). The IQ of children blind from retrolental fibroplasia was obtained from the verbal items only. Twenty-five of the 60 children tested (42%) had

IQs below 90 (and 16 of these IQs below 49). There were indications that many of the children who had intelligence quotients above 90 also had some handicap in their intellectual functioning. Twenty of the 35 children with normal intelligence were found to have experienced difficulties in their schooling. Reading difficulties, problems with numbers, or difficulty in learning were voluntarily cited by the parents of these children. Eleven children repeated one or more of the first three grades. Four others were not enrolled in kindergarten until they were six years old. Three had received speech therapy, and three others were considered emotionally disturbed.

Visual Problems

Permanent visual impairment due to retrolental fibroplasia was found in 16 children. Seven of these 16 children were blind and two were in sight-saving classes.

The use of liberal amounts of oxygen in the incubators of premature infants, was a routine practice during the years when these children were hospitalized. The flow meters were set routinely at five liters of oxygen per minute in order to produce a concentration of approximately 60% in the Gordon Armstrong type incubators. Oxygen administration was continued for a minimum of three weeks. Only seven infants received less than 21 days of oxygen, and there were three in whom the duration of oxygen administration was unknown.

Eye disorders, other than retrolental fibroplasia, were found in three children. Two had traumatic retinal detachments not due to retrolental fibroplasia, and one had evidence of macular degeneration. There was an unusual incidence of myopia and strabismus in the remainder of the 44 children—19 of these children were so affected. In summary, 19 of the 63 children had severe visual defects and 19 others had minor problems—an over-all visual morbidity of 60%.

Neurological Deficits

Spastic diplegia was the most frequently encountered central nervous system disturbance and was present in 22 of the 30 children with central nervous system lesions. A variety of other conditions was noted including mongolism, premature closure of the sagittal sutures, arrested hydrocephaly, and microcephaly.

The developmental histories in the children with spastic diplegia showed striking similarities. There was usually a delay in sitting, standing, and walking. After walking was established, it was poorly coordinated; the children were noted to be clumsy and had a tendency to walk on the toes. Muscle tone and coordination improved to near normalcy at school age.

Examination in all cases revealed bilateral symmetrical increase in muscle tone, which was only slightly more than normal in the upper extremities but much greater in the lower extremities. This increased tone frequently produced heel-cord shortening and pes cavus. There was very little, if any, weakness in the upper extremities, while weakness in the lower extremities in an elective distribution was readily demonstrable. The deep tendon reflexes of the upper extremities were normal or minimally increased, while those of the lower extremities were markedly hyperactive at both knee and ankle with sustained and unsustained ankle clonus frequently being present. Athetosis was not present, and no instance of clinical kernicterus was discovered.

Electroencephalograms

The incidence of abnormal electroencephalographic findings in these children was high—60% of the records were abnormal (33/55). This is in contrast to the incidence of abnormal electroencephalograms (6%) found in full-term infants followed in the Child Research Council. In 13 children, the electroencephalograms revealed only mild aberrations.

The most frequently observed disturbances were seizure discharges, disorganization of the record and 6 and 14 per second spikes. There were eight children with seizure discharges. Two of the eight children (patients 55 and 59) were considered to be entirely normal except for electroencephalographic abnormalities. Evidence of neurologic disease was noted in the other six children; only one of these had convulsions. Disorganization of the record was present most frequently in the children with severe intellectual retardation and usually was accompanied by other abnormalities such as focal or generalized slow waves and spikes.

There were 12 children who showed 6 and 14 per second spikes during sleep. The records of six contained no abnormality other than the 6 and 14 per second spikes. However, only half of the children with normal electroencephalograms (11/22) slept during the examination. The presence of 6 and 14 per second spikes was found predominantly in children with normal intelligence. There was no significant correlation between 6 and 14 per second spikes and emotional or behavioral problems in the children.

Two of the seven blind children in this series showed occipital spikes, but two children with normal vision and one with partial sight also had occipital spikes in their electroencephalographic records. Disruption of alpha activity was noted in three additional blind children. Only one blind child had a normal electroencephalogram. Four of the sighted children with retrolental fibroplasia (stages I–IV) had disorganization of their records, but acceptable alpha activity was present in all but one. One child with normal vision showed no alpha rhythm.

MATERNAL FACTORS AND NEONATAL COURSE

A review of perinatal events in the maternal and infant records revealed considerable pathology both in the mother prior to delivery and in the infant following birth.

Sixty-two per cent of the deliveries were complicated. Vaginal bleeding and premature rupture of the membranes were the most frequent obstetrical problems encountered. Multiple pregnancies, breech delivery, and prolonged labor were next in frequency and often were associated with the above complications. There was no correlation between obstetrical problems and the weight of the infant.

Illnesses in the infants were primarily respiratory difficulties and infection. Unlike obstetrical complications, their distribution was closely related to birth weight. The smaller the baby, the more frequent was illness present and the more severe was the disease process. Only five out of 23 infants with birth weights less than 1200 gm (2 lb 10 oz) had uneventful nursery courses, while one-half (20/40) of those with birth weights over 1200 gm were free of illness. Infants having a description of apneic periods (intervals of not breathing) in their records were reviewed for handicaps of intelligence or neurological disease. Of the nine infants having apnea, only two were seriously handicapped, four had normal intelligence, and three were normal.

Severity of Handicaps

To determine whether there was a relationship between the birth weight and the occurrence of handicaps later in life the following correlation was made: The severity of handicaps was defined and classified arbitrarily into four categories and then plotted according to birth weight. The severity of the handicaps at ten years of age in those children whose birth weights were below 1200 gm was significantly greater than in those with birth weights above 1200 gm. Only two of the 23 infants with birth weights of 1200 gm or less were considered normal, while 18 of the 40 with birth weights over 1200 gm were normal.

It may be argued that mild handicaps are not incapacitating to the child and should be disregarded. If these children are considered normal, half of the children in this study are still unquestionably handicapped. Rather than minimize the findings or continue to excuse the premature infant for subnormal functioning, all abnormalities, whether or not they were serious handicaps, were reported.

Physical Growth

The physical growth of the children was evaluated by plotting their heights and weights on the growth charts adapted from the Harvard School of Public Health and the Iowa Child Welfare Research Station Data. There were significantly smaller children among this group of premature children than in the general population. Forty-one percent of the prematures were below the tenth percentile for weight, and 47% were below the tenth percentile for height.

Social Situation

During the time when the children were admitted to the Premature Infant Center, all of the families were interviewed by a social service worker in order to evaluate social problems and to offer practical assistance when needed.

In the present study, approximately ten years later, the interviews were aimed toward finding out the effect on the families of having a premature infant. It was apparent that the rearing of a handicapped child, especially one with retrolental fibroplasia, added a strain to the adjustment of these families. Fourteen of the 63 sets of parents continued case work services after the children were discharged from the hospital. A few required intensive medical and social work counseling to make an adequate adjustment to the serious defects present in their children.

In general, by the time the premature infants reached ten years of age, most of the problems encountered by parents in rearing a seriously handicapped child were resolved or accepted. However, where the premature infants' handicaps were mild or unsuspected, many unresolved problems and anxieties persisted. This was particularly true of parents whose children had difficulty in learning. These children were considered normal throughout early childhood and only at school age were the intellectual deficits evident. It was necessary in several of these families to offer case work services as part of the follow-up study.

A few dramatic marital situations occurred in which the premature infants were purported to be the factors leading to divorce of the parents. However, the divorce rate for the entire group of premature infants' families was no greater than that in the general population.

COMMENT

The foregoing data leave little doubt about the high incidence of residual handicaps in small premature infants born between 1947 and 1950 and cared for in the Premature Infant Center in Colorado. These handicaps include visual defects primarily due to retrolental fibroplasia, brain damage, retarded growth, and social and emotional problems.

It has become clear that there is a significant correlation between birth weight and the presence of handicapping conditions later in life. The relationship is found for total or individual handicaps. For instance, there is also a greater incidence of individual problems such as retrolental fibroplasia, and most of the blind children were in the weight group below 1200 gm. The incidence of retarded children was greater, and there were more children with spastic diplegia and other neurological lesions in the smaller weight group. The incidence of difficulties in the neonatal period are more frequent and severe in infants weighing less than 1200 gm than in infants weighing more than 1200 gm at birth. Whatever the basic problem is in the premature infant which enhances the development of central nervous system damage, it is associated with the degree of immaturity as determined by birth weight. The poor outcome of the small premature infants is in general a depressing revelation, but the study did reveal some positive values.

One of the benefits of this study was the realization that infants diagnosed as having spastic diplegia improve in their physical abilities during the succeeding years and that many are nearly asymptomatic by school age. This knowledge was helpful in predicting the course of the disease and in interpreting the outcome of new cases to the parents. Another benefit of this study was the observation that parents with severely handicapped children responded well to social service and medical counseling. The early recognition of the severe defect was thought to be an important factor in the acceptance of counseling by the parents. If this is true, there is an increased need to discover less severe defects at an early age.

There was a troublesome lack of correlation between intelligence quotients and school performance, particularly in children with normal intelligence. It is not clear why many of these children are unable to complete the early school grades satisfactorily. Among factors suspected of playing a role in the poor performance are subtle brain damage, specific reading problems, and hearing losses. Immaturity of behavior was mentioned by the mothers of some of these children, and evidence of delay in social adaptation was noted by the psychologist in others. It is not clear whether or not these findings are related to overprotection in rearing of a premature infant.

Two-thirds of the children gave discrepant scores of ten points or more between verbal and performance items on the WISC. However, they are equally divided between those excelling in performance items and those excelling in verbal items, and there is no relation between discrepant scores and school failure. Specific reading problems are not necessarily detected by the tests administered. Partial hearing losses were not investigated in this study but could account for speech and learning difficulties.

Retardation in physical growth of premature infants has been described (Dann, Levine, & New, 1958; Alm, 1953; Drillien, 1961). Premature infants were found to be smaller than the general population during the childhood years and also as adults. The cause for physical retardation has not been determined. The children in this study were smaller at birth than the weight expected for their gestational ages. They remained relatively small throughout their childhood years. Undernutrition, so common in the first few weeks of the premature infant's life, is appealing as an explanation for growth retardation.

The high incidence of defects noted in the children in this study causes concern about the 12 children who did not return for the examinations because they were placed in adoptive homes. The adjustment of adoptive parents to unsuspected neurologic handicaps must have been difficult and accompanied by feelings uncomplimentary to the adoptive agencies. On the basis of the findings presented in this review, one would suggest that adoptive parents be fully informed of the possible later sequelae of premature birth. One can be reasonably sure of neurological damage by 40 weeks of age. The adverse effects on emotional growth of the child and the difficulties in adoptive home adjustment when placement is delayed until 10 or 12 months must also be considered.

One of the questions raised, in part by this survey and in part by the results reported by others, is whether there has been an actual increase in the incidence of handicapped premature infants in recent years and whether there are different types of defects noted in premature infants cared for in different centers. If such questions are answered in the affirmative, investigation of postnatal influences will become even more important than they have been in the past.

SUPPLEMENTARY READINGS

Alm, I. The long term prognosis for prematurely born children. *Acta Paediatric,* 1953, **42,** Suppl. 94.

Dann, M., Levine, S. Z., & New, D. The development of prematurely born children with birth weights or minimal postnatal weight of 1000 grams or less. *Pediatrics,* 1958, **22,** 1037–1053.

Drillien, C. M. The incidence of mental and physical handicaps in school-age children of very low birth weight. *Pediatrics,* 1961, **27,** 452–464.

Knobloch, H., Rider, R., Harper, P., & Pasamanick, B. Neuropsychiatric sequelae of prematurity. *Journal of the American Medical Association,* 1956, **161,** 581–585.

35 | Behavioral Differences Between Normal and Traumatized Newborns

FRANCES G. GRAHAM
RUTH G. MATARAZZO
BETTYE M. CALDWELL

What characterizes the behavior of children traumatized at birth? The authors present indices that reliably (and validly) differentiate between normal variation and the effect of birth trauma. They administered five separate procedures (pain threshold, maturation scale, vision scale, irritability scale, and muscle tension rating) to 265 "normal" babies and 81 traumatized infants. Each test reliably differentiated the traumatized infants from their normal peers. Older infants were found to be more sensitive than younger babies on the pain threshold, and to perform better on the maturation test and vision scales. Black babies were superior to whites on both the maturation and the vision tests; there were no race differences on the other scales.

While the desirability of considering the infant's response to trauma may be readily acknowledged, it is necessary to develop a satisfactory method of measuring newborn behavior before this variable can be introduced into experimental work. The present paper reports our efforts to do this. We have spoken of measuring "response" or "behavior," but this is an amorphous categorization which may be variously defined. For our present purpose, we are interested in measuring any response in the behavioral repertoire of the neonate which may be related to the kinds of trauma and the kinds of consequence which may be the result of birth injury. More specifically, we set as our goal the measurement of behavior which would differentiate a group of infants who were "normal" from those who might be candidates for "brain injury." We were interested primarily in differences between normal and abnormal or traumatized infants and not in variability among normal infants.

TEST PROCEDURES

The most seriously limiting factor was the relatively few abnormal Ss available. In the well-run modern obstetrical hospital, the percentage of babies who suffer severe birth injury is only 1 to 3 percent. This meant that an immediate check on the validity of a measure could not be made but had to wait until a sufficiently large number of traumatized Ss had accumulated. Probably the major effect of this was only to threaten the experimenters' morale, but it also meant that once a test procedure had been adopted and given to any appreciable number of abnormals, changes which might have im-

Adapted from Behavioral differences between normal and traumatized newborns, Psychological Monographs, 1956, 70(5), 427–428. Copyright © 1956 by the American Psychological Association, and reproduced by permission.

proved the procedure were not made since they entailed too great a loss of difficult-to-replace data. It was because of this scarcity of traumatized Ss that we also included infants with mild or questionable injury rather than using more widely separated criterion groups. . . .

Pain Threshold

A determination of pain threshold was employed for a number of reasons. Both pediatric and psychological examinations of the newborn have concentrated on motor ability and have neglected sensory functioning. Yet impairment of sensory functioning has been a useful sign of brain damage in the adult. . . . We selected pain as the sensory area on which to concentrate precise measurement, after preliminary experimentation revealed various practical difficulties in the other areas. One major advantage of using pain was that a specific, discrete response could be obtained which was relatively easy to differentiate from spontaneous movement. Another consideration was the possibility that sensitivity to pain has not reached a maximum at birth. If so, pain thresholds might prove a relatively sensitive indicator of brain damage, since many lines of investigation have suggested that functions which are not well established are especially susceptible to impairment. . . .

Our general procedure was to determine the stimulus intensity necessary to elicit a specified response within a specified time. . . . The apparatus (an electronic stimulator) delivers shocks whose intensity, duration, and frequency can be varied within the stimulating range for skin and peripheral nerves. For the present work, duration and frequency were held constant so that the shock consisted of a two-second impulse at a frequency of 14 per second which could be varied in intensity from 50 to 530 volts. . . .

The specific response required was a movement of the stimulated leg or the foot of that leg, with or without other bodily movement. . . .

Maturation Scale

The scale consists of nine items, which receive varying credits depending upon the level of the response. If more than one kind of response occurs, the infant is given credit for the higher-scoring response. The general distinction between low-scoring and high-scoring responses is between generalized, mass movements and more specialized, stimulus-oriented responses. The maximum possible score is twenty-one.

The nine items used are labeled and described briefly as follows:

1. reaction in prone position (turning and lifting the head);
2. crawling (alternating movement of the leg simulating crawling);
3. pushing feet in response to gentle pressure exerted against the feet;
4. auditory reaction (movement or any change in behavior in response to sound of rattle and bell);
5. response to stimulus of cotton lightly placed so that it covers the nostrils and touches the upper lip (credit given for head, mouth, and coordinated arm movement);
6. response to piece of cellophane lightly held so that it covers nostrils and mouth;
7. resistance (percentage of time during which infant responds to stimuli of items 5 and 6);
8. vigor (rating of rate and extent of movement in items 5 and 6);
9. grasp (measure of strength of infant's pull of rubber-covered objects placed in his palm).

Vision Scale

The stimulus is presented with the infant in a supine position. Either the examiner's hand, a bell, or a metal tape measure 1⅜ inches in diameter was used. . . .

The newborn usually does not turn head and eyes toward a stimulus at the periphery.

Fixation is limited to a relatively narrow range directly in front of the eyes, an area which is determined by the tonic-neck reflex. Stimuli are therefore initially presented in this area. The experimenter observes the direction in which one or both eyes appear to be turned and places the stimulus in line with the eyes. He then moves it slowly toward and away from the infant, since the distance from the eyes at which an object can be fixated is also limited, varying from about 3 inches to 12 inches (Gesell, Ilg, & Bullis, 1949).

After preliminary efforts to locate the position which is optimal for fixation, there are presented a number of trials in which the stimulus is moved slowly upward from the line of regard, or in either horizontal direction for as great a distance as the infant's eyes will follow. Each trial is begun with the stimulus in the place of regard. Visual items are scored both for the type of response which can be elicited and for ease of elicitation. As many trials may be given as are necessary to arrive at these judgments. . . .

Several aspects of the visual response are considered in making a classification: (a) presence or absence of a kind of response (such as fixation or pursuit); (b) the ease of eliciting the response; (c) the direction of eye movement (horizontal or vertical); (d) the distance the eye moves. . . .

Irritability and Muscle Tension Ratings

In pediatric discussions of the brain-injured newborn, there are frequent references to such symptoms as a high-pitched and feeble cry, excessive irritability, muscular rigidity or flaccidity, and poor muscle tonus. We attempted to provide a crude quantification of these characteristics by means of two ratings—a rating of irritability and one of muscle tension or tone. The ratings are based on observations of the infant while other tests are being administered, and on a few simple supplementary procedures. . . .

At the end of examination, the overall rating on muscle tension was made. A five-point scale, with numerical values from -2 to $+2$, was designed for the rating. The zero point represented the behavior of a normal infant and the endpoints (values -2 and $+2$) the extremes of flaccidity and rigidity, respectively, as seen in a grossly abnormal infant. The -1 and $+1$ points represented a "just perceptible" form of abnormal behavior. . . .

SUBJECTS

Our subjects (Ss) were full term infants born on the inpatient service of the St. Louis Maternity Hospital during the period from July, 1953, through October, 1955. . . .

The traumatized group was composed of almost the total population of traumatized infants born during the course of the study, with the exclusion of infants who were overlooked, and of a few infants whom we could not obtain permission to examine. We were informed by the pediatric staff of all infants who, either at birth or subsequently, might be classified as abnormal. Infants were tested, if possible, within 24 hours after birth or as soon after that as their condition permitted. Only infants 7 days old or younger are included in the study.

The kinds and degree of trauma present in the abnormal group are shown in Table 1. A pediatrician experienced in the neonatal field made the classification without the knowledge of psychological test results. . . .

TABLE 1 Classification of Traumatized Subjects According to Kind and Degree of Trauma

Kind of Trauma	Degree of Trauma		
	Mild	Moderate	Severe
Anoxia	21	26	11
Mechanical trauma	0	0	3
Infections or diseases[a]	3	12	5
Total N	24	38	19

[a] Erythroblastosis fetalis, hypoglycemia, meningitis.

TABLE 2   Comparison of Normal and Traumatized Groups on Five Tests

Test	N	Variables Controlled	Mean Scores	Comparison Statistic	p
Pain threshold					
normal	55	age	165	t test	.01
traumatized	55		270		
Maturation scale					
normal	28	age, race	13.0	F test	.05
traumatized	28		10.6		
Vision scale					
normal	37	age, race	6.8	t test	.01
traumatized	37		4.2		
Irritability					
normal	91	—	.12	chi-square	.01
traumatized	29		.61		
Tension					
normal	103	—	.08	chi-square	.01
traumatized	29		.48		

PROCEDURE

The Ss were examined in a hospital room maintained in the same manner as the regular nursery. No soundproofing was available in this room. Whenever extraneous noises were sufficiently loud to startle an S, test procedures were repeated. Examinations were carried out between 10:15 A.M. and 3:00 P.M. with most Ss seen during the morning. As pointed out previously, the number and kind of tests given varied during the course of the study. For those Ss who were tested with the final battery, the pain threshold was obtained first. Vision tests were given whenever the infant opened his eyes, and the maturation and tension scale items were given in whatever order best maintained the infant in a satisfactory state. Irritability was rated at the end of the examination. . . .

RESULTS

Differences Between Normal and Traumatized Groups

Mean difference   Table 2 shows the size of the groups, the variables on which they were equated by pairing, the mean scores of the two groups, the statistic used in estimating probabilities, and the probability that differences between groups are due to chance. The means are included on all five measures, although they were, of course, not used when chi-square was the comparison statistic. On all tests the performance of the traumatized groups was significantly poorer than that of the normal groups.

Cutting Points and Normative Data

In order to identify those Ss among whom we expect to find later evidence of brain damage, it is desirable to establish a cutting point. . . . The cutting point selected was at the extreme of the normal distribution, that point below which only 1 percent of the normal population would fall. . . . Table 3 shows the percentage of Ss who score on the abnormal side of the cutting point on any one or more tests and on each test separately. When Ss were retested, the poorest performance has been taken as the score on a test. These data are supplied for the normal and traumatized groups and for the three subsamples of traumatized Ss. Pain thresholds and the Vision Scale are superior, but all tests identify some Ss as abnormal. The percentage identified as abnormal appears to increase with the degree of trauma

TABLE 3   Percentage of Subjects Identified As Abnormal by Scores Below the Cutting Point on the Day of Poorest Performance

Test	Normal	Total Traumatized	Mild Trauma	Moderate Trauma	Severe Trauma
Maturation scale	0	25	(33)[a]	12	57
Pain	1	42	43	30	(50)
Vision scale	1	41	(17)	31	60
Irritability	1	28	(33)	8	46
Tension	3	34	(33)	23	46
Any one or more xxx	4	51	46	37	84

[a] Percentages in parentheses are based on an N of less than ten.

and, if scores on all tests are considered, is statistically significant at the .01 level when tested by chi-square.

DISCUSSION

The group of tests we have used samples much of the repertoire of an infant's response to his environment. All of the responses are relatively simple, but they represent a substantial portion of the most complicated behavior which an infant of this age can show. How complicated is such behavior? With the exception of the two rating scales, the tests can be described as measuring sensorimotor ability, i.e., (a) the capacity to respond at all to various kinds of sensory stimuli, and (b) the extent to which the response is specific to a particular stimulus. The ratings of irritability and of muscular tension provide two more dimensions along which all responses of an infant, both spontaneous and elicited, may be described. We should like to know whether measuring such behavior gives any information about either past or future development. . . .

The present work is not primarily concerned with predicting the relative superiority of "normal" individuals, but rather in determining whether external trauma has caused brain injury. We did find that a considerable percentage of traumatized infants show impaired functioning as compared with nontraumatized newborns, and that such impairment is related to clinical judgments of severity of trauma. But will measures of impairment of a newborn predict the extent of later impairment? The question cannot be answered at the present time. One can say only that it seems reasonable to assume that the greater the present trauma, the greater the likelihood that some cells will suffer irreversible damage.

REFERENCES

Gesell, A., Ilg, Frances L., & Bullis, G. D. *Vision, its development in infant and child.* New York: Hoeber, 1949.

CHAPTER TEN
EARLY
EXPERIENCE

Early experience has aroused considerable speculation and experimentation. The earlier an event occurs in the infant's life, the more influence it usually has on his later development. Very early effects are often strong and irreversible. Experiments on early experience have followed two lines: (1) modifications of the early environment of animals, including sensory deprivation, environmental enrichment, and variation of their family life. And (2) natural experiments with human infants.

The effect of early visual experience on ducks and geese is discussed in the first study. The young duck or goose will follow the first thing it sees, whether or not the object resembles its natural mother. The relations between imprinting and simple learning are of interest because human infants may develop attachments in the same manner as birds.

The second paper examines the effect of early visual or visual and motor experience on later performance by rats. One group of animals was raised in a cage where they could explore their environment visually; another group was raised in a cage which allowed them to see the environment and move about in it. Later tests showed that the type of early experience the rat received affected his later performance. However, the type of task required of the adult animal interacts with his early experience. Rats that received early visual experience were superior when many cues were present. However, when only restricted motor cues were present, the group of animals with early motor and visual experience were superior. What the animal learns from his early encounters must be known before we can understand its effect on later behavior.

In a witty account of early infant-mother attachment, Harlow discounts the learning theory notion that feeding and secondary reinforcement from feeding are the main determinants of mother love. He shows conclusively that the infant prefers contact with a soft, warm mother rather than one who feeds him. In another related study Harlow showed that the infant monkey is comforted by a soft mother surrogate, but not by one who only feeds him.

The final paper on early experience considers the later effects of modified mothering among several infants in an institution. From six to eight months of life, some (experimental) infants were cared for by one person while others were tended by several people. Immediately after the study, the experimental infants were more socially responsive than their control peers. However, one year later (following the infants' adoption into homes) the differences were insignificant.

36 Imprinting: An Effect of Early Experience

ECKHARD H. HESS

Imprinting results in a particularly strong attachment between the young of several species (for example, ducks, geese, chickens, and some mammals) and the first object they see that moves, makes noise, or is colored somewhat like their natural mother. There are genetic tendencies to follow certain stimuli; however, these natural preferences can be overcome by experience during a critical period. Studies on the wild mallard show a critical period for imprinting between eight and 24 hours after hatching. Before eight hours there is little imprinting, and after 24 hours there is no indication that the bird can be attached at all.

There are several differences between imprinting and simple association: (1) Learning a visual discrimination is quicker and more stable when practice trials are spaced, but imprinting is more rapid following massed trials. (2) Recency of experience is maximally effective in learning; for imprinting, primacy is more effective. (3) The administration of punishment increases the effectiveness of imprinting experience, while aversive experience leads to avoidance learning in other situations. (4) Finally, chicks and ducks (under the influence of meprobamate) are able to learn a color discrimination problem at their usual level; however, the administration of meprobamate reduces imprinting to zero.

Students of behavior generally agree that the early experiences of animals (including man) have a profound effect on their adult behavior. Some psychologists go so far as to state that the effect of early experience upon adult behavior is inversely correlated with age. This may be an oversimplification, but in general it appears to hold true. Thus, the problem of the investigator is not so much to find out *whether* early experience determines adult behavior as to discover *how* it determines adult behavior.

Three statements are usually made about the effects of early experience. The first is that early habits are very persistent and may

Adapted from Imprinting: An effect of early experience, imprinting determines later social behavior in animals. *Science*, 1959, **130**, 133–141.

prevent the formation of new ones. This, of course, refers not only to the experimental study of animals but also to the rearing of children. The second statement is that early perceptions deeply affect all future learning. This concept leads to the difficult question whether basic perceptions—the way we have of seeing the world about us—are inherited or acquired. The third statement is simply that early social contacts determine the character of adult social behavior.

Lorenz was the first to call this phenomenon "imprinting," although earlier workers had observed this effect. He was also the first to point out that it appeared to occur at a critical period early in the life of an animal. He postulated that the first object to elicit a social response later released not only that response but also related responses such as sexual behavior. Imprinting, then, was related not only to the problem of behavior but also to the general biological problem of evolution and speciation.

Although imprinting has been studied mainly in birds, it also has been observed to occur in other animals. Instances of imprinting have been reported in insects, in fish, and in some mammals. Those mammals in which the phenomenon has been found—sheep, deer, and buffalo (Grabowski, 1941; Darling, 1938; Hediger, 1938)—are all animals in which the young are mobile almost immediately after birth. Controlled experimental work with mammals, however, has just begun.

EXPERIMENTAL STUDIES

Our laboratory in Maryland had access to a small duck pond in which we kept relatively wild mallards. The birds laid their eggs in nesting boxes, so the eggs could be collected regularly. After storage for a few days, the eggs were incubated in a dark, forced-air incubator. About two days before hatching, the eggs were transferred to a hatching incubator. Precautions were taken to place the newly hatched bird into a small cardboard box (5 by 4 by 4 inches) in such a way that it could see very little in the dim light used to carry out the procedure.

Each bird was given a number, which was recorded on the box itself as well as in our permanent records. The box containing the bird was then placed in a still-air incubator, used as a brooder, and kept there until the bird was to be imprinted. After the young bird had undergone the imprinting procedure, it was automatically returned to the box, and the box was then transferred to a fourth incubator, also used as a brooder, and kept there until the bird was to be tested. Only after testing was completed was the duckling placed in daylight and given food and water.

The apparatus we constructed to be used in the imprinting procedure consisted of a circular runway about 5 feet in diameter. This runway was 12 inches wide and 12½ feet in circumference at the center. Boundaries were formed by walls of Plexiglas 12 inches high. A mallard duck decoy, suspended from an elevated arm radiating from the center of the apparatus, was fitted internally with a loud-speaker and a heating element. It was held about 2 inches above the center of the runway. The arms suspending the decoy could be rotated by either of two variable-speed motors. The speed of rotating and intermittent movement could be regulated from the control panel located behind a one-way screen about 5 feet from the apparatus. The number of rotations of both the decoy and the animal were recorded automatically. Tape recorders with continuous tapes provided the sound that was played through the speaker inside the decoy. A trap door in the runway, operated from the control panel, returned the duckling to its box.

Imprinting Procedure

The young mallard, at a certain number of hours after hatching, was taken in its box from the incubator and placed in the runway of the apparatus (Figure 1). The decoy at this time was situated about 1 foot away. By means of a cord, pulley, and clip arrangement, the observer released the bird and removed the box. As the bird was released, the sound was turned on in the decoy model, and after a short interval the decoy began to move about the circular runway. The sound we used in the imprinting of the mallard ducklings was an arbitrarily chosen human rendition of "*gock*, gock, gock, gock, gock." The decoy emitted this call continually during the imprinting process. The duckling was allowed to remain in the apparatus for a specified amount of time while making a certain number of turns in the runway. At the end of the imprinting period, which was usually less than 1 hour, the duckling was automatically returned to its box and placed in an incubator until it was tested for imprinting strength at a later hour.

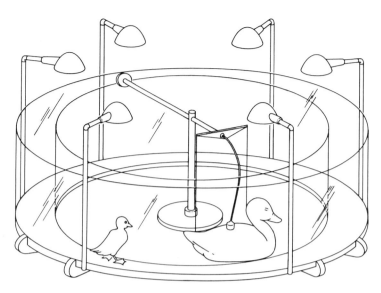

FIGURE 1 The apparatus used in the study of imprinting consists primarily of a circular runway around which a decoy duck can be moved. In this drawing a duckling follows the decoy.

Testing for Imprinting

Each duckling to be tested was mechanically released from its box halfway between two duck models placed 4 feet apart. One of these was the male mallard model upon which it had been imprinted; the other was a female model which differed from the male only in its coloration. One minute was allowed for the duckling to make a decisive response to the silent models. At the end of this time, regardless of the nature of the duckling's response, sound was turned on simultaneously for each of the models. The male model made the "gock" call upon which the duckling had been imprinted, while the female model gave the call of a real mallard female calling her young.

Four test conditions followed each other in immediate succession in the testing procedure. They were: (1) both models stationary and silent; (2) both models stationary and calling; (3) the male stationary and the female calling; (4) the male stationary and silent and the female moving and calling. We estimated these four tests to be in order of increasing difficulty. The time of response

and the character of the call note (pleasure tones or distress notes) were recorded. Scores in percentage of positive responses were then recorded for each animal. If the duckling gave a positive response to the imprinting object (the male decoy) in all four tests, imprinting was regarded as complete, or 100 per cent.

DETERMINATION OF THE "CRITICAL PERIOD"

To determine the age at which an imprinting experience was most effective we imprinted our ducklings at various ages after hatching. In this series of experiments the imprinting experience was standard. It consisted in having the duckling follow the model 150 to 200 feet around the runway during a period of 10 minutes. Figure 2 shows the scores made by ducklings in the different age groups. It appears that some imprinting occurs immediately after hatching, but a maximum score is consistently made only by those ducklings imprinted in the 13- to 16-hour-old group. This result is

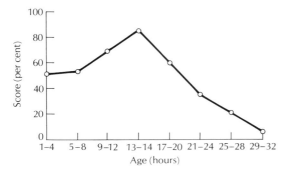

FIGURE 2 The critical age at which ducklings are most effectively imprinted is depicted by this curve, which shows the average test score of ducklings imprinted at each age group.

indicated in Figure 3, which shows the percentage of animals in each age group that made perfect imprinting scores.

Social Facilitation in Imprinting

In order to find whether imprinting would occur in those ducklings which were past the critical age for imprinting—that is, over 24 hours of age—we attempted to imprint these older ducklings in the presence of another duckling which had received an intensive imprinting experience. Ducklings ranging in age from 24 to 52 hours were given 100 feet of following experience during a period of

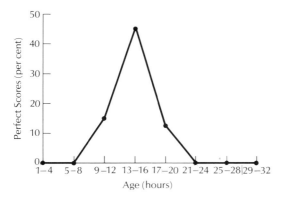

FIGURE 3 Another way of showing the critical age is by plotting the percentage of animals in each age group that made scores of 100 per cent in testing.

30 minutes. The average score for the ducklings was 50 per cent; this shows that some imprinting can occur as a result of social facilitation. Two conclusions can be drawn. (1) Social facilitation will extend the critical age for imprinting. (2) The strength of imprinting in these older ducklings is significantly less than that when the animal is imprinted alone at the critical age under the same time and distance conditions; under the latter circumstances the average score made is between 80 and 90 per cent. A further indication of this dissipation of imprintability with increasing age is obtained when we average the scores for those animals which were between 24 and 32 hours old. The average score for these animals was 60 per cent, while the score made by older animals ranging in age from 36 to 52 hours was 43 per cent. One last item points to the difference; even when the time and distance were increased during imprinting of the older ducklings there were no perfect scores. With such a large amount of distance to travel during the imprinting period, approximately 40 per cent of the animals would be expected to make perfect scores if they were imprinted during the critical period.

FIELD TESTS OF IMPRINTING

In this same exploratory vein we have also carried out some studies under more normal environmental conditions. To do this we took animals imprinted in our apparatus and placed them in the duck pond area, where they could either stay near a model placed at the water's edge or follow the model as it was moved along the surface of the duck pond, or go to real mallards which had just hatched their ducklings. Imprinted ducklings did not follow the live mallard females who had young of an age similar to that of the experimental animals. In fact, they avoided her and moved even closer to the decoy. Naive mallards, about a day old, from our incubator, immediately joined such live females and paid no attention to the decoys. These records, which we captured on motion-picture film, offer proof that what we do in the laboratory is quite relevant to the normal behavior of the animals and is not a laboratory artifact.

IMPRINTING AND LEARNING

The supposed irreversibility of imprinting has been particularly singled out by some investigators to show that imprinting is nothing but "simple learning"—whatever that is. We do have some isolated instances which point to a long-range effect, but systematic work is just now beginning in our laboratories. Canada goslings, imprinted on human beings for a period of a week or two, will from that time on respond to their former caretaker with the typical "greeting ceremony," as well as accept food out of his hand. This occurs in spite of the fact that they normally associate entirely with the Canada geese on our duck pond. A more striking case is that of a jungle fowl cock which was imprinted by me and kept away from his own species for the first month. This animal, even after 5 years—much of that time in association with his own species—courts human beings with typical behavior, but not females of his own species. This certainly is a far-reaching effect and is similar to the finding of Räber (1948), who reported on a male turkey whose behavior toward human beings was similar. An increased amount of homosexual courtship in mallards has been observed with some of our laboratory imprinted animals, which, while not a statistically valuable finding, perhaps points also to long-range, irreversible effects.

Our own experiments on the relation between association learning with food as a reward and imprinting during the critical period show four distinct differences.

In the first place, learning a visual discrimination problem is quicker and more stable when practice trials are spaced by interspersing time periods between trials than when practice trials are massed by omitting such intervening time periods. With imprinting, however, massed practice is more effective than spaced practice, as shown by our law of effort. Secondly, recency in experience is maximally effective in learning a discrimination; in imprinting, *primacy* of experience is the maximally effective factor. The second difference is illustrated by the following experiment. Two groups of 11 ducklings each were imprinted on two different imprinting objects. Group 1 was first imprinted on a male mallard and then on a female model. Group 2, on the other hand, was first imprinted on a female model and subsequently on a male model. Fourteen of the 22 ducklings, when tested with both models present, preferred the model to which they first had been imprinted, showing primacy. Only five preferred the model to which they had been imprinted last, showing recency, and three showed no preference at all.

In addition, it has been found that the administration of punishment or painful stimulation increases the effectiveness of the imprinting experience, whereas such adversive stimulation results in avoidance of the associated stimulus in the case of visual discrimination learning.

Finally, chicks and ducklings under the influence of meprobamate are able to learn a color discrimination problem just as well as, or better than, they normally do, whereas the administration of this drug reduces imprintability to almost zero.

Imprinting, then, is an obviously interesting phenomenon, and the proper way to approach it is to make no assumptions. To find out its characteristics, to explore its occurrence in different organisms, and to follow its effects would seem a worth-while program of study.

REFERENCES

Darling, F. F. *Wild Country*. London: Cambridge University Press, 1938.

Grabowski, K. Prägung eines Jungschafs aus dem Menschen (The adoption of a young lamb by man). *Zeitchrift fur Tierpsychologie*, 1941, **4**, 326–329.

Hediger, H. *Wild animals in captivity*. London: Butterworths, 1938.

Early Visual and Motor Experiences as Determiners of Complex Maze-Learning Ability under Rich and Reduced Stimulation

RONALD H. FORGUS

This paper reports a study that investigated early visual and motor experience and the maze-learning ability of adult rats. Two groups were reared under different conditions, from weaning until 85 days of age. One group lived in a large, complex environment that offered varied visual and motor experience, while a second group received visual experience but relatively little motor activity. As adults these rats were tested for maze-learning ability under conditions of rich and reduced visual cues. Group two was superior when many cues were present, while Group one was superior when the visual cues were reduced. It was concluded that the quality of early experience and the nature of the task to be solved are very important.

In a recent paper (Forgus, 1954) the writer reported evidence which he interpreted as indicating that early experience can be a hindrance or an aid to problem solving depending on the nature of the experience and its relationship to the problem. This interpretation is an extension of the theory of Hebb since in the work published so far by Hebb (1949) and his collaborators, Forgays & Forgays (1952) and Hymovitch (1952), they have stated that the "freer" the early experience of an animal is, the better it will be in solving a variety of problems. Up to now, however, most of the studies of these psychologists have dealt with performance on the Hebb-Williams intelligence test for rats.

In the paper referred to above we reported, among other facts, that a group of rats which had had extensive visual experience with inanimate objects learned to discriminate visual forms faster than another group of rats which also had had extensive visual experience with the same objects, but which had also been permitted to explore these objects physically. This result appears, at first sight, to be contradictory to Hebb's theory. However, it must be remembered that Hebb had dealt only with the gross aspects of perceptual experience and has not, as yet, dealt with the effect of varying the complexity of experience in different sensory channels. We have hypothesized that animals which had a varied experience, both visually and physically, with inanimate objects, would attempt various methods of solving the problem; e.g., they would respond to position and response cues as well as to visual cues. The animals whose motor experience with inanimate objects was relatively restricted, as compared with complex visual experience with the same

Adapted from Early visual and motor experiences as determiners of complex maze-learning ability under rich and reduced stimulation. *Journal of Comparative and Physiological Psychology*, 1955, **48**, 215–220. Copyright 1955 by the American Psychological Association, and reproduced by permission.

objects, should have a greater probability of responding exclusively to the visual cues earlier, and therefore should learn to discriminate visual forms more quickly. The longer learning time taken by the first group can be attributed to the time it takes these animals to abolish their wrong responses to the "irrelevant" cues. This "explanation" seems all the more plausible since there was no difference in form generalization after both groups had learned the discrimination. This hypothesis is consistent with Witkin's (1941) inference from his study that rats appear to display rather stable "reaction sets" when attempting to solve a problem.

The present study was performed to test further the hypothesis which was offered, viz., that whether a group of animals with more varied early experience will be superior in problem solving to a group with less varied early experience depends on the relationship of the experience to the requirements of the problem. We are arguing that the group of animals whose early experience was qualitatively more complex would be superior in solving a problem when external stimuli are reduced, i.e., they are able to change their reaction sets more readily when the solution requires such a change. We therefore specifically tested the following hypothesis: *If two groups of animals, one reared in a complex visual and motor environment and the other reared in a complex visual but relatively simple motor environment were to learn, partially, a complex open maze with visual cues present and were then tested for complete learning with the visual cues greatly reduced, then the first group would be superior in performance on the second test.*

METHOD

Rearing

Two groups of male hooded rats were reared under two different conditions from the age of 25 days until they were 85 days old.

There were 16 rats in each group. The rearing conditions were almost identical with those reported in the author's previous study (Forgus, 1954). The cage which housed group 1 was 5 ft. long, 5 ft. wide, and 15 in. high. The walls were painted a flat black, and the white objects were within 15 in. from the wall all around the sides of the cage. Group 1 was called the complex visual-motor group since the animals had complex visual as well as complex motor experience with the inanimate objects in their cage. They learned to explore and climb over the objects quite easily.

The cage which housed group 2 had the same dimensions as those of the cage that housed group 1, and the white objects were in the same relative position. However, these animals were permitted to live only in the inner 900 sq. in. of their cage. This was accomplished by inserting a plastic cage, 30 in. long, 30 in. wide, and 15 in. high, inside a large box, identical with that of group 1. Thus, these animals could only see the inanimate objects but were never permitted to traverse them. For this reason group 2 was called the complex visual but relatively simple motor group. Food and water were in the same relative positions in both cages. Both cages had very good lighting during the day.

Before we continue with the procedure we should point out certain limitations of this design. Because of the practical limitations imposed on us by the amount of laboratory space, cages, etc., we had to rear these animals in groups. Thus, it is incorrect to say that the animals of group 2 had restricted kinesthetic experience as such. Any differences in maze learning found between these groups cannot be attributed to differences in "kinesthetic learning" per se. The kinesthetic experience which the animals in group 2 derived from playing with their cage mates was probably comparable to the kinesthetic experience of the animals in group 1. The animals in both groups should have been equally good in reacting to internal postural, sequential stimuli. There is also no reason to believe that the visual learning of the two groups was significantly different, especially since the objects in the second cage were well within the rats' field of clear vision.

The experiences of the two groups were very different in one important respect, however. The animals in group 1, living in a complex, object-filled environment, had much motor experience in learning to negotiate elevated platforms, alleys, and blinds, etc. This kind of experience should improve their ability to solve complex mazes when visual cues are reduced since they had ample experience in exploring these kinds of environments in the dark.

In spite of the limitations of the design, it seems justifiable to state two things about the rearing conditions: First, the two groups were reared under similar conditions, especially with respect to visual experiences with inanimate objects. Second, the greatest difference in the rearing conditions was that the animals in group 1 had more opportunity for motor experience in negotiating a complex physical environment.

DISCUSSION

First, we may conclude that the hypothesis we set out to test has been confirmed. In this study the animals of group 1 were reared in a cage which afforded much opportunity for visual experience with inanimate objects and which also permitted physical exploration of this complex, object-filled environment. The animals of group 2 were reared under similar conditions with respect to breadth of visual experience but were not permitted physical exploration of the complex, object-filled environment which they saw. The problem is to explain why group 1 was poorer on the preliminary test but superior on the critical test. To interpret this fact, we will discuss three alternative explanations which immediately seem possible.

The first explanation is based on the assumption that the two groups had different emotional reactions to the task situation. Thus it might be argued that the group 2 animals, having little experience with elevated objects, are more frightened when they have to turn around after entering a blind on the elevated maze. Consequently they are more cautious not to re-enter the blinds, and thus avoid making errors more quickly in the preliminary test performed in the light. Furthermore, the animals in group 1 were quite used to falling off, climbing up, and turning around on elevated platforms since they presumably had much of this kind of experience in their living cage during the night when the lights were turned out. Group 2 animals were not. Thus it could be said that the group 2 animals were much more emotionally disturbed by the necessity of finding their way around a strange place, like the elevated maze, in the dark. This disturbance would account for their poorer performance in the dark. There are two reasons why this interpretation is not very plausible. The first is that we previously found no difference between two similar groups when we tested their emotionality on an elevated maze by using fairly standard emotionality tests (Forgus, 1954, pp. 332–333). Second, it seems difficult to believe that darkness per se would produce such startling differences since rats are normally dark adapted. We might add that the group 2 animals did not exhibit such disturbances. For example, there was not an obvious increase in defecation when the rats ran the maze in the dark. Moreover, no animal in either group ever fell off the maze.

The second alternative would assume that the animals in group 1 developed greater exploratory tendencies because of dealing with more varied inanimate objects. This greater exploratory behavior masks their learning in the preliminary test. But since they explored the maze more fully, they knew more about it. Thus they were better able to cope with the problem presented in the dark. This possibility is more appealing than the first, but again there is evidence which casts doubt on its validity. In our previous study (1954, pp. 332–333) we also found no differences in variability of behavior between two groups which were similar to the ones used in this study. Exploratory tendencies are usually revealed in variability of behavior.

We thus feel that the first two explanations taken alone are not adequate. We would like to suggest a more general type of explanation which probably includes aspects of the first two alternatives. This interpretation is based on the obvious fact that the animals in group 1 were more familiar with traversing elevated platforms. Thus they were less cautious when they ran on the elevated maze. This is supported by the fact that they ran much faster than group 2 animals. One of the reasons that the group 2 animals took a longer time per trial was the fact that they hesitated more at the bifurcation points on the maze. Now the arms of the maze were very short (15 in.) and the next T could vaguely be seen from the bifurcation point. Since the group 2 animals hesitated more frequently, they eliminated errors earlier and thus performed better during the preliminary test. We mentioned earlier that Ritchie et al. (1950) consider that the initial stage of maze learning is based primarily on visual cues. Because group 1 animals ran so much faster, they were not utilizing these cues as well as the animals in group 2. When the lights were turned out, however, both groups were forced to rely on nonvisual cues. Since group 1 animals had much experience in this kind of situation in their living cage, they were better able to negotiate the maze during the critical test.

In conclusion we wish to stress what we said in the introduction: In examining the effects of early experience on adult problem-solving behavior it seems to be the relationship between the kind of early experience and the demands of the problem task which is the important factor.

REFERENCES

Forgays, D. G., & Forgays, Janet W. The nature of the effect of free-environmental experience in the rat. *Journal of Comparative and Physiological Psychology,* 1952, **45,** 302–312.

Forgus, R. H. The effect of early perceptual learning on the behavioral organization of adult rats. *Journal of Comparative and Physiological Psychology,* 1954, **47,** 331–336.

Hebb, D. O. *The organization of behavior.* New York: Wiley, 1949.

Hymovitch, B. The effects of experimental variation on problem solving in the rat. *Journal of Comparative and Physiological Psychology,* 1952, **45,** 313–326.

Ritchie, B. F., Aeschliman, B., & Peirce, P. Studies in spatial learning: VIII. Place performance and the acquisition of place dispositions. *Journal of Comparative and Physiological Psychology,* 1950, **43,** 73–85.

Witkin, H. A. "Hypotheses" in rats: an experimental critique: II. The displacement of responses and behavior variability in linear situations. *Journal of Comparative Psychology,* 1941, **31,** 303–336.

38 The Nature of Love

HARRY F. HARLOW

One of man's most significant relations is love for his mother; how this attachment develops and what variables sustain it is a subject of considerable speculation and some experimentation. Harlow manipulated the relations between surrogate mothers and infant monkeys. The use of monkeys permits experimentation that would not be possible with human infants. His results indicate that feeding (which is postulated by learning theorists to be of primary importance in the development of mother love) is not significant. Rather, it is contact with a mother that determines infant attachment. Also, Harlow found that frightened infant monkeys stayed afraid in an open room or in the presence of a wire mesh surrogate mother. By contrast, infants who had a comfortable mother surrogate were able to overcome their fear.

Love is a wondrous state, deep, tender, and rewarding. Because of its intimate and personal nature it is regarded by some as an improper topic for experimental research. But, whatever our personal feelings may be, our assigned mission as psychologists is to analyze all facets of human and animal behavior into their component variables. So far as love or affection is concerned, psychologists have failed in this mission. The little we know about love does not transcend simple observation, and the little we write about it has been written better by poets and novelists. But of greater concern is the fact that psychologists tend to give progressively less attention to a motive which pervades our entire lives. Psychologists, at least psychologists who write textbooks, not only show no interest in the origin and development of love or affection, but they seem to be unaware of its very existence.

The apparent repression of love by

Adapted from The Nature of Love. *American Psychologist,* 1958, **13,** 673–685. Copyright © 1958 by the American Psychological Association, and reproduced by permission.

modern psychologists stands in sharp contrast with the attitude taken by many famous and normal people. The word "love" has the highest reference frequency of any word cited in Bartlett's book of *Familiar Quotations.* It would appear that this emotion has long had a vast interest and fascination for human beings, regardless of the attitude taken by psychologists; but the quotations cited, even by famous and normal people, have a mundane redundancy. These authors and authorities have stolen love from the child and infant and made it the exclusive property of the adolescent and adult.

Thoughtful men, and probably all women, have speculated on the nature of love. From the developmental point of view, the general plan is quite clear: The initial love responses of the human being are those made by the infant to the mother or some mother surrogate. From this intimate attachment of the child to the mother, multiple learned and generalized affectional responses are formed.

Unfortunately, beyond these simple facts we know little about the fundamental variables underlying the formation of affectional responses and little about the mechanisms through which the love of the infant for the mother develops into the multifaceted response patterns characterizing love or affection in the adult. Because of the dearth of experimentation, theories about the fundamental nature of affection have evolved at the level of observation, intuition, and discerning guesswork, whether these have been proposed by psychologists, sociologists, anthropologists, physicians, or psychoanalysts.

The position commonly held by psychologists and sociologists is quite clear: The basic motives are, for the most part, the primary drives—particularly hunger, thirst, elimination, pain, and sex—and all other motives, including love or affection, are derived or secondary drives. The mother is associated with the reduction of the primary drives—particularly hunger, thirst, and pain—and through learning, affection or love is derived.

It is entirely reasonable to believe that the mother through association with food may become a secondary-reinforcing agent, but this is an inadequate mechanism to account for the persistence of the infant-maternal ties. There is a spate of researches on the formation of secondary reinforcers to hunger and thirst reduction. There can be no question that almost any external stimulus can become a secondary reinforcer if properly associated with tissue-need reduction, but the fact remains that this redundant literature demonstrates unequivocally that such derived drives suffer relatively rapid experimental extinction. Contrariwise, human affection does not extinguish when the mother ceases to have intimate association with the drives in question. Instead, the affectional ties to the mother show a lifelong, unrelenting persistence and, even more surprising, widely expanding generality.

Oddly enough, one of the few psychologists who took a position counter to modern psychological dogma was John B. Watson, who believed that love was an innate emotion elicited by cutaneous stimulation of the erogenous zones. But experimental psychologists, with their peculiar propensity to discover facts that are not true, brushed this theory aside by demonstrating that the human neonate had no differentiable emotions, and they established a fundamental psychological law that prophets are without honor in their own profession.

The psychoanalysts have concerned themselves with the problem of the nature of the development of love in the neonate and infant, using ill and aging human beings as subjects. They have discovered the overwhelming importance of the breast and related this to the oral erotic tendencies developed at an age preceding their subjects' memories. Their theories range from a belief that the infant has an innate need to achieve and suckle at the breast to beliefs not unlike commonly accepted psychological theories. There are exceptions, as seen in the recent writings of John Bowlby, who attributes importance not only to food and thirst satisfaction, but also to "primary object-clinging," a need for intimate physical contact, which is initially associated with the mother.

As far as I know, there exists no direct experimental analysis of the relative importance of the stimulus variables determining the affectional or love responses in the neonatal and infant primate. Unfortunately, the human neonate is a limited experimental subject for such researches because of his inadequate motor capabilities. By the time the human infant's motor responses can be precisely measured, the antecedent determining conditions cannot be defined, having been lost in a jumble and jungle of confounded variables.

Many of these difficulties can be resolved by the use of the neonatal and infant macaque monkey as the subject for the analysis of basic affectional variables. It is possible to make precise measurements in this primate beginning at two to ten days of age, depending upon the maturational status of the individual animal at birth. The macaque infant differs from the human infant in that the monkey is more mature at

FIGURE 1 Response to cloth pad by one-day-old monkey.

birth and grows more rapidly; but the basic responses relating to affection, including nursing, contact, clinging, and even visual and auditory exploration, exhibit no fundamental differences in the two species. Even the development of perception, fear, frustration, and learning capability follows very similar sequences in rhesus monkeys and human children.

Three years' experimentation before we started our studies on affection gave us experience with the neonatal monkey. We had separated more than 60 of these animals from their mothers 6 to 12 hours after birth and suckled them on tiny bottles. The infant mortality was only a small fraction of what would have obtained had we let the monkey mothers raise their infants. Our bottle-fed babies were healthier and heavier than monkey-mother-reared infants. We know that we are better monkey mothers than are real monkey mothers thanks to synthetic diets, vitamins, iron extracts, penicillin, chloromycetin, 5% glucose, and constant, tender, loving care.

During the course of these studies we noticed that the laboratory-raised babies showed strong attachment to the cloth pads (folded gauze diapers) which were used to

cover the hardware cloth floors of their cages. The infants clung to these pads and engaged in violent temper tantrums when the pads were removed and replaced for sanitary reasons. Such contact-need or responsiveness had been reported previously by Gertrude van Wagenen for the monkey and by Thomas McCulloch and George Haslerud for the chimpanzee and is reminiscent of the devotion often exhibited by human infants to their pillows, blankets, and soft, cuddly stuffed toys. Responsiveness by the one-day-old infant monkey to the cloth pad is shown in Figure 1, and an unusual and strong attachment of a six-month-old infant to the cloth pad is illustrated in Figure 2. The baby, human or monkey, if it is to survive, must clutch at more than a straw.

We had also discovered during some allied observational studies that a baby monkey raised on a bare wire-mesh cage floor survives with difficulty, if at all, during the first five days of life. If a wire-mesh cone is introduced, the baby does better; and, if the cone is covered with terry cloth, husky, healthy, happy babies evolve. It takes more than a baby and a box to make a normal monkey. We were impressed by the possi-

FIGURE 2 Response to gauze pad by six-month-old monkey used in earlier study.

bility that, above and beyond the bubbling fountain of breast or bottle, contact comfort might be a very important variable in the development of the infant's affection for the mother.

At this point we decided to study the development of affectional responses of neonatal and infant monkeys to an artificial, inanimate mother, and so we built a surrogate mother which we hoped and believed would be a good surrogate mother. In devising this surrogate mother we were dependent neither upon the capriciousness of evolutionary processes nor upon mutations produced by chance radioactive fallout. Instead, we designed the mother surrogate in terms of modern human-engineering principles (Figure 3). We produced a perfectly proportioned, streamlined body stripped of unnecessary bulges and appendices. Redundancy in the surrogate mother's system was avoided by reducing the number of breasts from two to one and placing this unibreast in an upper-thoracic, sagittal position, thus maximizing the natural and known perceptual-motor capabilities of the infant operator. The surrogate was made from a block of wood, covered with sponge rubber, and sheathed in tan cotton terry cloth. A light bulb behind her radiated heat. The result was a mother, soft, warm, and tender, a mother with infinite patience, a mother available twenty-four hours a day, a mother that never scolded her infant and never struck or bit her baby in anger. Furthermore, we designed a mother-machine with maximal maintenance efficiency since failure of any system or function could be resolved by the simple substitution of black boxes and new component parts. It is our opinion that we engineered a very superior monkey mother, although this position is not held universally by the monkey fathers.

Before beginning our initial experiment we also designed and constructed a second mother surrogate, a surrogate in which we deliberately built less than the maximal capability for contact comfort. This surrogate mother is also illustrated in Figure 3. She is made of wire-mesh, a substance entirely

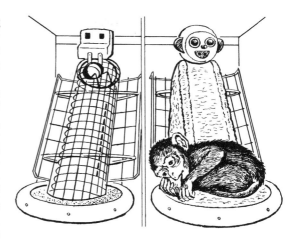

FIGURE 3 Wire and cloth mother surrogates.

adequate to provide postural support and nursing capability, and she is warmed by radiant heat. Her body differs in no essential way from that of the cloth mother surrogate other than in the quality of the contact comfort which she can supply.

In our initial experiment, the dual mother-surrogate condition, a cloth mother and a wire mother were placed in different cubicles attached to the infant's living cage for easy access. For four newborn monkeys the cloth mother lactated and the wire mother did not; and, for the other four, this condition was reversed. In either condition the infant received all its milk through the mother surrogate as soon as it was able to maintain itself in this way, a capability achieved within two or three days except in the case of very immature infants. Supplementary feedings were given until the milk intake from the mother surrogate was adequate. Thus, the experiment was designed as a test of the relative importance of the variables of contact comfort and nursing comfort. During the first 14 days of life the monkey's cage floor was covered with a heating pad wrapped in a folded gauze diaper, and thereafter the cage floor was bare. The infants were always free to leave the heating pad or cage floor to contact either mother, and the time spent on the

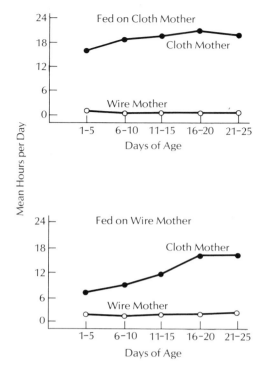

FIGURE 4 Time spent on cloth and wire mother surrogates.

surrogate mothers was automatically recorded. Figure 4 shows the total time spent on the cloth and wire mothers under the two conditions of feeding. These data make it obvious that contact comfort is a variable of overwhelming importance in the development of affectional responses, whereas lactation is a variable of negligible importance. With age and opportunity to learn, subjects with the lactating wire mother showed decreasing responsiveness to her and increasing responsiveness to the non-lactating cloth mother, a finding completely contrary to any interpretation of derived drive in which the mother-form becomes conditioned to hunger-thirst reduction.

We were not surprised to discover that contact comfort was an important basic affectional or love variable, but we did not

expect it to overshadow so completely the variable of nursing; indeed, the disparity is so great as to suggest that the primary function of nursing as an affectional variable is that of insuring frequent and intimate body contact of the infant with the mother. Certainly, man cannot live by milk alone. Love is an emotion that does not need to be bottle- or spoon-fed, and we may be sure that there is nothing to be gained by giving lip service to love.

One function of the real mother, human or subhuman, and presumably of a mother surrogate, is to provide a haven of safety for the infant in times of fear and danger. The frightened or ailing child clings to its mother, not its father; and this selective responsiveness in times of distress, disturbance, or danger may by used as a measure of the strength of affectional bonds. We have tested this kind of differential responsiveness by presenting to the infants in their cages, in the presence of the two mothers, various fear-producing stimuli such as the moving toy bear illustrated in Figure 5. A typical response to a fear stimulus is shown in Figure 6. It is apparent that the cloth mother is highly preferred over the wire one, and this differential selectivity is enhanced by age and experience. In this situation, the variable of nursing appears to be

FIGURE 5 Typical fear stimulus.

of absolutely no importance: the infant consistently seeks the soft mother surrogate regardless of nursing condition.

During the last two years we have observed the behavior of two infants raised by their own mothers. Love for the real mother and love for the surrogate mother appear to be very similar. The baby macaque spends many hours a day clinging to its real mother. If away from the mother when frightened, it rushes to her and in her presence shows comfort and composure. As far as we can observe, the infant monkey's affection for the real mother is strong, but no stronger than that of the experimental monkey for the surrogate cloth mother, and the security that the infant gains from the presence of the real mother is no greater than the security it gains from a cloth surrogate. Next year we hope to put this problem to final, definitive, experimental test. But, whether the mother is real or a cloth surrogate, there does develop a deep and abiding bond between mother and child. In one case it may be the call of the wild and in the other the McCall of civilization, but in both cases there is "togetherness."

In spite of the importance of contact comfort, there is reason to believe that other variables of measurable importance will be discovered. Postural support may be such a variable, and it has been suggested that, when we build arms into the mother surrogate, 10 is the minimal number required to provide adequate child care. Rocking motion may be such a variable, and we are comparing rocking and stationary mother surrogates and inclined planes. The differential responsiveness to cloth mother and cloth-covered inclined plane suggests that clinging as well as contact is an affectional variable of importance. Sounds, particularly natural, maternal sounds, may operate as either unlearned or learned affectional variables. Visual responsiveness may be such a variable, and it is possible that some semblance of visual imprinting may develop in the neonatal monkey. There are indications that this becomes a variable of importance

FIGURE 6 Typical response to cloth mother surrogate in fear test.

during the course of infancy through some maturational process.

John Bowlby has suggested that there is an affectional variable which he calls "primary object following," characterized by visual and oral search of the mother's face. Our surrogate-mother-raised baby monkeys are at first inattentive to her face, as are human neonates to human mother faces. But by 30 days of age ever-increasing responsiveness to the mother's face appears —whether through learning, maturation, or both—and we have reason to believe that the face becomes an object of special attention.

Our first surrogate-mother-raised baby had a mother whose head was just a ball of wood since the baby was a month early and we had not had time to design a more esthetic head and face. This baby had contact with the blank-faced mother for 180 days and was then placed with two cloth mothers, one motionless and one rocking, both being endowed with painted, ornamented faces. To our surprise the animal would compulsively rotate both faces 180 degrees so that it viewed only a round, smooth face and never the painted, ornamented face. Furthermore, it would do this as long as the patience of the experimenter in reorienting the faces persisted. The monkey showed no sign of fear or anxiety, but it showed unlimited persistence. Subsequently it improved its technique, compulsively removing the heads and rolling them into its cage as fast as they were returned. We are intrigued by this observation, and we plan to examine systematically the role of the mother face in the development of infant-monkey affections. Indeed, these observations suggest the need for a series of ethological-type researches on the two-faced female.

39 | The Later Effects of an Experimental Modification of Mothering

HARRIET L. RHEINGOLD
NANCY BAYLEY

The present study is a follow-up to work published a year earlier. The authors wanted to know whether experimentally produced differences in social responsiveness would be present a year later. The original differences were produced by a modification of mothering. Sixteen babies were involved, and half of them received the attentive care of one person from their sixth through their eighth month of life. This half was more responsive than the control infants at the end of the experiment, but they did not do better on tests of development. All infants were placed in foster homes over the next year. This follow-up study found no differences between the experimental and control infants, except that more experimental children vocalized during the tests. The experimental modification of mothering was enough to produce an immediate difference, but it was swamped by later events.

An extensive literature in psychology attests to the effect of early experience upon later behavior. For the human infant an important determiner of early experience is maternal care. Some of the dimensions of maternal care thought to be of consequence are amounts and kinds of care, interruptions of care, the number of persons giving care, as well as their attitudes. There is not yet, however, any considerable *experimental* literature on the effects of these variables upon the later behavior of children. The present study reports an attempt to discover the presence, a year later, of a change in behavior brought about in a group of infants by an experimental modification of maternal care (Rheingold, 1956).

Sixteen children, living in an institution for approximately the first nine months of

Adapted from The later effects of an experimental modification of mothering. *Child Development*, 1959, **30**, 363–372.

life, were the original subjects of study. From the sixth through the eighth month of life, half of them, the experimental group, were cared for by one person alone, the experimenter, for 7½ hours a day. They thus received more attentive care than the control subjects who were completely reared under institutional routine; and of course the number of different persons from whom they received care was markedly reduced. As a result the experimental babies became more responsive to the experimenter almost at once, while with time they became more responsive to other persons as well. They did not however do reliably better than the control subjects on the Cattell Infant Intelligence Scale or on tests of postural development and cube manipulation. At the conclusion of the study the experimental subjects returned to the full-time care of the institution. Details of the institutional care, of its experimental modification, of the tests used, and of the results may be found in the report referred to above.

One by one, all but one of both the experimental and the control subjects were placed outside the institution—in their own homes, or in adoptive or boarding homes. Approximately a year after the conclusion of the study, the children, then about 18 months of age, were seen again, in an attempt to detect the effects of the earlier treatment. Since the only clear difference between the groups at the time of the study had been an increase in social responsiveness among the experimental babies, it would be here that one would expect a difference, if any, to persist. Still, the possibility existed that differences might appear later as new functions matured. On the other hand, the subsequent, and more recent, experience of several months' duration in different life situations might reduce the chance of finding a difference.

The effects of experimental treatment were sought in two areas of behavior, the social and the intellectual. Would the experimental subjects be more socially responsive, that is, more friendly and outgoing than the control group to two examiners who visited the home? Would the experimental subjects, in addition, be more responsive to the original experimenter than to another person? If not, the variable under test is really their responsiveness to strangers. Second, would the experimental subjects now do better on a test of developmental progress?

PROCEDURE

Subjects

Fourteen of the original 16 children were located and tested; one from the experimental group and one from the control group could not be found.

The mean age of the experimental group was 19.8 months (range, 17.6–22.1), of the control group, 20.1 months (range, 17.5–21.7). The experimental group had spent an average of 9.2 months in the institution be-

fore being placed in homes (range, 4.0–13.6); for the control group the mean time was 10.4 months (range, 6.5–18.1). If the control subject who was still in the institution was omitted from the calculations, the average stay for the control group became 9.2 months (range, 6.5–12.2). In respect, then, to age and to duration of stay in the institution both groups were similar.

The children left the institution at different ages. Two experimental subjects left after only three weeks of treatment. One control subject left in the sixth week of the study, another in the seventh week. All the other subjects stayed at least through the eight weeks of treatment.

The home placements were varied. Three experimental and two control subjects returned to their own homes. With one exception, the own parents of these five subjects were of foreign birth and the homes were marked by poverty. Two of the experimental and four of the control subjects were in adoptive homes which, in general, were superior to the own homes in socioeconomic status. Two experimental subjects were living in boarding homes, pending a release for adoption. And one control subject, a Negro boy, remained in the institution only because a home could not be found for him. Furthermore, there was no difference between the experimental and the control groups in the intellectual stimulation provided by the homes or in the friendliness of the mothers, according to ratings made by the Experimenter and the Examiner after each visit. In type of home placement, therefore, there appeared to be no major difference. Rather, the difference between homes within each group appeared to be larger than any difference between the groups.

The Tests

Each child was seen in his own home. The homes were scattered widely through Chicago, its suburbs and neighboring cities, with one home in another state. Two persons, the original Experimenter and an Examiner, visited the homes together, with one exception: the child who lived out of the state was examined by the Experimenter alone. The Experimenter knew all the children but, of course, had been especially familiar with the experimental subjects. She served *only* as a stimulus person in the social test. The Examiner had no previous acquaintance with any of the children and did not know which had been the experimental subjects. She also served as a stimulus person in the social tests, but it was she alone who recorded the children's responses to both the Experimenter and herself, and who administered the test of developmental progress.

The social test resembled those reported in the first study, but was made more suitable for older children. It was composed of three parts, each of which set up a rather natural situation between adult and child, with an easy transition between the parts. In the first part, the responses to the stimulus person in the first few minutes after her entrance into the home were recorded. During this time the stimulus person did not talk to or approach the child but sat at some distance from him and talked to the mother, occasionally smiling at the child. The Examiner recorded the child's responses to whichever stimulus person happened first to engage his attention, then to the other person. At an appropriate moment one of the persons smiled and spoke warmly to the child, saying, "Hi (child's name) come to me," accompanying her words by stretching out her arms in invitation. This constituted the second situation. In the third situation, the stimulus person actually approached the child, smiling, talking, and gesturing as in the second situation. After the child's responses had been recorded, the other stimulus person presented herself to the child similarly. The order of stimulus persons was determined by the convenience of the moment: whoever was closer to the child or was receiving more glances was the first stimulus person.

The child's responses were recorded on a checklist under these categories: *positive facial expression,* which included seven items of behavior ranging from "stares with expression" to "laughs"; *physical approach* with nine items ranging from "shows toy" through "makes physical contact" to "makes social overtures while in the stimulus person's lap"; *vocalizations* for which a child received a score of one for each part of the test in which he vocalized, whether he said discrete sounds, jargon, or words; *negative facial expression,* which included eight items ranging from "a fleeting sober expression" to "cries"; *physical retreat* with six items ranging from "hangs head" to "leaves room"; and *response to mother* (during the social test period) which included a series of six items, from "turns toward mother" to "stays in contact with mother."

Within each category, items of behavior were thus arranged in what seemed a reasonable progression in terms of duration or amplitude of response. Each item within a category was arbitrarily assigned a value of one. Because the items were arranged in ascending order, the score for any item was one plus the value of all other items below it in that category. The scores for the categories of positive facial expression, physical approach, and vocalizations were summed to yield a measure of *positive social responsiveness.* Similarly, the sum of both negative categories gave a measure of *negative social responsiveness.* The sum of these two measures was the measure of *total social responsiveness.* The category of *response to mother* was calculated separately and not included in the other measures.

After the social tests, the Cattell Infant Intelligence Scale (1940) was administered by the Examiner, with the Experimenter *not* present. Lastly, the number of words in the child's vocabulary was calculated from his performance on the language items of the Cattell and from the mother's report.

RESULTS

The Effect of Treatment

Table 1 shows that both the experimental and the control subjects responded simi-

TABLE 1   Means and Ranges of the Social Test

Subjects	Experimenter		Examiner		Combined Score
	Mean	Range	Mean	Range	Mean
*Experimental Group**					
Total Social Responsiveness	32.1	27–39	30.9	27–38	31.6
Positive	17.4	2–30	16.0	2–37	16.7
Negative	14.7	1–37	14.7	3–29	14.7
Response to Mother	2.3	0–16	5.7	0–19	4.0
Control Group†					
Total Social Responsiveness	28.0	14–39	28.3	22–44	28.4
Positive	19.8	5–32	20.2	4–37	20.1
Negative	8.2	3–12	8.2	2–18	8.0
Response to Mother	4.5	0–11	4.8	0–10	5.4

* *N* is 7.
† *N* is 6 for responses to Experimenter and to Examiner, but 7 for Combined Score. See text for explanation.

larly to the Experimenter and to the Examiner. The close agreement of all means, and of the ranges, is apparent in the part, as well as in the total, scores. The only difference of any size between the two stimulus persons appeared in the experimental group's response to mother. But since only one subject of the seven gave a response to the mother when the Experimenter was the stimulus person, and only three subjects of the seven, when the Examiner was the stimulus person, this difference, as all the others, was not statistically significant. From the results we conclude that the experimental subjects did not appear to remember the Experimenter.

Furthermore, since the experimental and the control groups gave similar scores to both persons, it was assumed that they were of approximately equal stimulating value. Therefore, a combined score for each subject (the average of a subject's response to both stimulus persons) was used in the analyses which follow. This procedure made it possible to add to the control group the subject who was seen by the Experimenter alone. If every other subject responded similarly to both stimulus persons, it may be assumed that this subject would too. (It will be seen in Table 1 that the addition of this subject to the control group made the com-

bined means slightly different from the separate means.)

The combined scores showed that the experimental subjects were more responsive to both persons than the control subjects, but the difference was not statistically significant. The part scores, further, revealed that the control group gave more positive responses, the experimental group, more negative responses. Again, the differences were not statistically reliable. Moreover, inspection of the data revealed that the negative responses of only two of the seven experimental subjects were responsible for the difference between the groups. The findings therefore do not warrant the conclusion that the experimental subjects were either more or less responsive to the stimulus persons, positively or negatively.

Because some of the subjects made no response to their mothers during the social tests, the means for this category of behavior were not subjected to test. Only three of the seven experimental subjects and five of the control subjects made some contact with the mother during social stimulation by one or the other of the stimulus persons, a difference which permits no conclusive statement of difference.

Although vocalizations had been included in the measure of positive social responsiveness (as explained above), a measure which did not differentiate the groups, they were also analyzed separately. Inspection showed that five of the seven experimental subjects vocalized to one or the other of the stimulus persons but only one of the control subjects did. The difference was significant by the Fisher exact probability test at $p = .051$ (one-sided), a finding in agreement with the original study in which, at the end of the experimental treatment, the experimental subjects also vocalized more than the control subjects.

On the Cattell Infant Intelligence Scale the mean IQ for the experimental group was 97.4 (range, 82–110); for the control group it was 95.4 (range, 83–122). More attentive care given during a limited period in the first year of life therefore appeared to produce no difference in IQ on retest a year later.

The experimental subjects had a larger spoken vocabulary than the control subjects (17.9 and 13.7 words), but the difference was again not statistically significant.

The Effect of Home Placement

It early became clear that the adoptive homes were of a higher socioeconomic level than the own homes, and therefore it seemed desirable to look for differences in the performance of the children in these two types of home placement. The adoptive homes were also ranked higher than the own homes by the investigators on the basis of the friendliness of the mother during the visit and of the intellectual stimulation the home seemed to offer the child.

On the social test the children in adoptive homes gave more positive responses than those in own homes; the means were 21.6 and 15.6, respectively, but the difference was not statistically significant. It should be noted, however, that one subject in a boarding home and the subject still in the institution made higher positive scores than the mean of the adoptive home group.

Similarly, the mean IQ of the children living in adoptive homes was higher (98.8) than that of those living in own homes (95.4), but the difference was not reliable. The two children living in boarding homes had IQs of 95 and 102. And, while the child still in the institution obtained an IQ of only 83, two children in own homes had lower IQs, one of 79 and one of 82, and one child in an adoptive home had an IQ of 84.

Finally, the children in adoptive homes had a larger vocabulary than the children in own homes (means were 18.6 and 13.4, respectively), although again the difference was not significant.

In summary, there was no reliable evidence that the children in adoptive homes were more socially responsive or more developmentally advanced than those in own homes.

The Group as a Whole

We may now evaluate the performance of the group as a whole ($N = 14$), representing as it does a sample of children who spent approximately nine months of the first year of life in the care of an institution and who then experienced a major change in life situation.

In general, the group was marked by a friendliness which seemed warm and genuine. Eleven of the 14 Ss not only approached the stimulus persons but also allowed themselves to be picked up and held. Only two subjects, both boys, presented a different social response: they clung to their mothers and cried when the stimulus persons approached them. No comparable data are available for children who have lived all their lives in own homes, but in preliminary testing of the social test on three such children not one approached the examiners. Instead, they looked at the examiners from behind their mother's skirts and retreated whenever the examiners moved in their direction.

On the Cattell Infant Intelligence Scale the mean IQ of the group was 96.4. At six months of age the mean IQ for these 14 children was 93.8; at eight months it was 94.3. They continue therefore to score in the normal range. Furthermore, the mean number of words in their vocabulary was 15.5, which compares favorably with Gesell's (1941) norms of 10 words at 18 months and 20 words at 21 months. Certainly, the group showed no sign of mental dullness or of language retardation.

No child, furthermore, showed the marked apathy or attention-seeking behavior believed by some to characterize the behavior of children reared in institutions. Differences there were, to be sure, between the children, but none seemed to depart markedly from the normal in temperament or personality. In fact, several of the mothers spontaneously commented upon how easy these children were to handle in comparison with their other children. They mentioned, specifically, their good eating and sleeping habits and their ability to amuse themselves.

DISCUSSION

The discussion will take up three separate points: (a) the effect of the experimental treatment, (b) the effect of own home versus adoptive home placement, and (c) the characteristics of the whole group considered as a sample of institutionalized children.

On the basis of the changes in social behavior produced at the time of treatment, one might have expected that the experimental subjects on retest would have been more responsive to the Experimenter than to the Examiner. Instead, no reliable difference was found in their responses to either person. The Experimenter was not remembered. Further, we did not find, except in the vocalizing of the children, any evidence that the experimental subjects were more responsive than the control subjects. It seems, therefore, that the experiences provided by the more attentive mothering were not great enough to maintain the experi-

mentally produced difference over a year's time, except in one class of behavior.

The findings give rise to several speculations. First, it is possible that the verbal behavior of young children is more sensitive to changes in the environment than are other classes of behavior. In this connection, the responsiveness of vocalizations to conditioning in the three-month-old infant has already been demonstrated (Rheingold, Gewirtz, & Ross, 1959). Second, differences between the experimental and control groups may well have existed but in some untested area of behavior. Third, the expected (or some other) differences may make their appearance in the future in some more complex behavior incorporating the experiences of treatment. Finally, serious limitations to the study were imposed by the small number of subjects and by the diversity of home placements within each group. Differences would have to be very large indeed to surmount these limitations.

That no difference was found between the experimental and control groups in developmental status is not surprising, considering that no difference was found at the end of treatment. Some of the speculations about the course of social responsiveness may apply here, too.

We turn now to a consideration of the effect of home placement. The adoptive homes in general were of a higher socioeconomic level, the mothers were more sociable, and the homes were judged to offer more intellectual stimulation. For these reasons we would have expected the children in adoptive homes to be more socially responsive and more advanced in developmental status. But significant differences were not found. Possible explanations are that the differences between the two groups of home may have been not as great as they seemed, or that the number of cases was too small.

Lastly, the characteristics of the group as a whole may be assessed for the effects of a life experience usually thought of as deprived. All the children had been cared for in an institution for the first half of their lives, all but one had experienced a major "separation" in going from one life situation to another, and, furthermore, three children were now living in depressed socioeconomic environments, two were in boarding homes, and one was still in the institution. Yet, as a group, the children were healthy, of normal intelligence, and they appeared to be making a satisfactory adjustment. In addition, they seemed to be more friendly to strangers than children who have lived all their lives in own homes and, according to mothers' reports, were more adaptable than their other children. In no way, then, did they resemble the emotionally disturbed and mentally retarded children described in studies of the effect of institutional or hospital life or of separation from the mother. They did not show apathy or the inability to form relationships or make excessive bids for attention. Even earlier, at the beginning of the study when the infants were still in the institution, they were physically robust, mentally alert, and socially responsive.

It is true that in kind and duration of experience they resemble exactly no other group of children reported in the literature. There is a tendency among workers, however, to lump together studies of children who actually differ in age and experience and to generalize from them to all children who have experiences which may be similar in only one of many possible respects. It is to be hoped that as more prospective (in contrast to retrospective) studies are carried out, the dimensions of deprivation and of its effects can be clarified. Certainly, we may expect to find that the effects will depend upon the age of the child, the nature and duration of the deprivation, and the experiences prior to and subsequent to it (Ainsworth & Bowlby, 1954). The present study of the effects of early experience, limited as it is, emphasizes the need for more precise measurement both of deprivation and of its effects.

REFERENCES

Ainsworth, Mary D., & Bowlby, J. Research strategy in the study of mother-child separation. *Courrier of the Centre International de l'Enfance,* 1954, **4,** 105–131.

Cattell, Psyche. *The measurement of intelligence of infants and young children.* New York: Psychological Corporation, 1940.

Gesell, A., & Amatruda, Catherine S. *Developmental diagnosis.* New York: Hoeber, 1941.

Rheingold, Harriet L. The modification of social responsiveness in institutional babies. *Monographs of the Society for Research in Child Development,* 1956, **21,** No. 2 (Serial No. 63).

Rheingold, Harriet L., Gewirtz, J. L., & Ross, Helen W. Social conditioning of vocalizations in the infant. *Journal of Comparative and Physiological Psychology,* 1959, **52,** 68–73.

CHAPTER ELEVEN
SENSORY-MOTOR INTERACTION

What are the developmental stages of early sensory-motor integration and how can we study them? The first investigation in this section describes the development of visually directed reaching in the human infant. The progress of this important ability is followed from its earliest forms to the fully developed integrated behavior of the five-month-old.

The second paper shows another way to study sensory-motor integration, this time using mature adults fitted with goggles to invert or distort their visual fields. The resulting adaptation tells us about the plasticity and variability of visual and proprioceptive systems. Early studies by Stratton suggested that the visual system was very adaptable and that after a person wore the goggles for several weeks, perceptions would look normal. However, more recent work suggests that the perceptions are not nearly as normal as early introspective reports suggested. In fact, there is some evidence that the visual system does not change at all; instead, it is the proprioceptive system that undergoes adaptation. The second selection suggests that, at least for simple distortions, there is little or no visual adaptation; the results can easily be understood in terms of adaptation of the felt position of the arms.

40 Observations on the Development of Visually-Directed Reaching

BURTON L. WHITE
PETER CASTLE
RICHARD HELD

This paper reports the results of a normative study on the development of visually directed reaching during the first six months of life. Thirty-four normal infants born and reared under relatively uniform conditions in a state hospital were observed. The technique combined detailed longitudinal observations with a standardized testing procedure designed to elicit visual-motor responses including reaching. A sequence of development is described, categorized into eight stages of two weeks each. A number of separate visual-motor and tactual-motor behaviors make-up this sequence, culminating in the development of visually directed reaching just prior to five months of age.

The prehensory abilities of man and other primates have long been regarded as one of the most significant evolutionary developments peculiar to this vertebrate group. In man, the development of prehension is linked phylogenetically with the assumption of erect posture (thus freeing the forelimbs from the service of locomotion), the highly refined development of binocular vision, and the possession of an opposable thumb, among other specializations. One important accompaniment of the development of prehension is man's unique capacity to make and utilize tools. Considering the acknowledged importance of these developments in phylogeny, it is surprising how little is presently known about the ontogeny of prehension in man. The research to be presented here is focused on the behavioral ontogenesis of this vital function in the human infant during the first six months of life.

The detailed analysis of the develop-

Adapted from Observations on the development of visually-directed reaching. *Child Development,* 1964, **35,** 349–364.

ment of a sensorimotor function such as prehension inevitably raises a classic theoretical problem. The human infant is born with a diversified reflex repertoire, and neuromuscular growth is rapid and complex. In addition, however, he begins immediately to interact with his postnatal environment. Thus we face the complex task of distinguishing, to the extent that is possible, between those contributions made to this development by maturation or autogenous neurological growth and those which are critically dependent upon experience or some kind of informative contact with the environment. Previous work in the area of prehension has been variously oriented in regard to these polar alternatives, and it is important to note that the positions taken with regard to this theoretical problem have resulted in the gathering of selected kinds of data: namely, those kinds deemed relevant by each particular investigator to the support of his point of view on the development of prehension. Our own point of view is focused primarily around the role that certain kinds of experience have been shown to play in the growth and maintenance of sensorimotor coordinations (Held, 1961; Held & Blossom, 1961). Consequently, we have focused our attention on gathering detailed longitudinal data of a kind that would aid us in eventually testing specific hypotheses about the contributions of such experience to the development of prehension (Held & Hein, 1963).

Piaget (1952) made a number of original observations on the development of prehension, including the earliest stages of the process, which are prior to 3 months of age. His data are somewhat limited since his subject group consisted only of his own three children. And, as with Gesell, Piaget's interest in prehension was peripheral to another concern, namely, the sensorimotor origins of intelligence. Piaget's theoretical approach differs considerably from that of Gesell, being concerned primarily with the cognitive aspects of development. His work is focused on the adaptive growth of intelligence or the capacity of the child to structure internally the results of his own actions. As a result, he has formulated a theoretical point of view that centers around the interaction of the child with his environment, an approach similar to our own. This interaction is seen by Piaget as giving rise to mental structures (schemas) which in turn alter the way in which the child will both perceive and respond to the environment subsequently. This point of view avoids the oversimplified dichotomy of maturation versus learning by conceptualizing development as an interaction process. Without the aliment provided by the environment schemas cannot develop, while without the existence of schemas the environment cannot be structured and thus come to "exist" for the child.

Some primitive sensorimotor schemas are, of course, present at birth, the grasp reflex and visual-motor pursuit being two that are particularly relevant to prehension. Both Gesell and Piaget describe the observable development of the subsequent coordination between vision and directed arm and hand movements, part of which is clearly dependent on some kind of practice or experience. Gesell, however, contented himself with a vague acknowledgment of the probable role of experience in development, whereas Piaget attempted to determine in a loose but experimental fashion the role of specific kinds of experiences and structured his theorizing explicitly around the details of the interaction process.

It was with this general framework in mind that we undertook the study of prehension. In studies of animal development (Held, 1961) the technique of selective deprivation of environmental contact has been successfully used to factor out critical determinants. Since human infants obviously cannot be deliberately deprived, other experimental strategies must be employed. One approach would be to enrich in selective fashion the environment of a relatively deprived group of infants, such as might be found in an institutional setting. The rate of development of such a group could then be compared with that of a similar group not receiving such enrichment. Under such conditions the differences might well be small and consequently the techniques of observation and measurement should be as precise and as sensitive as possible to detect systematic differences. Consequently, our first task was to determine in detail the normal sequence of behaviors relevant to prehension spanning the first six months of life.

METHOD

Subjects

Our subjects were 34 infants born and reared in an institution because of inadequate family conditions. These infants were selected from a larger group after a detailed evaluation of their medical histories and those of their mothers along with relevant data on other family members whenever available. All infants included in the study were judged physically normal.

Procedure

For testing, infants were brought to a secluded nursery room where lighting, temperature, and furnishings were constant from day to day. After diapering, the infant was placed in the supine position on the examination crib. We used a standard hospital crib whose sides were kept lowered to 6 inches above the surface of the mattress in order to facilitate observation.

Our procedure consisted of 10 minutes of observation of spontaneous behavior (pretest) during which the observers remained out of view. This period was then followed by a 10-minute standardized test session during which stimulus objects were used to elicit visual pursuit, prehensory, and grasping responses. For the purposes of this report, the prehension-eliciting procedure is most germane. On the basis of several months of pilot work we selected a fringed, multicolored paper party toy as the stimulus object.

The infant's view of the object consists of a red and orange display, circular in form, with a diameter of about 1½ inches. He sees a dark red core, 1 inch square, surrounded by a very irregular outline. Two feathers, one red and one yellow, protrude 1 inch from the sides. We presented the object to the supine infant at three positions for 30 seconds each. Presentations were initiated when the infant's arms were resting on the crib surface. The infant's attention is elicited by bringing the stimulus into the infant's line of sight at a distance of about 12 inches and shaking it until the infant fixates it. The infant's head is then led to the appropriate test posture (45° left, 45° right, or midline) by moving the stimulus in the necessary direction while maintaining the infant's attention with renewed shaking of the stimulus when necessary. The object is then brought quickly to within 5 inches of the bridge of the nose and held in a stationary position. Infants over 2½ months of age do not require as much cajoling and the stimulus may be placed at 5 inches immediately.

This entire procedure takes no more than 10 seconds with most infants, but occasionally it takes much more time and effort to get young subjects to respond appropriately. The order of presentation was changed from test to test. In certain cases it was necessary to vary the position of the object to determine whether a response was accurately oriented or not.

RESULTS

The Normative Sequence

We found that under our test conditions infants exhibit a relatively orderly developmental sequence which culminates in visually-directed reaching. The following outline, based upon a frequency analysis describes briefly the spontaneous behaviors and test responses characteristic for each half month interval from 1 through 5 months.

The chronology of 10 response patterns is presented in Table 1. This chronology focuses on the test responses seen most consistently in our subject groups. The columns "Observed In" and "N" indicate that some of the responses are not shown by all subjects. Although 34 subjects were tested, the group size for each response is considerably smaller for several reasons. First, infants were not available for study for a uniform period of time. All of our subjects were born at the maternity section of the hospital. Usually they were transferred to the children's section at 1 month of age where they remained until they were placed in private homes. Aside from neonatal screening procedures, all tests and observations were performed at the children's section. Some infants arrived from maternity at 1 month of age and stayed through the next 5 or 6 months. Others arrived at the same age and left after a few weeks, and still others arrived as late as 3 months of age, etc. Since we were concerned with the time of emergence of the new forms of behavior, we were obliged

TABLE 1   Chronology of Responses

Response	Observed In	N	Median and Range of Dates of First Occurrence				
			2m	3m	4m	5m	6m
Swipes at object	13	13	(2:5)				
Unilateral hand raising	15	15	(2:17)				
Both hands raised	16	18	(2:21)				
Alternating glances (hand and object)	18	19	(2:27)				
Hands to midline and clasp	15	15		(3:3)			
One hand raised with alternating glances, other hand to midline clutching dress	11	19		(3:8)			
Torso oriented towards object	15	18		(3:15)			
Hands to midline and clasp and oriented towards object	14	19			(4:3)		
Piaget-type reach	12	18			(4:10)		
Top level reach	14	14			(4:24)		
			2m	3m	4m	5m	6m

to exclude a large number of datum because we could not be sure that a late-arriving infant would not have shown the response had we been able to test him earlier.

Another factor which guided us in the analysis of our test protocols was the ease of detection of responses. Each of the 10 items listed is relatively easy to pick out of the diverse behaviors shown by infants and therefore can serve as a developmental index. At times, the presence of a response was questionable. Such data were excluded from the analysis. It is likely therefore that the correct median dates are actually a few days earlier than those charted. A single clear instance of a response was con-

sidered sufficient for inclusion in the "observed" column, although multiple instances were by far more common. Another relevant consideration is the limiting effect of weekly testing. Although more frequent testing would have resulted in more accurate data, we felt the added exposure to test conditions might introduce practice effects into our subject groups.

Summary of the Normative Sequence

In summary, then, given the proper object in the proper location and provided that the state of the subject is suitable, our subjects first exhibited object-oriented arm movements at about 2 months of age. The swiping behavior of this stage, though accurate, is not accompanied by attempts at grasping the object; the hand remains fisted throughout the response. From 3 to 4 months of age unilateral arm approaches decrease in favor of bilateral patterns, with hands to the midline and clasped the most common response. Unilateral responses reappear at about 4 months, but the hand is no longer fisted and is not typically brought directly to the object. Rather, the open hand is raised to the vicinity of the object and then brought closer to it as the infant shifts his glance repeatedly from hand to object until the object is crudely grasped. Finally, just prior to 5 months of age, infants begin to reach for and successfully grasp the test object in one quick, direct motion of the hand from out of the visual field.

An Analysis of the Normative Sequence

When one examines the course of development of prehension, it becomes apparent that a number of relatively distinct sensori-motor systems contribute to its growth. These include the visual-motor systems of eye-arm and eye-hand, as well as the tactual-motor system of the hands. These systems seem to develop at different times, partly as a result of varying histories of exposure, and may remain in relative isolation from one another. During the development of prehension these various systems gradually become coordinated into a complex super-ordinate system which integrates their separate capacities.

During stages 1 and 2 (1 to 2 months), the infant displays several response capacities that are relevant to the ontogeny of prehension. The jerky but coordinated head and eye movements which are seen in *peripheral* visual pursuit are one such capacity. This form of pursuit is an innate coordination since it is present at birth. However, another form of pursuit is seen during the second month. The smooth tracking response present in *central* visual pursuit is a more highly refined visual-motor coordina-

tion. The path now followed by the eyes appears to anticipate, and thus predict, the future position of a moving target. Whether this response is in fact predictive at this early age remains to be conclusively determined. But this growing capacity of the infant to localize and follow with both his eyes and head is clearly an important prerequisite for the development of visually directed prehension. It should be noted that motion seems to be the stimulus property critical for eliciting attention during this stage.

Arm movements show little organized development at this stage and are limited in the variety of positions that they can assume, in large part because of the influence of the tonic neck reflex. The grasp reflex is present and can be elicited if the palm of the hand encounters a suitable object. But neither of these capacities is yet integrated with the more highly developed visual-motor tracking capacity. Infants of this age do not readily attend to near objects, namely those less than 9 inches distant. Thus, it is not surprising that objects which the infant is able to explore tactually, including his own hands, are not yet visually significant. At this stage, the tactual-motor capacities of the hands remain isolated from the visual-motor ones of the eye and head.

During stages 3 and 4 (2 to 3 months), the isolation of response capacities begins to break down, in part because the infant's eyes can now readily converge and focus on objects that are potentially within his reach. Central pursuit can be elicited from as near as 5 inches. One important consequence of this is that the infant now spends a good deal of time looking at his own hands. In addition, visual interest, sustained fixation, and related shifts in activity level are now readily elicited by a static presentation of the proper stimulus object. This indicates a growing capacity for focusing attention which is no longer exclusively dependent on motion.

In keeping with the above developments, it is at this stage that we see swiping, the first prehensory behavior. The appearance of this behavior indicates the development of a new visual-motor localizing capacity, one which now coordinates not only movements of the eyes and head but also those of the arms. Swiping is highly accurate, although it occasionally overshoots the target. It does not include any attempt at visually controlled grasping. Such grasping would indicate anticipation of contact with the object and is not seen at this stage. Instead, grasping is exclusively a tactually-directed pattern, which remains to be integrated into the growing visual-motor organization of prehension.

The next prehensory response, which develops soon after swiping, is that of raising a hand to within an inch or so of the stationary object followed by a series of alternating glances from object to hand and back. The crude but direct swiping response has been replaced by a more refined behavior. The visual-motor systems of eye-object and eye-hand are now juxtaposed by the infant and seem to be successively compared with each other in some way. This is the kind of behavior that Piaget refers to as the mutual assimilation and accommodation of sensorimotor schemas (Piaget, 1952).

During stages 5 and 6 (3 to 4 months), the infant exhibits mutual grasping, a new pattern of spontaneous behavior. This pattern, in which the hands begin to contact and manipulate each other, is particularly important for tactual-motor development. In addition, the visual monitoring of this pattern results in the linking of vision and touch by means of a double feedback system. For the eyes not only see what the hands feel, namely each other, but each hand simultaneously touches and is being actively touched.

In keeping with these developments, hands to midline and clasped is now seen as a test response. This is a tactual-motor response pattern during which the infant fixates the object while the hands grasp each other at the midline. Grasping is thus coming to be related to the now highly developed visual-motor coordination of the head and eyes. At this time, however, grasping is not yet directed towards the external object but remains centered on the tactual interaction of the infant's own hands.

During stages 7 and 8 (4 to 5 months), the infant finally succeeds in integrating the various patterns of response that have developed and coordinating them via their intersection at the object. Thus, alternating glances now become combined with the slow moving of the hand directly to the object which is fumbled at and slowly grasped. The visual-motor schemas of eye-hand and eye-object have now become integrated with the tactual-motor schema of the hand, resulting in the beginnings of visually directed grasping. This pattern has been described by Piaget (1952). It is not until the attainment of the highest level of reaching at the end of this stage, however, that one sees the complete integration of the anticipatory grasp into a rapid and direct reach from out of the visual field. Here all the isolated or semi-isolated components of prehensory development come together in the attainment of adult-like reaching just prior to 5 months of age.

The Role of Contact with the Environment

Having made a preliminary analysis of the normative sequence of behaviors, we may proceed to a detailed consideration of the question that originally motivated this study. How can we test for the contribution made by conditions of exposure to the development of prehension? At what stages of growth and in what manner can experimental techniques be applied?

Two factors are critical for providing this information. They are certain natural movements of the organism and the presence of stable objects in the environment that can provide sources of visual stimulation that will vary as a consequence of these movements. Deprivation studies with higher infra-human mammals have shown that, in the absence of either one of these factors, vision does not develop normally

(Riesen, 1961). No comparable systematic studies of the importance of such factors in the development of human infants are available. However, the complementarity of results between studies of adult rearrangement and of neonatal deprivation in animals (Held & Blossom, 1961) leads to specific suggestions as to the conditions of exposure essential for the development of the infant's coordination. For example, in the special case of eye-hand coordination, the work of our laboratory indicates the importance of visual feedback from certain components of motion of the arm, as well as from grosser movements of the body, as in locomotion. How shall we test the applicability of these findings to the development of the human infant? Obviously, we cannot experimentally deprive human infants, but the subjects of the present study are already being reared under conditions that seem to us deficient for optimal development. Thus, we are able to study the effects of systematic additions to the environments of our subjects. Moreover, since our research emphasis is on the importance of the exposure history of the human infant, the fact that our subjects are born and reared under uniform conditions is a distinct advantage. It assures us that previous and current extra-experimental exposure will not be a major source of variability as it might well be under conditions of home-rearing.

The everyday surroundings of our subjects are bland and relatively featureless compared to the average home environment. Moreover, the infants almost always lie in the supine posture which, in comparison to the prone position, is much less conducive to head and trunk motility. Furthermore, the crib mattresses have become hollowed out to the point where gross body movements are restricted. We plan to provide a group of these infants with enriched visual surrounds designed to elicit visual-motor responses. In addition, we will place these infants in the prone position for brief periods each day and use plywood supports to flatten the mattress surfaces. These changes should result in significantly greater motility in the presence of stable visible objects. We will assess the effects of such procedures by comparing the sensori-motor capacities of our experimental group with those of a control group reared under currently existing conditions.

REFERENCES

Held, R. Exposure-history as a factor in maintaining stability of perception and coordination. *Journal of Nervous and Mental Diseases,* 1961, **132,** 26–32.

Held, R., & Bossom, J. Neonatal deprivation and adult rearrangement: complementary techniques for analyzing plastic sensory-motor coordinations. *Journal of Comparative Physiological Psychology,* 1961, **54,** 33–37.

Held, R., & Hein, A. Movement-produced stimulation in the development of visually-guided behavior. *Journal of Comparative and Physiological Psychology,* 1963, **56,** 872–876.

Piaget, J. *The origins of intelligence in children.* (2nd ed.) Paris. International Universities Press, 1952.

Riesen, A. H. Stimulation as a requirement for growth and function in behavioral development. In D. W. Fiske and S. R. Maddi (Eds.), *Functions of varied experience.* Homewood, Ill.: Dorsey Press, 1961. Pp. 57–80.

41 | Perceptual Adaptation to Inverted, Reversed, and Displaced Vision

CHARLES SAMUEL HARRIS

A favorite technique of psychologists interested in the development of perception is to distort or invert visual input for considerable periods of time. They assume that the results will somehow tell us something about the plasticity of adult perceptual systems and indirectly about the development of infants' perceptions.

The first study of perceptual distortion was performed by Stratton, who wore goggles over his eyes for many weeks. His introspective reports suggested that the visual system adapted to the inversion, and his adapted perceptions appeared "normal." However, later replications of these early studies (Kohler, 1964) reported more ambiguous findings, and the search for the adapting component of our perceptual apparatus has continued.

The present selection reviews recent research showing that adaptation to inverting prisms consists primarily of a change in proprioceptive sensations (a change in the felt position of the arm seen through the prisms) rather than a change in the visual system. The author also suggests that more complex forms of the adaptation may be understood as the result of changes in the felt location of various parts of the body in relation to other parts. Contrary to early interpretations of the plasticity of the visual system, it now appears to be very stable; it is the proprioceptive system that is quite flexible. This makes some sense if we consider that the young child is continually growing and his proprioceptive system must compensate. He apparently uses the stable information from vision to correct proprioception.

For over a century, psychologists have been experimenting with optical devices that displace, reverse, or invert the retinal image. When a person first puts on such a device, he misses things he reaches for and bumps into things he is trying to walk around. But after a while he adapts. He ends up behaving normally despite the optical distortion.

Typically, experimenters have accepted this adaptation as evidence for or against various theories about the origin of visual space perception in the infant. But even if one hesitates to generalize from adult behavior to infant development, adaptation to optical distortions is of interest in revealing how perceptual-motor systems work and how they can be modified.

Recently there has been much concern with the mechanisms for adapting to optical distortions and with the conditions that are necessary for such adaptation to take place. Less attention has been given to the *end product* of adaptation. What change does the adaptation procedure produce

Adapted from Perceptual adaptation to inverted, reversed, and displaced vision. *Psychological Review*, 1965, **72**, No. 6, 419–444. Copyright © 1965 by the American Psychological Association, and reproduced by permission.

in the subject? How does the adapted subject differ from one who has not adapted?

Previous investigators have offered diverse answers to this question. For example, Kohler (1964) and Taylor (1962) believe that adaptation results in a change in visual perception. Smith and Smith (1962), on the other hand, claim that it consists mainly of learning specific motor responses. Held and Freedman (1963) say that adaptation "represents a change in state of the relevant sensorimotor control system" based on the storage of "newly correlated information" derived from "the one-to-one relation between movement and its sensory feedback [p. 457]."

This paper proposes another interpretation of adaptation: that it consists of changes in the position sense for various parts of the body. A change in position sense has been clearly demonstrated in one form of adaptation to displaced vision. The extension of this interpretation to other forms of adaptation is more speculative but seems to make sense out of a mass of otherwise perplexing data.

The Position Sense

Even in the dark we can perceive the relative locations of the various parts of our bodies. The sense that enables us to do this will be referred to as the *position sense,* and the perception of the position will be called a *felt position.* Changes in the position sense will be called, for want of a better adjective, *proprioceptive* changes. (The term *kinesthesis* will be restricted to the perception of movements of parts of the body.)

ADAPTATION TO DISPLACED RETINAL IMAGES

Arm Adaptation

Adaptation to inversion or reversal of the visual field may take many days or even weeks. However, as Helmholtz reported in 1866, a person can adapt to sideways displacement of the visual field in just a few minutes (Helmholtz, 1962b, p. 246).

If you look through prisms that displace the apparent locations of seen objects to the right, for example, and try to reach quickly for something, you will miss it by reaching too far to the right. But after just a few more attempts, your aim will improve considerably. When the prisms are then removed, however, you will reach too far to the left. For convenience, both the improved reaching while wearing prisms and the aftereffect when they are removed will be referred to as *adaptation* (i.e., adjustment to new conditions), since they are presumably manifestations of a single underlying change. The amount of adaptation (the *adaptive shift*) is indicated by the difference between a subject's responses on pre- and postadaptation tests. (During these tests the subject must not be allowed to see his hand; otherwise, by moving it slowly and guiding it visually, he would always be able to point correctly.)

Proprioceptive changes If a person's eyes are closed when he first puts on displacing prisms, he is surprised when he opens his eyes and looks at his hand. Because the prisms shift its visual image, his hand does not appear to be where he felt it was. If the discrepancy between the seen and felt locations of the hand is to be eliminated, either the person's visual perception or his position sense (or both) must shift.

According to the proprioceptive-change hypothesis, the subject comes to feel that his arm is where he saw it through prisms—even though this makes that arm's position sense erroneous (nonveridical). That is, after such a change, the subject's judgment of that arm's position relative to any other part of the body will be incorrect. If the prisms are removed and the subject tries (without seeing his hand) to reach for a target that he sees in a certain place, he will move his hand until he feels that it is in that place—but it will actually be off to one side of it. The same thing will happen if he tries to point at a sound or simply to point straight ahead. Only when judging the whereabouts of his hand relative to objects seen through prisms will he be accurate.

Other interpretations Five other simple, plausible conceptions of the nature of adaptation can also account for the rapid improvement in reaching for objects seen through prisms. Each, however, suggests a different set of predictions about other behavior. These five conceptions, which are often implicit rather than explicit in previous investigators' writings, have been presented in greater detail elsewhere (Harris, 1963a). They are described briefly below, together with some of their predictions about a subject who adapts by pointing with one arm, using a stereotyped arm movement, at a single target seen through prisms.

1. *Conscious correction of one's aim.* When the subject misses the target, he realizes that the prisms are deceiving him about the target's location and so deliberately aims to one side of visual targets; when the prisms are removed, he goes back to pointing normally.

2. *Altered visual perception.* A changed translation from retinal image to perception makes a target which at first looked off to the side appear to be straight ahead. This new perception can be demonstrated by any appropriate judgment of, or response to, a visual target seen with or without prisms.

3. *Reorientation of the perceptual frame of reference.* Perception of all external stimuli, visual or auditory, is shifted to one side; perception of the arms, however, is unaffected (if perception of the arm shifted too, the subject would show no adaptive shift in pointing at targets).

4. *Visuomotor recorrelation.* Visual perception does not change, but a given visual input is paired with a different motor output. Since only the visuomotor system used during adaptation is altered, the unexposed arm and all nonvisual targets are unaffected.

5. *Motor-response learning.* The practiced arm acquires a new motor response to stimuli from a given spatial location regardless of their modality. There is a generalization decrement when the subject uses arm movements that differ from the practiced one.

Experimental findings Harris (1963a, 1963b) carried out several tests. The subjects, whose heads were held stationary by a bite board, adapted by pointing for 3 minutes at a visual target seen through prisms that displaced its image 11° to the right or left. Adaptation was found to produce sizable and significant adaptive shifts, which were virtually identical whether measured by pointing at visual targets, at auditory targets, or "straight ahead." The shift was no smaller when subjects pointed at targets several inches from the one they had practiced on, even though the arm movements used then differed from the practiced one. However, adaptation had little or no effect on pointing with the unexposed hand. Nor did it affect judgments of whether a given auditory target sounded straight ahead. (Hein & Held, 1960, had previously reported that, with a similar adaptation procedure, there was no change in judged location of visual targets.) Others have independently demonstrated the adaptive shift with auditory test targets and with pointing straight ahead (Pick, Hay, & Pabst, 1963) and the absence of any shift in pointing with the unexposed hand (H. B. Cohen, 1963; Hamilton, 1964a; Mikaelian, 1963; Scholl, 1926). Subsequent studies have also confirmed these three findings (McLaughlin & Bower, 1965; McLaughlin & Rifkin, 1965).

The data can be accounted for only by the first interpretation: that adaptation consists of a change in the felt position of the adapted arm relative to the rest of the body.

Head Body Adaptation

Another way to adapt to displaced vision is simply to walk around while wearing prisms (Held & Bossom, 1961; Kohler, 1964; Taylor, 1962). The results are quite different from those of arm adaptation. When presented with a visual target after the prisms are removed, the subject points incorrectly with *both* arms, even if he saw neither one through prisms (Bossom & Held, 1957), and says the target *looks* straight ahead of him when it is actually somewhat off to one side (Held & Bossom, 1961; Kohler, 1964).

Is this type of adaptation, then, completely unlike arm adaptation? Probably not. Just as the felt relationship between arm and body is altered by moving the arm while wearing prisms, so perhaps the felt relationship between head and body is altered by moving the head while wearing prisms. The three investigators who independently proposed this hypothesis—Hamilton (1964a), Harris (1963a, 1963c), and Mittelstaedt (1964)—were unaware that Kohler (1951, p. 23) had already observed just such a phenomenon: A subject who wore prisms developed the "habit" of holding his head turned 6°–9° to the right of his body midline but was "completely unaware" of the deviation. He felt that his head was pointing straight ahead.

If a subject feels his head to be pointing straight ahead of his body when it is really somewhat turned, then when he sees an object directly in front of his nose he will incorrectly (if he is not wearing prisms) perceive that object to be straight ahead of his body. If he tries to point at it with either hand, he will point straight ahead of his body and thus point incorrectly. (Such misperception of head position would, of course, lead to improved accuracy of performance while the prisms are on.) Similar results will occur even if the test apparatus constrains the subject to hold his head straight relative to his body, as in Held and Bossom's (1961) procedure.

When Kohler forced his subject to point his head straight ahead, the subject felt that it was turned several degrees to the left (1951, pp. 23–24).

A change in the felt relationship between head and body necessarily entails a change in the perceived direction of visual targets relative to the body. But it would be inaccurate to describe such adaptation as solely a change in visual perception, since, for example, altered perception of head orientation would also result in altered auditory localization.

Intermanual transfer A number of investigators have found that if a subject watches one hand through prisms, with little head movement, the adaptation is completely or almost completely confined to the exposed hand. Helmholtz (1962a, p. 157), however, reported considerable adaptation of the unexposed hand as well. How can these findings be reconciled?

A plausible answer was suggested independently by Hamilton (1964b) and Harris (1963a, 1963c). They both noted (as did H. B. Cohen, 1963) that subjects whose heads were immobilized while they adapted showed little intermanual transfer, whereas those who were free to move their heads, as Helmholtz was, exhibited considerable transfer to the unexposed hand. Hamilton and Harris concluded that moving the head while wearing prisms leads to a change in the felt position of the head relative to the body, which would make the subject mispoint with both hands even if he never saw them through prisms. If he did see one arm through prisms, he would show a larger aftereffect with that arm than with the unexposed arm (since, in addition to the error caused by misperceiving the orientation of his head, there would also be a misperception of the exposed arm's orientation), thus manifesting "partial intermanual transfer."

If this analysis is correct, the term intermanual transfer is, in this context, something of a misnomer. Transfer implies that the adaptive change in one arm (or relevant parts of the nervous system) somehow spreads to or induces a similar change in the other arm (or contralateral part of the nervous system). Although this possibility has not been definitely ruled out (as Hamilton, 1964b, noted), it is simpler to assume that the measured adaptation in the unexposed arm results wholly from head-body adaptation, which affects both arms equally, and that there is in addition some arm adaptation of the exposed arm.

Half prisms Prisms that cover only the upper half of the eye displace the upper half of the visual field relative to the lower half, making a straight vertical line look discontinuous. Kohler (1964) reported that subjects who adapt to half prisms say that the line eventually looks straight and unbroken most of the time despite the discontinuous retinal image.

Although this adaptation sounds like a purely visual change—a change in perceived relationships *within* the visual field—Kohler's other observations indicate otherwise. When an adapted subject was asked to move his eyes straight up and down in the dark, Kohler says, the subject actually moved them in a jagged line, with a sideways jump approximately in the middle of the movement (*"einen seitlichen Sprung ungefähr in der Mitte der Bewegung"*—Kohler, 1951, p. 73; cf. 1964, p. 93). With more rapid eye movements, the path became diagonal. But the subject "always thought that his eyes moved vertically and without sudden deflections [1964, p. 94]." Apparently, the subject perceived a broken line as straight only because he felt that the jagged eye movement he made in scanning it was straight. What happened when the subject *fixated* the dividing line between the prism and nonprism areas? Kohler (1964, p. 83) says explicitly that, when fixated, vertical lines looked just as discontinuous after many days of adaptation as they had at first. Clearly, there was no change in the purely "pictorial" aspect of visual perception, but only in those perceptions of visual location that depend on

the registration of positions and movements of the eyes. Note that the adaptation did not entail any change in scanning *behavior:* When scanning the discontinuous line, the subject made essentaily the same eye movements after adapting as he had before. The only change was that a jagged eye movement was interpreted as straight. This is a perceptual change, not the acquisition of new motor responses.

ADAPTATION TO INVERTED RETINAL IMAGES

Is a proprioceptive-change interpretation appropriate when subjects adapt to optical transformations more drastic than displacement? Stratton's (1896, 1897) reports on his adaptation to "reinversion" of the retinal image indicate that the answer is yes.

Stratton's Experiments

Proprioceptive changes Stratton's reports are indeed difficult to comprehend—at times they sound bizarre, at times, self-contradictory. But it is clear that Stratton experienced proprioceptive changes similar to those considered above, though far more extensive and less stable.

When he first looked through inverting lenses, Stratton (1896) says,

> . . . the parts of my body were *felt* to lie where they would have appeared had the instrument been removed; they were *seen* to be in another position. But the older tactual . . . localization was still the *real* localization [p. 614].

Soon, however,

> . . . the limbs began actually to feel in the place where the new visual perception reported them to be. . . . The seen images thus became *real things* just as in normal sight. I could at length *feel* my feet strike against the *seen* floor, although the floor was seen on the opposite side of the field of vision from that to which at the begin-

ning of the experiment I had referred these tactual sensations. I could likewise at times feel that my arms lay between my head and this new position of the feet; shoulders and head, however, which under the circumstances could never be directly seen, kept the old localization they had had in normal vision, in spite of the logical difficulty that the shape of the body and the localization of hands and feet just mentioned made such a localization of the shoulders absurd [p. 615].

Proprioceptive changes such as these account for the behavioral aspects of Stratton's adjustment to inverted vision. If the felt locations and movements of his hands and feet came to agree with their seen locations and movements, he would have no trouble reaching for or kicking things, whereas before adapting he had to move the limb in a direction that felt wrong. When the new proprioceptive perceptions became stable enough to persist even when the limb was out of sight, responses with that limb would be completely normal with no need for conscious deliberation.

These proprioceptive changes also explain Stratton's feeling that he had achieved a "reharmonization" of touch and sight: Whenever he touched an object with an adapted limb, he felt it to be where he saw it, because he felt the limb to be in a new location that agreed with its visual location.

Upright vision   Stratton was not primarily interested in behavioral adjustments nor in proprioceptive or intersensory alterations. He wanted to find out whether the usual (inverted) orientation of the retinal image is necessary for seeing things as upright. If so, Stratton (1896) said, "it is certainly difficult to understand how the scene as a whole could even temporarily have appeared upright when the retinal image was *not* inverted [p. 616]." Yet, he claimed, this was precisely what happened. After several days of adaptation, the world seen through inverting lenses sometimes appeared to be "in normal position" (1896, p. 616), "right side

up" (1897, pp. 358, 469), "rather upright than inverted" (1897), p. 354). Some psychologists have taken these statements as conclusive evidence of a change in Stratton's visual system. Others have maintained that Stratton's assertions mean nothing at all. Walls (1951), for example, insisted that Stratton's descriptions of the scene as "upright" were "entirely metaphorical" (p. 191) and that actually all that Stratton achieved was a harmony between current perceptions and inverted eidetic imagery of objects outside the field of view (p. 200).

Stratton himself, on the other hand, thought it was quite natural for things to come to look upright again since he believed that "harmony between touch and sight, . . . in the final analysis, is the real meaning of upright vision [1897, p. 475]." But although "harmony between touch and sight" might indeed make the perceived orientation of the body and of the seen world agree, both body and world might still be perceived as *inverted* rather than upright. Perceived uprightness must depend on some other factor. That factor, as many investigators have pointed out, is the sensations of pressure and tension in the feet, legs, and body produced by the pull of gravity. Recently, experiments on subjects with labyrinthine defects led Clark and Graybiel (1963) to suggest that such pressure cues, rather than labyrinthine cues, may in fact be the major determinants of the perceived direction of gravity. Under zero-gravity conditions, for instance, subjects perceive the direction of the surface that their feet are touching as downward (Simons, 1959).

Kohler's Experiments

Kohler's accounts (1951, 1964) of adaptation to inversion help clarify the role of gravitational pulls on proprioceptively adapted body parts. When a partly adapted subject, who still saw the world as inverted, took hold of a string with a weight attached to the other end, he suddenly *saw* the weight as hanging from the string instead of floating upward like a balloon. The explanation may be that the hands and arms are often the first parts of the body to adapt (Taylor, 1962). So, when the weight pulled on the subject's arm and attracted his attention to it, he felt it pulling toward where he saw the floor and therefore perceived that direction as "down."

Several writers (e.g., Klein, 1960, p. 103) have assumed that gravitational cues provide a direct access to reality—a veridical standard to which visual perception, when shown the errors of its ways, conforms. According to the present interpretation, however, gravitational cues will make the inverted scene look upright only if they are felt by some proprioceptively adapted body part. Prominent gravitational cues in an *unadapted* area (produced, for instance, by a weight hanging from the subject's chin) might make the scene look even more clearly inverted.

Illusory Movements of the Visual Field

Ordinarily, when you move your head downward, objects enter your field of view from below and travel to the top. You perceive the external world as stationary. If you move your head downward while wearing inverting goggles, though, objects enter the visual field from the top and travel downward. As a result, the world appears to be moving rapidly downward. (With reversing goggles, sideways movements produce a similar illusion.) After a few days the illusory swinging diminishes, until eventually the world appears stationary during head movements (Kohler, 1964; Stratton, 1897; Taylor, 1962).

ADAPTATION TO REVERSED RETINAL IMAGES

Kohler (1953, 1964) has described in detail how subjects who wear right-angle prisms, which reverse their retinal images right for left, eventually achieve normal behavior and what he calls "correct seeing" (1964, p. 140). At first reading, his account is as bewildering as Stratton's.

"Piecemeal" Adaptation

When a person puts on reversing prisms, Kohler says, he initially reaches in the wrong direction for things, makes wrong turns, and sees all writing as mirror writing. In attempting to cope with reversed vision, the subject tries out various tactics, such as deliberately heading left when his goal appears to be on his right. As the subject adapts behaviorally, during the course of several weeks, he becomes able to walk, reach, and turn correctly without resorting to such "tricks." Concurrently, Kohler claims, his visual perception changes in a peculiar piecemeal fashion: Some parts of the visual field are perceived correctly while other parts remain reversed. For example, after 18 days:

> Inscriptions on buildings, or advertisements, were still seen in mirror writing, but the objects containing them were seen in the correct location. Vehicles driving on the "right" . . . carried license numbers in mirror writing . . . the subject is capable of localizing both sides of, say, a "3" correctly (open to the left, the curves to the right) and still see it mirrorwise [1964, p. 155]!

At this stage, even though the subject's spontaneous behavior is usually correct, he often becomes confused and makes "errors" when asked to attend to his "immediate visual experience."

After many weeks, Kohler, says, the subject's behavior and vision are both reoriented. He achieves "almost completely correct impressions, even where letters and numbers were involved [1964, p. 160]."

When one thinks of adaptation as a change in visual perception, these observations are incomprehensible. How can vision ever be partly right way round, partly reversed?

Determinants of Judgments

In attempting to make sense of Kohler's puzzling observations, it is helpful to bear in mind four different determinants of what a subject says when the experimenter tries to find out whether he sees things right way round. The first two determinants are distinguishable aspects of perception, whereas the other two are essentially irrelevant to spatial perception. Doubtless, people differ in which of these factors enter into their judgments in a given situation, and a given person may judge differently at different times. But it is often possible to find out operationally which factors the subject's report is based on and to design experiments that avoid the ambiguities of previous reports.

Directional perception   When asked "Does that object appear to be on your right or on your left?," many people probably make a directional judgment relative to their dominant hand. If the object is seen to lie on the same side of the body as the right hand, the subject says: "It's on my right" or "on my right-hand side." The same kind of judgment can be elicited whether or not the words right and left are used, whether or not the subject has a dominant hand, and whether or not he refers the judgment to his hand: The experimenter can simply touch any spot on the subject's body and ask whether an object appears to be on the same side of his body as the touched spot.

Such a judgment is based on one aspect of spatial perception—perception of the location of an object relative to some part of the body. This is the sort of perception that usually guides motor behavior such as reaching for an object or walking toward it (cf. the concept of "manipulable regions," Kohler, 1964, p. 163).

Pictorial perception   Most of the debate on adaptation to distorted vision has concerned this aspect of visual perception, though it has not been clearly differentiated from other determinants of subjects' judgments. Pictorial perception consists of "looking at" the "picture" received by the visual system (cf. Gibson's, 1950, concept of "the visual field"). It is most obvious in successive comparisons: For example, we can ask a subject whether an arrow he is looking at is pointing the same way as the locomotive in a painting he saw before the experiment began.

The perception of "clockwise" or "counterclockwise" notion and "east" or "west" on a map are probably pictorial perceptions for most people, based on purely visual memories. Thus, to test for changes in pictorial perception, we can keep a subject from seeing any clocks or maps during the experiment and then ask him whether something appears to be moving clockwise or counterclockwise, or whether it is on the same side as the 9 on a clock or the east coast on a map. As long as the subject has a visual image of a clock or a map, he need not even think about the labels "right" and "left," nor about any part of his body, when making his judgment. (Occasionally a subject may make a directional judgment when asked to make a pictorial one—for example, if he remembers that the locomotive in the painting was "going toward my right"—that is, toward his right hand. But such exceptions have no theoretical importance once recognized for what they are.) Even when he uses the terms right and left, which are often characteristic of directional judgments, the subject may be making a pictorial judgment: Some people habitually think of a certain part of the visual field as "the lower left corner" without referring at all to any part of the body.

Familiarity   A subject often describes his first perceptions through reversing goggles as "strange," "unusual," "unfamiliar," "new," or "mirror imaged." Later he describes them as "normal," "natural," "all right," "usual," "familiar," "right way round" (see Kohler, 1964, p. 142). Such descriptions are based almost entirely on past experience with particular stimuli or classes of stimuli and can be changed through repeated visual observation, even without distorting spectacles. For example, a person (perhaps an apprentice typesetter) who practices reading mirror writing may soon say that it is beginning to look "natural" or "all right." But neither his directional nor his pictorial perception has changed. If asked to judge the location of part of a letter (relative to part of the body or to visual memories), a person gives the same answer whether the letter looks "familiar" or "strange."

Labels It is risky to let a subject use the words right and left. First, the same word may be used to label two quite different sorts of perception, pictorial and directional. Second, a subject wearing reversing prisms could decide to start calling everything right that he formerly called left, even if he had not adapted at all. And third, he may be inconsistent or hesitant about which word to use even when his perception is completely determinate, stable, and clearcut; as Kohler (1964) put it, "there are people who always have trouble when asked to tell quickly where right or left is, but who never have difficulty in reaching for seen objects [p. 153]." Labels like right and left do not affect perception; it is irrelevant that the subject has learned to call a certain direction left and another direction right.

Proprioceptive Changes

With these distinctions in mind, it is possible to reexamine Kohler's observations and conclude that adaptation to reversed vision can be ascribed to a radical change in the felt location of the arms, legs, and body relative to the head and eyes, without any change in pictorial visual perception.

Kohler (1953, p. 110; cf. 1964, p. 153), in fact, did observe some proprioceptive and kinesthetic changes during the course of adaptation to reversal. After several days of wearing the goggles, he reported, there was:

> . . . a weakening of the right-left orientation of the body image, which becomes uncertain, especially in connection with movements that have been deliberately practiced in reverse. The subject may even turn left, with full confidence, when he does a "right face" with his eyes closed. When he moves his head and hands, the kinesthetic position- and movement-sensations are completely in accord with the

(reversed) visual field. Yet ultimately this leads to a "dead end" (two errors that cancel each other!).

In a footnote, Kohler added:

> . . . by touch, doors, for example, seem to open in a reversed direction (as compared with earlier), as if they had been turned around in the meantime. However, the pre-experimental "right-left" of the body image remains unchanged in the shoulder and upper-arm region, and from there it undertakes its new conquest. When the attention is concentrated on this region, there is almost never any error.

Clearly, Kohler regarded this kinesthetic and proprioceptive changes as temporary aberrations of no theoretical importance, leading only to a "dead end." Since proprioception and vision were *both* reversed, Kohler thought that both must proceed to a further, "correct" stage before adaptation could be complete.

With further adaptation, according to the proprioceptive-change hypothesis, the felt locations of the subject's legs, torso, and perhaps even his shoulders and most of his head, change. He again feels, as he felt before the experiment started, that the (physically) right half of his body is near the hand he writes with. Now he can reach accurately for objects seen through the reversing goggles, turn correctly, and correctly judge the directions of objects relative to his body.

Pictorial Perception

But still his pictorial visual perception remains unchanged. The letters on the blackboard and the license plates on cars look just the same as they did when he first put on reversing goggles. The only difference is that he now feels the right side of his body to be on the same side as the curve of the backwards R that he sees (Figure 1D), so he says the curve is "on my right."

Why, then, does writing eventually come to look "normal" through reversing goggles? Because, with practice, mirror writing becomes familiar and easy to read, whether the letters are actually printed in reverse or simply look reversed because one is wearing special goggles. Indeed, Kohler's (1964, p. 160) subject reported that "the first words to rectify themselves were the common ones," which were seen most often through the reversing goggles. But it is a mistake to conclude that pictorial perception reversed and "mirrorwise seeing" ("*spiegelbildliche Sehen*"—Kohler, 1953, p. 113) became established. We would not say that about someone who learned to read mirror writing without wearing reversing spectacles.

Given this interpretation of adaptation, it is not surprising to hear that one stubborn subject (Taylor, 1962, p. 180) "achieved satisfactory behavioral adjustment" but "denied that he ever perceived the world the right way round through his spectacles," even after 71 days of wearing them. When questioned closely, this subject said that all of his "incorrect" judgments were made by deciding whether his right temple or his left temple was closer to the part of the visual field he was judging. Stratton's reports–suggest that even after the felt location of the rest of the body has changed, the area around the eyes does not, so judgments made relative to the temples would remain unchanged. Or, the subject may have been trying to tell the experimenter that he was making a pictorial judgment, based on an unaltered visual memory of right and left. In either case, this subject's perceptions—visual and proprioceptive—were probably just the same as those of subjects who, according to Taylor, managed to "perceive the world the right way round."

Aftereffects

The "peculiar experiences" (Kohler, 1964, p. 158) that the adapted subject encounters when he takes off the experimental spectacles are just what one would expect if the subject has undergone proprioceptive changes, has become accustomed to the reversed appearance of particular stimuli, but has experienced no change in pictorial perception.

When Kohler (1964, p. 158) removed his reversing goggles, after weeks of adaptation, and looked at a picture which he had

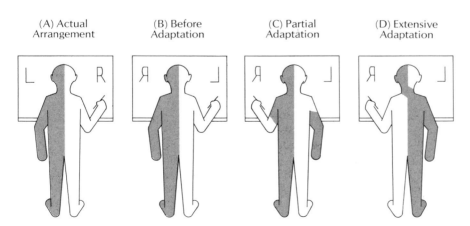

| (A) Actual Arrangement | (B) Before Adaptation | (C) Partial Adaptation | (D) Extensive Adaptation |

FIGURE 1 A subject's perceptions during the course of adaptation to reversed vision, according to the proprioceptive-change hypothesis. (In all cases perception of the letters is visual; perception of the subject's head and body is proprioceptive. A: The actual physical arrangement. B: The subject's perceptions when he first puts on reversing goggles. C: The subject's perceptions at an intermediate stage of adaptation, with only his arms adapted. D: The subject's perceptions at an advanced stage of adaptation.)

seen before but not during the experiment, the picture immediately looked familiar. The person in it appeared (pictorially) to be running, as before, from left to right. Nevertheless, the person was seen as running toward the *left* edge of the page; that is (as Kohler makes clear), toward where Kohler felt his (adapted) left shoulder to be.

Kohler (1964, p. 160) does report that another subject, the one who "achieved almost completely correct impressions" while wearing reversing goggles, *saw* the whole room mirrorwise when the spectacles were removed. But the evidence for this statement is that the subject read p's as q's, b's as d's, and 10:30 on a clock as 1:30—which is just what would happen, without any perceptual change, if one read nothing but mirror writing and saw nothing but backwards clocks for 37 days.

LIMITATIONS OF THE PROPRIOCEPTIVE-CHANGE HYPOTHESIS

Although changes in the position sense may underlie most of the phenomena of adaptation to optical distortions, there are some kinds of adaptation that cannot be so interpreted. For example, adaptation to the chromatic dispersion produced by prisms ("color fringes"—Kohler, 1964) seems to depend on changes in "contour detectors" within the visual system (Hay, Pick, & Rosser, 1963; McCollough, 1965a). Adaptation to bicolored spectacles (Kohler, 1964) has been shown to depend on retinal color adaptation and simultaneous contrast (McCollough, 1965b).

In the reports of Stratton (1897), Kohler (1964), and Taylor (1962), several passages seem to describe perceptual changes that cannot be attributed to altered position sense. Further work is needed to determine whether these statements are based on confusions about the various determinants of subjects' verbal reports or result from some complicated alterations in position sense or do in fact represent other sorts of adaptive change.

OTHER THEORIES OF ADAPTATION

Stratton

After reading Stratton's striking descriptions of the proprioceptive changes he underwent, one is surprised to find him saying in his theoretical discussion that "the tactual perceptions, as such, never changed their place," and "the restoration of harmony between the perceptions of sight and those of touch was in no wise a process of changing the absolute position of tactual objects so as to make it identical with the place of the visual objects [1897, p. 476]." He seems to be ignoring his own introspections when he claims that there is neither a change in proprioceptive localization nor a change in visual localization, but only a change in the relationship between the two. This noncommittal idea has proven quite appealing to many present-day psychologists.

Clearly a change either in vision or in the position sense would result in a changed relationship between the two. But saying that only the relationship between the two modalities changes is ignoring information about the changes *within* one (and only one) of the modalities.

Stratton's own reports make it clear that the first step in his adapting to inverted vision was to feel that his feet were in a new location relative to the rest of his body —a change within the position sense. Gradually, the felt locations of more and more of his body swung into line with that of his feet, that is, into line with the inverted visual scene. True, the final result was a new relationship between the position sense and visual perception, but this new relationship was brought about entirely by changes in the position sense, with no changes in vision.

In 1897, Stratton (pp. 472–475) theorized that adaptation is the attachment of new visual imagery to tactual sensations and, concurrently, the attachment of new tactual imagery to visual sensations. If we ignore the second half of this formulation and just postulate that adaptation consists of associating new visual imagery of parts of the body with proprioceptive stimuli from those parts, we can deal with much of the relevant data, provided we make one additional assumption: that the felt position of a limb is not directly connected with proprioceptive stimuli, but is a byproduct of where the limb is mentally pictured. The visual imagery notion, then, would make the same predictions as the proprioceptive-change hypothesis, but requires an extra step—a step that some subjects' introspections deny.

Kohler

Kohler's (1964) studies of adaptation to a wide variety of visual distortions have provided the inspiration, directly or indirectly, for much of the research in this field. He has concentrated on setting down his observations rather than on providing a detailed theory. It is clear that he agrees with Taylor that adaptation involves changes in directional perception, based on the acquisition of new behavioral responses to transformed retinal images (see, e.g., pp. 163–164). With prolonged exposure to reversing spectacles, Kohler says, there are eventually pictorial changes, with more and more stimuli "seen correctly" (pp. 140, 163–164). Unlike Taylor, however, Kohler thinks that verbal labeling is of no great significance in adaptation.

Although Kohler did mention (in a footnote) that "alterations in kinesthetic sensitivity" may be "of crucial importance" (p. 32) in adapting to displacement, he did not make much use of these alterations in explaining other aspects of adaptation. In fact, in his discussions of reversed vision, he regards such alterations as transitory—normal proprioception and kinesthesis are soon reinstated, and form the basis for the "correct" visual perception that ultimately emerges. In his theoretical discussions, Kohler did not attempt to explain the simpler phenomena of adaptation to displacement, inversion, and reversal of retinal images, but rather dealt with the complex "situational aftereffects."

Held

In an extensive series of carefully controlled experiments, Held and his co-workers have demonstrated the importance of active movement and movement-produced visual feedback ("reafference") in producing adaptation. These experiments set the pattern for most of the recent work in the area: brief adaptation periods with quantitative before-after measurements.

Held has been primarily concerned with the necessary preconditions for adaptation; he has said little about the nature of the adaptive change (see, e.g., Held, 1961). It is not clear whether Held believes that adaptation involves any perceptual changes, visual or proprioceptive. For instance, Held and Freedman (1963) say that adaptation "represents a change in state of the relevant sensorimotor control system, such that [after complete adaptation] the input-output or stimulus-response relation becomes identical to that which existed prior to rearrangement [p. 457]." Recently Efstathiou and Held (1964) proposed a tentative theory of arm adaptation to displacement, according to which "the change responsible for the shifts occurs in a representation, within the nervous system, of the spatial relation between the exposed arm and directions that are defined independently of that arm." Further elaboration of this model is necessary to determine how it differs from the proprioceptive-change intepretation.

IMPLICATIONS FOR PERCEPTUAL DEVELOPMENT

Psychologists have traditionally looked to studies of adaptation to distorted vision for clues about the development of visual perception in the infant. The usual, empiricist assumption (outlined by Berkeley in 1709 in his *New Theory of Vision;* see Berkeley, 1910) is that visual space perception is "secondary": It is based on the spatial sensations given by touch, kinesthesis, and position sense. As Dewey (1898) put it: "Ultimately visual perception rests on tactual. . . . Spatial relations are not originally perceived by the eye, but are the result of the association of visual sensations with previous muscular and tactual experiences [p. 165]."

This belief in the primacy of touch is so ingrained that experimental results are sometimes flagrantly misinterpreted in order to support it. Carr (1925), for instance, concluded: "It is thus obvious that the Stratton experiment involves no reconstruction or alteration of tactual . . . space. It is the visual system that is disrupted and then reorganized so as to conform to touch . . . [p. 141]." Stratton's, Kohler's, and Held's findings have been cited over and over as evidence that visual space perception is flexible and therefore must have been acquired through tactile-proprioceptive and motor experience. The reinterpretation of these findings that has been presented here suggests the opposite conclusion. Vision seems to be largely inflexible, whereas the position sense is remarkably labile.

The implication, if one dare draw any, is that the Berkeleyan notion should be turned around. It seems more plausible to assume that proprioceptive perception of parts of the body (and therefore of the locations of touched objects) develops with the help of innate visual perception rather than vice versa. A growing number of recent studies support the view that many aspects of visual perception are not influenced by experience and are largely innate (e.g., Bower, 1964; Fantz, 1965; Gibson & Walk, 1960; Hubel & Wiesel, 1963; Robinson, Brown, & Hayes, 1964). Furthermore, if the position sense were innate—if each spot on the skin were proprioceptively "preaddressed"—the local sign lodged in a baby's fingertip might go on forever signaling that his arm is 10 inches long.

So, when a baby stares raptly at his outstretched hand, he is probably finding out where his hand is, not what his visual sensations mean. He is making use of an adaptive mechanism that keeps his position sense accurate despite extensive and uneven growth of his body. This mechanism enables us to use the precise, detailed information that vision provides, as a means of continually readjusting our vaguer and more variable position sense.

REFERENCES

Berkeley, G. *An essay towards a new theory of vision.* New York: Dutton, 1910.

Bossom, J., & Held, R. Shifts in egocentric localization following prolonged displacement of the retinal image. *American Psychologist,* 1957, **12,** 454. (Abstract)

Bower, T. G. R. Discrimination of depth in premotor infants. *Psychonomic Science,* 1964, **1,** 368.

Carr, H. A. *Psychology: A study of mental activity.* New York: Longmans, Green, 1925.

Clark, B., & Graybiel, A. Perception of the postural vertical in normals and subjects with labyrinthine defects. *Journal of Experimental Psychology,* 1963, **65,** 490–494.

Cohen, H. B. Transfer and dissipation of aftereffects due to displacement of the visual field. *American Psychologist,* 1963, **18,** 411. (Abstract)

Dewey, J. *Psychology.* (3rd ed.) New York: American, 1898.

Efstathiou, Aglaia, & Held, R. Cross-modal transfer of adaptation to eye-hand rearrangement. Paper read at Eastern Psychological Association, Philadelphia, April 1964.

Fantz, R. L. Ontogeny of perception. In A. M. Schrier, H. F. Harlow, & F. Stollnitz (Eds.), *Behavior of nonhuman primates.* New York: Academic Press, 1965. Pp. 365–403.

Gibson, Eleanor J., & Walk, R. D. The "visual cliff." *Scientific American,* 1960, **202**(4), 64–71.

Gibson, J. J. *The perception of the visual world.* Boston: Houghton Mifflin, 1950.

Hamilton, C. R. Intermanual transfer of adaptation to prisms. *American Journal of Psychology,* 1964, **77,** 457–462. (a)

Hamilton, C. R. *Studies on adaptation to deflection of the visual field in split-brain mon-*

keys and man. (Doctoral dissertation, California Institute of Technology) Ann Arbor, Mich.: University Microfilms, 1964, No. 64-11,398. (b)

Harris, C. S. Adaptation to displaced vision: A proprioceptive change. (Doctoral dissertation, Harvard University) Ann Arbor, Mich.: University Microfilms, 1963, No. 63-8162. (a)

Harris, C. S. Adaptation to displaced vision: Visual, motor, or proprioceptive change? Science, 1963, 140, 812-813. (b)

Harris, C. S. The nature of adaptation to displaced vision. Paper read at Eastern Psychological Association, New York, April 1963. (c)

Hay, J. C., Pick, H. L., Jr., & Rosser, Edwenna. Adaptation to chromatic aberration by the human visual system. Science, 1963, 141, 167-169.

Hein, A. V., & Held, R. M. Transfer between visual-motor systems of adaptation to prismatic displacement of vision. Paper read at Eastern Psychological Association, New York, April 1960.

Held, R. Exposure-history as a factor in maintaining stability of perception and coordination. Journal of Nervous and Mental Disease, 1961, 132, 26-32.

Held, R., & Bossom, J. Neonatal deprivation and adult rearrangement: Complementary techniques for analyzing plastic sensory-motor coordinations. Journal of Comparative and Physiological Psychology, 1961, 54, 33-37.

Held, R., & Freedman, S. J. Plasticity in human sensorimotor control. Science, 1963, 142, 455-462.

Helmholtz, H. von. Popular scientific lectures. (Ed. by M. Kline) New York: Dover, 1962. (a)

Helmholtz, H. von. Treatise on physiological optics. (Trans. & Ed. by J. P. C. Southall) Vol. 3. New York: Dover, 1962. (b)

Hubel, D. H., & Wiesel, T. N. Receptive fields of cells in striate cortex of very young, visually inexperienced kittens. Journal of Neurophysiology, 1963, 26, 994-1002.

Klein, G. S. Cognitive control and motivation. In G. Lindzey (Ed.), Assessment of human motives. New York: Grove Press, 1960. Pp. 87-118.

Kohler, I. Über Aufbau und Wandlungen der Wahrnehmungswelt. Österreichische Akademie der Wissenschaften, Sitzungsberichte, Philosophisch-historische Klasse, 1951, 227, 1-118.

Kohler, I. Umgewöhnung im Wahrnehmungsbereich. Die Pyramide, 1953, 3, 92-96, 109-113, 132-133.

Kohler, I. The formation and transformation of the perceptual world. (Trans. by H. Fiss) Psychological Issues, 1964, 3(4).

McCollough, Celeste. Color adaptation of edge-detectors in the human visual system. Science, 1965, 149, 1115-1116. (a)

McCollough, Celeste. The conditioning of color perception. American Journal of Psychology, 1965, 78, in press. (b)

McLaughlin, S. C., & Bower, J. L. Auditory localization and judgments of straight ahead during adaptation to prism. Psychonomic Science, 1965, 2, 283-284.

McLaughlin, S. C., & Rifkin, K. I. Change in straight ahead during adaptation to prism. Psychonomic Science, 1965, 2, 107-108.

Mikaelian, H. Failure of bilateral transfer in modified eye-hand coordination. Paper read at Eastern Psychological Association, New York, April 1963.

Mittelstaedt, H. The role of movement in the origin and maintenance of visual perception: Discussion. In, Proceedings of the Seventeenth International Congress of Psychology. Amsterdam: North-Holland, 1964. P. 310. (Abstract)

Pick, H. L., Jr., Hay, J. C., & Pabst, Joan. Kinesthetic adaptation to visual distortion. Paper read at Midwestern Psychological Association, Chicago, May 1963.

Robinson, J. S., Brown, L. T., & Hayes, W. H. Test of effects of past experience on perception. Perceptual and Motor Skills, 1964, 18, 953-956.

Scholl, K. Das räumliche Zusammenarbeiten von Auge und Hand. Deutsch Zeitschrift für Nervenheilkunde, 1926, 92, 280-303.

Simons, J. C. Walking under zero-gravity conditions. United States Air Force, Wright Air Development Center, Technical Note No. 59-327, 1959. Cited by J. P. Loftus, Jr., &

Lois R. Hammer. Weightlessness. In N. M. Burns, R. M. Chambers, & E. Hendler (Eds.), *Unusual environments and human behavior*. New York: Free Press, 1963. Pp. 353–377.

Smith, K. U., & Smith, W. K. *Perception and motion*. Philadelphia: Saunders, 1962.

Stratton, G. M. Some preliminary experiments on vision without inversion of the retinal image. *Psychological Review,* 1896, **3,** 611–617.

Stratton, G. M. Vision without inversion of the retinal image. *Psychological Review,* 1897, **4,** 341–360, 463–481.

Stratton, G. M. The spatial harmony of touch and sight. *Mind,* 1899, **8,** 492–505.

Taylor, J. G. *The behavioral basis of perception*. New Haven: Yale University Press, 1962.

Walls, G. L. The problem of visual direction. *American Journal of Optometry,* 1951, **28,** 55–83, 115–146, 173–212.

CHAPTER TWELVE
PARENT-CHILD RELATIONS

There is little doubt that parents influence their children; the important point is *How?* This section considers three related questions: (1) the relation between parental attitudes and a child's personality adjustment; (2) the relation between childrearing practices and later intellectual development; and (3) the varying styles of childrearing practices as a function of time and social class.

Peterson *et al.* asked a simple question: Are fathers as important as mothers in shaping children's personalities? They compared a group of children receiving treatment from a child clinic with another group of "normal" children; interviews were taken from both mothers and fathers. The investigators wanted to know the relation between parental attitudes and child adjustment. They found that fathers of poorly adjusted children (conduct cases) tended to be ineffective, while the mothers tended to be maladjusted. In the case of children's personality disturbances (withdrawal), the mothers' behavior was independent of the children's problems, while the fathers' attitude tended to be cold.

Do children of high verbal ability (but low spatial or numerical skill) receive different early training than children of low verbal ability (but high spatial and numerical skill)? Bing surveyed several hundred children (boys and girls) in order to find four groups who possessed high verbal and low nonverbal abilities and the converse. She found that high verbal (with low nonverbal scores) ability was associated with mothers who gave strong verbal stimulation to their children during infancy and early childhood. Children who scored high on *non*verbal abilities and low on verbal abilities tended to have parents who let them explore their environment with few restrictions.

Fads in child rearing practices shift with the wind and whim of the times. The third paper shows trends in childrearing practices for differing social classes between 1940 and 1960. The investigators measured three groups with comparable socioeconomic status. Social class was related to two childrearing practices: Families of high social class tended to use suggestion in controlling their children, and they tended to impose less severe penalties for misbehavior. There is a cycle in child-rearing practices: In the thirties and the early forties middle-class parents were "strict," while during the fifties they were more permissive. Recently (1960) there has been a return to the middle ground.

42 Parental Attitudes and Child Adjustment

DONALD R. PETERSON   DONALD J. SHOEMAKER
WESLEY C. BECKER   HERBERT C. QUAY
LEO A. HELLMER

This study looked at the behavior of mothers and fathers of children who were undergoing treatment in a child clinic; they compared their behaviors with other parents of "normal" children from the community. The aim was to establish differential parental attitudes associated with two major areas of child disturbances: internal personality problems (withdrawal, feelings of inferiority) and conduct problems (stealing, fighting).

The investigators interviewed parents and then rated their answers. Both mothers and fathers of children in the clinic group were judged less well adjusted than parents of "normal" children. Clinic fathers were more likely to offer suggestions and tended toward the extremes of activity or disorganization. Personality problems were independent of mothers' attitudes in the clinic group but appeared to be related to an autocratic attitude on the part of fathers. Conduct problems were related to maladjustment on the part of the mothers and to permissiveness and ineffectuality on the part of the fathers.

Many contemporary personality theories attach great importance to the role parents play in determining the personality characteristics of children. Such emphasis is wisely placed. The primacy, the intimacy, and the extensive protraction of parental influences are likely to render them crucial to the formation of personality tendencies among children. In view of these considerations, there is a clear need for research in which important aspects of parental influence are examined, the behavior of children concurrently appraised, and relationships between the two sets of variables determined.

It is neither possible nor necessary to review here the mountainous literature on parent-child relationships which has emerged over the past 30 years, but certain

Adapted from Parental attitudes and child adjustment. *Child Development*, 1959, **30**, 119–130.

remarks concerning that literature can and should be made. A good deal of it consists of "expert" advice whose content changes with fashion (Stendler, 1950) and whose factual basis is obscure. Much of the rest is theory, which is sometimes a product of keen observation and closely reasoned thought, but which is seldom buttressed by carefully gathered, rigorously evaluated empirical data. There remain a number of excellent investigations on parent-child relationships, among which the works of Radke (1946), Baldwin and his collaborators (1949), and Sears et al. (1957) seem particularly outstanding, but it is no disparagement of these and similar studies to note that they leave large areas of the domain almost entirely untouched. A major hiatus exists, for example, in regard to the attitudes of fathers and their part in the formation of personality tendencies among children. A review of the literature on parent-child relationships over the years 1929 to 1956 revealed at least 169 publications dealing with relationships between mothers and their children. Available information on father-child relationships, by contrast, was encompassed in 10 articles, one convention address, and one book. This imbalance has ordinarily been justified through reference to an assumption that mothers play a more important part than fathers in the development of child personality. Levy's statement is typical: "It is generally accepted that the most potent of all influences on social behavior is derived from the social experience of the mother" (Levy, 1943). The present study permits evaluation of the validity of this assumption through examination of both parents and assessment of their relative influence on the behavior of children.

An analogous sampling restriction obtains in respect to most available investigations of child behavior. Attention has ordinarily been limited either to problem behavior or to "normal" activity. To our knowledge, there has been *no* research in which both fathers and mothers have been studied and their attitudes related to the behavior of disturbed as well as "normal" children, although the methodological advantage to be gained through expansion of variance among children is obvious. In this investigation, the families of both problem and nonproblem children have been examined. The study has two specific purposes. The first is to assess differences between parental attitudes in two groups of families, one in which the children display certain adjustment problems, and another in which they do not. The second is to establish, within the group of families where the children have problems, differential attitudinal patterns associated with two major dimensions of child behavior difficulty.

SUBJECTS AND PROCEDURES

Thirty-one families were selected for investigation from the clientele of a guidance clinic. All the children were from 6 to 12 years of age, of Caucasian extraction, and manifested difficulties in adjustment of sufficient severity to warrant treatment. Cases of known organic brain damage or other serious physical defect, families in which the parents were separated, and cases of intellectual retardation were excluded. We shall refer to this sample henceforth as the *Clinic* group. They were compared with 29 *Nonclinic* families in which the children had been judged by teachers to display acceptable adjustment tendencies in school. Age was again restricted to the range 6 to 12. Since no children with organic disturbances or intellectual defect appeared on the lists submitted by teachers, exclusion in terms of these criteria was unnecessary.

The groups do not differ significantly in respect to any of the dimensions examined (age and IQ of child, SES, and age, IQ, and education of mother and father), though there is an unequal representation of boys and girls in the Clinic group which approaches statistical reliability. The proportion of boys to girls in the latter sample is more than 2:1, while there are only a few more boys than girls in the Nonclinic group. Such disparity is typical of most clinic populations, but its possible effect on the results of this study will receive later comment. The discrepancy in child IQ also approaches significance ($.10 < pt < .20$), but the fact that the IQs of parents were not reliably different (means for Clinic parents were in fact numerically superior to those for the Nonclinic group) suggests that the lower functional intelligence of the Clinic children is part and parcel of the adjustment difficulty, and constitutes an interesting trend in its own right.

On the basis of a one-hour interview, parents were rated on 17 of the 30 Fels Parent Behavior Rating Scales (Baldwin, Kalhorn, & Breese, 1949). The 17 scales were selected on the basis of Roff's factor analysis (1949) in such a way that each factor was represented by at least two of the most heavily saturated rating scales.

Four staff psychologists and one advanced graduate student in clinical psychology performed the ratings immediately after each interview. Methodological ideals would have been most neatly met by rigorous structuring of the interview, but the need to allow parents of disturbed children to discuss problems in their own terms prevented such standardization. Rather free discussion was therefore permitted through much of the interview, but certain standard questions were asked, as needed, to insure collection of data relevant to the ratings. Distributions of scores on each of the attitudinal factors were then formed separately for fathers and mothers, and χ^2 analyses of discrepancy between the Clinic and Nonclinic groups conducted. Cutting points were set as close to the first and third quartiles as the distributions would permit, thus segregating the groups into those manifesting high, average, and low scores on each factor, and χ^2 calculated in accordance with the procedure suggested by McNemar (1949) for analysis of $2 \times k$ tables.

Information pertinent to reliability of the attitudinal factors was obtained by recording three interviews and comparing judgments made by the five interviewers after listening to the recordings. Over all comparisons, the judges were in agreement more than 80 per cent of the time in classifying subjects as high, average, or low on the factors, and *no* radical disagreements were found, i.e., in no case did a single judge regard a case as high on a given factor when another judge assigned the subject a low score. Such agreement seems quite remarkable in the light of commonly expressed views about the unreliability of clinical judgments. It appears that if raters are asked to judge certain well-defined variables at an appropriate level of differentiation, and are given enough information to do so, they can perform the rating task in a thoroughly acceptable way.

During the interviews with parents, information was also obtained about the nature of the problem which each child displayed. A rating schedule derived from Himmelweit's analysis (1952) of Ackerson's data (1942) on problem children was employed. The schedule required 3-point ratings of

8 behavior characteristics loading on a *personality problem* factor (sensitivity, absentmindedness, seclusiveness, day-dreaming, ineffciency in work, inferiority feelings, changeability of mood, and nervousness), and 11 tendencies loading on a *conduct problem* factor (truancy from home, truancy from school, stealing, fighting, lying, destructiveness, swearing, disobedience, rudeness, selfishness, and temper tantrums). Unit weights were assigned, and the two factor scores derived by direct addition of the appropriate elemental scores. The child problem scores were then correlated with each parent attitude factor to determine the kinds of attitudes associated with each problem dimension. This analysis was performed separately for mothers and fathers, and was restricted to the Clinic group. To reduce contamination, attitudes of mothers were correlated with judgments of child behavior based on the reports of fathers, and attitudes of fathers correlated with judgments based on the mothers' reports of child behavior.

Reliability of ratings on problem activity was estimated by correlating scores derived from the interviews of mothers with those based on the accounts of fathers. Correlations of .40 and .83 emerged for personality problem and conduct problem, respectively. Evidently the open behavior involved in conduct problems can be judged with fair accuracy, but the fine discriminations required in judging the severity of internalized difficulties, within such a homogeneous group as the present one, are too difficult to permit close agreement.

It is of methodological interest to note that gross classification of children into those manifesting personality problems and those manifesting conduct problems could be done in a highly reliable way. When classification was made simply by noting which of the two problem scores was higher, and designation based on father report compared with that based on mother report, only one case of actual disagreement was found. Classification was impossible in four cases, because the scores were equal, but independent judgments were in accord for the remaining 26 cases (84 per cent). Insufficiency of N in the two groups of problem children prohibited direct comparative study, and required use of the correlational analysis of dimensions described above, but investigators can be encouraged by the possibility of attaining respectably high agreement, not only in rating parental attitudes, but in rating child behavior, when variables are defined with proper care and the differentiations required are appropriate to the sensitivities of the judges.

Configural analyses of inter- and intra-parental patterns were considered, but on the basis of two pilot studies rejected in favor of the simpler, more straightforward, and evidently more powerful statistical techniques described above. A factor analysis drawn from the same basic data pool as the present one but dealing with a differently constituted set of variables is reported elsewhere (Becker, Peterson, Hellmer, Shoemaker, & Quay, 1959).

RESULTS

Results of comparison between the Clinic and Nonclinic parents are given in Table 1. Both mothers and fathers of problem children were judged to be less well adjusted and sociable, more autocratic, and to experience more disciplinary contention than were the parents in the Nonclinic group. No other reliable discrepancies were found for mothers, although a tendency for Clinic mothers to be either very strict or very permissive in disciplining their children approached significance. Fathers, however, differed reliably in respect to two dimensions which did not differentiate between the Clinic and Nonclinic mothers. The fathers of problem children were more prone to make suggestions than were the fathers of children without known problems, and were either highly active and rigidly organized or relatively inactive and disorganized in the conduct of their affairs. They also tended toward extremes in regard to concern for their children, but discrepancy along this dimension did not quite reach the level usually demanded for assertion of statistical significance.

In erecting hypotheses for study in future research, it is often fruitful to consider not only statistically significant results, but more modest data trends as well. If this is done by considering all parent attitudes for which r exceeds .20, the following patterns emerge. Personality problems seem largely independent of maternal attitude, but related to dictatorial attitudes and a lack of genuine concern among fathers. Conduct problems are related chiefly to maladjustment among mothers, and to democratic attitudes and heightened feelings of parental concern among fathers. Both parents appear overly permissive, and characterization of the fathers of children who present conduct problems as generally weak and ineffectual may not be far wide of the mark. Democratic qualities are esteemed in our culture, but when they are combined with laxity, unwillingness to issue orders, exaggerated concern for children, and a tendency to shelter them in the face of day-to-day problems the seeds of conduct disorders may be sown.

DISCUSSION

Probably the most significant finding to emerge from this study is that the attitudes of fathers are at least as intimately related as maternal attitudes to the occurrence and form of behavior problems in children. The popular choice of mothers as a focus of research attention and the general clinical tendency to offer psychotherapy to the mothers rather than the fathers of disturbed children are usually rationalized by noting that mothers generally spend more time with their children than fathers do, and by speculating that mother-child relationships are more intimate affairs than those between fathers and children. Whatever the validity of these assumptions, only the final effect is of fundamental concern, and we now have reason to believe that the emphasis in this effect is not as one-sided as it has previously appeared.

TABLE 1   Comparison between Clinic and Nonclinic Parents

Parent Attitude Factor	Mothers				Fathers			
	Clinic	Non-clinic	χ^2	p	Clinic	Non-clinic	$l\chi^2$	p
1. Concern for child			1.92	<.50			5.40	<.10
high	10	5			12	6		
average	15	16			9	17		
low	6	8			10	6		
2. Democratic guidance			8.58[a]	<.02			10.25[a]	<.01
high	5	11			4	13		
average	13	15			15	13		
low	13	3			12	3		
3. Permissiveness			4.79	<.10			1.17	<.70
high	8	6			8	9		
average	11	18			14	15		
low	12	5			9	5		
4. Parent-child harmony			21.13[a]	<.001			19.03[a]	<.001
high	2	11			4	13		
average	15	18			13	16		
low	14	0			14	0		
5. Sociability-adjustment			18.09[a]	<.001			7.14[a]	<.05
high	2	14			5	10		
average	15	13			14	16		
low	14	2			12	3		
6. Activeness			1.04	<.70			8.21[a]	<.02
high	10	6			10	4		
average	15	16			11	21		
low	6	7			10	4		
7. Readiness of suggestion			2.20	<.30			7.69[a]	<.05
high	10	5			13	3		
average	15	15			13	18		
low	6	9			5	8		

[a] Significant at or beyond .05 level.

The extent to which the present results were affected by sex disparity among children is difficult to assess. Surely the presence of twice as many boys as girls in the Clinic sample could have a bearing on any findings related to relative influence of the two parents on child behavior, and we may only have demonstrated that fathers play a more vital role in influencing the behavior of *boys* than has previously been assumed. Even this, however, would be a result worth noting, and, while there is an obvious need to find out whether the present results can be repeated in a study involving more nearly equal representation of boys and girls, the necessity for examining paternal influence remains as vital as before. The practical difficulties involved in securing the cooperation of fathers for a study such as this are considerable, but they can be overcome, and it is now clear that they must be overcome if the social environment, in its relationship to personality development in children, is ever to be understood.

The various relationships, as we have reported them, are probably better estimates of "true" association than some theory and previous research would lead one to expect. We have eliminated at least a little of the contamination-generated spuriousness of many earlier investigations, and as a consequence, relationships between parental attitudes and child behavior appear with generally lower magnitude. We would be the last to deny the importance of the relationships we have presented, no matter how small they seem, and in evaluating the importance of our results feel justified in Agreeing with Sears et al. (1957), who regard the location of any real (i.e., replicable) influence, however low its magnitude, as a contribution to knowledge. "If our general assumption is correct—i.e., that any given behavior is the product of many influences—it would be quite impossible to obtain high correlations between single child-rearing dimensions and the measures of child behavior." But the results pointedly indicate the operation of many factors other than the ones we chose to examine. Though certain general statistical tendencies emerged, we still found families in which the parents appeared maladjusted, evidently didn't get along, and exhibited the most abhorrent kinds of attitudes toward their children, but the children appeared to be getting along beautifully. We saw parents whose attitudes and other characteristics were in nearly perfect congruence with the stereotype of the "good parent," but whose children displayed problems of the most severe order. The need to expand the scope of studies on personality development, and to examine other parental characteristics, relationships with such influential adults as teachers, interactions with siblings and peers, in sum, a more complete matrix of social factors, is patently clear.

It is our belief, however, that even if all social influences could be encompassed, and absolutely perfect measurement of them attained, a sizeable share of the variance in child behavior would still be unexplained. Parents frequently reported that their children had displayed certain behavior consistencies very early in life, and that these tendencies had remained stable in the face of what often appeared to be very extensive changes in social environment. In a study of parent-child relationships of the present kind, we are not dealing with unidirectional causalities; we are dealing with interactions. We have reported a number of correlations and other relationships between parental attitudes and child behavior, and have sometimes implied that the former caused the latter. This inference seems the most likely of the several which might be made, but the tenability of other interpretations cannot be denied. To explicate the second most likely inference, it is often just as reasonable to assume that personality tendencies on the part of the children, appearing very early in life and possibly of constitutional origin, have engendered modification of parental attitudes. The parents of a stable, predictable, sensible child can afford to be democratic. As Escalona (1948) has suggested, the parents of an erratic, difficult, peculiar child may become apparently inconsistent out of sheer desperation. The direction of a causal relationship can only be established through determination of temporal priority, and the need to examine children very early in their development, and to explore the effects children may have on parents, is logically as critical as examination of the kinds of relationships with which this study is primarily concerned.

The extent to which the results have been influenced by rater bias is unknown. The interviewers made a conscious effort to avoid such bias, and it is entirely possible that estimates of "true" relationships were reduced rather than magnified through the operation of the systematic error such an effort could conceivably entail. In the correlational analysis, contamination was reduced by relating parental attitudes as measured on interview with one parent to child behavior as independently assessed by the clinician who saw the other parent. Throughout the study, however, interviewers knew which parents belonged to which group, they had rather firm ideas about the kind of behavior disturbance each child in the Clinic group presented, and there is a real possibility that some of the "significant" results reported above are spurious. Certain of the results were contrary to expectation, no obvious "bias factor" emerged on factor analysis of these and other data, and both considerations suggest that obtained associations were not completely generated by the preconceptions of the raters. Still the actual effect, even the probable direction of the effect of bias, is indeterminate, and will remain so until the appropriate methodological improvements are made. The need for direct, independent, objective measurement of parental attitudes and of child behavior is obvious. Much of our current effort is addressed to the development of such measures in the conviction that their proper application can determine some of the facts so urgently needed for adequate explanation, accurate prediction, and successful modification of developing personality trends in children.

REFERENCES

Ackerson, L. *Children's behavior problems.* Chicago: University of Chicago Press, 1942.

Baldwin, A. L. The effect of home environment on nursery school behavior, *Child Development,* 1949, **20,** 49–62.

Baldwin, A. L., Kalhorn, Joan, & Breese, Fay H. The appraisal of parent behavior. *Psychological Monographs,* 1949, **63,** Whole No. 4.

Becker, W. C., Peterson, D. R., Hellmer, L. A., Shoemaker, D. J., & Quay, H. C. Factors in parental behavior and personality as related to problem behavior in children. *J. consult. Psychol.,* 1959, **23,** 107–118.

Escalona, Sibylle. Some considerations regarding psychotherapy with psychotic children. *Bulletin of the Menninger Clinic,* 1948, **12,** 127–134.

Himmelweit, Hilde T. A factorial study of "Children's behavior problems." Unpublished manuscript, University of London, 1952. Cited in H. J. Eysenck. *The structure of human personality.* London: Metheun, 1953.

Levy, D. M. *Maternal overprotection.* New York: Columbia University Press, 1943.

McNemar, Q. *Psychological statistics.* New York: Wiley, 1949.

Radke, Marion J. *The relation of parental authority to children's behavior and attitudes.* Minneapolis, Minn.: University of Minnesota Press, 1946.

Roff, M. A factorial study of the Fels Parent Behavior Scales. *Child Development,* 1949, **20,** 29–45.

Sears, R. R., Maccoby, Eleanor E., & Levin, H. *Patterns of childrearing.* Evanston, Ill.: Row, Peterson, 1957.

Stendler, Celia B. Sixty years of child training practices. *Journal of Pediatrics,* 1950, **36,** 122–134. (1950).

43 | Effect of Childrearing Practices on Development of Differential Cognitive Abilities

ELIZABETH BING

The present study searched for relations between early childrearing practices and later intellectual abilities; by separating groups of boys and girls into those who possessed high verbal and low nonverbal intelligence, and those who possessed high nonverbal and low verbal intelligence, the author was able to examine differences in childrearing practices and their relation to intellectual abilities. She used 60 fifth-grade children in her sample. Comparison of the groups through an interview and a mother-child interaction situation showed several variables related to children's intellectual capacity.

Mothers whose children were low in spatial or number ability but high in verbal ability gave their children more verbal stimulation during early infancy and childhood, let their children participate in conversations more, punished them less for poor speech, bought them more books, criticized them for poor academic achievement, and perceived their husbands as strict. Also, mothers of high verbal children helped them more in an interview situation than did mothers of low verbal children. The findings suggest that high verbal ability (coupled with low numerical and spatial ability) is fostered by a close relation with a demanding and intrusive mother, while high nonverbal abilities (coupled with low verbal abilities) are enhanced by allowing the child considerable freedom to explore on his own.

Individual differences in cognitive development have come to be considered the result of interactions between a child's life experiences and the set of genes with which he has been endowed. Relations have been found between cognitive abilities and perceptual and cognitive style on one side and personality traits on the other side, and some investigators have made efforts to identify antecedent conditions in the home which might be responsible for differences in children's personality as well as cognitive development. Thus "democratic homes"

Adapted from Effect of child rearing practices on development of differential cognitive abilities. *Child Development*, 1963, **34**, 631–648.

(Baldwin, 1955), "maternal acceleration" (Moss & Kagan, 1958), and a "warm, positive family atmosphere" (Milner, 1951) have been reported to increase the rate of growth of children's intelligence, especially verbal ability. Results of investigations of the effect of institutionalization, and prolonged hospitalization of infants, summarized by McCarthy (1954, pp. 584–585), uniformly indicate retardation in language development. On the other hand, there has been suggestive evidence that certain conditions favor disproportionately the development of verbal ability and possibly impede the development of nonverbal skills, like numerical and spatial ability. Suggested as antecedents for such differential development in favor of verbal ability were "growth restricting" childrearing practices such as parental overlimitation and excessive control, "maternal overprotection" (Levy, 1943), "emphasis on verbal accomplishment" (Levinson, 1958), and a "demanding discipline with emphasis on academic achievement" (Kent & Davis, 1957). Similarly, overanxious discipline and tense parent-child relationships were postulated to be responsible for low nonverbal, especially spatial, ability in children.

While the consistently found superiority of boys over girls in spatial ability may be considered innate (Emmet, 1949), there has been suggestive evidence that this may be the result of differences in roles assigned to males and females in our culture (Bieri, 1960).

Most of these studies, while yielding intriguing leads, failed to measure children's verbal and nonverbal abilities with relatively "pure" tests. Also, these studies investigated primarily parents' present-day childrearing behavior and did not attempt to investigate the very early mother-child relationships. Furthermore, the sole measure of parents' behavior used was the interview of the parent.

In the present study, specifically designed tests were used to measure children's verbal and nonverbal abilities, such as spatial and numerical, as well as their total IQ in order to identify groups of children with discrepant abilities. An effort was made to investigate not only present, but also early childrearing practices as far as they may be assumed to be antecedents to differential cognitive development in children. And, finally, the mother's actual mode of interaction with the child was observed in a fairly structured situation.

From the theoretical considerations and available research findings, it was assumed that childrearing practices which stimulate, reward, and encourage verbal or nonverbal abilities should increase either one of these abilities and that fostering dependency should favor verbal ability while

at the same time depressing nonverbal ability, whereas fostering independence should have the opposite effect. While not consistent over all age groups, some studies indicate female superiority in verbal and male superiority in numerical ability (Kuckenberg, 1962). It was therefore thought worthwhile to test the hypothesis that emphasis on sex-typing should reinforce verbalism as a sex-appropriate trait in girls and spatial and numerical ability in boys.

METHODS AND PROCEDURES

Subjects

The subjects of the sample consisted of 60 mothers who had children who were in the fifth grade and had discrepant cognitive abilities. The selection was made from a total of 1214 children representing the universe of fifth grade children in the public school system of Redwood City and San Carlos, two communities in the San Francisco Bay Area. The basic discrepancy that was of interest for the purpose of the study was the comparison of high verbal children with low verbal children of similar IQ, the complementary nonverbal abilities being either spatial or numerical ability.

Verbal and nonverbal mental abilities were partly assessed on the basis of results of the Thurstone's SRA Primary Mental Abilities for ages 7 to 11 (Form AH) which was administered to all fifth grade children in their classrooms. The scores obtained by each child on the verbal, spatial, and numerical parts of this test were supplemented by scores from the Iowa Achievement Test or the California Mental Maturity Test. Cases with total PMA scores below 125, cases with visual or hearing impairment, cases from foreign language homes, and cases whose "high" ability was below the population median, and those whose "low" ability was above the population median were dropped from the sample.

With this selection procedure the following four major groups could be established: 16 high verbal boys, 16 low verbal boys, 12 high verbal girls, and 16 low verbal girls. The contrasting ability was spatial ability for one half and numerical ability for the other half of these groups with the exception of the group of the 12 high verbal girls. Eight of these were low in space and four were low in number. Cases of girls with high verbal, low number ability were surprisingly difficult to find.

Measurement of Antecedent Variables

Questionnaire The mother was asked to fill in a questionnaire which consisted of 20 groups of questions referring to factual material in relation to the mother's caretaking activity of the child, the child's first verbal and nonverbal accomplishments, kinds of toys, number of story books, and the mother's as well as her husband's interest in reading and manual activities. The mother was also asked to estimate age levels at which she thought the average child would have usually learned a variety of listed behaviors, some of these based on Winterbottom's scale (1953), such as feeding himself, keeping room tidy, shopping for own clothing, crossing busy street, etc.

Interview The interviews with the mothers were semistructured with open-ended questions similar to the type developed by Sears, Maccoby, and Levin (1957) and by Bandura and Walters (1959). It was attempted to cover in the interviews the child's early history as well as the present with respect to the mother's behavior regarding her relationship with the child, verbal stimulation provided by her, fostering dependency or independence in the child, verbal freedom allowed, permission for object experimentation, emphasis on sociability, academic achievement and sex-typing, and restrictiveness. The interviews lasted from 1 to 2 hours, were tape recorded, and conducted by one graduate student in psychology and the author. Neither of the two interviewers knew to which group the mother belonged.

Three graduate students in psychology and the author rated the interviews from the tape recordings according to preconstructed rating scales comprising 41 dimensions. Most of these scales were 5-point scales, specifying five different levels of behavior or attitudes. All 60 interviews were rated by various combinations of two of the four raters, and none of the raters knew to which group the case belonged.

Interaction situation Either before or after the interview, the child was called in and the mother was asked to read some verbal problem questions to the child, and, following the completion of this task, the child was requested by the observer to perform two nonverbal tasks.

While seemingly the child's performance was the focus of attention, the situation was devised to obtain firsthand observational data on the mother's mode of interaction with the child. The situation was so constructed that the mothers could demonstrate a great variability of behavior, from no intervention at all to a high degree of helping, pressuring, or disapproving types of behavior.

For the verbal task, a comprehension type test was used. It contained five problem situations which were rather difficult for 10-year-old children to answer satisfactorily. The questions were also worded in such a way that several solutions were possible. Two of the questions required the child to give reasons to explain a fact; the reasons being manifold, it gave the mother an opportunity to prompt, encourage, or pressure the child to improve his answer. (Example: Why should children not be out in the street alone at night?)

The mother's behavior with the child during the verbal and nonverbal tasks was analyzed according to pre-established categories which were thought to represent different degrees and manners of stimulating and helping the child with his tasks. The following nine categories could be distinguished for both verbal and performance tasks: Focusing, Approval, Encouragement, Prompting, Giving answers (instead of letting child answer), Pressure for improvement, Disapproval, Withholding help, and Helping after request from child. One category covering the number of questions the mother asked the experimenter was devised as yielding a possible measure of the mother's dependency needs, or at least her need for more structure. Three additional categories were established for the nonverbal tasks, dealing with the mother's physical help-giving behavior, such as the mother's own handling of puzzle pieces, showing of her own copy to child, and the time elapsed until the mother made her first help-giving response. This resulted in a total of 22 categories.

Reliabilities of Ratings

As a measure of the reliabilities of the ratings for the questionnaire and the interview, the percentage of cases with perfect agreement between two raters and the percentage of cases with 1 and with more than 1 point difference was computed for every scale. Perfect agreement of ratings ranged from 62 to 100 per cent of the cases for the questionnaire scales and from 48 to 88 per cent for the interview scales. Agreement within 1 point ranged from 89 to 100 per cent for questionnaire scales and from 87 to 100 per cent for the interview scales.

Correlational Analysis and Combination of Variables

From the questionnaire, the interview, and the interaction situation, a total of 79 variables was obtained. In cases where variables were assumed to belong to the same complex of behavior, but to represent different aspects of it, the scores of these variables were combined if the variables also actually showed a correlation of at least .26 which corresponds to the .05 level of significance for our sample of 60 cases. As a result of these combinations the 16 questionnaire and 41 interview variables were reduced to a total of 34 variables and the 22 interaction categories or variables to a total of 15.

The differences between the means of all variables for the high verbal children as compared to the low verbal children and for the high verbal boys and girls as compared to the low verbal boys and girls had to be tested for significance. This was done by the t technique for testing differences between independent means for small samples. For two variables showing extreme skewed distributions, the chi square method for testing the significance of the differences between the distributions for two contrast groups was used.

RESULTS

Interview and Questionnaire

Of the 34 single and combined variables of the interview and questionnaire, 10 were found to distinguish significantly between high and low verbal groups (see Table 1).

Antecedents of Verbal Ability

Verbal stimulation and interest shown by mother For the early childhood period, a combination of measures relating to the child's early verbal stimulation (amount of playtime mother had with infant, verbal stimulation of infant, mother's responsiveness to child's early questions, taking young child on outings, early reading to child, tutoring before school, interest shown in child's good speech habits) differentiated on a highly significant level between high verbal and low verbal groups for boys and for sexes combined as predicted, $p < .001$ in favor of more verbal stimulation during infancy occurring with high verbal than with low verbal groups. While for the girls, taken by themselves, the mean of this variable was higher for the high verbal than for the low verbal group, the difference was not large enough to be significant.

Verbal freedom Two of the seven scales assumed to measure different aspects of verbal freedom differentiated significantly between groups as predicted. Punishment for poor speech differentiated significantly in favor of LoV as compared to HiV girls, and amount of meal conversation distinguished HiV from LoV groups significantly for boys and for sexes combined. None of the differences on the measures dealing with permissiveness or punishment for verbal aggression, permissiveness to listen and participate in adult conversation, and freedom for democratic discussion to discuss "adult" topics was significant.

Emphasis on academic achievement The hypothesis that verbal ability should be associated with emphasis on academic achievement was confirmed when criticism for poor academic achievement was taken as a separate measure, but not for a combination of this measure with rewarding academic achievement, level of schooling desired by parents, and amount of present tutoring. Criticism for poor academic achievement, taken by itself, discriminated significantly between HiV and LoV groups for boys, girls, and for sexes combined, the means of criticism of poor academic achievement being higher for all high verbal groups.

Sex-role differentiation and parent's own verbal interest It was hypothesized that, for girls, verbal ability should be positively associated with mother's emphasis on the girl's adopting a feminine role and sex-appropriate behavior and with father's relative strictness and that for both sexes it would be associated with like-sex parent's amount of time spent reading. The hypothesis with respect to father's strictness was partly confirmed; significant results were obtained though not predicted for girls with respect to father's reading time. None of the other variables of this cluster distinguished significantly between groups.

While mothers of the high verbal group girls reported on the average that their husbands were stricter than themselves, this difference failed to reach significance. However, further analysis of the data indicated that, for those of the HiV girls whose low ability was space, the difference was significant at the .05 level, the stricter father being associated with the HiV girl group.

One assumption had been that the mother's perception of the father as the "Master" would enhance the masculinity of the male role and implicitly the feminine role of the girl in the family and might reveal the importance that the mother attaches to appropriate sex-typing and thereby strengthening girls' verbal ability. This was borne out with respect to the HiV-LoS girls and their contrast group.

The fact that father's reading time discriminated highly in favor of high verbal ability only for girls and not for boys was just as surprising as the fact that mother's reading time did not differentiate between any of the groups. The latter fact may be due to lower dispersion of scores of reading time for mothers. The assumption that with respect to verbal and nonverbal ability children would model themselves after the like-sex parent was not borne out. Many of the mothers' behavior patterns and attitudes that were investigated through the interview seemed to influence boys' cognitive development, but not girls'; on the other hand, of the very few behavior patterns pertaining to fathers that were evaluated, two proved to be significantly associated with girls' cognitive development. This points to the possible importance of the influence of the opposite-sex parent on the child's cognitive development. Such an influence is hard to account for in terms of our present knowledge of personality development, but merits further investigation.

Antecedents of Nonverbal Ability

Nonverbal stimulation and freedom of exploration It was hypothesized that nonverbal ability should be associated with opportunity and freedom for exploration and object experimentation at preschool age and at present. This hypothesis was confirmed with respect to boys for a combination of the measures of permissiveness for object experimentation at preschool age, availability to child of tools, gadgets, and objects for experimentation at present, and lack of restrictions indoors and outdoors. It was not confirmed for the measures of number of toys at preschool age and strictness of time schedules.

While the number of toys that children have before school age did not seem to be a significant antecedent to nonverbal cognitive development, the freedom the children have in playing with these toys and in exploring their environment was the condition that discriminated significantly between HiV and LoV groups of boys, the greater freedom being associated with the low verbal boys who are high either in space or number.

Sex-role differentiation and parent's own nonverbal interest It was hypothesized that nonverbal ability should be positively associated for boys with mother's emphasis on the boy's adopting a masculine role and sex-appropriate behavior and for both sexes with parents' time spent with child in arts, crafts, hobbies, and do-it-yourself activities. None of these hypotheses was confirmed.

Dependency-Independence

It was hypothesized that verbal ability was associated with mother's behavior fostering dependency and nonverbal ability with behavior fostering independence. Dependency-fostering behavior was measured by (a) encouragement of emotional dependency and lack of punishment for dependency; (b) permissiveness for instrumental dependency; (c) anxiety arousal in cautiousness training; (d) continuity of mother-child relationship; and (e) continuity of caretaking activity. One of these five measures, anxiety arousal in cautiousness training, differentiated between the high and low verbal group, greater anxiety

arousal being associated with the HiV group for boys and sexes combined.

The assumption was thus borne out, at least for boys, that the mother who tried to impress the child more with the potential dangers of the environment would make the child more anxious, insecure, and dependent and thus less capable of dealing with cognitive tasks presumably requiring more independence, such as arithmetic and spatial relations.

Interaction Situation

1. The hypothesis that high verbal mothers should be more active in all categories of help-giving behavior (focusing, encouragement, approval, prompting and answering problems for child) was confirmed, at least when these categories were combined. The differences were significant at the $< .01$ level for girls and for sexes combined. However, the differences were not significant for boys alone. When the help-giving behavior on the nonverbal tasks alone was considered, the differences in favor of the high verbal mothers were highly significant for the same groups, in addition to a difference at the $< .05$ level for the boys. On the other hand, if one considers some of the help-giving activities on the verbal tasks alone, they did not yield significant differences. This was true for approval and for the combination of focusing and prompting and giving answers, where the differences for the means were for all groups in the predicted direction, but did not reach significance. However, with respect to helping the child focus on the verbal task as a separate variable, the mothers of HiV girls were significantly higher on this behavior category than the mothers of the LoV girls.

2. The hypothesis that high verbal group mothers should be higher in pressure for improvement was confirmed for HiV girls as compared to LoV girls. This held true for nonverbal tasks as well as for the combination of verbal and nonverbal tasks, but not for verbal tasks alone.

3. The hypothesis that high verbal group mothers should give help more often after request was confirmed for girls and sexes combined. There were no differences for any of the boys' groups. The number of times a mother helped a child after request was partly a function of the child's asking for help. It appeared that the child who had learned to expect an answer, at least intermittently, would ask more questions. The child's asking questions in the observed interaction situation may then be partly a measure of the mother's past (unobserved) behavior in interaction with the child; this category may thus reflect not so much temporary behavior specific to the experimental situation, but rather usual interaction patterns between mother and child.

4. The hypothesis that high nonverbal mothers should disapprove and withhold help more often was not only not confirmed, but the observed differences were significant in the opposite direction. High verbal group mothers disapproved and withheld help more often. This was true for girls and sexes combined, while the difference for boys was in the same direction but failed to reach significance. On this measure of "negative" interaction, just as on "help after request," a measure of "positive" interaction, high verbal mothers scored significantly higher. It appears, therefore, that what is important seems to be the degree of interaction between mother and child rather than its content.

5. As predicted, high verbal group mothers asked the observer more questions. This was true for girls' mothers with respect to HiV as compared to LoV groups. Again, no significant differences were found for boys' mothers. It was thought that the mother's need to ask questions about procedure would be a measure of one aspect of her dependency needs. That this measure yielded significant results for girls' mothers, but not for boys' mothers, came as a surprise, but was consistent with results for the other categories where mother's behavior was found to be significant mainly for girls' discrepancy groups.

6. The hypothesis that high verbal group mothers should give more physical help was confirmed when the chi square method of analyzing the data instead of the comparison of means was used. Twelve of the 32 LoV group mothers abstained completely from giving any physical help as compared to four of the 28 HiV group mothers ($\chi^2 = 4.19$; $df = 1$), a difference significant at the $< .05$ level for a one-tailed test.

7. The hypothesis that on performance tasks HiV mothers should give help sooner was also confirmed, when they were compared with LoV mothers for the whole sample as to whether they waited 30 seconds or less (8 HiV and 6 LoV), 30 seconds to 5 minutes (15 HiV and 12 LoV), or more than 5 minutes (5 HiV and 14 LoV) before helping physically. The difference was significant ($\chi^2 = 4.73$; $df = 2$) at the .05 level for a one-tailed test.

The pattern of behavior of the high verbal girls' mothers was thus quite different from the behavior of the low verbal group. The HiV mothers showed on the average more positive and negative interaction with the child, the child asking more often for help and getting the help part of the time. Most of the help was given without being requested by the child, and these mothers helped their children, especially on the performance tasks, in all categories of helping behavior. Their motivation might very well have been their eagerness for the child to do well on the tasks, since these were also the mothers who, on the average, pressured their children more for improvement of responses than the mothers of the high nonverbal children. While thus attempting to help their children, these mothers of high verbal children revealed themselves to be rather controlling and pressuring while the mothers of the high nonverbal group left their children more on their own and interfered less with their responses.

Comparison of Results of Interview and Interaction Situation

Comparing the results of the interview with those of the interaction situation, it appeared that the interview variables that distinguished significantly between groups did so mainly for boys, while the observation situation variables did so mainly for girls.

Implication of Results

Considering all the results which indicate that the HiV groups have received more and earlier help, physical or verbal, on nonverbal tasks as well as verbal tasks, a possible question arises about interpreting the mother's behavior as an antecedent to the child's cognitive functioning. One might argue that mothers of the HiV group whose children are low in space or number have developed a pattern of helping their children more on performance tasks because their children showed more difficulties with such problems. However, one of our nonverbal tasks, the Healy Picture Completion, did not involve spatial ability. Furthermore, if the child's ability had consistently determined the mother's degree of help-giving behavior, the mothers of high verbal children would have presented verbal tasks to them without any admonishment, realizing that their children have little difficulty with verbal tasks. Nevertheless, mothers of HiV girls scored significantly higher on "focusing" their children's attention on these verbal tasks than mothers of LoV girls.

We therefore felt entitled to interpret the mother's behavior in the interaction situation as a sample of the kind of behavior which in the past was antecedent to the child's cognitive development.

The data do not support the contention that a child develops a particular ability because his parents are selectively training him in it. Rather, the high level of inter-action between mother and child must produce some intervening conditions which enhance verbal more than number or spatial performance.

The essential condition for the development of verbality is probably the close relationship with an adult, and verbal ability is fostered by a high degree of interaction between mother and child. In contrast, the development of number ability requires, above all, concentration and ability to carry through a task by oneself. Similarly, spatial ability is probably developed through interaction with the physical rather than the interpersonal environment. A marked pattern of help seeking and help giving interferes with the development of an independent and self-reliant attitude, which may be the intervening condition for a high degree of development of spatial and numerical ability.

It seems therefore likely that the mother of a child in the HiV-Low nonverbal group is much more emotionally involved with her child, having given more attention and stimulation to the baby, but tending to pressure, restrict, and control the child more later than the low verbal, high nonverbal mother.

REFERENCES

Baldwin, A. L., *Behavior and development in childhood,* New York: Dryden, 1955.

Bandura, A., & Walters, R. H. *Adolescent aggression,* New York: Ronald Press, 1959.

Bieri, J. Parental identification, acceptance of authority, and within sex differences in cognitive behavior. *Journal of Abnormal and Social Psychology,* 1960, **60,** 76–79.

Emmet, W. C. Evidence of a space factor at eleven and earlier. *British Journal of Psychology,* 1949, **2,** 3–16.

Kent, M., & Davis, D. R. Discipline in the home and intellectual development. *British Journal of Medical Psychology,* 1957, **30,** 27–34.

Kuckenberg, L. Effects of early father absence

on subsequent development of boys. Unpublished doctoral dissertation, Harvard University, 1962.

Levinson, B. M. Cultural pressure and WAIS scatter in a traditional Jewish setting. *Journal of Genetic Psychology,* 1958, **93,** 277–286.

Levy, D. M. *Maternal overprotection.* Columbia University Press, 1943.

McCarthy, D. Language development in children. In L. Carmichael (Ed.), *Manual of child psychology.* (2nd Ed.) New York: Wiley, 1954. Pp. 492–630.

Milner, E. A study of the relationships between reading readiness on grade one school children and patterns of parent-child interactions. *Child Development,* 1951, **22,** 95–112.

Moss, H. A., & Kagan, J. Maternal influences on early IQ scores. *Psychological Reports,* 1958, **4,** 655–661.

Sears, R. R., Maccoby, E. E., & Levin, H., *Patterns of child rearing,* Evanston, Ill.: Row, Peterson, 1957.

Winterbottom, M. R. The relation of childhood training in independence to achievement motivation. Unpublished doctoral dissertation, University of Michigan, 1953.

44 | Social Class and Observed Maternal Behavior from 1940 to 1960

ELINOR WATERS
VAUGHN J. CRANDALL

By studying variations in childrearing practices, we gain two types of information about children. We discover how styles of child training shift with time, and we have a natural experiment (although a confounded one) in which variation in childrearing practices can be related to other behaviors of the infant and child. The present study measured relations between socioeconomic status and childrearing practices over a 20-year period (1940–1960). Waters and Crandall found that family socioeconomic status (SES) was unrelated to maternal nurturance, nor was it consistently related to maternal affection. The amount of coercion displayed by mothers was related to social class: Higher social class families employed less coercive pressures than did their lower-class peers. In addition, the families of higher social class tended to use less severe penalties for misbehavior.

Comparison of middle-class maternal behaviors over the 20-year period showed that before 1940 mothers were more restrictive; a period of permissiveness followed during the fifties (when baby-care books generally suggested permissiveness as the best method of rearing children). There was a more recent swing (1960) toward a middle ground in which the limits of behavior are outlined but severe restrictions are not used.

Almost all theories of personality stress the importance of a child's nuclear family in his social learning experiences and personality development. Early personality theories, however, primarily discussed parent-child relations and children's personality development as though the child and his family lived in a social and cultural vacuum. Some of the more recent research addressed to this general question, in contrast, has attempted to assess directly various cultural and social factors influencing child-

Adapted from Social class and observed maternal behavior from 1940 to 1960. *Child Development*, 1964, **35**, 1021–1032.

rearing practices and child development. During the last 15 years, for example, numerous articles have appeared in sociological and psychological journals assessing relations between social class membership of American families and their childrearing attitudes and behaviors. Results of these studies, however, have often been contradictory or equivocal. For example, while the oft-quoted Chicago study of Davis and Havighurst (1948) found that middle class mothers were more restrictive than lower class mothers, several recent investigations including the Harvard Project (Sears, Maccoby, & Levin, 1957) and a California studies Bayley & Schaefer, 1960; (Bayley & Schaefer, 1960) have reported the opposite to be true. Still a third conclusion was reached by Littman's study of an Oregon sample of mothers (1957) which found that social class status was essentially unrelated to a variety of child socialization practices. Several reasons have been suggested for the discrepancies among these studies and other similar investigations. These include the fact that data were gathered at different periods of time and in various parts of the country, that the studies often employed samples differing in their socioeconomic composition, that different assessment methods were used, and that analogous findings have sometimes been interpreted differently by investigators with varying points of view.

The current study had two general aims. The first was similar to the previously mentioned research, i.e., to assess the influence of socioeconomic status on maternal childrearing practices. The second was concerned with evaluating changes in maternal behaviors and socialization techniques during the last 20 years to ascertain if consistent trends are evident and, if so, whether these patterns parallel changing currents in recommended childrearing procedures.

Changes in the types of advice given by "experts" to American parents over the years have been reported by Stendler (1950) and by Wolfenstein (1953), and possible concomitant changes in childrearing practices have been discussed in two excellent summaries by Bronfenbrenner (1958). In the 1930's, rigid schedules of caretaking, discipline, and training were strongly espoused, probably as the result of Watsonian behaviorism. This was followed by a pendulum swing during the 1940's and early 1950's to a "permissive era" influenced by psychoanalytic dicta. By the early 1960's, a shift back toward a middle ground was evident and parents were enjoined to establish the limits of acceptable behavior for their children.

METHOD

Sample

All Ss were mothers of families enrolled in the Fels Research Institute's longitudinal study of human development. From its inception in the early 1930's, this research project has studied social, psychological, and physical factors influencing normal children's growth and development from birth to maturity (Kagan & Moss, 1962). An integral part of this longitudinal assessment has been the Institute's home visit program. From 1937 until the present time, specially trained home visitors have made semiannual visits to the homes of all families with preschool age children participating in the Fels study. During these visits, the home visitors have observed *in situ* mother-child interactions and have rated mothers' behaviors using the Fels Parent Behavior Rating Scales (Baldwin, Kalhorn & Breese, 1945).

In conducting the present study, it was decided that all data must be based on direct observation of overt maternal behaviors rather than mothers' self reports. In this respect, it might be noted that most current information on social class differences in American childrearing practices comes from research based on mothers' verbal—and often retrospective—reports rather than their actual behaviors. The credibility of the findings of such studies rests on two basic assumptions: first, that mothers' contemporary reports of their behaviors with their children are free from distortion, defensive or otherwise; and, second, that retrospective reports are essentially uninfluenced by selective memory. A substantial body of general psychological knowledge, e.g., recent research on the social desirability factor in subjective reports (Christie & Lindauer, 1963), suggests that uncritical acceptance of these assumptions may be unwarranted. Moreover, one recent study has reported that mothers' subjective evaluations of their maternal behaviors may reflect their actual actions in certain areas, but bear little or no relation to their child-rearing practices in other areas (Crandall & Preston, 1961).

The decision to use only data based on observed maternal behaviors in the current investigation limited the study to mothers who had nursery-school-age children at the time they were observed. Children of elementary school age and older are not characteristically in their homes in interaction with their mothers for reasonably long periods except during the dinner and evening hours, when home visit observations are impractical.

In order to assess changes in childrearing practices over three different time periods it was, of course, mandatory that the three subsamples of mothers representing these time periods should not differ in their socioeconomic composition.

Finally, within each of the three subsamples, it was thought desirable to include approximately equivalent numbers of mothers of 3-, 4-, and 5-year-old children, as well as an equal proportion of mothers of boys and girls.

On the basis of the preceding criteria, all available home visit data of the Fels Research Institute obtained during the last 25 years were evaluated before the study was begun. From this preliminary perusal, 107 mothers were selected who met all of the three criteria. A 1940 group was made up of 40 mothers who were observed by Fels home visitors in interaction with their nursery-school-age children between 1939 and 1941; a 1950 subsample consisted of 32 mothers on whom similar observations and ratings had been made between 1948 and 1952; and a final group, designated the 1960 subsample, contained 35 mothers on whom maternal behavior data had been obtained between 1959 and 1961. All mothers in this final sample were white, and resided in communities within a 30-mile radius of the Fels Institute in southwestern Ohio. The three subsamples did not differ significantly in their socioeconomic distributions as measured by the Hollingshead Index of Social Position discussed below.

Assessment of Socioeconomic Status

The socioeconomic status (SES) of the families of the study was determined by Hollingshead's Two Factor Index of Social Position, an index based on the type of occupation and amount of education of the head of the family (Hollingshead, 1957). Scores ranged from 11 for families with the highest social status to 77 for families having the lowest socioeconomic position. These raw scores can be divided into five groups using cutting points suggested by Hollingshead. When this was done with the present sample of 107 families, 10.3 per cent fell in class I (scores 11 to 17), 17.8 per cent in class II (scores 18 to 27), 36.5 per cent in class III (scores 28 to 43), 30.8 per cent in class IV (scores 44 to 60), and 4.7 per cent in class V (scores 61 to 77). Since Hollingshead has not specified how his categories relate to the lower, middle, and upper class distinctions usually employed in sociological research, illustrative families of the current study falling into each of the Hollingshead classifications are briefly described. Class I contained heads of households who were, for example, a dentist, an aeronautical engineer, and a college professor, all with graduate degrees. Class II included a high level—but not top management—executive with some college training and a high school principal with an M.A. degree. Class III encompassed a broad grouping including, among others, the owner of a medium sized business who had a high school education, a farmer with a college degree, and an insurance adjustor and a machine tool manufacturing supervisor, both of whom had some college training. Examples of class IV were a clerical worker with a high school education and a carpenter and a television repairman who had some formal technical training in addition to a high school education. Class V was represented by heads of households such as a construction laborer who had gone to high school for two years and a truck driver with a grade school education.

Unfortunately, the sample is not as representative of the American population as would be desirable. While the over-all sample produced a distribution of families on the SES variable that closely approximated a bell-shaped curve, this is not a typical SES distribution. In New Haven where Hollingshead's indices were developed and in other parts of the country where SES has been evaluated by other means, the distribution of families has consistently been skewed with the preponderance of families falling toward the lower class end of the scale. Thus, the current sample is "top-heavy" as compared with usual SES distributions and almost entirely lacking in lower-lower class families. It is important, then, to keep the characteristics of the sample and its limitations in mind when the results and discussion of this study are presented later.

Assessment of Maternal Behaviors

The basic maternal behavior data were the home visitor's ratings of the mothers. Here the Fels Parent Behavior Rating Scales (PBRs) were used. Each scale has a verbal definition of the variable under consideration and five or more cue-point descriptions placed on a 90-millimeter line along which a rater distributes the mothers. The PBR scales and their intra- and interrater reliabilities have been reported in detail elsewhere (Baldwin, Kalhorn & Breese, 1945) and will not be duplicated here. Suffice it to say, acceptable inter- and intrarater reliabilities for the variables studied in the present investigation have been consistently reported over the years.

Not all PBR variables were investigated in this study.

The present study limited its analysis of maternal behaviors to nine of these variables (the tenth, "general adjustment of the home," was not a maternal behavior variable per se and was, therefore, excluded).

Of the remaining nine variables, three pairs represent three broad dimensions of parent behavior, i.e., nurturant, affectionate, and coercive behaviors, which were identified in previous research (Crandall & Preston, 1955). The additional three PBR variables do not satisfy statistical requirements for inclusion in any one of these three clusters of maternal behaviors and, for the purpose of this study, have been designated as "miscellaneous" PBR variables.

A brief description of the nine PBR variables used in this study follows. The two scales representing *nurturant maternal behaviors* were entitled Protectiveness and Babying. The Protectiveness scale contained cue points running from extreme sheltering of the child to frequently exposing him to actual or potential psychological and physical frustrations and dangers. The Babying scale was concerned with the degree to which a mother offered instrumental help to her child and ranged from behaviors of mothers who consistently helped their offspring whether they needed it or not to mothers who rarely assisted their children even in difficult situations. The two scales concerned with *affectionate maternal behaviors* pertained to overt displays of maternal affection and to the characteristic direction of criticism used by the mother. The former, Affectionateness, ranged from extremely affectionate to consistently hostile maternal behaviors. The second, Direction of Criticism, focused on whether a mother typically approved or criticized her child's everyday actions. The two PBR scales concerned with *coercive maternal behaviors* were entitled Coerciveness of Suggestions and Severity of Penalties. The first covered the degree to which a mother's suggestions to her child regarding his behaviors required mandatory or optional compliance. The other, Severity of Penalties, referred to punitive maternal behaviors and ranged from severe punishment to mild reprimand for various infractions of maternal rules and prohibitions. The final three scales—which did not represent any of the three above-mentioned dimensions of maternal behavior but are still a part of PBR assessment of maternal behaviors—were designated *miscellaneous maternal behaviors*. The first of these, Restrictiveness of Regulations, was concerned with the number of restrictions a mother characteristically imposed on her child's actions. A second miscellaneous scale was entitled Clarity of Policy and was based on home visitors' judgments of how clear or vague a mother's sanctions and proscriptions were. Finally, maternal Accelerational Attempts were observed and rated. Here, the observers evaluated the degree to which a mother attempted to foster and facilitate her child's development of independent problem solving techniques and achievement skills.

Data Analysis

Nonparametric statistical procedures were used for all data analyses of the study. Mann-Whitney U tests were applied to data requiring tests of difference, and rank difference correlations were employed as measures of association. Two-tailed tests of significance are reported throughout the Results section which follows.

RESULTS AND DISCUSSION

Social Class and Maternal Behavior

Relations between family socioeconomic status and observed maternal behaviors for the three time periods and for the total sample of mothers are presented in Table 1. Before discussing the results summarized in this table, two comments are in order. First, it will be noted that SES-maternal behavior correlations in Table 1 do not differentiate maternal actions toward boys and girls. Correlations were run separately by sex of the child, but, since neither the direction nor the significance of the associations were found to differ appreciably, they are not reported separately. Second, since Hollingshead's Index of Social Position uses a rating system in which smaller numbers represent higher socioeconomic status, correlation signs were reversed in the present study to avoid unnecessary confusion. Relations can thus be interpreted in the usual manner, i.e., positive correlations indicate that increased social status is associated with a greater amount of the maternal behavior

TABLE 1 Socioeconomic Status and Maternal Behaviors at Three Periods of Time and for Total Sample: Rank Difference Correlations

PBR Variables	1940 (N = 40)	1950 (N = 32)	1960 (N = 35)	Total Sample (N = 107)
Nurturant Behavior				
Babying	.12	.07	.31	.14
Protectiveness	.21	.16	.10	.16
Affectionate Behavior				
Affectionateness	.17	.18	−.02	.08
Direction of Criticism				
(Approval)	.38**	.14	.28	.26**
Coercive Behavior				
Coerciveness of Suggestions	−.54**	−.13	−.45**	−.43**
Severity of Penalties	−.21	−.15	−.44**	−.25**
Miscellaneous PBR Scales				
Restrictiveness of Regulations	−.55**	−.37**	−.39**	−.43**
Clarity of Policy	.40**	.18	.13	.26**
Accelerational Attempt	.63**	.31	.02	.34**

** p < .01.

under consideration. Returning to Table 1, no significant correlations were found between social class and *nurturant maternal behaviors* for the total sample of mothers nor for mothers representing any of the three separate time periods studied. Neither the mothers' tendency to over- or under-help their children nor their general protectiveness was associated with family social class status.

Family social position was also found to bear little relation to *affectionate maternal behavior*. At none of the time periods studied was the amount of spontaneous affection displayed by mothers related to their social class level. Around 1940, mothers in higher status homes were more likely to approve, and less likely to disapprove, of their children's actions than were mothers of relatively low SES. However, similar associations, while in the same direction, were not significant in either 1950 or 1960, and the significance of the correlation for the total sample seems to be mainly a function of the larger N of the total group of mothers.

In contrast to the negligible relations found between SES and nurturant and affectionate behaviors, *maternal coerciveness* was more clearly associated with social position. In the sample in general, and in the 1960 subsample in particular, SES was positively correlated with noncoercive maternal childrearing practices. The higher the family status, the less dictatorial were mothers' attempts to influence their children's behavior, and the less severe were their penalties for misbehaviors. The maternal behavior variable which was most consistently related to SES was Restrictiveness of Regulations, which is conceptually related to coerciveness although the Crandall and Preston study (1955), previously referred to, indicated that it did not meet statistical requirements for inclusion in the coerciveness category used here. At all three time periods sampled, the higher the family status, the less a mother was prone to impose restrictive regulations on her offspring's behavior.

In summary, for whatever reasons, maternal coerciveness seems to be more class-linked than either maternal affection or maternal nurturance. In this respect, it is of some interest to note that a previous study evaluating the influence of personal needs of mothers on their childrearing practices (Crandall & Preston, 1961) found that related needs *were* predictive of mothers' affectionate and nurturant behaviors toward their children, but *were not* predictive of the degree of coerciveness they characteristically employed with their children. The combined findings of that study and the present one, both based on PBR data from home visit observations, suggests a tentative generalization. To understand and predict mothers' behaviors with their children, both types of variables are helpful—social class membership and personal needs. Moreover, when one set of variables is operative, the other may be less predictive and vice versa.

The final two PBR variables, Clarity and Accelerational Attempts, were class linked in 1940 and for the total sample. Mothers of higher SES families employed more clearly formulated policies of childrearing and more often attempted to accelerate their children's achievement development than mothers of lower social status. It is interesting to note that the SES-maternal behavior relations of these variables have progressively decreased over the last 20 years.

Before comparing the results of this study with those of previous investigations, several differences should be mentioned. First, this study used maternal behavior data based entirely on assessments of overt mother-child interactions. Hopefully, the procedures employed provided a more direct and accurate assessment of actual childrearing practices than interviews. The only other study of social class and childrearing practices in which observed maternal behaviors have been evaluated is the Bayley and Schaefer (1960) investigation in which data were based partially on such observations, but also on interviews. Second, while analogies are drawn to variables of other investigations which are relatively similar to those used in the present study, behavioral referents are not always exactly the same. These differences will be pointed out as the variables are discussed. Third, there are also sample differences between this study and many of the others. Lower class families were not sufficiently represented in the present sample (as was true in the Bayley and Schaefer study), and this sample cannot be divided into representative middle and lower class groups. With these differences in mind, let us consider the relations of the findings of this study to those reported in previous research.

Variables used in earlier research bear very little similarity to the *maternal nurturance* variables in the present study. None seems to pertain directly to the Babying PBR which focused solely on the amount of instrumental help given a child by his mother and which was found to be unrelated to SES in our research. Previous findings relevant to the maternal Protectiveness variable studied here are somewhat contradictory. Davis and Havighurst (1948) have reported that lower class mothers imposed fewer restrictions on the movements of their children outside of the home than did middle class mothers. For example, lower class children were allowed to go to the movies at an earlier age and to stay out later at night than middle class children. Sears *et al.,* on the other hand, found that middle class mothers allowed their children more freedom to cross the streets or go to visit friends than lower class mothers and less frequently checked on their whereabouts. While both of these findings represent protectiveness, the second maternal nurturance variable included in the present study, they both differ from the present study in that they refer to protectiveness, or lack thereof, outside of the house while the current rating assesses maternal protectiveness solely within the home and yard. As mentioned earlier, no association between maternal protectiveness in the home environment and family social position was found in the present study.

The results of at least four studies are pertinent to the *maternal affection* dimension investigated in the current research. A suggestion that a positive relation between SES and maternal affection might exist comes from a study by Duvall (1946) in which she asked mothers to describe their ideal picture of a good mother. In this research, middle class mothers expressed more concern with the affectional bond between mother and child than lower class mothers, while the latter seemed to be more interested in obedience and cleanliness training. Also, Sears *et al.* (1957) found that middle class mothers reported in interviews that they had warmer relations with their preschool children than did working class mothers. The lack of consistent associations between social class and maternal affection found in the present study may be a function of sample differences with the above-mentioned research. Reports of studies based on samples which were more comparable to the present one agree with those results reported here. For example, Bayley and Schaefer (1960), whose distribution was very similar to the present one, report no class differences in maternal affection. And an incidental finding in a study by Kagan and Freeman (1963) on early childhood experiences and later adolescent behavior, which also used the Fels Institute's longitudinal sample, was that maternal affection and acceptance were essentially unrelated to mothers' education, a variable closely associated with social position. Why should the findings of Duvall and Sears differ from those of Bayley and Schaefer, Kagan and Freeman, and the present study? Two possibilities suggest themselves. First the SES samples of Duvall and Sears *et al.* were such that they could be neatly divided into middle and working class dichotomies, and they also had a larger proportion of lower class families than the other three studies. Second, the Sears and Duvall studies used mother interviews, while the data of the remaining three studies were based, at least in part, on direct observations of maternal behavior.

The negative associations found in the current study between social class position

TABLE 2 Median Ratings of Maternal Behavior at Three Time Periods and Differences between Periods

PBR Variables	1940 (N = 40)	Direction of Diff.	p	1950 (N = 32)	Direction of Diff.	p	1960 (N = 35)
Nurturant Behavior							
Babying	59.5	<	ns	61.5	>	.01	45.1
Protectiveness	57.5	<	ns	64.5	>	.01	50.0
Affectionate Behavior							
Affectionateness	69.0	<	ns	71.5	>	.01	58.0
Direction of Criticism (Approval)	53.0	<	.05	62.5	>	.01	45.0
Coercive Behavior							
Coerciveness of Suggestions	58.5	>	.05	48.0	>	.05	43.7
Severity of Penalties	52.0	>	ns	48.0	>	ns	44.8
Miscellaneous PBR Scales							
Restrictiveness of Regulations	54.5	>	ns	54.0	>	.01	42.8
Clarity of Policy	58.5	<	ns	64.5	>	.01	55.0
Accelerational Attempts	54.0	=	ns	54.0	>	ns	53.2

and *maternal coerciveness* are consistent with other reports of class differences in disciplinary techniques used by American families. There is agreement from a variety of source that lower class mothers use more forceful and punitive methods of discipline than middle class mothers. Bronfenbrenner's (1958) summary of recent research reports on middle vs. lower class disciplinary techniques is relevant. He states that middle class parents are "in the first place, more likely to overlook offenses, and when they do punish they are less likely to ridicule or inflict physical pain. Instead they reason with the youngster, isolate him, appeal to guilt, or show disappointment." Our study, despite its more restricted SES range, found the same to be true, with lower social status mothers especially prone to use coercive suggestions and severe penalties.

Changes in Maternal Behavior over Time

Table 2 presents median maternal behavior scores for the nine PBR variables at each of the three time periods investigated. Direc-

tion of changes between the periods are also given, along with the levels of significance of the differences. Two basic trends are apparent. First, several of the maternal behavior variables exhibit curvilinear trends between 1940 and 1960 paralleling changing advice by child-care experts during this time. The so-called "permissive era" in child care literature probably reached its peak in the early 1950's. This was the period in which mothers in the present study were observed to display the most nurturance and affection toward their children. During this period these mothers also made the greatest efforts to make their policies clear to their offspring, possibly in response to advice to give children reasons for demands put upon them. By 1960, the mothers studied were more similar to the 1940 sample and displayed less babying, protectiveness, affection, and approval than the 1950 mothers.

It is interesting to note that Spock, perhaps the single most influential adviser of American parents, made changes and additions to his book on child care and training which preceded, and predicted, changes in maternal practices found in the current study. While it is impossible to determine whether Spock or other "experts" were actually instrumental in bringing about any of the changes in maternal behaviors reported here, the congruence of advice and behaviors is interesting. In this respect Spock's introduction to the 1957 revision of his book lucidly describes his conscious efforts to influence American childrearing practices, first toward permissiveness and later toward a more moderate position (Spock, 1957).

A second trend which is evident in other maternal behaviors in the present study can be characterized by a progressive, rather than a curvilinear, change over time. This trend is primarily seen in the degree of coerciveness the mothers employed in their socialization techniques. From 1940 through 1950 to 1960 maternal coerciveness gradually decreased. During the last 20 years the mothers studied have become less prone to make coercive suggestions requiring mandatory compliance from their children, employ less restrictive regulations of their children's activities, and are less severe in the way they punish misbehaviors.

REFERENCES

Baldwin, A., Kalhorn, J., & Breese, F. Patterns of parent behavior. *Psychological Monographs*, 1945, **58,** No. 3 (Whole No. 268).

Bayley, N., & Schaefer, E. Relationships between socio-economic variables and the behavior of mothers toward young children. *Journal of Genetic Psychology*, 1960, **96,** 61–77.

Bronfenbrenner, U. Socialization and social class through time and space. In E. Maccoby, T. Newcomb, & E. Hartley (Eds.), *Readings in social psychology.* (3rd ed.) Holt, 1958. Pp. 400–425.

Christie, R., & Lindauer, F. Personality structure. *Annual Review of Psychology*, 1963, **14,** 201–207.

Crandall, V., & Preston, A. Patterns and levels of maternal behavior. *Child Development*, 1955, **26,** 267–277.

Crandall, V., & Preston, A. Verbally expressed needs and overt maternal behaviors. *Child Development*, 1961, **32,** 261–270.

Davis, A., & Havighurst, R. Social class and color differences in child rearing. *American Sociological Review*, 1948, **11,** 698–710.

Duvall, E. Conceptions of parenthood. *American Journal of Sociology*, 1946, **52,** 193–203.

Hollingshead, A. *The two factor index of social position.* New Haven: Privately printed, 1957.

Kagan, J., & Freeman, M. The relation of childhood intelligence, maternal behaviors, and social class to behavior during adolescence. *Child Development*, 1963, **34,** 899–911.

Kagan, J., & Moss, H. *Birth to maturity.* Wiley, 1962.

Littman, R., Moore, R., & Pierce-Jones, J. Social class differences in child rearing: a third community for comparison with Chicago and Newton. *American Sociological Review*, 1957, **22,** 694–704.

Sears, R., Maccoby, E., & Levin, H. *Patterns of child rearing.* Row, Peterson, 1957.

Spock, B. *Baby and child care.* Pocket Books, 1957.

Stendler, C. Sixty years of child training. *Journal of Pediatrics*, 1950, **36,** 122–134.

Wolfenstein, M. Trends in infant care. *American Journal of Orthopsychiatry*, 1953, **23,** 120–130.

CHAPTER THIRTEEN
LANGUAGE

Language is a particularly human function; how a child learns the rules that allow him to string morphemes into sentences is a fundamental problem for psychology. These selections examine how children learn names, the effect of social reinforcement on their use of speech, and the clues available to help a child learn his language.

In the first selection Brown suggests that children learn names for objects because they listen to adults. Adults use two criteria in naming things: their frequency of occurrence and their usefulness to the child. Concrete terms are learned before abstract names, probably because the adult gives a concrete name for an object first.

Social reinforcement changes the types of utterances we produce, but can it influence our learning of utterances or does it merely control performance? The second selection looks at this question indirectly. It shows that an extremely infrequent response (the passive construction) is not influenced by modeling or reinforcement. However, children generate significantly more simple prepositional phrases (which they already know) following reinforcement and modeling. These findings show that modeling, attentional set, and reinforcement can increase the frequency of an already existing response; however, they do not allow the child to learn a new construction.

The third selection considers "what is learned" when children begin to speak. Braine proposes that children learn the position of words and use this position as a marker of grammatical class. Experiments in which children were trained to use artificial languages show that they can generalize the position of noun and verb from one sentence to another. He also showed that children code morphemes into phrases; this coding enables them to use phrases in the same way as single morphemes. Finally, Braine analyzes what we know about natural language to see if his notions are tenable. In general, the facts are consistent with the idea that children learn the position of words and generalize this rule to help them learn grammar.

45 | How Shall a Thing Be Called?

ROGER BROWN

Though we often think of each thing as having a single name, in fact each thing has many equally correct names. When some thing is named for a child, adults show considerable regularity in their preference for one of the many possible names. This paper is addressed to the question: "What determines the name given to a child for a thing?" The first answer is that adults prefer a shorter to a longer expression. This gives way to the frequency principle. Adults give a thing the name it is most commonly given. We have now come full circle and are left with the question: "Why is one name for a thing more common than another?"

It seems likely that things are first named to categorize them in a maximally useful way. For most purposes Referent A is a spoon rather than a piece of silverware, and Referent B is a dime rather than a metal object. The same referent may have its most useful categorization on one level (*Prince*) for one group (the family) and on another level (*dog*) for another group (strangers). The categorization that is most useful for very young children (*money*) may change as they grow older (*dime* and *nickel*).

With some hierarchies of vocabulary the more concrete terms are learned before the abstract; probably the most abstract terms are never learned first, but it often happens that a hierarchy develops in both directions from a middle level of abstraction. Psychologists who believe that mental development is from the abstract to the concrete, from a lack of differentiation to increased differentiation, have been embarrassed by the fact that vocabulary often builds in the opposite direction. This fact need not trouble them, since the sequence in which words are acquired is not determined by the cognitive preferences of children so much as by the naming practices of adults.

The most deliberate part of first-language teaching is the business of telling a child what each thing is called. We ordinarily speak of *the* name of a thing as if there were just one, but in fact, of course, every referent has many names. The dime in my pocket is not only a *dime*. It is also *money*, a *metal object*, a *thing*, and, moving to subordinates, it is a *1952 dime*, in fact, a *particular 1952 dime* with a unique pattern of scratches, discolorations, and smooth places. When such an object is named for a very young child how is it called? It may be named *money* or *dime* but probably not *metal object, thing, 1952 dime, or particular 1952 dime*. The dog out on the lawn is not only a *dog* but is also a *boxer*, a *quadruped*, an *animate being*; it is the *landlord's dog*, named *Prince*. How will it be identified for a child? Sometimes it will be called

Adapted from How shall a thing be called? *Psychological Review*, 1958, **65**(1). Copyright © 1958 by The American Psychological Association, and reproduced by permission.

a *dog,* sometimes *Prince,* less often a *boxer,* and almost never a *quadruped,* or *animate being.* Listening to many adults name things for many children, I find that their choices are quite uniform and that I can anticipate them from my own inclinations. How are these choices determined and what are their consequences for the cognitive development of the child?

Adults have notions about the kind of language appropriate for use with children. Especially strong and universal is the belief that children have trouble pronouncing long names and so should always be given the shortest possible names. A word is preferable to a phrase and, among words, a monosyllable is better than a polysyllable. This predicts the preference for *dog* and *Prince* over *boxer, quadruped,* and *animate being.* It predicts the choice of *dime* over *metal object* and *particular 1952 dime.*

Zipf (1935) has shown that the length of a word (in phonemes or syllables) is inversely related to its frequency in the printed language. Consequently the shorter names for any thing will usually also be the most frequently used names for that thing, and so it would seem that the choice of a name is usually predictable from either frequency or brevity. The monosyllables *dog* and *Prince* have much higher frequencies according to the Thorndike-Lorge list (1944) than do the polysyllables *boxer, quadruped,* and *animate being.*

It sometimes happens, however, that the frequency-brevity principle makes the wrong prediction. The thing called a *pineapple* is also *fruit. Fruit* is the shorter and more frequent term, but adults will name the thing *pineapple.* Similarly they will say *apple, banana, orange,* and even *pomegranate;* all of them longer and less frequent words than the perfectly appropriate *fruit.* Brevity seems not to be the powerful determinant we had imagined. The frequency principle can survive this kind of example, but only if it is separated from counts like the Thorndike-Lorge of overall frequency in the printed language. On the whole the word *fruit* appears more often than the word *pineapple* (and also is shorter), but we may confidently assume that, when pineapples are being named, the word *pineapple* is more frequent than the word *fruit.* This, of course, is a kind of frequency more directly relevant to our problem. Word counts of general usage are only very roughly applicable to the prediction of what will be said when something is named. What we need is referent-name counts. We don't have them, of course, but if we had them it is easy to see that they would improve our predictions. Bananas are called *banana,* apples, *apple,* and oranges, *orange* more often than any of them is called *fruit.* The broad frequency-brevity principle predicts that *money* and *dime* will be preferred to *metal object, 1952 dime,* and *particular 1952 dime,* but it does not predict the neglect of the common monosyllable *thing.* For this purpose we must again appeal to imagined referent-name counts, according to which dimes would surely be called *dime* or *money* more often than *thing.*

While the conscious preference for a short name can be overcome by frequency, the preference nevertheless affects the naming act. I have heard parents designate the appropriate objects *pineapple, television, vinegar,* and *policeman;* all these to children who cannot reproduce polysyllabic words. Presumably they use the names because that is what the referents are usually called, but the adult's sense of absurdity of giving such words to a child is often evident. He may smile as he says it or remark, "That's too hard for you to say, isn't it?"

Some things are named in the same way by all adults for all children. This is true of the apple and the orange. Other things have several common names, each of them used by a specifiable group of adults to specifiable children. The same dog is *dog* to most of the world and *Prince* in his own home and perhaps on his own block. The same man is a *man* to most children, *policeman* to some at times, *Mr. Jones* to the neighborhood kids, and *papa* to his own. Referent-name counts from people in general will not predict these several usages. A still more particular name count must be imagined. The name given a thing by an adult for a child is determined by the frequency with which various names have been applied to such things in the experience of the particular adult. General referent-name counts taken from many people will predict much that the individual does, but, for a close prediction, counts specific to the individual would be needed.

The frequencies to which we are now appealing have not, of course, been recorded. We are explaining imagined preferences in names by imagined frequencies of names. It is conceivable, certainly, that some of these specific word counts might be made and a future naming performance independently predicted from a past frequency. Probably, however, such frequencies will never be known, and if we choose to explain particular naming performances by past frequencies we shall usually have to infer the frequency from the performance.

BEYOND THE FREQUENCY PRINCIPLE

A frequency explanation is not very satisfying even when the appeal is to known frequencies. The question will come to mind: Why is one name more common than another? Why is a dog called *dog* more often than *quadruped* and, by some people, called *Prince* more often than *dog?* Perhaps it just happened that way, like driving on the right side of the road in America and on the left in England. The convention is preserved but has no justification outside itself. As things have worked out, coins are usually named by species as *dime, nickel,* or *penny* while the people we know have individual names like *John, Mary,* and *Jim.* Could it just as easily be the other way around? Might we equally well give coins proper names and introduce people as types?

The referent for the word *dime* is a large class of coins. The name is equally appropriate to all members of this class. To name a coin *dime* is to establish its equivalence, for naming purposes, with all other coins of the same denomination. This equivalence for naming purposes corresponds to a more general equivalence for all purposes of economic exchange. In the grocery one dime is as good as another but quite different from any nickel or penny. For a child the name given an object anticipates the equivalences and differences that will need to be observed in most of his dealings with such an object. To make proper denotative use of the word *dime* he must be able to distinguish members of the referent category from everything else. When he learns that, he has solved more than a language problem. He has an essential bit of equipment for doing business. The most common names for coins could not move from the species level to the level of proper names without great alteration in our nonlinguistic culture. We should all be numismatists preparing our children to recognize a particular priceless 1910 dime.

Many things are reliably given the same name by the whole community. The spoon is seldom called anything but *spoon,* although it is also a piece of *silverware,* an *artifact,* and a *particular ill-washed restaurant spoon.* The community-wide preference for the word *spoon* corresponds to the community-wide practice of treating spoons as equivalent but different from knives and forks. There are no proper names for individual spoons because their individuality seldom signifies. It is the same way with pineapples, dimes, doors, and taxicabs. The most common name for each of these categorizes them as they need to be categorized for the community's nonlinguistic purposes. The most common name is at the level of usual utility.

People and pets have individual names as well as several kinds of generic name. The individual name is routinely coined by those who are disposed to treat the referent as unique, and is available afterwards to any others who will see the uniqueness. A man at home has his own name to go with the peculiar privileges and responsibilities binding him to wife and child. But the same man who is a one-of-a-kind *papa* to his own children is simply a *man* to children at large. He is, like the other members of this large category, someone with no time to play and little tolerance for noise. In some circumstances, this same man will be given the name of his occupation. He is a *policeman* equivalent to other policemen but different from *bus drivers* and *Good Humor men.* A policeman is someone to "behave in front of" and to go to when lost. To the kids in the neighborhood the man is Mr. Jones, unique in his way—a crank, bad tempered, likely to shout at you if you play out in front of his house. It is the same way with dogs as with people. He may be a unique *Prince* to his owners, who feed and house him, but he is just a *dog* to the rest of the world. A homeless dog reverts to namelessness, since there is none to single him out from his species. Dimes and nickels have much the same significance for an entire society and their usual names are fixed at this level of significance. People and pets function uniquely for some and in various generic ways for others. They have a corresponding variety of designations, but each name is at the utility level for the group that uses it. Our naming practices for coins and people correspond to our nonlinguistic practices, and it is difficult to imagine changing the one without changing the other.

The names provided by parents for children anticipate the functional structure of the child's world. This is not, of course, something parents are aware of doing. When we name a thing there does not seem to be any process of choice. Each thing has its name, just one, and that is what we give to a child. The one name is, of course, simply the usual name for us. Naming each thing in accordance with local frequencies, parents unwittingly transmit their own cognitive structures. It is a world in which *Prince* is unique among dogs and *papa* among men, *spoons* are all alike but different from *forks.* It may be a world of *bugs* (to be

stepped on), of *flowers* (not to be picked), and *birds* (not to be stoned). It may be a world in which *Niggers,* like spoons, are all of a kind. A division of caste creates a vast categorical equivalence and a correspondingly generic name. *Mr. Jones* and *Mr. Smith* do not come out of racial anonymity until their uniqueness is appreciated.

Adults do not invariably provide a child with the name that is at the level of usual utility in the adult world. An effort is sometimes made to imagine the utilities of a child's life. Some parents will, at first, call every sort of coin *money.* This does not prepare a child to buy and sell, but then he may be too young for that. All coins are equivalent for the very young child in that they are objects not to be put into the mouth and not to be dropped down the register, and *money* anticipates that equivalence. A more differentiated terminology can wait upon the age of storegoing. Sometimes an adult is aware of a child's need for a distinction that is not coded in the English lexicon. A new chair comes into the house and is not going to be equivalent to the shabby chairs already there. A child is permitted to sit on the old chairs but will not be permitted on the new one. A distinctive name is created from the combinational resources of the language. *The new chair* or *the good chair* is not to be assimilated to *chairs* in general.

Eventually, of course, children learn many more names for each thing than the one that is most frequent and useful. Sometimes a name is supplied in order to bring forward an immediately important property of the referent. A child who starts bouncing the coffee pot needs to be told that it is *glass.* Sometimes a name is supplied to satisfy the child's curiosity as to the place of a referent in a hierarchy of categories. Chairs are *furniture* and so are tables; carrots are a *vegetable* but apples are not. Probably, however, both children and adults make some distinction among these various names. *The* name of a thing, the one that tells what it "really" is, is the name that constitutes the referent as it needs to be constituted for most purposes. The other names represent possible recategorizations useful for one or another purpose. We are even likely to feel that these recategorizations are acts of imagination, whereas the major categorization is a kind of passive recognition of the true character of the referent.

THE CHILD'S CONCRETE VOCABULARY

It is a commonplace saying that the mind of a child is relatively "concrete" and the mind of an adult "abstract." The words "concrete" and "abstract" are sometimes used in the sense of subordinate and superordinate. In this sense a relatively concrete mind would operate with subordinate categories and an abstract mind with superordinate categories. It is recorded in many studies of vocabulary acquisition (e.g., Smith, 1926) that children ordinarily use the words *milk* and *water* before the word *liquid;* the words *apple* and *orange* before *fruit; table* and *chair* before *furniture; mama* and *daddy* before *parent* or *person;* etc. Very high-level superordinate terms like *article, action, quality,* and *relation,* though they are common in adult speech, are very seldom heard from preschool children. Presumably this kind of vocabulary comparison is one of the sources of the notion that the child's mind is more concrete than the mind of the adult. However, the vocabulary of a child is not a very direct index of his cognitive preferences. The child's vocabulary is more immediately determined by the naming practices of adults.

The occasion for a name is ordinarily some particular thing. In the naming it is categorized. The preference among possible names seems to go to the one that is most commonly applied to the referent in question. That name will ordinarily categorize the referent so as to observe the equivalences and differences that figure in its usual utilization. There are not many purposes for which all liquids are equivalent or all fruits, furniture, or parents; and so the

names of these categories are less commonly used for denotation than are the names of categories subordinate to them. It is true that words like *article, action, quality,* and *relation* are rather common in adult written English, but we can be sure that these frequencies in running discourse are not equaled in naming situations. Whatever the purposes for which all articles are equivalent, or all actions, or qualities, they are not among the pressing needs of children.

It is not invariably true that vocabulary builds from concrete to abstract. *Fish* is likely to be learned before *perch* and *bass; house,* before *bungalow* and *mansion; car* before *Chevrolet* and *Plymouth* (Smith, 1926). The more concrete vocabulary waits for the child to reach an age where his purposes differentiate kinds of fish and makes of cars. There is much elaborately concrete vocabulary that is not introduced until one takes courses in biology, chemistry, and botany. No one has ever proved that vocabulary builds from the concrete to the abstract more often than it builds from the abstract to the concrete. The best generalization seems to be that each thing is first given its most common name. This name seems to categorize on the level of usual utility. That level sometimes falls on the most concrete categories in a hierarchy (proper names for significant people), and vocabulary then builds toward the more abstract categories (names for ethnic groups, personality types, social classes). Utility sometimes centers on a relatively abstract level of categorization (fish) and vocabulary then builds in both directions (perch and vertebrate). Probably utility never centers on the most abstract levels (thing, substance, etc.), and so probably there is no hierarchy within which vocabulary builds in an exclusively concrete direction.

In the literature describing first-language acquisition (McCarthy, 1946) there is much to indicate that children easily form large abstract categories. There are, to begin with, the numerous cases in which the child over-generalizes the use of a conventional word. The word *dog* may, at first, be applied to every kind of four-legged animal. It sometimes happens that every man who comes into the house is called *daddy*. When children invent their own words, these often have an enormous semantic range. Wilhelm Stern's (1920) son Gunther used *psee* for leaves, trees, and flowers. He used *bebau* for all animals. Lombroso (Werner, 1948) tells of a child who used *qua qua* for both duck and water and *afta* for drinking glass, the contents of a glass, and a pane of glass. Reports of this kind do not suggest that children are deficient in abstracting ability. It even looks as if they may favor large categories.

There are two extreme opinions about the direction of cognitive development. There are those who suppose that we begin by discriminating to the limits of our sensory acuity, seizing each thing in its uniqueness, noting every hair and flea of the particular dog. Cognitive development involves neglect of detail, abstracting from particulars so as to group similars into categories. By this view abstraction is a mature rather than a primitive process. The contrary opinion is that the primitive stage in cognition is one of a comparative lack of differentiation. Probably certain distinctions are inescapable; the difference between a loud noise and near silence, between a bright contour and a dark ground, etc. These inevitable discriminations divide the perceived world into a small number of very large (abstract) categories. Cognitive development is increasing differentiation. The more distinctions we make, the more categories we have and the smaller (more concrete) these are. I think the latter view is favored in psychology today. While there is good empirical and theoretical support (Lewin, 1935) for the view that development is differentiation, there is embarrassment for it in the fact that much vocabulary growth is from the concrete to the abstract. This embarrassment can be eliminated.

Suppose a very young child applies the word *dog* to every four-legged creature he sees. He may have abstracted a limited set of attributes and created a large category, but his abstraction will not show up in his vocabulary. Parents will not provide him with a conventional name for his category, e.g., *quadruped,* but instead will require him to narrow his use of *dog* to its proper range. Suppose a child calls all elderly ladies *aunt.* He will not be told that the usual name for his category is *elderly ladies* but, instead, will be taught to cut back *aunt* to accord with standard usage. In short, the sequence in which words are acquired is set by adults rather than children, and may ultimately be determined by the utility of the various categorizations. This will sometimes result in a movement of vocabulary toward higher abstraction and sometimes a movement toward greater concreteness. The cognitive development of the child may nevertheless always take the direction of increasing differentiation or concreteness.

The child who spontaneously hits on the category four-legged animals will be required to give it up in favor of dogs, cats, horses, cows, and the like. When the names of numerous subordinates have been mastered, he may be given the name *quadruped* for the superordinate. This abstraction is not the same as its primitive forerunner. The schoolboy who learns the word *quadruped* has abstracted from differentiated and named subordinates. The child has abstracted through a failure to differentiate. Abstraction after differentiation may be the mature process, and abstraction from a failure to differentiate the primitive. Needless to say, the abstractions occurring on the two levels need not be coincident, as they are in our quadruped example.

REFERENCES

Lewin, K. A *dynamic theory of personality.* New York: McGraw-Hill, 1935.

McCarthy, Dorothea. Language development in children. In L. Carmichael (Ed.), *Manual of child psychology.* New York: Wiley, 1946. Pp. 477–581.

Smith, M. E. An investigation of the development of the sentence and the extent of vocabulary in young children. *University of Iowa Studies in Child Welfare,* 1926, **3** (5).

Stern, Clara, & Stern, W. *Die Kindersprache.* Leipzig: Barth, 1920.

Thorndike, E. L., & Lorge, I. *The teacher's word book of 30,000 words.* New York: Bureau of Publications, Teachers College, Columbia University, 1944.

Werner, H. *Comparative psychology of mental development.* Chicago: Follett, 1948.

Zipf, G. K. *The psycho-biology of language.* Boston: Houghton-Mifflin, 1935.

46 | Modification of Syntactic Style

ALBERT BANDURA
MARY BIERMAN HARRIS

Several authors believe that language acquisition is simply another example of learning. This study tries to show that variables controlling "social learning" also modify the child's production of passive and prepositional constructions in his native language. For an extremely *infrequent* response (the passive construction), neither reinforcement nor modeling were effective. In the case of a *common* syntactic category (prepositional phrases), reinforcement combined with modeling and attention cues increased the children's use of these familiar phrases. These findings indicate that modeling, attentional set, and positive reinforcement are sufficient for an increase in an already well learned transformation; however, in the case of a little known construction (passive) the child must learn it before he can perform. Reinforcement and modeling control performance.

Much of the research in psycholinguistics has been concerned with formulating categories of syntactic structures and determining usage of grammatical categories in language development under naturalistic conditions (Menyuk, 1963, 1964; Miller and Ervin, 1964; Templin, 1957). Although these approaches have provided systems for describing the basic rules used to generate sentences, they have furnished little information about the variables governing the acquisition and alteration of syntactic structures which might form the basis for an adequate theory of language learning.

Research conducted within the framework of social-learning theory (Bandura, 1967; Bandura and Walters, 1963) provides substantial evidence that modeling variables play a highly influential role in the development of social response patterns, and their position with respect to language

Adapted from Modification of syntactic style. *Journal of Experimental Child Psychology*, 1966, **4**, 341–352.

seems almost unique. Since children cannot acquire words and grammatical structures without exposure to verbalizing models, it is obvious that some amount of modeling is indispensable for language acquisition.

Because of the highly generative character of linguistic behavior, it is generally assumed in psycholinguistic theories that modeling variables cannot possibly play much of a part in language development and production. The main reasoning, which is based on the mimicry view of imitation (Brown and Bellugi, 1964; Menyuk, 1964) is as follows: Children can obviously construct an almost infinite variety of sentences that they have never heard; consequently, instead of imitating and memorizing specific utterances that they may have heard at one time or another, children learn sets of rules which enable them to generate an unlimited variety of grammatical sentences. The limitations typically attributed to modeling processes are largely due, however, to the erroneous assumption that exposure to the verbal behavior of others can produce at the most mimicry of specific responses that are modeled.

Results of recent experiments (Bandura and McDonald, 1963; Bandura and Mischel, 1965) demonstrate that generalized behavioral orientations, judgmental standards, and principles for generating novel combinations of responses can be transmitted to observers through exposure to modeling cues. In these experiments the models and observers respond to entirely different sets of stimuli in the social-influence setting, and subsequent tests for generalized effects are conducted by different experimenters in different settings with the models absent, and with different stimulus items.

It seems extremely unlikely that rules about grammatical relations between words could ever be learned if they were not exemplified in the verbal behavior of models. An important question therefore concerns the conditions that facilitate abstraction or generalization of rules from verbal modeling cues. The principle underlying a model's specific responses can be abstracted if its identifying characteristics are repeated in responses involving a variety of different stimuli (Bandura, 1967). Thus, for example, if one were to place a series of objects on tables, chairs, boxes, and a variety of other places and simultaneously verbalize the common prepositional relationship between objects, a child would eventually discern the grammatical rule. He could then easily generate a novel grammatical sentence if a toy hippopotamus were placed on a xylophone and the child were asked to describe the depicted stimulus event.

In addition to the existence of modeling variables that are indispensable for acquisition of highly complex response patterns, there is no doubt that some form of reinforcement is usually contingent upon grammatical speech and that language is extremely functional in controlling the social environment. The informative properties of differential reinforcement may enhance acquisition by facilitating discrimination, whereas its rewarding properties may function to strengthen and increase existing linguistic responses.

Unlike nonverbal behavior, which is often readily acquired, language learning is considerably more difficult because sentences represent complex stimulus patterns in which the identifying features of syntactic structures cannot be easily discriminated. The present experiment was designed to investigate the role of modeling, reinforcement, and discrimination processes in modifying the syntactic style of children who had no formal grammatical knowledge of the constructions that were manipulated.

The grammatical categories chosen to be modified were the passive voice and the prepositional phrase. These constructions were selected because they are both relatively unambiguous and because both appear relatively free of any semantic connotations. The primary difference between them is that the production of a passive requires the use of one of Chomsky's (1957) postulated transformational rules and thus a higher level of linguistic development and organization than the construction of a prepositional phrase. Another important difference for the purpose of this study is the fact that the passive voice is utilized far less frequently than the prepositional phrase.

Young children generated sentences in response to simple nouns prior to, during, and after experimental treatments designed to increase passive and prepositional constructions. In order to determine the relative contributions of several learning variables to the modification of different classes of linguistic behavior, three variables, applied singly and in combination, were chosen for study. These included exposure to an adult model who generated a high proportion of sentences containing the appropriate syntactic structure; informative feedback provided by positive reinforcement of correct utterances of the model and subjects; and induction of an attentional set to identify the characteristics of "correct" sentences.

It was assumed that contingent reinforcement would be necessary for syntactic discrimination, and that an attentional set would further facilitate recognition of the identifying properties of passive and prepositional constructions. For a syntactic category as common as prepositional phrases it was predicted that high occurrence of attending responses combined with differential reinforcement would be sufficient to increase prepositional constructions. On the other hand, it was expected that the latter conditions alone would have no significant effect upon passive grammatical productions which have a very low probability of occurrence in young children. It was predicted that, in addition to factors that increase syntactic discriminability, appropriate modeling cues would be necessary in order to create passive features in children's speech productions.

METHOD

Subjects

The Ss were 50 boys and 50 girls drawn from second-grade classrooms in schools serving a middle-class community.

Verbal Stimuli

The basic stimulus words selected for the children were 65 simple nouns commonly known at the first or second grade level and printed on index cards.

The model's sentences were prepared in advance in order to ensure comparability of verbal modeling cues between subjects and across treatment conditions. If all of a model's linguistic performances contain only the syntactic structure to be manipulated in a given phase, an observer is provided with little or no basis for distinguishing, within the complex verbal pattern, the identifying characteristics of the desired syntax. Therefore, in order to increase syntactic discriminability, particularly in conditions employing selective reinforcement, seven of the model's sentences, which contained neither passives nor prepositional phrases, were interspersed among the experimental items, primarily in the first half of the set.

Procedure

For all children the basic paradigm was the same. They were told that the experimenter was interested in how people make up sentences and that they would be shown a card with a word written on it and asked to make up a sentence using the word. For conditions involving the model, the children were informed that the E was interested in both adults and children and that he and the model would be taking turns in making up sentences. The model and the child were then introduced to each other, and instructions were given to them both. Children were instructed to tell the E if they could not read a particular word, and that she would identify it for them. The children were also told that any sentence at all was acceptable as long as it contained the word on the card. The 65 stimulus cards for the subject were shuffled and a random 60 were used; if a child did not know the meaning of one of the words or could not use it in a sentence after a reasonable length of time, one of the five remaining words was substituted.

Base rate measure   All children were first presented 20 words, one at a time, with no reinforcement given except mild encouragement for the first sentence or two for those Ss who had difficulty in composing sentences at the outset. The S's sentences were recorded verbatim and later scored for the frequency of passives and prepositional phrases.

Experimental treatments   Immediately following the base-rate assessment, Ss were again presented 20 words and one construction was manipulated. In the conditions involving modeling procedures, the model first completed 13 sentences and then the S and the model alternated generating sentences in five-trial blocks. After a short break, another set of words was presented in which the second construction was manipulated. The modeled performances were interspersed among the children's trials in the same manner as in the preceding experimental phase.

Subjects in each condition were counterbalanced for sex and order of construction (i.e., half the boys and half the girls received the passive treatment first and prepositional condition second; the other half of the Ss were administered the experimental treatments in reversed order).

Five different conditions were used, with 20 Ss, equally divided between boys and girls, in each group. The control condition consisted of having the Ss continue to make up sentences to the stimulus words, without any attempt being made to modify the syntactic properties of their sentence construction. For the purpose of the analysis only, however, one half of the children of each sex in the control condition were randomly assigned to each order and treated as if one construction had been influenced in each period, although no manipulation was actually done.

In the reinforcement + set condition, children were given both reinforcement and a problem-solving set. It was decided to have no group exposed to only reinforcement because results of a previous investigation (Bierman, 1964) as well as preliminary studies indicated that reinforcement alone was not effective in altering linguistic structure.

Reinforcement consisted of telling the child that for some of his sentences the E would give him a star to paste on a card and that he would have to figure out what kind of sentence would gain a star. After the experiment was over, he was told, he would receive a present, with the particular present dependent upon the number of stars he earned. For every correct construction uttered, the child was given a colored star accompanied by social reinforcing comments such as "very good," "right," etc. Problem-solving set consisted of telling the S to pay close attention to the sentences which did and did not gain stars

and try to figure out just what it was about a sentence that earned a star. Throughout the procedure, he was urged to try to earn as many stars as possible, and asked occasionally to repeat sentences which were rewarded.

In the modeling condition an adult male model was introduced to the child, and they were told that he and the child would be taking turns in making up sentences. The model read his sentences in a clear voice, pausing to make it appear that he was inventing them on the spot. The model and the children alternated in constructing sentences in the order described previously.

In the modeling + reinforcement condition, modeling cues and positive reinforcement of syntactic structure were combined. Both the model and the child were rewarded for all the correct constructions; however, no instructions designed to produce strong attentional responses were given.

In the modeling + reinforcement + set condition, the factor of set was added to the experimental procedures described above. The children were instructed to pay close attention to the sentences that earned stars, and both children and the model were rewarded for correct constructions.

The frequency of passives and prepositional phrases in each block of 20 sentences was scored by the E. Use of the appropriate grammatical structure in the sentence was considered: 1 the stimulus word did not have to be included as part of the critical phrase. A set of 600 sentences, drawn at random from the various groups, was also scored independently by a second judge to provide an estimate of interscorer reliability. The two judges were in virtually perfect agreement (99.7%).

RESULTS

The results for the two linguistic constructions were analyzed separately, as the frequency of passives in several of the treatment conditions was extremely low and could not be evaluated by parametric techniques.

Passives

A Kruskal-Wallis one-way analysis of variance computed on change scores between the base-rate level and the frequency of passive constructions in the manipulated phase of the experiment disclosed a highly significan treatment effect ($H = 20.3$; $p < .001$). Comparisons between pairs of conditions, evaluated by the Mann-Whitney U test, showed that children who had the benefit of modeling cues, reinforcement feedback, and an active attentional set generated significantly more passives than either the controls ($U = 82$; $p < .001$), or children who were provided reinforcement ($U = 87$; $p < .001$), modeling cues ($U = 76.5$; $p < .001$), or modeling combined with reinforcement ($U = 94.5$; $p < .01$). The latter three groups, however, did not differ significantly from each other.

Prepositional Phrases

A $5 \times 2 \times 2 \times 2$ analysis of variance was performed on the difference scores with the main factors representing the 5 conditions, 2 treatment phases, 2 orders of grammatical constructions, and the sex difference. This analysis yielded a highly significant condition effect ($F = 3.92$; $p < .01$). As might be expected, children constructed more sentences containing prepositional phrases in the manipulated phase than in the non-manipulated period ($F = 13.73$; $p < .01$); they also generated more prepositional phrases when the experimental treatments were administered in the prepositional-passive order than in the reversed sequence ($F = 4.12$; $p < .05$).

The highly significant interaction between phases and experimental conditions ($F = 4.37$; $p < .01$) indicates that the various treatment variables were differentially effective in increasing children's use of prepositional phrases primarily in the ma-

nipulated period. The specific differences contributing to the treatment effect were therefore investigated by comparison of pairs of conditions. These analyses revealed that the reinforcement + set and the model + reinforcement + set groups, which did not differ from each other, were superior at the .05 level of significance or better to the control and the model conditions.

Additional evidence of the relative efficacy of the different variables in augmenting prepositional constructions is furnished by within-group analyses of the increase from base rate to the manipulated phase of each condition separately. The increase was found to be highly significant for children in both the reinforcement + set ($t = 3.03$; $p < .01$), and the model + reinforcement + set groups ($t = 3.47$; $p < .01$), and of borderline significance for the model + reinforcement treatment ($t = 1.65$; $.10 > p > .05$). The control and the model conditions, on the other hand, did not display increments in prepositional constructions.

The significant phases × order interaction effect shows that children in both syntactic orders achieved comparable increases in prepositional phrases in the manipulated phase of the study; however, Ss receiving the prepositional-passive sequence generated significantly more prepositional phrases than children assigned to the passive-prepositional order.

DISCUSSION

The results of this study provide evidence supporting the proposition that syntactic style, although difficult to modify, can nevertheless be significantly altered by appropriate social-learning variables.

As predicted, reinforcement procedures, even when combined with a strong attentional set, were ineffective in increasing the use of passives in sentences freely generated by children. The majority of Ss did not produce a single passive phrase and consequently, there were no responses that could be reinforced. Nor were the children able to discern, within the relatively brief exposure period, the critical syntactic category simply from observing a model construct a series of passive sentences. On the other hand, children were able to generate passives when verbal modeling cues were combined with procedures designed to increase syntactic discriminability. The most powerful treatment condition was one in which the attentional set was induced, modeled passive constructions were interspersed with some sentences in the active voice so as to enhance differentiation of relevant grammatical properties, and both the model and the children were rewarded for all passive constructions.

Although the actual content of the constructions was not analyzed, the passive sentences generated by the children were varied, and only rarely duplicated the model's verbal productions. Indeed, some of the sentences reflected notable inventiveness (e.g., "The tea was dranked" . . . "Ice are put in boxes sometimes"). These findings thus provide further evidence that people can acquire observationally principles exemplified in a model's behavior and use them for generating novel combinations of responses.

In the case of the syntactic category of prepositional phrases, which has a relatively high base rate of occurrence, reinforcement combined with an active attentional set was sufficient for increasing children's usage of prepositions, but modeling cues were not an important contributory factor. However, the fact that Ss in the reinforcement + set condition continued to produce prepositional phrases when this construction was no longer appropriate, whereas children in the model + reinforcement + set group showed no such perseverative effect, suggests that the modeling cues mainly served a discriminative function signifying the change in reinforcement contingencies. These data would seem to indicate that under conditions where the desired patterns of behavior are already well established, modeling cues may facilitate flexibly adaptive behavior.

In the present experiment the model merely generated sentences with the appropriate grammatical structure while the experimenter controlled both the informative feedback and the administration of reinforcement. On the other hand, in naturalistic situations the model not only exemplifies the behavior, but also conducts any necessary discrimination training and serves as the reinforcing agent. The traditional training practice usually takes the form of parental repetitions of modeled verbal behavior accenting the elements that may have been omitted or inaccurately reproduced by the child (Brown and Bellugi, 1964).

The results clearly indicate that brief exposure (i.e., 20 observational trials) to verbal modeling cues alone has no demonstrable effect upon children's syntactic style. It would be interesting to determine whether children could eventually acquire implicit rules of syntax from repeatedly hearing the grammatical utterances of adult models over an extended period of time without the benefit of selective reinforcement or other forms of corrective feedback.

There is some recent corroboratory evidence (Lovaas, 1967) from studies designed to establish complex functions of speech in mute schizophrenic children that the social-learning variables manipulated in the present experiment govern syntactic learning as well as performance. After children acquire verbal responses and an adequate labeling vocabulary through a combined modeling-reinforcement procedure, grammatical speech is developed by rewarding discriminative responsivity in children to events that are modeled either verbally or behaviorally. In prepositional training, for example, the model gives a verbal instruction involving a preposition (e.g., "Put the block inside the box"), and the child is positively reinforced for performing the motor response appropriate to the verbal stimulus. Objects are then arranged in a particular way and the child verbally describes the relationships between the objects using the proper prepositions. For the third step, the child gives grammatical responses to sentences spoken by the model. As in the present experiment, children are gradually taught to abstract or generalize the linguistic rule by modeling a variety of objects in a variety of prepositional relationships.

REFERENCES

Bandura, A. Social-learning theory of identificatory processes. In D. A. Goslin and D. C. Glass (Eds.), *Handbook of socialization theory and research.* Chicago: Rand McNally, 1967.

Bandura, A., & McDonald, F. J. The influence of social reinforcement and the behavior of models in shaping children's moral judgments. *Journal of Abnormal and Social Psychology,* 1963, **67,** 274–281.

Bandura, A., & Mischei, W. Modification of self-imposed delay of reward through exposure to live and symbolic models. *Journal of Personality and Social Psychology,* 1965, **2,** 698–705.

Bandura, A., & Walters, R. H. *Social learning and personality development.* New York: Holt, Rinehart and Winston, 1963.

Bierman, Mary. The operant conditioning of verbal behavior and its relevance to syntax. Unpublished B.A. Thesis, Harvard University, 1964.

Brown, R., & Bellugi, Ursula. Three processes in the child's acquisition of syntax. *Harvard Educational Review,* 1964, **34,** 133–151.

Chomsky, N. *Syntactic structures.* The Netherlands: Mouton, 1957.

Lovaas, O. I. A program for the establishment of speech in psychotic children. In J. K. King (Ed.), *Childhood autism.* Oxford: Pergamon Press, 1967.

Menyuk, Paula. Syntactic rules used by children from preschool through first grade. *Child Development,* 1963, **34,** 407–422.

Menyuk, Paula. Alteration of rules in children's grammer. *Journal of Verbal Learning and Verbal Behavior,* 1964, **3,** 480–488.

Miller, W., & Ervin, Susan. The development of grammar in child language. In Ursula Bellugi and R. Brown (Eds.), The acquisition of language. *Monographs of the Society for Research in Child Development,* 1964, **29,** No. 1 (Serial No. 92).

Templin, Mildred C. *Certain language skills in children.* Minneapolis: University of Minnesota Press, 1957.

47 | On Learning the Grammatical Order of Words

MARTIN D. S. BRAINE

What is learned when children begin to speak? Have they learned associations among words, or have they learned the deep structure of language? Braine says that, whatever else they learn, young children note the position of words and use this position as an adequate marker of grammatical class. He believes "contextual generalization" (a form of stimulus generalization) carries this rule to novel sentences. In this study, children were taught an artificial language; the results show that children can learn generalizations of position between the first and second words in a simple sentence. They also learn phrases that occur before other phrases. A second study suggests that morphemes are coded into phrases. When compared with the facts of English grammar, the theory is tenable, provided its scope is narrowed and the additional assumption is made that children learn closed-class morphemes to help them slice the language into phrases and positional units.

Just how virtually every human child contrives to learn his native language probably constitutes the most arresting mystery in psychology. A salient feature of the development is the relative rapidity with which the complexity of sentence structure increases during the initial period of acquisition. The purpose of the present paper is to explore the potentialities of the concept, "contextual generalization," for explaining the acquisition of grammatical structure, especially those aspects of grammatical structure which have to do with word order (which constitute much of the grammar in English).

For verbal learning, contextual generalization may be defined informally as follows: when a subject, who has experienced sentences in which a segment (morpheme, word, or phrase) occurs in a certain position

and context, later tends to place this segment in the same position in other contexts, the context of the segment will be said to have generalized, and the subject to have shown contextual generalization.

Thus defined, contextual generalization falls within the general rubric of stimulus and response generalization. One speaks of "stimulus generalization" when a subject, who has learned to make a certain response to a stimulus S_1, later makes the same response to a new stimulus S_2 which is like S_1. In stimulus generalization, the mediating property (the way in which S_2 is like S_1) is usually conceived to be some intrinsic property of S_1 and S_2, e.g., color, shape, etc. Similarly, in response generalization, the mediating property of R_1 and R_2 is usually thought of as some intrinsic property of the responses. Although the properties mediating generalization are usually intrinsic ones, there seems to be no particular reason why this should be so, and contextual generalization appears to be a special case where the mediating property is an extrinsic one,

Adapted from On learning the grammatical order of words. *Psychological Review*, 1963, **70,** No. 4, 323–348.

329

namely, temporal location in an utterance.

In any explanation of the learning of grammatical structure it seems to the writer that some such generalization mechanism will have to occupy a central position. The present paper explores whether contextual generalization is a serious candidate for this role.

The paper is divided into two parts. The first part reports a series of experiments in which children learn some miniature artificial languages with nonsense syllables as words. Contextual generalization is first demonstrated as a phenomenon, and then various problems associated with the concept are explored. From the experiments, the general lines are sketched of a theory of the learning of grammatical structure based on contextual generalization—based, that is, on the notion that "What is learned" are primarily the proper locations of words in sentences.

Although experiments with artificial languages provide a vehicle for studying learning and generalization processes hypothetically involved in learning the natural language, they cannot, of course, yield any direct information about how the natural language is actually learned. The adequacy of a theory which rests on findings in work with artificial languages will therefore be judged by its consistency with data on the structure and development of the natural language. In the second part of the paper an attempt is made to confront the theory developed with known facts about the grammatical structure of natural languages, especially English, so as to discover the limitations of the theory, the stumbling blocks it faces, and the resources it can draw upon to meet the stumbling blocks.

EXPERIMENT I: THE A + P LANGUAGE WITH WORD CONSTITUENTS

This experiment demonstrates, for a very simple language, that the position of a word in a verbal array can be the "functional stimulus" mediating generalization.

Method

Description of the language There were two classes of words, A words and P words, and sentences were always two words long and consisted of an A word followed by a P word. The words were low-association value nonsense syllables. KIV, JUF, and FOJ were the A words, and BEW, MUB, and YAG the P words. Two words of each class were used during the initial learning, and the third was introduced in generalization trials.

Procedure The subject was told that he was going to play a sort of word game in which he would learn a bit of a new language which might seem strange because he would not know what any of the words meant. The words (written on 1.5 × 3 inch cards) were shown to him and a consensus about their pronunciation was reached.

The "language" was taught through a series of sentence-completion problems. A word was presented on the ledge of a board, either preceded or followed by a vacant position; A words were always presented on the left, and P words on the right of the vacant position. In each problem, the subject was given two words, one of each class, to choose from to complete the sentence by placing his selection in the vacant position. Before each problem the subject was asked "Do you remember how this one goes?" or "How do you think this one should go?" If he chose the correct word he won a poker chip (eight poker chips were worth a chocolate); if he chose wrongly he was shown the correct answer. After each problem, the correct sentence was read aloud by him, and repeated by the experimenter.

In the initial learning two A words (KIV and JUF) and two P words (BEW and MUB) were used. Four sentences can be formed from these, and eight sentence-completion problems can be constructed since each sentence can be formed either by filling in the first word or by filling in the last word.

The initial learning had two stages. Four of the eight problems were first selected and were presented in random order until learned to a criterion of seven successive correct responses (not including the first presentation of the first problem, which was used to demonstrate the procedure to the subject). Then the remaining four problems were presented once each, followed by all eight problems in random order until correct responses to seven successive presentations were made.

After the initial learning four generalization problems were each presented once to discover whether the subjects had registered the positions of the words used in the initial learning. A new A or P word was presented, with the alternatives always being words used in the initial learning. The generalization problems were (with the alternatives in parenthesis): FOJ ―― (KIV, BEW); ―― YAG (MUB, KIV); ―――― YAG (JUF, BEW); FOJ ―――― (MUB, JUF).

Subjects The subjects were 16 children, aged 9–6 to 10–5, 8 boys and 8 girls. Non-readers were excluded.

Results

The initial learning was accomplished quite rapidly, two subjects making no errors whatever following the initial demonstration problem. As a demonstration of contextual generalization, the main interest of the experiment lies in the performance on the generalization problems. In 78% of these problems the subjects filled the vacant position with the word that had occupied this position in the initial learning. Using the binomial expansion, one would expect by chance that, among 16 subjects, 5 subjects would respond correctly on either all four or three of the four generalization problems, 6 subjects on two problems, and 5 subjects on one problem or none. The obtained figures were 12, 4, and 0 subjects, respectively. The tendency to respond correctly is highly significant ($\chi^2 = 15.5$, $df = 2$, $p < .001$).

Discussion

Extrapolating from the above conclusion, it is possible to hazard a guess about the infant's learning of grammatical word order. Perhaps he constantly hears the same expressions recurring in the same positions in his verbal environment; these therefore come to sound familiar and therefore "right" to him in these positions, and consequently in his own language he reproduces the same positional relationships. Such a theory would make the learning of grammatical word order a special case of "Gibsonian" perceptual learning (Gibson & Gibson, 1955), i.e., a process of auditory differentiation, or of becoming familiar with, the temporal positions of expressions in utterances. Perceptual learning is usually assumed to be a rather primitive process and there is therefore no reason to suppose that it demands much in the way of intellectual capacity in the learner. Learning of this sort would therefore satisfy at least one requirement of any process postulated to be involved in first language learning, namely, that it not require intellectual capacities obviously beyond the reach of the 2-year-old.

The most immediate problem in the above line of thought concerns the definition of position. In the learning of a language more complex than the one used in this experiment, two closely related questions arise. One question concerns whether it is the absolute positions of expressions (e.g., first, second, etc.) that are learned, or the positions of expressions relative to other expressions. A less obvious but probably more important question concerns the nature of the elements that fill positions. It is perhaps most natural to assume that the word is the principal element whose position is learned. If the word is the only element whose position is learned, then for English, position must be defined relatively and not absolutely, since almost any English word can occur in any absolute position in a sentence.

However, some exploratory work suggested that the relative positions of words were rather difficult to learn. It seemed, therefore, that it might be fruitful to question the assumption that there is anything inevitable about the word as the sole or principal element whose position is learned.

An alternative assumption is that the elements are hierarchically organized: a sentence would be assumed to contain a hierarchy of elements in which longer elements (e.g., phrases) contain shorter elements (e.g., words) as parts, with the positions that are learned always being positions within the next larger element in the hierarchy. A hierarchy of elements would require that expressions of any length can be elements whose position is learned; words (or morphemes) would be merely the smallest elements in the hierarchy. At each level in a hierarchical scheme position could be defined either absolutely or relatively. A simple example of a hierarchical scheme in which position is defined absolutely is provided by binary fractionation. In this scheme a sentence contains just two positions, a first and a last, and each expression in these positions can itself contain two positions, a first and a last, and each resulting expression is potentially divisible in turn in like manner, etc. It may be noted that this method of defining position seems relevant to English structure, e.g., the verb in English generally constitutes the first part of the last section of a sentence. A hierarchical organization of elements is assumed in immediate constituent analysis in structural linguistics (cf. Chomsky, 1957).

EXPERIMENT II: THE A + P LANGUAGE WITH PHRASE CONSTITUENTS

This experiment was designed to investigate whether the ease and effectiveness of learning is related to the way in which position is defined for the subject. The learning of the same language was compared under conditions (a) when words were the units and the positional cues were relative, and (b) when phrases (either one or two words long) were the units and the positional cues were absolute—first and last. It was expected that Condition b would prove simpler. The initial learning procedure was designed to match that of Experiment I, so that the learning scores could be compared with those for the apparently simpler language of Experiment I.

Method

Description of the language The language was that of Experiment I, except that an additional word (GED) always preceded two of the three A words (JUF and FOJ), and another additional word (POW) always followed one of the P words (BEW). Sentences could thus vary from two to four words in length, and the A and P words were sometimes first and second, and sometimes second and third; the relative ordinal positions were, however, the same as in Experiment I, i.e., A words (KIV, JUF, and FOJ) always immediately preceded P words (BEW, MUB, and YAG).

An alternative way of specifying this language is to say that any of three A phrases (KIV, GED JUF, GED FOJ) could be followed by any of the three P phrases (BEW POW, MUB, YAG). When described in this way the grammar is an exact replica of the grammar taught in Experiment I, but with phrases instead of words as the immediate constituents.

Procedure The procedure had four parts: initial learning, second learning, learning test, and recall test. To match Experiment I, the initial learning used only two A terms (KIV, and JUF preceded by GED) and two P terms (BEW followed by POW, and MUB). Using a sentence completion procedure as before, the language was taught in two ways. For one group of subjects (Group 1) only the position of the A or P word was left vacant in a problem, and the choices available for sentence completion were always an A and a P word. (For this group the two new words GED and POW never had to be filled in.) For another group of subjects (Group 2), the sentences were presented in each problem lacking the whole A or P phrase (i.e., either one or two words as the case might be), and the choices available for completing the sentence were always a whole A and P phrase. (When the choices were of unequal length, these subjects of course were not given any cues as to the length of the sentence to be constructed.) The initial learning was exactly parallel to the initial learning in Experiment I: to every sentence completion problem used then there corresponded a problem for each group in this experiment, and the order of administration of problems and the learning criteria were the same. Subjects who failed to complete the initial learning in 60 trials were not included in the remaining parts of the experiment.

The purpose of the second learning was to introduce and provide practice with the A term (FOJ preceded by GED) and the P term (YAG) not used in the initial learning. Nine problems combined these new items with previously used words or phrases, and with each other; in a further six problems, each A and P word (or phrase) occurred twice, once as the correct alternative and once presented in the sentence for completion. In the second learning, as in the initial learning, Group 1 filled in A and P words only, and Group 2 the full A or P phrase.

In the learning test, each of the eight sentence completion problems of the initial learning were administered in turn to both groups with only the A and P words to be filled in. For Group 1 the learning test was simply a repetition of the same eight problems they had already learned to criterion.

In the recall test, the eight words of the language were handed to the subjects and they were asked to try to make a complete sentence of the language that they remembered. The request was repeated until they had offered four sentences.

Subjects In each group there were 12 children, aged 9–7 to 10–7, 6 boys and 6 girls. Nonreaders were excluded.

Discussion

The similarity between the learning scores for Group 2 and for the language of Experiment I indicates that it matters little whether the elements in first and last position are words or variable length phrases (one or two words).

The results also indicate that the same language is learned more easily and effectively when the response units are phrases of variable length and the positional cues are first and last, than when the response units are words and the positional cues are provided by the relative positions of the words to each other. This result is probably due to the greater informational economy of a first-last dichotomy; that is, to learn the absolute positions of the phrases fewer items of information would have to be registered than to learn the positional relationships between the words taken individually. Consider, for example, the complexity of a relative definition of the position of BEW: BEW precedes POW; it follows either KIV, JUF, or FOJ, whichever of these appear; and it occurs next but one after GED, when GED is present. Obviously it is much simpler to take BEW POW as a unit and state only that this occurs last. (Within a hierarchical scheme the position of BEW could then be specified as the first member of a BEW-POW unit.)[1]

The results of this experiment therefore

---

[1] One way (which would apply only to a language more complex than the one taught here) in which the complexity of a relative definition of position could be reduced, would be to arrange that a few elements recur in a very large number of sentences of the language. The subject might quickly learn to recognize these elements and they might then serve him as reference points in the sentence; the positions immediately preceding or following such elements would then be defined in a fairly simple manner. The familiar element would, so to speak, serve as a "tag" (cf. the discussion of "closed-class" morphemes, below).

suggest that learning is easier with a simple definition of position, and that a variable length element does not impair learning. Such a result would be expected under the assumption that position can be defined through a hierarchical scheme, since a hierarchical scheme permits a simple definition of position, but does so at the cost of a complex element.

GENERAL DISCUSSION

The remainder of the paper will consider how far a theory based on contextual generalization may provide a plausible account of the learning of the grammatical structure of natural languages, particularly English. As developed in the preceding experiments the theory consists of three proposals. (a) "What is learned" are the locations of expressions in utterances. (b) Units (i.e., expressions whose position is learned) can form a hierarchy in which longer units contain shorter units as parts, the location that is learned being the location of a unit within the next-larger containing unit, up to the sentence. (c) The learning is a case of perceptual learning—a process of becoming familiar with the sounds of expressions in the positions in which they recur.

With respect to Proposal (b), probably the simplest hierarchial scheme is provided by the binary-fractionation model. This model, in which position is defined through successive first-last dichotomies, is the one used in the design of Experiment II and can serve as a basis for discussion where a specific model is required.

One direct way in which the theory might be examined is by collecting data on the development of grammatical structure. The first word combinations of three children 18–24 months old studied by the writer have been shown to have a characteristic structure which was interpreted as indicating that what had been learned was that each of a small number of words belonged in a particular position in a word combination (Braine, 1963). Occasional reference to the subsequent development of these children will be made in the discussion.

The discussion will be concerned with some obvious facts about the structure of natural languages, English especially, which raise difficulties for the theory proposed. Each difficulty will be discussed in turn. Since it is hardly to be expected that the learning of all of the many kinds of grammatical regularities that exist will prove amenable to interpretation in terms of the above proposals, a purpose of the discussion will be to determine the range of phenomena to which the theory can hope to apply, and suggest ways of extending its scope.

Contrasting Word Order

Of the conceivable arrangements of any given set of morphemes, usually only a few are grammatically possible (e.g., THE MAN. is possible in English, whereas MAN THE. is not); the word-order is said by linguists to be "restricted" to those that can occur (e.g., Harris, 1951, p. 184). When two (or more) arrangements are grammatically possible, sometimes the two orders are equivalent (e.g., BOYS AND GIRLS, GIRLS AND BOYS), in which case the order is said to be "free"; more often the two orders are nonequivalent (e.g., GEORGE HIT JOHN, JOHN HIT GEORGE, or THE CHILD IS INSIDE THE CAR, THE CAR IS INSIDE THE CHILD), in which case the orders are said to "contrast."

It seems clear that the theory developed is not relevant to the learning of contrasts between word orders, and that its scope must be confined to the learning of restrictions on word order. This exclusion from the theory may be quite far-reaching: it seems probable that features of English word order which have to do with the difference between transitive and intransitive verbs, and with the distinction between the prepositional and adverbial use of words like INSIDE, ON, OFF, DOWN, etc. (e.g., THE CAR OUTSIDE, OUTSIDE THE CAR, or THE LIGHT [IS]

ON, ON THE TABLE) may not develop until the appropriate contrasts have been learned.

Positional Regularities in English?

Since colloquial English constitutes both the terminal point of the child's own development and the verbal environment in which he develops, a theory which proposes that what is learned are the locations of words must suppose that rigid rules define what parts of speech can occur in what phrase- and sentence-positions in ordinary English grammar.

In discussing the extent to which such a correlation exists, it is convenient to follow recent work in linguistics which divides English grammar into two parts. According to Harris (1957) and Chomsky (1957), the grammar of a language can be hierarchized into an elementary part, called the "kernel" of the language, and a second part which consists of a set of transformational rules for deriving complex sentences from simple ones. The kernel grammar contains the definitions of the main parts of speech and describes rules for constructing simple declarative statements without complex noun or verb phrases. The transformational rules then carry these kernel sentences into other sentences, or into phrase or clause segments of sentences, which could not be derived in the kernel grammar. Thus from the kernel of English one could generate THE MAN IS BITING THE DOG. The transformational rules would then show how to turn this into the passive, or into the negative, or into any of several questions (e.g., WHY IS THE MAN BITING THE DOG?), or into a relative clause (e.g., . . . WHO IS BITING THE DOG . . .), or into a noun phrase (e.g., THE MAN'S BITING THE DOG, as subject perhaps of IS CAUSE FOR SURPRISE), etc.

Obviously no set of rules defining the positions of words and phrases in simple declarative sentences like THE LIGHT IS ON or GEORGE WALKED ACROSS THE STREET, will also fit the part-of-speech positions in complex sentences of transformational origin like SHE FOUND THEM HELPING THE MAN MAKE IT GO with its successive noun-verb sequences, or THE BOY'S PUSHING THE LAWNMOWER WOKE THE BABY where the arrangement of words in the initial noun phrase is more like that of a normal sentence than of an ordinary noun phrase. Correlations of parts of speech and sentence positions must therefore be discussed separately for kernel sentences and for the derived transforms. Within the simple declarative kernel sentence there appears to be a standard arrangement of words and phrases which is normal for this type of sentence. (Whether this arrangement actually shows the detailed correlations of words and phrases with positions which is required by the theory proposed will be considered in the next section.) Similarly, in each type of transform there seem to be definite rules governing the positional arrangements of parts of speech which is standard for that type of transform. For example, all interrogatives are constructed according to a plan which is standard for interrogatives; similarly questions beginning with WHAT, WHERE, WHY, WHEN, HOW, WHO have a common arrangement; relative clauses follow one of two main arrangements according to whether the pronoun is object or subject of its verb; transforms which occupy noun positions in other sentences follow one of several standard arrangements (e.g., THE BOY'S PUSHING THE LAWNMOWER, THE LIGHT'S BEING ON, HIS BRAKING THE CAR AT THAT MOMENT, etc., or THE READING OF BOOKS, THE ACTING OF PLAYS, etc., or FOR THE LIGHT TO BE ON, FOR HIM TO BRAKE THE CAR AT THAT MOMENT, etc., and several other forms); the same is true for the several other types of transform. In general, therefore, within the kernel and within each of the various types of transform there is a standard arrangement of parts of speech; the various standard arrangements are, however, all different from each other.

One way to formulate this state of affairs would be to regard English not as a unitary language, but as a family of sublanguages. The sentences in some of the sublanguages are complete English sentences; in others they do not occur alone, being merely clauses or phrases of English. The sublanguages differ in that the sequential arrangement of morphemes in each sublanguage is peculiar to that sublanguage. The languages have in common the fact that they all share the same vocabulary, and that any class of words which constitutes a part of speech in one sublanguage constitutes a part of speech in all the others. Moreover there are sentence-by-sentence correspondences between the sublanguages: to every sentence in each of the transformations there corresponds a sentence in the kernel (e.g., to JOHN WAS HIT BY GEORGE in the passive transformation, there corresponds GEORGE HIT JOHN in the kernel). However, the converse, that to every sentence in the kernel there corresponds a sentence in each transformation, is not true since many of the transformations are defective vis-a-vis the kernel (e.g., there are no passive transforms of kernel sentences containing the verb TO BE or intransitive verbs). The kernel therefore has a privileged status since the sentences in each sublanguage apparently constitute a mapping of some large group of sentences of the kernel (cf. Harris, 1957, Footnote 61). It is worth noting that the changes in arrangement made in the various transformations are usually rather minor ones, and much of the normal word order of the kernel grammar tends to be retained (e.g., in the interrogative there is merely an inversion of subject and auxiliary verb; noun transforms like THE BOY'S PUSHING THE LAWNMOWER differ little in arrangement from the kernel sentences to which they correspond, i.e., THE BOY WAS PUSHING THE LAWNMOWER, etc.).

In attempting to account for the child's learning of this intricate set of structures, it seems to the writer that it would be sound strategy to aim first at finding an explanation for the learning of the kernel of the language, i.e., for the learning of the structure of the simple declarative English sentence. This constitutes enough of a problem already. Moreover, any proposed theory which fails to account for the learning of the kernel will, a fortiori, fail to account for the learning of the structure of the language as a whole. If a viable account of the learning of the kernel can be found, then the fact that all the sublanguages have so very much in common (the same vocabulary and parts of speech, and many of the same word arrangements) suggests that there may be some hope of treating the learning of the other sublanguages as a problem in transfer of training. In any case the remainder of this discussion will consider only whether the proposals advanced earlier can be worked into a defensible account of the learning of the kernel grammar.

Even with the scope of the proposals narrowed in this way, there still remains the problem that the verbal environment in which the child learns contains both kernel and transforms, and therefore does not consistently present to him the same parts of speech in the same positions. It is difficult to evaluate this problem. On the one hand, it is noticeable that adults tend to simplify their language when speaking to very young children; also, since transforms usually change the normal word order in minor ways, it is probably true that most stretches of speech exemplify the normal positional arrangements more than they distort them. On the other hand, in the early stages of development the positional relationships in the child's own language obviously do not simply mirror the relationships in the adult English around him, but must be related to them in a much more complex manner. Almost nothing is known about the sequence in which various structures of English develop, so there is no point in discussing this question further.

Conclusion

The preceding discussion indicates that the line of thought developed from the experiments described certainly cannot provide a general theory of the learning of grammatical word order. However, the gross facts of English structure reviewed appear to be compatible with a modified version of the theory, restricted in scope. The necessary restrictions in scope are the limitation of the theory to the learning of the kernel grammar (although further study may permit extension to transformations), and the exclusion of the learning of contrasts between word orders.

As modified the theory proposes: (a) "What is learned" are the locations of units, and associations between pairs of morphemes. (b) The location learned is the location of a unit within the next-larger containing unit of a hierarchy of units. There are hierarchies at two levels: within sentences the units are primary phrases and sequences of primary phrases; within primary phrases the ultimate units are morphemes. (c) The learning of locations is a case of perceptual learning—a process of becoming familiar with the sounds of units in the temporal positions in which they recur.

REFERENCES

Braine, M. D. S. The ontogeny of English phrase structure: The first phase. *Language,* **39,** 1963, 1–13.

Chomsky, N. *Syntactic structures.* The Hague: Mouton & Co., 1957.

Gibson, J. J., & Gibson, Eleanor J. Perceptual learning: Differentiation or enrichment? *Psychological Review,* 1955, **62,** 32–41.

Harris, Z. S. *Methods in structural linguistics.* Chicago: Chicago University Press, 1951.

Harris, Z. S. Co-occurrence and transformation in linguistic structure. *Language,* 1957, **33,** 283–340.

CHAPTER FOURTEEN
INTELLIGENCE AND CREATIVITY

How can we know that one child is brighter than another? Binet answered this difficult question when he stopped measuring discrimination and other elementary abilities in favor of a more global approach. This chapter describes how Binet came to develop his tests and the items that appeared on the original Binet-Simon scale of intelligence. Next, it explores the stability of mental test performance over age. The last article suggests that our conception of intelligence as a single dimension—the ability to manipulate symbols in the solution of problems (Binet's definition)—is too constrained. Guilford argues for at least three faces to intellect and he thinks we should look at them all.

Binet broke a tradition in developing his famous scale. Instead of trying to measure the several faculties (for example, memory, threshold, span of apprehension, reaction time, size estimation), he developed questions that duplicated real-life situations; problems that required intelligence to solve. He arranged the questions in an age-related sequence, with simple items for young children and more difficult items for adults. Binet introduced the notion of age-relevant questions (using age as a criterion of validity) and revolutionized the field of mental testing.

There is little question that behavior changes with development. The interesting thing is: How stable are behaviors and how systematic is their variation? Honzik, Macfarlane, and Allen show systematic relations between age of testing, time since testing, and reliability of intelligence measures. The older the child and the closer are testing sessions, the higher the relation between scores of intelligence.

Guilford suggests that we look at intellect in all its happy diversity, instead of placing a straitjacket of preconceptions on it. He sees the mind as composed of three dimensions: operations, products of these operations, and contents of the operations. Only by considering all aspects of the mind can we understand how the child comes to think. In this article, Guilford also emphasizes the importance of productive thinking.

48 | Binet's Method of Measuring Intelligence

LEWIS M. TERMAN

Beginning about 1890 there were several attempts to measure intelligence by tests. Early tests failed because they tried to measure intelligence through simple items like two-point threshold, memory span, reaction time, size estimation, and speed of association. Binet developed the first successful intelligence test to differentiate feeble-minded children from their more normal peers in the French public school system. He included in the Binet-Simon scale a diverse set of items (for example, knowledge of common objects, words, tests of memory and judgment). This article by Terman suggests that Binet was not measuring school learning but native intelligence. The reader should ask himself: How is it possible to measure potential for intelligence independently of what has been already learned? Are we merely measuring rate of growth of acquired knowledge and assuming that rate will continue?

ESSENTIAL NATURE OF THE SCALE

The Binet scale is made up of an extended series of tests in the nature of "stunts," or problems, success in which demands the exercise of intelligence. As left by Binet, the scale consists of 54 tests, so graded in difficulty that the easiest lie well within the range of normal 3-year-old children, while the hardest tax the intelligence of the average adult. The problems are designed primarily to test native intelligence, not school knowledge or home training. They try to answer the question, "How intelligent is this child?" How much the child has learned is of significance only in so far as it throws light on his ability to learn more.

Binet fully appreciated the fact that intelligence is not homogeneous, that it has many aspects, and that no one kind of test will display it adequately. He therefore

Adapted from *The measurement of intelligence*. Boston: Houghton Mifflin Company, 1916.

assembled for his intelligence scale tests of many different types, some of them designed to display differences of memory, others differences in power to reason, ability to compare, power of comprehension, time orientation, facility in the use of number concepts, power to combine ideas into a meaningful whole, the maturity of apperception, wealth of ideas, knowledge of common objects, etc.

HOW THE SCALE WAS DERIVED

The tests were arranged in order of difficulty, as found by trying them upon some 200 normal children of different ages from 3 to 15 years. It was found, for illustration, that a certain test was passed by only a very small proportion of the younger children, say the 5-year-olds, and that the number passing this test increased rapidly in the succeeding years until by the age of 7 or 8 years, let us say, practically all the children were successful. If, in our supposed case, the test was passed by about two-thirds to three-fourths of the normal children aged 7 years, it was considered by Binet a test of 7-year intelligence. In like manner, a test passed by 65 to 75 per cent of the normal 9-year-olds was considered a test of 9-year intelligence, and so on. By trying out many different tests in this way it was possible to secure five tests to represent each age from 3 to 10 years (excepting age 4, which has only four tests), five for age 12, five for 15, and five for adults, making 54 tests in all.

LISTS OF TESTS

The following is the list of tests as arranged by Binet in 1911, shortly before his untimely death:—

Age 3:
1. Points to nose, eyes, and mouth.
2. Repeats two digits.
3. Enumerates objects in a picture.
4. Gives family name.
5. Repeats a sentence of six syllables.

Age 4:
1. Gives his sex.
2. Names key, knife, and penny.
3. Repeats three digits.
4. Compares two lines.

Age 5:
1. Compares two weights.
2. Copies a square.
3. Repeats a sentence of ten syllables.
4. Counts four pennies.
5. Unites the halves of a divided rectangle.

Age 6:
1. Distinguishes between morning and afternoon.
2. Defines familiar words in terms of use.
3. Copies a diamond.
4. Counts thirteen pennies.
5. Distinguishes pictures of ugly and pretty faces.

Age 7:
1. Shows right hand and left ear.
2. Describes a picture.
3. Executes three commissions, given simultaneously.
4. Counts the value of six sous, three of which are double.
5. Names four cardinal colors.

Age 8:
1. Compares two objects from memory.
2. Counts from 20 to 0.
3. Notes omissions from pictures.
4. Gives day and date.
5. Repeats five digits.

Age 9:
1. Gives change from twenty sous.
2. Defines familiar words in terms superior to use.
3. Recognizes all the pieces of money.
4. Names the months of the year, in order.
5. Answers easy "comprehension questions."

Age 10:
1. Arranges five blocks in order of weight.
2. Copies drawings from memory.
3. Criticizes absurd statements.
4. Answers difficult "comprehension questions."
5. Uses three given words in not more than two sentences.

Age 12:
1. Resists suggestion.
2. Composes one sentence containing three given words.
3. Names sixty words in three minutes.
4. Defines certain abstract words.
5. Discovers the sense of a disarranged sentence.

Age 15:
1. Repeats seven digits.
2. Finds three rhymes for a given word.
3. Repeats a sentence of twenty-six syllables.
4. Interprets pictures.
5. Interprets given facts.

Adult:

1. Solves the paper-cutting test.
2. Rearranges a triangle in imagination.
3. Gives differences between pairs of abstract terms.
4. Gives three differences between a president and a king.
5. Gives the main thought of a selection which he has heard read.

It should be emphasized that merely to name the tests in this way gives little idea of their nature and meaning, and tells nothing about Binet's method of conducting the 54 experiments. In order to use the tests intelligently it is necessary to acquaint one's self thoroughly with the purpose of each test, its correct procedure, and the psychological interpretation of different types of response.

HOW THE SCALE IS USED

By means of the Binet tests we can judge the intelligence of a given individual by comparison with standards of intellectual performance for normal children of different ages. In order to make the comparison it is only necessary to begin the examination of the subject at a point in the scale where all the tests are passed successfully, and to continue up the scale until no more successes are possible. Then we compare our subject's performances with the standard for normal children of the same age, and note the amount of acceleration or retardation.

Let us suppose the subject being tested is 9 years of age. If he goes as far in the tests as normal 9-year-old children ordinarily go, we can say that the child has a "mental age" of 9 years, which in this case is normal (our child being 9 years of age). If he goes only as far as normal 8-year-old children ordinarily go, we say that his "mental age" is 8 years. In like manner, a mentally defective child of 9 years may have a "mental age" of only 4 years, or a young genius of 9 years may have a mental age of 12 or 13 years.

SPECIAL CHARACTERISTICS OF THE BINET-SIMON METHOD

Psychologists had experimented with intelligence tests for at least twenty years before the Binet scale made its appearance. The question naturally suggests itself why Binet should have been successful in a field where previous efforts had been for the most part futile. The answer to this question is found in three essential differences between Binet's method and those formerly employed.

1. The use of age standards. Binet was the first to utilize the idea of age standards, or norms, in the measurement of intelligence. It will be understood, of course, that Binet did not set out to invent tests of 10-year intelligence, 6-year intelligence, etc. Instead, as already explained, he began with a series of tests ranging from very easy to very difficult, and by trying these tests on children of different ages and noting the percentages of successes in the various years, he was able to locate them (approximately) in the years where they belonged.

2. The kind of mental functions brought into play. In the second place, the Binet tests differ from most of the earlier attempts in that they are designed to test the higher and more complex mental processes, instead of the simpler and more elementary ones. Hence they set problems for the reasoning powers and ingenuity, provoke judgments about abstract matters, etc., instead of attempting to measure sensory discrimination, mere retentiveness, rapidity of reaction, and the like. Psychologists had generally considered the higher processes too complex to be measured directly, and accordingly sought to get at them indirectly by correlating supposed intelligence with simpler processes which could readily be measured, such as reaction time, rapidity of tapping, discrimination of tones and colors, etc. While they were disputing over their contradictory findings in this line of exploration, Binet went directly to the point and succeeded where they had failed.

3. Binet would test "general intelligence."

Finally, Binet's success was largely due to his abandonment of the older "faculty psychology" which, far from being defunct, had really given direction to most of the earlier work with mental tests. Where others had attempted to measure memory, attention, sense discrimination, etc., as separate faculties or functions, Binet undertook to ascertain the *general level* of intelligence. Others had thought the task easier of accomplishment by measuring each division or aspect of intelligence separately, and summating the results. Binet, too, began in this way, and it was only after years of experimentation by the usual methods that he finally broke away from them and undertook, so to speak, to triangulate the height of his tower without first getting the dimensions of the individual stones which made it up.

The assumption that it is easier to measure a part, or one aspect, of intelligence than all of it, is fallacious in that the parts are not separate parts and cannot be separated by any refinement of experiment. They are interwoven and intertwined. Each ramifies everywhere and appears in all other functions. The analogy of the stones of the tower does not really apply. Memory, for example, cannot be tested separately from attention, or sense-discrimination separately from the associative processes. After many vain attempts to disentangle the various intellective functions, Binet decided to test their combined functional capacity without any pretense of measuring the exact contribution of each to the total product. It is hardly too much to say that intelligence tests have been successful just to the extent to which they have been guided by this aim.

BINET'S CONCEPTION OF GENERAL INTELLIGENCE

In devising tests of intelligence it is, of course, necessary to be guided by some assumption, or assumptions, regarding the nature of intelligence. To adopt any other course is to depend for success upon happy chance.

However, it is impossible to arrive at a final definition of intelligence on the basis of a priori considerations alone. To demand, as critics of the Binet method have sometimes done, that one who would measure intelligence should first present a complete definition of it, is quite unreasonable. As Stern points out, electrical currents were measured long before their nature was well understood. Similar illustrations could be drawn from the processes involved in chemistry, physiology, and other sciences. In the case of intelligence it may be truthfully said that no adequate definition can possibly be framed which is not based primarily on the symptoms empirically brought to light by the test method. The best that can be done in advance of such data is to make tentative assumptions as to the probable nature of intelligence, and then to subject these assumptions to tests which will show their correctness or incorrectness. New hypotheses can then be framed for further trial, and thus gradually we shall be led to a conception of intelligence which will be meaningful and in harmony with all the ascertainable facts.

Such was the method of Binet. Only those unacquainted with Binet's more than fifteen years of labor preceding the publication of his intelligence scale would think of accusing him of making no effort to analyze the mental processes which his tests bring into play. It is true that many of Binet's earlier assumptions proved untenable, and in this event he was always ready, with exceptional candor and intellectual plasticity, to acknowledge his error and to plan a new line of attack.

Binet's conception of intelligence emphasizes three characteristics of the thought process: (1) Its tendency to take and maintain a definite direction; (2) the capacity to make adaptations for the purpose of attaining a desired end; and (3) the power of auto-criticism.

How these three aspects of intelligence enter into the performances with various tests of the scale is set forth from time to time in our directions for giving and interpreting the individual tests. An illustration which may be given here is that of the "patience test," or uniting the disarranged parts of a divided rectangle. As described by Binet, this operation has the following elements: "(1) to keep in mind the end to be attained, that is to say, the figure to be formed; (2) to try different combinations under the influence of this directing idea, which guides the efforts of the subject even though he may not be conscious of the fact; and (3) to judge the combination which has been made, to compare it with the model, and to decide whether it is the correct one."

Much the same processes are called for in many other of the Binet tests, particularly those of arranging weights, rearranging dissected sentences, drawing a diamond or square from copy, finding a sentence containing three given words, counting backwards, etc.

However, an examination of the scale will show that the choice of tests was not guided entirely by any single formula as to the nature of intelligence. Binet's approach was a many-sided one. The scale includes tests of time orientation, of three or four kinds of memory, of apperception, of language comprehension, of knowledge about common objects, of free association, of number mastery, of constructive imagination, and of ability to compare concepts, to see contradictions, to combine fragments into a unitary whole, to comprehend abstract terms, and to meet novel situations.

49 | The Stability of Mental Test Performance Between Two and Eighteen Years

M. P. HONZIK
J. W. MACFARLANE
L. ALLEN

Behavior changes with age; this is the point of developmental studies. The relation between early and later intellectual behavior is of considerable interest. Many studies have shown that behavior increases in stability over age; the present work finds that correlations between measures of intelligence also increase systematically as a function of age. Also, if two measures of intelligence are taken close together, their correlation is higher. In addition to age trends, the authors found marked individual changes in IQ scores, in some cases as much as 30 points (9 percent of the group tested).

In an earlier study, the constancy of mental test performance was reported for a group of normal children during their preschool years (Honzik and Jones, 1939). These children are now young adults, and it is possible to show the relative stability or lability of their mental test scores over the entire period of testing, 21 months to 18 years, inclusive. The contribution of the present study lies in the fact of repeated individual tests given at specified ages over a 16-year period to more than 150 children; and, second, in the fact that this group of children was selected so as to be a representative sample of the children born in an urban community during the late 1920's. Furthermore, since the Guidance Study has as its primary purpose the study of personality development and associated factors, it has been possible to note the relation of fluctuations or stability in rate of mental growth to

Adapted from the *Journal of Experimental Education*, 1948, **17,** 309–324.

physical ills, unusual environmental strains or supports, and to evidences of tension or serenity within the individual child.

THE SAMPLE

The Guidance Study has been described in detail in previous publications (Macfarlane, 1938, 1939, and 1943). Suffice it to say here that the two groups, which are referred to as the Guidance and Control Groups, constitute representative subsamples of the Berkeley Survey. The names of every third child born in Berkeley between January 1, 1928, and June 30, 1929, were included in the Berkeley Survey (Welch, 1928–1929). A total of 252 children from the Berkeley Survey Group were asked to come to the Institute for their first mental test at the age of 21 months. At this age level, the group of 252 children was divided into two matched subsamples of 126 children on the basis of socio-economic factors (parents' national derivation, income, father's occupation, socio-economic rating, neighborhood, and mother's age and education). One of these subsamples (of the Berkeley Survey) has been called the "Guidance Group" because of the program of intensive interviews had with the parents and children; the second group, which has had physical examinations and mental tests but fewer and less intensive interviews and these at a much later age of the child, has been called the "Control Group." The children in both groups were given mental tests at the age of 21 months. At ages 2 and 2½ years, only the children in the Guidance Group were tested. Thereafter, the testing program was the same for the two groups.

Every effort was made to test the children as nearly as possible on or near their birthdays. Actually, from 72 to 95 per cent of the children were tested within one month of their birthdates at the various ages up to and including 8 years (Honzik and Jones, 1939).

As was to be expected in a longitudinal study, a number of children were unable to come in for one or more of the mental tests. The most frequent cause of a missed test was the family being "out of town." However, a number of families lost interest or became uncooperative as their children grew older; one child was killed in an automobile accident. Table II shows the number of children tested at each age level. It will be seen that at 18 years 153 of the 252 children were tested on the Wechsler-Bellevue. The reasons that the remaining 99 did not come in for a test are listed in the following table:

	Guidance n	Control n
"Out of town"	24	26
Uncooperative	17	16
Died	—	1
Case closed early, cause unknown	—	6
Missed 18-year test (due to changes in staff, illness, or transportation difficulties)	5	4
	46	53

THE TESTING PROGRAM

The testing program followed in the Guidance Study is summarized in the following table:

Ages	Test
21 months-5 years	California Preschool Schedule I or II
6 and 7 years	Stanford-Binet, 1916 Revision
8 years	Stanford Revision, Form L
9-15 years	Stanford Revision (either Form L or M; see Table I)
18 years	Wechsler-Bellevue

GROUP TRENDS IN MENTAL TEST STABILITY

Pearsonian coefficients of correlation between test scores earned at specified ages between 21 months and 18 years were computed. These correlation coefficients are based on the scores of the children in the combined Guidance and Control Groups for all but two age levels (2 and 2½ years) when only the children in the Guidance Group were tested.

Correlations for adjacent ages indicate a fair degree of mental test constancy when the interval between tests is at a minimum. The range of correlations for adjacent ages varies from $r = .71$ (between ages 21 months × 2 years; 2 × 2½ years; 3 × 3½ years; and 5 × 6 years) to $r = .92$ for the ages 12 × 14 years on the Stanford Revision, Form L. However, the correlations decrease markedly with the interval between tests but tend to increase with the age of the children when tested.

Comparison of the correlation coefficients for three-year intervals shows clearly the increase in mental test constancy with age:

2 × 5	years	$r = .32$
3 × 6	years	$r = .57$
4 × 7	years	$r = .59$
5 × 8	years	$r = .70$
7 × 10	years	$r = .78$
9 × 12 or 13	years	$r = .85$
14 or		
15 × 18	years	$r = .79$

The correlation between tests given at 2 and at 5 years ($r = +.32$) suggests a prediction which is not much better than chance, but the magnitude of the test-retest correlation increases markedly with age.

The importance of both age and interval between tests on the test-retest correlation is shown by the relation of these correlations to the age ratio (age at first test/age at second test), = .85 (Honzik and Jones, 1937).

The relation of test scores earned at four specified ages (21 months, 3 years, 6 years, and 18 years) to test scores earned at all other ages is of interest. We note a marked decrease in the size of the correlation coefficients with age, especially during the preschool years. However, the correlation between the 21-month and 2-year test ($r = .71$) indicates that the first test given the children at the age of 21 months was fairly reliable.

The correlations of the 3-year test with scores at the adjacent ages 2½ and 3½ years are fairly high (r's are .71 and .73) but decrease to values which indicate poor prediction by 9 years ($r = .43$).

Since Stanford tests are frequently given to children in the first grade, the results given in the lower left quadrant should be of interest to educators. The 6-year I.Q.'s are fairly constant, but the correlation coefficients are not sufficiently high so that the possibility of marked changes in the I.Q.'s of individual children is precluded.

If changes in I.Q. of 20 points can occur between the 6- and 7-year tests, it would be reasonable to expect rather marked changes in scores over the entire test period, 21 months to 18 years. We have, therefore, prepared distributions of the range of sigma score changes for the entire 16-year period of testing. We find that the scores of three children have increased between 4 and 4½ sigma (roughly between 70 and 79 I.Q. points, assuming an approximate standard deviation of 17.5 I.Q. points); and the scores of two children have decreased a similar amount. The most interesting aspect of these tremendous changes in scores is the fact that the changes are not made abruptly but consistently over a long period of time. However, the greatest changes do occur on the preschool tests. We have, therefore, prepared distributions showing the range of changes in sigma scores and I.Q.'s between 6 and 18 years. No child's sigma score changes as much as 4 sigma during the school years. But the scores of one child changes 3 sigma; and those of four others between 2.5 and 2.9 sigma.

Since educators and clinical workers use I.Q.'s rather than standard scores, we have prepared a distribution of the range of changes in I.Q. during the 12-year period 6 to 18 years for the two groups, Guidance and Control:

I.Q. Changes between 6 and 18 years	Guidance $n = 114$	Control $n = 108$	Total $n = 222$
	%	%	%
50 or more I.Q. pts.	1	—	.5
30 or more I.Q. pts.	9	10	9
20 or more I.Q. pts.	32	42	35
15 or more I.Q. pts.	58	60	58
10 or more I.Q. pts.	87	83	85
9 or less I.Q. pts.	13	17	15

Although it is extremely important to point out the possibility of marked changes in scores in individual cases, it is equally important to emphasize that the scores of many children change only slightly with respect to the group from one age period to the next. And it is only when the changes are consistently in one direction, or the other, over a period of years that the range of variation becomes as great as 3 or 4 sigma (or over 50 I.Q. points).

SUMMARY AND CONCLUSIONS

A group of 252 children, who comprise a representative sample of the children living in an urban community, were given mental tests at specified ages between 21 months and 18 years. These data have been analyzed to show the extent of the stability of mental test performance for this age period. The results may be summarized as follows:

1. Mental test constancy for the age period 21 months to 18 years is markedly dependent upon the age at testing and the interval between tests. That is, group prediction is good over short age periods, and mental test scores become increasingly predictive after the preschool years.

2. Test-retest correlations are as high for children tested on different forms (L or M) of the 1937 Stanford Revision as for children tested on the same form over the same age periods.

3. Distributions of the extent of the changes in I.Q. for the age period 6 to 18 years show that the I.Q.'s of almost 60 per cent of the group change 15 or more points; the I.Q.'s of a third of the group change 20 or more points; and the I.Q.'s of 9 per cent of the group change 30 or more points. The I.Q.'s of 15 per cent of the group change *less* than 10 points of I.Q. The group averages, on the other hand, show a maximum shift in I.Q. over this age period of from 118 to 123.

In conclusion, it should be re-emphasized that, whereas the results for the group suggest mental test stability between 6 and 18 years, the observed fluctuations in the scores of individual children indicate the need for the utmost caution in the predictive use of a single test score, or even two such scores. This finding seems of especial importance since many plans for individual children are made by schools, juvenile courts, and mental hygiene clinics on the basis of a single mental test score. Specifically, it could be noted that a prediction based on a 6-year test would be wrong to the extent of 20 I.Q. points for one out of three children by the age of 18 years, and to the extent of 15 I.Q. points for approximately six out of ten children.

REFERENCES

Honzik, M. P. & Jones, H. E. "Mental-Physical Relationships During the Preschool Period," *Journal of Experimental Education,* 1937, **6,** 139–146.

Macfarlane, J. W. "Studies in Child Guidance, I. Methodology of Data Collection and Organization," *Monograph Society for Research in Child Development,* 1938, **3,** 1–254.

Macfarlane, J. W. "The Guidance Study," *Sociometry,* 1939, **2.**

Macfarlane, J. W. "Study of Personality Development," from *Child Behavior and Development,* Barber, Hounin, and Wright, (Eds.). New York: McGraw-Hill, 1943.

Welch, F. M. *The Berkeley Survey: A Study of the Socio-Economic Status of Four Hundred Berkeley Families in Years 1928–1929.* Manuscript (Institute of Child Welfare, University of California, Berkeley).

50 | Three Faces of Intellect

J. P. GUILFORD

New conceptions of intelligence are elaborated in this article by Guilford. In place of a unidimensional intellect which permeated earlier writings about thought, he suggests the mind is composed of at least three dimensions: operations (composed of evaluation, convergent and divergent thinking, memory, and cognition), products (composed of units, classes, relations, and systems), and contents (composed of figural, symbolic, semantic, and behavioral aspects). Guilford suggests that we develop particular tests to tap each type of thought. In place of a single number to describe intelligence, he would substitute several numbers. The article includes many sample tests that describe the character of each dimension.

Of particular interest is the author's insistence that both convergent and divergent thinking be considered in our evaluation of the child. So far tests have concentrated on the child's abilities to learn simple rules and memorize items. However, Guilford says we should measure and encourage productive thinking—creativity of the mind. He argues for a new approach in our educational system, one in which the child is given a chance to explore his environment and produce new information instead of merely accepting what is fed to him on a spoon.

My subject is in the area of human intelligence, in connection with which the names of Terman and Stanford have become known the world over. The Stanford Revision of the Binet intelligence scale has been the standard against which all other instruments for the measurement of intelligence have been compared. The term IQ or intelligence quotient has become a household word in this country. This is illustrated by two brief stories.

A few years ago, one of my neighbors came home from a PTA meeting, remarking: "That Mrs. So-And-So, thinks she knows so much. She kept talking about the 'intelligence *quota'*, imagine. Why, everybody knows that IQ stands for 'intelligence *quiz.*' "

Adapted from Three faces of intellect, *American Psychologist*, 1959, **14.** Copyright © 1959 by the American Psychological Association, and reproduced by permission.

The other story comes from a little comic strip in a Los Angeles morning newspaper, called "Junior Grade." In the first picture a little boy meets a little girl, both apparently about the first-grade level. The little girl remarks, "I have a high IQ." The little boy, puzzled, said, "You have a what?" The little girl repeated, "I have a high IQ," then went on her way. The little boy, looking thoughtful, said, "And she looks like such a nice little girl, too."

It is my purpose to speak about the analysis of this thing called human intelligence into its components. I do not believe that either Binet or Terman, if they were still with us, would object to the idea of a searching and detailed study of intelligence, aimed toward a better understanding of its nature. Preceding the development of his intelligence scale, Binet had done much research on different kinds of thinking activities and apparently recognized that intelligence has a number of aspects. It is to the lasting credit of both Binet and Terman that they introduced such a great variety of tasks into their intelligence scales.

Two related events of very recent history make it imperative that we learn all we can regarding the nature of intelligence. I am referring to the advent of the artificial satellites and planets and to the crisis in education that has arisen in part as a consequence. The preservation of our way of life and our future security depend upon our most important national resources: our intellectual abilities and, more particularly, our creative abilities. It is time, then, that we learn all we can about those resources.

The discovery of the components of intelligence has been by means of the experimental application of the method of factor analysis. It is not necessary for you to know anything about the theory or method of factor analysis in order to follow the discussion of the components. I should like to say, however, that factor analysis has no connection with or resemblance to psychoanalysis. A positive statement would be more helpful, so I will say that each intellectual component or factor is a unique ability that is needed to do well in a certain class of tasks or tests. As a general principle we find that certain individuals do well in the tests of a certain class, but they may do poorly in the tests of another class. We conclude that a factor has certain properties from the features that the tests of a class have in common. I shall give you very soon a number of examples of tests, each representing a factor.

THE STRUCTURE OF INTELLECT

Although each factor is sufficiently distinct to be detected by factor analysis, in very recent years it has become apparent that the factors themselves can be classified because they resemble one another in certain ways. One basis of classification is according to the basic kind of process or operation performed. This kind of classification gives us five major groups of intellectual abilities: factors of cognition, memory, convergent thinking, divergent thinking, and evaluation.

Cognition means discovery or rediscovery or recognition. Memory means retention of what is cognized. Two kinds of productive-thinking operations generate new information from known information and remembered information. In divergent-thinking operations we think in different directions, sometimes searching, sometimes seeking variety. In convergent thinking the information leads to one right answer or to a recognized best or conventional answer. In evaluation we reach decisions as to goodness, correctness, suitability, or adequacy of what we know, what we remember, and what we produce in productive thinking.

A second way of classifying the intellectual factors is according to the kind of material or content involved. The factors known thus far involve three kinds of material or content: the content may be figural, symbolic, or semantic. Figural content is concrete material such as is perceived through the senses. It does not represent anything except itself. Visual material has properties such as size, form, color, location, or texture. Things we hear or feel provide other examples of figural material. Symbolic content is composed of letters, digits, and other conventional signs, usually organized in general systems, such as the alphabet or the number system. Semantic content is in the form of verbal meanings or ideas, for which no examples are necessary.

When a certain operation is applied to a certain kind of content, as many as six general kinds of products may be involved. There is enough evidence available to suggest that, regardless of the combinations of operations and content, the same six kinds of products may be found associated. The six kinds of products are: units, classes, relations, systems, transformations, and implications. So far as we have determined from factor analysis, these are the only fundamental kinds of products that we can know. As such, they may serve as basic classes into

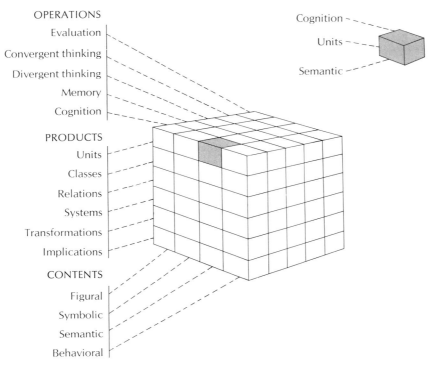

FIGURE 1 A cubical model representing the structure of intellect.

which one might fit all kinds of information psychologically.

The three kinds of classifications of the factors of intellect can be represented by means of a single solid model, shown in Figure 1. In this model, which we call the "structure of intellect," each dimension represents one of the modes of variation of the factors. Along one dimension are found the various kinds of operations, along a second one are the various kinds of products, and along the third are various kinds of content. Along the dimension of content a fourth category has been added, its kind of content being designated as "behavioral." This category has been added on a purely theoretical basis to represent the general area sometimes called "social intelligence." More will be said about this section of the model later.

In order to provide a better basis for understanding the model and a better basis for accepting it as a picture of human intellect, I shall do some exploring of it with

you systematically, giving some examples of tests. Each cell in the model calls for a certain kind of ability that can be described in terms of operation, content, and product, for each cell is at the intersection of a unique combination of kinds of operation, content, and product. A test for that ability would have the same three properties. In our exploration of the model, we shall take one vertical layer at a time, beginning with the front face. The first layer provides us with a matrix of 18 cells (if we ignore the behavioral column for which there are as yet no known factors) each of which should contain a cognitive ability.

The Cognitive Abilities

We know at present the unique abilities that fit logically into 15 of the 18 cells for cognitive abilities. Each row presents a triad of similar abilities, having a single kind of product in common. The factors of the first row are concerned with the knowing of units. A good test of the ability to cognize figural units is the Street Gestalt Completion Test. In this test, the recognition of familiar pictured objects in silhouette form is made difficult for testing purposes by blocking out parts of those objects. There is another factor that is known to involve the perception of auditory figures—in the form of melodies, rhythms, and speech sounds—and still another factor involving kinesthetic forms. The presence of three factors in one cell (they are conceivably distinct abilities, although this has not been tested) suggests that more generally, in the figural column, at least, we should expect to find more than one ability. A fourth dimension pertaining to variations in sense modality may thus apply in connection with figural content. The model could be extended in this manner if the facts call for such an extension.

The ability to cognize symbolic units is measured by tests like the following:

Put vowels in the following blanks to make real words:

$$P\_\_\_W\_\_\_R$$
$$M\_\_\_RV\_\_\_L$$
$$C\_\_\_RT\_\_\_N$$

Rearrange the letters to make real words:

R A C I H
T V O E S
K L C C O

The first of these two tests is called Disemvoweled Words, and the second Scrambled Words.

The ability to cognize semantic units is the well-known factor of verbal comprehension, which is best measured by means of a vocabulary test, with items such as:

GRAVITY means _____
CIRCUS means _____
VIRTUE means _____

From the comparison of these two factors it is obvious that recognizing familiar words as letter structures and knowing what words mean depend upon quite different abilities.

For testing the abilities to know classes of units, we may present the following kinds of items, one with symbolic content and one with semantic content:

Which letter group does not belong?
XECM   PVAA   QXIN   VTRO

Which object does not belong?
clam   tree   oven   rose

A figural test is constructed in a completely parallel form, presenting in each item four figures, three of which have a property in common and the fourth lacking that property.

The three abilities to see relationships are also readily measured by a common kind of test, differing only in terms of content. The well-known analogies test is applicable, two items in symbolic and semantic form being:

JIRE : KIRE : FORA :
KORE KORA LIRE GORA GIRE
poetry : prose : dance :
music walk sing talk jump

Such tests usually involve more than the ability to cognize relations, but we are not concerned with this problem at this point.

The three factors for cognizing systems do not at present appear in tests so closely resembling one another as in the case of the examples just given. There is nevertheless an underlying common core of logical similarity. Ordinary space tests, such as Thurstone's Flags, Figures, and Cards or Part V (Spatial Orientation) of the Guilford-Zimmerman Aptitude Survey (GZAS), serve in the figural column. The system involved is an order or arrangement of objects in space. A system that uses symbolic elements is illustrated by the Letter Triangle Test, a sample item of which is:

$$
\begin{array}{llll}
 & & \overline{} & \\
 & d & \underline{} & \\
 & b & e & \underline{} \\
a & c & f & ?
\end{array}
$$

What letter belongs at the place of the question mark?

The ability to understand a semantic

system has been known for some time as the factor called general reasoning. One of its most faithful indicators is a test composed of arithmetic-reasoning items. That the phase of understanding only is important for measuring this ability is shown by the fact that such a test works even if the examinee is not asked to give a complete solution; he need only show that he structures the problem properly. For example, an item from the test Necessary Arithmetical Operations simply asks what operations are needed to solve the problem:

A city lot 48 feet wide and 149 feet deep costs $79,432. What is the cost per square foot?

A. add and multiply
B. multiply and divide
C. subtract and divide
D. add and subtract
E. divide and add

Placing the factor of general reasoning in this cell of the structure of intellect gives us some new conceptions of its nature. It should be a broad ability to grasp all kinds of systems that are conceived in terms of verbal concepts, not restricted to the understanding of problems of an arithmetical type.

Transformations are changes of various kinds, including modifications in arrangement, organization, or meaning. In the figural column for the transformations row, we find the factor known as visualization. Common measuring instruments for this factor are the surface-development tests, and an example of a different kind is Part VI (Spatial Visualization) of the GZAS. A test of the ability to make transformations of meaning, for the factor in the semantic column, is called Similarities. The examinee is asked to state several ways in which two objects, such as an apple and an orange, are alike. Only by shifting the meanings of both is the examinee able to give many responses to such an item.

In the set of abilities having to do with the cognition of implications, we find that the individual goes beyond the information given, but not to the extent of what might be called drawing conclusions. We may say that he extrapolates. From the given information he expects or foresees certain consequences, for example. The two factors found in this row of the cognition matrix were first called "foresight" factors. Foresight in connection with figural material can be tested by means of paper-and-pencil mazes.

The Memory Abilities

The area of memory abilities has been explored less than some of the other areas of operation, and only seven of the potential cells of the memory matrix have known factors in them. These cells are restricted to three rows: for units, relations, and systems. The first cell in the memory matrix is now occupied by two factors, parallel to two in the corresponding cognition matrix: visual memory and auditory memory. Memory for series of letters or numbers, as in memory span tests, conforms to the conception of memory for symbolic units. Memory for the ideas in a paragraph conforms to the conception of memory for semantic units.

The formation of associations between units, such as visual forms, syllables, and meaningful words, as in the method of paired associates, would seem to represent three abilities to remember relationships involving three kinds of content. We know of two such abilities, for the symbolic and semantic columns. The memory for known systems is represented by two abilities very recently discovered (Christal, 1958). Remembering the arrangement of objects in space is the nature of an ability in the figural column, and remembering a sequence of events is the nature of a corresponding ability in the semantic column. The differentiation between these two abilities implies that a person may be able to say where he saw an object on a page, but he might not be able to say on which of several pages he saw it after leafing through several pages that included the right one. Considering the blank rows in the memory matrix, we should expect to find abilities also to remember classes, transformations, and implications, as well as units, relations, and systems.

The Divergent-Thinking Abilities

The unique feature of divergent production is that a *variety* of responses is produced. The product is not completely determined by the given information. This is not to say that divergent thinking does not come into play in the total process of reaching a unique conclusion, for it comes into play wherever there is trial-and-error thinking.

The well-known ability of word fluency is tested by asking the examinee to list words satisfying a specified letter requirement, such as words beginning with the letter "s" or words ending in "-tion." This ability is now regarded as a facility in divergent production of symbolic units. The parallel semantic ability has been known as ideational fluency. A typical test item calls for listing objects that are round and edible. Winston Churchill must have possessed this ability to a high degree. Clement Attlee is reported to have said about him recently that, no matter what problem came up, Churchill always seemed to have about ten ideas. The trouble was, Attlee continued, he did not know which was the good one. The last comment implies some weakness in one or more of the evaluative abilities.

The divergent production of class ideas is believed to be the unique feature of a factor called "spontaneous flexibility." A typical test instructs the examinee to list all the uses he can think of for a common brick, and he is given eight minutes. If his responses are: build a house, build a barn, build a garage, build a school, build a church, build a chimney, build a walk, and build a barbecue, he would earn a fairly high score for ideational fluency but a very low score for spontaneous flexibility, because all these uses fall into the same class. If another person said: make a door stop, make a paper weight, throw it at a dog, make a bookcase, drown a cat, drive a nail, make a red powder, and use for baseball bases, he would also receive a high score for flexibility. He has gone frequently from one class to another.

A current study of unknown but predicted divergent-production abilities in-cludes testing whether there are also figural and symbolic abilities to produce multiple classes. An experimental figural test presents a number of figures that can be classified in groups of three in various ways, each figure being usable in more than one class. An experimental symbolic test presents a few numbers that are also to be classified in multiple ways.

A unique ability involving relations is called "associational fluency." It calls for the production of a variety of things related in a specified way to a given thing. For example, the examinee is asked to list words meaning about the same as "good" or to list words meaning about the opposite of "hard." In these instances the response produced is to complete a relationship, and semantic content is involved. Some of our present experimental tests call for the production of varieties of relations, as such, and involve figural and symbolic content also. For example, given four small digits, in how many ways can they be related in order to produce a sum of eight?

One factor pertaining to the production of systems is known as expressional fluency. The rapid formation of phrases or sentences is the essence of certain tests of this factor. For example, given the initial letters:

W____c____e____n____

with different sentences to be produced, the examinee might write "We can eat nuts" or "Whence came Eve Newton?" In interpreting the factor, we regard the sentence as a symbolic system. By analogy, a figural system would be some kind of organization of lines and other elements, and a semantic system would be in the form of a verbally stated problem or perhaps something as complex as a theory.

In the row of the divergent-production matrix devoted to transformations, we find some very interesting factors. The one called "adaptive flexibility" is now recognized as belonging in the figural column. A faithful test of it has been Match Problems. This is based upon the common game that uses squares, the sides of which are formed by match sticks. The examinee is told to take away a given number of matches to leave a stated number of squares with nothing left over. Nothing is said about the sizes of the squares to be left. If the examinee imposes upon himself the restriction that the squares that he leaves must be of the same size, he will fail in his attempts to do items like that in Figure 2. Other odd kinds of solutions are introduced in other items, such as overlapping squares and squares within squares, and so on. In another variation of Match Problems the examinee is told to produce two or more solutions for each problem.

A factor that has been called "originality" is now recognized as adaptive flexibility with semantic material, where there must be a shifting of meanings. The examinee must produce the shifts or changes in meaning and so come up with novel, unusual, clever, or farfetched ideas. The Plot Titles Test presents a short story, the examinee being told to list as many appropriate titles as he can to head the story. One story is about a missionary who has been captured by cannibals in Africa. He is in the pot and about to be boiled when a princess of the tribe obtains a promise for his release if he will become her mate. He refuses and is boiled to death.

In scoring the test, we separate the responses into two categories, clever and nonclever. Examples of nonclever responses are: African Death, Defeat of a Princess, Eaten by Savages, The Princess, The African Missionary, In Darkest Africa, and Boiled by Savages. These titles are appropriate but commonplace. The number of such responses serves as a score for ideational fluency. Examples of clever responses are: Pot's Plot, Potluck Dinner, Stewed Parson, Goil or Boil, A Mate Worse Than Death, He Left a Dish for a Pot, Chaste in Haste, and A Hot Price for Freedom. The number of clever responses given by an examinee is his score for originality, or the divergent production of semantic transformations.

Another test of originality presents a very novel task so that any acceptable response is unusual for the individual. In the Symbol Production Test the examinee is to produce a simple symbol to stand for a noun or a verb in each short sentence, in other words to invent something like pictographic symbols. Still another test of originality asks for writing the "punch lines" for cartoons, a task that almost automatically challenges the examinee to be clever. Thus, quite a variety of tests offer approaches to the measurement of originality, including one or two others that I have not mentioned.

Abilities to produce a variety of implications are assessed by tests calling for elaboration of given information. A figural test of this type provides the examinee with a line or two, to which he is to add other lines to produce an object. The more lines he adds, the greater his score. A semantic test gives the examinee the outlines of a plan to which he is to respond by stating all the details he can think of to make the plan work. A new test we are trying out in the symbolic area presents two simple equations such as $B - C = D$ and $z = A + D$. The examinee is to make as many other equations as he can from this information.

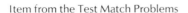
Item from the Test Match Problems

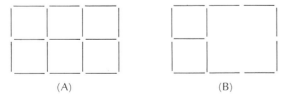

(A)   (B)

Take away four matches in A, leaving three squares and nothing more. *Answer:* B

FIGURE 2 A sample item from the test Match Problems. The problem in this item is to take away four matches and leave three squares. The solution is given.

The Convergent-Production Abilities

Of the 18 convergent-production abilities expected in the three content columns, 12 are now recognized. In the first row, pertaining to units, we have an ability to name figural properties (forms or colors) and an ability to name abstractions (classes, relations, and so on). It may be that the ability in common to the speed of naming forms and the speed of naming colors is not appropriately placed in the convergent-thinking matrix. One might expect that the thing to be produced in a test of the convergent production of figural units would be in the form of figures rather than words. A better test of such an ability might somehow specify the need for one particular object, the examinee to furnish the object.

A test for the convergent production of classes (Word Grouping) presents a list of 12 words that are to be classified in four, and only four, meaningful groups, no word to appear in more than one group. A parallel test (Figure Concepts Test) presents 20 pictured real objects that are to be grouped in meaningful classes of two or more each.

Convergent production having to do with relationships is represented by three known factors, all involving the "education of correlates," as Spearman called it. The given information includes one unit and a stated relation, the examinee to supply the other unit. Analogies tests that call for completion rather than a choice between alternative answers emphasize this kind of ability. With symbolic content such an item might read:

pots   stop   bard   drab   rats ____

A semantic item that measures education of correlates is:

The absence of sound is _____ .

Incidentally, the latter item is from a vocabulary-completion test, and its relation to the factor of ability to produce correlates indicates how, by change of form, a vocabulary test may indicate an ability other than that for which vocabulary tests are usually intended, namely, the factor of verbal comprehension.

Only one factor for convergent production of systems is known, and it is in the semantic column. It is measured by a class of tests that may be called ordering tests. The examinee may be presented with a number of events that ordinarily have a best or most logical order, the events being presented in scrambled order. The presentation may be pictorial, as in the Picture Arrangement Test, or verbal. The pictures may be taken from a cartoon strip. The verbally presented events may be in the form of the various steps needed to plant a new lawn. There are undoubtedly other kinds of systems than temporal order that could be utilized for testing abilities in this row of the convergent-production matrix.

In the way of producing transformations of a unique variety, we have three recognized factors, known as redefinition abilities. In each case, redefinition involves the changing of functions or uses of parts of one unit and giving them new functions or uses in some new unit. For testing the ability of figural redefinition, a task based upon the Gottschaldt figures is suitable. Figure 3 shows the kind of item for such a test. In recognizing the simpler figure within

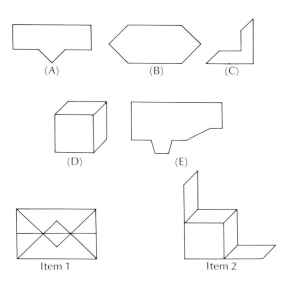

(A)   (B)   (C)

(D)   (E)

Item 1   Item 2

FIGURE 3 Sample items from a test of Hidden Figures, based upon the Gottschaldt figures. Which of the simpler figures is concealed within each of the two more complex figures?

the structure of a more complex figure, certain lines must take on new roles.

In terms of symbolic material, the following sample items will illustrate how groups of letters in given words must be readapted to use in other words. In the test Camouflaged Words, each sentence contains the name of a sport or game:

I did not know that he was ailing.

To beat the Hun, tin goes a long way.

For the factor of semantic redefinition, the Gestalt Transformation Test may be used. A sample item reads:

From which object could you most likely make a needle?

A. a cabbage
B. a splice
C. a steak
D. a paper box
E. a fish

The convergent production of implications means the drawing of fully determined conclusions from given information. The well-known factor of numerical facility belongs in the symbolic column. For the parallel ability in the figural column, we have a test known as Form Reasoning, in which rigorously defined operations with figures are used. For the parallel ability in the semantic column, the factor sometimes called "deduction" probably qualifies. Items of the following type are sometimes used.

Charles is younger than Robert
Charles is older than Frank
Who is older: Robert or Frank?

Evaluative Abilities

The evaluative area has had the least investigation of all the operational categories. In fact, only one systematic analytical study has been devoted to this area. Only eight evaluative abilities are recognized as fitting into the evaluation matrix. But at least five rows have one or more factors each, and also three of the usual columns or content

categories. In each case, evaluation involves reaching decisions as to the accuracy, goodness, suitability, or workability of information. In each row, for the particular kind of product of that row, some kind of criterion or standard of judgment is involved.

In the first row, for the evaluation of units, the important decision to be made pertains to the identity of a unit. Is this unit identical with that one? In the figural column we find the factor long known as "perceptual speed." Tests of this factor invariably call for decisions of identity, for example, Part IV (Perceptual Speed) of the GZAS or Thurstone's Identical Forms. I think it has been generally wrongly thought that the ability involved is that of cognition of visual forms. But we have seen that another factor is a more suitable candidate for this definition and for being in the very first cell of the cognitive matrix. It is parallel to this evaluative ability but does not require the judgment of identity as one of its properties.

In the symbolic column is an ability to judge identity of symbolic units, in the form of series of letters or numbers or of names of individuals. Are members of the following pairs identical or not:

825170493_____825176493
dkeltvmpa_____dkeltvmpa
C. S. Meyerson_____C. E. Meyerson

Such items are common in tests of clerical aptitude.

There should be a parallel ability to decide whether two ideas are identical or different. Is the idea expressed in that one? Do these two proverbs express essentially the same idea? Such tests exist and will be used to test the hypothesis that such an ability can be demonstrated.

No evaluative abilities pertaining to classes have as yet been recognized. The abilities having to do with evaluation where relations are concerned must meet the criterion of logical consistency. Syllogistic-type tests involving letter symbols indicate a different ability than the same type of test involving verbal statements. In the figural column we might expect that tests incorporating geometric reasoning or proof would indicate a parallel ability to sense the soundness of conclusions regarding figural relationships.

The evaluation of systems seems to be concerned with the internal consistency of those systems, so far as we can tell from the knowledge of one such factor. The factor has been called "experiential evaluation," and its representative test presents items like that in Figure 4 asking "What is wrong with this picture?" The things wrong are often internal inconsistencies.

A semantic ability for evaluating transformations is thought to be that known for some time as "judgment." In typical judgment tests, the examinee is asked to tell which of five solutions to a practical problem is most adequate or wise. The solutions frequently involve improvisations, in other words, adaptations of familiar objects to unusual uses. In this way the items present redefinitions to be evaluated.

A factor known first as "sensitivity to problems" has become recognized as an evaluative ability having to do with implications. One test of the factor, the Apparatus Test, asks for two needed improvements with respect to each of several common devices, such as the telephone or the toaster. The Social Institutions Test, a measure of the same factor, asks what things are wrong with each of several institutions, such as tipping or national elections. We may say that defects or deficiencies are implications of an evaluative kind. Another interpretation would be that seeing defects and deficiencies are evaluations of implications to the effect that the various aspects of something are all right.

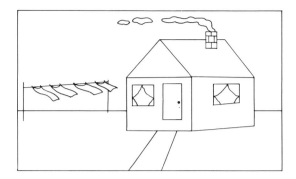

FIGURE 4   A sample item from the test Unusual Details. What two things are wrong with this figure?

other, in other words, to discover traits, the results also tell us much about how individuals are alike. Consequently, information regarding the factors and their interrelationships gives us understanding of functioning individuals. The five kinds of intellectual abilities in terms of operations may be said to represent five ways of functioning. The kinds of intellectual abilities distinguished according to varieties of test content and the kinds of abilities distinguished according to varieties of products suggest a classification of basic forms of information or knowledge. The kind of organism suggested by this way of looking at intellect is that of an agency for dealing with information of various kinds in various ways. The concepts provided by the distinctions among the intellectual abilities and by their classifications may be very useful in our future investigations of learning, memory, problem solving, invention, and decision making, by whatever method we choose to approach those problems.

SOME IMPLICATIONS OF THE STRUCTURE OF INTELLECT

For Psychological Theory

Although factor analysis as generally employed is best designed to investigate ways in which individuals differ from one an-

For Education

The implications for education are numerous, and I have time just to mention a very few. The most fundamental implication is that we might well undergo transformations with respect to our conception of the learner and of the process of learning. Under the prevailing conception, the learner is a kind of stimulus-response device, much on the order of a vending machine. You put in a coin, and something comes out. The machine learns what reaction to put out when a certain coin is put in. If, instead, we think of the learner as an agent for dealing with information, where information is defined very broadly, we have something more analogous to an electronic computer. We feed a computer information; it stores that information; it uses that information for generating new information, either by way of divergent or convergent thinking; and it evaluates its own results. Advantages that a human learner has over a computer include the step of seeking and discovering new information from sources outside itself and the step of programing itself. Perhaps even these steps will be added to computers, if this has not already been done in some cases.

At any rate, this conception of the learner leads us to the idea that learning is discovery of information, not merely the formation of associations, particularly associations in the form of stimulus-response connections. I am aware of the fact that my proposal is rank heresy. But if we are to make significant progress in our understanding of human learning and particularly our understanding of the so-called higher mental processes of thinking, problem solving, and creative thinking, some drastic modifications are due in our theory.

The idea that education is a matter of training the mind or of training the intellect has been rather unpopular, wherever the prevailing psychological doctrines have been followed. In theory, at least, the emphasis has been upon the learning of rather specific habits or skills. If we take our cue from factor theory, however, we recognize that most learning probably has both specific and general aspects or components. The general aspects may be along the lines of the factors of intellect. This is not to say that the individual's status in each factor is entirely determined by learning. We do not know to what extent each factor is deter-mined by heredity and to what extent by learning. The best position for educators to take is that possibly every intellectual factor can be developed in individuals at least to some extent by learning.

If education has the general objective of developing the intellects of students, it can be suggested that each intellectual factor provides a particular goal at which to aim. Defined by a certain combination of content, operation, and product, each goal ability then calls for certain kinds of practice in order to achieve improvement in it. This implies choice of curriculum and the choice or invention of teaching methods that will most likely accomplish the desired results.

Considering the very great variety of abilities revealed by the factorial exploration of intellect, we are in a better position to ask whether any general intellectual skills are now being neglected in education and whether appropriate balances are being observed. It is often observed these days that we have fallen down in the way of producing resourceful, creative graduates. How true this is, in comparison with other times, I do not know. Perhaps the deficit is noticed because the demands for inventiveness are so much greater at this time. At any rate, realization that the more conspicuously creative abilities appear to be concentrated in the divergent-thinking category, and also to some extent in the transformation category, we now ask whether we have been giving these skills appropriate exercise. It is probable that we need a better balance of training in the divergent-thinking area as compared with training in convergent thinking and in critical thinking or evaluation.

The structure of intellect as I have presented it to you may or may not stand the test of time. Even if the general form persists, there are likely to be some modifications. Possibly some different kind of model will be invented. Be that as it may, the fact of a multiplicity of intellectual abilities seems well established.

There are many individuals who long

for the good old days of simplicity, when we got along with one unanalyzed intelligence. Simplicity certainly has its appeal. But human nature is exceedingly complex, and we may as well face that fact. The rapidly moving events of the world in which we live have forced upon us the need for knowing human intelligence thoroughly. Humanity's peaceful pursuit of happiness depends upon our control of nature and of our own behavior; and this, in turn, depends upon understanding ourselves, including our intellectual resources.

REFERENCES

Christal, R. E. Factor analytic study of visual memory. *Psychological Monographs,* 1958, **72,** No. 13 (Whole No. 466).

CHAPTER FIFTEEN
SOCIAL RELATIONS

Children's social relations cover three main topics: play, the child's perception of others' personality characteristics, and the relations of children in various group atmospheres.

Children's play was a neglected aspect of behavior until recently. Early theories assumed an instinctive base; play was supposed to derive from a need to practice skills required later in life. More recently, Freud and Piaget proposed other explanations. Freud wrote that children play to handle their anxieties. He believed that strong anxieties cause rejection of toys, while weaker anxiety leads to counterphobic activities (in which the child tries to work through his fears). Piaget, on the other hand, suggested that the child is primarily interested in toys for their intellective function. He predicted that children will play with novel as opposed to familiar toys. The article by Gilmore tested these opposing notions. His results showed that children's choices are determined *both* by anxieties and toy novelty.

The accuracy with which a child can estimate others' personality characteristics affects his interpersonal relations. The accurate child can form immediate ties with those most like himself; however, the child who cannot perceive social characteristics correctly often finds himself in difficulties. The second study of this chapter explored the accuracy of person perception among young children. The main finding was that older children are more accurate than their younger peers in describing other persons. Interestingly, large differences appeared between the children's descriptions of their peers and adult raters' descriptions of the same children. Whether this discrepancy resulted from adult attitudes, or whether the actual behavior was different, is unknown.

The atmosphere of a group can affect a child's satisfaction and productivity. Lippitt studied groups that were democratic, groups that were authoritarian, and groups without structure. He measured the satisfaction and productivity of boys in these differing situations. The productivity of both authoritarian and democratic groups was quite high, but the authoritarian group produced less identification and satisfaction among members. The laissez-faire group was characterized by low productivity and little satisfaction.

51 | The Role of Anxiety and Cognitive Factors in Children's Play Behavior

J. BARNARD GILMORE

Theorists differ in their interpretation of play's function; Piaget views play as a way of learning about novel or complex objects and events, but Freud sees play in terms of motivation. Psychoanalytic theory suggests that when a child is anxious, he plays with toys on the basis of their relevance to the source of his anxiety. When he is not anxious, he plays with toys on the basis of their relative novelty.

Children about to undergo surgery and a matched group of school children showed the following effects: (1) Novelty does *not* interact with anxiety to determine toy preferences; (2) anxiety does affect a child's preferences for toys; but (3) anxiety is by no means as strong a determinant as relative novelty.

Play is considered the most typical activity of childhood. Because in play a child expresses so much of what he thinks, play is perhaps unique in affording potential insights into the cognitive structure of the developing child. Yet, to date, developmentalists in psychology and biology have reported fewer than a dozen truly experimental investigations of play behavior itself (e.g., Beach, 1945; Britt & Janus, 1941; Hurlock, 1934; Levin & Wardwell, 1962). The great bulk of play research in the past has been observational. Almost certainly, one reason that play behavior has been so little explored experimentally can be traced to the lack of clear and testable theories of play. There are a great many theories of play, to be sure, but most of them are arbitrary in scope, vague in outline, and global rather than specific in their approach (Gilmore, 1965).

Adapted from The role of anxiety and cognitive factors in children's play behavior. *Child Development*, 1966, **37**, 397–416.

Two theories stand as exceptions to this general rule, however, and they point in turn to two variables which might be important determinants of play behavior. This paper reports an initial attempt to measure the influence of these two variables (anxiety and toy novelty) in a series of three related studies. Although some new questions are raised by the data we reported below, these data clearly show that anxiety and toy novelty *do* influence play behavior to a large degree, while their interaction does *not* do so, contrary to our predictions. Consider, then, the theories of play put forward by Piaget and by the psychoanalysts, from which our predictions can be derived.

Piaget theorizes that play is the product of a certain developmental stage of thinking through which all normal children must pass (Piaget, 1951). Piaget holds that adults respond to reality both by bending reality to fit their current moods and expectations (assimilation), and by bending their moods and expectations to fit reality (accommodation). In the adult, these processes of assimilation and accommodation invariably are complementary and automatic. In the child, these two processes are often neither complementary nor automatic, and play is seen whenever *assimilation* dominates. According to Piaget, the child has an inherent tendency both to seek out objects and to bend them to fit any new response system ("schema"). Piaget has also said that, at least in the earlier developmental stages, play occurs only in conjunction with signs of pleasure and not when the child is "serious" or is striving to master or learn. It seems likely, then, that strong needs or affects would preclude all play which reflects assimilation of newly acquired skills. Given this likelihood together with Piaget's basic theoretical position, one would predict that when a child is free from strong needs and affects, he will play most with objects which are as yet somewhat novel, unfamiliar, and unmastered. Throughout this paper the reader should keep in mind that the word "novelty" will always refer to a rather broad concept, a concept for which "complexity" might also be one appropriate label. "Novel" materials elicit the play that Piaget has called "pure assimilation" because, being new to the child and less than completely mastered, these materials have to be fit to available schemata.

The psychoanalytic theory of play holds play to be cathartic response, one which reduces psychic tension and affords the child both mastery over his wishes to be grown up and mastery over those experiences which have been overwhelming. This latter aspect of play has been summarized by Erikson (1959) as follows:

> Individual child play often proves to be the infantile way of thinking over difficult experiences and of restoring a sense of mastery, comparable to the way in which we repeat, in ruminations and endless talk, in daydreams and dreams during sleep, experiences that have been too much for us.

Freud (1959) observed:

It is certain that children behave in this fashion toward every distressing impression they receive, that is by reproducing it in their play. In this changing from passivity to activity they attempt to master their experience psychically.

On the basis of the psychoanalytic theory of play, then, one would predict that when a child experiences strong affects he will play with objects relevant to the perceived source of his anxiety.

The two predictions put forward above can be restated as follows: When a child is relatively free from anxiety, he will prefer to play with toys on the basis of their novelty, whereas when a child is anxious he will prefer to play with toys on the basis of their relevance to the source of his anxiety. This hypothesis was tested in each of the three studies reported below by allowing children to play with various sets of toys while anxious and while not anxious. Each set of toys contained novel and simple items and items relevant and irrelevant to the child's anxiety state. One study was observational, insuring a truly anxious population seen in a natural setting; two studies were experimental, insuring control of a number of potentially influential variables. Since the data of all three studies are crucial for drawing conclusions from this research, discussion of the studies will be deferred until after presentation of the results from all the studies.

THE HOSPITAL-SCHOOL STUDY

Previous studies have given strong indication that children facing tonsillectomy are highly anxious about the experience, especially as regards their helplessness during the period of hospitalization (Levy, 1945; Prugh, Staub, Sands, Kirschbaum, & Lenihan, 1953). In the present study, children who were facing surgery, and in whom there could be little doubt about the presence of great anxiety, served as anxious subjects.

Method

Subjects There were two groups of subjects in this study: a group of 18 children hospitalized for tonsillectomy in the children's ward of the Grace-New Haven Hospital and a group of 18 matched controls from the lowest four grades of a public elementary school in New Haven. Control subjects were individually matched to hospitalized subjects on the basis of their sex, birth date, and grade in school (see Gilmore, 1964). There were nine boys and nine girls in both the hospital and school groups. The Ss ranged in age from 5 years and 4 months to 8 years and 11 months. There were five children at the kindergarten, first-, and second-grade levels, as well as three children at the third-grade level, for both groups in this study.

Play materials Each S played with three different sets of toys, one set at a time. Each set of toys was composed of four individual toys chosen to represent the dimensions of novelty and relevance to hospitalization. Thus, in each set of toys there were four toy items which were designated "novel-relevant," "novel-irrelevant," "simple-relevant," and "simple-irrelevant" toys. Toys were assigned to these categories on the basis of agreement among three independent judges. Toys were then assigned to a set on the basis of pilot research which indicated the interest of all the toys for children of both sexes. Three sets of toys were used in this study so that all findings might reasonably be attributed to the underlying variables of novelty and hospital relevance rather than to characteristics specific to one certain set of toys. For toy sets "A," "B," and "C," respectively, the following toys were classified as novel-relevant: one brand of "doctor's kit," a toy syringe and stethescope, a second brand of "doctor's kit"; classified novel-irrelevant were: a "magic slate," a small pinball game, a three-dimensional maze puzzle; classified simple-relevant were: a pair of scissors and

a cutout figure, a toy thermometer, a toy ambulance; and classified simple-irrelevant were: a plastic pig, a pipe cleaner, a pencil and pad of paper.

Procedure Hospital subjects were seen on their ward. The experimenter would say, with some variation from child to child:

> I'm not a doctor, *Child*. The hospital thought that some of the boys and girls who come here might like to have some toys to play with, and so I've brought some that you could play with if you like. Would you like to see the toys that I brought?

All but four of the 28 potential Ss approached by E indicated a desire to see the toys, either immediately or after a short time. Testing took place on S's bed. Frequently S's mother would come along as well. No attempt was made to isolate S from the sight of parents, roommates, or hospital routine, although social interactions were minimized. Once S was seated comfortably on his bed, E placed the first set of four toys (selected at random) in front of S and said: "If you'd like to play with those for a few minutes, you go right ahead. Then I have some other toys I will show you."

The Ss were allowed 6 minutes of playing time with each set of toys. The time of onset and completion for play with each toy was recorded by E. A small hand-held stopwatch was used for this purpose. The formal criterion for "play" was the touching of a toy or its parts. All Ss used the toys in what would generally be considered a playful manner.

When each S had spent 6 minutes with the first set of toys, E said:

> *Child*, which one of these four toys is the most fun toy? [S responds.] Which toy is the next best? [S responds.] And next best? [S responds.] Fine. I brought, you some other toys you can play with if you like. Let me show them to you.

The *E* then removed the first set of toys and introduced the second toy set (selected at random from the remaining two sets) as before. The *S* was given 6 minutes of playing time with these toys; then *E* asked for toy preferences as noted above. The procedure was repeated one more time with the third set of toys, concluding the procedures on the hospital *S*s.

At the school, *E* was introduced by the principal to each class from which control *S*s were drawn. Then *E* said: "Good morning boys and girls. I brought some toys to school today that some of you could play with if you like. Who would like to play with the toys?" All children indicated a desire to play. First *E* explained that he could only see a very few of the children, then he "chose" the *S*, seemingly at random. Next, *E* led school subjects to a familiar vacant classroom and seated them at a small table. Then *E* said:

My job is working with toys, which I think you'll agree is a pretty nice job to have. I brought some toys you can play with today. First, I brought this [*E* places the first toy, corresponding to the first toy presented to this *S*'s hospital counterpart, in front of *S*]. The next thing I brought you is this.

The *E* continued exactly as with hospital *S*s, introducing the toys, recording play for 6 minutes, recording stated preferences, and then introducing the next set of toys. When each *S* had completed this procedure with all three toy sets, *E* thanked him and walked with him back to the classroom where the next *S* was met.

RESULTS

Analysis of predictions The measure of response used throughout these analyses was the time spent with toys of each category during the three 6-minute periods when toys were available for play. An analysis of the *S*s' stated ranked preferences among toys and of the rank order with which toys were played revealed significant trends parallel to those reported below.

The mean time spent on novel and simple toys under the hospital and school conditions is shown in Figure 1. Hospital *S*s played more with novel toys and less with simple toys than did school *S*s. An analysis of variance showed this novelty-by-condition interaction to be a significant one ($f = 8.22$; $p < .01$; $df = 1/32$). It should be noted that the direction of this change in preference strength is contrary to the prediction that nonanxious *S*s would prefer novel toys more and simple toys less than would anxious *S*s. Furthermore, a general preference for novel toys was significant over both the anxious and nonanxious condition ($F = 48.85$; $p < .001$; $df = 1/32$).

The mean time spent on the hospital-relevant and hospital-irrelevant toys for each toy set, under the hospital and school conditions revealed that the hospital *S*s showed a greater preference for hospital-relevant toys and a lesser preference for

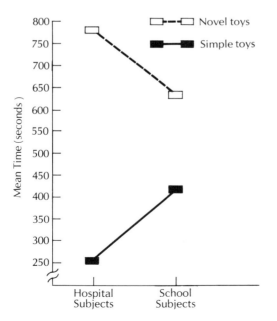

FIGURE 1 Mean time spent in play with novel and simple toys by subjects in the hospital and school conditions.

hospital-irrelevant toys, as compared with their school-subject counterparts. This interaction is a significant one ($F = 26.66$; $p \mathbin{/} < .001$; $df = 1/32$), and it is congruent with the prediction advanced that play will reflect the presence of anxiety.

It might seem as if the amount of play on one type of toy would necessarily be inversely related to the amount of play on the opposite type of toy, thus casting doubt on the validity of testing an interaction effect which could capitalize on such a restriction. The reader should note, however, that children could and did abstain from play with either type of toy, so that the effects of no play were also being tested. Further, the predictions are little changed if we restrict them only to the amount of play with novel (or relevant) toys and then proceed to test such predictions with *t* tests of the *slopes* of the relevant lines shown in the accompanying figure. In every case such tests show results parallel to those reported above.

DISCUSSION

The first finding of consequence in the hospital-school study was that children who were experiencing the anxiety of hospitalization preferred novel (or complex) toys over simple toys to a *greater* degree than did similar Ss in school. This finding was opposite to the predicted relation, that is, that nonanxious Ss would choose toys more on the basis of novelty than would anxious Ss. Data from this study offered no support at all for this hypothesis. School Ss might have *satiated* on all toys before each 6-minute play period was over, for instance. This would have made novel and simple toys less different and discriminable on the novelty dimension for school Ss, producing the effects pictured in Figure 1. However, a careful analysis of shifts in play and durations of play showed nothing to support the hypothesis that uncontrolled variations of this sort could have led to the observed results. On the basis of all the data it

seems likely that the presence or absence of anxiety does not generally affect the child's preference for novel toys versus simple toys.

All groups of Ss in these studies showed a strong preference for novel toys at all times. The absence of the predicted interaction between novelty and anxiety, however, makes the main effect less relevant to the Piagetean theory of play. While these data do not seriously call into question Piaget's theory of play, they do suggest that if anxiety affects the child's play preferences for novelty at all, it must do so at younger ages.

Perhaps the most striking finding of the hospital-school study was that children who were experiencing the anxiety that goes with hospitalization preferred to play with toys relevant to hospitalization more than did a similar population of children in school. This finding supports the hypothesis that under conditions of anxiety children prefer to play with toys on the basis of toy relevance to the anxiety being experienced.

REFERENCES

Beach, F. A. Concepts of play in animals. *American Naturalist*, 1945, **79**, 523–541.

Britt, S. H., & Janis, S. Q. Toward a social psychology of human play. *Journal of Social Psychology*, 1941, **13**, 351–384.

Erikson, E. H. Growth and crises of the healthy personality. *Psychological Issues*, 1959, **1**, 50–100.

Freud, S. Inhibitions, symptoms, and anxiety [1926]. (Standard ed., vol. **20**.) London: Hogarth, 1959. Pp. 77–178.

Gilmore, J. B. The role of anxiety and cognitive factors in children's play behavior. Unpublished doctoral dissertation, Yale University, 1964.

Gilmore, J. B. Play: a special behavior. In R. N. Haber (Ed.), *Current Research in Motivation*. New York: Holt, Rinehart & Winston, 1965.

Hurlock, E. B. Experimental investigations of

childhood play. *Psychological Bulletin,* 1934, **31,** 47–66.

Levin, H., & Wardwell, Elinor. The research uses of doll play. *Psychological Bulletin,* 1962, **59,** 27–56.

Levy, D. Psychic trauma of operations in children and note on combat neuroses. *American Journal of Diseases of Childhood,* 1945, **69,** 7–25.

Piaget, J. *Play, dreams, and imitation in childhood* [1945]. London: Heinemann, 1951.

Prugh, D., Staub, Elizabeth M., Sands, Harriet H., Kirschbaum, Ruth M., & Lenihan, Ellenora A. A study of the emotional reactions of children and families to hospitalization and illness. *American Journal of Orthopsychiatry,* 1953, **23,** 70–106.

52 | Person Perception in Children

MARIAN RADKE YARROW
JOHN D. CAMPBELL

How accurately a child perceives others must affect his peer relations. The present study explores how children view others and what role the child's own feelings play in his perceptions. This study explores the accuracy of children's perceptions of people and the biases introduced by their feelings about those people. The authors also examine the relation between children's perceptions of acts and adult descriptions of the same acts.

Children appraise others in interactional terms—words that describe the actions between children (for example, aggressive, dependent, supportive, friendly). The most organized descriptions are given of children hated by their peers. Some variation in perceptual reports is caused by the sex of the observer and his age. Older children give more organized descriptions.

Large differences exist between children's and adults' perceptions of the same child. The reasons for this discrepancy are complex; some differences derive from methodological considerations, while others reflect real changes in the behaviors that occur when adults are present.

How do people "perceive" one another? This question continues to invite research of many kinds. In many of these studies, behavioral responses are taken as perceptual indicators, but the meaning of the other person and the cognitive processes involved in achieving such meaning are left an inference. A needed extension of the work in this area is an inquiry into the ways in which other persons are experienced, as represented by the perceiver's description or conceptualization of the "other." In what dimensions is the other experienced; how

uniquely and complexly is he comprehended? How do constant tendencies of the perceiver bring a screen into the situation? How do qualities of the particular other and the particular situation affect perception?

In research on person perception, investigators have proceeded along several different lines. One approach has emphasized *judgmental* aspects of person perception and has focused on factors correlated with an individual's empathic ability, insight, or accuracy in appraising the responses of others. Common to this research is a focus on a discrete judgment, an appraisal of the person perceived along specified dimensions preselected by the investigator, for example, prediction of a person's responses

Adapted from Person perception in children. *Merrill-Palmer Quarterly of Behavior and Development*, 1963, **9**, 57–72.

to a picture frustration test, a technique employed by Bieri (1953); prediction of the stimulus person's self description by an adjectival Q-sort, used by Baker and Block (1957); or prediction of another's sociometric choices, in work by Tagiuri, Kogan and Bruner (1955).

Another approach less commonly employed was pointed to by MacLeod (1945) when he emphasized the need to ask the phenomenological question "What is there?"

This study uses a meaningful real-life social situation as a setting for examining the characteristics of children's perceptions of one another as they occur in a behavioral context. The basic aims of the research are: (a) to examine the dimensions in terms of which children conceptualize and organize their impressions of others; (b) to explore ways in which characteristics of the perceiver and of the perceptual object contribute to interpersonal perceptions; and (c) to assess effects of continued contact (the transition from stranger to acquaintance) on children's cognitive appraisals.

The setting and design of the research utilized the essentially natural laboratory of children's summer camps. The 267 boys and girls, white and Negro, who served as subjects ranged in age from eight to 13. They came from low-income families in the greater Washington area. The children were placed in cabin groups of eight children per cabin. The cabins were homogeneous in age and sex. In half the cabins, groups were racially homogeneous; in half, biracial. The groups were composed of children who were initially strangers to one another. The setting was isolated from familiar surroundings of family and friends. Children of the cabin were, therefore, the child's primary social group for two weeks of camp.

The data on children's perceptions derive from interviews with each child at the beginning and at the end of the two weeks of camp. In the interviews, individual snapshots of all the cabin members were spread out in front of the child, and he was asked to choose one child whom he felt he knew most about. He was encouraged to "tell all

about him, as if you were telling a friend back home." The questions were designed to learn what was most salient to the child (whom he selected, and what dimensions he used for description) and the quality of his interpretations. From sociometric questions, each child's ranking of his cabin mates on their desirability as friends was obtained.

For 20 of the 32 cabins studied, systematic behavior observations were made using a sampling of periods and locations in the camp day, on days at the beginning, middle, and end of camp. The observer made detailed running accounts of the behavior of each child in the cabin. This was done by observing for five minutes, followed by five minutes for additional writing-up of observations. In each five-minute record, the observer was required to account for each child present. There were 1,010 such observational records, representing slightly more than four hours in the life of each group studied.

CHARACTERISTICS OF CHILDREN'S PERCEPTIONS OF PERSONS

In order to present the data on children's perceptions of persons it will be necessary first to describe ways in which their "perceptual" reports have been analyzed. Descriptions were divided into psychological units, a unit being defined as a discrete action; or a single characteristic or evaluation. For example, the following response is broken up into twelve units:

> He is nice—and plays all right,—but he likes to fight people.—Says he can beat anybody in the cabin.—He likes to tell jokes a lot. He makes you laugh.—O.K.—but he likes to fight other kids.—Acts all right—except when gets mad, then he wants to punch on people.—Most of the time he is on his bed telling jokes.—He says he don't like to play baseball but he likes to play horseshoes.—That's all I know.

A report was scored on: (a) number of psychological units present, (b) content of the units, and (c) nature of interpretation in the total description.

Content of Perceptual Report

The desire to examine content by using a framework that did not deviate too greatly from the children's phenomenal reports guided the development of a classification scheme. The one evolved has antecedents in the conceptualization of interaction formulated by Coffey and his associates (Freedman, Leary, Ossorio & Coffey, 1951), but the categories were tailored to the content in the children's reports.

When asked to tell all they knew about another, children showed two very strong tendencies: (a) broad positive or negative judgments were given by 85 per cent, and (b) these judgments were elaborated primarily in terms of peer actions having direct interpersonal consequences. In contrast, noninteractive qualities appeared in only one-half of the reports, as relatively minor fractions of the descriptions. Physical appearance was the most frequently reported noninteractive aspect.

Individual children contributed differently to the distribution of characteristics about others. On the average, children reported 11 units of description, some reported as many as 27, others a single unit. When each child's description of another was summarized in terms of four major categories of interaction—aggressive, affiliative, assertive and submissive—forty-six per cent of the children concentrated their descriptions entirely in one of these broad dimensions. Thirty-one per cent were able to see opposite or contradictory features in the other child (i.e., both affectionate and hostile behavior, dominating and passive-dependent actions). Only two per cent of the children described the other child in terms of all four categories. The remaining children, in using more than one dimension of content, did not present both ends of any given continuum.

Children's perceptions on the two interviews (in the first or second day at camp

and at the end of camp) demonstrated noteworthy stability; content areas appeared in relatively the same frequency positions on the two interviews. Within this consistency, some shifts occurred; emphasis on interaction rather than noninteraction (proportion of interaction units in each description) became even more pronounced. Among children mentioning noninteractional factors in either interview, 56 per cent showed lessened emphasis and 35 per cent increased emphasis. This shift over time was statistically significant. Decline in noninteraction was primarily accounted for by the lesser emphasis on a child's appearance. In descriptions of interaction, reports of dominating and aggressive, rebellious and nonconforming behavior increased and reports of affiliative behavior decreased on the second interview.

Comparisons of the individual child's reports revealed intra-individual consistency. A child's descriptions on the second interview were by no means repetitions of his first interview; however, if a child used a given dimension of personality on his initial description, he was more likely to report it on the second occasion than was a child who did not mention it initially. This self-consistency occurred regardless of whether the same or a different child was being described on the two occasions.

Quality and Complexity of Perceptual Report

Consider these two descriptions of the same child:

> I have been with this guy name of Mark. He always talks back to the chief, and gets me to tie his shoes. I wake him up in the morning . . . He is a funny guy, likes to play around a lot. I get along real good. He acts okay . . . Every five minutes he has to be told something. He likes to act simple, too.

> He is simple. When he talks, he makes me laugh, and he always talks back to the chief (counselor). Yesterday he said that "camp, it looks pretty good, and we look

like jackasses." He likes for you to have manners. He likes to play with people. He eats a lot. He always wants food passed around the table. Don't want anybody to put their arms across his plate . . . I think he could get along with others all right. He gets along with me, but everybody picks on him. I like to help out people who everybody pick on, something is wrong with them . . . Last night the man say "have your father been pounding on you a lot?" I would think that, because something is wrong with him. It might make him worser.

These descriptions have used similar categories of content, yet they differ markedly in how they have organized and synthesized the "parts," and in the extent to which they have attempted interpretation of motives or causes of behavior. The description which arrives at a picture-of-a-person or a "theory" of personality may be regarded as more complex than the description which is an atomistic collection of discrete variables.

A seven-point scale of complexity of organization was used to measure the extent to which children gave systematically organized descriptions. Descriptions rated at the top of the scale painted well-integrated personality portraits involving implicit and explicit inferences about behavior. Those in the intermediate range were typified by more superficial generalizations supported by congruent behavioral detail. At the lower end of the scale of organization were the reports that consisted either of vague global generalizations that were inadequately supported (e.g., "He's OK." "She's nice." "He's all right.") or a congeries of specific details without a stated or implied theme.

The individual child tended to give descriptions at similar levels of complexity on both interviews, regardless of whether the same or a different peer was described on both interviews. However, there was a significant trend for the group toward more highly organized impressions on the second interview. The qualitative superiority of the later descriptions may derive from the fact

that the child had more opportunity to collect many diverse bits of information about another child and to observe more occasions of given kinds of behavior in the child which might aid in the synthesizing process.

From the examination of children's perceptions, several conclusions have emerged: (a) Children's descriptions of others were dominated by social relevance; the emphasis on interaction and the very common use of evaluative appraisals gave evidence of this. (b) There was stability over time both in content and quality of the individual child's perceptual report, whether reporting on the same or a different child. (c) Within this stability, there were certain systematic changes over time toward increased emphasis on interaction and more fully organized descriptions.

There were marked individual variations in children's reports. The next portions of this paper attempt to account for some of these variations by examining certain characteristics of the perceiving child and certain characteristics of the child perceived.

CHARACTERISTICS OF THE PERCEIVING CHILD AND HIS PERCEPTION OF PERSONS

In looking for links between the perceiving child and his appraisal of others, variables of age, sex, and the perceiver's behavior have been considered.

Age and Sex

One would anticipate that the child's conceptions of his human world change as greatly with increasing maturity and experience as do his conceptions of the physical world. There have been very few studies, however, concerning the development of the child's sensitivity to phenomena of human characteristics and behavior. . . . The present study deals with only a limited cross-section spanning middle childhood (eight to 13 years). By this time most children have had experience with a fairly wide range of personalities in the family, neighborhood and school life; also, the differential roles of boys and girls in society are certainly well defined. To what extent are age and sex differences related to variability in children's person perceptions?

Age related trends in categories used in describing others did not appear except in reports of aggression and domination, which tended to be more frequent among the older children. There was, however, a sex-linked pattern of differences, consistent with the different experiences of boys and girls, and with adult values for boys and girls. Thus, distinctly nurturing behaviors were emphasized more by girls than boys (especially at the end of camp). The boys, on the other hand, were more attentive to acting-out nonconformities and withdrawn behavior. Attending to the conforming actions in the other child ("She's polite." "He doesn't say bad things.") was also more frequent in boys than girls.

When perceptual complexity is considered, there were no consistent sex differences, but age trends appear. Older children tended to give more complex perceptual reports. A relevant, but unavailable, measure in the present study is the child's intelligence, which might bear a significant relation to his characteristic ways of perceiving others. The relatively small developmental trends are surprising for functions as complex as the perceiving of persons and interpersonal relations. This may be a reflection of the early development of sensitivities to interpersonal relations. Also, more specific differences by age may have been undetected by the analysis (e.g., concrete *details* of aggressive or nurturant behavior might be quite different at different age levels, though the generic categories would be the same). A more detailed developmental study is needed.

Personality as Reflected in Behavior Patterns

The personality of the perceiving child, as expressed through his actions, was also examined in relation to cognitive responses.

Behavioral records on each child were divided into units of action. Each unit was classed in one of four broad categories: (a) friendly, sociable, and nurturing behavior (49 per cent of all units), (b) aggressive, rebellious, and disruptive actions (20 per cent), (c) assertive and influencing behavior (21 per cent), and (d) submissive, dependent, fearful behavior (10 per cent). Two coders independently classified 89 per cent of 298 units in identical fashion. Each child was scored in terms of the relative frequency with which he initiated these interactions. Combination of the three most frequently occurring kinds of interaction gave behavioral types defined as follows: "active" children scored in the upper third of their cabin group on friendly as well as aggressive interaction, with assertion ranging from high to average; "withdrawn" children rated in the bottom third on at least two of these three dimensions, and high on none; "aggressive" children rated high on aggressive, disruptive, and rebellious action, *not* high on friendliness, and varied from high to low on assertion scores; and "friendly" children ranked high on sociable, affiliative and nurturing interaction and average or below on both aggression and assertion. Analyses by age and sex revealed no systematic differences in the frequency of these behavior types among boys and girls in the three age groups.

Active and friendly children gave more complex descriptions of others than did withdrawn or hostile children. Active children made explicit inferences to a greater extent than did the withdrawn (measured only at the end of the session). In comparing friendly with hostile children, there was a consistent, but nonsignificant, tendency on both interviews for the friendly children to describe others in a more organized fashion, and they were significantly more likely than the hostile children to make inferential statements.

These comparisons suggest that the active participant brings his awareness of others into sharper judgmental focus than does the child who remains on the sidelines. Intentional or not, some degree of manipulation of interaction seems to facilitate obtaining a clear picture—accurate or inaccurate—of the social environment. That descriptions by the more sociable and affiliative children were generally more complex than those of the withdrawn children might be accounted for on similar grounds. That descriptions given by the friendly children are not strikingly superior in quality to those given by the hostile aggressive children might suggest that the general equivalence in their amounts of contact with peers tended to outweigh any possible influences of differences in the affective flavor of their behavior.

BEHAVIOR OF THE PERCEIVED CHILD AND OTHERS' DESCRIPTIONS OF HIM

The portrait of a child reported by his peers would not be expected to reflect his behavior with his peers with complete fidelity, but would be expected to show some correspondence. It was possible in this study to examine the closeness or divergence of these two pictures by comparing peer descriptions with records of behavior on each child made by trained observers, covering four hours of interaction. Descriptions and observations of behavior were both reduced to the four broad classes of action—friendly, aggressive, assertive, and submissive. Presence of a given class of action in a peer's descriptions of a child was compared with relative frequency with which the child initiated such action in his group. In this comparison, peer image and recorded behavior showed a remarkable absence of correspondence. In other words, in the child's synthesized picture of another child, the relevance or salience of a characteristic does not appear to be determined by the sheer frequency of its display in the behavior by the perceived child. This lack of correspondence is open to several possible interpretations. In part, it might be a function of the way in which the data were gathered. Thus, the "sample" of behavior available to the adult observer might not adequately represent the "universe" of peer behavior available to the perceiving child. It is possible, too, that the perceiving child selects from the total behavior of the object child only the direct behavioral interchange between himself and the perceived child, whereas the adult observer is attuned to interactions occurring among all the cabin group. This latter explanation is unlikely—because the reporting child frequently referred to the perceived child's relations with others.

While methodological factors may account for some of the discrepancies between the adult's and the child's "conclusions" about the nature of another child, these discrepancies might also derive from "real" differences in their selection from and interpretation of the same raw materials of children's behavior which are important in the understanding of the perceptions of children and which have importance also as a methodological issue in research with children.

Adults and children, while observing the same actions, might attribute quite different meaning to these actions. The values of scientist-observers and those of children—in this instance children from lower socioeconomic groups—may differ. It would not be surprising, therefore, if concomitant differences were also reflected in cognitive interpretation of action. Thus, the adult-asscientist may impute meaning to particular behavior differing from the interpretation given it by a participating child. Behavioral data may be reliably coded, but still such reliability does not eliminate the possibility of the differential perspective suggested. If such possible differences in cognitive interpretations are real and considerable ones, then this would clearly suggest the need for caution in the utilization of adult observers' reports of children's behavior as suitable "objective" indices in some child development research.

A second potential source of discrepancy between adults' records of behavior and children's perceptual reports is that of selective screening. Here the data shed some light and partially support a hypothesis of perceptual selectivity on the child's part.

Feelings of the perceiver enter into the level of organization of his descriptions about the perceived child and into the content of his descriptions. Affect of the reporting child and complexity of organization of description were related curvilinearly; disliked children were described in a more systematic fashion than liked children, and liked children were described more systematically than children in a more neutral range of friendship. This relationship was much less pronounced after two weeks of interaction. The interesting qualitative superiority with which disliked children were described may in part reflect the perceiver's personal concern; it may come as the result of intense negative interactions which furnished conspicuous experiences; it may reflect the need to rationalize a negative evaluation.

Content of the reports reflects the affect of the perceiver in the expected manner. Liked children were described in terms that document "good guy" labels; reports of aggressive, fearful and dependent behavior were less often included. Similarly, the least liked children were reported as less affiliative and less nurturant. The extent to which affect is selectively shaping the perception can be seen by considering simultaneously the affect of the reporting child, the content of his report and the adult observer's behavior record of the perceived child. Even when one controls on the amount of recorded friendly behavior of the object child, the more the child is liked by his describer, the more likely is he to be seen as affiliative. The amount of reported affiliation decreases systematically, from highest reported on children liked best, to lowest reported on children liked least. In a similar fashion, still controlling on observed friendly behavior of the object child, children most strongly liked are seen as least aggressive; those least well liked, most aggressive. Now controlling on recorded aggressive behavior of the object child, children strongly liked are systematically seen as more affiliative than children less well liked. And those most strongly liked are seen as least aggressive; those least well liked, most aggressive. Affect appears to in-

fluence significantly and systematically the child's selection and interpretation of behavioral information from his peers, resulting in peer assessments quite markedly at variance with the assessments arrived at through the perspectives of scientist-observers.

DISCUSSION

We have examined children's perceptions of persons in a new social situation. Their perceptions, as represented by their reports to the investigator, are generally not unrelated congeries of elements but rather syntheses of varied and sometimes disparate characteristics about the other person. Children appraise others in interactional terms, along lines of personal significance. The most highly organized descriptions are given about children who have affective value for the observing child, particularly negative affective value. The sizable variations found in children's cognitive reports, both in content and level of organization, present a dimension of individual differences about which there is relatively little information and relatively little understanding as to its significance for interpersonal relations. Some of the variations in perceptual reports were accounted for in terms of characteristics of the child reporters, such as age and sex differences and differences in the behavioral qualities of the perceivers. Older children and the more active and friendly children were somewhat more likely to give complex person perceptions. Differences in content of descriptions by boys as contrasted with girls are consistent with the differences in the experiences of childhood for the two sexes.

It would be misleading, however, to point only to differences in children's perceptions. Children's appraisals of their peers in many respects showed shared sensitivities, with repeated thematic emphasis on certain salient relationships, such as sociability, affiliative tendencies, potentially hostile acts. The same themes, with few exceptions, were characteristic of both initial and considered impressions at each age level studied. Thus, the *variations* among children are within this broad common framework. These similar sensitivities (unchanged by age) may possibly be attributable to a common culture of childhood and to similar learning of the significant interpersonal cues, those that are differentially rewarding or punishing in nature.

The particular characteristics of children's person perceptions obtained in this study in unknown ways may derive from the characteristics of the population being studied (children from lower socio-economic classes), and from the particular circumstances under which the testing was carried out. The children were in a new situation in which the other children, the environmental setting, and the adults in charge were all unfamiliar to them. These factors may possibly have heightened children's sensitivities to particular kinds of qualities in other persons. Lack of correspondence between children's reported impressions of another child and adult observors' behavioral records of the child was far greater than one might have anticipated in advance. The children's personal perceptions, fashioned, we assume, from expectations, past experiences and personal needs, resulted in "realities" quite different from the assessments of children based on the observations and codings of the researchers. The coexistence of such discrepant "realities" poses a complicated problem in understanding children's responses to interpersonal stimuli, and one calling for more research. It is a truism to state that person perception is a complex process, yet the evidence of the present study indicates the need for emphasizing this fact.

REFERENCES

Baker, Bela O., & Block, J. Accuracy of interpersonal prediction as a function of judge and object characteristics. *Journal of Abnormal and Social Psychology,* 1957, **54,** 37–43.

Bieri, J. Changes in interpersonal perceptions following social interaction. *Journal of Abnormal and Social Psychology,* 1953, **48,** 61–66.

Freedman, M. B., Leary, T. F., Ossorio, A. G., & Coffey, H. S. The interpersonal dimension of personality. *Journal of Personality,* 1951, **20,** 143–161.

MacLeod, R. B. The phenomenological approach to social psychology. *Psychological Review,* 1945, **54,** 193–210.

Tagiuri, R., Kogan, N., & Bruner, J. S. The Transparency of interpersonal choice. *Sociometry,* 1955, **18,** 624–635.

53 | The "Social Climate" of Children's Groups

RONALD LIPPITT

Can the social atmosphere of a children's group influence the productivity, satisfaction, and interpersonal relations of its members? Social psychologists asked this question during World War II; they were particularly concerned about German efficiency under authoritarian control. The author of this study created "democratic," "authoritarian," and "laissez-faire" atmospheres. Individual satisfaction, group productivity, interactions among members, and the effect of leader removal were studied.

The results showed that a "democratic" atmosphere produces more satisfaction, more identification with group goals, and more productivity when the leader is absent than do the other social climates. Goals were defined by the democratic group, but they were imposed on the authoritarian group by a leader. However, the output of a submissive authoritarian group was superior to the democratic group. The group atmosphere chosen must depend on the goal; if production is the only criterion, then authoritarian methods work fine. However, if individual satisfaction is important (as it usually is), then democracy is superior.

THE AIM OF THE STUDY

The study herein reported was carried out in two different parts. The primary aim of the first study was to develop techniques for creating and describing the "social atmosphere" of children's clubs and for quantitatively recording the effects of varied social atmospheres upon group life and individual behavior. Chiefly because of practical interests two degrees of adult social control of group life, labeled "democratic" and "authoritarian," were selected as the experimental variables. The second experiment, utilizing in large measure the most fruitful techniques of the first study, had as its primary aims:

Adapted from an experimental study of the effect of democratic and authoritarian group atmospheres. *University of Iowa Studies in Child Welfare*, 1940, **16,** No. 3, 43–195.

(a) the intensive study of the effects upon individual and group behavior of three variations in social atmosphere, labeled "democratic," "authoritarian," and "laissez-faire"; (b) the study of the transition from one atmosphere to another of the same group of children; and (c) the relationship between the individual child's home "social climate" and his adjustment to a particular club atmosphere. It should be clear at the outset that these experiments were developed as a contribution to experimental social psychology rather than with any aim of proving the values of one or another kind of educational system or political organization. The actual meaning of the adjectives used to label the experimental social atmospheres ("authoritarian," "democratic," "laissez-faire") is necessarily somewhat different from what the same terms usually mean in political and economic discussions. No confusion will result, however, if the reader lets the terms be operationally defined by the quantitative descriptions which follow of the various behavioral characteristics of the group situations in question.

THE TECHNICAL METHODOLOGY OF THE PRESENT STUDY

Selection of Groups, Experimental Manipulations, and Controls

Three different degrees or types of leader control of club life constituted the major experimental variable. The tabulation below describes briefly the chief characteristics of these three treatment variations.

Obviously other aspects of the experimental situation besides leader treatment might cause variations in the social atmosphere of the club. It was necessary to make sure that differences in group behavior attributed to different types of leadership were not actually due to other factors. The experimenters, on the basis of the preliminary experiment and their own previous experience, felt that the following factors were potential variables which would have to be experimentally controlled or varied systematically if the results of the study were to be definitive in regard to the variations in leader treatment: (a) the type of club activity; (b) the physical setting in which the clubs met; (c) special characteristics of a particular club personnel (controlled to some extent by selection); (d) personality differences of the leaders (as a separate variable from leader treatment); (e) sequence of experimental club treatments (democratic treatment coming after an authoritarian experience rather than before it, etc.).

It was possible to equate the *club activities* by arranging it so that the democratic clubs should meet first and decide what their activities would be. The authoritarian leaders could then dictate the same activities to the controlled clubs. In the laissez-faire situation the same materials (plaster of paris, soap for soap carving, model airplanes, etc.) were supplied as in the other situations for use by the boys as they pleased.

The *physical setting* was the same for all

Authoritarian	Democratic	Laissez-faire
1. All determination of policy by the leader	1. All policies a matter of group discussion and decision, encouraged and assisted by the leader	1. Complete freedom for group or individual decision, with a minimum of leader participation
2. Techniques and activity steps dictated by the authority, one at a time, so that future steps were always uncertain to a large degree	2. Activity perspective gained during discussion period. General steps to group goal sketched, and, where technical advice was needed, the leader suggested two or more alternative procedures from which choice could be made	2. Various materials supplied by the leader, who made it clear that he would supply information when asked. He took no other part in work discussion
3. The leader usually dictated the particular work task and work companion of each member	3. The members were free to work with whomever they chose, and the division of tasks was left up to the group	3. Complete nonparticipation of the leader
4. The dominator tended to be "personal" in his praise and criticism of the work of each member; remained aloof from active group participation except when demonstrating	4. The leader was "objective" or "fact-minded" in his praise and criticism and tried to be a regular group member in spirit without doing too much of the work	4. Infrequent spontaneous comments on member activities unless questioned and no attempt to appraise or regulate the course of events

clubs. The groups met, two at a time, in adjacent clubrooms which were similar in size and arrangement and which allowed for easy interaction between the groups.

It was possible to ascertain the influence of the variable of *peculiarities of club personnel* by comparing the variation of the behavior of the same group under different treatments (leadership techniques) with the variation of the behavior of different clubs under the same type of treatment.

Several avenues for finding a possible distinction between *leader personality and leader treatment* are open for analysis. Inasmuch as leaders shifted from one type of treatment to another it was possible to find whether the different treatments by one leader tended to be more alike than the same types of treatments by different leaders. It was also possible to find from interviewing the children whether certain of the adults tended to be regarded as good leaders no matter what their leadership technique while other leaders were persistently unpopular. Comparisons of the same leader repeating the same technique with different leaders giving the same treatment also shed some light upon the importance of this variable.

The fifth probable variable mentioned above, *sequence of club experience,* is also amenable to rather systematic analysis in the plan of the present experiment. (For instance, some of the 6-week periods of "autocracy" followed periods of "democracy" and sometimes the opposite sequence occurred.)

The observation techniques were broad enough in scope to throw into bold relief other unplanned-for variables which might affect in an appreciable way the experimental results.

Observation techniques and other records

Just as mechanical recording instruments in the physics laboratory may be roughly or highly calibrated, so the human organism as a recording instrument may reflect the behavior of others with refined accuracy or only with rough approximations. It is probably correct to say that the more interpretive and meaningful the units of behavior are which are being recorded the more highly trained or "sensitized" must be the observer to get reliable records. In the present experiment, which called for the grouping of diverse behavioral symptoms having the same psychological meaning into one category, it was important that observers have preliminary training as well as be trained students of child behavior. The University of Iowa preschools were used for this training purpose until our human instruments had become sufficiently refined to record the behaviors called for by our observation categories.

Eight types of club records were kept. The four most important were as follows; at least one observer specialized in each type.

1. A quantitative running account of the *social interactions* of the five children and the leader, in terms of symbols for directive, compliant, and objective (fact-minded) approaches and responses, including a category of purposeful refusal to respond to a social approach.

2. A minute-by-minute *group-structure* analysis giving a record of activity subgroupings, the activity goal of each subgroup, whether the goal was initiated by the leader or spontaneously formed by the children, and rating on degree of unity of each subgrouping.

3. An *interpretive* running account of strikingly significant member actions and changes in the atmosphere of the group as a whole. This was the basis of the most significant interaction data—difficult to quantify but extremely suggestive as to the underlying dynamic factors involved.

4. Continuous *stenographic records* of all conversation. This was the basis of the most significant data.

These data were synchronized at minute intervals so that placed side by side they furnished a rather complete and integrated picture of the ongoing life of the group.

The introduction of observers into such a club situation without affecting the naturalness of behavior is itself an interesting re-search problem. In the first experiment it was found that four observers grouped around a table in a physically separated part of the clubroom attracted virtually no attention if it was explained to the boys at the first meeting that "those are some people interested in learning how a mask-making club goes; they have plenty to do so they won't bother us and we won't bother them." In the second experiment the physical ar-rangement was even more advantageous and seemed to make for equally unself-conscious behavior on the part of the clubs. From the drift of the group conversations while the leaders were out of the room it was clear to even the most skeptical guest observers that, as a rule, they "hardly existed at all" so far as the behavior of the children was concerned.

Reliability, validity, and categorization of data   The validity of social-behavior records, the extent to which they actually conform to the realities of the behavior they repre-sent, can be judged only by agreement with other attempts to measure the same vari-ables, or by the fruits, in terms of correct predictions and hypotheses which result from the use of the measurements. The au-thors believe that a more valid picture of social-behavior data is possible with this present field-theoretical approach to be-havior measurement than is possible with some of the other more widespread child-behavior recording techniques.

It is possible to consider three different types of reliability: (a) agreement between the records of two observers making simul-taneous observations of the same phenom-ena; (b) agreement between categorizers of behavior from the same behavior record (the same person twice or two different per-sons); (c) adequacy of the behavior sample as a reliable (stable) representation of the total behavior range concerning which the researcher wishes to generalize.

With 11 trained observers required to carry on the regular observations in the pres-ent experiment it was found impossible to get additional trained volunteers to work out simultaneous observer reliabilities with each one. It was possible to make prelim-inary checks and indirect estimates. Simul-taneous observations by two group-struc-ture analysts yielded an index of agreement on subgroupings of 85 per cent, which would have been higher if degrees of disagreement rather than an all-or-none method of com-puting agreement had been used. From the preliminary training of stenographic record-ers the index of agreement for conversation records ranged from .78 to .95 with an aver-age reliability of .84. Checks of the other techniques indicate the same range of ob-server agreement.

LEADER BEHAVIOR

The planned differences in leader behavior have been indicated above. We shall con-fine ourselves here to some illustrations of the data on how the leaders actually be-haved and how homogeneous the actions were of leaders delegated to behave in the same manner.

Figure 1 presents a comparison of the behavior of the average authoritarian, dem-ocratic, and laissez-faire leaders in terms of incidents of behavior in an equated unit of time (6 club meetings of 50 min. each). The reader will note that the first three cate-gories, "leader orders," "disrupting com-mands," and "non-constructive criticism," may be thought of as representing leader behavior which has a limiting effect upon the scope and spontaneity of child activity. About 60 per cent of all the behavior of the average authoritarian leader was of this sort, as compared to 5 per cent for the demo-cratic and laissez-faire leaders. The author-itarian leader usually initiated a child's ac-tivity with an order; often disrupted the ongoing activity by an order which started the child off in a new direction not spon-taneously chosen; and sometimes criticized club work in a personal manner which car-ried the meaning, "It's a bad job because I say it's a bad job" rather than "It's a poor job because those nails are bent over instead of driven in" (objective criterion). These are statistically significant differences and conform with the planned leader behavior patterns.

The next three categories may be thought of as representing leader behaviors that extend a child's freedom and mastery of his environment. In "guiding suggestions" the authoritarian and laissez-faire leaders were both significantly lower than the democratic leaders, which is again in line with the planned behavior.

The category "praise and approval" indicates the functioning of the adult as a dispenser of social recognition. This was a function of the authoritarian leader significantly more often than the democratic leader, in whose club situation recognition flowed from all members rather than just the leader.

The "jovial, confident" items of behavior are a good index of the extent to which the leaders got "on the same level" as the boys and established friendly personal relationships with them. The democratic leaders exhibited eight times as much of such behavior as the authoritarian and laissez-faire leaders.

GROUP MORALE: COHESIVE AND DISRUPTIVE FORCES

The level of morale in autocracy, democracy, and laissez-faire   In the limited space available, we can give only a sample of the actual results of the experiment. The sample which we have chosen includes data on two specific problems: group morale and the determination of group goals.

The morale of the democratic groups was strikingly superior in the number of friendly remarks made by the average group member to other group members in a 1-hr. meeting.

Some reasons for group disruption in autocracy   Looking behind these data and trying to find the psychological factors which ac-

counted for them, we must ask two major questions: (a) Why was morale usually higher in democracy than in autocracy? (b) Why was morale usually higher in democracy than in *laissez-faire*, which was, at least superficially, at the opposite extreme from autocracy?

On the basis of our quantitative and qualitative records, three factors emerge as probably most important in answering our first question; i.e., in accounting for the comparatively low morale associated with both types of reaction to autocracy:

1. Restricted space of free movement (with resultant frustration of the need for autonomy—if this need is not "given up"—and a generalized dissatisfaction with the total situation).

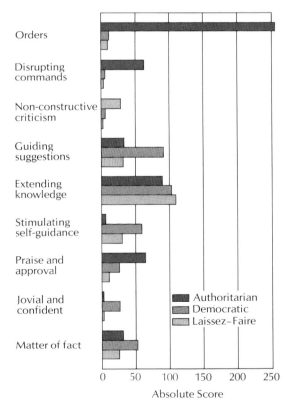

FIGURE 1   Comparison of behavior of average authoritarian, democratic and laissez-fair leader.

2. Frustration of the need for sociability.

3. Opposition to (or at least a psychological detachment from) the leader and his goals.

It is obvious that any type of autocracy which did not produce these particular effects might coincide with a very high morale. (In the present-day German army, for instance, it is at least conceivable that there may be a high degree of "identification" with, rather than detachment from, the "Leader" and his goals.) The fact remains, however, that in our own culture, and on the ten-year age level, our particular sort of autocracy did seem to have these effects.

1. The first factor, "restricted space of free movement," is quantitatively represented in our data by the large proportion of restrictive behavior by the leader (e.g., 256 "orders" in autocracy in 6 meetings as contrasted with 11 in democracy, and 63 "commands disrupting boys' previous activity" as contrasted with 4 in democracy). It is represented also by the high proportion of dependent reactions to the leader in the conversation analysis (13.7 and 15.8 in the two reactions to autocracy, as contrasted with 5.8 in democracy). It is best represented, however, by the boys' own statements, in the interviews, about their own feelings toward their autocratic leaders: "He was too strict," "He didn't let us do what we wanted to do," "He made us make masks, and the boys didn't like that," etc.

There were several indications that this frustration was reduced to a minimum in some of the autocratic atmospheres in which the submissive reaction was shown. In at least two of these groups, the boys apparently "gave up," to a large extent, their normal wish for autonomy, independence, or self-determination, and to that extent they ceased to be frustrated by the autocratic restrictions. This giving-up process seems to have been facilitated by the fact that in these cases the leader was viewed as work-minded, rather than arbitrary and personal, in the restrictions he imposed. To give in to a master workman, who was intent upon getting an important job done well, was apparently not a great blow to the boys' pride and was more easily accepted by them. Frustration reached a high point when the boys felt that their leader imposed arbitrary demands upon them which were not required by the objective character of the job that had to be done.

2. A quite unexpected result of autocratic leadership, in our experiments, was the extent to which it apparently inhibited normal free-and-easy sociability between the boys. In the four examples of "submissive reaction" this nonsociability was particularly striking. It was illustrated, for example, by the low total volume of child-to-child conversation (126 conversation units per six 50-min. meetings as contrasted with 220 in democracy), and by the small proportion of "out-of-club-field" conversation; i.e., outside of the range of topics directly related to club activities (4.6 conversation units as contrasted with 13.6 in democracy). Whatever the psychological reasons for it may have been, the fact was obvious that the repressive influence of the autocrat was carried over or generalized, somehow, so as to inhibit types of sociability which he never overtly prohibited in any way.

In the case of both of the above factors the inference from our data would be that the dissatisfaction with one aspect of the total situation (e.g., lack of independence or lack of sociability) has spread to the situation as a whole. Because the boys were dissatisfied with one aspect of the club situation, they tended to become dissatisfied with all of it, *including the group itself and the work on which it was engaged.* This is, at least, one way in which we can logically link the data on specific frustrations with the data on lowered group morale.

3. The third factor is psychologically quite different. Instead of involving a spreading of dissatisfaction from a part of the situation to the situation as a whole, it involved a dividing of a boy's psychological field into two sharply opposed portions; the portion which belongs to the adult leader and the portion which belongs to the boy himself (or, in some cases, to the boys considered

collectively, in opposition to their leader). Through this sharp dichotomizing of the field, there results a lack of relationship, or even an inverse relationship, between what is perceived in one portion of the field and what is perceived in the other. Specifically, the leader's goals, as perceived by the boy, are not automatically taken over by him (as they often are in democracy, where the boys "identify" with their leader), but are ignored or actively rebelled against. It is "what *he* wants me to do and what *I* want to do"—with the implication that the two things are necessarily different or even opposite—rather than simply "what we all want to do." It is understandable that any sharp cognitive differentiation between leader and followers —any stressing of the differences between them—would tend to provide a basis for this sort of psychological response. The evidence on this factor is largely circumstantial, but it is fairly convincing. It consists partly of the data showing how sharply differentiated the behavior of leader and followers were in autocracy (e.g., the ratio of leader's ascendant behavior to boy's ascendant behavior was 11.3 in the submissive reaction to autocracy and only 0.8 in democracy). It consists partly, also, of the boys' own verbalized feelings about their leader; e.g., the boy who said his democratic leader "worked right along with us, and thinks of things just like we do."

Some reasons for group disruption in laissez-faire There seemed to be three factors, again, which were primarily responsible for the low group morale in *laissez-faire:*

1. Restricted space of free movement (restricted by ignorance and mutual interference and resulting in frustration of the need for worth-while cooperative achievement).

2. Frustration of the need for clearness of structure.

3. The vicious circle of frustration-aggression-frustration.

1. There is much evidence indicating that the boys in the laissez-faire situation became dissatisfied with their own lack of efficiency and of solid accomplishment. They wanted to accomplish things, and they wanted the satisfaction of accomplishing them cooperatively as a harmonious working group. Both needs—the workmanlike need and the social need—were frustrated in *laissez-faire.* This was shown, for instance, by the high frequency of proposals for united action: "We gotta have some plans to work on," "Let's make a map or something," "Let's draw plans of a gun or a building or something"—proposals which usually remained abortive because of incapacity to cooperate in carrying them out. Such proposals account for the surprisingly high proportion of group-minded conversation and the surprisingly high We-I ratio that was always found in the highly individualistic laissez-faire groups. The frustrated needs were apparent also in the boys' evaluation of their laissez-faire leaders: " He was too easygoing," "He had too few things for us to do," etc.

2. There was evidence that at least a majority of the boys had a need for "clearness of structure" in their psychological environment. There was a tendency to be dissatisfied by chaos, confusion, uncertainty. This was shown both by many of their remarks during the meetings (e.g., the attempt to set up a military type of organization when things became too anarchic) and by remarks in the interviews (e.g., "He let us figure things out too much," while the autocrat "told us what to do, and we had something to do all the time").

3. In the running accounts of the laissez-faire meetings there was evident a vicious circle involving frustration which led to aggression and aggression which led, in turn, to mutual frustration. Both the psychological tension which resulted from frustration and the idleness which resulted from the absence of any organized constructive group activity, were apparently conducive to a large amount of more or less good-natured bickering and competitive horseplay. This aggression, then, tended to "frustrate" the persons who were attacked, especially if these persons were sincerely attempting to start some construc-

tive work. Thus, the work-minded boys who wanted to exercise their "freedom" to do constructive work found it almost impossible to do so. Mutual interference proved to be a highly effective disrupting force.

Differences in acceptance of the group goal It was possible to make judgments concerning individual and group acceptance of club goals from the following criteria: (a) change of behavior when the leader left the club; (b) presence or absence of motivation when the leader arrived late; (c) expressions of discontent for the club work; (d) carefulness of work; (e) creative suggestions in regard to club projects; (f) pride in the products of club effort.

In the submissive autocracies 74 per cent of the time while the leader was in the room was spent in serious work, but with the leader out this proportion dropped to 29 per cent and "distracted work atmosphere" increased from 6 to 20 per cent. In the atmosphere of aggressive reaction to autocratic leadership serious work periods dropped from 52 per cent with the leader present to 16 per cent while the leader was out of the room, with a corresponding rise in distracted work and horseplay. As compared to these striking evidences of lack of identification with the coercively induced work goals in the autocratic atmospheres the data on the democratic clubs indicate a negligible shift from 50 per cent "serious work atmosphere" with the leader in to 46 per cent with the leader out. A similar lack of effect of the adult leader upon the pattern of the club atmosphere was discovered in the laissez-faire clubs.

Data concerning the third criterion, overt expressions of discontent with club activities, were cited in the previous section. They showed that there were about three times as many expressions of discontent in *laissez-faire* and submissive autocracy as in the democratic clubs and about ten times as much in the atmosphere of aggressive overt reaction to authoritarian leadership.

Quantitative work output (in which the submissive autocracies led the other groups) cannot be taken as an evidence of group goal acceptance in comparing groups which differ in regard to the amount of coercive force exerted by central persons, but probably the care with which work is carried through and the number of suggestions for the improvement of group effort should furnish some valid clues. Comparisons, such as photographs of murals painted by all the clubs, indicate much more care for detail and less "slopping of paint" in the products of the democratic clubs, and it was found that boys in the groups with democratic leaders made 7 suggestions for group action to every 3 such remarks by members of the aggressive autocracies and laissez-faire groups and 1 similar contribution by members of the submissive autocracies.

The conflict of cooperative group goals and individual ego goals Besides the fact that enforced group goals were not enthusiastically accepted by the members of the authoritarian clubs another constellation of forces was discovered which hampered the progress of the autocratic clubs toward their group goals. In the previous section on disruption of group morale it was noted that the authoritarian group atmosphere produced (in the case of the aggressive reaction) more ego-centered competitive behavior than did the democratic social climates. These conflicts seemed to focus largely upon a competition for social recognition and approval from the adult leader. As the social structure of the situation was analyzed more completely it was concluded that motivation to contribute effort to the group goal was derived to some extent from reinforcing social approval for efforts already made. Because of the rigid status hierarchy in the authoritarian situation which set the adult leader off as the only person who could do any leading, the adult leader was the chief source of recognition for good work, as contrasted to a shifting boy leadership in the other two atmospheres. In democracy the boys more freely praised each other's work, while in autocracy the only way to get praise was to get it from the adult.

A "vicious circle of ego involvement" developed in the aggressive reaction to authoritarian situations, for as competition for social approval from "the source" increased the boys became less inclined to recognize with approval the work of one another. This insecurity tended to result in a continually increasing preoccupation with ego competitions and a loss of orientation toward joint group goals. In the democratic situation, where "recognition security" could be more readily gained, cooperative efforts more easily emerged and were maintained by continuing reinforcement. In the laissez-faire situation child leadership efforts were readily rewarded with group recognition, but lack of adult guidance usually meant that the leadership efforts to develop cooperation broke down.

On the basis of the observations reviewed in this section it has been concluded that cooperative group activity in the direction of group goals was impeded in the authoritarian situation not only by a *lack of identification with the group aims* (as induced by the leader) but also because the social structure of the situation produced *ego-centered ingroup conflicts* which resulted in individual efforts tangential to the direction of cooperative group progress.

CHAPTER SIXTEEN
PERSONALITY DEVELOPMENT

A child's personality embodies many processes. Perception, learning, thinking, motivation, early experience, will, and the various social and cultural influences all interact to produce a total person. A major process of personality development is identification between a child and significant others. Identification is strengthened by love and perceived similarities between the model and child. In addition, the child increases these similarities by acquiring personality characteristics of the model.

The first paper presents an analysis of identification in terms of learning theory. Identification is seen as a cognitive response; it is strengthened by perceived similarities between the child and the model. In addition, the child strives for mastery of the environment and for love from the model; both these secondary goals are served by acquisition of the model's characteristics. Once the child identifies with a model, he acquires more and more model characteristics; the child is vicariously affected more and more by successes and failures of the model.

The relation between model and child affects imitation. Bandura and Huston tested this notion directly by producing a warm, nurturant relation between model and children in one group, and a cold, distant relation between the model and children in another group. Children who experienced a warm, nurturant relation with the model produced much more imitative behaviors in a two-choice learning situation than did children who experienced a cold relation with the model.

Often, personality development does not follow an ideal course to health and productivity. What then? Must we wring our hands and say, "Better luck next time"? Levitt looked at the effectiveness of psychotherapy with children. He found no evidence to support its effectiveness. However, before we give up treating children's personality disorders, we should consider three facts. First, the children with whom he compared his treated patients were not an adequate control group. Second, the methods of data collection and analysis are primitive.

Finally, finding no difference between groups does not imply that there is no effect of therapy. Before we accept the proposition that psychotherapy has no effect, we need more careful attention to design and analysis of data.

Freud was a giant, and he produced several intricate formulations of personality. In this charming little essay about children's dreams he suggests that all dreams fulfill wishes, both in children and in adults. The point is that children's dreams show the process of wish fulfillment much more clearly than do the distorted and hidden dreams of adults.

54 | The Concept of Identification

JEROME KAGAN

How do children learn personality characteristics? Through identification with their parents and other models of mature behavior. The present paper suggests that identification is a learned cognitive response supported by a child's perceived similarity with significant others. Identification is viewed as a gradual process; a child can associate himself more or less with the model and he can acquire some or all of the model's characteristics. The motives for identification are a desire for the resources of the model, mastery of the environment, and love. Reinforcement for modeling comes from perceived similarity between the child and the model; a child strives to create similarities. He then acts as if the goals of the model belong to him and is vicariously satisfied with successes and disappointed with failures of the model, much like any spectator sport!

Several years ago Sanford (1955) presented an analysis of the concept of identification. In brief, Sanford suggested that the term be applied to situations in which "an individual may be observed to respond to the behavior of other people or objects by initiating in fantasy or reality the same behavior himself . . . the individual strives to behave in a way that is exactly like that of the object" (p. 109). Sanford further suggested that the motive for this imitative behavior was a threat to the person's self-esteem. By limiting the term "identification" to those imitative behavioral sequences in which the motivation for the act was anxiety over self-esteem, Sanford emphasized two points: (a) mere similarity in overt behavior between a subject and a model was not necessarily a measure of identification, and (b) the motive for the imitative behavior was one of

Adapted from The concept of identification. *Psychological Review*, 1958, **65** (5), 296–305. Copyright © 1958 by the American Psychological Association, and reproduced by permission.

the defining characteristics of an identificatory response.

The various behavioral phenomena which have been labeled "identification" differ in their manifest properties and motivations. The following four classes of behavior have been described as related to the process of identification because they all can lead to similarities in behavior between a subject and a model.

IMITATION LEARNING

This term refers to the initiation and practice of certain responses (gestures, attitudes, speech patterns, dress, etc.) which are not subject to prohibition by the social environment and which are assumed to be the result of an attempt to imitate a model. The behavior has been labeled either "matched-dependent behavior" or "copying" by Miller and Dollard (1941). Miller and Dollard posit that initially the imitative act occurs by chance and the act can only be reinforced if some drive is reduced following the execution of the response. According to this view only direct reward from the social environment, like praise or affection, can strengthen the person's tendency to imitate a model. Mowrer (1950) distinguishes between developmental and defensive identification. In the former process, the person imitates or reproduces the behavior of a model in order to "reproduce bits of the beloved and longed-for parent" (p. 615). Mowrer suggests that most imitation of a model is the result of the desire to reproduce responses which have acquired secondary reward value through association with a nurturant and affectionate model. Thus, Mowrer emphasizes the self-rewarding aspect of certain imitative acts as opposed to Miller and Dollard's emphasis on direct reward from the social environment.

PROHIBITION LEARNING

This term refers to the adoption and practice of the prohibitions of the parents and parent substitutes. The acquisition of these prohibitions bears some relation to the process of superego development as described by psychoanalytic theory (Freud, 1933). Several investigators have suggested that a major motivation for the acquisition of some prohibition is anxiety over anticipated loss of love (Kagan, 1958). Sanford labeled this process "introjection" and suggested that the learning and maintenance of this class of behavior might be explained without use of the concept of identification.

IDENTIFICATION WITH THE AGGRESSOR

This phrase refers to the adoption of behaviors which are similar to those of an aggressive or threatening model. The motivation for this "imitation" is assumed to be anxiety over anticipated aggression or domination by the threatening model. It is difficult to explain this behavior as a product of either prohibition or imitation learning, since the motive and reinforcement do not seem related to anxiety over anticipated loss of love or desire for a direct, social reward like praise or affection. Anna Freud (1937) has labeled this phenomenon "identification with the aggressor," Mowrer has called this process "defensive identification" (as distinct from developmental identification), and Sanford has suggested that the term "identification proper" be restricted to this class of behavior.

VICARIOUS AFFECTIVE EXPERIENCE

This phrase refers to the experience of positive or negative affect on the part of a person as a result of an event which has occurred to a model. Salient examples of this phenomenon are (a) a child's elation or depression at learning that his parent is a success or failure, or (b) a mother's elation following the success of her child in school. This phenomenon of vicarious, affective experience has been attributed to a person's identification with a model, but this affective response has been difficult to explain and often neglected by psychologists investigating the identification process. These four phenomena (imitation learning, prohibition learning, identification with the aggressor, and vicarious, affective experience) appear to be mediated by different motives and rewards, and an analysis of each of them is one purpose of this paper.

In different contexts, social scientists have used the term "identification" to refer to three different sets of variables: (a) the process of identification; (b) individual differences in the content of the behaviors, motives, and attitudes acquired as a result of the identification process; and (c) the differential effect of various models that are used during the identification process. This paper recognizes the relevance of the model and content dimensions but is primarily concerned with the process of identification, and will attempt to analyze this process in behavioral terms. It is suggested that the process remains the same regardless of the models used or the specific behavioral content that is acquired as a result of an identification.

DEFINITIONS OF IDENTIFICATION

The concept of identification originated in psychoanalytic theory, and Freud (1935) made a distinction between primary and secondary identification. Primary identification referred to the initial, undifferentiated perception of the infant in which an external object was perceived as part of the self, while secondary identification began after the child had discriminated a world of objects separate from the self. Freud implied in his later writings that the process of secondary identification was motivated primarily by the motives and anxieties created by the Oedipal situation. In order to reduce the anxiety over anticipated aggression or rejection from the same-sex parent and obtain vicariously the affection of the opposite-sex parent, the child identified with the former. Identification was described by Freud as "the endeavor to mould a person's own ego after the fashion of one that has been taken as a model" (1949, p. 63).

Mowrer's concept of "defensive identification," Sanford's definition of "identification proper," and Anna Freud's description of "identification with the aggressor" are all related to the earlier psychoanalytic hypothesis that the threat value of the same-sex parent motivated the child to identify with him in order to reduce the anxiety associated with this threat. However, it is suggested that an individual may identify with a model not only to reduce anxiety over anticipated aggression from a model but also to experience or obtain positive goal states which he perceives that the model commands. The thesis of this paper is that the motivation to command or experience desired goal states of a model is salient in the development and maintenance of an identification. It will be suggested later that two major goal

states involved in identification behavior are (a) mastery of the environment and (b) love and affection. However, it is not implied that these are the only goals which an individual desires to command.

DEFINITION

Identification is defined as an acquired, cognitive response within a person (S). The content of this response is that some of the attributes, motives, characteristics, and affective states of a model (M) are part of S's psychological organization. The major implication of this definition is that the S may react to events occurring to M as if they occurred to him.

THE ACQUISITION AND MAINTENANCE OF AN IDENTIFICATION

Although identification has been defined as a cognitive response, it is not implied that the content of the response is available to consciousness or easily verbalized. Thus the terms "cognitive response," "belief," "wish," or "assumption" will be used in this text to include cognitive processes not always available through verbal report. Identification is not viewed as an all-or-none process. Identification is a response that can vary in strength and there will be differences in the degree to which an S believes that the characteristics of a model, whether assets or liabilities, belong to him. In addition, the S may become identified, to differing degrees, with a variety of models. The motives and reinforcements that are involved in the acquisition and maintenance of this cognitive response are elaborated in the following assumptions.

Assumption 1   Initially the S perceives that the M possesses or commands goals and satisfactions that the S desires. This perception leads to a wish to possess these desired goal states.

Assumption 2 This wish to command the goal states of the M leads to the desire to possess the characteristics of the M because S believes that if he were similar to the M he would command the desired goals. That is, the S assumes that the more similarity there is between the S and M the more likely S is to possess or command the desired goal states of the M.

Assumption 3 The identification response (i.e., "some of the characteristics of the model are mine") is reinforced each time S perceives or is told that he is similar to the M. One type of reinforcement for the identification response occurs when an S is told directly that he and the M are similar in temperament or appearance. It is suggested that a second type of reinforcement for this cognitive response is S's own perception of similarity to the M. Once again, consider the case of the small child and his parent. Although the child may perceive marked differences in size, strength, and skills between himself and the M, he may perceive a similarity in affective states, such as joy, anger, or sadness. The importance of the perception of similarities in affective states between the S and M is stressed because a major motive for identification is a desire to experience positive affective states of the model. Thus, perception of similarity in affect is assumed to have saliency as a reinforcement. If the parent becomes angry, sad, or happy and communicates these affects to the child, the child has the opportunity to perceive that he and the M experience similar feelings. This perception reinforces the belief that there is similarity between the S and M. In addition to similarity in affective states, perception of similarities in external characteristics will reinforce the identification response. With specific reference to the child-parent relation, it is assumed that perception of similarities in sexual anatomy, dress, amount and distribution of hair, and other external attributes are potential reinforcements of the identification. Thus, while the identification response is being learned, the major rein-

forcements for the response are perceptions of similarity between the S and M.

Assumption 4 In order for the identification belief to be maintained, the S must not only perceive similarity between the S and M but he also must experience some of the desired, affective goal states of the M. Thus, if the M were successful or happy and S believed that M was experiencing positive affect, the S would also feel positive affect appropriate to the success, and this experience would reinforce his identification. The S also may experience affect appropriate to events occurring to M as a result of the expectation that the social environment will respond to him the same way it responds to the M. That is, when the S has developed some degree of identification with the M he may anticipate that when the social environment praises or rewards the M, it will behave similarly to him. If, on the other hand, the M were sad or criticized, S might experience negative affect because of the identification belief that he and the M were similar and the expectation that the environment might react to him as it did to M. However, if no vicarious command of desired goals or positive affect were experienced as a result of the identification, then the response should extinguish just as any other habit does in the absence of positive reinforcement. That is, some degree of identification should be maintained as long as S perceives that the M commands desired goals. When the S no longer perceives the M in this fashion, then both the motivation for the identification and the intensity of the positive reinforcement should decrease.

THE ACQUISITION OF BEHAVIOR SIMILAR TO A MODEL: THE MOTIVES FOR IMITATION, IDENTIFICATION, AND PROHIBITION LEARNING

Since perceptions of similarity between the S and M reinforce the identification response, the S may imitate the M during the acquisition phase of an identification in order to increase the degree of similarity. It is acknowledged that the social environment rewards imitative behaviors with affection and praise, and these direct, social reinforcements may strengthen the tendency to imitate adults independently of any identification motives. However, it is suggested, along with Sears et al. (1957), that direct, social reinforcement of imitative behavior cannot account for all of the imitative responses that the S initiates. A 4-year-old child may simulate adult behaviors when the child is alone or in situations where the parents discourage or punish the imitative response. However, despite the punishment or absence of social reward for some imitative behaviors, the behavior continues to be practiced. Sears et al. (1957), call this behavior "role practice" and assume that it is motivated by the "desire to reproduce pleasant experiences" (p. 370). Consider the 3-year-old girl who plays the role of mother alone in her room. It is hypothesized that a potential reinforcement for this behavior is the creation, in fantasy, of perceptual similarity between the behaviors of the S and M. This perception strengthens S's identification with the M and allows S to share vicariously some of the positive goal states which M commands.

A somewhat different phenomenon is the behavior called "identification with the aggressor" by Anna Freud or "defensive identification" by Mowrer. Anna Freud (1937) describes a girl who was afraid of ghosts and suddenly began to make peculiar gestures as she ran in the dark. She told her brother, "there is no need to be afraid, you just have to pretend that you're the ghost who might meet you" (p. 119). The present theory assumes that the child desired the threatening power of the feared object and this motive elicited the imitative behavior. The fantasied perception of similarity to the feared model gave S a vicarious feeling of power and reduced her anxiety over attack. It is suggested that "identification with the aggressor" does not differ from other identification responses with respect to the basic mechanism of acquisition but does involve a specific motive and goal state. Identification with the aggressor involves a specific relationship between the S and M in which S fears the M. Thus, S desires the aggressive power or threat value of the M in order to reduce his own anxiety over anticipated attack. It may be misleading to classify "identification with the aggressor" as qualitatively different from other identificatory behavior merely because the motive and goal differ from those involved in other identifications.

A third motive which can lead to behavioral similarity between an S and M is anxiety over anticipated loss of love or nurturance. It is suggested that many social prohibitions which the M practices are learned by the S in situations in which this anxiety motivates the acquisition and maintenance of the response. The reinforcement for the learned prohibition is continued acceptance and a consequent reduction in anxiety over rejection. The research of Sears et al. (1957) suggests a relationship between "high conscience" in a child and a pattern in which the mother is nurturant and uses withdrawal of love as a disciplinary technique. In summary, any one response which is imitative of a model may be mediated by three different motive-reinforcement sequences, and in many instances all three may be involved in producing behavioral similarity between S and M. Thus, "eating neatly," "getting good grades," or "being nonaggressive" could be motivated by the desire for praise as in imitation learning, by anxiety over loss of love as in prohibition learning, or by the desire to create perceptual similarity between the S and M as in identification. Thus, mere similarity in overt behavior between an S and M may not be the most sensitive measure of degree of identification.

At a more speculative level, it is suggested that the behaviors which have been called "self actualizing" (Goldstein, 1939) could be motivated and reinforced by a desire for perceptual similarity to an M and be an indication of early identification tendencies. Even the most orthodox supporters of the importance of simple imitation learning find it difficult to explain the child's initial imitations of a model. Once the child has begun to imitate a model it is likely that praise and recognition from adults could maintain this behavior. However, why does the child suddenly want to dress himself, sit on the toilet alone, or put on Daddy's shoes? It is difficult to account for the initial display of this imitative behavior, and the term "self actualization" implies that the child has some biological drive to use his potentialities. This hypothesis seems no more parsimonious than the suggestion that the initiation of these "self actualizing" behaviors is motivated by S's desire to create perceptual similarity between himself and a model.

TWO GOALS MOTIVATING IDENTIFICATION: MASTERY AND LOVE

It has been assumed that S's desire to command certain goal states motivates his identification with a model. It is suggested, for the child especially, that two important goal states that the S desires to command are (a) a feeling of power or mastery over the environment and (b) love and affection. Attainment of these goals should lead to diminution in anxiety over helplessness or loneliness. The young child perceives that he is not able to gratify all of his needs while the parental model is perceived as more capable of dealing with the environment. This discrepancy between the S's perception of his own relative helplessness and the power that he perceives M to possess motivates the wish to have M's power and the search for perceptions of similarity between himself and the M.

Unfortunately, there are no empirical studies which directly test these hypotheses because most of the research on identification has used similarities in behavior between an S and M as the measure of identification. However, there are some results which are at least consistent with the view that the child identifies with the more powerful parent and the one who is perceived to command important sources of gratifica-

tion. Payne and Mussen (1956) reported that adolescent boys who perceived the father as rewarding on projective tests were more highly identified with the father (based on similar answers to a personality inventory) than boys who pictured their fathers as nonrewarding. In addition, boys with dominant and "masculine" mothers tended to be poorly identified with the father. P. S. Sears (1953) reported a finding that is more difficult to explain without use of the concept of identification. She found, in a doll-play situation, that kindergarten girls used the mother doll as agent significantly more often than the father doll, while boys used both mother and father dolls with more nearly equal frequency. Since the mother is initially the major controller of gratifications for both sexes, one might expect an initial identification with her for both boys and girls. P. S. Sears also reports that the kindergarten boys who used the mother doll most often had mothers who were (a) more nurturant than the father, (b) more critical of the father, and (c) more restrictive of the child's mobility outside the home. This result is consistent with the hypothesis that the child is predisposed to identify with the parental model who is perceived as controlling important goal states.

FACTORS INFLUENCING THE STRENGTH OF IDENTIFICATION

The strength of the identification habit, following a basic behavioral law, should be a function of the strength of the motive and the quality and frequency of the reinforcement (Hull, 1943). It would be predicted, therefore, that the most intense identification would occur when the S had strong needs for love and power, felt incapable of gratifying these motives through his own skills, and perceived similarity between himself and an M who commanded these goals. Utilizing this hypothesis, two generalized predictions can be made concerning the strength of identification for different ages and models.

1. The strength of identification tendencies should decrease with age because, in general, the individual's ability to gratify his needs for mastery and love through his own behavior, rather than through a vicarious mechanism, should increase with development. Thus, the identifications of a young child should be more intense than the identifications of older individuals.

2. An identification with an M with whom S was in direct contact should be stronger than with an M with whom S was not in contact, assuming that the motivation for identification was constant and the models were perceived as equally potent. This statement is based on the assumption that the reinforcements of perceived similarity are stronger when S perceives the affects and attributes of the M directly as opposed to instances in which he is merely told that he is similar to the M. Thus, degree of identification with a father with whom S was in contact should be greater than with an imagined fantasy father whom S had never seen. Only very indirect evidence is available to support this prediction. However, reports by P. S. Sears (1951) and Sears et al. (1946) suggest that absence of the father from the home tends to decrease the degree of "masculine" doll play in preschool boys while this experience has little effect on the doll play of girls. The results are open to alternative interpretations but are not inconsistent with the present hypothesis.

REFERENCES

Freud, Anna. *The ego and the mechanisms of defense.* London: Hogarth, 1937.

Freud, S. *New introductory lectures in psychoanalysis.* New York: Norton, 1933.

Freud, S. *The ego and the id.* London: Hogarth, 1935.

Freud, S. *Group psychology and the analysis of the ego.* London: Hogarth, 1949.

Goldstein, K. *The organism.* New York: American Book, 1939.

Hull, C. L. *Principles of behavior.* New York: Appleton-Century-Crofts, 1943.

Kagan, J. The child's perception of the parent. *Journal of Abnormal and Social Psychology,* 1956, **53,** 257–258.

Kagan, J. Socialization of aggression and the perception of parents in fantasy. *Child Development,* 1958, **29,** 311–320.

Miller, N. E., & Dollard, J. *Social learning and imitation.* New Haven: Yale University Press, 1941.

Mowrer, O. H. *Learning theory and personality dynamics.* New York: Ronald, 1950.

Payne, D. E., & Mussen, P. H. Parent-child relations and father identification among adolescent boys. *Journal of Abnormal and Social Psychology,* 1956, **52,** 358–362.

Sanford, R. N. The dynamics of identification. *Psychological Review,* 1955, **62,** 106–118.

Sears, Pauline S. Doll play aggression in normal young children: influence of sex, age, sibling status, father's absence. *Psychological Monographs,* 1951, **65,** No. 6 (Whole No. 323).

Sears, Pauline S. Child rearing factors related to playing sex-typed roles. *American Psychologist,* 1953, **8,** 431. (Abstract)

Sears, R. R., Maccoby, Eleanor E., & Levin, H. *Patterns of child rearing.* New York: Harper & Row, 1957.

Sears, R. R., Pintler, Margaret H., & Sears, Pauline S. Effect of father separation on preschool children's doll play aggression. *Child Development,* 1946, **17,** 219–243.

55 | Identification as a Process of Incidental Learning

ALBERT BANDURA
ALETHA C. HUSTON

This study was designed to explore the child's ability to imitate behavior shown by a model; the authors proposed that a nurturant interaction between model and child would enhance the model's secondary reward properties and thus facilitate imitative learning.

They asked 48 preschool children to learn a two-choice discrimination problem. A model displayed distinctive behaviors (for example, "march, march") which were irrelevant to the task. With the experimental subjects, the model performed these irrelevant tasks; with the control subjects, she merely took a circuitous route to the box. Half the subjects experienced a rewarding (warm, nurturant) interaction with the model prior to testing, while the other subjects experienced a cold, distant relation. The experimental children produced behaviors resembling the irrelevant behaviors of the model. The warm relation between child and model facilitated imitation (except in the case of aggression, which was facilitated in all conditions). Nurturance did not directly influence imitative learning, but the amount of predecision conflict was greater in the nurturant group.

Although part of a child's socialization takes place through direct training, much of a child's behavior repertoire is believed to be acquired through identification with the important adults in his life. This process, variously described in behavior as "vicarious" learning, observational learning, and role taking appears to be more a result of active imitation by the child of attitudes and patterns of behavior that the parents have never directly attempted to teach than of direct reward and punishment of instrumental responses.

While elaborate developmental theories

Adapted from Identification as a process of incidental learning. *Journal of Abnormal and Social Psychology,* 1961, **63** (2), 311–318. Copyright © 1961 by the American Psychological Association, and reproduced by permission.

have been proposed to explain this phenomenon, the process subsumed under the term "identification" may be accounted for in terms of incidental learning, that is, learning that apparently takes place in the absence of an induced set or intent to learn the specific behaviors or activities in question (McGeoch & Irion, 1952).

During the parents' social training of a child, the range of cues employed by a child is likely to include both those that the parents consider immediately relevant and other cues of parental behavior which the child has had ample opportunity to observe and to learn even though he has not been instructed to do so. Thus, for example, when a parent punishes a child physically for having aggressed toward peers, the intended outcome of the training is that the child should refrain from hitting others. Concurrent with the intentional learning, however, a certain amount of incidental learning may be expected to occur through imitation, since the child is provided, in the form of the parent's behavior, with an example of how to aggress toward others, and this incidental learning may guide the child's behavior in later social interactions.

The use of incidental cues by both human and animal subjects while performing nonimitative learning tasks is well documented by research. In addition, studies of imitation and learning of incidental cues by Church (1957) and Wilson (1958) have demonstrated that subjects learn certain incidental environmental cues while imitating the discrimination behavior of a model and that the incidental learning guides the subjects' discrimination responses in the absence of the model. The purpose of the experiment reported in this paper is to demonstrate that subjects imitate not only discrimination responses but also other behaviors performed by the model.

The incidental learning paradigm was employed in the present study with an important change in procedure in order to create a situation similar to that encountered in learning through identification. Subjects performed an orienting task, but, unlike most incidental learning studies, the experimenter performed the diverting task as well, and the extent to which the subjects patterned their behavior after that of the experimenter-model was measured.

The main hypothesis tested is that nursery school children, while learning a two-choice discrimination problem, also learn to imitate certain of the experimenter's behaviors which are totally irrelevant to the successful performance of the orienting task.

One may expect, on the basis of theories of identification (Bronfenbrener, 1960), that the presence of affection and nurturance in the adult-child interaction promotes incidental imitative learning, a view to which empirical studies of the correlates of strong and weak identification lend some indirect support. Boys whose fathers are highly rewarding and affectionate have been found to adopt the father-role in doll play activities (Sears, 1953), to show father-son similarity in response to items on a personality questionnaire, and to display masculine behaviors to a greater extent than boys whose fathers are relatively cold and unrewarding.

One interpretation of the relationship between nurturance and identification is that affectional reward increase the secondary reinforcing properties of the model and, thus, predispose the imitator to reproduce the behavior of the model for the satisfaction these cues provide (Mowrer, 1950). Once the parental characteristics have acquired such reward value for the child, conditional withdrawal of positive reinforcers is believed to create additional instigation for the child to perform behaviors resembling that of the parent model, i.e., if the child can reproduce the parent's rewarding behavior, he can, thus, reward himself (Sears, 1957). In line with this theory of identification in terms of secondary reward, it is predicted that children who experience a warm, rewarding interaction with the experimenter-model should reproduce significantly more of the behaviors performed by the model than do children who experience a relatively distant and cold relationship.

METHOD

Subjects

The subjects were 24 boys and 24 girls enrolled in the Stanford University Nursery School. They ranged in age from 45 to 61 months with a mean age of 53 months. The junior author played the role of the model for all 48 children, and two other female experimenters shared in the task of conducting the study.

General Procedure

Forty subjects were matched individually on the basis of sex and ratings of dependency behavior, and subdivided randomly in terms of nurturant-nonnurturant condition yielding two experimental groups of 20 subjects each. A small control group comprising 8 subjects was also studied.

In the first phase of the experiment half the experimental and control subjects experienced two nurturant rewarding play sessions with the model while the remaining subjects experienced a cold nonnurturant relationship. For the second phase of the experiment subjects performed a diverting two-choice discrimination problem with the model who exhibited fairly explicit, although functionless, behavior during the discrimination trials, and the extent to which the subjects reproduced the model's behavior was measured. The experimental and control procedures differed only in the patterns of behavior displayed by the model.

Matching Variable

Dependency was selected as a matching variable since, on the basis of the theories of identification, dependency would be expected to facilitate imitative learning. There is some evidence, for example, that dependent subjects are strongly oriented toward gaining social rewards in the form of attention and approval (Cairnes, 1959), and one means of obtaining these rewards is to imitate the behavior of others. Moreover, such children do not have the habit of responding independently; consequently they are apt to be more dependent on, and therefore more attentive to, the cues produced by the behavior of others (Kagan & Mussen, 1956).

Measures of subjects' dependency behavior were obtained through observations of their social interactions in the nursery school. The observers recorded subjects' behavior using a combined time-sampling and behavior-unit observation method. Each child was observed for twelve 10-minute observation sessions distributed over a period of approximately 10 weeks; each observation session was divided into 30-second intervals, thus, yielding a total of 240 behavioral units.

The children were observed in a predetermined order that was varied randomly to insure that each child would be seen under approximately comparable conditions. In order to provide an estimate of reliability of the ratings, 234 observation sessions (4,680 behavior units) were recorded simultaneously but independently by both observers.

The subjects' emotional dependency was assessed in terms of the frequency of behaviors that were aimed at securing a nurturant response from others. The following four specific categories of dependency behavior were scored: seeking help and assistance, seeking praise and approval, seeking physical contact, and seeking proximity and company of others.

The dependency scores were obtained by summing the observations made of these five different types of behaviors and on the basis of these scores, the subjects were paired and assigned at random to the two experimental conditions.

Experimental Conditions

In the *nonnurturant* condition, the model brought the subjects to the experimental room and after instructing the child to play with the toys that were spread on the floor, busied herself with paper work at a desk in the far corner of the room. During this period the model avoided any interaction with the child.

In contrast, during the nurturant sessions, the model sat on the floor close to the subject. She responded readily to the child's bids for help and attention, and in other ways fostered a consistently warm and rewarding interaction.

These experimental social interactions, which preceded the imitation learning, consisted of two 15-minute sessions separated by an interval of approximately 5 days.

Diverting Task

A two-choice discrimination problem similar to the one employed by Miller and Dollard (1941) in experiments of matching behavior was used as the diverting task which occupied the subjects' attention while at the same time permitting opportunities for the subjects to observe behavior performed by the model in the absence of any instructions to observe or to reproduce the responses resembling that of the model.

The apparatus consisted of two small boxes, identical in color (red sides, yellow lid) and size (6" x 8" x 10"). The hinged lid of each box was lined with rubber stripping so as to eliminate any auditory cues during the placement of the rewards which consisted of small multi-color pictures of animals and flowers. The boxes were placed on small chairs approximately 5 feet apart and 8 feet from the starting point.

At the end of the second social interaction session the experimenter entered the room with the test apparatus and instructed the model and the subject that they were going to play a game in which the experimenter would hide a picture sticker in one of the boxes and that the object of the game was to guess which box contained the sticker.

The model and the subject then left the room and after the experimenter placed two stickers in the designated box, they were recalled to the starting point in the experimental room and the model was asked to take the first turn. During the model's trial, the subject remained at the starting point where he could observe the model's behavior.

Although initially it was planned to follow the procedure used by Miller and Dollard in which one of two boxes was loaded with two rewards and the child made his choice immediately following the leader's trial, this procedure had to be modified when it became evident during pretesting that approximately 40 percent of the subjects invariably chose the opposite box from the model even though the nonimitative response was consistently unrewarded. McDavid (1959) in a recent study of imitative behavior in preschool children, encountered similar difficulties in that 44 percent of his subjects did not learn to imitate the leader even though the subjects were not informed as to whether the leader was or was not rewarded.

In order to overcome this stereotyped nonimitation, the experimenter placed two rewards in a single box, but following the model's trial the model and the subject left the room and were recalled almost immediately (the intratrial interval was approximately 5 seconds), thus, creating the impression that the boxes were reloaded. After the subject completed his trial, the model and the subject left the room. The experimenter recorded the subject's behavior and reloaded the boxes for the second trial. The noncorrection method was used throughout. This procedure was continued until the subject met the learning criterion of four successive imitative discrimination responses, or until 30 acquisition trials had been completed. The slight modification in procedure proved to be effective as evidenced by the fact that only 9 of the 48 children failed to meet the criterion.

In order to eliminate any position habit, the right-left placements of the reward were varied from trial to trial in a fixed irregular order. This sequence was randomly determined except for the limitation that no more than two successive rewards could occur in the same position.

The number of trials to criterion was the measure of the subjects' imitation behavior on the discrimination task.

Although initially it was planned to follow the procedure used by itself, of some theoretical interest, the discrimination problem was intended primarily as an orienting or distraction task. Thus, on each discrimination trial, the model exhibited certain verbal, motor, and aggressive behaviors which were totally irrelevant to the performance of the task to which the subject's attention was directed. At the starting point, for example, the model remarked, "Here I go," and then marched slowly toward the box containing the stickers repeating, "March, march, march." On the lid of each box was a small rubber doll which the model knocked off aggressively when she reached the designated box. She then paused briefly, remarked, "Open the box," removed one sticker and pasted it on a pastoral scene that hung on the wall immediately behind the boxes. The model terminated the trial by replacing the doll on the lid of the container. The model and the subject then left the room briefly. After being recalled to the experimental room the subject took his turn, and the number of the model's behaviors reproduced by the subject was recorded.

Control Group

In addition to the two experimental groups, a control group, consisting of eight subjects, comparable to the experimental groups in terms of sex distribution, dependency ratings, and nurturant-nonnurturant experiences was studied. Since the model performed highly novel patterns of responses unlikely to occur independently of the observation of the behavior of the model, it was decided to assign most of the available subjects to the experimental groups and only a small number of subjects to the control group.

The reasons for the inclusion of a control group were twofold. On the one hand, it provided a check on whether the subjects' behavior reflected genuine imitative learning or merely the chance occurrence of behaviors high in the subjects' response hierarchies. Second, it was of interest to determine whether the subjects would adopt certain aspects of the model's behavior that involved considerable delay in reward. With the controls, therefore, the model walked to the box, choosing a highly circuitous route along the sides of the experimental room; instead of aggressing toward the doll, the model lifted it gently off the container and she left the doll on the floor at the completion of a trial. While walking to the boxes the model repeated, "Walk, walk, walk."

Imitation Scores

On each trial the subjects' performances were scored in terms of the following imitation response categories: selects box chosen by the model; marches; repeats the phrases, "Here I go," "March, march," "Open box," or "Walk, walk"; aggresses toward the doll; replaces doll on box; imitates the circuitous route to the box.

Some subjects made a verbal response in the appropriate context (for example, at the starting point, on the way to the box, before raising the lid of the container) but did not repeat the model's exact words. These verbal responses were also scored and interpreted as partially imitative behavior.

In order to provide an estimate of the reliability of the experimenter's scoring the performances of 19 subjects were scored independently by two judges who alternated in observing the experimental sessions through a one-way mirror from an adjoining observation room.

RESULTS

Reliability of Observations of Dependency Behavior

The reliability of the observers' behavior ratings was estimated by means of an index of agreement based on the ratio of twice the number of agreements over the combined ratings of the two observers multiplied by 100. Since small time discrepancies, due to inevitable slight asynchronism of the observers' timing devices, were expected, a time discrepancy in rating a given behavior category greater than two 30-second intervals was interpreted as a disagreement.

The interobserver reliabilities for the dependency categories considered separately were as follows: Positive attention seeking, 84 percent; help seeking, 72 percent; seeking physical contact, 84 percent; and seeking proximity, 75 percent.

Reliability of Imitation Scores

Except for *other imitative responses*, the subjects' behavior was scored with high reliability and, even in the latter response category, the scoring discrepancies arose primarily from the experimenter's lack of opportunity to observe some of the behaviors in question rather than from differences of interpretation.

Incidental Imitation of Model's Behavior

Since the data disclosed no significant sex differences, the imitation scores for the male and female subgroups were combined in the statistical analyses.

Ninety percent of the subjects in the experimental groups adopted the model's aggressive behavior, 45 percent imitated the marching, and 28 percent reproduced the model's verbalizations. In contrast, none of the control subjects behaved aggressively, marched or verbalized, while 75 percent of the controls and none of the experimental subjects imitated the circuitous route to the containers. Except for replacing the doll on the box, which was performed by most of the experimental and control subjects, there was no overlap in the imitative behavior displayed by the two groups (see Table 1).

Effects of Nurturance on Imitation

In order to make comparable the imitation scores for the subjects who varied somewhat in the number of trials to criterion, the total imitative responses in a given response category were divided by the number of trials. Since only a small number of subjects in the nonnurturant condition displayed imitative nonaggressive behavior and the distributions of scores were markedly skewed, the sign test was used to estimate the significance of differences between the two experimental groups.

The predicted facilitating effect of social rewards on imitation was essentially confirmed. Subjects who experienced the rewarding interaction with the model marched and verbalized imitatively, and reproduced other responses resembling that of the model to a greater extent than did the subjects who experienced the relatively cold and distant relationship. Aggression, interestingly, was readily imitated by subjects regardless of the quality of the model-child relationship.

While nurturance did not seem to influence the actual choices the subjects made, it nevertheless affected their predecision behavior. A number of the children displayed considerable conflictful vacillation, often running back and forth between the boxes, prior to making their choice. In the analysis of these data, the vacillation scores were divided by the total number of trials, and the significance of the differences was estimated by means of the sign test since the distribution of scores was markedly skewed. The results of this test revealed that the subjects in the nurturant condition exhibited more conflictful behavior than subjects in the nonnurturant group ($p = .03$). This finding is

TABLE 1   Amount of imitative behavior displayed by subjects in the experimental and control groups

Response Category	Experimental Subjects N=40		Control Subjects N=8	
	Percentage Imitating	Mean per Trial	Percentage Imitating	Mean per Trial
Behaviors of experimental model				
marching	45	.23	0	0
verbal responses	28	.10	0	0
aggression	90	.64	13	.01
other imitative responses	18	.03	0	0
partially imitative verbal behavior	43	.11	0	0
replacing doll	90	.60	75	.77
Behaviors of control model circuitous route				
circuitous route	0	0	75	.58
verbal responses	0	0	13	.10

Note. The mean number of trials for subjects in the experimental group (13.52) and in the control group (15.25) did not differ significantly.

particularly noteworthy considering that one has to counteract a strong nonimitation bias in getting preschool children to follow a leader in a two-choice discrimination problem as evidenced by McDavid's findings as well as those of the present study (i.e., 75 percent of the subjects made nonimitative choices on the first trial).

Dependency and Imitation

Correlations between the ratings of dependency behavior and the measures of imitation were calculated separately for the nurturant and nonnurturant experimental subgroups, and where the correlation coefficients did not differ significantly the data were combined. The expected positive relationship between dependency and imitation was only partially supported. High dependent subjects expressed more partially imitative verbal behavior ($r_t = .60$; $p < .05$) and exhibited more pre-decision conflict on the discrimination task ($r = .26$; $p = .05$) than did subjects who were rated low on dependency.

Dependency and total imitation of nonaggressive responses was positively related for boys ($r_t = .31$) but negatively correlated for girls ($r_t = -.46$). These correlations, however, are not statistically significant. Nor was there any significant relationship between dependency and imitation of aggression ($r = .20$) or discrimination responses ($r = -.03$).

DISCUSSION

The results of this study generally substantiate the hypotheses that children display a good deal of social learning of an incidental imitative sort, and that nurturance is one condition facilitating such imitative learning.

The extent to which the model's behavior had come to influence and control the behavior of subjects is well illustrated by their marching, and by their choice of the circuitous route to the containers. Evidence from the pretesting and from the subjects' behavior during the early discrimination

trials revealed that dashing toward the boxes was the dominant response, and that the delay produced by marching or by taking an indirect route that more than doubled the distance to the boxes was clearly incompatible with the subjects' eagerness to get to the containers. Nevertheless, many subjects dutifully followed the example set by the model.

Even more striking was the subjects' imitation of responses performed unwittingly by the model. On one trial with a control subject, for example, the model began to replace the doll on the box at the completion of the trial when suddenly, startled by the realization of the mistake, she quickly replaced the doll on the floor. Sure enough, on the next trial, the subject took the circuitous route, removed the doll gently off the box and, after disposing of the sticker, raised the doll, and then quickly replaced it on the floor reproducing the model's startled reaction as well!

The results for the influence of nurturance on imitation of verbal behavior are in accord with Mowrer's autism theory of word learning. Moreover, the obtained significant effect of nurturance on the production of partially imitative verbal responses indicates that nurturance not only facilitates imitation of the specific behaviors displayed by a model but also increases the probability of responses of a whole response class (for example, verbal behavior). These data are essentially in agreement with those of Milner (1951), who found that mothers of children receiving high reading readiness scores were more verbal and affectionately demonstrative in the interactions with their children than were the mothers of subjects in the low reading ability group.

That the incidental cues of the model's behavior may have taken on positive valence and were consequently reproduced by subjects for the mere satisfaction of performing them, is suggested by the fact that children in the nurturant condition not only marched to the containers but also marched in and out of the experimental room and marched about in the anteroom repeating, "March,

march, march," etc. while waiting for the next trial. While certain personality patterns may be, thus, incidentally acquired, the stability and persistence of these behaviors in the absence of direct rewards by external agents remains to be studied.

A response cannot be readily imitated unless its components are within the subjects behavior repertoire. The fact that gross motor responses are usually more highly developed than verbal skills in young children, may explain why subjects reproduced the model's marching ($p = .05$) and aggression ($p < .001$) to a significantly greater extent than they did her verbal behavior. Indeed several subjects imitated the motor component of speech by performing the appropriate mouth movements but emitted no sound. The greater saliency of the model's motor responses might also be a possible explanation of the obtained differences.

"Identification with the aggressor" or "defensive identification," whereby a child presumably transforms himself from object to agent of aggression by adopting the attributes of an aggressive, punitive model so as to allay anxiety, is widely accepted as an explanation of the imitative learning of aggression. The results of the present study, and those of a second experiment now in progress, suggest that the mere observation of aggressive models, regardless of the quality of the model-child relationship, is a sufficient condition for producing imitative aggression in children. A comparative study of subjects' imitation of aggressive models who are feared, liked and esteemed, or who are more or less neutral figures would throw some light on whether or not a more parsimonious theory than the one involved in "identification with the aggressor" can explain the modeling process.

Although the results from the present study provide evidence that nurturance promotes incidental learning, the combination of nurturance followed by its withdrawal would be expected, according to the secondary reinforcement theory of imitation, to furnish stronger incentive than nurturance alone for subjects to reproduce a model's behavior. It is also possible that dependency may be essentially unrelated to imitation under conditions of consistent nurturance, but may emerge as a variable facilitating imitation under conditions where social reinforcers are temporarily withdrawn.

REFERENCES

Bronfenbrenner, U. Freudian theories of identification and their derivatives. *Child Development,* 1960, **31,** 15–40.

Cairns, R. B. The influence of dependency-anxiety on the effectiveness of social reinforcers. Unpublished doctoral dissertation, Stanford University, 1959.

Church, R. M. Transmission of learned behavior between rats. *Journal of Abnormal and Social Psychology,* 1957, **54,** 163–165.

Kagan, J., & Mussen, P. H. Dependency themes on the TAT and group conformity. *Journal of Consulting Psychology,* 1956, **20,** 29–32.

McDavid, J. W. Imitative behavior in preschool children. *Psychological Monographs,* 1959, **73** No. 16 (Whole No. 486).

McGeoch, J. A., & Irion, A. L. *The psychology of human learning.* New York: Longmans, Green, 1952.

Miller, N. E., & Dollard, J. *Social learning and imitation.* Yale University Press, 1941.

Milner, Esther. A study of the relationship between reading readiness and patterns of parent-child interaction. *Child Development,* 1951, **22,** 95–112.

Mowrer, O. H. Identification: A link between learning theory and psychotherapy. In *Learning theory and personality dynamics.* New York: Ronald, 1950. Pp. 573–616.

Sears, Pauline C. Child-rearing factors related to playing of sex-typed roles. *American Psychologist,* 1953, **8,** 431. (Abstract)

Sears, R. R. Identification as a form of behavioral development. In D. B. Harris (Ed.), *The concept of development.* Minneapolis: University of Minnesota Press, 1957. Pp. 149–161.

Wilson, W. C. Imitation and learning of incidental cues by preschool children. *Child Development,* 1958, **29,** 393–397.

56 | The Results of Psychotherapy with Children: An Evaluation

EUGENE E. LEVITT

Many activities directed toward the betterment of society are assumed to be good because they have a humanitarian purpose. For this reason, many of these activities (for example, education, psychotherapy) are not subjected to criticism, even though critical investigation might produce significant improvement. The present paper takes an objective look at current evidence on the effectiveness of child psychotherapy. The author finds little support for its effectiveness; however, these studies raise several problems. For one thing, the control subjects he compared with the treated patients differed in at least two ways: they were not treated and they were self-selected. Those children who originally ask for therapy and then do not take it are most likely to experience spontaneous remissions. Another problem is the variability in methods and procedures and the unsystematic methods of data collection. The best we can say from these data is that psychotherapy is not proven effective; to accept the converse proposition that there is no effectiveness to psychotherapy is premature and probably wrong.

A compendium of results of psychotherapy with adults, published a few years ago by Eysenck (1952), resulted in the conclusion that ". . . roughly two-thirds of a group of neurotic patients will recover or improve to a marked extent within about two years of the onset of their illness, whether they are treated by means of psychotherapy or not." He concludes further that "the figures fail to support the hypothesis that psychotherapy facilitates recovery from neurotic disorder."

The purpose of this paper is to summarize available reports of the results of psychotherapy with children using Eysenck's article as a model. Certain departures will

Adapted from The results of psychotherapy with children: An evaluation. *Journal of Consulting Psychology*, 1957, **21**, 189–196.

be necessitated by the nature of the data, but in the main, the form will follow that of Eysenck.

BASELINE AND UNIT OF MEASUREMENT

As in Eysenck's study, the "Unit of measurement" used here will be evaluations of the degree of improvement of the patient by concerned clinicians. Individuals listed as "much improved, improved, partially improved, successful, partially successful, adjusted, partially adjusted, satisfactory," etc. will be grouped under the general heading of Improved. The Unimproved cases were found in groupings like "slightly improved, unimproved, unadjusted, failure, worse," etc.

Various difficulties arise in the selection of a control group to provide a baseline for comparison. However, a common phenomenon of the child guidance clinic is the patient who is accepted for treatment, but who voluntarily breaks off the clinic relationship without ever being treated. In institutions where the service load is heavy and the waiting period between acceptance and onset of treatment may range up to 6 months, this group of patients is often quite large. Theoretically, they have the characteristics of an adequate control group. So far as is known, they are similar to treated groups in every respect except for the factor of treatment itself.

Nevertheless, the use of this type of group as a control is not common in follow-up evaluations of the efficacy of treatment. Three studies report follow-up data on such groups. Of these, the data of Morris and Soroker (1953) are not suitable for the purposes of this paper. Of their 72 cases, at least 11 had treatment elsewhere between the last formal contact with the clinic and the point of evaluation, while an indeterminate number had problems too minor to warrant clinic treatment.

The samples in the remaining two studies appear satisfactory as sources of baseline data. Witmer and Keller (1942) appraised their group 8 to 13 years after clinic treatment, and reported that 78% were Improved. In the Lehrman study (1949), a one-year follow-up interval found 70% Improved. The overall rate of improvement for 160 cases in both reports is 72.5%. This figure will be used as the baseline for evaluating the results of treatment of children.

THE RESULTS OF PSYCHOTHERAPY

Studies showing outcome at close of treatment are not distinguished from follow-up studies in Eysenck's aggregation. The distinction seems logical, and is also meaningful in the predictive sense, as the analyses of this paper will indicate. Of the reports providing data for the present evaluation, thirteen present data at close, twelve give follow-up results, and five furnish both types, making a total of eighteen evaluations at close and seventeen at follow-up. The data of two reports (Jacobsen, 1948, and Johnson and Reid, 1947) are based on a combined close-follow-up rating. Results for the three kinds of evaluations will be presented separately.

The age range covered by all studies is from preschool to 21 years at the time of original clinic contact, the customary juncture for the determination of age for the descriptive data. However, very few patients were over 18 years at that time, and not many were over 17. The median age, roughly estimated from the ranges, would be about 10 years.

The usual psychiatric classification of mental illnesses is not always appropriate for childhood disorders. The writer has attempted to include only cases which would crudely be termed neuroses, by eliminating the data on delinquents, mental defectives, and psychotics whenever possible. The latter two groups constituted a very small proportion of the clinic cases. The proportion of delinquent cases is also small at some clinics but fairly large at others. Since the data as presented were not always amenable to these excisions, an unknown number of delinquent cases are included. However, the outcomes for the separated delinquents are much the same as those for the entire included group.

The number of categories in which patients were classified varied from study to study. Most used either a three-, four- or five-point scale. A few used only two categories, while one had twelve. Classification systems with more than five points were compressed into smaller scales. The data are presented tabularly in their original form, but the totals are pooled into three categories. Much Improved, Partially Improved, and Unimproved. A summation of the former two categories gives the frequency of Improved Cases. Combined percentages in the Much Improved and Partially Improved categories is 67.05. It is not quite accurate to say that the data are consistent from study to study. A chi-square analysis of improvement and unimprovement yields a value of 230.37, which is significant beyond the .001 level for 17df. However, as in the case of Eysenck's data, there is a considerable amount of consistency considering the interstudy differences in methodology, definition, etc.

The average percentage of improvement in the follow-up studies is 78.22. The percentage for the combined close-follow-up evaluations is 73.98, roughly between the other two. The percentage of improvement in the controlled studies was 72.5, slightly higher than the improvement at close and and slightly lower than at follow-up. It would appear that treated children are no better off at close than untreated children, but that they continue to improve over the years and eventually surpass the untreated group.

This conclusion is probably specious, perhaps unfortunately. One of the two control studies was an evaluation one year after the last clinic contact, the other 8 to 13 years after. The former study reports only 70% improvement while the longer interval provided 78% improvement. The figure for the one-year interval is similar to the results at close, while the percentage of improvement for the control with the 8- to 13-year interval is almost identical with that for the follow-up studies.

TABLE 1   Improvement as a Function of the Interval between Last Clinic Contact and Follow-up

Estimated Median Interval in Years	Number of Reports	Total N	N Improved	Per Cent Improved
1–1½	4	437	261	59.73
2–2½	6	1,167	929	79.61
5–6½	3	742	583	78.57
10	2	1,189	958	80.57
12	2	684	569	83.19
All cases	17	4,219	3,300	78.22

The point of the analysis is more easily seen if the results at close and at follow-up are pooled. This combination gives the same sort of estimate as that furnished by the two control groups pooled since one of them is a long-interval follow-up while the other was examined only a short time after clinic contact. The pooled percentage of improvement based on 7,987 cases in both close and follow-up studies is 73.27, which is practically the same as the percentage of 72.5 for the controls.

It now appears that Eysenck's conclusion concerning the data for adult psychotherapy is applicable to children as well; the results do not support the hypothesis that recovery from neurotic disorder is facilitated by psychotherapy.

The discrepancy between results at close and at follow-up suggests that time is a factor in improvement. Denker's report (1946) also indicated the operation of a time factor. He found that 45% of the patients had recovered by the end of one year, 72% had recovered by the end of two years, 82% by three years, 87% by four years, and 91% by five years. The rate of improvement as a function of time in Denker's data is clearly negatively accelerating.

The data of Table 1 indicate that most of the correlation between improvement and time-interval is accounted for by the studies with the shortest intervals, and those with the largest. The curve is more or less the same as that of Denker's data, negatively accelerating with most of the improvement accomplished by 2½ years. It is peculiar that the improvement after 1½ years is about 60%, less than the 67% improvement at close. However, the difference is not too great to attribute to variations in methodology and sampling among the concerned studies. Another potential explanation will be offered shortly.

There are a number of different kinds of therapies which have been used in the studies reported here. The therapists have been psychiatrists, social workers, and teams of clinicians operating at different points in the patient's milieu. Therapeutic approaches included counseling, guidance, placement, and recommendations to schools and patients, as well as deeper level therapies. In some instances the patient alone was the focus of attention. In others, parents and siblings were also treated. The studies apparently encompassed a variety of theoretical viewpoints, although these are not usually specified. Viewed as a body, the studies providing the data are therapeutically eclectic, a plurality, perhaps, reflecting psychoanalytic approaches.

Thus we may say that the therapeutic eclecticism, the number of subjects, the results, and the conclusions of this paper are markedly similar to those of Eysenck's study. Two-thirds of the patients examined at close and about three-quarters seen in follow-up have improved. Approximately the same percentages of improvement are found for comparable groups of untreated children.

As Eysenck pointed out (1955) in a sequel to his evaluation, such appraisal does not *prove* that psychotherapy is futile. The present evaluation of child psychotherapy, like its adult counterpart, fails to support the hypothesis that treatment is effective, but it *does not* force the acceptance of a contrary hypothesis. The distinction is an important one, especially in view of the differences among the concerned studies, and their generally poor caliber of methodology and analysis. Until additional evidence from well-planned investigations becomes available, a cautious, tongue-in-cheek attitude toward child psychotherapy is recommended.

REFERENCES

Denker, P. G. Results of treatment of psychoneuroses by the general practitioner. *New York State Medical Journal,* 1946, **46,** 2164–2166.

Eysenck, H. J. The effects of psychotherapy: an evaluation. *Journal of Consulting Psychology,* 1952, **16,** 319–324.

Eysenck, H. J. The effects of psychotherapy: a reply. *Journal of Abnormal and Social Psychology,* 1955, **50,** 147–148.

Jacobsen, Virginia. Influential factors in the outcome of treatment of school phobia. *Smith College Studies in Social Work,* 1948, **18,** 181–202.

Johnson, Lillian J., & Reid, J. H. An evaluation of ten years work with emotionally disturbed children. *Ryther Child Center Monographs,* IV, 1947.

Lehrman, L. J., Sirluck, Hilda, Black, B. J., & Glick, Selma J. Success and failure of treatment of children in the child guidance clinics of the Jewish Board of Guardians, New York City. *Jewish Board of Guardians Research Monograph,* 1949, No. 1.

Morris, D. P., & Soroker, Eleanor. A follow-up study of a guidance-clinic waiting list. *Mental Hygiene, N. Y.,* 1953, **37,** 84–88.

Witmer, Helen L., & Keller, Jane. Outgrowing childhood problems: a study in the value of child guidance treatment. *Smith College Studies in Social Work,* 1942, **13,** 74–90.

57 | Desires Expressed in Children's Dreams

SIGMUND FREUD

To understand a child we need to know his goals, desires, and wishes—his motivations. Freud, in this delightful collection of children's dreams, argues that all dreams satisfy ungratified wishes. There is plenty of evidence for this hypothesis in the dreams presented; however, we do not know how much selection Freud exercised to produce this set. A random sampling might look different. However, the wish-fulfillment in these dreams is strong evidence for his point.

The most simple dreams of all, I suppose, are to be expected in the case of children, whose psychic activities are certainly less complicated than those of adults. The psychology of children, in my opinion, is to be called upon for services similar to those which a study of the anatomy and development of the lower animals renders to the investigation of the structure of the highest classes of animals. Until now only a few conscious efforts have been made to take advantage of the psychology of children for such a purpose.

The dreams of little children are simple fulfillments of wishes, and as compared, therefore, with the dreams of adults, are not at all interesting. They present no problem to be solved, but are naturally invaluable as affording proof that the dream in its essence signifies the fulfillment of a wish. I have been able to collect several examples of such dreams from the material furnished by my own children.

For two dreams, one of my daughter, at that time eight and half years old, the other of a boy five and a quarter years of

Adapted from *The interpretation of dreams*. London: George Allen and Unwin Ltd., 1913. Pp. 109–112.

age, I am indebted to an excursion to the beautiful Hallstatt in the summer of 1896. I must make the preliminary statement that during this summer we were living on a hill near Aussee, from which, when the weather was good, we enjoyed a splendid view of the Dachstein from the roof of our house. The Simony Hut could easily be recognized with a telescope. The little ones often tried to see it through the telescope—I do not know with what success. Before the excursion I had told the children that Hallstatt lay at the foot of the Dachstein. They looked forward to the day with great joy. From Hallstatt we entered the valley of Eschern, which highly pleased the children with its varying aspects. One of them, however, the boy of five, gradually became discontented. As often as a mountain came in view, he would ask: "Is that the Dachstein?" whereupon I would have to answer: "No, only a foot-hill." After this question had been repeated several times, he became altogether silent; and he was quite unwilling to come along on the flight of steps to the waterfall. I thought he was tired out. But the next morning, he approached me radiant with joy, and said: "Last night I dreamt that we were at Simony Hut." I understood him now; he had expected, as I was speaking of the Dachstein, that on the excursion to Hallstatt, he would ascend the mountain and would come face to face with the hut, about which there had been so much discussion at the telescope. When he learned that he was expected to be regaled with foot-hills and a waterfall, he was disappointed and became discontented. The dream compensated him for this. I tried to learn some details of the dream; they were scanty. "Steps must be climbed for six hours," as he had heard.

On this excursion wishes, destined to be satisfied only in dreams, had arisen also in the mind of the girl of eight and a half years. We had taken with us to Hallstatt the twelve-year-old boy of our neighbor—an accomplished cavalier, who, it seems to me, already enjoyed the full sympathy of the little woman. The next morning, then, she related the following dream: "Just think, I dreamt that Emil was one of us, that he said papa and mamma to you, and slept at our house in the big room like our boys." Then mamma came into the room and threw a large handful of chocolate bars under our beds." The brothers of the girl, who evidently had not inherited a familiarity with dream interpretation, declared just like many authors: "That dream is nonsense." The girl defended at least a part of the dream, and it is worth while, from the point of view of the theory of neuroses, to know which part: "That about Emil belonging to us is nonsense, but that about the bars of chocolate is not." It was just this latter part that was obscure to me. For this mamma furnished me the explanation. On the way home from the railway station the children had stopped in front of a slot machine, and had desired exactly such chocolate bars wrapped in paper with a metallic lustre, as the machine, according to their experience, had for sale. But the mother had rightly thought that the day had brought enough wish-fulfillment, and had left this wish to be satisfied in dreams. This little scene had

escaped me. I at once understood that portion of the dream which had been condemned by my daughter. I had myself heard the well-behaved guest enjoining the children to wait until papa or mamma had come up. For the little one the dream made a lasting adoption based on this temporary relation of the boy to us. Her tender nature was as yet unacquainted with any form of being together except those mentioned in the dream, which are taken from her brothers. Why the chocolate bars were thrown under the bed could not, of course, be explained without questioning the child.

From a friend I have learnt of a dream very similar to that of my boy. It concerned an eight-year-old girl. The father had undertaken a walk to Dornbach with the children, intending to visit the Rohrerhütte, but turned back because it had grown too late, and promised the children to make up for their disappointment some other time. On the way back, they passed a sign which showed the way to the Hameau. The children now asked to be taken to that place also, but had to be content, for the same reason, with a postponement to another day. The next morning, the eight-year-old girl came to the father, satisfied, saying: "Papa, I dreamt last night that you were with us at the Rohrerhütte and on the Hameau." Her impatience had thus in the dream anticipated the fulfillment of the promise made by her father.

Another dream, which the picturesque beauty of the Aussee inspired in my daughter, at that time three and a quarter years old, is equally straightforward. The little one had crossed the lake for the first time, and the trip had passed too quickly for her. She did not want to leave the boat at the landing, and cried bitterly. The next morning she told us: "Last night I was sailing on the lake." Let us hope that the duration of this dream ride was more satisfactory to her.

My eldest boy, at that time eight years of age, was already dreaming of the realization of his fancies. He had been riding in a chariot with Achilles, with Diomed as charioteer. He had, of course, on the previous day shown a lively interest in the *Myths of Greece,* which had been given to his elder sister.

If it be granted that the talking of children in sleep likewise belongs to the category of dreaming, I may report the following as one of the most recent dreams in my collection. My youngest girl, at that time nineteen months old, had vomited one morning, and had therefore been kept without food throughout the day. During the night which followed upon this day of hunger, she was heard to call excitedly in her sleep: "Ann Freud, strawberry, huckleberry, omelette, pap!" She used her name in this way in order to express her idea of property; the menu must have included about everything which would seem to her a desirable meal; the fact that berries appeared in it twice was a demonstration against the domestic sanitary regulations, and was based on the circumstance, by no means overlooked by her, that the nurse ascribed her indisposition to an overplentiful consumption of strawberries; she thus in the dream took revenge for this opinion which was distasteful to her.

If we call childhood happy because it does not yet know sexual desire, we must not forget how abundant a source of disappointment and self-denial, and thus of dream stimulation, the other of the great life-impulses may become for it. Here is a second example showing this. My nephew of twenty-two months had been given the task of congratulating me upon my birthday, and of handing me, as a present, a little basket of cherries, which at that time of the year were not yet in season. It seemed difficult for him, for he repeated again and again: "Cherries in it," and could not be induced to let the little basket go out of his hands. But he knew how to secure his compensation. He had, until now, been in the habit of telling his mother every morning that he had dreamt of the "white soldier," an officer of the guard in a white cloak, whom he had once admired on the street. On the day after the birthday, he awakened joyfully with the information which could have had its origin only in a dream: "He(r)-man eat up all the cherries!"

What animals dream of I do not know. A proverb for which I am indebted to one of my readers claims to know, for it raises the question: "What does the goose dream of?" the answer being: "Of corn!" The whole theory that the dream is the fulfillment of a wish is contained in these sentences.

NAME INDEX

A

Ackerson, L., 289, *293*
Ainsworth, M., *259*
Alm, I., 228, *229*
Anastasi, A., 1
Apostel, L., 144, *147*
Archer, E., 149, *153*
Aronson, E., 198, *202*
Attneave, F., 104, 105, 176, *178*

B

Baker, B., 372, *378*
Baldwin, A., 287, *293*, *294*, *301*, 304, *311*
Bandura, A., 173, *174*, 296, *301*, 322, *328*, 398
Barker, R., *18*
Bartlett, F., 175, *178*
Bartoshuk, A., 66, *68*, 70, *75*
Battig, W., 149, *153*
Bayley, N., 304, *311*
Beach, F., 17, *18*, 365, *369*
Becker, W., 290, *293*
Berkeley, G., 281, *282*
Berlyne, D., 144, *147*, 175, *178*
Bernard, J., 219
Bieri, J., 295, *301*, 372, *378*

B

Bierman, M., 325, *328*
Bindra, D., 169, *174*
Bing, E., 294
Bossom, J., 273, *282*
Bower, T., 89, 90, *93*, *282*
Brackbill, Y., 70, *75*
Braine, M., 329, *337*
Brian, C., 183, *188*
Bridger, W., 66, *68*, 70, 75
Britt, S., 365, *369*
Bronfenbrenner, U., 304, *311*, 399, *405*
Bronshtein, A., 65, *69*, 70, *75*
Brown, R., 315, 322, *328*
Bruner, J., *105*
Brunswik, E., *105*, 126, *129*
Butler, R., 175, *178*

C

Cairnes, R., 400, *405*
Cannon, W., 160, *161*
Cantor, G., 74, *76*
Carr, H., *282*
Cattel, P., 255, *259*
Child, I., 42, *43*, 198, *202*
Chomsky, N., 323, *328*, 334, *337*
Christal, R., 354, *361*

NOTE: Page entries in italics indicate complete reference citations.

415

SUBJECT INDEX